Mark

A Biography

Mark

James E. B. Breslin

Rothko

A Biography

The University of Chicago Press   Chicago & London

James E. B. Breslin is professor of English at the
University of California, Berkeley, and author of *From
Modern to Contemporary: American Poetry, 1945-1965*
and *William Carlos Williams: An American Artist,* both
published by the University of Chicago Press.

Publication of this book has been aided by a grant from
the John Simon Guggenheim Memorial Foundation.

The University of Chicago Press, Chicago 60637
The University of Chicago Press, Ltd., London
© 1993 by The University of Chicago
All rights reserved. Published 1993
Printed in the United States of America
02 01 00 99 98 97 96 95 94   3 4 5

ISBN: 0-226-07405-6 (cloth)

Library of Congress Cataloging-in-Publication Data
Breslin, James E. B., 1935–
    Mark Rothko : a biography / James E. B. Breslin.
      p.   cm.
    Includes bibliographical references and index.
    1. Rothko, Mark, 1903–1970.   2. Painters—United States—
Biography.   3. Abstract expressionism—United States.   I. Title.
ND237.R725B74   1993
759.13—dc20
  [B]   93-14966

∞ The paper used in this publication meets the minimum
requirements of the American National Standard for
Information Sciences—Permanence of paper for Printed
Library Materials, ANSI Z39.48-1984.

For Ramsay

Contents

List of Illustrations ix
1 Parnassus on 53rd Street 3
2 Dvinsk/Portland 9
3 New Haven/New York 47
4 Starting Out in the Depression 81
5 Working for the WPA 119
6 "All-Out War" 151
7 "'Globalism' Pops Into View" 179
8 "A New Life" 207
9 "An Art That Lives and Breathes" 231
10 Rothko's New Vision 271
11 Recognitions 297
12 The Dark Paintings 329
13 The Seagram Murals 371
14 Rothko's Image 411
15 The Harvard Murals 445
16 The Houston Chapel 459
17 Rothko's Aneurysm 489
18 The Gift to the Tate 513
19 Rothko's Suicide 521
   Afterword 545
   Documentation 561
   Notes 565
   Acknowledgments 681
   Index 685
   Photo Credits 700

Illustrations

Color Plates (*following p. 244*)

1. *Street Scene*
2. *Portrait of Rothko's Mother*
3. *The Rothkowitz Family*
4. *Untitled, early 1930s*
5. *Untitled, early 1930s*
6. *Sculptress*
7. *Self-Portrait*
8. *Subway Scene*
9. *The Omen of the Eagle*
10. *Untitled, c. 1940*
11. *The Syrian Bull*
12. *Slow Swirl at the Edge of the Sea*
13. *Untitled, 1948*
14. *Number 10, 1950*
15. *Number 12, 1951*
16. *Red, Brown and Black, 1958*
17. *Red on Maroon, 1959*
18. Harvard Murals, Panel Four
19. Houston Murals, east triptych
20. *Untitled, 1967*
21. *Black on Grey, 1969*

Illustrations

Figures (*following p. 116*)

1. View of Shosseynaya Street, Dvinsk, 1903
2. Jacob Rothkowitz
3. Albert, Kate, and Moise Rothkowitz
4. Marcus Rothkowiz, age 10, his mother and his sister
5. Albert and Sonia, Marcus and Moise
6. The Fortress, Daugavpils, 1991
7. View from bridge across Dauga River, 1991
8. View from bridge across Dauga River, 1991
9. Holocaust site, woods north of Daugavpils, 1991
10. Downtown Portland, c. 1910
11. View from the Portland Hills, c. 1910
12. Shattuck School
13. Lincoln High School
14. Graduation from Lincoln High School
15. Yale, 1921–23
16. 1920s
17. Drawing by Mark Rothko from Lewis Browne, The Graphic Bible
18. 1930s
19. Edith Sachar
20. Edith Sachar
21. 1930s
22. 1930s
23. Mark Rothko, mural sketch, c. 1939
24. Mark Rothko, drawing, c. 1939
25. Mark Rothko, drawing, c. 1939

(*following p. 340*)

26. Mell Beistle at Skidmore, 1940
27. 1945–46
28. Yorktown Heights, c. 1949
29. With Mell Rothko and Clyfford Still, 1947
30. With Mell Rothko, East Cleveland, Ohio, 1949
31. Betty Parsons Gallery, New York, 1949
32. "The Irascibles," 1950
33. Jackson Pollock, 1950

Illustrations

34. *Mark Rothko, East Hampton, 1964*
35. *Mell and Mark Rothko, early 1950s*
36. *With his daughter Kate, early 1950s*
37. *53rd Street Studio, early 1950s*
38. *Mid-1950s*
39. *Partial floor plan, Four Seasons Restaurant*
40. *1960, at 222 Bowery*
41. *1960, at 222 Bowery*
42. *118 East 95th Street*
43. *With son Christopher, summer, 1964*
44. *Exterior, 69th Street Studio*
45. *Houston Chapel project, 69th Street studio, 1965–66*
46. *Houston Chapel paintings, 1965*
47. *Exterior of Houston Chapel, 1971*
48. *Houston Chapel, interior with original skylight, 1971*
49. *In the garden of Dimitri Hadzi's studio, 1966*
50. *Living area, 69th Street studio, 1969*
51. *Black on Grey paintings, 1969*
52. *1969*

Mark Rothko

A Biography

1 Parnassus on 53rd Street

That [Museum of Modern Art] show was to him like being invited to dwell on Parnassus.

Stanley Kunitz

For eight months during the winter of 1958 and the spring of 1959, Mark Rothko worked, eight hours daily, on a set of murals he had been commissioned to produce for the Four Seasons restaurant in the new Seagram Building being constructed on Park Avenue, between 52nd and 53rd Streets, in New York City. Designed by Philip Johnson, the Four Seasons was to be an exclusive and expensive restaurant where, in Rothko's words, "the richest bastards in New York will come to feed and show off."

"I accepted this assignment as a challenge, with strictly malicious intentions," Rothko declared. "I hope to paint something that will ruin the appetite of every son of a bitch who ever eats in that room." More than that, he hoped to make his "viewers feel that they are trapped in a room where all the doors and windows are bricked up, so that all they can do is butt their heads forever against the wall."[1] Rothko, who had been butting his own head against the walls of New York's art world for more than thirty years, wanted to make the well-heeled Four Seasons patrons feel just as he did.

His malice was being enacted in a large, "cavernous" studio, in a former YMCA building. To approximate the interior of the restaurant, Rothko had covered three of the studio's walls, for about two-thirds of the room's twenty-three-foot height, with plasterboard, then built a fourth, movable wooden wall. He had also installed pulleys on the ceiling to allow him flexibility in adjusting the height at which the paintings could be hung. This studio was kept *very* dark. Of its eight windows—all about fifteen feet from the floor—four were blocked off by a storage area Rothko had constructed for his paintings, the lower halves of two more windows were cut off by the plasterboard walls. Only the two northern windows admitted a very dim light. Robert Motherwell described the room as "a darkened movie set." Rothko's friend Dore Ashton found "the great space" as "dim as a cathedral."[2] Rothko himself, when he wasn't stressing the malice behind his project, was proclaiming its exalted,

Chapter One

even sacred character, as if he were executing paintings for a cathedral rather than a restaurant. When, in the summer of 1959, he visited Pompeii, he claimed "a deep affinity" between his own murals and those in the House of Mysteries there—"the same feeling, the same broad expanses of somber color."[3] At the end of a long afternoon in which he showed the murals to Ashton, Rothko declared: "They are not pictures." "I have made a place."[4]

At the time of the Four Seasons project, Rothko lived, with his wife, Mell, and nine-year-old daughter, Kate, in a midtown Manhattan flat, at 102 West 54th Street, around the corner from the Museum of Modern Art. Rothko did not like to work in neighborhoods where there were many other painters. Nor did he like to work at home where, he said, he felt he was under "surveillance."[5] So his studio was located far downtown, at 222 Bowery, between Prince and Spring streets, in the old YMCA building; the cathedral-like space in which Rothko was painting had once been its gymnasium—its hardwood floor then (and, in 1991, still) covered with splotches of the blood-red paint Rothko was using in his murals. Painting for (or against) the rich, Rothko worked in a neighborhood of poverty, hunger, dereliction, homelessness. During the winter months, he would arrive at the studio wearing "an old overcoat that came down to the ground" and "a great big black hat that had a mouse hole eaten in the crown"—in short, looking more like a citizen of the Bowery than, say, a patron of the Four Seasons.[6]

At fifty-six, Rothko, always a hefty bearlike man with a voracious appetite, had grown portly. Although he suffered from gout, he liked to eat rich foods, he liked to drink, and he liked to smoke. His physician, Dr. Albert Grokest, commented that Rothko's "greatest sources of consolation were calories and alcohol."[7] Around this time, there were also signs of trouble in his marriage, with many arguments, and Mell Rothko, too, was developing a drinking problem.

With his paintings Rothko could create a place for himself. Within the last few years he had also made a place for himself in the world—an increasingly preeminent one. In late January of 1961, the Rothkos attended the inauguration of President John F. Kennedy. Getting Rothko into the proper clothes for such an occasion was, said one nephew, "always an adventure." Rothko rented the required tuxedo and, because of the alphabetical seating arrangement, was placed next to Walt Rostow, a member of the Kennedy "brain trust" whom Rothko decided was "mad." Rothko himself, as one friend recalled, "was riding high."[8]

Just three days before the inauguration, he had opened a two-month show at the Museum of Modern Art, becoming the first living member of his generation to have a one-man show at the museum. In the next two years, the exhibit would travel to London, Amsterdam, Basel, Rome, and Paris. Publicized by interview-articles in *Time* and *Newsweek* prior to the opening, the show received generally enthusiastic reviews, with one, by Robert Goldwater, providing what Rothko regarded as the most penetrating account ever written of his work. By 1960 Rothko's position in the art world and his financial position were secure enough so that he could, once he decided that the Four Seasons could not be transformed into the kind of "place" he wished to create, return what he had been paid of his commission and withdraw the paintings.

For many years a kind of impoverished urban wanderer in New York, and still often dressing to look like one, Rothko, now receiving as much as $10,000 to $15,000 for his paintings, had just purchased his first home, a $75,000 four story painted brick house at 118 East 95th St., near Park Avenue. His wardrobe even improved—somewhat. "Now that I have a bank account, I have a banker's coat," he joked.[9] At fifty-eight Rothko was a proclaimed master and well-to-do. He had every reason to feel satisfied with himself.

Yet Rothko was a "combative" person "with an adversary view of human nature." As an outsider, he had long felt bitter and deprived. Now as an insider he felt uneasy and contaminated. He had experienced "anxiety about buying a house, becoming a property owner, no longer being poor." To some of his friends, he complained that his wife and his accountant, Bernard Reis, had pressured him into buying the house.[10] After all, if he was no longer poor, wronged, and marginal, then who was he? Moreover, a restless, lonely and gregarious person, Rothko had enjoyed hanging out in the bars and drugstores near his midtown 54th Street flat. Of his new neighborhood on New York's affluent Upper East Side, he complained that there were "no friendly bars, no interesting jaunts or joints."[11] Success was producing its own headaches. "He'd been fighting the world for so long," said Anne-Marie Levine, "he felt severely compromised by situations when the world paid him homage."

Turning back the Seagram's commission reassured him that he had not compromised and was still the embattled outsider. Another consequence of success was the loss of friendships with some of the painters in his own generation to whom he had felt closest—men like Clyfford Still and Barnett Newman. "There's no one to hang out with any more," he complained. "They're too busy achieving things." Younger painters, particularly the Pop artists, Rothko feared as eager to displace him: "Those young artists are out to murder us," he warned.[12] He may not have been entirely comfortable with the place he had made for himself in the world, but it had taken him so long to make it that he wasn't about to give it up.

The Museum of Modern Art show provided a crucial turning point. During the 1950s Rothko had lived in two flats, both of which were just a short walk from the museum; he spent many hours with its collection, he liked to hang out and hold forth in its coffee shop, and he often ran into Director Alfred Barr and Curator Dorothy Miller at the Valmor, a local Italian restaurant; "he would often join us," Ms. Miller recalled, and "sit and talk for a while."[13] But he had long resented the museum's failure to give him the recognition he thought he deserved, when he had needed it most. The Modern "has no convictions and no courage," he declared. "It can't decide which paintings are good and which are bad. So it hedges by buying a little of everything." Now he responded to the Museum's offer of a one-man exhibit with an angry grandiosity: "They need me. I don't need them. This show will lend dignity to the Museum. It does not lend dignity to me."[14]

Yet Rothko also felt a triumphant "euphoria," as if the exhibit did confer position, even dignity.[15] In fact, he was sufficiently aware of, and involved with, the museum's power to confer place in the art world to threaten withdrawing from the show if he couldn't get the particular floor in the museum he wanted.[16] "Of course, this was the biggest event in his life up to then," his friend Stanley Kunitz recalled, adding that Rothko behaved "like a man obsessed during the whole period" before and during the exhibit. Originally scheduled for April–June 1960, the show had been twice put back on the museum's schedule; and Rothko had been planning the exhibit for at least eighteen months. Yet two days before the opening, he withdrew six works and added seven new ones to the exhibit.[17] On the last day of the show, Rothko, who had tried to persuade the museum to extend it, "was very reluctant for his show to end."[18] But, Kunitz added, Rothko also felt that his involvement "was to a degree an act of self-betrayal because his caring so much about this show negated all that he'd been saying about the museum world."[19]

Regina Bogat, a young painter whose studio was across the hall, helped Rothko prepare for the exhibit. She recalled that "his feeling about the Museum of Modern Art show was very intense. He became very busy and involved with his past, with his past work," and he had to take old paintings out of storage, unroll them, examine them and, for the ones he selected, he had to restore them, get them measured, and have stretchers made for them "and it became a tremendous physical labor and time-consuming. He wondered what he was doing it for." She finally asked why he was doing the show if it was causing him so much grief, and Rothko replied, "I want to prove to my family that it was a good thing that I became a painter." Both of Rothko's older brothers did attend the show, and one of them commented, after viewing fifty-seven of Rothko's works, "I didn't know this place was so big." So much for impressing the family.

After it opened, Rothko spent a great deal of time, almost daily, at the show. One young painter told him, "Mark, it's a beautiful show"—to which Rothko replied, "It's not a show, it's an event."[20] Yet Rothko hovered anxiously about, starting conversations with skeptical-looking strangers, trying to convert them. For all his grandiosity, Rothko himself was the doubter he was most struggling to convince. The January 16 opening was what newspapers call "a gala event." The invited guests included older artists from Albers to Hofmann, Davis to Duchamp, Dali to Hopper; it included all the living painters from Rothko's own generation (de Kooning and Kline, Motherwell and Newman), some younger painters such as Jasper Johns and Ray Parker, a few art critics (Clement Greenberg, Meyer Shapiro, Robert Goldwater), and more than a few dealers and collectors (Joseph Hirshorn and Paul Mellon).[21] Rothko, who once said that "when a crowd of people looks at a painting, I think of blasphemy," occupied the center of this profane rite.[22]

"For all his gregariousness," writes John Hurt Fischer, remembering the opening, Rothko "was shy; and since he was on display as much as his paintings, he began the evening in an agony of stage fright. Later, as one guest after another came to congratulate him—and usually to express an almost reverent admiration for his work—he relaxed and started to glow with affability."[23] After the black-tie reception at the museum, there were drinks at a bar on University Place. Then at five o'clock that morning, he showed up at a friend's apartment. "I'm in despair," Rothko said. He was distraught, and he said, "It's because everyone can see what a fraud I am." With what he had chosen as the best of his life's work in front of him, his friends, and the public, Rothko felt exposed as worthless, empty. "The whole enterprise was nothing," he declared, and Rothko's artistic enterprise *was*, after all, a something that was dangerously close to nothing. At the Museum of Modern Art opening, the moment of triumph he had worked so long and hard for had gone from stage fright through elation to humiliating despair.

Rothko's desire to create artistic works that would provide a place for him, his difficulty in accommodating these creations to the real world of restaurants, museums, and viewers, his combativeness, his prophetic ambitions, his intense desire for success, his guilt about success, his uncompromisingness, his compromises, his propensity to isolate himself, his wish for community, his mixed feelings about both wealth and poverty, his suspicions, his suspicions about himself, his vulnerability to despair—all these conflicting feelings in the Mark Rothko of the early 1960s had their origins in the life of Marcus Rothkowitz, born in Dvinsk, Russia, a despised Jew in the infamous Settlement of Pale, in the first years of the twentieth century.

2 Dvinsk/Portland

Mark Rothko was very conscious of his sources, both as a location and as a cultural heritage.

Stanley Kunitz

In 1902, Major W. Evans-Gordon, a member of the English Parliament concerned with the "problems" created by the increasing number of "alien immigrants"—i.e., Jews—in London's East End, decided he might better understand these aliens by visiting their places of origin. His journey began in St. Petersburg, Russia, from which he traveled by train to Dvinsk.

He found the Dvinsk railroad station "spacious," with "an excellent restaurant." But "as soon as one leaves it one steps into another world," one predominantly Jewish, filled with a "prevailing misery."

The cabs pulled up to the station are "driven by Jewish drivers clad in filthy rags," their horses "mere bags of bones." The drive into the town "gave me a first idea of what Russian country roads are—heart-breaking cobbles varied by patches of unfathomable black mud." On either side of the road Evans-Gordon saw "mournful wooden houses and shanties, mouldy and crumbling," "inhabited by a few dejected women, children, and pigs." "The sanitary arrangements are better imagined than described."

It is Saturday, and no shop is open. "The Jewish Sabbath puts the whole trade of the place to sleep." "Large crowds of respectably dressed Jews were promenading in front of the synagogue—a sort of church parade." A police officer with whom the major strikes up a friendly conversation tells him "that the Jewish people had the upper hand here, and that the entire trade of the place was in their possession."

The Jews are not only tradesmen; they are thieves, their young women are prostitutes, they run gambling and drinking dens. The police chief has tried to reform the city, but found it an "impossible task."

Evans-Gordon admires the Dvina River, where "there is a handsome boulevard and an avenue of trees on the bank of this fine stream," and he liked the public park, filled, on Saturday evening, with "well-dressed and apparently well-to-do" Jews.

Chapter Two

But Dvinsk "is, for its size, the most backward town I have ever seen." There are no tram lines, few public conveyances. The streets are lit "by wretched oil lamps." "There are no public buildings of any size." "Many of the dwellings are crumbling and squalid."

"I left Dvinsk without regret," he concludes.[1]

• • •

To get to Dvinsk today, you must travel by railroad from St. Petersburg, arriving at the Riga Station, at the center of town, now called Daugavpils. As you walk out of the station's main entrance, you are facing southwest, down the city's main commercial street, toward the Dauga River, about a mile and a quarter away. To the north, the city is bounded by a military base called "The Fortress." To the south, it is bounded by the river, along which a dike has been built to prevent floods.

"Where the dike ended," writes Yudel Flior in his memoir of early twentieth-century Dvinsk, "a tarred road curving away from the Dvina . . . became a paved highway that carried on to St. Petersburg"; this was Evans-Gordon's "handsome boulevard." "On the other side of this main highway," Flior continues, "was the suburb of Gayok, where was to be found a fair concentration of Jews," one of whom, in early 1913, living on the road that became the highway to St. Petersburg, was Marcus Rothkowitz, ten years old, living in a flat with his sister and mother; his father and two older brothers had already emigrated to the United States.[2] Part of the Settlement of Pale, to which most of Russia's 5 million Jews were confined, Dvinsk was then a city of about 75,000, about half of them Jewish. Rothko had been born there on September 26, 1903, the youngest, by about eight years, of four children.[3]

• • •

"Daugavpils" means "Castle by the Dauga." The city originated as a fortified castle, built by the ancient Latgallians just north of the point where the 640-mile-long Dauga River, which has been flowing westward, turns north to empty, eventually, into the Baltic Sea.[4] In the late thirteenth century, Teutonic knights captured, destroyed, and rebuilt the castle, calling it "Dunaburg." A settlement grew up nearby, which, with the protection of the fortress and the proximity of the river, became a flourishing center of trade. Under Ivan IV, the Russians captured and destroyed the castle, then began to build a new one a bit south. By the time this new fortress was complete, the town had come under the rule of the Kingdom of Poland and Lithuania. Except for four years of Russian control in the seventeenth century, the city remained under Poland —until 1772 when the town was annexed by the Russians, who later, in 1893, renamed it Dvinsk.

"In this city East and West face each other most closely, so that Daugavpils has long been an object of dispute and more than once has been destroyed by fire and wars."[5] Dvinsk—as I will be calling it, since that is the name Rothko knew—has for centuries been a (more or less) fixed point surrounded by countries with fluctuating borders, imperial designs, and migratory populations; historically, the city has known violence, followed by oppressive nationalization programs—Russification, in Rothko's time.

Outside the city, the countryside is flat, with some distant rolling hills, many lakes, and forests of pine, spruce, and birch trees. In the early twentieth century, there were many small farms, worked by peasants. All of the land north of the town, stretching as far as 135 miles to Riga, formed Count Zybert Platov's estate, worked by serfs, as if it were still the Middle Ages.[6] But the city of Dvinsk, still a trading center and now an important railroad junction, was lurching its way into the industrial age. The town had three railroad stations— the Riga Station, the Libau Station and the new St. Petersburg Station, where seven rooms were reserved for Czar Nicholas II, who sometimes stopped in Dvinsk on trips from St. Petersburg to Warsaw.[7]

But railroads symbolize modern industrialization and mobility. As one of the town's historians told me, "the railroad brought people here, and it took those who wanted to achieve anything away."[8] During the ten years before Rothko left, the trains were certainly bringing people *to* Dvinsk, as the city's population grew by 50 percent between 1905 and 1913.[9] The railroad was also bringing trade to, and from, the town.

"Commerce was the soul of Dvinsk," recalls Yudel Flior, whose autobiography vividly recreates the town's factories, manufacturers, wholesalers, shopkeepers, workers, lumpen-proletariat, beggars.[10] Twice a week, peasants brought vegetables, fish, poultry, and diary products in carts and wagons, to be sold at open markets. In the spring, after the ice broke up on the Dvina, rafts of fifty-foot timbers began to drift by, floating down the river to Riga, where the logs would be sold. Farming and logging continued as they had for centuries. But by 1912, there were a hundred factories, employing over 6,000 workers, in Dvinsk. There were two large railroad repair shops, many textile factories, plants manufacturing leather goods, matches, bricks. "Trade is concentrated in the hands of the Jews," says the *Dvinchanin*, a 1913 guidebook to the town. Since Jews, forbidden to own land, were restricted to urban occupations, they ran haberdasheries, restaurants, printing houses, confectioneries, jewelry stores, hardware stores, shoemakers' shops, tailor shops, and (like Rothko's father) pharmacies.

But if commerce was the soul of Dvinsk, its easily activated conscience was its formidable Russian military presence. "The fortress consisted in the main of solid, towering walls, surrounded by ramparts made up of sand-mounds to render the shells of the enemy ineffective," Flior writes. "The walls served as emplacements for the cannons. Around the fortress a deep moat had been dug, the flooding of which would halt the attacker. The moat was spanned by four wooden bridges, which could be demolished at short notice."[11] To Rothko's brother Moise, the Fortress did not represent protection against foreign invaders but the status of the town's Jews: "The army was stationed out there and they were the elite of the state and we were the other half."[12] Altogether, 25,000 troops were stationed in Dvinsk, some at the Fortress, others housed in the town and its suburbs. Along the eastern and southern edges of the city, there were practice fields for the cavalry, and storage depots for gunpowder.[13] In Dvinsk, the means of political repression were everywhere, and everywhere visible. Rothko's family lived down the street from a food-storage building for the military.[14]

Most of the people of Dvinsk, and thus most of its Jews, were quite poor. "Well-to-do persons, even by local standards, were few and far between. The majority lived on scanty bread and water."[15] For those who were employed, working conditions were miserable. The eight hundred workers in the town's match factory—half of them female, many as young as ten—began their day when the factory's siren sounded at 6 A.M. and did not quit until 8 P.M., earning fifty kopeks a week for their fourteen hour days. Many lost fingers or hands in their machines; many died of phosphorous consumption. In 1901, these workers went on a six-month strike they eventually won, their success inspiring a series of strikes by workers in other industries over the next several years, with these strikes inspiring, in turn, arrests and harassment by the police.[16]

The city's many workers and its even more numerous paupers made it an active center of political dissidence in the early years of the twentieth century, the town's Old Park a frequent site for political speeches and demonstrations. The Social Democrats, the Social Revolutionaries, the Bund (a Jewish socialist group), and various Zionist organizations all developed strong followings. "A new spirit descended on Dvinsk," Flior says.[17]

Or, from the point of view of its Russian rulers, Dvinsk generated plenty of dangerous activity; official repression was often required. "The political parties were beginning to stir," says Flior. "Not a day passed but arrests took place." The town's red-brick jail, nicknamed the "Dvinsker Bastille," expanded from one to two to four to six stories. "It was quite a common sight now to see the mounted soldiers charge into the crowd at the Old Park, and use their knouts at random." In Dvinsk, there were no pogroms; but in 1904, in response to the brutal pogroms in Kishinev, Bialystok, and several other cities ("these pogroms hung like a pall of doom above the heads of the people of Dvinsk and elsewhere") a mass demonstration, its participants singing a funeral march for the victims of the pogroms, was attacked by police and soldiers as it reached the Old Park. Strikes were now forbidden; meetings were forbidden, initiating a period of raids, arrests, assassinations, spies, counterspies.[18] Many Dvinsk Jews began to emigrate to the United States.

"The year 1904 slid painfully into 1905—the bloody year, as it has gone down in Russian history. And January 9, has gone down as Bloody Sunday," on which the Czar's soldiers killed over two hundred of the peasants, workers, students, liberals in a peaceful St. Petersburg political march. "On Saturday, the 15th January, there took place a tremendous demonstration outside the Old Park." As a result Dvinsk was placed under martial law, a 9 P.M. to 6 A.M. curfew was imposed, gatherings of more than three persons were forbidden. "The Cossack on his horse, armed with sabre, knout and revolver, became the master of the town. They used their knouts and whips very liberally." Later, in October of 1905, a Dvinsk mass meeting, called to celebrate the new liberal constitution declared by Nicholas II, was fired upon and nine people were killed; military order was again imposed.[19] The ensuing reactionary period (1906–11)—Rothko's third through eighth years—were, according to one historian, "the worst in the history of Russian Jewry."[20] "Destroy the Jews, and save Russia," became the Russian nationalists' slogan, while laws were tightened, anti-Semitic rhetoric was intensified, and the pogroms, often led by police or the vigilante Black Hundreds groups, became more frequent and more violent.[21]

"We escaped pogroms," Moise recalled. "We did have Cossacks; they would come in with whips and do what they wanted and scare the life out of people."[22] "We had many scares. We had to all of a sudden run home and close the windows and shutters and be on the look-out all the time."[23] When Rothko himself recalled the first ten years of his life, he was most likely to remember Russian persecution. He was "very strongly interested" in "his Russian background," according to his friend Herbert Ferber, and often repeated stories of his childhood—"being carried in the arms of his mother or a nurse at one time when a Cossack rode by and slashed at them with a whip. And he had a scar on his nose which he claimed had been caused by the whip of a Cossack."[24]

· · ·

Chapter Two

> *Michalishek, village of my mighty ancestors.*
>
> Menke Katz, "Gold Diggers"

Among those the railroad did bring to Dvinsk, sometime in the mid-1890s, were Jacob and Kate Rothkowitz, and their two children, Sonia and Moise.

Jacob Rothkowitz had been born in 1859 in Michalishek, a shtetl of two hundred and fifty families (about half of them Jewish), about sixty miles southwest of Dvinsk, in Lithuania, along the Viliya River.[25] Menke Katz's poem "Gold Diggers," after praising the "bearded rivermen," potato farmers, lumbermen, and potters of the village, goes on to lament the corrupting influence of dreams of American riches on its pious, earthy life.[26] Jacob Rothkowitz left, but with ambitions for more than riches. Somehow he managed to obtain a high school education and, despite quotas limiting the number of Jews—not to mention other forms of anti-Semitism—he had received, in Vilna, the training and certification then required to become a pharmacist. Moise remembered "a highly educated man" who "left the little village he was born in and starved to go to school so that he could achieve what he wanted."[27]

The family of Rothko's mother, Kate Goldin, came from East Prussia; they spoke German at home. She had been born in 1870 in St. Petersburg—which means that, since she lived outside the Settlement of Pale, her family was probably well-off. Jacob Rothkowitz and Kate Goldin met in St. Petersburg and they were married in 1886, when he was twenty-seven and she just sixteen, a gymnasium student. At first they lived in Michalishek, where their daughter, Sonia, was born on March 19, 1890, and Moise on November 2, 1892.[28] Sometime between 1892 and 1895, the family moved to Dvinsk, where Albert was born in 1895 and Marcus in 1903.

At Rothko's birth, his sister was thirteen and his brothers eleven and eight; he constituted a kind of second generation, a figure apart, in his own family—a position he both cherished and resented. Moreover, in a city filled with poor workers and paupers, the family itself was set apart by Jacob's profession, by his original disaffiliation from orthodox Judaism, and by the family's unusually intense commitment to politics and education. At home the family spoke Russian, one sign of their educated status.[29] The one surviving photograph of Rothko's father (fig. 2) suggests a man of slight build, studious disposition, and mild temper—a man more sensitive than powerful. His children recalled him as quiet, intellectual, scrupulously moral, passionately political—a man more idealistic than practical. According to Sonia, "we were a reading family, very interested in literature—all of us. I remember that when we left Russia, we left behind a library of 300 books." After Sonia came to the United States, she learned English by reading translations of the many books she had already read in Russian.[30]

Jacob Rothkowitz was "an avid reader," "a well-read man." He enjoyed sitting quietly to read or just sitting quietly. Later in Portland, Oregon, on Sundays, Jacob would walk over to the house of a male relative and the two men would "sit silently" together on the front porch. Moise described his father as a "quiet dreamer" and "idealist" who was more political than religious.[31] Both parents and sometimes the children attended synagogue; they all followed the dietary practices at home, at least until they came to Portland. But Moise remembered that in synagogue on Yom Kippur his father would "get tired of it" and read political pamphlets hidden inside his prayer book. Rothko himself once claimed that his father's relation to formal religion was much more openly oppositional: "My father was a militant social democrat of the Jewish party, the Bund, which was the social democracy of that time. He was profoundly Marxist and violently anti-religious, partly because in Dvinsk . . . the orthodox Jews were a repressive majority." Other members of the family all relate that Jacob Rothkowitz was a "strong Zionist."[32] He could hardly have belonged to both the rival Bund and Zionist groups; and the weight of family opinion has him a Zionist. But he was certainly committed to dissident politics, holding "meetings all the time in our house," according to Moise, even when such activities had been "forbidden" by the Russian authorities. "He was strong for any liberal movement. He was active in it."

Rothko always spoke with "reverence" of his father, as a "man of great character, great intelligence," Rothko's nephew Kenneth Rabin recalled. Jacob Rothkowitz was "some sort of icon up there" for his youngest child. Because Jacob Rothkowitz died relatively young and so long ago, family stories have preserved a more legendary than human figure. But that legend does have a particular shape. "When I got married I was sixteen years old," Kate Rothkowitz said. "I didn't know anything. He taught me everything."[33] All of Jacob's children similarly stressed their father's role, in the family and in the community, as a teacher and moral counselor. Educated, able "to read and write Russian as well as Hebrew," Jacob was "extremely popular" among both Jews and non-Jews in Dvinsk. His pharmacy "was the place where they all came for advice; to write letters; to read letters." "He would make up the letters for them; they wouldn't know what to say but he would talk it over with them," and then write down what they had decided to say. Jacob was especially close to Sonia, who "adored him, absolutely worshipped him." He "kept straightening her out, telling her how to behave." Once, Sonia asked her father if the Rothkowitzes couldn't, like some of their friends, have a Sabbath goy—a Christian to come on the Sabbath, when Jews were forbidden to work, and light the fire, cook, etc. Jacob asked, "Why don't you light fires on the Sabbath?" Sonia replied that she had been taught that she'd go to hell if she did. Jacob: "And what about that boy, you don't care about his soul, whether he goes to hell?" Jacob Rothkowitz, it appears, was as much Jewish patriarch as he was political radical.[34]

Literate guide for the community, instructor in "moral lessons" for his children, Jacob also made sure that his children received formal educations, as he had. The family, though, was "not all that well-off." Kate Rothkowitz would do her laundry at night so the neighbors wouldn't see her, because "a druggist should have maids doing it." But the family was "farsighted" with such money as they had, saving enough to send Sonia, after she completed gymnasium, to study dentistry at the University of Warsaw. Moise followed his father into the pharmacy, attending Jewish schools in Dvinsk and then the University of Vilna, where he had to be coached for his certifying exams because "examiners would try to cut down on the numbers of Jews that passed." Albert, too, became a pharmacist, though he was not certified until after he came to Portland.[35] Marcus, however, was singled out for a religious education—a distinction he grew to despise.

Jacob Rothkowitz was one of a generation of Russian Jewish intellectuals who had substituted secular education and political zeal for religious fervor; his life reflects some of the conflicts created by this process of modernization that was taking place, in the late nineteenth and early twentieth centuries, among many Eastern European Jews. Jacob's boyhood and adolescence coincided with the rule of Czar Alexander II (1855–81), whose relaxation of anti-Jewish measures had brought larger numbers of Jews into the Russian public schools. Feeling liberated from rabbinical scholasticism, many sought assimilation, or Russification. Jacob's secular education; his migration from village to city; his commitment to secular education for all his children (daughter as well as sons); his family's use of Russian rather than Yiddish (the language of Michalishek) as the language spoken in their home: all these marked Rothko's father as secular, modern—*haskalah*.[36]

Yet his exacting moral sense, his role as community "wise man" and family teacher, his belief in Zionism all placed him with the young Jewish intellectuals who, after the assassination of Alexander and the pogroms of 1881, wished to remain Jewish and develop a progressive politics; the Bund was one eventual solution, Zionism another. These tensions in Jacob Rothkowitz's life, between modernization and ethnic identity, later reappeared in the struggles of his youngest son who, as an adult, struggled to find a way of being American without being *merely* assimilated. But while the family lived in Dvinsk, Jacob's conflicts created problems, and inspired resentments, for his youngest son, Marcus.

• • •

As a boy, Marcus Rothkowitz was fragile, sensitive, sickly.

His brother Moise recalled "a highstrung, noticeably sensitive child."[37] "He was a very, very sick child," Sonia said. "We didn't expect him to live until [he was] about four years old." The problem, according to Moise, was an undiagnosed calcium deficiency: "the doctor gave up on him because he was very ill. At that time they did not know what the lack of calcium meant. We had plaster walls and he ate the plaster off the walls because he craved calcium. And that was the only way he could get it." Afterwards, Rothko was sent to a nearby village to recover, drinking a quart of milk a day. The boy who ate the plaster off the walls grew up, in Albert's description, with a "perpetually ravenous" appetite, and into a hypochondriacal adult, constantly fretting over his body.[38]

No Marc Chagall or Jean Jacques Rousseau, Rothko seldom reminisced, in paint or words, about his boyhood, his native town, its Jewish community. His daughter Kate observed that he "was sort of closed about it." He did tell her of being allowed to sleep on top of the brick stove, and of ice skating to school on the Dvina River—both memories alluding to the cold Russian winters. Talking with Robert Motherwell, Rothko remembered the "glorious" Russian sunsets. Talking with a student, Rothko complained that he always had to wear a schoolbag on his back because anti-Semitic boys would throw rocks at him as he walked to school.[39]

One story that he did repeat involved an early memory of his family and relatives talking about a czarist pogrom. "The Cossacks took the Jews from the village to the woods and made them dig a large grave. Rothko said he pictured that square grave in the woods so vividly that he wasn't sure the massacre hadn't happened in his lifetime. He said he'd always been haunted by the image of that grave, and that in some profound way it was locked into his painting." In another version of this story Rothko himself witnessed the digging of the grave and the ensuing massacre.[40]

It's tempting, especially for a biographer, to conclude that this story offers an allegorical key with which we can unlock the mystery of Rothko's later obsession with the rectangle, as if his paintings of the 1950s and 1960s transformed his memory of Jewish victimization into a space of transcendent freedom and sensual pleasure. Yet, there are some reasons to doubt Rothko's story.

There were no pogroms in Dvinsk, and so Rothko certainly never witnessed any such execution. He *may* have heard adults discussing pogroms elsewhere, and he *may* have heard a story of a mass grave, but the mass grave was a phenomenon of the holocaust, not of pogroms.[41]

Rothko's close friend Herbert Ferber believes stories like this one, or Rothko's account of being struck on the nose by a Cossack's whip, are self-dramatizing fictions, and it is true that Rothko, whose paintings are commanding and theatrical, yet silent and understated, alternately kept quiet about his past or narrated it in a theatrical, even melodramatic way. "Look at the pain I had to bear, the dangers I was exposed to as a child," his stories assert. Yet he did belong to a stigmatized social group ("we were the other half," as Moise put it), in a city that often confronted Jews, particularly political Jews (like Rothko's family), with *real* violence. Rothko experienced these dangers through the consciousness of a child, apt to exaggerate, distort, blend reality with fantasy. The adult Rothko may have related such stories for dramatic effect; they may or they may not have happened. True or false, they convey real fears of real dangers.

There were the insecurities of political life in the Pale; and there were the insecurities of physical life, of the body. The domestic order offered no sure protections against either; in fact family life, responding to external pressures, often replicated their coercions. An "idealist" known in his community as a generous man—he spent many hours in volunteer work at a local hospital—Jacob Rothkowitz could also assert his paternal authority at home. He "insisted" that Sonia, then twenty, come to the United States, although she didn't want to go because she "had a sweetheart" in Dvinsk, had established a dental practice there and believed that Americans were "all mercenary, all money and nothing else. And I kind of leaned to the other side."[42]

Rothko's sister had attended Russian public schools, his brothers attended Jewish schools, but not religious ones. But in reaction to the 1905 pogroms, the political and "liberal" Jacob turned orthodox, thereby creating "a lot of conflict" with his wife over dietary rules.[43] He also decided to send his youngest son to *cheder,* thereby creating a lot of conflict with his youngest son.[44] Once again, Rothko was being set apart—and again with mixed feelings, this time because he was the one being forced to act out his father's politically inspired orthodoxy. Whether Rothko attended a traditional *cheder* or one of the reform *cheders* then popular among middle-class Zionists, as the "chosen son" he was subject to a strict, tedious regime, possibly starting as early as the age of three, of reading instruction, prayer, translation of Hebrew texts and rote memorization of Talmudic law.

When Rothko recalled *cheder,* he spoke angrily against his father for imposing the regime upon him, and yet with a feeling of loss for his early sense of Jewish community. During a 1965 lunch Philip Guston mentioned a book which argued that all people were originally Jewish:

> Mark suddenly asked: "Doesn't it make you feel lonesome?" Being brought up as the youngest child when his father was an orthodox Jew, Mark during the first nine years of his life was an hebrew infant prodigy. All the rules and rigor of religion were never sufficiently observed by his mother, not sufficiently to Mark's rigid father. And then a complete blank came into his life—oblivion of the hebrew language and a complete break with temple rigor—after having gone 100 times to the temple during holidays[,] one day at the age of 9 he came home and announced to his mother he would never set foot into a temple again.[45]

Rothko's account of his break with *cheder,* like other of his narratives, certainly exaggerates, may fictionalize. After his emigration to Portland, Oregon, at ten, he kept a notebook in which he composed some poems, a story, and a play—all in Hebrew. Not only do these works reveal no sign of any disaffiliation with Judaic religion, they mark Jewish holidays (Passover, Hanukkah) and envision the coming of the messiah or the triumph of the Jews over the Gentiles; they affirm tribal loyalty and celebrate the heroic Jewish survival of oppression.[46]

Moreover, this story of his refusal even to enter a synagogue contradicts another story in which Rothko located his break with religion after his father's death in 1914. Yet, as with the story of the mass grave, Rothko's *cheder* narrative conveys an emotional reality: he experienced his father as severe and impositional—the sort of man who made his son all the more angry by subjecting him to a cheerless religious regime toward which he himself had previously been antagonistic.

But if Rothko was nine when he boldly refused to return to the temple, he was declaring his independence in the literal absence of his father, who had emigrated to the United States two years before.

. . .

The tarred road which began at the Dvina River and ended in St. Petersburg was called Shosseynaya (or "highway-like road") in 1913. Rothko lived at 17 Shosseynaya, one long block from the Dvina, in an L-shaped, three-story apartment house, looking across a wide, tree-lined boulevard with a promenade along the center (fig. 1).[47] "The flat question is the most difficult question," says a 1913 Jewish guidebook to the town, as if early twentieth-century Dvinsk resembled late twentieth-century New York.

Dvinsk *was* moving into the industrial age. In 1901 the first "horseless carriage," driven by a Russian colonel, had appeared in the town; in 1904 the first movies were shown. The first plane would appear during World War I, when the Germans bombed the Petersburg Railway Station and the Fortress. But in Rothko's time, day-to-day living conditions remained premodern: flats had no electricity, no inside bathrooms, no inside water. Bathing was done at public baths. More important, housing was not increasing as rapidly as the city's population, so flats were hard to find, expensive (rents increasing by two or three times in the years just prior to 1913), and they were crowded.[48] Sonia's dentistry was done in this flat (providing her younger brother with occasional gruesome background noises).

When Rothko's brother Albert was asked about Dvinsk, he remembered "military post," "agriculture, farming," "flat plains," "heavily forested," "very cold," "snow, long winters," "severe climate."[49] A northern city, Dvinsk, while not as far north as St. Petersburg or Helsinki, is almost as far north as Juneau, Alaska. Winters are long and bleak, with average temperatures descending below freezing by the beginning of December and staying there—the river frozen—until early March. The breakup of the ice in spring still caused serious flooding in Rothko's time, despite the dike, with the river flooding the Gayok district in 1906.[50] Summers bring a good deal of rain, especially in July, and throughout the year the sky is often overcast, gray. Yet because Dvinsk is so far north, days are long—in the summer, there are only three hours of darkness—and the light soft. "The Latvian painter has a special love for diffused outdoor light which seems to penetrate the bodies and emanate from them," a light that reappears within, and from behind, Rothko's paintings, an illumination glimpsed through a hazy doorway or window, a light longed for but beyond reach.[51]

Not all of life in Dvinsk consisted of unrelenting struggle with the flat question, the Jewish question, the money question, the weather question. A quarter of a mile south of Shosseynaya, a wooden bridge for carts and pedestrians crossed the river and provided a vantage point from which to contemplate the Dvina and the "flat plains" around the city—a flat landscape with a strong horizon. Rothko's brothers remembered skating on the river in winter, swimming in it during the summer; there were family picnics, walks after dinner, the weekly peasant markets, stealing rides to school on peasant carts, and an active social life with friends who shared their political views.[52]

Political and economic pressures, however, forced Jacob Rothkowitz to emigrate. He feared conscription of his two oldest sons into the czar's army; and Dvinsk, while it had no pogroms, did have its terrors. "We all lived in fear," said Moise. According to one family story, the beheading of a relative by a Cossack also influenced their decision to leave. In fact, so many of their relatives had already emigrated to the United States that "we had more family here than we had in Russia." But mainly Jacob left because his business was failing. "He went broke and couldn't make a go of it," said Moise. "He couldn't make a living," Sonia recalled. "My father was a druggist and you never saw a bigger-hearted man. Anybody that came with a hard luck story, he helped them out." Jacob Rothkowitz was a "wise man," an avid reader, a quiet dreamer, a political idealist, the neighborhood philanthropist; but "he was not a great businessman."[53]

. . .

Mark described vividly to me once: you don't know what it is to be a Jewish kid dressed in a suit that is a Dvinsk not an American suit travelling across America and not able to speak English.

Robert Motherwell

Jacob Rothkowitz did have a younger brother who was an able businessman. In 1891, at nineteen, Sam Rothkowitz had emigrated to Portland, Oregon. By 1899 he had married; his wife, Bessie, was from New York City, and they eventually had two children, Sylvia and Hazel. Sam Rothkowitz changed his name to Weinstein when he formed a partnership in the clothing business (New York Outfitting Company) with Nate Weinstein, the oldest son in a family of twelve that also came from Michaleshek. Three of Nate's brothers (Moe, Abe, and Joe) eventually came to Portland; they did not get along with Nate—"nobody liked him," one nephew recalled, "he was the oldest brother and the rich one"—so they started their own clothing business, Weinstein Brothers, with branches in Seattle and Tacoma, Washington.[54] By the time Jacob arrived in Portland, he had a large extended family on the west coast, some of whose members, like his brother Sam, were quite well-off.

Choosing America over Palestine, where his Zionist beliefs might have led him and where some Dvinsk Zionists were already settling, Jacob was valuing family attachments and economic opportunity over his historic Jewish identity—a step toward modernization. The rest of the Rothkowitz family remained in Dvinsk, so that the young Rothko had at once been freed from a paternal authority that consigned him to *cheder* and abandoned to the economic uncertainties and political dangers of the Pale. In 1912 Moise and Albert left Dvinsk, but without passports; they made part of the trip in a railroad car and "travelled through Poland in a covered wagon," bribing soldiers along the way. After their long, anxious journey—and a wait for several days in a baggage room before they could get on a ship—the two were so relieved to get a place that they threw overboard a trunk of books and food their mother had packed for them. Now "they didn't want to have anything to do with Russia." On December 31, 1912, Moise and Albert sailed, steerage, from Bremen, Germany, arriving January 16, 1913, at Ellis Island, where they were met by relatives.[55]

In the early summer of 1913, three years after Jacob's departure, Kate, Sonia, and Marcus Rothkowitz paid one kopek each to cross the Dvina by ferry, then boarded a train at the Libau Station, to travel to Libau, a port on the Baltic Sea. Avoiding the dangerous illegality of the journey of Moise and Albert, and avoiding the cramped conditions and miserable food of steerage, they sailed second class on the SS *Czar*, from Libau to Brooklyn, landing on August 17, 1913.[56] After a ten-day visit with a branch of the Weinstein family in New Haven, Connecticut—where Marcus was introduced to baseball—the three, all wearing "badges that said we couldn't speak English," made the two-week journey to Portland.[57]

Later in life Rothko remembered an "exhausting, unforgettable journey." He wondered "whether they were ever going to get to the end of it." On his arrival, he felt painfully self-conscious—ashamed. He often told his first wife, Edith Sachar, how "his mother had fixed him up with one of these Buster Brown shirts and he was very embarrassed by it when he came to this country." Rothko told Robert Motherwell: "You don't know what it is to be a Jewish kid dressed in a suit that is a Dvinsk not an American idea of a suit travelling across America and not able to speak English."[58] Shame is a social emotion, usually experienced as a sense of public exposure, nakedness, being looked at and seen through; Rothko, however, felt ashamed of his clothing. Yet it's not as if he disembarked at Ellis Island in the tattered rags of a passenger in steerage. Traveling second class and landing in Brooklyn, Rothko wore his Buster Brown Dvinsk suit. What embarrassed *him* was the parental effort, coercive and excessive, to "civilize" the boy from the Pale and transform him into a model bourgeois child, an effort that only succeeded in marking him as out of place, an alien. He was embarrassed, in short, by *both* his poor Russian-Jewish origins *and* their denial.

Most of all, he resented his enforced migration. He "was never able to forgive," he angrily declared, his "transplantation to a land where he never felt entirely at home."[59] A strong sense of displacement informs a powerful painting of the 1930s, *Street Scene* (1936; color plate 1). The painting's title leads us to expect a realistic treatment of human activities—working, playing—of people at home in their urban environment; but Rothko's people are still, almost frozen, caught between two juxtaposed environments that are rendered symbolically. The three human figures—an adult and two children—are a family dressed warmly against the dark cold, and they are dressed and grouped formally, placed atop four gray steps which form a stage or pedestal. In this very frontal painting, they are displayed as if they were public statuary. The adult, who can be seen either as a bearded Jewish wise man or as a woman wearing a fur coat, combines mother and father in a single powerful presence who enfolds, protects, and directs the children forward into the picture plane. The children, gently but firmly coerced, look grim and worried. Some movement—along a diagonal line from right rear to left front—is suggested by the positions of the children's legs; but it looks as though any forward movement would merely drop them into the dark brown space at the left of the steps.

At the left a series of tan horizontal rectangles, with four vertical rectangles inside, creates a classical facade: blank, impersonal, geometrical. The structure appears flat, as if it might be a stage set; its architecture suggests some kind of public building—a government office, a railroad station, a prison, or a mausoleum. This monumental structure is replicated by another behind it, beginning an infinite regress; there are suggestions of death in its tomblike appearance and in the way the dark brown behind the human figures seems to reveal what is really behind these classical facades, namely, a dark void.

At the right a purely abstract, freely painted area creates a bleak, chilly, dense, confused environment, from which the human figures appear to be emerging. The curved dark brown shape descending from the top right corner makes it look as though a dark curtain has been pulled back to expose a thick gray substrate that is deeper, more primitive, and more powerful than the shaped areas. Like the monumental architecture, this formless space seems to recede toward infinity; yet it also rolls forward, absorbing the left arm of the adult, casting a gray light on the left sides of the children and enveloping the stairs.[60] Both sides of the painting, then, create environments that are anonymous and alien to human feeling. Each side does have its attractions: the tan gives warmth, the geometrical order a soothing regularity to the left; a mysterious glow emanates from within the cool gray. Yet each side also points up what the other lacks: the structure's rigid formality offers peace without vigor; the thick gray creates a force without order or clarity. As a result, the family, haunted by what is behind them, shadowed by what is to come, is radically displaced, caught between two worlds, neither of which is comfortable, familiar, homelike.

Street Scene, painted during the Depression, painted in fact while Rothko was working for the WPA, has a clear social dimension. Confronted with a blank, impersonal, public order, the family becomes a haven, but one which, in its own parentally imposed structure, ends up by replicating the heartless public world. Seen clearly, the family looks like public statuary situated in a dark void, but even then it remains vulnerable to obscure, perhaps interior, forces. *Street Scene* sharply divides public from interior, only to pull them together in the human figures, who cannot successfully integrate them. But in making his public, social comment, Rothko gained resonance by drawing on his own inner experience, most of all on his forced "transplantation." His painting thus conveys homelessness; it dramatizes apprehensions of moving out of a cold, chaotic world (which cannot be fully put behind) and moving toward a new and mysterious—perhaps grand, perhaps stifling—environment. Finally, the painting's evocation of a displacement possibly culminating in death had been Rothko's actual experience of migration.

Despite Sonia's reluctance to come, the elation of their journey to the New World was what stuck in her memory: "We all thought we were coming to Heaven."[61] Certainly, Rothko, his sister, and his mother were leaving the insecurities and terrors of life in the Pale; they could look forward to a joyful reunion with Jacob, Moise, and Albert; and they had been sent enough money to travel second class, thus avoiding the general immigrant fate in steerage and the indignities of Ellis Island.

By the time they arrived in Portland, Sam Weinstein's family had prepared a two-story wooden frame house for the Rothkowitzes at 834 Front Street. Located at the southern end of the Jewish ghetto (known as "Little Russia") in southwest Portland, the house looked west toward the forested hills of Portland and east toward the Willamette River and, beyond, to the misty, snow-topped grandeur of Mount Hood.[62] "We had a big party the night they came," Moise recalled.[63]

But whatever hopes for a freer and more stable life Rothko brought to the United States were soon upset. Jacob, who had suffered from chronic stomach problems for many years, was already seriously ill by the time his wife, daughter, and youngest son arrived in Portland. Seven months later—on March 27, 1914—Jacob died of a colon cancer. "We took care of him to the very last day, all of us," said Moise. "We were all around his bed when he died. We watched him die."[64]

On Sunday, March 29, a funeral service was held at the Front Street house and Jacob Rothkowitz, aged fifty-five, was buried in the cemetery of the Ahavai Shalom synagogue, where both Sam and Nate Weinstein were prominent members. The more secular Rothkowitz family, not being members, were voted the "burial privilege" at a special meeting of the synagogue's board of trustees.[65]

. . .

Dvinsk/Portland

To be rooted is perhaps the most important and least recognized need of the human soul.

Simone Weil

Dore Ashton noticed Rothko's fondness for words that have the prefix "trans," words like "transcend," or "translate," or "transplant."[66] In Latin, the preposition "trans" means "across, to or on the farther side of, beyond, over." The English prefix suggests a crossing, a movement over boundaries—as in a migration. In 1913, more than a million immigrants entered the United States; many of them came from Eastern Europe; many of these were Jewish; some of these Eastern European Jews were children; many of these children came one or two or three years after their fathers had preceded them; and possibly some of these children lost their fathers soon after being reunited with them. Rothko nonetheless experienced his migration as an event unique to him; it affected him profoundly.

Rothko's stories of Russia—schoolboys throwing rocks, Cossacks' whips, mass graves—mainly emphasized persecutory violence. From this point of view, leaving Dvinsk was justified as a necessary move toward both security and freedom. In fact, as I will suggest later on, had Rothko and his family remained in Dvinsk, they would have been uprooted or killed during the First World War; and had they survived that and continued in Dvinsk, they would have been exterminated by the Nazis in the Second World War. Yet, leaving Dvinsk created a rupture in Rothko's life, severing him from his native place just as his childhood was ending. "Doesn't it make you feel lonesome?" In America, he had been liberated from czarist oppression, but he also had been removed from his flat, his street, his school, his town, from relatives and close friends, from his language, his culture, his climate; all of these, no matter how oppressive or frightening they sometimes felt, were now lost.

Rothko had never, as he later said, been "able to forgive this transplantation to a land where he never felt entirely at home." As a child, Rothko had no voice in the family decision to leave; nor did he have the choice of staying. Even Sonia, who was twenty when Jacob left in 1910, had been told by her father that she *must* leave. "Parents may be voluntary or involuntary emigrants, but children are always 'exiled': they are not the ones who decide to leave, and they cannot decide to return at will."[67] Imposed upon him partly by czarist harassment and partly by his father's failures as a businessman, Rothko's migration *felt* like exile, a fate he did not choose and one that made him angry as well as sad.

An immigrant child may be vulnerable to helplessness and confusion; but being less formed, more curious and flexible, more open to new sensations, a child is also better able to learn a new language, adopt new customs, absorb a new culture than is, say, a middle-aged adult. A child, in short, can evolve a new life, a new home, a new identity. Yet Rothko resisted such assimilation, as if he wished to preserve what he had left, keeping it silently alive inside him. About this much, he *could* choose.

A self can emerge only from within a context—a family, a society, a culture. Migration, which moves the self beyond its stabilizing structures, its familiar supports, creates an inner diffusion, a fear the self may simply disperse into the new environment, so that it, too, will be lost. In Dvinsk, Rothko had belonged to a social group itself marked as not belonging, and one—given his father's original antagonism toward the town's rabbis and his own eventual antagonism toward *cheder*—he did not quite belong to. In his family, Rothko had been set apart by the eight years between himself and Albert, by his "sensitive" nature and fragile health, by his *cheder* education, his standing as the resident "hebrew infant prodigy." In America, he could experience some sense of continuity, a feeling that he was still himself, by setting himself slightly apart, viewing his new world warily, with suspicions he had developed in a Settlement of Pale town where there *had* been dangerous enemies. It's as though he could best hold himself together by holding himself apart: melancholy, distrustful, inwardly removed, somewhere else—a boy in America writing poems in Hebrew on Old Testament themes. *Street Scene,* in fact, shows him frozen, suspended between two worlds, belonging to neither.

A child migrating with his or her family has the possible advantage of a warm, protective structure with which to help manage this (literally) unsettling experience, except that the parents are likely to be distracted by their own upheaval. In Rothko's case, he had in effect been abandoned by his father three years before his own migration, three years in which to prepare to leave, hope to leave, fear to leave. And when he finally did arrive in Portland, the father who had forced the family move was preoccupied with his own illness, which also required the attention of Rothko's mother. Then, after six months, Jacob Rothkowitz died.

Moise believed that his father died "due to lonesomeness and leaving the family and going through an ordeal of being broke," as if Jacob had heroically sacrificed his own life to save his family. Albert felt, on the other hand, that the family had been "left in the lurch" by Jacob's death.[68]

Marcus attributed great importance to his father's death. In his biography for the Yale yearbook for the class of 1925, where his classmates listed academic prizes, social clubs, and athletic teams, Rothko mentioned the date of his father's death. At Yale, his friend Aaron Director recalled, Rothko was still "bitter about poverty" and his "father's dying."⁶⁹ Rothko told his daughter, Kate, that, after his father died, "he felt compelled to go to synagogue every day for a year"—"apparently the rest of the family did not participate"—as if such strict submission to the rules and rigor of religion made him feel that his father was still alive. "But he did not finish the year and finally just swore that he would never go into a synagogue again." This story both contradicts and resembles Rothko's account of his "complete break" from *cheder* and temple attendance at the age of nine. In both stories, Rothko suddenly, in the absence of his father, refuses a rigid religious regime, leading him to reject the Jewish religion itself.

Both narratives at first sound somewhat suspect, because of their insistence on an *absolute* break. Yet Jacob Rothkowitz's departure from Dvinsk would have seemed to his seven-year-old son, and his death *was,* such an absolute rift. His father's absence freed Rothko to respond, to retaliate, in kind, by turning his back on the religious order imposed by the father. So Rothko's grieving for his father eventually turned into an open rebellion, as if he found it easier to be angry than sad; Jacob's death also intensified his youngest son's feeling that life was treating him unjustly, that he couldn't rely on or trust people, especially males in authority.

Dr. Albert Grokest became Rothko's physician in the late 1950s; he also became a friend, one of the few to whom Rothko ever spoke about these painful events. What struck Dr. Grokest about Rothko was his mistrust, a quality that made him a difficult patient; he would not even let Grokest touch him during his first examination. "What impressed me about Mark Rothko and his distrust was his referrals to his father's departure from Dvinsk," Dr. Grokest recalled.

> That bothered him a great deal and he would make references to it without giving specifics except that he was very much upset by it. [And] once Rothko and his mother and brothers and sister came here to the States to Portland and were all united with his father, the next thing his father does is die. . . . And he made reference to that as a terrible experience.

At ten, transplanted to a wholly new environment, Rothko had been left in the lurch—financially and emotionally.

But within the family Jacob, dead, became the revered father who had sacrificed his own life in saving his family from the Pale—a family icon that was difficult to criticize. So other male authorities, beginning with Rothko's oldest brother, Moise, who now assumed the paternal role in the family and from whom Rothko expected financial support during his early years in New

York, provided the target for Rothko's angry disappointment. At the same time, his father's death left Rothko eager to find a reliable male authority, a desire that would sometimes make him too dependent, or too passively trusting.

Rothko later conceived of his art as a kind of romanticized migration, "an unknown adventure in an unknown space," a journey to freedom.[70] Yet, he also spoke of his work as "tragic." During the 1930s, Rothko said, and he said it more than once, that "the only serious thing is death; nothing else is to be taken seriously." In a 1958 lecture at the Pratt Institute, he declared the first ingredient of his work to be "a clear preoccupation with death—intimations of mortality."[71] His paintings of the 1950s and 1960s—works such as *Number 12, 1951* (color plate 15)—contain no people, no places, no objects, none of those parts of the world to which we feel attached, on which we affectionately, or anxiously, rely. In Rothko's paintings, we are confronted with solitude, emptiness, diffusion, loss. Yet we are also pulled into a new world, an unknown space, filled with a sensuous, colored light. If, as in the mural projects he began to produce in 1958, Rothko could fill the walls of a room with such works, he would transplant himself (and others) into an environment where he *did* feel at home. "I have made a place."

. . .

Jacob Rothkowitz's death left the young Rothko solely in the care of his mother, the place he had mostly occupied from the age of seven, when his father had left Dvinsk. By the time he began high school in 1918, Rothko, his older sister and brothers now married, was living alone with his widowed mother. There are good reasons to think that, all along, Kate Rothkowitz had been the most powerful person in the family. The differences between his parents were suggested by Moise: "My father was a quiet dreamer. He'd dream a lot. My mother was the woman behind him."[72] Jacob was strict, quiet, philanthropic, idealistic; Kate was energetic, forceful, and practical, a contrast that stuck in the mind of their youngest child.

As an adult Rothko perceived his mother as "very powerful" and "a little amusing." He would make "friendly fun" of "her accent, her way of bustling around." "She didn't know what he was doing as an artist, but he loved her." Affectionate kidding covered up social, cultural, and, once Rothko left Portland, physical distance. Kenneth Rabin tells the poignant story of his grandmother, Kate Rothkowitz, eagerly awaiting Rothko's arrival for a Portland visit: "from early morning to late night she sat on the sofa," often pulling back the curtain and "looking out." "She just couldn't wait to see her baby." And if she did not understand her son's work, she was "*very* supportive" of him, "defensive and protective" of Rothko, "whatever he did." According to Rabin, she even referred to him, proudly, as "my son, the painter."[73]

But if Jacob became an icon, Kate was remembered more as an elemental force, one very difficult to contend with on any but a kidding basis. Kenneth Rabin recalled that the "classic story" of his grandmother was that "you wake her up at four in the morning and say, 'we're climbing Mt. Hood, grandma, you want to go?' And she would say, 'I'll be right there.' She didn't want to be left out of *anything*." All members of the family stress her "bustling" energy and force. She was "very passionate, very strong willed"; "a very determined woman"; "a good manager" who was the "driving force" behind the family; "a very controlling person"; "a tough cookie," "very strong"; "a very powerful woman, center stage in every group." When forced to move in with her daughter's family during the Depression, Kate "took over." "She gave my mother fits; she wanted to run everything," according to one grandson.[74] Rothko told many people that he had been raised by his sister and that he was closer to her than to his brothers. "My mother adored him," said Kenneth Rabin. "It was her baby brother that she raised and he could do no wrong." But at least one of her grandchildren doubts that Kate Rothkowitz, "a very jealous woman," would have permitted her daughter to replace her.[75] The very determined mother of an equally determined son, Kate Rothkowitz was the woman behind Rothko—perhaps, he felt, a little too close behind.

Two photographs (figs. 3, 4), probably taken in 1912 when Kate was in her early forties, reveal a short, sturdy, sensuously beautiful and straightforward woman. The picture with her two older sons conveys melancholy depths; the second photo, emphasizing the proud upward tilt of her chin, expresses a stubborn determination. About twenty years later, in a rare attempt to explore his own emotional backgrounds, Rothko painted *Portrait of Rothko's Mother* (n.d.; color plate 2). What he produced was a painting which conveys a complex sense of his mother as a woman both oppressed and oppressive. By the time of the *Portrait,* Kate Rothkowitz's melancholy had hardened, through age and adversity, into a lonely, bitter determination.

At forty, in Russia, she possessed a proud, almost aristocratic bearing. At sixty, in America, the thick mass of her body, the masculine shape of her face, her deep-set, heavily shadowed eyes, her tightly shut lips, the grim downward curve of her mouth all give her an attitude of tough resentment. More resistant than yielding, she conveys no softness. Plain, direct, and straightforward, she conveys no sophistication, no intellectuality, no playfulness—little, in short, with which her son the painter might connect.

Yet Rothko does connect with her, looking empathetically, going deeper than the powerhouse grandmother of family story. He depicts his usually bustling mother in a moment of inwardness, as she looks away from him (and us) and into herself. But she is no dreamer like her husband; her heavy lids and sad eyes with bags under them reveal a person by no means defeated, but one worn, preoccupied with losses remembered from the past or anticipated in the future. In portraying his mother, then, Rothko emphasized her determination, her lack of warmth, and her sorrow. Rothko's idealism and intellectuality derived from his father; his brooding melancholy and strength of will derived from his mother. Like her, he liked to occupy stage center, and he later liked to speak of "controlling the situation" in reference to the reception of his paintings.[76] To follow his own ambitions and to separate himself from a mother who didn't like to be left out of anything, Rothko eventually made a transcontinental move, a migration to New York City. Rothko's closeness to his powerful mother required a literal distancing.

This play of closeness and distance provides the central drama in Rothko's only explicitly autobiographical work, *The Rothkowitz Family* (c. 1936; color plate 3).[77] Here, the mother holds up her chubby, sleeping infant for the father's adoring gaze, as if in a painting of the Holy Family. Rothko binds his three figures together by enclosing them within a single, long, curving line that starts upward along the top of the mother's head, moves down her forehead, up across the father's right arm and back, then down his left arm to her hands. Expressionistic distortions also pull the family members together. The mother's grotesquely elongated arms enfold the child; the father's unrealistically bent head emphasizes his intense contemplation of his son; and the infant's right hand seems pressed to his father's cheek.

Yet this web of familial interconnections contains strong tensions and separations. The intense bond between father and son excludes the mother; and if the son becomes the center of the father's attention, the father's gaze seems more grimly searching than warmly loving. The center of the mother's attention, however, is the father, toward whom she looks apprehensively, as if fearing his disapproval. Her pained expression also suggests that she feels burdened by the weight of her child; and her right arm has been disjoined from her body, as if she were a puppet producing her baby on her husband's command. Meanwhile, the well-fed infant sleeps, blissfully oblivious to the family drama. Yet the white baby blanket draped over the mother's arms ominously suggests a stone altar; the infant's splayed limbs, fleshy nudity, pure white innocence, and peaceful sleep qualify him as a vulnerable, even luscious, offering. Is the child held up for adoration or for sacrifice?

But what preoccupies the painter in this familial drama is not the child but the mother, whom Rothko has made the focus of emotional interest by giving her massive size, foreground position, and psychological complexity. At first her face appears to be a flat, pale mask with a look of pained apprehension; but the blue-gray areas within and around the edges of the mask suggest a brooding sorrow that contrasts with the pink-cheeked unawareness of the father. As in *Street Scene,* the family forms a tight but artificial and coerced unity, with some hints of potential tragedy.

With his death, Jacob Rothkowitz became a simplified but powerful icon in the mind of his son. Jacob may have pulled the strings, but Kate Rothkowitz, strong-willed, sad, and energetically alive, loomed as a complex and *real* presence. In both the *Portrait* and *The Rothkowitz Family,* Rothko depicted his mother as more melancholy than warm. Yet he paints as *very* aware of how *she* feels. Both mother and son were, after all, victims of the father's severity ("all the rules and rigor of religion were never sufficiently observed by his mother, not sufficiently to Mark's rigid father"), victims of his business failures, his money troubles, his absence, his illness, and finally his death. Rothko's sense of deprivation, his empathetic identification with his mother, and his need to separate from her would all inform his creative enterprise. After 1949— shortly after his mother's death—he would begin to create works that were large, commanding presences, beautiful and seductive, aggressive and invasive, works that address a solitary viewer, works that evoke a relation that is silent and empathetic, yet distanced and separate.

• • •

> *You are not from the Castle, you are not from the village, you aren't anything. Or rather, unfortunately, you are something, a stranger.*
>
> Kafka, *The Castle*

In Dvinsk the Rothkowitz family had some professional status but not much money. In Portland, after Jacob's death, they had neither status nor money. In Portland, Marcus—without an American past, without the English language— was a "nobody." Or rather, unfortunately, he was something, a "greenhorn," as new immigrants were then derisively called. Initiation to America entailed a series of humiliations.

His Weinstein uncles had accumulated both position and money, and, adding to the sting, the proud Rothkowitzes were at first forced into economic dependence on them. "The class distinction in Russia was so great; if you had any kind of education, you were above the laborer, you wouldn't even talk to them," Sonia recalled. So when she was offered a job in a Weinstein alteration room, she found the position demeaning: "I was so insulted that I came home and never went back to work." Portland was no "heaven." Albert and Marcus worked for the Weinsteins at various times, as had Jacob before his family arrived. But Rothko "resented the Weinstein family terribly. They were rich and he was poor. He thought they treated him like a poor relation." They belonged; he did not. He felt patronized, embarrassed, angry. The Weinsteins came to stand for a Jewish philistinism that Rothko, feeding off his deprivation, loved to hate—"vilifying his relatives because he had to work selling newspapers and piling pants."[78]

Still, the Rothkowitzes were able to make do. Sonia worked as a dental assistant. Moise opened a pharmacy. Albert worked for Moise for a while, then opened his own pharmacy. Kate Rothkowitz, who had circumspectly laundered at night in Dvinsk, took in boarders. In September of 1913 Marcus, less than a month in America and knowing no English, was enrolled at Failing School, where no formal instruction in English was provided. Immigrant children were all placed in the first grade and expected to learn the language simply by listening to it. At the end of his first day of school, the ten-year-old first grader came home bloodied and harassed because he couldn't speak the language.[79]

"We were all so green," Sonia said. "We didn't know anything."[80] Rothko had a new language, new gestures, foods, styles of dress, codes of behavior—a whole new culture to absorb. For a young boy, perhaps especially for one saddened by the loss of his father, this meant a flood of sensations from a new physical environment. At the northern end of a long, flat agricultural valley, Portland has rainy winters and a wet, hazy atmosphere much of the rest of the year. The young Rothko liked to hike through the forested Portland hills, climbing to the top and looking out across the valley, a kind of vantage point he did not have in Dvinsk. Here, he could see the snow-covered summits of Mount Hood to the east and Mount St. Helen's to the north, peaks that, in the hazy summers, seem to float above the valley floor. Rothko later recalled the time he'd spent "in his youth in front of the endless space of the landscape of Oregon lying covered by wintry snows, in front of the monumental emptiness that is nothingness and at the same time a part of 'all' "—a memory that seems to combine Portland and Dvinsk, as if the new environment merged with the old and as if both cities persisted in the painter's memory primarily as natural, rather than social, environments and as landscapes of emptiness, loss.[81]

The young Rothko also had to work, selling newspapers on street corners in downtown Portland. Max Gordon, a Rothko cousin, recalled that he and Rothko sold papers on opposite corners at ten o'clock at night, when the morning papers would come out. It was a job that Rothko "hated." With good reason. He vividly remembered the cold.[82] Sometimes there were fights for the best locations, and the boys were also exploited by distributors who refused to buy back unsold newspapers. As one contemporary of Rothko's remembered, "I was ten years old when I started selling papers. It wasn't very safe to go downtown and sell papers before you could handle yourself on the street. The boys were very jealous of the corners on which they sold and interlopers were made unwelcome. . . . Competition was very heavy; it sometimes resulted in fights, black eyes and bloody noses. Each one had to bring money back to his family." Rothko was a frequent victim: "Mark was a little chubby boy and he used to come home beaten up every time," his sister recalled.[83] Marcus Rothkowitz had been freed from the Cossacks of Dvinsk to learn democratic capitalism on the streets of Portland.

The strangeness of the New World was tempered by the strong sense of familiarity created by Portland's Jewish community. In the Portland of 1910 Jews constituted about 5,000 out of the total 207,000 population. The German Jews, who had begun to settle in the city as early as the 1860s, were generally now rather prosperous; the Eastern European Jews, beginning to arrive in the 1890s, had moved into the southwest section of downtown Portland. There were numbers of Italians, too, but the neighborhood was intensely Jewish, with four synagogues, a Jewish Shelter House, a B'nai B'rith, a settlement house called Neighborhood House, delicatessens, kosher markets, bakeries, drug stores, tailor shops, and many other Jewish-owned and run small businesses.[84]

By September of 1914, the start of Rothko's second year in the school system, the Rothkowitzes had moved from Front Street to a similar two-story wooden frame house at 232 Lincoln Avenue. The next year they moved around the corner to a flat at 538 2nd Street, where they lived until after Rothko's graduation from high school.[85] Along with the rest of the southwest Portland ghetto, both of these houses have vanished, razed in order to build the twenty-five-story luxury apartments now occupying the site. On Lincoln Avenue, the Rothkowitzes were living in a neighborhood slightly more crowded and commercial than that of their Front Street house; but both the Lincoln and 2nd Street addresses were just one block across the boundary separating the Failing from the Shattuck school district. Now, instead of attending Failing, "located in the immigrant district along the southwest waterfront," Rothko was enrolled at the Shattuck School, "located to the north and west in a district" where "slightly more affluent families were likely to reside."[86] Shattuck was a better school, and the Rothkowitzes, continuing to value education, apparently moved in order to take advantage of that.

Many children respond to the death of a parent by having trouble at school; not Rothko, who, while he may have rejected the synagogue, remained intensely committed to his father's faith in education. In 1913 at Failing he was a ten-year-old first grader who spoke no English. In the fall of 1914, he

Chapter Two

was placed in the third grade at Shattuck, then advanced to the fifth grade for the spring term. At the time the Portland elementary schools continued through the ninth grade. Rothko completed the last four years in just three (1915–18). By June 1921, eight years after his arrival in Portland, he had graduated from Lincoln High School in just three and a half years and he had been admitted to Yale University with a scholarship. Looking back, Rothko pronounced the program at Lincoln "ridiculously easy."[87]

Like many immigrants, like many Jewish immigrants, Rothko confidently and energetically adapted to his new environment, as if migration and the death of his father *had* freed him. His superior verbal and intellectual gifts set him apart, transforming the "hebrew infant prodigy" into an American adolescent prodigy.

• • •

While in high school Marcus was a good student, interested more in literature and social studies, well versed with the English language, an excellent speaker and loved to debate; he was quite outspoken and didn't hesitate to voice his opinions, which were quite on the liberal tone and at the time not too acceptable by many.

Max Naimark

As an adolescent, Rothko was smart, articulate, contentious. His classmate Aaron Director described the Rothko of Lincoln High School as an "assertive" boy who "liked to talk a lot."[88] Rothko's graduation photograph (fig. 4) reveals a chubby, earnestly intellectual, and slightly aggrieved young man, one more likely to impress in the classroom than on the dance floor or the athletic field. If there were any romantic involvements or sexual episodes, no memory of them survives. His energies, beyond work and school, were turned toward loftier cultural and political concerns.

Rothko had been responsive to music from the time he was a boy, and he remained so throughout his life. Both of his brothers played the mandolin; Rothko could play both mandolin and piano by ear, claiming to be self-taught. Like his father and sister, the young Rothko was an avid reader, especially engaged by the Greeks and by the theater. At Lincoln High he elected a special course in the dramatic arts.[89]

What experience, if any, did the young Rothko have with art? He later declared that he was "not exposed to paintings at all as a boy," "or even in college." As he told one art critic, "he learned painting from his contemporaries in their studios." In painting, as in music, he liked to think of himself as self-taught. He didn't like to acknowledge dependence on male authority; and he liked to stress the humanistic content, rather than the craft, of his painting. He did not take any of the children's art classes given by the Portland Art Museum; he did not study art at Lincoln High School, or later at Yale.[90] Yet during Rothko's time in elementary school, the Portland school district initiated an innovative art program, involving museum visits, slide talks, and photographic reproductions of works that were displayed in the halls and classrooms.[91] So Rothko did have *some* early awareness of art. Relatives recall that, during high school and college, he liked to draw, particularly when he was supposed to be doing something else. While at Lincoln High, Rothko worked in the shipping department of Sam and Nate Weinstein's New York Outfitting Company. "At times," said Ed Weinstein, "Mark would occupy himself by drawing and sketching on the store wrapping paper." One day Rothko was discovered drawing by his Uncle Nate, who "shook his head and observed, 'Marcus, why are you wasting your time? You will never be able to earn a living that way'."[92]

Succeeding academically, as if eager to adapt to American society, Rothko was also engaged with dissident politics, as if seeking a way to assimilate without betraying family and Jewish involvements with leftist causes. His whole family, Rothko later said, "followed and applauded the Russian Revolution." But its youngest son gave the family's left views a unique twist, by substituting the romantic individualism of anarchism for the collective consciousness of socialism. He "grew up as an anarchist," Rothko said. "While I was still in grade school I listened to Emma Goldman and to the I.W.W. orators who were plentiful on the West Coast in those days." Goldman spoke in Portland on her annual tours, one time provoking a local scandal. In August 1915, she lectured Portlanders on "Anarchism," "Free Love," "Nietzsche," and "Birth Control." Rothko did attend at least some of these talks. Her August 7 birth-control speech, however, was stopped by the police, who arrested her for distributing birth-control pamphlets. She was tried and fined $100.[93] A Russian Jewish emigré like himself, Emma Goldman appealed powerfully, because her romantic politics abolished all political, family, or temple authority.

At Lincoln High, Rothko's "College Preparatory Course" offered a conventional program of English, math, language (he took French), science, and arts (he elected Dramatic Arts) courses.[94] But some lasting intellectual interests were either formed or pursued in these classes. There, Rothko read the Greeks, with Greek tragedy and myth providing sources for many of his paintings in the early 1940s. As a high school student, he particularly admired Herodotus (whom, as late as 1949, he could quote from memory) because, rejecting

Thucydides' efforts at rational understanding of history, Herodotus viewed events as irrational and thus attributed them to the gods.[95] Many experiences in Rothko's first eighteen years—anti-Semitism, migration, the death of his father—had prepared him to accept a vision of life as irrational.

Socially, Lincoln High also helped sharpen the young Rothko's political sensitivities. Of the school's approximately nine hundred students, probably no more than 10 percent were Jewish; tensions, based on ethnic and class differences, were clear. WASPs from affluent families in the Portland hills controlled the school's social clubs and athletic teams. Some of the Jews, like Rothko, were recent immigrants who came from poorer families in southwest Portland; others, like Aaron Director, came from families who were somewhat better off. Either way, Jews were excluded from the social clubs. In a letter to *The Cardinal,* the school magazine, Rothko's friend Max MacCoby complained of "race prejudice" in selection of club members: "Anyone who has a name ending in 'off' or 'ski' is taboo and branded a Bolshevik."[96] Rothko himself was the target of anti-Semitic slurs. In the June 1921 issue of *The Cardinal,* which served as a yearbook for his graduating class, Rothko's classmates sneeringly predicted that he would become a "Pawn Broker." Back pages of this issue were filled with advertisements and old jokes enlivened by inserting student names—e.g., "M. Rothkowitz: 'Oh, I am so sleepy'. D. Piper: 'Give me a rock and I'll rock you to sleep'." The exchange is not very funny, but it is very hostile. Elsewhere in *The Cardinal,* stereotypes about Jewish clannishness inspired bad jokes about the close friendships between Rothko and Max Naimark and between Director and MacCoby.[97]

As a high school student and after, Rothko, as Naimark remembered, was "an excellent speaker" who "loved to debate."[98] At Lincoln, however, Jews were excluded from the Tologeion Debating Society. Looking for an alternative, Rothko, at the beginning of his senior year, revived *The Cardinal*'s "Contributors' Club," a letters-to-the-editor section which he hoped to make "an open forum for the expression of ideas, opinions of everyone in the school." Rothko launched the project with a youthful, high-minded idealism:

> The ability to think clearly and to set our thoughts in convincing order is always useful, is always a necessity, no matter what walk of life we choose as our own.
>
> It is that ability which we must have in order to perform well the sacred duties of every member of society. It is that which will safeguard our political institutions, which will irradicate [sic] our social evils and, in short, which will solve the great mass of problems confronting society. If we have the power of intelligent thinking and expression, we shall not

fall a prey to the smooth tongues of politicians or self-seeking economists.[99]

The viewpoint here is more Jeffersonian liberal than Emma Goldman radical; but the first installment, containing letters from the editor's buddies Max MacCoby and Max Naimark, did insert a critical perspective into *The Cardinal*'s usual accounts of athletic deeds and tea parties. MacCoby, calling it "absurd that a high school should spend more time and energy on athletics than it does in debating," urged a course in debating. Naimark complained of the hardship on students, like himself, who were working their way through school but who were always forced to buy new books because the school board constantly changed texts.[100] But open forums, training in debate, and economic realities had no wider audience than Rothko and his circle of friends, and the Contributors' Club soon folded.

At the Weinstein business, Sonia Rothkowitz, conscious of her family's former status, felt the role of laborer to be demeaning; at Lincoln High her youngest brother, even further displaced, was joked about and discriminated against by status-conscious WASP students. *Cheder* imposed a harsh discipline but offered a sense of Jewish community; Lincoln was more liberal but made Rothko an outsider, making his cultural difference not something he chose to preserve but a fate he could not escape.

Still, whatever his resentments from Russian persecution, from his forced emigration, the death of his father, his family's poverty, the exclusions and insults he was subject to at Lincoln High, the seventeen-year-old Rothko was no social rebel. His anarchism seems to have been more romantic attitude than serious political program. By the time he was seventeen, Jackson Pollock, for example, had already determined to be "an Artist of some kind," had discovered alcohol and occult mysticism, and had twice been expelled from Manual Arts High School in Los Angeles, once for his contributions to the *Journal of Liberty* (which attacked the school's faculty) and once for getting into a fistfight with a physical education teacher.[101] Next to the adolescent Pollock, the young Rothko looks straight and dutiful, which he was.

"Monday at Lincoln," an essay which Rothko published in *The Cardinal* at the end of his junior year does, however, reveal deep resistance to the demands of school. Rothko starts by observing the "sleepiness and laziness" felt by himself and many others on Monday mornings.

> I set off to school on Monday morning with the sad thought of a week's hard work in my mind. And [as I] approach the school, the vision of a long, long road arises before me. The road is rough and bumpy. Milestones, marked Monday, Tuesday, Wednesday, Thursday, Friday, are

lined along the road. The last one is far, far away, beyond that point where the horizon meets the earth.

Rothko experiences the school week as a tedious routine, empty and meaningless, as if it were *merely* duty. But his response is less angry or combative than depressed and despairing. Rather than denouncing the authorities or the educational system, he blames himself, explaining boredom as the result of his lack of preparation. Over the weekend he usually postpones homework until Sunday night, but when that time comes around, he goes out. So he can't enjoy either the weekend (his lessons being on his mind "all the time") or the school week. As a solution, he proposes that homework be done on Friday, leaving the student free to enjoy the weekend and "fresh" on Monday morning.[102]

Rothko's discontent issues in no grand refusal of the sort that may have ended his days at *cheder*. Instead, he calls for a personal and superficial reform. He avoids the deeper issue—i.e., why he resists doing homework in the first place—but he does give moving expression to a feeling not just about school but about life: a depressed sense of grim necessity, of an endless and hollow task stretching out toward, and even beyond, "that point where the horizon meets the earth," as if life were a migration that could *never* be completed. At seventeen Rothko felt the emptiness and despair which would make him vulnerable to depressions throughout his life, but which, beginning in 1949, he would transform into empty bands of colored light.

Despite his resistance, despite his despair, Rothko was successful enough as a high school student to be awarded a Yale scholarship. And despite his success at Lincoln, Rothko remained a social outsider, a pariah subject to exclusions (the Tologeion Debating Society) and sneering jokes ("Pawn Broker"). He was "assertive," "quite outspoken and didn't hesitate to voice his opinions," but his anger about injuries was mainly intellectualized as political dissent and verbal debate. He was not yet ready to make a "complete break" with the American educational system or with the social assimilation it might provide.

For many of the Jews in southwest Portland, Neighborhood House, built in 1905 through the cooperation of Rabbi Stephen Wise and the Council of Jewish Women, provided a center for social and civic activities. Begun in an effort to promote Bible study among Jewish women, Neighborhood House by 1915 had shifted from religious to philanthropic aims. The Portland Hebrew School was there, but the settlement house—run by Ida Lowenberg, from one of the city's older German-Jewish families—also offered cooking and sewing classes for girls, manual arts for boys, sports, social events, English-language and American citizenship classes. Neighborhood House was now an institution for integrating the new immigrant population—largely Eastern European and orthodox—into American society. Moise and Albert learned English there; and at one point Rothko and his friends Max Naimark, Aaron Director, Gus Solomon, and Gilbert Sussman started a debating team there because the club at the high school excluded them.[103] Still, Rothko's relation to this community center was tangential; "he was outside that world," said Max Gordon. Rothko was as little interested in Jewish as in goyish social and athletic activities.

. . .

How does migration threaten the identity of the immigrant?

How does the immigrant threaten the identity of his or her new community?

In America, as Rothko was learning, social and political freedoms, like economic opportunities, had their ambiguities. Portland had a reputation as a progressive city, one reason Jewish immigrants settled there; but in the late teens and early twenties, the city, like the rest of the country, was dominated by reactionary politics. Certainly, there were no pogroms; but espousing radical positions at that time in Portland was *quite* dangerous.

American entry into the First World War in the spring of 1917 had bred a strenuous nationalism that demanded political loyalty and social conformity. "Huns" and "alien slackers" were the culprits, to be eliminated by the militant "Americanization" movement, led by such nativist drum-thumpers as the American Legion and the Daughters of the American Revolution. Earlier, assimilation of white immigrants had been permitted to proceed "naturally." In the late 1890s, however, settlements like Neighborhood House began to provide a friendly push toward Americanization; they were institutions of genteel absorption, but they were local, humane, and voluntary. But with the beginning of the First World War assimilation began to be coerced. The 1917 Espionage Act effectively made political dissent a crime, while the Sedition Act of the following year meted out a twenty-year prison term for anyone who, for example, spoke disparagingly of the U.S. government, its Constitution, or its flag. And these laws were enforced, particularly against members of the IWW, one of the few organizations in the country to express any skepticism about American participation in the war. In such a "highly charged" atmosphere, John Higham writes in *Strangers in the Land*, "a foreigner was well-advised to conduct himself with unusual circumspection."[104]

Foreigners needed to be circumspect—because patriots certainly were not. Portland was the same as the rest of the country, only more so. According to the city's historian, E. Kimbark MacColl, Portland "became the patriotic center of the Northwest" during the war, "achieving a per capita record of war bond sales unequalled in the United States."[105] So zealous was this nationalism that a pacifist city librarian who announced her refusal to buy war bonds was forced to resign. Oregon had its own "Americanization" organizations, such as the Guardians of Liberty and the Oregon Federation of Patriotic Societies. "We must hereafter have an Americanized America," declared the *Oregon Journal,* supporting the tough 1919 criminal syndicalism bill which made it a crime, among other things, to join the IWW. George Baker, a belligerent reactionary who was elected mayor of Portland in 1917, instigated a series of militant efforts to purify and unify his city. One of his professed goals was "the extermination of the IWW members congregated in this city." In September of that year a young Socialist met a train being loaded with soldiers and announced to them that they were going to fight in order to protect the Rockefeller fortune; he was arrested for violating the Espionage Act, tried in Portland, convicted, and sentenced to eighteen months. Another local radical, Dr. Marie Equi, called the war "The Big Barbecue" and ended up serving time in San Quentin. In February of 1919 a man was jailed simply for carrying an IWW banner in Portland. The union's headquarters were then raided and the mayor issued an order prohibiting meetings of workers and the carrying of banners announcing strikes. Just a few weeks later the IWW hall at 109 2nd Avenue—just four blocks from Rothko's home—was raided.[106]

When the war ended in late 1918, the Americanization crusade was left without its original demons ("Huns" and "slackers"), but thanks to the Bolshevik revolution welcomed by Rothko, his family, and many other Russian immigrants, new demons were not hard to find. "Reds" now became the national menace and, like the "slackers," many of the "reds" happened to be Jewish. In November of 1919 Attorney General J. Mitchell Palmer organized a series of raids across the country that resulted, the following month, in the deportation of 249 suspected radicals, who were dispatched, naturally, to Russia. Among them was Rothko's hero, Emma Goldman. According to MacColl, "there was actual fear, even in Oregon, that a Red revolution might begin, patterned after the successful Bolshevik revolution of November 1917." In Portland a flu epidemic in late 1918 was widely interpreted as a red plot. A new criminal syndicalism bill, "one of the strongest and most flexible anti-radicalism statutes in the United States," was passed in early 1921 by the Oregon legislature. A week later, at the start of Rothko's last term in high school, Lincoln Steffens, recently back from the Soviet Union, was denied use of the school auditorium for a speech, mainly because of pressure from Mayor Baker.[107]

The First World War, Americanization, and antiradicalism were not just happenings in some remote public world; they affected Rothko's life, directly and indirectly. His brother Albert was drafted and spent two years in the U.S. Army, stationed in nearby Vancouver, Washington.[108] Rothko's "transplantation," moreover, saved him from becoming a victim or casualty of the war, which began just a year after he left Dvinsk and effectively ended Russian emigration to the United States. During the war, the Jews of Dvinsk endured "unending trials and tribulations," Yudel Flior recalls. Men, up to the age of forty-three, were mobilized in the summer of 1914, and then sent to Vilna, a major assembly point for the czar's army. In the early stages of the war, trainloads of soldiers, canons, guns, ammunition were constantly passing through Dvinsk, headed west, to the front. Soon, the town's hospitals began to fill with wounded soldiers; schools were converted into hospitals; new structures were built for hospitals. During the spring and summer of 1915, as the Russians retreated and the Germans advanced, "Dvinsk became an important military centre," now filling up with fresh soldiers and their equipment.[109]

The defeats of the Russian army required an explanation, which is to say, a scapegoat; the Jews were assigned this role, and soon trainloads of Jewish refugees, evacuated from Lithuania as potential collaborators with the Germans, were passing through Dvinsk, headed east, away from the front, into the interior of Russia. Yet the German army continued to advance. In the north, the Kaiser's Eighth Army moved across Lithuania toward Dvinsk, capturing and, in Menke Katz's words, reducing "to ash the comely/village of Michalishek."[110]

In Dvinsk, meanwhile, reinforcements were brought in, fortifications built. "Masses of artillery were placed in position to defend the Dvina at all costs," Flior writes. The Germans bombarded the town with planes and artillery. Beginning in August 1915, strategic industries and their workers were evacuated; the families of military officers were evacuated; and Dvinsk Jews were evacuated, "the coaches, cattle-trucks and freight cars . . . jammed with fleeing humanity like barrels with herrings."[111]

The Germans were finally stopped on the other side of the Dvina, which for two years formed part of an eight-hundred-mile-long front line, stretching south from Riga. The czar's Fifth Army, under General Ruzski, was now garrisoned along Shosseynaya Street.

Only about 12,000 of Dvinsk's 55,000 Jews survived the war.[112]

Rothko's migration protected him from the physical dangers of the war, but it also brought him to a country where, as a leftist Jew, his loyalty was suspect, his position insecure. At Lincoln High he encountered intense pressures toward patriotism and political conformity. By June, 1918—the end of Rothko's first term at the school—two hundred and sixty students had already enlisted in the armed services.[113] *The Cardinal* printed stories and letters from local boys at the front and urged students to correspond with them. There were continuous food, clothing, and War Savings Stamps drives, patriotic posters and essays ("What We Can Do To Help Win the War") and assemblies featuring military and Liberty Loan speakers. Students not participating were condemned as "slackers."

After the war, *Cardinal* writers turned their sights on subversives. One student warned that the members of the IWW "wish to control the upper and middle and lower classes, so that they can systematically starve, murder and destroy them in order that they may obtain the fruits for which others have strived and worked." Another proposed tightening immigration laws as a way of combatting IWW control over workers and concluded by echoing Mayor Baker: "Education can and will exterminate Bolshevism, anarchy and tyranny."[114] Rothko sought to create an "open forum" in *The Cardinal*; his fellow students wished to "exterminate" dissent.

. . .

I became a painter because I wanted to raise painting to the level of poignancy of music and poetry.

Mark Rothko

As a young man, Mark Rothko played the piano and mandolin; he also wrote poems, a few of which have survived.[115] Self-consciously poetic, their language discretely vague and conventional, their rhythms stiff, their attitudes charged with romanticism, these are the literary productions of a young man.

Salutation

As a mother mourns for her child
I mourn.
She will see her child,
And she comforts herself
With pictures of it in Paradise.

But I cannot comfort myself
And I mourn for my child—
The child of my dream—
My picture of the world—beautiful and free!
And as a mother's arms
Are hungry for her child,
I am hungry for that World;

And dreams of Paradise do not assuage me;
Nor hope of joy in any world but this.

Heaven is like a lamp in the fog
At the end of a long, dark road.
It has a wan glimmer.
And if flame-winged figures roam
In other worlds than this—
Figures of joy, flame-winged, exquisite—
I do not care.
It is here in this world
Where Spring comes beautifully
And birds spread their wings in blue air
And sing—
It is here in this world,
Silvered with playing streams
And pink with blossoms—
In this world—
I would be joyous and free.

Oh, beautiful World—beautiful World!
No mother ever yearned
Over the limbs of her milk-white, perfect child
As I yearn over you.
You break through the mist of my dreams
Oh, People of the Future
Pink and golden!
Life seems to flow
In the steady rhythm of music for you.
Young men like mountain lions,
And girls like young saplings—
I see you in a golden mist.
Empty the cup of joy,
Oh, People of the Future,
For whom life is a game
Taking your superbest strength.

"Heaven is like a lamp in the fog / At the end of a long dark road": the lines anticipate the distant, obscure light that shines from within Rothko's mature paintings. But here that spiritual light is rejected as a "wan glimmer." Writing about loss, Rothko compares himself to a mother mourning for her child. She can compensate for the loss by imagining that her child has ascended to paradise, but Rothko, refusing any such religious dispensation, must seek happiness "here in this world."

Yet his generalized and literary evocations of this world—"Spring comes beautifully / And birds spread their wings in blue air / and sing," or "silvered with playing streams / and pink with blossoms"—suggest a very attenuated contact with natural life. Physical reality fails to "break through the mist of [his] dreams." In fact, according to the poem's basic analogy (Rothko = mourning mother; world = dead child), he laments the loss of this world, from which he is alienated because it does not now (though it may in some utopian future) conform to his dream, his ideal vision of it. The poem reveals a young romantic's separation from this world.

 Walls of Mind: Out of the Past

> Heavy tonight with the weight of invisible chains
> I sink by the fire and dream.
> All the past seems to rush up over me—
> All the sad past of the race.
> Those primitive barbarous people
> They live again in my blood,
> And I feel myself bound to the past
> By invisible chains.
> A woman comes crouching beside me
> A primitive mother,
> And I feel the fierce darkness within her,
> And all the primitive fears
> Rustling and slipping about me—
> Powers of darkness.
> She brings with her the feel of the cave,
> And danger ever at hand.
> The feel of the cave—the cave.
> From a cave they looked out on the world,
> And struggled to understand,
> And slowly the flicker of their intelligence
> Grew and consumed the dusk with their mind,
> And the Brute-Man stood erect and knew himself[.]

Rothko here writes about what he *can't* lose, his racial (Jewish) past, epitomized in the figure of the mother, to whom he remains bound by "invisible chains." His people are "primitive barbarous," and his mother holds a "fierce darkness," as if Rothko's racial and familial attachments at once embarrassed and threatened him. When the "primitive mother" crouches beside him, he feels "the primitive fears / Rustling and slipping about me—/ Powers of darkness," a description that suggests both that the mother herself experiences such fears and that her "crouching" proximity awakens such fears of *her* in him. The ancient racial awareness of "danger ever at hand" produces withdrawal, retreat into the safety of the "cave," a maternal, womblike space which holds its own "fierce darkness." In the 1950s Rothko would claim that his apparently serene paintings actually grew out of and contained such a fierce, primitive darkness. Here, he wishes for a way out, to leave the cave, transcend racial fears, and enter *this* world through the light of "mind." "Salutation" wishes for freedom through nature; "Walls of Mind" seeks freedom through the intelligence, education.

Jacob Rothkowitz had migrated from Michalishek to Dvinsk, then from Dvinsk to Portland. Marcus Rothkowitz migrated from Dvinsk to Portland, then from Portland to the east coast. In the late summer of 1921, he traveled from Portland to New Haven, Connecticut, to enroll at Yale University.

3 New Haven/New York

Mark was completely scornful of the Yale establishment and the students—I suppose this is one reason he left.

Simon Whitney

As I remember him, Marcus was a big, amiable, delightful Falstaffian character, with a streak of amused cynicism about the Yale of those days, a broad sense of humor, and devoid of the crusading spirit that motivated [Aaron] Director.

Morris Gitlitz

When Marcus Rothkowitz—along with his close friends Aaron Director and Max Naimark—left Portland to begin study at Yale, he was making a second journey toward a new life, this one stirred by even higher hopes than whatever expectations he had brought to the United States. Now, rather than being "transplanted," he was striking out on his own, leaving behind the immigrant Jewish community and provincial Portland for the glamour and sophistication of the Ivy League.

Once again, however, his new world fell short of his dream. In Portland, while anti-Semitic stereotypes were part of the popular imagination, and discrimination was a reality at Lincoln High, Eastern European Jews were not in the "stigmatized class position" of their fellows, say, on the Lower East Side of Manhattan. In fact, many Portland Jews of Rothko's generation report that their first conscious experiences of anti-Semitism occurred at eastern colleges and universities.[1] By moving from the Portland ghetto to the Yale campus, Rothko was exchanging reactionary politics and latent prejudice for enlightened gentility and institutionalized anti-Semitism. In New Haven, he *was* in a stigmatized class position.

Indeed, the beginning of Rothko's college education in 1921 coincided with a period of intensifying anti-Semitism throughout the country, and Ivy League campuses were one of the main battlegrounds. Enrollments of Jewish students had been rising dramatically, most of them Eastern European immigrants (or their children) from working-class backgrounds. By 1920 80 to 90 percent of the students at Hunter College and City College of New York were Jewish.[2] Ivy League schools, to repulse the "Jewish invasion," responded with secret quota systems. Yale was known to be one of the least friendly environments for Jews.

Although a fair number of German-American Jews had entered Yale and assimilated with relative ease before the turn of the century, there was a strong backlash when the sons of Eastern European immigrants began to arrive after the war. In 1918 Frederick S. Jones, dean of Yale College, warned a meeting of the Association of New England Deans that "a few years ago every single scholarship of any value was won by a Jew. I took it up with the Committee and said that we could not allow that to go on. We must put a ban on the Jews." For Jones, not only do the Jews dominate scholarship funds; they also, in the view of Yale administrators, "demand" financial assistance as if it were owed to them, violate the honor code because of their shabby ethics, and "contribute very little to class life." Materialistic, dishonest, and clannish, the Jews, according to Roswell Angier, the dean of freshmen at Yale, are "a foreign body in the class organism."[3]

By the fall of 1922 Dean Jones had completed an elaborate statistical study of all the Jewish students in the Yale classes from 1911 to 1926; Jones's tables listed name, home address, place of birth, father's place of birth, extracurricular activities, scholarship support, high school(s) and future plans for each student thought to be Jewish. One of Jones's statistics was Marcus Rothkowitz, of the class of 1925. Ironically, the size of Rothko's entering class—its 866 students then the largest freshman class to arrive at Yale—provided the university administration with a means of solving the "Jewish problem": the need to limit enrollment would provide a cover for the desire to limit Jewish enrollment.[4]

For those Jews, like Rothko, who were admitted, discrimination became overt. In the early 1920s Yale, like other Ivy League institutions, conceived of itself as a "gentleman's college," aptly defined by Thorstein Veblen as "an establishment in which scholarship is advisedly made subordinate to genteel dissipation." "Prep school patricians" formed the social elite. If you belonged, the literary critic F. O. Matthiessen wrote, "you aimed for the right social goals, you wore the right Brooks suit, your soft white shirt had a buttoned-down collar, and you did nothing—except possibly drinking—to excess."[5] Yale was Lincoln High writ large and eastern. The chimera of social status was pursued through an intricate system of eating clubs, athletic teams, fraternities, and senior secret societies—all ruled by the Protestant upper classes. Jews, excluded from these organizations and others, were the untouchables.

Ethnic prejudice, reinforced by the fears of a privileged group confronting an upwardly mobile class, was mystified as a problem of decorum. At Lincoln, the elite might fantasize about exterminating radicals through education; but for Yale's Dean Corwin, the Jews, especially New Haven Jews, were simply hopeless.

> The serious phase of the problem here as at Harvard is the local Jew, who lives at home, knows nothing of dormitory associations, sees nothing

of Chapel or Commons, and graduates into the world as naked of all the attributes of refinement and honor as when born into it.[6]

More academic than social, Jews were "pushy" or "grinds." Working-class and immigrant, they were also "crude" and "foreign." Clearly, they were not material for the Whiffenpoofs.

Still, "the public high school mythology that held that America's great universities were temples of learning attracted the East Europeans to 'worship' at Yale." During Rothko's senior year, Max Naimark recalled, "Dr. Angier, Dean of Yale University, visited Lincoln High School apparently to promote applications to Yale from Oregon. Mr. Thorne, our chemistry teacher, was a Yale 1902 graduate and very popular with the students. He arranged for a private session with the students," during which they were assured that "*money was no object as long as we had brains and were good students.*"[7] Besides, the east coast Weinsteins had already made Yale something of a family tradition.[8] So Rothko, too, was attracted to this temple, but if he worshiped there at all, it was not for long. During his first year, living off-campus to cut expenses, Rothko became, in effect, one of those irredeemable "local" Jews who lived beyond the civilizing associations of campus life. Jews, it seems, either formed a foreign body *in* the class organism or a foreign body *outside* the class organism.

In his first year Rothko lived with Naimark at 840 Howard Avenue, on the third floor of Dr. Herman Grodzinsky's home and office. Located across the street from a parochial school, the brick house was one of several physicians' residences on the street; the Yale Medical School and the New Haven Hospital were one block south on Howard. In the early 1920s Howard Avenue was also one of the borders of the New Haven Jewish ghetto—smaller, tougher, more congested, more squalid than Portland's "Little Russia." Among New Haven's population of about eight thousand Jews, most of whom had emigrated to America in the last thirty years, was a local branch of the ever-present Weinstein family, just three blocks away, at 510 Howard.[9]

Jacob Rothkowitz's brother Sam had provided the link to the Portland Weinsteins; his sister Esther provided the link to the New Haven Weinsteins. In Russia she had married Abraham Hirsch, who later changed his name to Weinstein. In 1892—the year after Sam Rothkowitz emigrated to Portland—Abraham Weinstein emigrated to New Haven. He became a junk dealer and eventually the father of nine children, four of whom—Jacob, Daniel, Edward, and Louis—graduated from Yale.[10]

According to one of Abraham's sons, Edward Weinstein, "Mark would just come to [our] house and have his evening meal. Then my mother would fill up a bag with sandwiches and fruit. She knew it was tough by the way he ate his evening meal, that he didn't have much to eat during the day." At the Weinsteins, dinner table conversation covered culture and politics. Rothko met some musician friends of Jacob's, with whom he "seemed to enjoy himself very much because these people spoke a language which he enjoyed"—the language of "art, music, literature."[11] Among the Weinsteins Rothko was once again the poor relation; but they also offered him a place to eat, some family atmosphere, friends who shared his interests, spoke his language, and provided a comforting Russian Jewish familiarity.

A poor relation off-campus, on the campus Rothko was a pariah. The financial troubles of all three Portlanders worsened when, at the end of their first semester, their tuition scholarships were converted into loans. Once again authority had betrayed Rothko and he was forced to work, just as he had been when his father died. Now, however, finding a job was made difficult by the anti-Semitism on Yale's Board of Appointments which, in Naimark's memory, gave Jewish students a "hell of a time." At the end of his first year an angry Naimark left Yale. Rothko, however, found work, probably in a campus dining hall or with local cleaning businesses.[12]

Rothko later liked to joke that he would deliberately spill food on students in the dining commons in order to promote business for the cleaners. At the time, however, his position was more painful than amusing. Rothko was a Russian Jew among Yankee WASPs; he was a western public school graduate among the East Coast prep school elite; he lived in a rented room, not a dormitory; and he was forced to take menial jobs in a college community devoted to leisure, sport, and "the right social goals." Worst of all, in basic ways—his poverty, a job he resented, living in the Jewish ghetto, dependence on Weinstein relatives who were better-off—Rothko's life resembled what he thought he had left behind in Portland.

His Yale friends recalled Rothko as a "brilliant," "well-read" young man convinced that his "genius" "destined" him "for great things." "As far as I was concerned," said Naimark, "Mark was brilliant. He did not have to study much, didn't pay much attention to some of the subjects of the professors he didn't particularly like."[13] At Yale, Rothko continued to draw and sketch, but his announced ambitions were professional. He considered law; he considered engineering.[14] The year before Rothko's arrival, Yale had instituted a "common" freshman program; Rothko took freshman English, second-year French, European history, elementary mathematics, and elementary physics. In his second year, he studied sophomore English, advanced French, general biology, elementary economics, history of philosophy, and general psychology. He was apparently working toward the Ph.B. degree offered to public high school graduates who lacked the Latin requirements for a B.A. His grades averaged about a C+, slightly better in the first year than in the second. Gradually, Rothko "lost interest completely" in his courses, getting C's, as if he were one of his gentleman classmates.[15]

During his second year, despite losing his scholarship, Rothko lived in a dormitory; his room in 161 Lawrence Hall was near Director's in 171. Living inside the university, however, did little to reconcile Rothko with its customs and values. By the spring of 1923, he had become disillusioned with the idea of education as a route to professional security, and he was becoming increasingly antagonistic toward Yale, and especially toward his fellow students. In February of 1923 Rothko, along with Aaron Director and another friend, Simon Whitney, launched *The Yale Saturday Evening Pest*, a kind of underground newspaper, copies of which were slid "under the doors of the rooms in the college dormitories early Sunday mornings when the students were either away for the weekend or slept late." Contributions to the *Pest* were anonymous, so, except for the issue on "False Gods," which Whitney identified as Rothko's, we don't know for certain which pieces Rothko himself wrote, but the paper's point of view is quite consistent and it seems fair to associate Rothko with that perspective.[16]

"We believe that in this age of smugness and self-satisfaction destructive criticism is at least as useful, if not more so, than constructive criticism," the first issue began.[17] With its "destructive criticism" and its provocative slogan ("The Beginning of Doubt is the Beginning of Wisdom"), the *Pest* was a more aggressive version of the idealism which had produced the Contributors' Club project at Lincoln High; its critical perspective was, roughly, H. L. Mencken crossed with Henry David Thoreau.

Rothko and his friends were not, however, solitary prophets crying out in a country club. At the start of the jazz age the Yale campus was often the scene of boisterous drinking parties, brawls, and even riots which the New Haven police were called to quell. But more serious students, faculty, and administrators were also raising fundamental questions about the nature and goals of education. During the spring of 1923, in particular, articles in the *Yale Daily News*, the *Yale Literary Magazine* and the *Yale Alumni Weekly* were asking, "What are we here for? What is the purpose of Yale?" The *Pest*, along with several other anonymous, short-lived sheets, grew out of that ferment.[18]

Students debated about compulsory chapel, the cut system, a curriculum at once rigid and fragmentary, and the charged issue of limitation of enrollment; but what was really at stake was the modernization of the American university in the years following the First World War. Yale, originally a religious institution, was now run and supported by businessmen, drew its students from an increasingly wider geographical, social, and ethnic spectrum and aimed its graduates toward Wall Street rather than public service. Jews, mythologized as at once too crudely primitive and too graspingly modern to become Old Blues, became scapegoats for the fears aroused by these changes. Yale's new president, James R. Angell, was a modernist, pushing to build up the graduate and professional schools. Many students adopted a conservative position; they attacked faculty-administrative "paternalism," blamed it on the increased enrollment, and called for student independence and higher standards. "For Yale is not stamping her undergraduates as indelibly as in the past with the old Yale tradition and ideals, which turned out the thoughtfully conservative type of men who are leaders in this country," the editor of the *News* worried.[19] Sensing the university's drift toward the modern, impersonal institution now familiar to us, Yale students espoused traditional ideals as a defense of their own elite status.

While the opening issue of the *Pest* promised critiques of international politics, capitalism, socialism, immigration, and poverty, subsequent issues focused on campus issues and introduced a new voice, at once skeptical and romantic, into the debate about education at Yale. With administrative modernists to the one side and student traditionalists to the other, the *Pest* urged neither democratization nor the old elites but "an aristocracy of the mentally alert and curious"—a meritocracy. The target of the *Pest*'s attack, however, was less university authority than the "mentally lazy and intellectually sloven" students—less fathers than brothers. "Today at Yale there is no central force, other than that of utility to guide its policy," with the result that students attend "not to get educated but to become engineers."[20] So much for modernization, not to mention Rothko's projected career as an engineer.

"False gods! Idols of clay!" Rothko declaimed in his issue on "False Gods." "There is only one way to smash them, and that is a revolution in mind and spirit in the student body of Yale University. Let us doubt. Let us think." Rothko's impassioned rhetoric sought to smash the idols of athletics, extracurricular success, social success, majority opinion, the cult of grades: all forms of prestige which Rothko ironically exposed as a leveling conformity. "Some day," he writes, "we shall see what is as plain as daylight—that blind conformity to the custom of the majority, to the average, brings mediocrity, and crushes genius." In Rothko's utopian vision of Yale—"an educational institution, with the library as its core"—"the individual and his individualism will be respected."[21] The university will provide a home for romantic genius.

What the present Yale lacks, according to the *Pest,* is "a desire for learning . . . based upon more than material necessity." Commerce had been the soul of Dvinsk; genteel affluence was now the soul of Yale. If one *Pest* theme was this pervasive spirit of utility and materialism, another was the substitution of social for intellectual life. "Instead of talking about art and literature," as Rothko did with his New Haven relatives and friends, "Yale students spend their evenings in basketball discussion, bridge-playing and dancing." So "the whole institution is a lie and serves only as a cloak of respectability for a social and athletic club."[22] What study does occur is mere memorization designed to pass an exam, a form of education Rothko knew from his days at *cheder*.

The root problem, however, was that such student "docility" led to an existence that was "soul-less," "lifeless," "empty," like Rothko's vision of the high school week as an endless grind. The year following the publication of T. S. Eliot's *The Waste Land*, three Yale undergraduates looked at contemporary campus life and found it a "semi-conscious slumber," a "sleeping sickness," a "vacuum."[23] Passively accepted, university authority (or any other) deadens. The *Pest* provides us with the attitude, in its formative stage, that invented the grand but blank public facade in *Street Scene*. At Yale the institution was not animated by any inward "*desire* for learning." The beginning of doubt is the beginning of desire—and life. In its ultimate assumptions the *Pest* leaned away from both modernism and traditionalism toward a romantic idealism. Within, the editors assert, man does have "nobler instincts." Through questioning, provocation, doubt, the *Pest* sought to open a space, within the institution, for bringing such nobler instincts to life.

The idealistic premises of the *Pest* are particularly apparent in "The House of the Dead," an essay which transforms the kind of experiences Rothko had known both in Portland and New Haven into a parable more romantic then Dostoyevskian. An innocent young man "loved life and sang his love," but "his songs found no sympathetic ear" "among those who had lost their hearts in the whirlpool of material strife." "I have lived in the House of the Dead," he grandly concludes. Now he is drawn to "the spires of a great university." "Here I shall find a new life." But "no one shared his enthusiasm"; many mocked him. At first he blames himself: "I am green." But he eventually decides, "Again I am in the House of the Dead," among "phantoms" who have succumbed to "mediocrity." For even the rare few to survive that "pestilence," a "prodigious strength" is required. Still, hope for a general "resurrection of the dead" is held out; "the living can awaken the sleeping," the gifted individual can animate the crowd.[24]

The *Pest* did achieve a certain notoriety. In the "Campus Views and News" section of the *Yale Alumni Weekly* there were frequent, usually favorable, references to it. But no resurrections of the dead occurred. Instead, an alumni reminded *Pest* editors that Yale's ideal of "gentlemanliness" meant that "the attitude of the pessimist, the radical, muckraker, has no place in the halls of Old Eli," and a New Haven newspaper identified the *Pest* staff as "'foreign intellectuals' who have a reputation for radicalism." In his pious two-volume history of Yale, George Pierson later dismissed "the morosely critical *Saturday Evening Pest,* which died unlamented." Failing to raise the dead, the *Pest* itself expired.²⁵

In the fall of 1923, Rothko quit college, making another "complete break," this time with a temple of learning rigid in its social values but not intellectually rigorous.

· · ·

Then one day I happened to wander into an art class, to meet a friend who was taking the course. All the students were sketching this nude model—and right away I decided that was the life for me.

Mark Rothko

Leaving Yale, a key turning point in Rothko's life, was a difficult and dramatic act for several reasons. Sacrifices had been made to send him there, and his mother, impressed by his ability "to talk you out of anything," had hoped "he would become an attorney." Such an attorney might well help support a widowed mother. In fact, Rothko's brother Moise, by this time married, the father of two children and working daily from 8 A.M. to midnight in his downtown Portland pharmacy, was already contributing to the support of Kate Rothkowitz.²⁶ Now, however, Rothko was breaking with family needs and expectations, with the traditional Jewish emphasis (especially strong in his own family) on education, and with the standard immigrant hopes for professional success and economic security.²⁷ Among Rothko's Lincoln High friends, Gus Solomon became a lawyer and eventually a federal judge, Max Naimark became a doctor, Max MacCoby a rabbi, and Aaron Director a professor of legal economics (a field he invented). By leaving Yale, Rothko was refusing to become a "soulless" character in a conventional American narrative, the kind of Jewish Ben Franklin that had already been criticized by Abraham Cahan in his novel *The Rise of David Levinsky* (1917).

But Rothko was doing something more radical than refusing to submit to the Rothkowitz faith in formal education. If he had decided to return to Portland to become, say, a pharmacist or a union organizer, either of these choices would have made some kind of sense to his family. Rothko was quitting Yale, leaving Portland, moving to New York City, and considering a career in the arts. He later said that he went to New York to "wander around, bum about, starve a bit," and that he had only discovered painting accidentally when he went to meet a friend at the Art Students League, saw the students sketching a nude model, and "decided that was the life for me."[28] This apocryphal-sounding story presents Rothko's discovery of his vocation as a complete conversion, a pure and absolute change, with no history. He, again, often insisted that he had not been "exposed to paintings at all as a boy" or "even in college." "I was passionate about many things, books, music, things of the world," but not about painting.[29] Attributing his conversion to his response to a nude model suggests the origin of his *passion* for painting, which he locates *outside* painting, in erotic desire.

Compare Rothko with Henri Matisse, who also came late to painting. At twenty, Matisse was a lawyer recovering from an attack of appendicitis, when a neighbor suggested he try a "chromo," a Victorian version of painting by the numbers. "Before, I had no taste for anything. I was filled with indifference to everything that people wanted me to do," Matisse said. "But the moment I had this box of colors in my hands, I had the feeling that my life was there."[30] Matisse responded to the paints, Rothko to the female body, a response that, as we shall see, came from the core of his involvement with painting. Of drawing and painting the nude—something he was to do very frequently in his early career—Rothko commented: "I thought it was marvelous. I was intoxicated by it."[31]

However intoxicated, Rothko wavered between painting and the theater. After just two months as a student at the Art Students League, Rothko returned in early 1924 for several months to Portland, where he studied acting in a company run by Josephine Dillon, soon to become Clark Gable's first wife.[32] Rothko's brief experience in the theater produced one contribution to his self-mythologizing: he loved to tell people the story that Gable had been his understudy, that "I was a better actor than Clark Gable." Gable was a member of Dillon's group at this time, but Rothko's claim is very improbable, partly because Gable had already emerged as her leading pupil and partly because the theater was a very strange choice of career for Rothko.[33] It's not just that he had no acting experience. The problem was that Rothko, a plump 5'11", looked more like Franz Schubert than a leading man; and he was notoriously clumsy, a man who, as one sister-in-law later put it, couldn't pass down a hallway without bumping into both walls. Still, Rothko's interest in theater was not just passing. He had elected a drama course at Lincoln High; he had talked about a career in the theater while at Yale. Back in New York after his acting experience in Portland, he tried, unsuccessfully, to win a scholarship to the American Laboratory Theater.[34] He admired first Greek and then, later in life, Shakespearean tragedy; and, from the late 1940s on, he often spoke of his pictures as "dramas," with his "shapes" as the "performers."[35] And if Rothko

Chapter Three

lacked the sex appeal of a Gable, he was, in Kenneth Rabin's description, a "spellbinder," a brilliant, witty talker who enjoyed occupying center stage. Both Rothko and his works were to be theatrical.

By early 1925, however, Rothko had returned to New York and enrolled at the New School of Design, a small commercial art school on Broadway near 52nd Street.[36] There, Rothko took one class from Arshile Gorky. "He taught as well as saw to it that the students were on good behavior," Rothko recalled. "And he expected good performance. He was strict. Perhaps I shouldn't say this, but Gorky was overcharged with supervision." In class Gorky brought copies he had made of paintings by Monticelli and Franz Hals, and he would "lecture to us and expound on the techniques used by the artists." Some of Rothko's memories of Gorky sound remarkably like self-descriptions: listening to Gorky's stories "it was difficult to tell where reality ended and imagination began," Rothko says; or, Gorky "appeared to be a sad and melancholy person. And I wonder if perhaps his love for art furnished him with his single greatest source of happiness. I believe it did." Visiting Gorky's studio only once, Rothko remembered "taking out his garbage. I'm afraid I still thought of him as my class monitor."[37]

In October of 1925 Rothko enrolled at the Art Students League, in Max Weber's still-life class, which he took for six of the next seven months. During his term at the League, Rothko listed three addresses on his registration card—102nd Street in New York, his cousin Jacob's address in New Haven, and his mother's flat in Portland. In the mid-1920s Rothko spent substantial time at all three locations. At 19 West 102nd Street Rothko had been given, at first rent-free, a spare room by Mrs. Goreff, a distant relative of his mother's, to whom he had appealed: "I'm a struggling artist. I need a place to sleep." While living there, Rothko did charcoal and pencil drawings of nearby Central Park, Harlem, and the El. He also "played a lot of Bach on our phonograph and painted."[38]

During this period, Rothko often hitchhiked to New Haven. "I don't think he was in a position to afford train rides," his cousin Ed Weinstein said. Rothko would visit for a week or two. "I strongly suspected, at the time, that this was the only place where he could get real food."[39] However romantic the life of a bohemian wanderer might have seemed from a dorm window in Lawrence Hall, however intoxicating the act of drawing or painting the nude might be, Rothko was a twenty-two-year-old living in a spare room in a West Harlem apartment, starving for art; and he was still not entirely sure where his home was.

Breaking away from his family was a slow, difficult, yet necessary struggle. He certainly had not quit Yale to return to Portland. Later in life Rothko claimed that had he "remained in Portland, he would have been a bum," whereas in New York he found the "freedom to develop." "He hated Portland," calling it "dull and provincial." He felt "he didn't belong." In Sonia's recollection, "he wanted bigger horizons," and his desire to leave had begun at Lincoln. "He said when he gets out of high school, he is going to someplace else."[40] Portland would have smothered him, making him a "bum," a nobody. By leaving he could disengage himself from the constricting demands of his family; and in New York he would occupy a stage large enough for his most grandiose ambitions.

Painting gave Rothko an intoxicating physical pleasure; in making art his vocation, he was affirming emotional and sensual values over the "soul-less" material existence (for him) of an engineer or lawyer. Art provided a noble ideal in which Rothko could have faith and which he felt he could choose freely; it delivered him from the House of the Dead and elected him to an "aristocracy of the mentally alert and curious." Art awakened *desire*—perhaps partly because it was transgressive. Not only did Rothko's choice defy family expectations for a bourgeois career: "Marcus, why are you wasting your time? You will never be able to earn a living that way." Painting also defied the traditional Jewish taboo against iconic images. Such religious prohibitions were less strong for Rothko—or for Adolph Gottlieb or Barnett Newman, to name just two Jewish artistic contemporaries of Rothko's—than they were, say, for Marc Chagall or Chaim Soutine, both of whom, born about ten years before Rothko, had grown up in the Settlement of Pale, where their interest in art confronted severe political harassment and religious taboos. When the young Soutine, for example, had asked a rabbi to sit for a portrait, the rabbi's son had beaten him.[41]

In this context, Rothko's "transplantation" to the United States was liberating, helping to free him from the pressure of a religious stricture of which, as a *cheder* student, he was well aware. Chagall and Soutine went to Paris; Rothko went to New York. There, Rothko was a poor immigrant *Jewish* artist. As Irving Howe points out in *The World of Our Fathers,* "to become an artist, the young Jewish aspirant had to possess exceptional strength of will, a stubborn insistence that he would go his own way whether or not his family approved."[42] Twenty-two years old, Rothko was a latecomer to art, entering a suspect, unknown field, an alien, gentile tradition, without the support of any tradition or training of his own.

. . .

Anonymous, mobile, urban, secular, skeptical, a self-made proletarian, Rothko, like many young men from the American provinces in the twenties, was now a modern. The dream of modernity has always been the dream of a "complete break" with the ties of family, class, religion, ethnicity; many of Rothko's stories of his life dramatized him as the modern rebel repudiating traditional authority. Yet Rothko, who would later identify the modern with the archaic, had deep attachments to his past. In fact, his route to modernity—a spiral rather than a linear progress—was *by way of* his familial and ethnic origins. Jacob Rothkowitz had, at first, replaced religious with political fervor; his youngest son replaced politics with art and completed the process of secularization, except that, for Rothko, art was a sacred calling and his temple would become very much a Jewish temple. The abstract, sacred spaces of his mature works are not violated by graven images; his Jewishness helped Rothko become an *abstract expressionist*. Stanley Kunitz aptly called him "the last rabbi of western art."[43]

Rothko's father, a young man from the Lithuanian provinces, had "left the village he was born in and starved to go to school so that he could achieve what he wanted." Rothko left the small American city he was raised in and starved so that he could teach himself to be what *he* wanted. Rothko imposed upon himself the same "lonesomeness and leaving the family and going through an ordeal of being broke" that Moise attributed to his father. Refusing the success ethic of the Portland ghetto only, in the long run, to exceed it by becoming an internationally famous and wealthy artist, Rothko at once defied, repeated, and completed the life of a father who died young.

During the Roaring Twenties—a time of national prosperity, bohemian rebellion and hedonistic excess—Rothko, combining his mother's determination with his father's quiet idealism, imposed upon himself an almost monastic ordeal of poverty, hunger, and solitude, sleeping in a bathtub at one point, in the subways at another.[44] Later in the 1920s, while sharing a cold-water flat with Gordon Soule, a young pianist from Portland, Rothko told Arthur Gage, "I've got to become a great painter because I've found a way to live for three days on a can of sardines and a loaf of bread and the milk that I stole from somebody down the hall." "He meant," commented Gage, "that if he could make that much sacrifice, he *had* to become a great painter." Rothko's conviction that self-sacrifice would produce greatness, as if the gods would be moved by his pain, proved a deep and abiding one; he would always have trouble finding ways of liberating himself that did not turn out to be self-punishing.

In his later manifesto "The Romantics Were Prompted," Rothko generalized his own earlier experience into a program for psychological and social redemption through suffering and deprivation:

> The unfriendliness of society to his activity is difficult for the artist to accept. Yet this very hostility can act as a lever for true liberation. Freed

from a false sense of security and community, the artist can abandon his plastic bank-book, just as he has abandoned other forms of security. Both the sense of community and of security depend on the familiar. Free of them, transcendental experiences become possible.

Rothko's mature paintings, begun just two years after this statement, express such "transcendental experiences." The blurry edges of the rectangles, the softly diffused shapes within them, the way they float over the ground, the absence of any line that might define volume, a luminosity that seems to come from within the painting, the intense but disembodied colors, even the thin application of a very thin paint—these features create a free space, in which our "familiar" physical world has been dematerialized.

But neither in his paintings nor in "The Romantics Were Prompted" does Rothko, who associated his attraction to the female body with the origins of his art, wish to sever physical from spiritual. His paintings are themselves sensual and seductive, even as they draw us into an empty and ethereal space. Social hostility, isolation and economic need, Rothko writes in "The Romantics Were Prompted," are the preconditions for "true liberation," just as the Bowery might be the ideal locale in which to make mural-scale paintings with a sacred aura.

In the 1920s, by going to New York and deciding to become an artist, Rothko freed himself from such conventional forms of security as family, religious tradition, professional career. Yet to free himself he joined a socially marginal group, elected poverty and dislocation, insecurity and lack—the rankling circumstances of his life almost from the beginning. Only now *he* was choosing them. Liberating the self required *self*-sacrifice, entering an open and uncertain future by preserving a painful and uncertain past.

· · ·

I saw a child playing all by itself with stones. It made two lintels and an arch. Right there primarily it made more architecture than these blusterers. An arch, an aperture, the heavens over the arch, what more can you want?

Max Weber

The year that Rothko arrived in the United States, 1913, was also the year of the Armory Show, in which European artistic modernism came to the United States and was denounced as "Ellis Island art."[45] By the mid-1920s Rothko was not yet a modern artist; he was hardly an artist at all. "Provincial about art," as he later described himself, he was living in a city that, by Parisian standards, was itself provincial about art; and he was beginning his career as a painter in a period of conservative reaction against what had come to be viewed as the excesses of modernist experimentation.[46]

Yet Rothko's position had distinct long-term advantages. As a Jewish "outsider," he felt no strong ties either to the American or the European artistic traditions. As an American artist starting out in the twenties, he was not burdened with intimidating American predecessors; figures like Picasso and Matisse were formidable but distant European presences. Like many painters of his generation, Rothko developed slowly; but his provincial situation also created some free space in which to grow. "Due to [the] provincial position in which the American artist was pushed," Rothko later said, "he had nothing to lose and everything, a world, to gain."[47]

Asserting that he had "learned painting from his contemporaries in their studios," Rothko claimed to be self-educated, and mainly he was.[48] His formal education as a painter was certainly brief, probably because, even under the best of circumstances, he had trouble submitting to institutional authority. There was his short time at the New School of Design and then, at the Art Students League, two months in George Bridgman's life-drawing class, and six months in Max Weber's still-life class. But those eight months at the League had an important impact; Rothko came to see that it was possible for him to be a painter, and he began to clarify his ideas about painting, especially with Weber.

Located on 57th Street between Broadway and 7th Avenue, the Art Students League provided an alternative, American-style academy of art—vital, free-wheeling, and democratic. The League might be accused of a lot of things—Anthony Comstock had once raided its classrooms because of the nude models—but no one would accuse it of "paternalism." "The Art Students League is organized on a sound democratic principle, being run for students by students," the 1925–26 catalogue announced. "Because the students direct its policy, the interest of no outside group or individual is served. Its very life, therefore, comes from the needs of those who compose it." The faculty consisted of practicing artists hired annually. There were no requirements for admission, or after admission; there were no grades and no degrees. For low fees—Weber's class cost Rothko $13 a month—students were able to register, on a monthly basis, for whatever classes interested them.[49] At the Art Students League the students, including Rothko, *were* animated by a desire for learning.

Yet however progressive the League's organization, in the 1920s it was a "stronghold of the realist tradition."[50] A Canadian who had studied at the Ecole des Beaux-Arts, George Bridgman had been teaching at the League for thirty years. Originally "an innovator in teaching anatomy and figure drawing," about which he wrote several books, Bridgman had a reputation at the League as a kind of hard-nosed, cigar-smoking, W.C.Fields–type character whose classes were so popular that candidates for admission were asked to gather in a room and produce a drawing; Bridgman then picked fifty for his class.[51]

Though his instruction was given individually, it was also highly routinized. "Bridgman walked into his class at the precise time and class started at the precise time. And he finished with every student on an individual basis by the time the class was over." Students were arranged in three rows—the first on low chairs, the second on regular chairs, the third on stools—in front of the model. "If you weren't there when he got there you just lost a criticism."[52] Over the years neither Bridgman's teaching methods nor his artistic theories (stressing a kind of simplified anatomy he learned from Matisse) changed. That he "had a formula" made him popular; but some students found his classes a "deadly routine." Lloyd Goodrich, later director of the Whitney Museum, remembered his first criticism from Bridgman. "He took my drawing and just rubbed it all out with a chamois cloth and began to draw it himself. I said, 'Mr. Bridgman, I don't see it that way.' He said, 'Consult an oculist!' "[53]

If George Bridgman represented American academicism in the 1920s, Max Weber represented American modernity—and its fate. In 1905, at twenty-four, Weber had gone to Paris. Dissatisfied with the three private art-academies he entered there, Weber ended up as a student of Matisse and a friend of Picasso, Rousseau, and Apollinaire. Weber admired the work of Cézanne at the Salon d'Automne of 1906; he became interested in primitive art, especially African sculpture; and he studied the European masters, especially El Greco. When he returned to New York in 1909, Weber was a sophisticated painter who had modernized himself on his own; he soon produced the first Cubist painting done by an American, joining the group of avant-garde artists around Alfred Stieglitz.

Weber was also a man of broad general culture with musical and literary interests. He was a gifted singer who considered a musical career while in Paris; he professed "a great reverence for literature, especially if it is prophetic," publishing *Cubist Poems* (1914) as well as an oracular-sounding theoretical treatise, *Essays on Art* (1917).[54] But Weber's advanced position as a painter subjected him to critical ridicule; one reviewer of Weber's 1911 show at Stieglitz's 291 Gallery declared his paintings to be "a strange, insane obsession" whose "ugliness is appalling," while another described his human figures as "emanations" "such as one might expect from the inmate of a lunatic asylum." Even at the Art Students League, whose structure he praised as "a little soviet,"

Chapter Three

Weber felt looked upon "with suspicion," "with no respect," "with very polished derision."⁵⁵

A cultivated and articulate man, a pioneer of modern art who had actually *been there* at the founding of modernist art in Paris, yet who had been derided for his efforts to assimilate the European advances, the forty-four-year-old Weber—a heroic figure victimized for his artistic transgressions—was the kind of authority with whom the twenty-two-year-old Rothko *could* connect. More than that, Weber had been born in Bialystok, Russia, of orthodox Jewish parents, had emigrated to Brooklyn at the age of ten, lived there "in near poverty conditions," entered the first grade knowing no English, and then, after skipping several grades, completed high school at sixteen.⁵⁶ Weber was also a political leftist who became president of the American Artists' Congress during the 1930s. Weber proved that a Russian-Jewish immigrant like Rothko *could* become a modern artist.

In one former student's recollection, Weber, "a small, plump man with a full, pale face,"

> would enter the classroom and seat himself at an easel before the model and paint on a fresh canvas as if in the privacy of his own studio. As a concession to his pupils, he would formulate his thoughts in words as the picture progressed, but these were uttered in so dreamlike a way that one felt one was not hearing words but actually reading a mind as it pondered the problems of painting.⁵⁷

What he taught, Weber later emphasized, "wasn't only *that* painting, *that* model; it was art, related to music, related to literature, but of course it was a new plastic approach, a sense of construction."⁵⁸ He urged his students to "go to Cézanne for composition," but he also invited them "to write poetry around a painting," declaring that "painting was a kind of poetry." Weber's combination of demonstration and oracular pronouncement, which might make students seeking more precise direction anxious, was ideal for someone, like Rothko, apt to resist a more aggressive style of authority.

Of course, Weber did supplement his meditations with comments on student work, doing "a 'round-robin,' where he would talk to each student about his work, often painting over the student's work."⁵⁹ In fact, several years later, Rothko received some free, postgraduate instruction from Weber, when he visited a WPA show in which Rothko was exhibiting. Weber examined his former student's painting of a ghostly string quartet.⁶⁰ He "eyed it indulgently and yet a mite critically," Joseph Solman recalled. "Then, flicking some ashes from his lit cigarette into the palm of his hand, went over and rubbed them over the face of one of the players, saying 'This spot should be toned down a little'." Rothko laughed.[61] The often-prickly student's amused reaction reveals his respect for his old teacher. "He said he learned a lot from him," said Solman.[62]

Rothko's work of the late twenties, rendering domestic and urban scenes in a thickly impastoed, murky expressionist style, reveals Weber's impact. What Weber taught, Rothko was prepared to hear, for by this time Weber had evolved a humanistic reaction against what he now viewed as modernist formalism. "Many ancient sins are covered with the cloak of modernity," he warned. "Ideals ferment art. Emotion is as the sunlight to the seed of art, and the seed in time is fruit." Weber's paintings now renounced Cubism and moved toward the expressionism of Rouault, sometimes applied to specifically Jewish subjects. In *Essays on Art* Weber had gone back to a broadly romantic idealism already familiar to Rothko. Weber emphasized the divine indwelling spirit of the creator and the emotional force of the work. "Always it is expression before means," he stressed. "Art is not mere representation"; it is "revelation," "prophecy," making "of dead or indifferent matter the very abode for the spirit."[63] Max Weber was a not-so-quiet idealist; his conception of the artist as prophet, his emphasis on emotion and spirit over construction, had lasting impact on Rothko.

• • •

Rothko was a lonely man who chose a profession that cut him off from his family and which was itself solitary. "I think he was probably the loneliest man I ever met," said Regina Bogat. "I never met anybody who was that lonesome, really desperately lonely." The paintings in the Western tradition that most moved him, he wrote in "The Romantics Were Prompted," "were the pictures of the single human figure—alone in a moment of utter immobility." The act of painting was solitary, fraught with the kind of self-doubt that overcame Rothko on the night of his Museum of Modern Art opening. Painting was also contemplative and quiet, the more so after Rothko purged all recognizable subject matter from his work. At the same time, Rothko was one of the "people of the book," for whom God is the Word. Verbal, dramatic, and combative, Rothko was famous in his family for first coming down on one side of an issue and then with equal vehemence on the opposite side.[64] He liked talk and verbal sparring; he considered law as a career. As a young man, he said, he had thought about becoming a writer.[65]

Yet as both the Contributors' Club at Lincoln and the *Pest* at Yale showed, words did not strike deeply enough, either to awaken the sleeping or to convey the writer's own emotional life. That they didn't was one reason for Rothko's hyperbolic style of narrating his past. As he went on to say in "The Romantics Were Prompted," the crowds gathered "on beaches and streets and in parks" only "form a *tableau vivant* of human incommunicability," like the family group in *Street Scene*. Direct, visual, nonverbal, painting offered a possible "ending to this silence and solitude." Expressionism, with its emotionally vehement distortions of ordinary reality, was Rothko's first attempted solution. But not until he arrived at his mature format could he create a space in which that solitary immobile figure could be freed for "breathing and stretching [his] arms again." In these later paintings the heavy, constricting social and physical worlds have been "pulverized," allowing feeling to be communicated immediately, without the mediation of real or symbolic incident.[66] These canvases ("they are not pictures") breathe feeling, enfolding the artist (and the viewer) in an atmosphere of deep emotion. Here, Rothko, the victim of so many dislocations and humiliations in his own life, could feel alive and at home.

Rothko could be contentious. "Yet he was so friendly," partly because he was so lonely. As a beginning painter in New York in the mid-1920s he was not utterly isolated in a strange city. There was Gordon Soule, the young pianist who was Rothko's roommate and, Rothko later said, his closest friend in the 1920s. There was, of course, a New York branch of the Weinstein family, though it is not known what contacts Rothko had with these rather distant relations.[67] Two of Rothko's Weinstein cousins from the West Coast lived in New York at this time. Harold Weinstein was a graduate student of history at Columbia; Arthur Gage spent two years studying acting at the American Laboratory Theater, the school which had rejected Rothko. Max Naimark, Rothko's old friend from Portland and Yale, was then a student at Columbia, as was Gus Solomon from Lincoln High; and another Lincoln friend, Max MacCoby, was a New York rabbi by the late twenties.[68] But if painting isolated Rothko, it also made him part of a community. At the Art Students League he formed close friendships with Lewis Ferstadt, Lou Harris, Nathan Israels, and Hirsch Stein.[69]

Arthur Gage recalled that he and Rothko would spend Saturday afternoons at the Russian Bear, a Second Avenue "hang-out for Russian exiles," where, not able to afford a meal, the two young men ordered tea and rye bread and sat and talked and listened to the balalaika orchestra. The cold-water flat that Rothko shared with Gordon Soule, said Gage, "had no furniture, just a chair or two." The two young men slept on mattresses on the floor. In the fall of 1926 Rothko was living on just five dollars a week. Yet the economic prosperity of the twenties did supply low-paying jobs which enabled members of its bohemian subculture, like Rothko, to survive. One reason the Depression was so devastating for artists was that it made finding such work nearly impossible.

In the twenties, Rothko worked as a cutter and at other jobs in the garment district; he was a bookkeeper for an in-law of the New Haven Weinsteins, Samuel Nichtberger, a CPA and tax attorney; he may have painted signs for a summer camp.[70] He illustrated a *Menorah Journal* essay called "Jungle Jews" (on the fate of the first Jewish city in the Western hemisphere, in Dutch Guiana), and he accumulated "three years of illustrative work in the advertising field" between 1925 and 1928.[71] One of his employers, the Federal Advertising Agency, specialized in appropriating modernist art methods in designing its ads.[72]

• • •

Jews have hurt me the most.

Mark Rothko

Yet as a rule all our cases are foregone conclusions.

Kafka, *The Trial*

Like many artists of his generation, Rothko distinguished absolutely between high art and popular or commercial art—one reason he would later so dislike Pop art and one reason he repressed his experience as an illustrator from later accounts of his life. Indeed, Rothko's involvement with commercial art resulted, in late 1928, in a law suit which dramatizes in especially clear form many of the issues of his early life and beginning career. Rothko sued Lewis Browne, a rabbi turned popular author, who had hired Rothko to assist him with the illustrations for a book called *The Graphic Bible*. Browne, Rothko contended, had failed to give him the full acknowledgment and full payment he had been promised.

The hearing for the suit produced seven hundred pages of testimony, three hundred of them from Rothko himself—the most elaborate record we have of Rothko as a young man.[73] More important, the legal confrontation between Rothko and Browne posed many of the deeper issues of Rothko's identity: the questions of who he was, who he was in relation to authority, who he was as a painter, who he was as a Russian Jew in America.

Rothko and Browne had first met on the 1921 train ride that had taken Rothko and his friends Director and Naimark from Portland to New Haven; Browne, six years older than Rothko, was Director's cousin. He had been born in London in 1897, been educated in the primary and elementary schools

Chapter Three

there, and had immigrated to the United States in 1912. Like Rothko's, Browne's family settled in Portland. After a brief attempt to start a career in business, Browne decided to attend college, receiving a B.A. from the University of Cincinnati in 1919 and, then, choosing a religious vocation, a Bachelor of Hebrew from Hebrew Union College in 1920. While a student, Browne became involved with the Reform movement led by Rabbi Stephen Wise, and in 1920 Browne was ordained by Wise as rabbi of the Temple Israel congregation in Waterbury, Connecticut.[74] When he met Rothko on the train, Browne was returning to his congregation and was about to begin what turned out to be his only year of graduate study at Yale. During that year, he and Rothko saw each other occasionally and "became friendly."

Both left the New Haven area in 1923, however, and did not see each other again until the fall of 1926, when Rothko, looking for work, came to Browne, now living on New York's Upper East Side. In the intervening three years the lives of the two men had diverged markedly. Browne had resigned his position at Temple Israel in defense of "a radical who had been denied free speech"; he then, with no immediate source of income and living in a Connecticut farmhouse, wrote a history of the Jews published as *Stranger Than Fiction* (1925). Wise helped Browne become rabbi at the Free Synagogue of Newark, where he served from 1924 to 1926.[75] Browne's second book, *This Believing World* (1926), an account of world religions, was a popular and even critical success, selling a hundred thousand copies and winning an honorable mention from the American Institute of Graphic Arts as one of the most beautifully illustrated books of 1926. As a result of his success, Browne resigned the rabbinate to devote all of his time to writing.

Rothko, meanwhile, having chosen high art, was living on five dollars a week—which now put him in the uncomfortable position of having to turn to a man whose pursuit of commercial art had quickly made him affluent. At first Browne responded helpfully. *The Graphic Bible* project was mentioned in their talk, but Browne's first response was to refer Rothko to four advertising agencies, all of which, according to Browne, rejected Rothko because of "inexperience" and "inability." Browne also recommended the young painter to Lloyd Goodrich, then associate editor of *Arts Magazine*: "I have a young friend named Mr. Rothkowitz, who is working in art. If you can do anything to give him publicity in his work, or if you can give him any work reviewing books for your magazine, I should consider it a personal favor," Browne told Goodrich on the phone. Book reviews by the young Rothko would be nice to have today, but Goodrich turned him down, thus planting some of the seeds for Rothko's later battles with Goodrich, when he was director of the Whitney Museum.

Several months later, on August 27, 1927, Rothko and Browne met again at the home of their mutual friend, Rabbi Max MacCoby. Just four days before, Browne had signed a contract for *The Graphic Bible* with Macmillan, an agreement that included five hundred dollars for someone to assist with the illustrations for the book. *The Graphic Bible*—aimed primarily at younger readers—was to recreate the events of both the Old and New Testaments through text and illustrated maps. Rothko's participation in the project was discussed at MacCoby's and then later that night at Browne's apartment; the next morning, after Rothko produced a sample of the work he would do, the two men agreed that Rothko would be hired for the five hundred dollars allotted Browne, to be paid out at ten dollars a week.

For the next four months Rothko worked seven days a week, four or five hours a day, completing the project in late December. He did the lettering for all of the maps and decorated many of them; he also worked on the book's jacket and end pieces. On December 16 Browne gave Rothko an IOU for the $195 still owed him. Browne began paying the remainder in installments, but in mid-January, when Rothko came to collect his last fifty dollars, Browne demanded that he sign a release certifying that he had been paid in full for the job. Rothko refused. Both men became angry, with Rothko finally declaring "I will see you in hell" before he would sign the release and Browne finally ordering Rothko out of his apartment. At this point Rothko hired a lawyer.

On so much—not very much, as it turns out—there was agreement. Otherwise the two men disputed what work Rothko had been expected to do, what he actually did, what payment and what credit he had been promised, how closely Browne had supervised the work, not to mention their numerous disagreements over matters of detail. According to Rothko, he had been hired to do the lettering on 150 maps, with Browne to do the illustrating and decorating. Sometime in late September or early October, Browne asked Rothko to do the lettering on the jacket and to provide some designs for the end pieces. So pleased was Browne with the results that he then promised to pay Rothko a hundred dollar bonus and to put his name on both the jacket and end pieces. A week later Browne asked Rothko to produce four maps of Jerusalem. Now Browne was so impressed that he announced he wished to make Rothko his "coworker" and have him make a substantial number of the maps. In return, Rothko's name would appear on the title page and on all maps where he did more than the lettering, and he would receive an unspecified share of the book's royalties.

Under these new terms Rothko proceeded with his now expanded task. But when some of the work returned from the printer in late October or early November Rothko pointed out to Browne that his name did not appear on the maps; Browne assured him that this "oversight" would be corrected. When

Chapter Three

some more maps came back printed without Rothko's name in early December, he again raised the issues of payment and credit and was again put off. A third version of this exchange took place shortly after the dummies were returned. Rothko did not abandon hope of receiving his due, he testified, until his final meeting with Browne, in January, when Browne refused to pay the last fifty dollars unless Rothko signed a release.

In his testimony, then, Rothko presents himself as the innocent victim of Browne's greedy exploitation; his only mistake was in his prolonged willingness to believe in Browne's good faith. Browne, of course, saw things differently; he portrays himself as a kindly benefactor whose only error was his generosity toward an impoverished artist who, in his view, turned out to be sloppy, lazy, surly, and even dangerous. Rothko was hired, Browne claimed, "out of sympathy, and not recognition of his work." And when he started the job, the project included 250 maps, subsequently reduced to 150 in mid-September and then to 100 in October. At some points in his testimony Browne states that, from the beginning, the lettering Rothko had been hired to do included the inking in of drawings and illustrations; at other points he says that as the number of maps diminished, Rothko's responsibilities increased, so as to justify Rothko's still receiving the original five hundred dollars. Browne denied ever promising Rothko a share of the royalties or a place on the title page. He added the hundred-dollar bonus and placed the "R" on several maps when, early on, he was pleased with Rothko's work and in a "good mood."

From his perspective, Browne was the "creator" of the maps, with Rothko a mere "mechanical" aid executing his boss's conceptions. The question of authorship—i.e., just whose creations were the maps?—proved to be one of the deeper and more vexing issues raised by the suit. Browne contended that, for the most part, Rothko's responsibility was to ink in letters and illustrations that Browne himself had already penciled onto tissue-paper tracings; in some cases, Browne would write "ship" or "camel" where he wanted Rothko to draw a ship or camel, but even then Rothko relied on models in books provided by Browne, some of them his own earlier books. Browne and his attorney, Arthur Garfield Hays, both insisted that in all cases Rothko was producing a mere "copy."

According to Browne, his difficulties with Rothko reached a crisis point when the dummies returned and Rothko asked, "Won't my initials appear on these maps?" Browne replied, "No, these plates have already been done. I put your initials on some others at a time I felt particularly good. I have since found your attitude is particularly reprehensible, and I shall not put your name on any of the other maps, and furthermore I have a good mind to take it out where I put it before on the jacket." Ill feeling had been building between the two men for some time. Browne was irked by his assistant's "slackness and a general attitude of unpleasantness" as early as September. He subsequently complained about finger stains on the maps and Rothko's "littering my apartment with his clothing"—for example, "he would throw off his coat and vest in the apartment, and I would always insist that he hang up his clothes, as I did my own clothes, in the closet." Nevertheless, Browne was moved to play patron of the arts.

> "You say you need money. Perhaps I can find some of my wealthy friends who will purchase some of your paintings. I myself need one. I should like to have one for my apartment. I have never seen your work. I should like very much to see it. Will you bring me one of your paintings? I prefer a landscape." He said, "I shall" and within a short time he brought me a painting. I looked at it, and I said, "This won't do." He said, "No, you would not like this sort of painting."

One day, Browne testified, his criticisms about the finger stains so enraged Rothko that he picked up an unloaded revolver used as a paperweight on Browne's desk and pointed it at him. Despite their deteriorating personal relations, Browne kept Rothko on, even giving him the IOU in mid-December (for the remaining salary) in case something should happen to him. Like Rothko, Browne dated their final break as the angry January meeting when he asked Rothko to sign the release.

The dispute then became a legal one. Rothko's attorney wrote to Browne, requesting the last fifty dollars, which Browne quickly sent. On April 28 Rothko left New York for one of his trips to Portland, this time for six months. *The Graphic Bible* was released for publication in August 1928 and Rothko saw it for sale in Portland in early September. Within two weeks of his return to New York—on November 10—Rothko started legal proceedings against both Browne and the Macmillan Company, asking for twenty thousand dollars and a temporary injunction against further sale of the book. A hearing was held before Judge Isadore Wasservogel on December 5; to speed up the litigation—necessary because of the request for the injunction—the case was turned over to a referee, Herman Joseph, who presided over eight sessions between December 26 and January 7.

When Rothko, living on five dollars a week, had been hired by Browne, he had every reason to feel, perhaps not great expectations, but at least some solid hopes. Rothko had been forced to rely on commercial art to support his beginnings as a painter, but he was now working for a man who was the relative of an old friend, a New Haven acquaintance and a former rabbi connected with the reform Judaism and progressive politics of Stephen Wise; in short, an employer with whom he might have much in common. Rothko also had the promise of a steady and, for him, substantial salary, plus the advantages of Browne's connections in the publishing and artistic worlds and whatever work might develop out of the likely commercial success of *The Graphic Bible*. Instead, Rothko was betrayed by Browne and then publicly humiliated by losing a lawsuit covered by the *New York Times,* whose stories played up Browne's characterization (misquoted) of Rothko's drawings as "monkey-doodles."[76] As one final turn of the screw, Rothko, obliged to pay court costs, was left over nine hundred dollars in debt.[77]

In fact, the relation between Browne and Rothko was doomed from the start; each of them embodied what the other was striving to reject. In his Upper East Side apartment Browne was occupying a very familiar and fairly lucrative space. His soggy prose, avuncular tone, sloppy scholarship, and many elements of his graphic style were all lifted from his mentor, Hendrik Willem van Loon, a bestselling popular historian and illustrator of the twenties.[78] In *Stranger Than Fiction,* Browne, characterizing Jewish history as "the immortal epic of a people's confused, faltering, insatiable hunger for a nobler life in a happier world," at once secularizes and trivializes that history by sentimentalizing its anguish and suffering.[79] If *Stranger Than Fiction* takes the reality out of Jewish history, *The Graphic Bible* takes the sacred out of the holy scriptures. In his introduction, Browne, plagiarizing himself, describes the Bible as "the immortal epic of a people's confused, faltering, but indomitable struggle after a nobler life in a happier world." At the Rothko hearing, Browne testified that he had written the fifty-thousand-word text of *The Graphic Bible* in one month. Commerce was the soul of Lewis Browne.

Moreover, the Marcus Rothkowitz of 1928 was a kind of person particularly disturbing to Browne, and not just because he had chosen high over commercial art. Browne complained at the hearing of Rothko's "slackness"; the term was taken from the popular demonology of World War I ("alien slackers") and had provided Browne with the central issue for his first publication, "The Jew Is Not a Slacker," which appeared in the genteel, conservative pages of the *North American Review.*[80] Quoting an anti-Semitic sentence from a selective service manual, Browne wonders why, "even in official circles," the stereotype of the Jew as slacker has so persisted. To explain this anti-Semitism, however, Browne turns not to the official circles but to the Jews. For this reason his essay provides not an analysis but an instance of anti-Semitism.

Not all Jews are slackers, Browne asserts; the trouble is that those who are manifest their dissent with such "zeal and passion" that they create a public impression out of proportion to their actual numbers. They are, in Browne's term, "un-Americanized Jews." Foreign-born, "usually from Russia," a "newly arrived immigrant" who has lived here for a decade or perhaps two, "the un-Americanized Jew is one who lives in this country but is not yet essentially a part of it." He is, then, an *alien* slacker, a category that, given Browne's definition of it, gradually expands to embrace most of the Jews then living in the United States.

Browne deplores these slackers and admits that "I am thoroughly ashamed of them." Still he proposes "kindly sympathy" rather than "harsh censure." "Teach him your ways and your thoughts," he exhorts the WASP readers of the *North American Review;* "Americanize him." Where there were matzo balls, let there be Wonder Bread. Jewish slackers (by now a redundant phrase) constitute a group that Browne sentimentalizes. "You, who walk free and lightly through the terrors of the hour, remember that he, poor foreign Jew, stumbles heavily beneath the burden of twenty centuries of unremitting woe." Yet they are also a group from which Browne (speaking of "we occidentals") wishes to dissociate himself. His Americanization program is designed to delegitimatize dissent and drain it of ideological zeal and passion—its life.

The young man Browne hired to assist him with *The Graphic Bible* was foreign-born, a Russian Jew, an immigrant who had lived in this country about fifteen years, and a political dissident—an ideal candidate for a Brownean educational experiment in Americanization. In fact, Browne's own testimony establishes that he conceived of his relationship with Rothko not as a professional one in which Rothko exchanged his time, talent, and expertise for money but as a more "humane" and personal one. From the beginning, Rothko, hired "out of sympathy and not recognition of his work," was treated as a "charity" case. "I would like, as much as possible, to encourage you," Browne told Rothko, "because I think any man who has devoted himself for four years and has starved at art is a man worthy of encouragement."

By personalizing his relationship with Rothko, Browne could think of himself as generous while enlarging Rothko's duties from graphic artist to factotum. "He also performed errands for me, answering the phone, bringing up mail," and picking up packages. "He was very handy about the place and a most amiable chap." Later, Browne placed Rothko's name on the jacket of *The Graphic Bible* because he was "so pleased with Rothkowitz as a boy in the place." Similarly, Browne placed Rothko's initial ("R") into the margins of a dozen maps not out of recognition for the work but out of a "feeling of generosity," when he was in a "good mood." "One day—generous—I won't give the reason," Browne added a hundred dollars of his own to Rothko's pay, telling him, "This is in return for the fine way you have acted around here." This, of course, now makes Rothko's pay or recognition a function of what Browne's mood happens to be or of how closely Rothko conforms to his employer's notions of decorum.

But like good men, good boys are hard to find; the most amiable chaps can turn surly or sloppy or both. There were Rothko's dirty finger-marks on the maps, his "littering" the apartment with his clothes, his "slackness" and "general attitude of unpleasantness." When philanthropic methods did not work, Browne became coercive. Because Rothko's attitude had become "reprehensible," Browne was not going to put Rothko's name on any more maps and he might remove it from the jacket—a threat he eventually carried out. Rothko—resistant to an authority he had once invested some hopes in—proved a poor candidate for Americanization.

Rothko's sharpest exchanges at the legal hearing were with Browne's attorney, Arthur Garfield Hays. At forty-seven Hays was then probably the most successful and certainly the best-known criminal attorney in America. Born in Rochester, New York, Hays descended on both sides of his family from German Jewish families who, like Rothko's Weinstein relatives, had become wealthy in the clothing business. In fact, Hays's maternal grandfather had been Emma Goldman's first employer in the United States, paying her $2.50 a week for ten and a half hours a day at sewing overcoats. So assimilated was the family by Hays's time that when he was a boy he called a friend a "little Jew" and his parents had to take him aside and explain that *he* was Jewish.[81] Like Rothko, Hays identified with the victims of oppression; he was an ardent civil libertarian who defended, often gratis through the ACLU, many of those stigmatized as radical by the government during the 1910s and 1920s. He had defended Sacco and Vanzetti in Boston and Scopes in Tennessee; he had defended the right of H. L. Mencken to publish the *American Mercury,* the rights of Pennsylvania coal miners to organize, and the rights of blacks in Chicago to live where they chose. Active in progressive politics, Hays had participated in the founding of the Farmer-Labor party in 1920 and in the LaFollette campaign in 1924.

Often reviled as a dangerous radical, Hays was actually a classic American liberal. In his *Let Freedom Ring* (published the year of the Rothko hearing), Hays passionately condemned contemporary American society: "Order has become the fetish; prosperity its handmaiden; respectability its emblem. Conformity is the watchword. Production, possessions, material success, the end. . . . A dominating complacence, a comfortable obliviousness, an ignorant pretense, mark the Babbitry of those who govern."[82] The indictment here, focusing on materialism and hypocrisy as the basic social problems, refuses to move on to any systematic account of the many threats to freedom Hays's book describes. These derive, rather, from certain regrettable but permanent features of the human mind: "ignorance, bigotry, and intolerance," a line of argument elaborated in Hays's later *Trial by Prejudice* (1933).[83] In fact, for Hays, political and religious ideologies constitute instances of prejudice, not ways of understanding or dealing with it. But though a liberal in politics, Hays was a cultural conservative. At the beginning of his autobiography, *City Lawyer,* he presents himself as an unabashed philistine: "I like melody in music, content in a picture, terseness and point in a poem."[84] The Browne-Rothko hearing exposed some of the civil libertarian's own cultural prejudices. His cross-examination of Rothko joined one of the hearing's most provocative issues: a debate over the nature of art.

At the hearing Browne and the defense lawyers developed a reductive and self-contradictory position on art. On the one hand, they advanced a very literalistic concept of art as mimesis, insisting that good art is accurate copying, and they used this notion to criticize and ridicule Rothko's drawings. On the other hand, they belittled his work as *mere* copying from sources provided by Browne. Henry W. Taft, the attorney for Macmillan, pretended to be unable to identify one of Rothko's fish and mockingly commented: "I have seen all the varieties in the aquariums at Naples, and I do not think there is one like that there." Taft later called another Rothko fish "grotesque," and when Rothko asked what was meant by "grotesque," Taft defined it as "unusual and not in accord with nature."

In a November 1927 letter, Browne had urged Rothko, "Use your genius, boy!"—i.e., in decorating the maps. At the hearing, however, Browne insisted that he had given Rothko sources for all the drawings and had typically instructed him, "Copy this out exactly." Browne was the master, Rothko the apprentice. Hays continually sought to establish Rothko's reliance on Browne's superior knowledge—for example, did Rothko know what was the sea, what were the mountains on a given map?—as well as his dependence on the graphic sources provided by Browne from his extensive collection. Some of these sources were historical studies such as Friedrich Delitzch's *Babel and Bible;* others were decorative design books such as the *Handbook of Ornamental and Natural Form;* others were illustrations from Browne's earlier books, some of them taken, in turn, from still earlier books by Browne, who seems to have had a peculiar fondness for verbal and visual self-quotation.

The defense maintained, however, that Rothko was simply copying work by Browne and other authorities, while Browne, making no secret of his reliance on these same authorities, claimed that the drawings were somehow *his* creations because he owned the books. Rothko, for instance, testified that he had drawn the map on page 43 of *The Graphic Bible* (fig. 17). Hays countered that Rothko had traced the olive tree at the lower right from one in the map on

Chapter Three

page 105 of Browne's *Stranger Than Fiction*. Rothko, freely admitting that he had Browne's work in front of him when he did his own drawing, argued that he had reproduced such sources "in my own style."[85] The differences of both visual detail and style in the two drawings are quite clear. Rather than copying Browne exactly, Rothko had used perhaps not his genius but at least his talent. Unfortunately, these differences were difficult to establish in a legal context.

From Rothko's perspective, judicial authority in New York proved as inflexible as academic authority at Yale. Instead of vindication, the hearing provided Rothko with a painful public attack on his integrity, his artistic ability and knowledge, and even his intelligence. He did not always suffer the ordeal patiently. When Hays wanted to know if Rothko could tell what was to be sea and what was to be mountain on a map, Rothko replied, "Yes, I am not that stupid." When Hays later inquired whether Browne hadn't told Rothko "where to put your ships and sea animals and where to put your decorations," an exasperated Rothko declared, "That is so stupid." And in answer to Hays's efforts to demonstrate that Rothko had copied a camel from a picture postcard, Rothko testily retorted, "I can draw camels at any time without postal cards."

In many respects the hearing itself replicated Rothko's relation with Browne. Genteel lawyers exposed ethnic and class bias: "You are trained in English, aren't you?" Taft sarcastically inquired at one point. There were moments of condescension; Hays referred to Rothko as "a boy expecting," and the idea that he had "starved for art" provoked general "merriment" among the members of the court. The hearing placed Rothko in conflict with authorities who, complacently pretending to know more, actually knew a lot less about the subject at hand than Rothko did. With comic naiveté, Taft asked Rothko whether his "drawings would be of such a character as to portray perspective." Rothko explained that "perspective is a tool that artists use in expressing their ideas." "That is a little too technical for my mind," Taft remarked, then tried to get back on his feet by advancing a safe generality: "Of course, perspective is a modern development of art, is it not?" "No, it is not, sir," countered Rothko, who proceeded to argue that both the Greeks and the Egyptians had "an idea of perspective." But Taft refused to back away: "In any case, their idea of perspective was not what the modern idea of perspective is; is not that so?" Again Rothko countered, now by asserting that "the modern idea is quite to eliminate perspective altogether," a view that inspired Taft to move in with what he thought would be his knockout punch: "That is a jazz artist, isn't it?"

At one point Hays sought to expose Rothko's ignorance by giving him a kind of oral exam on the representative symbols of various ancient civilizations—Babylonian, Egyptian, Persian, Chaldean; Rothko passed the test and in the process revealed that he was now quite familiar with the ancient art collections at New York's Metropolitan Museum. Rothko, moreover, not only knew about art but had developed a more sophisticated account of it than had the defense. On the issue of creativity Rothko testified that he respected artistic authority: "I don't abhor learning from others." As he amusingly pointed out to Hays, dependence on sources is sometimes inevitable: "I myself had never seen Christ. I had to take him from some source." On the other hand, such reliance is not copying: "Nothing is ever a copy which changes the original," and "there is always some change."

In part Rothko's own premises were formalist, stressing not the literal accuracy but the structural unity of the work. In producing his maps, Rothko created "the whole unit, the decoration as a unit. It is a picture, and everything in the map goes toward making the picture." Hays questioned: "Wasn't that unit taken from an Atlas?" but Rothko disagreed: "No, the decorative unit was not taken from an Atlas." Similarly, when the referee asked Rothko his definition of a creative work, he emphasized formal unity: "Creative work is creating a unit, a pictorial unit, in which all the various parts are harmonized." The artist may begin from his own imagination or from "observation, both from the work of predecessors, and also from nature," says Rothko, but it is through its internal relations that a work "becomes a creation."[86]

Rothko spoke of his desire to give "form and grace" to the maps; even "the lettering was made with a feeling of beauty on my part for filling that space." But the young Rothko was no more a mere formalist than he was a jazz artist; his ultimate assumptions even at this time included but went beyond formalism. They can be delineated by juxtaposing the different definitions of the graphic that Rothko and Browne formulate. Says Browne: "By graphic I mean pictorial and therefore, easily assimilateable to the mind unacquainted with the thing in nature itself." Browne understands the graphic not by way of the creator but by way of the audience; in *The Graphic Bible* the pictorial therefore is a *means,* specifically, a means of making his text—which is not exactly opaque—"easily assimilateable." Verbal and visual media were the vehicles that powered Lewis Browne down the road to social assimilation and commercial success.

Rothko's notion of the graphic emerges during his cross-examination by Taft.

> *Taft:* I suppose that the graphic consists in making what is pictured true, as natural as possible, doesn't it?
> *Rothko:* To draw as naturally as possible, yes; to give the pictorial idea of the things involved.
> *Taft:* To reproduce the objects which are sought to be portrayed?

Rothko: Or to so create the objects that they give the idea of the thing, yes.

Taft urges closeness to nature; Rothko insists on an *idea* of the thing—not a realistic representation of the thing but what he elsewhere calls its "adequate suggestion." A picture for Rothko is neither an accurate mimesis nor an easily assimilable illustration; for this recent student of Max Weber, a picture is an expressive object, its unity a unity of feeling: "All things have to appear as done at the same time, under a single motion, and with the same feeling," he says. From this point of view Rothko eloquently distinguishes Browne's work from his own.

> Mr. Browne has taken his entire area of the map, and has filled it with very fine straight lines that go here and there in every direction, and filled the page himself entirely. Now, his lines do not express any ships; they do not express any sort of picture; they do not express any sort of idea. They simply fill the page.

His own work, however, attempts

> to make a certain area alive with lines to express an idea of waves, an idea of sea, and an idea of ships, that may be around in the water, and give a graphic idea, a living idea of the territory which this space is supposed to enclose.

While Browne was sapping religious feeling from the scriptures in order to turn them into easily consumed prose and pictures, Rothko, the old *cheder* student, was subverting Browne's intention by making the biblical text a "living idea."

Rothko's position on art at the hearing suggests that, even at the beginning of his career, his interest lay less in mimesis than in the expressive "idea," less in material appearance than in inner essence. It would take another twenty years for Rothko to evolve an artistic theory and practice that were at once radical and faithful to these assumptions. Certainly his artistic views of the late twenties, while often eloquently stated, leaned upon a tradition of thinking about art that was at least a couple of hundred years old. Ironically, even this position, conventional as it was, scandalized the American bourgeois literalism that had been assimilated by Browne and Hays. Throughout the hearing the defense sought not just to refute but to ridicule Rothko's thought and practice. He was accused of what he abhorred—mere copying; Browne accused Rothko of doing exactly what Browne was doing—mere copying. The books introduced by Hays as the graphic sources provided for Rothko by Browne were books that Browne himself stated were his own sources for *The Graphic Bible*, yet none of these works are cited in Browne's introduction. Browne made unacknowledged use of scholarly and artistic authorities. All of which raises a key question: when Browne was quoting himself, just who was he quoting? The answer is: in one sense, nobody in particular.

In one of his more flabbergasting admissions, Browne, asked about his graphic style, said: "I have no style. . . . I wish I could acquire one." At times, he later adds, he has used a particular style, but "it was not my style. I had not that style. Style did not have me. I had it . . . I had fifty styles." In wishing he could "acquire" one, Browne conceives of style as if it were a new suit; he had "fifty" suits in his closet, but none of them quite fit because underneath them there was—nothing. "Style did not have me" because there was no "me" to have. Lacking one himself, Browne was made anxious—in fact, vengeful—by anyone with the "zeal and passion" of an authentic self, whether they were Eastern European slackers, starving young artists, or, horribly, some combination of both. As long as Browne could imagine himself as benefactor, roles were defined and Rothko was a "boy" in his place, but when Rothko began "littering" the apartment with his vest and jacket and showing that he had a style of his own, those roles collapsed and Browne became openly vengeful, withholding some of Rothko's pay for as long as two months after the job was finished.

The battle between Rothko and Browne, then, was much more than a legal one; it pitted Rothko against the legal system (since he had to rely on it to right his wrongs), against politically liberal authority (since both Browne and Hays were liberals), against Jewish authority (since both Browne and Hays were Jews) and even against a certain kind of artistic authority (since both Browne and Hays—well-off, cultivated liberals—were precisely the kind of people to whom Rothko might hope to sell his works). Rothko lost the case, just as Browne decided that one of Rothko's landscapes would not "do."

Indeed, on Rothko's theory that the "unfriendliness of society" acted as "a lever for true liberation," then by the late 1920s Rothko ought to have been one of the most liberated men in the United States. All through the first three decades of his life, Rothko felt, authority—political, familial, academic, legal—betrayed and victimized him. His father had saved him from charging Cossacks and Russian anti-Semitism—then died; Yale saved him from Portland—then dropped his scholarship; Browne saved him from poverty—then cheated him. Just a few years after leaving New Haven, Rothko had replaced its genteel WASP anti-Semitism with Browne's genteel Jewish anti-Semitism.

The Browne episode confirmed Rothko's suspicions of affluent authority—of the very people his choice of profession had forced him into economic reliance on. Yet if Rothko did accept Browne's spoken promise of an unspecified share of royalties—and the whole legal debate hinged on this issue—then he was all too trusting. To Rothko, who often complained about his older brothers' failure to help support him when he was "starving" for art, Browne had appeal as a potential *kindly* older brother. So, later, did Bernard Reis, the accountant and collector upon whom Rothko became increasingly dependent in the last ten years of his life. Reis was eight years older than Rothko, well-to-do, politically left, a self-styled benefactor of artists, and a businessman who liked to operate on a personal basis. Like Browne, Reis betrayed Rothko (and his heirs) by selling Rothko's paintings to his own employer, the Marlborough Galleries, while also acting as an executor of Rothko's estate.[87] Rothko, it seems, had some propensity for putting himself in the way of wolves, the better to assure himself that he was a lamb. Wolves were not hard to find.

In fact, given that the Browne case came down to believing the word of an eminent author against that of an unknown artist and that the author was defended by Arthur Garfield Hays, Rothko's suit seems to have been doomed from the start. Why then did he undertake it? Probably he was convinced he was right; possibly he *was* right. He certainly needed the money; for all his strenuous efforts, then and later, to "transcend" material pressures, the Browne suit shows Rothko's entanglement with them. The courtroom, moreover, provided the theatrical and combative Rothko with a stage on which to dramatize his conflict with authority. His zealous pursuit of what was likely to be a "tragic" lost cause was also entirely characteristic, all the more so if his side of the case were in any sense, consciously or unconsciously, fabricated. Suing Browne was at once a self-assertive and a self-destructive act.

Yet if Rothko later converted his moment of triumph at the Museum of Modern Art into a moment of despair, he turned his defeat in the Browne case into something like liberation. Social copying (assimilation) and artistic copying (mimesis) triumphed, leaving Rothko feeling more marginalized, and more uncompromising. He did no more commercial art. The outcome confirmed who he was: a poor, marginal, victimized artist, a man set apart.

4 Starting Out in the Depression

When I was a younger man, art was a lonely thing: no galleries, no collectors, no critics, no money.

Mark Rothko

In the summer of 1932, Marcus Rothkowitz was enjoying himself far from the heat, the crowded streets and subways, the contentious courtrooms, and the steel and concrete skyscrapers of New York City. He was 160 miles north, living in a tent with a painter-friend, Nathaniel Dirk, at Hearthstone Point, a primitive camping ground along the shore near the south end of Lake George. Located in a beautiful pine and hemlock forest, Hearthstone Point offered an expansive view of the mile-wide lake, a few of its many small islands, and the forested Adirondack mountains. Most campers came to swim, hunt, fish; Rothko swam, took walks, did watercolors, and met his first wife.[1]

Rothko had brought along his mandolin; one evening as he was playing it at the campfire, the music attracted Edith Sachar, a young woman from Brooklyn who was also camping at Hearthstone. Forty years and one divorce after their first meeting Edith still remembered the "beautiful setting" and Rothko's "classical mandolin."[2] Despite the romantic setting, Edith was not that impressed. But shortly after they met again in Albany, New York, she was writing to Rothko, "You have no idea how much I learned to care for you and how my opinion altered and my affection grew." But she wanted to live on her own for a while.[3] By September, she had become intensely involved with Christianity, and while, she wrote Rothko, "my love for you [as] I said is complete—yet it is not restful as the love I feel for God." She experienced Rothko's intense love as a threat to her freedom and separateness: "you consume me body and soul with your love," a worry she expressed several times in one of her letters.[4]

Just two months later, on November 12—two days before Edith's twentieth birthday—they were married, by Rothko's old high-school friend Rabbi Max MacCoby, in Rothko's apartment at 314 West 75th Street, with Rothko's Seattle cousin Harold Weinstein and his wife, Barbara, as the witnesses.[5]

The couple's new life was quite impoverished. Their two-room basement apartment had once served as the dog kennel for the wealthy Ochs family, whose mansion the building had once been. The new occupants bathed in a small tub formerly used for the dogs, and they cooked on a hot plate. But even back in the city, there was the romance of art. Rothko painted; Edith remembered him "with paint in his hair, on his face and clothes. He would smoke cigarettes and paint brush alike while painting in complete absorption." Before meeting Rothko, Edith "was more interested in writing, in poetry, than in art," she said, but when they were first married, she began to produce clay sculptures. There was painting, sculpture—and music. Edith recalled that their "first possession was a piano with a harpsichord attachment—which Rothko would play by ear." He "would play the piano hours and hours and hours" because of the "sensual pleasure" he said it gave him. "He said he could've been a musician, he should have been a musician; he had no formal training, but on the piano he could play almost anything just by ear," as he could on the mandolin. He especially liked to play Mozart, occasionally declaring that "Mozart was a Jew" and then playing a Mozart theme in a Yiddish style. But eventually Rothko "had to get rid of the piano because he said it was occupying too much of his time."[6]

So far as we know, the acutely lonely Rothko had had only one previous romantic-sexual relationship—with a woman remembered only, by a few of his friends, as Ida from Staten Island. Now twenty-nine, Rothko was nine years older than his new wife, exactly the age difference between his own parents. Rothko was tall, burly, physically awkward, with a wide nose, sensual lips, steel-rimmed glasses, and a receding hairline; Edith was of medium height (5'4½"), slender, with long brown hair usually pulled into a bun. She was attractive and graceful.[7]

Physically opposite, they shared artistic aspirations and similar backgrounds. Like Rothko, Edith came from a Russian Jewish family which was more political than religious. Both of Edith's parents—Meyer Sachar and Bella Korris—had been born near Kiev, Russia; both had emigrated to New York City as adolescents. They met there, married in 1907 and eventually had five children: Pauline (1909), Willie (1911), Edith (1912), Lilian (1919) and Howard (1927). Before he left Russia, Meyer Sachar had worked with an itinerant crew doing interior decoration in the homes of the rich. When he came to New York, he first operated a furniture store; he gave that up to open a small tea and coffee shop; he went bankrupt and moved to Union City, New Jersey—where Edith was born—to run a secondhand furniture store with a brother. Within a few years the family had moved to Brooklyn, living at a series of addresses in the predominantly Jewish Crown Heights section. Meyer Sachar tried manufacturing toy horses, manufacturing gloves, making upholstery for cars. By the mid-1920s, however, he had started the Empire Upholstery Company and bought a building at 611 Nostrand Avenue, where the family lived on the second floor, over his shop.[8]

Edith attended the local public school and then—two trolley rides away, at the corner of Flatbush and Church Avenues—Erasmus High School, starting there in February of 1927. At Erasmus Edith received her highest grade in an art appreciation course, but her record was generally poor, averaging just under a C, and in September of 1930, six months short of graduation, she was "discharged" for reasons her transcript does not specify.[9] Like Rothko's, Edith's family "lived a hard life; they had a kind of difficult time making a living." From the age of twelve Edith worked, first as an usher in a movie theater, later selling dresses for a commission in neighborhood shops. "The Sachars were all free spirits," the oldest, Willie, recalled; the Sachar women, in particular, were strong-willed, independent, and adventurous. At nineteen, Edith's older sister Pauline had hitchhiked around the country, stopping in cities to work for a while, then moving on.[10]

In the spring of 1931 Edith admonished herself in her diary: "I realize how love means everything in life to everyone and I do not want it to be everything in my life. I want to go out and do things. I don't want to settle down. Not ever." As did the young Rothko, she liked politics, debate, and literature, listing her interests, with adolescent seriousness, as "socialism, communism, public speaking, poetry, science." Her diary entries often convert radical politics into the stuff of teenage romance: "in and out again in love with socialism," she noted. By May of 1931 she was enough in love with the left to be saving "money to go to Commonwealth College" in Arkansas.[11] Rothko had been drawn to anarchism—and then went to Yale. Edith saved her money to go to Commonwealth College, a small experimental school in the Ozark hills of western Arkansas devoted to educating labor leaders. With a girlfriend, Edith hitchhiked there from New York in the fall of 1931.

The college, an offshoot of a Louisiana leftist utopian colony which had split off from a similar colony in southern California, had found a site on an isolated, mile-long valley floor, with woods, meadows, a creek, and plenty of farm land; it opened in the fall of 1925, at just about the time that Rothko was living in West Harlem and beginning to take courses from Max Weber.[12] Commonwealth was an experiment in worker's education, educational self-support, pedagogical democracy, and cooperative living. The style was intellectually freer but physically more rigorous than what Rothko had experienced at Yale.

Usually there were about forty-five students and ten to twelve faculty; classes averaged four students, met in the cottage where the instructor lived, and followed an informal discussion format. There were no exams, no grades, no required attendance, no degrees. The day began at 6:15 A.M. and proceeded through five morning classes. In the afternoon students and faculty were required to *do* labor, divided, even in this educational utopia, along quite traditional lines: men did farm work, carpentry, masonry, hauling, while the women worked in the kitchen, library, or laundry. By 1931, however, the Depression had caused a liberal-radical division at the school. As Edith was saving her money that spring, the more militant faction gained ascendancy, and during her time there students became more activist, helping, for instance, to found the Arkansas Socialist party.[13]

"The adventure of hitchhiking to Commonwealth was thrilling," she wrote in her diary. The college turned out to be less so. She stayed, apparently, just for the fall and winter quarters, 1931–32, and, even though she had vowed not to allow love to mean everything in her life, her diary allocates much more time to her romantic relations than to her political development. She had so many boyfriends that she feared her high school reputation was following her all the way to Arkansas. Edith wanted, she wrote, "to live alone and to write," but when one of her boyfriends, the young poet Kenneth Patchen, proposed going to live on a Texas mountain, she declined, declaring him too "idealistic." So in the spring of 1932 Edith and her friend hitchhiked back home, getting a ride from two young men who started out to go coon hunting but ended up driving the two women all the way to New York City.

Not quite ready to settle down in Brooklyn, or anywhere else, Edith soon left for the Adirondacks. By the late summer of 1932, after she had met Rothko, she was living alone, outside the small town of Prattsville, New York—in a cave. She was reading, and urging Marcus Rothkowitz to read, J. Middleton Murry's *Jesus, Man of Genius*. Jesus, she wrote, was a "man truly beautiful—a man with great love and truth in him."[14] She had become, according to her second husband, "a kind of small-time evangelist on the street." But her career as a Christian hermit and wandering prophet ended when she accidentally started a forest fire. "They were going to sue her but they found that she didn't have anything."[15] Like Rothko, Edith wanted to "do things," as she wrote in her diary, and went about doing them audaciously, even impulsively. A romantic herself, she was attracted to and skeptical about "idealistic" males. At Commonwealth, when she was deciding whether or not to take up Patchen's offer, she wrote: "He is good looking,—almost everything about him except his unhappy disposition appealed to me—he is an artist—a literary artist—Perhaps that is one reason I cared—He had such a beautiful feeling about him. . . . But he hasn't any money—can people live on air [?]" Having fallen in and out of love with socialism, Patchen, and Jesus, Edith Sachar now met Marcus Rothkowitz playing classical mandolin in front of a Lake George campfire. He was not good-looking; he had a *very* unhappy disposition; he was an artist; and he had such a beautiful feeling about him that she married him just a few months later. But neither one of them had any money. Could they live on air?

Edith and Rothko had been married, in fact, just three days after the election of Franklin D. Roosevelt. "The interval between Roosevelt's election in November, 1932, and his inauguration in March, 1933, proved the most harrowing four months of the depression"; one historian has called those months the "winter of despair." Just a couple of hundred yards from the couple's 75th Street apartment, hundreds of squatters camped below Riverside Drive along the Hudson River from 72nd Street to 110th Street.[16] Even during the prosperous twenties Rothko's economic state was, in Edith's word, "horrendous." He had told Ann Wolverton, a friend of Lewis Browne's, "I can teach you how to live on ten dollars a week"; she replied, "I don't wish to know."[17]

In the Depression, Rothko's finances, while never as desperate as they had been in his early New York years, were still spartan, and money was to become a major source of friction in his first marriage. Throughout the 1920s the art market in America had gradually expanded; true, American collectors typically purchased European work, but "for the last two years of the twenties, a minor boom had developed in American art," a boom that collapsed in 1929 along with the stock market.[18] All during the harrowing winter of 1932–33 banks were closing; by March 4, the day of Roosevelt's inauguration, they had shut down in forty states and that day the New York Stock Exchange did not open. Not that Rothko was worried about his investment portfolio. In fact, the old radical in Rothko might have viewed the decline of capitalism with some satisfaction; but the Depression effectively denied him and his fellows of what they needed most—collectors.

On the way back from Lake George, Rothko had stopped in Albany to see his New Haven cousin Ed Weinstein, then working for the State of New York. Rothko showed his new watercolors, and Weinstein said, " 'Very nice.' I knew his intent. His intent was to get me interested in [buying] at least one," but "I would say, 'Here, Mark. Take some money.' And he would say, 'No. No. No.' Then I would insist." But Weinstein never bought. "I said to him, 'No, Mark. Next time you're in New Haven, you'll drop off one or two to my sister, Sylvia.' And then I turned and gave him a ten dollar bill."[19] That fall, in New York, Rothko took the watercolors "around the galleries and he hadn't gotten any reaction," Edith recalled. She believed that the work was not "presented very well; he didn't frame them." "He had great faith in those watercolors"; but no one else did.[20] Rothko's cousin was willing to give a handout but not to make a purchase; dealers were just not interested. In the Depression, a watercolor by an unknown artist was a luxury item not likely to find a place in anybody's budget.

The Lake George pastoral was over; Rothko and Edith could not live on air. Sometimes, Edith later recalled, they were "so poor that all they had to eat was bean soup." To support their artistic ambitions, both of them were forced to find alternative work. Since 1929 Rothko had been teaching art two days a week to children at the Center Academy, a progressive Yeshiva attached to the Brooklyn Jewish Center on Eastern Parkway. At first Edith "was an occasional sales girl in a dress shop."[21] Later she worked for the WPA, and she taught crafts part-time at the Center Academy. Eventually, she started her own jewelry business.

Yet, if they lived at the edge of the poverty line, they never fell over it. Edith "used to talk about how she and Mark used to move frequently; she used to kid about they used to move every October," the beginning of the rent year in New York City.[22] But the series of flats they rented in Manhattan and Brooklyn were not hovels or even tenements. Even at the beginning they were able to afford the piano with a harpsichord attachment and later they bought a Ford coupe with a rumble seat. Not that the unworldly Rothko was interested in accumulating material possessions. "He told me he disdained material things," recalled Edith's younger brother, Howard. "What came across was that he never really wanted anything more than he had." Rothko was not greedy but he was ambitious; and the collapse of the art market, along with the national economy, made survival a hardship and recognition very difficult. Rothko's teaching job, moreover, took valuable time and energy away from his painting.

But the job did give him summers off, and in the summer of 1933 Rothko and Edith took the first of a series of low-budget Depression vacations, hitchhiking across the country, camping along the way, to visit Rothko's family. They stopped in Dufur, a town of about 500 in north-central Oregon, where Rothko's brother Albert, after opening a drugstore there in the mid-1920s, had become mayor, fire chief, and head of the Masons. After a brief visit in Dufur, Rothko and Edith were driven by Albert and his family to Portland. There, they camped in a tent in Washington Park in the hills above the city, "made breakfast on a sterno stove" and took some of their dinners with Rothko's mother. According to one family story, the police eventually rousted the young couple for public nudity, but Rothko was able to talk the officers out of making an arrest. At least one of Rothko's nephews was "very very impressed" with his uncle's boldness; "that was a scary thing to do in those days—to hitchhike out of New York and he didn't have a dime."[23] In 1933 Rothko was hardly the only impoverished hitchhiker along the U.S. highways, but from the conservative perspective of southwest Portland, Rothko was turning poverty into bohemian adventure.

While camping in the Portland hills, Rothko produced a number of watercolors, giving one to each of his brothers and his sister. The gifts, shows of affection and strategies to gain family approval, represented the natural landscape around Portland. By the time he evolved his mature painting style, Rothko had become a thoroughly urban personality; he told Stanley Kunitz that "he didn't want to be associated with nature. In fact, one of his statements that shocked me most was saying that he really hated nature, that he felt uncomfortable in the natural world."[24] The young Rothko, while no Monet, was responsive to the pleasures of the outdoors, and he often painted them, as he did at Lake George and in the Portland hills. A Rothko nephew remembered seeing a closet of Sonia's filled with "hundreds" of his uncle's watercolors—presumably from this and earlier trips to Portland.[25] Typical of these is an untitled work (color plate 4), in which Rothko adopts a vantage point in the hills south of Washington Park and the city itself, to look across the Willamette toward the still-rural eastern side of the river. If, as a boy, Rothko had climbed the Portland hills and gazed out at the "monumental emptiness" of the valley, this conservative watercolor seems to give little sense of such a mystical response. A long curved line established by the trees, bushes, and the edge of the steep hill in the foreground creates a bowl-like shape within which Rothko has framed and enclosed the prospect before him. He *is* partly drawn by the feeling of distance; what appears to be a dock in the lower center creates a strong arrowlike shape, which points us into the distance, and Rothko has taken care to suggest how far away the two hills are on the further shore. But just as he has framed, Rothko has also shortened, the panorama of the valley. He has tilted the plane of the valley floor slightly upward, shortening the expansive view—an effect reinforced by the way the Portland haze and clouds obscure both the blue sky and the landscape behind the hills. The sky itself is flattened by Rothko's rapid horizontal strokes, which let plenty of white paper show through. Rothko's treatment thus transforms what might have been a sublime landscape into a more conventionally beautiful and pleasing one.

From the first, even before his class with Max Weber, Rothko had been intrigued not with the sharply contoured details of a realistically rendered landscape but with what he called at the Browne trial "adequate suggestion," the landscape's expressive idea. In the Portland watercolor he has been attentive to certain parts of the scene—the pier on the far side of the river, the cows and trees at the left center; but he does not render particulars precisely. Nor, despite his rather stagy framing device, is he primarily interested in formal unity. Some areas interest him more than others. Moreover, the more we look at this piece, the more the tree at the right attracts our attention and begins to dominate the scene it is supposed to frame. Its top branches float free of the tree's trunk, itself severed, about halfway up, by a blank white space. These mysterious qualities, plus the earth tones, pull our eye toward the tree and away from the river and valley. At times the tree resembles a giant female figure gazing out and presiding over the Portland landscape. Yet what remains most striking, and most expressive, about this watercolor are Rothko's light, feathery strokes and the luminosity which shines through his thin, transparent washes. This execution owes something to Cézanne, but it lacks his formal severity; Rothko's mood is light, cheerful, enthusiastically blending natural and human into a harmonious, genteel landscape. Just as these early watercolors avoid the rugged, dangerous, awesome aspects of nature, so they fail to reflect Rothko's brooding, melancholy depths. This one, though done with an appealing youthful buoyancy, domesticates nature and romanticizes Cézanne. Yet its luminosity also suggests that behind this conventionalized landscape Rothko sensed a light that reminded him of a deeper happiness which his art could not yet fully confront.

On his trip west Rothko had brought along a portfolio of his own work and that of some of the children in his Center Academy art classes. That summer, Rothko, who liked to revile Portland for its provinciality, had his first one-man show, at the Portland Art Museum, exhibiting his own drawings, watercolors and temperas as well as a selection of his students' work. His work was reviewed favorably in the *Oregonian*. Yet his visit, not all bohemian adventure and artistic triumph, had its strains. Albert found Edith "difficult." Albert's son Richard recalled that Edith had a "hard time" in Dufur and mysteriously "stayed in their room" during most of the visit. Albert's wife, Bella, reported that Edith wore flour sacks for underwear. In Portland, Kate Rothkowitz declared her new daughter-in-law lazy.[26]

And, like any family reunion, this one brought to the surface old affections, along with old tensions and grudges. Moise, Albert, and Sonia had all married within the Portland ghetto. By 1933 the family, like many of those from southwest Portland, had dispersed across the city and, in Albert's case, about seventy miles east of it. But Albert would return to Portland not long after Rothko's visit, and as Moise's son Julian put it, "we were a very close-knit family. It was a rare weekend that we weren't either at Sonia's or Sonia at our house, and when Albert lived in Portland, all the children played together. Grandma was always with us." Rothko was no longer part of this circle. Not only did he live two thousand miles beyond its borders, his vocation placed him in a strange world which his family did not particularly understand or value. Moreover, he seldom wrote. He did feel close to Sonia—less so to his two brothers. When they were all together there was a "strong family tie and they picked up as if the conversation had had a brief pause." But resentments persisted on both sides. Moise's wife, Clara, angrily criticized Rothko for not writing to his mother, who "used to send him stuff and never know whether he got it or not." Rothko expected help from his family, especially from Moise whom, as the oldest male, Rothko perceived as the "father." But the Depression affected pharmacists as well as artists; Albert's Dufur business folded, and Moise, to open his Portland store, had given an "on demand" note for a loan from one of the Weinstein brothers. "During the Depression they haunted him to death" for the money.[27]

Moreover, the Portland family resented Rothko's failure to send money to his mother, who at this time was dependent upon her less than well-off children for support. Eventually she was forced to move in with Sonia. Worst of all, Rothko felt, correctly, that his family did not understand his art. "I don't think they knew what it was about," Moise said. "Especially in the beginning we didn't know what it was all about anyhow. . . . At that time it looked to us like we didn't know what it was. Of course, it wasn't that the world accepted him so well." In Rothko's absence, bewildered disapproval was sometimes expressed as ridicule. By camping at Washington Park while visiting Portland, Rothko established some necessary distance from these tensions. He was showing, in the words of one nephew, that "he was independent; he made his own decisions as to when he was going to entertain the family."[28]

When Rothko and Edith returned to New York, they rented the top floor of a three-story brownstone at 1000 Park Place, Brooklyn.[29] The living room, which got northern light and overlooked the small Brower Park across the street, served as Rothko's studio. This new location, in a quiet residential and mainly Jewish neighborhood, had two geographical advantages: it was just a four-block walk south to the Center Academy and just a five-block walk west and north to Edith's parents' place on Nostrand Avenue. The Rothkowitzes prided themselves on being educated; the Sachars prided themselves on being free spirits. Their newest in-law prided himself on being a self-educated free spirit.

At first, he stretched the limits of Sachar family tolerance. Rothko was an impoverished artist, he was nine years older than Edith, and he had been living with her prior to their marriage—all of which had inspired Meyer and Bella Sachar's initial disapproval, which, in turn, had inspired the young couple to "elope" by getting married in the apartment where they were already living together. But after the marriage, Rothko, according to both Edith's sister Lilian and her brother Howard, "was taken right into the family."[30] During the two years when they lived on Park Place and the following six months when they lived at 724 Nostrand Avenue (just three blocks from the Sachars), Rothko and Edith not only participated in all family functions; they took many of their daily meals with her parents.[31] As Lilian pointed out, "It was the only family he had," at least in New York. More than that, it was a family with which Rothko felt comfortable for several reasons.

They were Russian, Jewish, and secular; they were not, like the Weinsteins, well-off; they ran a family business. Meyer Sachar, of whom Rothko was particularly fond, was "a very lovable man; the kids all loved their father," according to Edith's second husband, George Carson. After Meyer retired from his upholstery business, he took up painting and commented that "if he had started to paint as a young man, he would have given up everything for it." But Bella "was all business—no jokes; no time for that, we have to make a living." She ran the family and perhaps the Empire Upholstery Company as well; "she was sort of a businesswoman."[32] The Sachar family circumstances and structure were familiar to Rothko; but the Sachars lacked the complex history of expectations and gripes that came with his original family, that sense of forced closeness and the tensions he depicted in *The Rothkowitz Family*.

"I really feel that Marcus enjoyed the sense of family because we had a diversity, and the thing that he liked were the discussions," Howard remembered. Sachar family discussions covered a wide range of topics, with politics a leading subject during the 1930s. While "there was a lot of joking around," these discussions were highly competitive. The three oldest children—Pauline, Willie, and Edith—were "very forceful people. It was always argument time when the three of them were together, because each one had his or her own ideas and had to express them. So it was really a knockdown time."[33]

Verbal combat was congenial enough to Rothko, though the Sachars differ on his participation. Lilian remembered Rothko as "a very reserved person; he was thinking all the time; things were going on in his head; he wasn't looking for any horsecrap—*ever*. But he entered into it, to have a good meal." But Howard recalled that "Marcus would hold sway; everybody loved the range of his thought—the subjects. Particularly, he had a marvelous sense of humor, a wry sense of humor." "Marcus would be in the limelight and if my brother [Willie] was there, it would be between Marcus and my brother," and if Pauline were also there, all three would be "trying to upstage each other." It is easy to imagine that Rothko was both thoughtfully reserved and eager for the limelight. With the Sachars he was neither the poor relation, as he was with the Weinsteins, nor the wunderkind over whom people rolled their eyes and shook their heads, as he was with his own family. His new family attachments were less deep but less complicated, and they helped mollify both the economic and emotional force of the Depression.

. . .

> *Rothko explained to me that [Milton] Avery was the first person that Rothko knew who was a professional artist twenty-four hours a day. And he gave Rothko the idea that that was a possibility.*
>
> Elaine de Kooning

Rothko sought domestic attachments as intensely as he sought to free himself of them, and the Sachars were not his only or even his most important surrogate family during the 1930s. In 1927, his roommate, Gordon Soule, had put Rothko in touch with Louis Kaufman, a young violinist whose family had known Rothko's in southwest Portland. Kaufman was interested in painting, and he had already met Milton Avery and bought a still life from him, for $25. "I took Marcus to Milton," said Kaufman, "and then he became a real fanatic on the work of Milton."[34]

In the fall of 1928, just as he was launching his ill-fated suit against Lewis Browne, Rothko was accepted for his first group show, at the Opportunity Gallery, a small city-subsidized gallery which held month-long shows of young artists selected by a more established painter, in this case Bernard Karfoil, a progressive turned conservative who also chose Rothko's friends Louis Harris, Lewis Ferstadt, and Milton Avery.[35] Rothko, who had been betrayed and humiliated by Browne, now came under the influence of Avery, whose style of authority was relaxed and restrained. "Marcus, like the rest of us, began to haunt the place and visit [Milton] regularly," said Kaufman. Rothko was "at our house every night," Sally Avery recalled.[36]

Born in 1885, Milton Avery was eighteen years older than Rothko, almost old enough to be his father.[37] The last of four children, Avery had been born in Sand Bank (now Altmar), a village in north-central New York, about ten miles inland from Lake Ontario. Unlike Rothko, Avery descended from an old and prosperous Yankee family, which had emigrated from England in the early eighteenth century. Avery's side of the family, however, was downwardly mobile, and by his day they were working class, his father laboring as a tanner in a local factory. During Avery's boyhood, the family's fortunes continued to decline. When Avery was thirteen the Sand Bank tanning factory folded and the Averys moved to Wilson Station, a village near East Hartford, Connecticut. By 1903, the year of Rothko's birth, Milton Avery had already been working for two years at the Hartford Machine and Screw Company. Sometime after 1905 Avery began taking courses at the Connecticut Art Students League, combining eight hours of manual labor by day with art study by night. By 1915, Avery's father, two older brothers, and a brother-in-law had all died. At thirty, now living in a poor section of Hartford, Avery was the only male and one of only two sources of income in a household of nine women, "all of whom doted on Milton."[38] Avery's beginnings as a painter thus combined severe financial constraints with female emotional support.

As Rothko was beginning his two years at Yale, Avery, who never attended college, had switched his schedule, so that he now painted by day and worked nights as a file clerk at the Travellers Insurance Company. In 1920 he had begun spending his summers in the art colony at Gloucester, Massachusetts, where in 1924 he met Sally Michel, a twenty-one-year-old painter from an orthodox Jewish family in Brooklyn. To be near Sally, Avery moved, the following year, with his painter-friend Wallace Putnam, to New York City, and the year after that—on May 1, 1926—they were married.

Sally, too, doted on Milton. In fact, Avery's new domestic life was modeled on his old one, except that he was now relieved of the need to do anything but paint. Milton, a reticent Yankee with a "dry wit," was quiet. "Why talk when you can paint?" he liked to say.[39] Sally was more social and loquacious; and she was more worldly and ambitious, at least for her husband. She "guided their relationship in a manner that created a supportive environment in which he could work freely, unimpeded by economic or social responsibilities."[40] She pursued a career as an illustrator, refusing even to let her husband teach (as Rothko did) because she believed it would waste his time. In the words of their friend Putnam, Sally "supplied the drive to a large extent and also the worldly wisdom enough to deal with people. I'm quite sure that [Milton] couldn't have done it alone."[41]

In the early years of his friendship with the Averys, Rothko himself was struggling to do it alone. With the quietly confident Milton and his effervescent young wife, Rothko was the bumbling bachelor who one day served the Averys some tea that tasted funny—because it had been made in a pot in which Rothko had cooked some glue. Rothko soon became part of an Avery coterie that included Adolph Gottlieb, John Graham, Jack Kufeld, Barnett Newman, Wallace Putnam, Joseph Solman, and Louis Schanker. More than that, Rothko became a family intimate, dropping by daily to see Avery's new work.[42] The month before their own marriage, Rothko and Edith helped the Averys bring their new daughter, March, home from the hospital; and not long after their wedding, Rothko and Edith moved from West 75th to West 72nd Street, just across the street from the Averys' apartment.[43]

Rothko may have visited the Averys in Gloucester either before or after his 1932 Lake George camping trip. He and Edith did spend a few summers at Gloucester with the Averys during the 1930s and at least one summer in the early 1940s. Adolph and Esther Gottlieb and, later, Barnett and Annalee Newman were also part of these working vacations. "Everybody had a space to work by themselves," said Sally Avery. In the afternoons "we'd meet on the beach every day and go swimming and play handball and we had a lot of good, nice, wholesome times." In the evenings "they'd look at Milton's paintings" and talk, for example, "about the color and the shapes and the forms and how Milton could make a brilliant color recede when it would normally come forward and things like that."[44] During *these* vacations Rothko did not find it necessary to encamp himself and his wife on a distant hill. Back in New York, the Averys held a once-a-week sketch class, with a nude model, at their apartment; and they also conducted occasional evening poetry readings ("Milton liked to read poetry out loud") which included the writings of T. S. Eliot and Wallace Stevens. Rothko attended both the sketching classes and the readings. Avery produced at least four paintings and one etching of Rothko.[45] Rothko's sketchbooks of the 1930s contain several drawings of Avery, a few of Milton and Sally, and one of Milton, Sally, and himself; his *Woman and Child* represents Sally and March.[46]

"The instruction, the example, the nearness in the flesh of this marvelous man—all this was a significant fact—one which I shall never forget," Rothko recalled at Avery's funeral in 1965.[47] It is not hard to understand the intensity of his bond with Avery. Both came from backgrounds that were working class and provincial; both had an early familiarity with economic hardship and human mortality. Yet they also reacted from these shared circumstances in opposite directions. "Rothko was very verbal," Sally Avery said, "and he used to tell fabulous stories. He was a continual raconteur," whereas Milton "was not verbal at all." Louis Kaufman found the Averys to be "natural charmers, without trying to be anything except themselves"; Sally Avery thought Rothko to be a "natural sufferer"—no doubt without trying to be anything but himself.[48]

Dislocation, loss, and poverty had given Rothko a bitter conviction of lack, Avery "an unrelenting compulsion to work, as if work itself would provide a deliverance from the terrors of everyday reality." Rothko, who associated the origins of his motive for painting with his erotic response to the female nude, "hated to paint," according to Sally Avery. Not that painting did not give Rothko pleasure; but as Edith recalled, "painting was sort of a tormented act for him. He was tortured when he painted and when you watched him when he painted, the expressions on his face, he seemed to go through agony."⁴⁹ Rothko eventually conceived of the artist as a self-sacrificial prophet whose painful process agonized him into a kind of transcendence. Avery's conception was more modest: "his approach was that of an artisan and his attitude without pretension or agony." In the 1930s, both Milton and Sally arose every morning at 6 A.M. and worked until 6 P.M. Avery produced quickly and regularly. "I can't keep up with my ideas for pictures," he said. "Often I paint a big oil in the morning and another one in the afternoon." Avery "would say himself, that if he had to struggle and work with things, they generally didn't come out." He criticized Rothko for not working enough.⁵⁰

Yet these differences were precisely what made Avery so attractive to someone who, in Rothko's own words, was "younger, questioning, and looking for an anchor." Being young, uncertain, and alone left Rothko feeling "at sea." By the time he had encountered Max Weber in the mid-1920s, Weber was embittered and grandiose, directive and somewhat pompous. He was no *real* anchor. Avery, on the other hand, "was the most unassertive, the least bombastic person that you can think of," said Louis Kaufman. He "taught not by what he said but what he did," but, unlike Weber, he did it quietly: "Avery," said Rothko, "had that inner power in which gentleness and silence proved . . . audible and poignant." Gentleness and silence, to become leading qualities in his mature work, were buried in the twenty-five-year-old Rothko, who, according to Edith, had "a tremendous emotional capacity for despair." At the time he met Avery, Rothko was sharing a small, seedy tenement apartment with Louis Harris on 15th Street, just west of Union Square. "I cannot tell you what it meant for us during those early years to be made welcome in those memorable studios on Broadway, 72nd Street, and Columbus Avenue," Rothko said. "The walls were always covered with an endless and changing array of poetry and light."⁵¹ Avery represented psychological calm, domestic stability, a life devoted to the poetry and light of pure art.

Together, the Averys represented an idealized transformation of Rothko's original family. Milton was a quiet dreamer who was not a failing pharmacist but, already by the early 1930s, an assured, independent painter. Sally was the woman behind him—not pushing but protecting him, allowing Milton to work in a world largely severed from material concerns and obligations. Rothko's first marriage was, in fact, modeled on Avery's: a patriarchal arrangement in which the wife emotionally and financially supports her artist-husband. Like Avery, Rothko married a much younger woman whom he met in a romantic summer-vacation setting. At least in the beginning Edith doted on Rothko; she "really respected his ability, even though he wasn't making any money at it.

She really felt that he was doing something that was very important"—so much so that in the mid-1930s when she started her business designing and selling silver jewelry, she became the family's main source of income.[52] Edith was doing what Rothko's older brothers were not—supporting him. Like Sally Avery, she turned to commercial art to free her husband for high art. But the dream of emulating the Averys collapsed, partly because Marcus was not Milton, and Edith was not Sally, but also because Avery's marriage was an extension of his earlier family life, while Rothko's attempted to compensate for what he felt was lacking in his own emotional past.

Of course, Avery affected Rothko most through his work. Max Weber had brought artistic modernism to the United States, then, in the 1920s, joined most American painters of his generation by abandoning it. Milton Avery, a Hartford provincial who had missed the invasion of "Ellis Island" art during the 1910s, developed a unique and fruitful relation to European modernism during the 1920s, by looking not to the cubes of Picasso but the colors of Matisse. Avery simplified natural landscape and the human figure into flat, lyrical areas of opaque color, and by doing so he became the historical link between European modernism and the "color field" wing of American Abstract Expressionism. As Rothko's friend Alfred Jensen put it, "Avery brought color to America."[53]

His timing was important. Social, political, and economic crises made American painting not just conservative but artistically reactionary in the 1930s. Painters of the American Scene, such as Thomas Hart Benton, responded with heroized images of our agrarian past; the Social Realists, such as William Gropper, responded by satirizing contemporary political authority or lamenting its working-class victims. Benton was nationalistic and nostalgic; Gropper was aggressively critical. Despite their opposed politics, however, both groups were programmatically antimodern: by substituting social for aesthetic values and adopting a style of figurative illustration, they aimed at a large audience.

Asked whether modern painting was beautiful or ugly, Milton Avery wryly told a journalist in 1931: "Olives taste ugly, too, until you learn to enjoy them." Avery was no populist. His paintings began with subjects—landscapes, human figures—which remained recognizable; but Avery always insisted that the artist's obligation was not to mimetic exactitude but to aesthetic design. As the reporter continued:

> Mr. Avery believes that paintings need not be "literary"; but rather, they should express a more or less abstract idea, largely of an aesthetic nature. To get this effect, he said, the canvas must be completely organized

through the perfect arrangement of form, line, color and space. Objects in the subject matter, therefore, cannot be painted representatively [sic], but they must take their place in the whole design."[54]

To painters who were young, questioning, and looking for an alternative, Avery's emphasis on aesthetic design provided an artistic anchor. "When social realism and the American scene were considered the important thing," said Adolph Gottlieb, Avery "took an esthetic stand opposed to regional subject matter. I shared his point of view; and since he was ten years my senior and an artist I respected, his attitude helped reinforce me in my chosen direction. I always regarded him as a brilliant colorist and draftsman, a solitary figure working against the stream."[55]

"Meeting Milton really changed [Rothko's] idea of what art was all about," said Sally Avery.[56] Milton also changed his young friend's practice. Some of these changes emerged slowly; Rothko's mature works, though produced when he no longer saw very much of Avery, owe something of their simplified, buoyant forms, their expressive use of color, their thinned paints, and even their quiet, to Avery. But Avery had an immediate impact as well. He did beach scenes; so did Rothko, as in the untitled watercolor (color plate 5) probably done in the early 1930s. Rather than a cheerful prospect of a Portland landscape, Rothko here presents four human figures in a rather somber beach scene. Gray sand and an even darker-gray sky suggest a chilly, overcast day. Except for the transparent light blue dress on the woman at the forward left, the figures' clothing is also dark. In fact, Rothko's people, still fully dressed, seem urban, and the white borders of exposed paper that surround most of three of them lift them off the sand, as if they were not entirely at home there. The work communicates some of Rothko's stated discomfort with nature. Like the long, flat valley east of Portland, beaches can be scenes of expansive emptiness, but Rothko, evoking sea and sky with rough narrow bands of green and gray, gives most space to the sand which, like many rectangular areas in these early works, becomes a ground which almost but does not quite contain the human figures.

Here, people, not the sublime vastness of the ocean, engage Rothko. He renders them as flat colored shapes, without detail, without even facial features, just as Avery rendered the people in the beach scenes he was doing at this time. But Rothko adopted his mentor's subject and manner in order to push them in his own direction. Rothko's rough application, differing from both his light touch in the Portland watercolor and Avery's elegant color tones and clean outlines, aims less at an aesthetic idea than what Rothko later called "the human drama."[57]

The two rear figures, apparently a woman and a man, sit in similar positions; facing the water, resting on their left elbows, both look toward and extend their right arms in the direction of the top right corner, with their legs, feet crossed, also extending toward the top right. Their legs and arms are unrealistically elongated, as are the legs of the woman lying on her stomach in the front left. She turns to her left, looking past the smaller figure at our right, a girl who has curled up into a fetal-like position. The three adults are familiar enough with each other to be physically close; the lower body of the woman in blue touches and merges with the upper bodies of the two rear figures. Together, the three create a single shape. Yet in spite of their physical intimacy, no contact is made among these four silent figures. In Rothko's later words, they "form a *tableau vivant* of human incommunicability" and solitude.[58] As in many of Rothko's works of the 1930s, a tight physical proximity is crossed with emotional distance.

Avery's beach scenes are elegant and light; Rothko's are gloomy and ponderous. Here, the heads of all four figures are highlighted as heavy smudges of dark brown and gray, as if, in their separateness, they shared a brooding melancholy. In *Moby Dick* Herman Melville wrote that "meditation and water are wedded for ever"; beaches inspire reflection and reverie, and Rothko's people have come to meditate and to look, not to plunge in or to take a long walk. The two rear figures gaze toward something, in the expanse of water and sky, that is of mutual interest but outside the borders of the picture. The woman in the front looks past the child toward the bottom right, while the child looks into herself. The strong diagonal established by the elongated legs of the three adults, the way the man's legs break into the plane of the water, suggest a sense of strain and longing in figures whose physical postures are otherwise relaxed. The arrow in the Portland picture directed us into the landscape; the diagonal in the beach scene directs us outside the work. More strictly unified than the earlier watercolor, this one nevertheless conveys the feeling that something is missing.

· · ·

A few months after returning from the 1933 summer trip to Portland, Rothko had his first one-man show in New York, from November 20 to December 9, at the Contemporary Arts Gallery. Rothko showed fifteen oils, mostly portraits, four watercolors—three of them (*Portland*, *The Oregon Forest*, and *Mount Hood*) from his trip west—and six works using black tempera on white paper. Reviews were mildly favorable, preferring the watercolors to the oils, with one writer shrewdly declaring that Rothko's "peculiarly suggestive style, with its dependence on masses and comparative indifference to establishing any markedly definite form, seems better adapted to landscape, and to landscape in watercolor at that."[59]

But an exhibit at Contemporary Arts was a mixed blessing. The only New York gallery that "favored romantics and expressionist painting with free or dramatic brushwork," Contemporary Arts' policy was to give young artists only their first one-man show, with the ironic result that "the chosen painters had in a way the mark of the damned on them and were homeless in the art arena."[60] Rothko did show in special Christmas exhibits in 1933 and 1934 at Contemporary Arts, as well as in two of their annual reviews of the artists the gallery had introduced. By May of 1934, however, he was exhibiting with Robert Godsoe's Uptown Gallery, with paintings included in three of the gallery's group exhibits during that spring and summer.[61]

While Rothko's watercolors may have been more advanced at this point in his career, he declared oil on canvas his favorite medium; his favorite subject in any medium was the human, particularly the female, figure. Edith was a frequent model, as she was in *Sculptress* (color plate 6), a painting which reveals many of Rothko's preoccupations at the time. Edith, head bent, body turned to our left, ponders one of her sculptures. She sits on a high-backed wooden chair placed in front of a dark screen, which contains a rust-colored, Matisse-like decorative design. The flesh of her face and hands is gray, outlined in thick black; her face, merged with her left hand, is flat and masklike, and even though Edith was slender, her body is represented as large and heavy. Her lower body, in particular, recedes too far to the back right and has been widened by pushing her legs quite far apart. Wearing a white gown covered by a pink coat or smock, Edith is placed close-up, in front of the screen, which sits, in turn, in front of a solid, bare wall. Partly enclosed by the screen, she fills the picture, but with her head seemingly squeezed down by the painting's top edge. Her right hand hangs down, passively, toward her work.

The pedestal on which her sculpture sits, however, has been tilted away from her, toward us. Edith's work may be a couple making love, but it remains too vague to identify confidently. Rothko looks at Edith, not her sculpture, and Edith is important to him not as an artist but as *his* subject, though what interests Rothko about his wife is that her attention is directed *away* from him. As in the portrait of his mother, Rothko places himself (and us) close to a large, melancholy, distracted woman. By the time of this painting, done less than eighteen months after their marriage, the honeymoon with Edith was over. Attempting to emulate the Avery family, Rothko would end up—as this painting suggests—by replicating the Rothkowitz family.

All during the 1930s, in a variety of mediums—pencil-and-ink drawings, watercolors, tempera on colored construction paper, oil paintings—Rothko struggled with the female figure, most often the nude. His sketchbooks contain a few still lifes, occasional landscapes, some couples, a number of males and, later on, a series of subway scenes; but the female body predominates. When asked what Rothko liked to do when he wasn't working, Edith replied that he liked to look at women; he also liked to look at them *while* he was working.[62] Yet Rothko's women are not sexy or seductive; they are imposing and bulky—drawn in thick, heavy, agitated lines, without much detail or modeling. His nudes adopt a wide range of poses but they generally look away, sadly or angrily; clothed women are shown sewing or reading or playing a musical instrument or simply brooding. Rothko's women are both imposing and self-preoccupied; physically bulky and yet abstracted, they are at once oppressed and oppressive. In his story of his chance viewing of a nude model at the Art Students League, Rothko equated the origins of his art with his fascination with the female body. In his sketchbooks and paintings of the 1930s, he struggles with female distance and absence.

In *Sculptress* Edith is at once pulled up close and held in place, as if Rothko needed *some* distance—as if the distance were his own. Like the sand in Rothko's beach scene, the screen here forms a rectangular shape which frames and contains the human figure, whose head has been bent into near alignment with its top edge. The interior space she fills is shallow and compressed. Later, in "The Romantics Were Prompted," Rothko would speak "of ending this silence and solitude, of breathing and stretching one's arms again." *Sculptress* offers no hints of a missing open space, as Rothko's beach scene had; Edith is confined, solitary, immobile—here the only way out is inward. Nor is there any hint of an exchange between the artist and his model. Rothko reveals no sexual passion, no romantic longing, not even any friendly affection for his wife. When Rothko had first brought Edith to meet the Averys, Sally Avery recalled, "he thought she was the most beautiful woman alive."[63] Here, Rothko's fuzzy gaze, his expressionistic distortions, cut through the realistic surface to the emotional core. Edith *looked* slender and attractive; she *felt* massive, removed.

At the same time, this painting, like many of Rothko's 1930s paintings, combines emotional sincerity with a kind of self-conscious theatricality. The screen behind Edith looks like a theatrical backdrop; her face resembles a mask; Rothko's expressionist distortions have an exaggerated, melodramatic quality—all of which make the scene appear staged and artificial. In the absence of genuine human exchanges, people, Rothko suggests, become characters in a drama, unreal. Still, the silent distance between husband and wife is crossed by Rothko's identification with, or projection upon, his sculptress.

Rothko himself was physically large and heavy, melancholy, solitary, involved with his artistic productions, inward. The female body became a kind of mirror in which he explored his own emotions and thus a representation of what blocked and confined him—his own psyche.

For Rothko, the self-preoccupied husband of a self-preoccupied wife, cannot really feel his way inside her. Edith's face is a ghostly, averted mask; her body is hidden within the thick folds of what are sometimes two layers of clothing. Edith's gown and coat are brightly lit, dramatically contrasted with the dark screen, and painted in long sloping lines; her clothes are visually quite powerful, another hint of the effect of Matisse. In fact, the white area covering her lap and her legs becomes an abstract space which holds our attention because it is the only *open* space in this cramped, shallow painting. This opaque white shape pulls our eye toward, while it impedes our view of, the space between Edith's widely separated legs, as if Rothko were struggling to look inside the female, but her physicality and his melancholy kept them apart.

His expressionism took Rothko beyond the deceptive surfaces of realism; but it didn't take him far enough. Rothko himself had to become not less but more abstract to find his way into and then beyond silence and solitude. Only then could he transform his screen/backdrop into a large, luminous, and transparent rectangle, emptied of bulky bodies and material objects but filled with emotion. In these solitary, contemplative spaces, he could begin to breathe and stretch his arms again.

Sculptress had first been shown at the Uptown Gallery in May 1934. Uptown's director Robert Godsoe was a dissident "who wanted to fight all the museums at once, a kind of a rather overweight Don Quixote." He saw no conflict in operating as both art critic and gallery owner, so in April he reviewed an invitational for Brooklyn artists and sculptors at the Towers Hotel, praising "M. Rothkowitz's evocative, loose and delicately orchestrated 'Annunciation'."[64] Godsoe was impressed enough to give Rothko a show.

By the end of the year, however, Godsoe had moved the Uptown downtown, to West 12th Street, and provocatively renamed it Gallery Secession. As Joseph Solman put it, Godsoe took "the illegitimates," and he produced a series of one-man shows for them in the front room of the gallery while in the back room he kept "one example each of the stable mates." Godsoe "was full of encouragement for his new entourage," and "for a time the gallery acted as an informal and amiable cooperative. Artists who had not known each other before then met, exchanged ideas, and became acquainted with each other's work." But Godsoe began to admit painters whom some of his artists—Rothko and Solman among them—"considered too slight or specious for the character of the place" so the dissatisfied group, now doubly illegitimate, "seceded from

Secession" and, at a late 1935 meeting at Solman's 2nd Avenue studio, they formed The Ten.[65]

"So we decided to go forth on our own, so to say leave momma and take to the road," said Solman. "We were sort of a vagabond group, vagabond modern group." "We were homeless."[66] Possibly, The Ten had their sights on a specific home. At the time of the group's formation, the city of New York had announced plans for a Municipal Art Gallery, to show only self-organized groups of ten to fifteen artists. In January of 1936 The Ten became one of the four groups in the gallery's opening exhibit.[67] But The Ten, never establishing a permanent relation with any gallery, remained vagabonds. Moreover, they were not even ten; they were actually nine: Ben-Zion, Ilya Bolotowsky, Adolph Gottlieb, Louis Harris, Yankel Kufeld, Louis Schanker, Nahum Tschacbasov, Marcus Rothkowitz, and Joseph Solman—with the tenth a rotating position. Why The *Ten,* if there were only nine regular members? Perhaps the group liked the idea of a rotating position as a way to introduce new work, a fresh perspective. Perhaps the Municipal Art Gallery's requirement of at least ten members played a part. But all nine regular members were Jewish, and ten is the number of Jews required for a minyan, to hold religious services. Ten constitutes a sacred band, and these men, the first generation of Jewish painters in America, would bond against the goyim, against the 1930s alliance between the aristocracy (Gertrude Vanderbilt Whitney) and the "folk" (American regionalist painting) in the Whitney Museum's espousal of regionalist work.

Milton Avery, a close friend of several members, did not join The Ten because he had just been taken on by the prestigious Valentine Gallery and therefore "didn't need a group like The Ten." Rothko did. Just as Rothko sought a familial closeness that he at least thought he had once had, so he looked to his fellow painters for what Robert Motherwell later called "a collective intimacy. He would have liked a group of supportive colleagues, but not in an institutional setting."[68] The Ten was Rothko's first attempt to fill that lack.

The group, moreover, made possible a kind of collective strength and active presence in the art arena that was not available to the individual modern vagabond. Their exhibition at the Municipal Art Gallery suggests that the group may have been drawn by the thirties' dream of finding an alternative to the existing gallery system that would bring art closer to "the people." If so, they were disappointed. At the opening, Mayor Fiorello La Guardia revealed that his feeling was "somewhat lukewarm toward a few of the modern paintings" shown; and the day before the opening one of the men who had worked at converting the old brownstone into a gallery, looked at the floor where the works of The Ten were hung and commented, "I guess this is the floor for goofs. These paintings ain't supposed to tell you anything except what's the matter with the guys that painted them."[69] By the time of their next exhibit, at the Galerie Bonaparte in Paris (November 1936), The Ten were following the more conventional method of establishing a Continental reputation as a way into the New York art market. Subsequently, delegations were appointed to go uptown and show photos of the members' work to gallery owners, and during its four years on the road The Ten did succeed in getting eight group shows, two of them at the conservative Montross Gallery.[70]

Once a month the group met at a member's studio to discuss business, current shows, reproductions of European work in magazines like *Cahiers D'Art*. At the end of the session they had the member in whose studio they had gathered "drag out his new work." "The spirit," said Solman, "was one of comradeship and fight to go on with our work."[71] At the time of The Ten's founding, Rothko was thirty-two, with just a few shows and probably even fewer sales behind him. But Rothko was not only fighting the marketplace, he was also fighting himself. Avery knew what he wanted and achieved it with sureness and ease; but Rothko was struggling, doubting and questioning himself, looking for the expressive means that would take him to the core of his involvement with painting. His questioning deepened and strengthened Rothko's work in the long run, though he couldn't have known that in 1935. His marriage, moreover, was providing no tranquil haven from either his worldly discouragements or his inner struggles. He and Edith "were not getting along very well at that time. They were scrapping," Solman recalled. Rothko, a "natural sufferer" whose life was providing him with plenty of grist for his melancholy mill, needed the practical help and supportive comradeship of "The Nine Who Were Ten."

Their meetings also provided Rothko with the kind of freewheeling intellectual forum he had sought from the time he was at Lincoln High School. At least according to Solman, he and Rothko were "the most articulate," "the current leaders." Sometimes Rothko played the provocateur. During one discussion of a recent Picasso exhibit, Rothko asked, "Boys, do you know why he's so great?" and then answered his own question: "Because he's three-dimensional"—not exactly the standard account of Picasso's greatness. "What do you mean?" Solman wanted to know, and Rothko replied, "Look at some of those monumental nudes."[72] Of course, Rothko had been looking at Picasso's bulky, primitive nudes (and those of Max Weber) as part of his own struggle to find an expressive representation of the female body.

According to Solman, Rothko "was a very good talker. He could talk for hours," and in struggling to convey just how "persuasive" his old friend had been, Solman compared him first to a Bible salesman, then to a lawyer, finally to a Talmudic student.[73] Avery, for example, would "just say, 'Oh, Klee, I like him very much' and that was that." But "Rothko was a little more probing, debating and arguing and questioning a lot of things and studying the qualities of each master, so that you could have a whole discussion on Matisse or Cézanne or Soutine or Picasso." But Rothko's intellectual provocations also had a kind of angry edge. "He could be bitter and argue about things when he disagreed with you. There was no room for easy latitude; he'd get kind of grim about the argument." At the same time that his marriage was becoming a battleground, Rothko turned his means of collective intimacy into another occasion for combat.

Whatever their internal disputes, however, The Ten did share a set of common antagonists, for which their chief symbol became the Whitney Museum. The Whitney had opened in November of 1931, the personal creation of Gertrude Vanderbilt Whitney, great-granddaughter of Cornelius Vanderbilt, who had accumulated a fortune in shipping and railroads. In 1896, at twenty-one, Gertrude had married Harry Whitney, "the boy next door," the adjacent doors in this case leading into mansions on Fifth Avenue at 57th Street. Harry took up race horses, polo, and womanizing; Gertrude took up art and artists. At her Greenwich Village studio she produced public sculpture on commission, with titles like *Aspiration*. She also collected American art, being an early advocate of the realism of The Eight (the "Ashcan School"), and she became a philanthropic patron who formed the Society of Friends of Young Artists, the Whitney Studio Club, and the Whitney Studio Galleries. When Rothko had come to Lloyd Goodrich in 1926 looking for a job writing reviews for *The Arts*, he was applying to a magazine then subsidized by Mrs. Whitney.

Of course, the Depression affected the Whitneys, too, reducing Harry's worth from $200 to $100 million and Gertrude's from $20 to $10 million. In fact, just before the stock-market crash, Mrs. Whitney had offered her entire collection of six hundred American paintings, along with a new wing to house it, to the Metropolitan. The museum declined; so Gertrude Whitney built her own museum, devoting it to the support of "contemporary liberal artists" who "have had difficulty 'crashing the gate'."[74] To that end the Whitney Museum initiated a series of biennial invitational exhibits of contemporary American artists.

But a liberalism founded on the values of The Eight mainly excluded The Ten. Instead of trying to crash the gate, the group, in November of 1938, nailed some theses to it in the form of the catalogue statement for a show called "The Ten: Whitney Dissenters," at the Mercury Galleries, just two doors away from the museum on West 8th Street and running concurrently with one of its biennials. "A new academy is playing the old comedy of attempting to create something by naming it," began the stern catalogue polemic, written by

Rothko and the Mercury's two owners, Bernard Braddon and Sidney Schectman, who went on to identify the foe: "In this battle of words the symbol of the silo is in ascendancy in our Whitney museums of modern American art."[75]

The Whitney gave authority to the Regionalist aesthetic of artists like Benton. To help publicize the protest, Braddon, Schectman, and Louis Harris spoke about "What's Wrong with American Art?" on WNYC radio. Yet the Whitney Dissenters themselves were trying to create something by naming it—i.e., the "new academy" that any embattled avant-garde group requires for its passion and justification. For by no means was all of the work in the Whitney biennials the kind of painting of the American Scene sneered at by "the symbol of the silo." Among numerous other abstract artists, Milton Avery and Max Weber had been included; in fact, The Ten's own Ilya Bolotowsky had one painting in the current Whitney exhibit.[76]

Attacking the Whitney was a way to grab some of what little public attention was then paid to art, and it worked; the "Whitney Dissenters" show attracted a WPA adult art-tour and several reviews.[77] But the Whitney was mainly important as a convenient, nearby symbol of a complex set of issues, especially for Rothko. According to Schectman, the reason The Ten "talked about the Whitney so much is because we were so near them and there were these glittering shows going on, famous people coming in and fine openings, and where were they?"—i.e., The Ten. "Out in the cold somewhere."[78] Rothko was still the poor relation, but now, instead of being beaten up for selling newspapers on cold Portland street corners, he was *not* selling paintings. The Whitney signified economic and social privilege. The Whitney also stood for a liberal authority whose blandness masked real limits and exclusions. In their catalogue, the dissenters condemned the museum for espousing the "equivalence of American painting and literal painting." Of course, Benton's silos were more nostalgic idealizations than literal representations. The Whitney symbolized the way the Americanization program had, in the nationalistic 1930s, been translated into an aesthetic program.

In fact, The Ten were Jewish, with immigrant backgrounds. One reviewer of the group's May 1938 show at the Georgette Passedoit Gallery remarked that "practically all of the men paint in somber tones and this may be merely a coincidence or it may be racial, for the names of the artists suggest recent acclimatization and it is not always at once that newcomers pass into the glories and joys of living in America"—such as they were in 1938.[79] Yet it was not so much the derivativeness of The Ten that bothered the critics; it was their derivation from *European* modernism, as if that made them "aliens" who deserved to be out in the cold. The Ten were, in Lewis Browne's term, "un-Americanized."

Both Braddon and Schectman remembered Rothko as a man "full of ideas and full of strong convictions about the condition of American art in general, about his own work." They also found him "very introspective." As with his Sachar in-laws, Rothko was at times "silent" and "not communicative," at others "he would come out and they would all listen to him." But what most impressed the two men about Rothko was how "very serious" he was ("he never smiled"): "it was really an unalloyed seriousness about what everybody in that group and ourselves felt was a misguided view of American art." The Ten, according to the owners of the Mercury Gallery, "was not a particularly cohesive organization and he sort of pulled it together . . . whereas the others tended to wander off."[80] One reason for Rothko's grimly intense commitment was that the group's disputes—with privilege; with art as copying; with Americanization—were, for him, old, private, and very bitter battles.

Yet The Ten resisted a very attractive offer to come in out of the cold. Just after the Whitney Dissenters show, in December of 1938, Braddon and Schectman proposed that the Mercury be "devoted *exclusively*" to The Ten, promising that the work of its members would be "*continuously* exhibited" for the "*entire year*," that the group would receive the "equivalent of two shows *every month*" and that the gallery would undertake an elaborate program of advertising and salesmanship.[81] Writing as secretary for The Ten, Rothko replied on December 16, 1938, that "since our exhibition in your gallery certain problems of reorganization have arisen, which has made it necessary to abandon all exhibition activities for the present season."[82] Given the utopian character of the Mercury's proposal, the vague, bureaucratic character of Rothko's rationale for refusing it ("certain problems of reorganization") sounds suspiciously like a polite fiction.

Perhaps The Ten preferred to remain vagabonds, the better to assure themselves of their modernity. More likely, The Ten—never "a particularly cohesive organization"—were beginning to succumb to what Solman later called "the pressures of individuality."[83] The group would have just one more show, at the Bonestell Gallery, in the fall of 1939; but in February of that year, just two months after the Mercury offer, Solman, then teaching on a WPA program in Spokane, Washington, had written to his friend Jacob Kainen that "The Ten have suffered an organic split. It seems man is not equal to the collective life as yet."[84]

In fact, the pressures of individuality (as opposed to the bonds of the collective life) were organic to the aesthetic point of view that provided such internal cohesion as The Ten were able to achieve. As Solman put it, "We were allied to the broad spring of Expressionism," an alliance that separated them not only from the American Scene and the social realist painters but also from the American Abstract Artists, a group oriented toward geometric abstraction that started about a year after The Ten. "The term expressionist was aesthetically subversive at the time," recalled Solman.[85] The Ten were denounced as "dirty expressionists," their paintings as "silly smudges."[86] What made their work subversive was less its somber tones or its loose brushwork than its inwardness, its origins in the private self—precisely what made expressionism congenial to the "very introspective" Marcus Rothkowitz.

• • •

During the 1930s Rothko read two books titled *Expressionism in Art,* one by Oskar Pfister, a psychoanalyst influenced by Freud, and the other by Sheldon Cheney, an art critic influenced by Hans Hofmann.[87] Together, Pfister and Cheney reflect the expressive and formalist concerns in art that we have already seen Rothko beginning to formulate in his testimony at the Lewis Browne hearing. Here, the psychoanalyst and art critic do arrive at opposite evaluations of expressionists: Pfister condemns them for a pathological "introversion," which gives their pictures a feeling of "painful imprisonment," while Cheney praises their ascent to "a new stage" in "art's upward climb."[88] Yet both authors view expressionism as "the art of inwardness," a rejection of mimetic exactitude for emotional depth and an attempt—against impressionism's engagement with material surfaces—to penetrate to the essences of objects and people.[89] In this sense Rothko had been an expressionist, at least in theory, from the beginning.

Both Pfister and Cheney, moreover, understand *all* modern art to be expressionist, an art of the self. So did Rothko: "At the moment of lay art, when men discarded the myths and the methods developed to describe them, the artist looked into himself and found himself using his own emphasis (emotional) rather than visual, and using the geometric shape," he wrote in "The Scribble Book," a notebook he kept in the late 1930s. For Rothko the problem was not that man is not yet equal to the collective life; it's that modern man has rejected the religious and social myths that once sustained collective life, just as Rothko himself "discarded" both the orthodox Judaism imposed on him by his father and the secular myth of success adopted by many of his immigrant contemporaries. When Rothko later claimed to have made a "complete break" with *cheder* and the Jewish religion, he did so in the context of lamenting his loss of a sense of community ("Doesn't it make you feel lonesome?"). Again and again in his paintings of the 1930s, Rothko represents a rootless solitude, a painful imprisonment which is the cost of modernity.

In Rothko's early watercolors, nature—in rural or in seaside scenes—had offered an external grounding for art and for the self. But Rothko's landscapes, often artificially framed and held off at a distance, lack the freshness that comes from deep involvement; something is missing. In his oil paintings of the 1930s, however, Rothko concentrated on "the human drama" available to him in the city.[90] His interior scenes create a shallow, cramped, and airless space, occupied by tormented figures whose looming physical size often suggests that they are being viewed from the vantage point of a young child. Most are female; all are solitary, silent, and withdrawn, as if, despite their imposing physical presence, they are *not there*. When there are domestic groupings—couples; parent and child—their bodies touch, are joined, or even squeezed together while their faces look off in anguished distraction; human relations, it seems, are simultaneously too close and too distant.

Rothko's exterior scenes—modern street scenes, symbolic classical plazas, subway stations—confront the social reality of a bleak city from which all of the energies and openness of the natural world have been banished. In this enclosed and stony urban environment without trees, plants, hills, rivers, beaches, without even earth or very much sky, his people are typically thin, attenuated, faceless, and constricted within a space ruled by the blank rectangular walls of shops, apartment buildings, and looming skyscrapers. As in *Street Scene* (color plate 1), the flat facades of the buildings make them resemble stage sets, stressing the empty artificiality of urban life. But whether the space is interior or exterior, domestic and private or urban and public, "the human drama" for the Rothko of the 1930s is a drama of lack; his paintings convey silent isolation, emotional deprivation, and stifling enclosure.

If collective life is dead, the condition of the private self is more ambiguous, as Rothko reveals in his only *Self-Portrait,* painted probably in the mid-1930s (color plate 7). Many self-portraits are cropped just below the shoulders, but Rothko represents himself as no mere bust, rendering much more of his body and emphasizing an impressive physical size and a barrel-chested, animal power. Standing out from the turmoil of a vigorously brushed brown and yellow background, Rothko appears immovable, even monumental. By turning his head one quarter to the right and toward the light, he has brought out a bony facial structure which also conveys definition and force of character. Yet the painting communicates a tension between Rothko's strength and his vulnerability. Along with his bulky physical power, he reveals a sensitivity suggested partly by the intensely worked yet delicate juncture of his forehead and his (receding) hairline. Rothko's left ear, moreover, is represented as a raw, woundlike splotch; and his mouth is pulled back into an angry red curl. Unlike many artists painting their own image, Rothko does not hold a brush or a palette in his hand, does not place himself in his studio, does not represent himself *as an artist*. The only hint of this role comes from the white on his right hand, the dark red on the upper left hand and right fingers; perhaps the white and red are paint stains.

But Rothko does stress the physical parts of himself most intimate to the act of painting: his eyes and hands, both of which are rendered as impaired or damaged. Self-portraits, in which the artist paints his eyes in the act of looking intensely at himself, often make the eyes quite prominent, as, in a striking variation, does Rothko. Aggressively painted out with a blue that drips down onto his cheeks, his eyes are dark voids. His right arm looks to be detached from his body; his right hand is oversized. But what appears to be his right hand is actually his left since Rothko, painting a self-portrait, is looking into a mirror and producing a reversed image of himself. Thus his actual painting hand—on *our* right—appears as a flat, yellow stub, with what could be reddish-brown blood running along the top and over onto the fingers of his left hand whose curled fingers, in turn, protect, stroke, console the right. Rothko portrays a self powerful yet hurt, massive yet split; a man who paints because he suffers and suffers because he paints.

Yet this highly self-conscious work cannot simply be taken as yet another "innocent" version of the familiar myth of the wounded artist. During the 1930s Rothko did one pencil drawing of himself nude; but for his oil portrait this impecunious and dissident artist got himself dressed up, with a beautiful plum/blue/brown jacket, a white shirt, and a red tie.[91] To make his private self public, Rothko adopts a deliberate *pose:* formal clothing; a stiff, awkward positioning of his upper body; a rigid, squared-off look to his right arm; a blue covering his glasses which makes it look as though he is hiding behind "shades." His bony, skull-like face, with high, pale forehead and darkened eye sockets, looks like a mask—a *death* mask. Frozen, formally dressed, and uneasily posed, this adult Rothko resembles the little boy in Street Scene (color plate 1), with the difference that his persona is here consciously adopted, not a parental imposition.

In some literal respects, too, Rothko's painting constructs rather than copies a self. Covering his right hand with his left, Rothko solves the self-portraitist's problem of how to represent the hand with which he is in fact painting. Similarly, his eyes were not actually blacked-out while he was painting his portrait. As a reader of both Pfister's *Expressionism in Art* and his *Psycho-analysis in the Service of Education,* Rothko was aware of the Freudian symbolism of a self-blinding or a severed limb. As a modern painter, he was certainly aware of the allusive meaning of a damaged ear. "I'd like to have money; I'm not crazy like Van Gogh," he said in the 1930s.[92] Yet, one myth that Rothko was not willing to discard was that of the tortured and wounded artist. In his *Self-Portrait* he constructed a self—a kind of modern, post-Freudian Van Gogh.

Like Rothko's self-mythologizing stories about the mass grave or about *cheder,* his *Self-Portrait* fabricates a theatrical self, the only means by which the self-conscious Rothko could express real feeling. Just as the right side of his suit jacket is pulled too far across his chest and the left side pulled too far back, Rothko's mythic disguise both covers and exposes his private self—a tension between the desire to be seen and the desire to remain hidden that will become central to his art. Here, giving himself no specific background, he confronts us as a commanding physical presence while also defining himself as beyond any particular spatial or temporal context, as if he had somehow managed to transcend those circumstances that wounded him; *or,* as if his wounds were precisely what made him transcendent. At the same time, his twisted, dark red lip gives him a belligerent, almost pugilistic edge. Similarly aggressive, his paintings in these years distorted "nature" in order to look inside and expose hidden qualities in his human subjects, as in his painting of Edith. The kind of angry or "malicious" intent with which Rothko later tried to charge his murals for the Four Seasons restaurant had been part of his work from early on.

Rothko forcefully asserts himself, but he also shields his apparently damaged right hand with his left, conceals himself behind his Sunday clothing and mythic identity, and withdraws behind his dark glasses, keeping himself shadowed, enigmatic, and private, as if to protect himself from the very kind of invasive looking that produced his paintings. Angry, he remains silent and held in. Hurt, he withdraws. Or so it seems, until we realize that behind his blue glasses we can make out two small flat black discs, Rothko's eyes, gloomy, haunted, and impenetrable, but looking *out.* According to Pfister, expressionism was pathologically inward. Rothko, however, experiences his inwardness as both a liberation from the (to him) claustrophobic physical and social worlds and as itself a painful imprisonment. In his early work, his women, like Kate Rothkowitz in her portrait and in *The Rothkowitz Family* or like Edith in *Sculptress* typically look away; they are distracted and *merely* inward. In his *Self-Portrait* Rothko's body is turned away from us, but his head is turned slightly back to us, and his eyes look directly at us. From behind his gloomy veil, he engages the other.

Of course, Rothko, gazing into his mirror, is first of all gazing into himself, as if the person he were angry with, afraid of, and haunted by was Marcus Rothkowitz—a Marcus Rothkowitz who is not at ease with his body, not at ease with his clothing, not at ease with himself. In "The Romantics Were

Prompted," Rothko, identifying his pictures as "dramas" and their shapes as "the performers," writes of "the need for a group of actors who are able to move dramatically without embarrassment and execute gestures without shame." In his *Self-Portrait* of the mid-1930s, Rothko, the one-time aspiring actor, adopts a theatrical posture partly because he has not freed himself from a painful self-consciousness. Shame, which Rothko recalled feeling when he arrived in this country in his Buster Brown suit, is the agonizing, and paralyzing, sense of being *seen through* and exposed as *lacking*.

Looking at and into himself, Rothko sees a person who is hefty, fierce, hurt, painfully self-conscious and self-protective. Combining self-concealment with self-exposure, the introspective Rothko could protect himself from himself, shielding his eyes as he looks, willing to probe so far, but no further. The *Self-Portrait* thus achieves a *veiled* self-expression, one in which Rothko represents his interior not just through his physical being and social appearance but also by displacing parts of that interior onto the painting's abstract background, as if these parts of him were separate from his physical nature.

Rothko's expressionist paintings of the 1930s are frontal and shallow. Often their backgrounds are solid, heavy, blank walls, placed close up to the picture plane, an effect doubled in both *Sculptress* and *The Rothkowitz Family* by the placement of a screen in front of a close back wall. Occasionally, human figures are backed, or have withdrawn, into a corner. Ceilings in these stifling and quiet rooms are so low that the people are sometimes bent at the neck in order to fit into their cramped environments. Rothko was claustrophobic; in the 1930s, his melancholy heavy-set characters look walled-in, trapped in physical matter.[93]

In his *Self-Portrait,* however, Rothko occupies a shallow but abstract and delocalized space which, rather than confining him, presents him as a man beyond *any* specific context. His environment is built up out of a vehemently and thickly painted brown, with varying densities, which appears to have been applied over a yellow/gold color. The shadows on Rothko's face locate the source of light at the upper left; but the area along the right side of his head and shoulder, where we look through the brown to a golden luminosity, suggests a light within or behind the painting. The solid, formal, immovable physical presence of Rothko stands out from the turmoil of what turns out to be not exactly a *back*ground. For the boundaries between figure and ground are imprecise, especially along Rothko's arms, where the brown/gold comes forward and gently enfolds him. Here, the "transplanted" Rothko inhabits a self-created environment that is turbulent yet warm and glowing, almost solicitous.

The same could hardly be said about Rothko's actual environment. In a

March 1935 letter, Rothko's later friend, the painter Bradley Walker Tomlin, observed,

> I have been rather jumpy and nervous this winter. Somehow the strain of the depression seems to have worn everyone out, I think. I have of course been fortunate in having a [teaching] job but one never sells a canvas and painting more pictures seems at times a futile business. The exhibitions all have a tired uninspired look—the impulse seems to have been deadened.[94]

In "The Romantics Were Prompted," Rothko would declare that social "hostility can act as a lever for true liberation. Freed from a false sense of security and community, the artist can abandon his plastic bank-book, just as he has abandoned other forms of security,"—say, the bankable value of a Yale degree. But such attempts to convert the marginality of the artist into an advantage only came after society had warmed up enough to buy a few of his paintings, so that the artist had at least some balance in the plastic bank-book he was abandoning. In the 1930s, when one seldom sold a canvas and painting could seem a futile business, the problem was less hostility than social indifference, an enervating historical "background" that could nevertheless slip forward, seep inside the individual and replicate the social as a psychic depression.

. . .

"Passing by on Eastern Parkway at the number 667 you will see a gracefully impressive building of white stone. It is somewhat reminiscent of the Metropolitan Museum of Art, and you will think that it is indeed an art institution, or at least some exclusive town club." More town club than art institution, the white stone building was the Brooklyn Jewish Center. "Should you now go up the wide stone steps and cross the flagged terrace"—as Rothko did twice a week from 1929 to 1946—"you will find yourself in a beautiful, high-vaulted foyer, a pillared marble staircase at one side leading to the floors above. The chiseled stone walls bring to you a feeling of dignity and repose, and you are grateful that a Jewish institution can impress a visitor with such qualities."

In the basement, a gymnasium, pool, and Turkish bath were available; on the main floor there was a large auditorium "designed in the manner of a salon," and one flight up, "a mellow lounge and reading room" (such as "you might find in an English mansion"), a private dining room, club rooms, and a two-story synagogue with "a great dome" and "walls ranged with stained-glass windows." On the top third floor were located the "educational departments," staffed with instructors "of the highest standing obtainable."[95] One of these departments was the Center Academy; and one of these instructors was Marcus Rothkowitz, affectionately known by teachers and students as "Rothkie."[96]

During the prosperous 1920s and even the depressed 1930s, many New York Jews moved, as Rothko did, out of Manhattan and into the newly developed, still suburban sections of the Bronx and Brooklyn. This new migration usually meant a step across the border dividing the working from the lower-middle class. One result was that the Orthodox synagogue of the Lower East Side and the Reform temple of Central Park West were replaced by the Jewish center, whose recreational, social, educational, and cultural facilities defined the religious as one among many Jewish activities. To a young man who had grown up in the southwest Portland ghetto, the Brooklyn Jewish Center would appear as Neighborhood House writ bourgeois. In their religious observances, these centers adopted a Conservative middle ground between Orthodox and Reform Judaism. In their politics, they were liberal and Zionist.

Completed in 1920, at a cost of around $1 million, the Brooklyn Jewish Center had a largely second-generation, Eastern European membership. Having passed through the building's monumental exterior, observed its chiseled stone walls and climbed its pillared marble staircase, an American Jew, a professional or businessman whose parents had lived in fear of Cossacks and pogroms, could sit in the center's "mellow lounge" feeling grateful that a Jewish institution could offer that "dignity and repose" experienced, say, by members of Fifth Avenue's Yale Club. The center symbolized Jewish community, security, and arrival. With mass immigration over and the Americanization process largely completed, this new Jewish bourgeoisie turned to preserving its ethnic origins by redefining Jewishness as a *cultural* inheritance.[97]

To this end, Jewish schools, like the synagogues, had to be transformed. Combining middle-class aspirations, progressive theories of education, and an ardent Zionism, Center Academy had been organized, in the fall of 1927, by a group of Brooklyn Jewish Center parents who were looking for a "cultural synthesis" between Americanism and Judaism. For the previous generation, either the Talmud Torah had tacked Hebrew onto the end of a public-school day or the Yeshiva had tacked secular studies onto the end of a day of Hebrew. The "dualism" built into both these approaches, according to one Center Academy founder/historian, created "inner conflicts," "maladjustments," and "emotional strains," whereas a program integrating secular and Jewish studies would produce "inner security." Yet in this synthesis the Americanism came close to absorbing the Judaism. At Center Academy, Hebrew was taught but only to create a "link with the new Palestine." "The theological or doctrinal aspect of religion" was eliminated. Jewish faith and history became "traditional customs and ceremonials," taught for their "beauty and poetry."[98] Jewishness was culture. By following this route, Center Academy's parents hoped to realize "our dream of a new type of Jew—steeped in Jewish culture yet thoroughly at home in his American milieu."[99]

As the talk of "maladjustment" reveals, the school's parents and staff were also educational reformers committed to the "modern progressive" principles of John Dewey. As one former student put it, "the staff believed that Dewey was God and came down from heaven to reveal his theory of education."[100] Critical of the American public school system's "formalism and regimentation," its emphasis on "the acquisition of facts rather than on the development of native powers," Center Academy instead sought "to preserve the spontaneity, the joyousness and emotional freedom which should characterize all genuine growth." Instruction was organized around practical "centers of interest" and Jewish festivals. Second-graders, for example, learned reading, writing, and arithmetic skills by running an imaginary department store. Palestine figured prominently in these class projects, with its own department in the second-graders' store, where only Hebrew was written and spoken, where the walls were decorated with "Jewish motifs and Eastern scenes," and where exhibits of Palestine art were held. The academy exchanged gifts with a Jewish public school in Haifa, and from that time "we date the strong prevalence of oriental hues and motifs in the 'art' of Center Academy: camels and palm trees, shepherds and water carriers—all in a riot of color," and all supplied by the students of the former illustrator of *The Graphic Bible*. Jewish festivals were observed with plays or pageants on biblical subjects (in English or Hebrew) written and staged by the children, who also produced, under Rothko's supervision, the sets and songs. Ancient Jewish law prohibiting graven images was eroded by a new emphasis on "the poetic and romantic element in Jewish life." Lewis Browne had militarized Jewish history; at Center Academy, that history was aestheticized.[101]

In February of 1928, just as Rothko was hiring a lawyer to recover his final $50 from Browne, Center Academy opened.[102] By 1935, the school, enrolling about ninety students from 8:45 A.M. to 3:15 P.M. daily, extended from kindergarten through eighth grade.[103] Beginning in 1929, Rothko taught forty-five-minute sessions in painting and clay sculpture, for two days a week, probably making about $800 a year during the 1930s. Rothko did not much participate in faculty political discussions, but he was a "good businessman" who "negotiated a good salary for his wife," when she briefly taught crafts there, getting her portal-to-portal pay.[104]

"The progressive school is a symbol of liberalism," Rothko wrote in "The Scribble Book." In the radical thirties, Rothko, insofar as he was political, was a liberal who shared the academy's commitment to progressive methods in education. His classes worked on specific projects, such as sets for the Purim play or a dramatization of the legend of Siegfried, or "the children were taken on trips to see things," and "afterwards 'went down to see Rothkie', where they would paint pictures of what they had seen." Either way, the classes were, said one former student, "very freewheeling—not a confining or a conforming kind of activity at all."[105]

A 1934 essay Rothko wrote about teaching children's art ("New Training for Future Artists and Art Lovers") describes how his classes worked:

> They enter the art room. Their paints, paper, brushes, clay, pastels—all the working material is ready. Most of them, full of ideas and interests, know just what they want to portray. Sometimes it is something from the history lesson, sometimes from Hebrew history; at other times, something they might have seen in the movies, on a summer trip, on a visit to the docks or at a factory, or some scene observed on the street; often it is a subject that is born entirely in their own minds as a result of reflection, or of particular sympathies and dreams.
>
> They proceed to work. Unconscious of any difficulties, they chop their way and surmount obstacles that might turn an adult grey, and presto! Soon their ideas become visible in a clearly intelligent form.

"The function of the instructor," Rothko continues, is not to impart technique but "to stimulate and maintain" the "emotional excitement" of the children, "to inspire self-confidence on their part," "always, however, taking the utmost care not to impose laws which might induce imaginative stagnation and repetition."[106] Center Academy was no Dvisnk *cheder*.

It is doubtful that Rothko, looking up at the building on his way to teach, ever mistook the Brooklyn Jewish Center for the Metropolitan Museum of Art. More likely, in spite of its creeping secularism, he viewed the center itself as far too much the pretentious and *arriviste* town club to satisfy his yearnings for "collective intimacy." Most of its members, having chosen the route of upward mobility he had rejected, were making much more than $800 a year. "Transplanted" and poor as a boy, the adult Rothko had chosen to remain the outsider, refusing to become thoroughly at home in his American milieu. So when Rothko climbed the center's pillared marble staircase, he was not going to plunge in the pool or relax in the lounge; he was going to work, with his position at the affluent Center reminiscent of his "poor relation" role with his Weinstein relations in Portland and New Haven. Yet teaching children's art was better than producing commercial art for an ad agency or *The Graphic Bible,* so much better that for a few years in the late 1930s, Rothko also taught at a similar school in Far Rockaway.[107] If he complained about the demands teaching made on his time—the more so as time went on—he performed his job with an idealistic enthusiasm.

"He was friendly, funny, warm, encouraging and very very much loved as I remember," recalled one of Rothko's students.[108] Not the grimly dialectical Marcus Rothkowitz of the gatherings of The Ten, "Rothkie" was admired by both staff and students at Center Academy for his warmth and good humor.

> He was a big bear of a man, the friendliest, nicest, warmest member of the entire school.
>
> Martin Lukashok, student

> I liked him very much. He was very intelligent and he had a wonderful sense of humor. He was very good company.
>
> Frieda Prensky, music teacher

> He was a genial, gentle, dear man, fun, easy-going and a wonderful teacher. He was very serious about his teaching but gave kids a free hand.
>
> Judith Eisenstein, music teacher

> A very fine art teacher. As for talent at that school, it was zero. Rich little kids who were terrible at art. He had to put up with those kids, but he was extremely gentle with kids, very friendly, one of only two men on the staff, much beloved by the students.
>
> Howard Adelson, student

> I was never good at art. A couple of boys or girls in the class had more art or technique than I did. But he was very supportive, very kind. He liked my colors. He made you feel that you were really producing something important, something good.
>
> Gerald Phillips, student

With parents and staff at the school, as with the children, Rothko showed the "easy latitude" which Joseph Solman found missing in his character. When Irene Dash's parents rejected a Rothko portrait of their daughter they had commissioned—they thought it "too gloomy"—he was not particularly disturbed. When one of his fellow teachers returned from a Rothko show with the comment, "Rothkie, I saw the exhibition and I didn't understand what it was all about even after I read the little pamphlet," he answered, "Neither do I know." At another show one of the Center Academy staff overheard some women ask Rothko, "What kind of brushes do you use?" with him replying,

Chapter Four

"I buy them in the 5 & 10." "He took everything in stride," Frieda Prensky recalled.[109]

If he resented the job's demands on his time, he often did more than he had to. He participated in the school's PTA activities. In October of 1933, he acted as "lecturer and guide" for a group of Center Academy parents on an "art pilgrimage" to the Brooklyn Museum, the Metropolitan Museum, and the Museum of Modern Art. On other occasions he spoke at PTA meetings, talking about "Art Education for Children," for instance, in February of 1932.[110] To help inspire student self-confidence, he arranged exhibits of the children's work. As we have seen, he brought some of their work with him when he and Edith hitchhiked across the country in the summer of 1933, including it in his show at the Portland Art Museum. Early the following year—from February 8 to 21, 1934—he organized an exhibit of about 150 of his students' paintings and sculptures at the Brooklyn Museum, several blocks down Eastern Parkway from the school. The children's art was also shown at the Neumann Gallery, the New York Young Men's Association, the Jewish Welfare Board, and the Jewish Theological Seminary.[111] As a teacher, Rothko gave his students the freedom and support he wished he had had as a child.

In fact, it was the Brooklyn Museum exhibit that produced Rothko's first published writing since his contributions to the Yale *Pest*—an essay called "New Training For Future Artists and Art Lovers" which appeared in the *Brooklyn Jewish Center Review* in early 1934.[112] Beyond its description of Rothko's working methods in the classroom, this polemical essay reveals the intellectual, political, and psychological bases of Rothko's passionate commitment to the teaching of children's art. Rothko, the political and artistic liberal, humanizes the activity of painting by viewing it not as a craft acquired through training and discipline but as an innately human form of expression.

"Painting is just as natural a language as singing or speaking," he insists. "We all tell stories, narrate events, indulge in correspondence, sometimes with great feeling and artistry. Yet we do not feel that our expression in this medium is dependent on our knowledge of grammar, syntax or the rules of rhetoric." Similarly, "we sing melodies and improvise tunes for ourselves and I am sure we can do both without voice culture and a knowledge of harmony and counterpoint." Not a set of conventions to be learned, painting, then, is "a method of making a visible record of our experience, visual or imaginative, colored by our own feelings and reactions and indicated with the same simplicity and directness as singing or speaking."

Hence, if you watch the children in his art classes at work, "you will see them put forms, figures, views into pictorial arrangements, employing of necessity most of the rules of optical perspective and geometry, but without the

Fig. 1. View of Shosseynaya Street, Dvinsk, 1903. The Rothkowitzes lived in the three-story white building in the middle left (Gesel Maimin).

Fig. 2. Jacob Rothkowitz (Kenneth Rabin).

Fig. 3. Albert, Kate, and Moise Rothkowitz (Kenneth Rabin).

Fig. 4. Marcus Rothkowitz, age 10, seated at the front, his mother seated behind him, at the right, and his sister standing, second from the right (Kenneth Rabin).

Fig. 5. Albert and Sonia standing at the left; Marcus and Moise seated at the right (Kenneth Rabin).

Fig 6. Right, top: The Fortress, Daugavpils [Dvinsk], 1991 (Author photo).
Fig. 7. Bottom: View from bridge across Dauga [Dvina] River, 1991 (Author photo).

Fig. 8. View from bridge across Dauga [Dvina] River, 1991 (Author photo).

Fig. 9. Holocaust site, woods north of Daugavpils [Dvinsk], 1991 (Author photo).

Fig. 10. S.W. Washington Street, downtown Portland, c. 1910; Rothko worked at New York Outfitting Co., owned by his uncle Sam Weinstein (Oregon Historical Society).

Fig. 11. View, including Mt. Hood, from the Portland Hills, c. 1910 (Oregon Historical Society).

Fig. 12. Shattuck School (Oregon Historical Society).

Fig. 13. Lincoln High School (Oregon Historical Society).

Fig. 14. Graduation from Lincoln High School (Kate Rothko Prizel and Christopher Rothko).

Fig. 15. Yale, 1921–23 (Kate Rothko Prizel and Christopher Rothko).

Fig. 16. 1920s (Kate Rothko Prizel and Christopher Rothko).

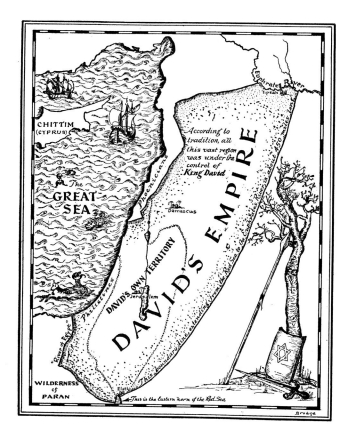

Fig. 17. Drawing by Mark Rothko from Lewis Browne, *The Graphic Bible* (New York, 1928).

Fig. 18. 1930s (George Carson).

Fig. 19. Edith Sachar (George Carson).

Fig. 20. Edith Sachar (George Carson).

Fig. 21. 1930s (George Carson).

Fig. 22. 1930s (George Carson).

Fig. 23. Mark Rothko, mural sketch, c. 1939 (National Archives).

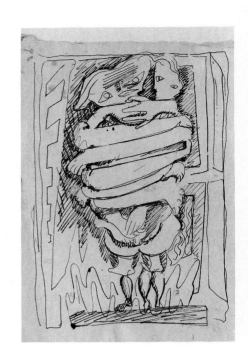

Fig. 24. Mark Rothko, drawing, c. 1939 (National Gallery of Art).

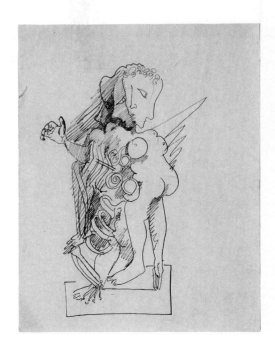

Fig. 25. Mark Rothko, drawing, c. 1939 (National Gallery of Art).

knowledge that they are employing them," just as they speak "unconscious that they are using the rules of grammar." Refusing to "impose laws" and seeking "to inspire self-confidence," the instructor provides a style of authority more in the manner of a Milton Avery than a George Bridgman. As a result, each child "develops a style of his own," while a "community spirit" pervades the class. The students, moreover, do not "occupy themselves with precious themes, such as still life" subjects, but render "factories, docks, streets, crowds, mountains, lakes, farms, cattle, men, women, ships, water—everything conceivable." "Here," Rothko stresses, "is a social art."

In the 1930s, of course, art was pressured to be social; Rothko himself met this expectation by conceiving of painting as a "natural" human expression, in short, by adhering to the expressive theory of art which he had formulated by the late 1920s and had practiced from the start. For him, art ultimately became social by becoming inward, speaking a shared human language of feeling. Rothko's own style in 1934 can be described as a kind of somber Fauve expressionism. Of the children's works in the Brooklyn Museum exhibit, he wrote that "they are complete realizations of a subject that moves us by the beauty of its moods, by the fullness of its forms, and the excitement of its design. In short, many of these pieces are capable of moving us emotionally," a quality which makes them "intrinsically works of art."

Rothko's involvement with children's art thus grew out of his expressive aesthetic, which led him to idealize the unself-conscious spontaneity, the "simplicity and directness" of children. In "The Scribble Book" he defined "expressionism" as "an attempt to recapture the freshness and (naiveté) of childish vision," "a nostalgia for the innocence of childhood." But Rothko's memories of his own childhood dwelt on racial victimization, hunger, poverty, and abandonment. He complained that he had been *deprived* of a childhood.[113] Believing this, he could easily have dismissed his pupils as the children of privilege and merely put in his time to collect his paycheck. Instead, he took his family's faith in education in a new direction by creating a warm, good-humored, freewheeling "community spirit" that might save his students from the lacks and impositions which he felt had characterized his own beginnings.

5 Working for the WPA

Hell, they got to eat just like other people.

Harry Hopkins

"Rothkowitz, the easel painter, whose wife is employed, was in this morning and is going to try to be certified for relief. I told him that if he did we would consider his work on the strength of the information on his card," wrote Cecil Jones, the business manager for the Treasury Relief Art Project (TRAP), in a July 14, 1936, memo to his chief, Olin Dows.[1]

Initiated by a grant from the Works Progress Administration (WPA) to the Treasury Department, TRAP had been formed in July of 1935 to hire five hundred artists to decorate about 1,900 government buildings, mostly post offices. "Ours was considered a privileged program, and indeed it was," Dows has written.[2] TRAP, in fact, was called "the Ritz" of the federal art projects, its purpose conceived less as the feeding of impecunious painters than the production of "quality" work for public buildings. So selective were its administrators that the program came far short of meeting its quota of five hundred artists, thereby inspiring attacks from artists' organizations more concerned with the material conditions of their members than the quality of post-office art.[3] Partly in response to such criticisms and partly because skilled American muralists were not easy to find in 1935, the program began accepting easel painters like Rothkowitz.

In June of 1936 Rothko had thus been one of five hundred artists invited to apply for a place on TRAP.[4] On June 30 he had called the New York office to request a nonrelief position but was told "we could only use him" on relief.[5] At first 90 percent, later 75 percent, of TRAP's employees had to qualify for relief, so that to enjoy the privileges of a place at the Ritz, most painters had to declare themselves paupers and endure a humiliating investigation by Emergency Relief Bureau social workers whose zeal sometimes led them to examine the contents of the family refrigerator. To be eligible, applicants could not exceed prescribed allowances—e.g., $9.30 a month to feed an adult male, $7.70 for an adult female. Adolph Gottlieb recalled "the degrading requirement of taking the poverty oath," "followed by an investigation which in most cases involved much duplicity," as it certainly did in Rothko's case. Applicants had to be unemployed; Rothko was teaching both at the Center Academy and the Far Rockaway school, and Edith had probably started her jewelry business by this time. Later, after July 1937, WPA workers had to be U.S. citizens; Rothko was not.[6]

By mid-August Rothko was still trying to convince the bureaucracy of his poverty: "A man named Rothkowitz, whose work you have seen and approved, is trying to get on relief and I will put him on if possible," reads a memo to Dows from Alice Sharkey, TRAP's New York supervisor. Funding problems required, Dows decided later that month, that we "close our employment on the Project now," "and we will put on no more new people unless something extraordinarily good comes up on relief." Nevertheless, Rothko was appointed to TRAP at $95.44 (later $103.40) a month, for fifteen hours of work a week. His position was precarious, partly because of the duplicity required to get it and partly because of the continual threat of cutbacks. Yet, while on one of the federal art programs, the easel artist could eat better fare than bean soup, have some free time in which to paint, and for the first time feel himself, in Joseph Solman's words, "a self-esteemed citizen of his country [whose] product was a viable commodity and beneficial to it."[7]

Rothko submitted at least one painting to the project's administrators.[8] But just four months after his appointment, "TRAP began a slow phase-out." In general, muralists were kept on, while, beginning in February of 1937, easel painters were let go.[9] With the Ritz now a condemned building, Rothko was soon evicted, but, due to protests of the early dismissals by the Artists' Coordination Committee, he did not end up on the street.[10] Instead, on May 16, 1937, Rothko—along with forty-one other New York artists—was relocated to the Easel Division of the WPA Federal Art Project.[11]

At the time of his transfer, 2,100 artists worked on the New York project and there was a waiting list of 2,000 more, some of whom vehemently protested the priority given the TRAP appointments. For the past several months, funding cutbacks, a hiring freeze, layoffs, welfare investigations, conflicts between artists and administrators, and rumors of the project's termination had made the New York 34th Street office the scene of verbal protests, picketings, and a sit-in which produced police beatings and the arrest of 219 artists. A month after Rothko's transfer, an ordered 25 percent reduction in personnel provoked a massive work stoppage, sit-ins, and other demonstrations.[12] Over the next two years economic pressures on the WPA mounted, along with political investigations of suspected bolshevism. In the words of Jacob Kainen, "after 1937 artists anticipated the dreaded pink slip every payday"—"a demoralizing experience."

On July 12, 1938, Rothko's pay was reduced to $91.10 per month; on August 17, 1939, a month short of three years after his appointment to TRAP, he received his pink slip.[13]

Among the painters and sculptors taken on by the WPA were Milton Avery, William Baziotes, James Brooks, Willem de Kooning, Arshile Gorky, Philip Guston, Lee Krasner, Louise Nevelson, Jackson Pollock, Ad Reinhardt, David Smith—plus eight of the nine core members of The Ten.[14] In the early days of the project, easel painters had to punch in at their local office by 8 A.M. and punch out at 4 P.M.; otherwise they would lose the day's pay. Jacob Kainen remembered Jackson Pollock, still dressed in pajamas, rushing in to make the morning deadline.[15] By the time of Rothko's transfer from TRAP, however, working conditions had somewhat improved. Artists made substantially more than the $60 a month averaged by WPA workers, and the project provided free materials and models. To collect his paycheck Rothko was required to submit an oil painting every four to six weeks (depending on size) for allocation to public buildings. Easel painters worked without supervision, in their own studios, and—unlike the muralists, who were often expected to produce in the "American Scene" manner—they were generally free to develop their own styles. It is likely that many painters submitted, as Adolph Gottlieb said he did, his "most bland and neutral work, to avoid difficulties in allocation," and probably in order to hold onto their stronger work.[16]

Still, while the program provided economic support and enhanced the self-esteem of artists, it could also prove demeaning. Artists on relief, like Rothko, were subject to home inspections. "Once in a while," Maurice Sievan recalled, "they'd come to your place to look at your icebox and see how much food you'd got."[17] Supervisors could be intrusive and demanding, as Rothko's friend Milton Avery had discovered while working for the Public Works of the Art Project (PWAP) in early 1934. After viewing three Avery landscapes, an administrator commented: "oil work submitted very poor. Gouaches seen elsewhere and artist's reputation suggest that his work is better than examples submitted would indicate." Avery then began a 32" × 48" painting of an "industrial scene." But the reviewing committee recommended that he "not exceed 40 inches" in oils and wondered "if you would not prefer to work in washes which they feel you are more suited and experienced in executing." PWAP's assistant director, the Whitney Museum's Lloyd Goodrich, also requested a "smaller scale." Avery turned to a 28" × 36" oil of what he described as an "industrial scene: factory buildings, barges, big boats, Queensboro bridge, in distance." But Avery's progress report on the work was returned because he had not specified a completion date. Two weeks later he was terminated.[18]

Despite the demoralizing threat of the pink slip and the equally demoralizing directives from art bureaucrats, most of the participants later emphasized what David Smith described as the "unity," "friendship," and "collective defensiveness" of the project.[19] In addition, the WPA supported art instruction programs, community art centers, art tours (one of which visited The Ten's "Whitney Dissenters" exhibit), and local art galleries (it was at the Federal Art Gallery in New York that Max Weber had "corrected" one of Rothko's works). Through this commitment to cultural democracy, the WPA helped broaden the audience for American painting.

Nevertheless, the project's deepest impact was more private and individual than social or collective. By awarding what were in effect large numbers of grants based on need, the WPA provided an important defense against the economic and psychic depressions of the thirties. Rothko thought the WPA "a Godsend to so many artists who really needed help," Edith recalled. Jackson Pollock said that he was "grateful to the WPA, for keeping me alive during the thirties." Less melodramatically, Jacob Kainen put it that, on the WPA, "I did what I chose to do and thus came to rely on my personal feelings rather than on the pressures of the market, which might have resulted in a loss of faith in my own identity. Early success based upon clever adaption to current styles is fatal for an artist."[20] Rothko, who did not have to worry about the dangers of early success, was now being paid not to draw advertisements, not to illustrate the Bible, not to teach children, but to make paintings. In this case, it was the *friendliness* of society toward the artist that was liberating.

Ironically, the collapse of the art market diminished rivalries among painters and helped to create a solidarity based on the sense of a common fate. The WPA paid easel painters to work alone in their studios; but economic circumstances also forced them to perceive mutual interests and the advantages of collective dependence. The Ten and the American Abstract Artists were two such responses, but these small groups were traditional in nature, mainly concerned to find opportunities for their members to exhibit. More political, and more politically radical, was the leftist Artists Union, which had first pressured the federal government to support the art programs and then, in response to cutbacks, organized mass demonstrations, sit-ins, and strikes. The union became the WPA artists' collective bargaining agent; but beyond its concern with bread-and-butter issues, the union envisioned a new integration between the American artist and his national culture.

In the union's account, the economic crisis exposed the failure of the old patronage system; the union proposed permanent government patronage, a Federal Bureau of Fine Arts. Now, the painter would be supported not by the privileged classes but by "the people as a whole," a relationship which would, in turn, demand "a growth within the art movement itself toward the entire people." In the words of the union's president, "The face of American art at last was turned toward the entire population through economic and cultural necessity."[21] No longer a bohemian producing luxury items for the few, artists would *belong* to their society.

But the politics of the thirties combined such utopian hopes with fears of a world cataclysm. On January 30, 1933—two and a half months after Rothko's marriage to Edith—Adolf Hitler had been sworn in as chancellor of the Third Reich. That spring Nazi terror began, with book burnings, street beatings, political arrests of communists and Jews and their incarceration in the regime's first concentration camp, at Dachau. By the mid-1930s, the rise of Hitler and Mussolini, their expansionist policies, and the revolt of the army against the Republican government in Spain had created an international political crisis which seemed more and more likely to end in a second world war. In response, the Soviets developed the strategy of the popular front, a coalition of the working and middle classes which achieved unity by emphasizing the dangers not of capitalism but of fascism.

In particular the front sought the allegiance of bourgeois intellectuals and artists; one result was the First American Artists' Congress Against War and Fascism, which met at New York's Town Hall in February of 1936. Like other artists' organizations, the congress held exhibitions and ran symposiums. Like the Artists Union, the congress was a left, activist political organization, national in scope, lobbying for artists' economic issues and their political rights. But whereas the earlier John Reed Clubs had advocated proletarian art and the Artists Union journal, *Art Front,* espoused Social Realism, the congress, in keeping with the popular front desire for unity, admitted "artists of all esthetic tendencies" in the war against fascism both here and in Europe.[22]

"Marcus in those days was very perturbed about whether or not joining a group was going to make him change his art and would he lose his identity," Juliette Hays recalled. "He was very, very aware of I, Marcus Rothkowitz."[23] He did join the American Artists' Congress, at least occasionally attended their meetings, exhibited *Street Scene* in their second annual membership show (May 1938) and, for the Brooklyn Heights branch of the congress, contributed four canvases to an art auction raising funds for children who were victims of the war in Spain.[24] Rothko was almost certainly a member of the Artists Union and he participated in some of the decade's political demonstrations. At a protest of the threatened closing of a federally supported dance project, Juliette Hays lined up with others along 44th or 45th Street, then looked back toward Broadway "and suddenly coming around the corner, these banners appeared. They were Artists Union banners and Marcus was carrying a banner and he was on the line."[25]

Chapter Five

"Mark had no objection to picketing for immediate preservation of jobs," said Juliette's husband, H. R. Hays, "but he strenuously opposed the injection of politics into art which he felt simply resulted in bad art."[26] Too involved in an inward struggle to find his identity, Rothko was not tempted to lose it in a political ideology and he was not much of a political activist. Insofar as he sought "collective intimacy," he did so outside an institutional or political setting. He did later claim to have been arrested a few times in the political demonstrations of the 1930s, though no record of any such arrests exists.[27]

According to his brother-in-law, Howard Sachar, "He wasn't a marcher. My brother and sisters were the marchers and the protestors; they went in May Day parades and all that sort of thing. I don't recall his being like that." Neither does anyone else. Jacob Kainen said: "Rothko never involved himself in any of the organizations that I remember. I can't even remember him in the Artists Union. He steered clear of all entanglements. He was more single-minded than most of the artists I met." While Rothko did join the congress and probably the union, Kainen's memory seems essentially right. In aesthetic terms, Rothko "felt very strongly about art not being political."[28]

One of Rothko's most passionate statements in "The Scribble Book" separates creativity from history and repudiates Marxist Social Realism.

> I wish to protest against the historical viewpoint[;] as living creative beings we must contribute to history in whatsoever fashion we function. But we have no particular obligation to fulfill the logic of history just in order to prove their point. We must follow in the logic of art; and if history did not anticipate it, it is history which must change. History is not demonstrated by pictures, nor should pictures be demonstrated by history.

Accordingly, Rothko "hated" the Social Realist Gropper, calling his satiric painting, *The Senate,* a cartoon. In fact, along with Solman and some others, Rothko in 1935 mounted a successful protest against the strict leftist code which predominated at *Art Front*.[29] Like his expressionism, Rothko's politics were a liberal affirmation of the individual self.

In "The Scribble Book," just after calling "the progressive school" "a symbol of liberalism," Rothko goes on to praise "the courage of liberalism" for making "a positive virtue of scepticism and inquiry," an echo of the *Pest*'s advocacy of doubt as the beginning of wisdom. In fact, Rothko, the young idealist who had gone to Yale hoping to become a labor lawyer, later said that he had "lost all faith in the idea of progress and reform" during the 1920s. "Perhaps we were disillusioned because everything seemed so frozen and hopeless during the Coolidge and Hoover era," Rothko later said.[30] The "tremendous emotional capacity for despair" which Edith observed in her husband sensitized him to the unfriendliness of a society which he could no longer hope to change. In the politicized thirties, the one-time anarchist was now a skeptical liberal, focused on expressing an "I," which, as in his self-portrait, he wished to locate outside the entanglements of *any* historical context.

Yet Marcus Rothkowitz was a political liberal who was also a Russian Jew familiar with anti-Semitic persecution. Rothko, whatever his yearnings, had a history—several histories, in fact. While in Portland in April 1924, he had started but then never completed the process of becoming a U.S. citizen. In January 1935, he reinstituted the process; two years later, in November of 1937, he submitted a petition for naturalization; and finally on February 21, 1938, he took the oath of allegiance to the United States.[31] Rothko's actions may have been partly influenced by the "alien rule" requiring U.S. citizenship for status on the WPA; but he began the legal procedure before that rule was passed. Like many other American Jews who became citizens in the late 1930s (among them, his mother), Rothko was likely concerned about both the rise of Nazi racism and the current revival of American anti-Semitism, led by the German-American Bund and the radio broadcasts of Father Charles Coughlin. American citizenship meant safety.

And like many other American Jews in this period, Marcus Rothkowitz changed his name, probably in 1940.[32] One story has it that Edith appointed herself Rothko's manager and decided he should shorten his name; another has it that the dealer J. B. Neumann told Rothko, "Marcus, I have so many Jewish painters, why don't you make your name Rothko?"[33] Whoever first suggested it, Rothko's new name, which would coincide with a dramatic change in his painting style, was chosen, rather than imposed, and it reflected the new "I" in his work. And just as Rothko would be hesitant about showing this new work, he hedged his name change, using "Marcus Rothko" in some contexts in the early and mid-1940s.[34]

"Marcus Rothkowitz" is an Eastern European, Jewish name. More than twenty years before, Rothko's two older brothers had both changed their names to "Roth"—a common name and a common Jewish-American name. "Mark Rothko" is an unusual name which differentiates the painter from his pharmacist brothers and preserves his standing as a special figure both in his family and beyond it. *This* "I" is unique.[35] "Mark Rothko" does not particularly sound like an American name (or like a Russian or Jewish name, for that matter), as if its bearer transcended ethnic or national identity. The name does have a strong, solemn sound: this "I" is unique, ethnically elusive, a bit awesome. With his new citizenship and his new name, Rothko made two steps toward Americanization. As a boy, he had repudiated the temple and Talmudic law. As a young man, he had repudiated the path of social assimilation taken, say, by the members of the Brooklyn Jewish Center. Eventually, he would find a way of Americanizing himself and his painting that at once concealed and incorporated his Jewish origins.

• • •

George Okun, the first of two young men to rent a small bedroom in Rothko's Park Place apartment, remembered that "most mornings when I got up to perform my ablutions, Mark would be sitting in the living room studio with his pajama tops on, smoking a cigarette and looking at his latest painting."[36] Okun's memory has an intimate feel to it, as if we were suddenly granted a glimpse of Rothko, at work, in an unguarded moment. We don't see the grimly combative Rothkowitz of political and aesthetic debate, or the warm, funny "Rothkie" presiding over his Center Academy art classes. This is Rothko alone, not yet dressed, but already silently and completely absorbed in his work. Yet the anecdote also dramatizes our distance from this man, whose private feelings and ruminations can only come to us indirectly, mainly through his words and his paintings, both of which were highly theatrical.

Rothko had taught himself to play the mandolin and the piano. He loved classical music, particularly opera, particularly Mozart, and in the 1930s he liked to work with his radio tuned to WQXR, New York City's classical music station. As a boy, he had written Hebrew poems; later, he contributed to high school and college publications. During the thirties he wrote two essays about children's art, planned another, and, for several years, was writing a book about art. He was an active reader, with Nietzsche's *The Birth of Tragedy* and, later, Kierkegaard's *Fear and Trembling* important texts for him. Rothko carefully read, transcribed quotations from, and made occasional comments on Freud's *The Interpretation of Dreams*.[37] Rothko enjoyed music, talking, writing, reading. In fact, he may have had a greater "natural" gift for verbal and musical expression than he did for painting. He came to painting relatively late, mainly taught himself, and mastered it only after a twenty-year, backbreaking effort.

When he wrote that "painting is just as natural a language as singing or speaking," the thirty-one-year-old Rothko was trying to convince himself as much as his reader. In his *Self-Portrait* (color plate 7), he represents his eyes and his right hand, the two parts of his body most intimately connected with painting, as damaged. The act of painting, as Edith remembered, "tormented" even as it "completely absorbed" her husband. In "The Scribble Book," Rothko declared that expressionism attempts "to recapture the freshness and (naiveté) of childish vision." His own expressionism, like his own remembered childhood, was melancholy, oppressed, tortured. The act of painting, for Rothko, was a painful struggle to recover a sensual, emotional aspect of the self that had been repressed, lost, or damaged in childhood, and it left him feeling depressed and walled-in (like the people in his paintings), stiff and ill at ease (like the boy in *Street Scene* or the man in the *Self-Portrait*).

In *Street Scene* (color plate 1) a sharply drawn line, defining the edge of the public building against the black background for the human figures, splits the work into public and private spaces. The classical architecture of the building associates it with art and suggests that *Street Scene* explores self-expression *as a problem*. Can private feeling be made public, the painting asks, without becoming blank, impersonal, dead, without becoming mere theatrical facade? The freely painted, abstract gray space at the right in the painting anticipates Rothko's later solution: the dissolution of physical objects enabling the communication of deep emotion not through real or symbolic incident but immediately, through colored shapes. Eventually Rothko quit the mandolin and got rid of his piano; he abandoned his book on art and, after 1950, he generally avoided making public statements about his art. The language for his core self was the language of abstract painting.

Just as The Ten was forming in late 1935, Rothko began to explore an alternative to expressionism. Like many other painters, Rothko often carried a sketchbook with him, drawing urban scenes, beach scenes, rural scenes, an occasional still life, but mostly the human figure and mostly female nudes, many of them probably done at the sketching class which met on Saturday mornings at the Averys'. At some point Rothko began drawing subway stations, a subject which had already engaged his friend Solman. Rothko produced at least five subway paintings, one of which, *Subway Scene,* c.1938 (color plate 8), became "one of the few canvases he ever brought out of the racks" in later years, when "visitors asked to see his early work."[38] Rothko, then, attached some lasting importance to this painting.

This "scene," specifically, is the Nostrand Avenue stop on the IRT/New Lots line, the station where Rothko got off the train when, in the early and late 1930s, he commuted from Manhattan to his job at Center Academy. As in all his subway paintings, Rothko's interest is not in the trains but the platforms: modern, public, urban spaces where strangers come and go—or wait. His stations are not grimy, dark, hellish underground spaces; nor are they filled with quick-moving, shoving, noisy, rush-hour crowds. Rather, they are bare, compressed areas which contain a slow, quiet, and solitary mobility.

Here, on the left, a brown sliver of a person climbs the stairs to the street, while two more cheerfully dressed figures in the foreground descend to (or one rises from and one descends to) the lower station where the trains going to Manhattan depart. Toward the rear, as one wide-shouldered person in gray approaches the turnstile, another, who looks like a turn-of-the-century policeman, approaches the change booth. Other paintings in the subway series people the stations with well-dressed, middle-class figures who, unlike the massive, bulky figures inhabiting Rothko's domestic interiors, are elongated and attenuated, as if prosperous but spiritually deprived, and the posts of the subway platforms lock them into a series of vertical compartments which dramatize their isolation. In these works, dreamlike distortions (one of them is titled *Subterranean Fantasy*) make a social critique.

"A limited space and limited objects," Rothko writes in "The Scribble Book," "are more likely to express action and a communicable experience of movement." In *Subway Scene* the ceiling is low; the floor is slightly tilted upward; the back wall pushes forward. Space is compressed. The people, composed of thin splotches of color and lacking facial features, are mobile, flat, and anonymous. Ironically, the station is specified—by the repeated "N"s—while the humans are not. Modern city-dwellers on the move, these faceless figures go about their business with silent passivity, held within an elaborate grid of vertical and horizontal rectangles established by entrance/exit ways, gray cement floor, the green door on the left, four cream and green steel posts, ceiling beams, brown squares with decorative "N"s, blank walls, advertising signs, a brown change booth, its window, and a jail-like pattern of blue iron bars.[39]

Within this grid the man in the change booth occupies a strong focal point. Seated in a glowing brown enclosure, he is the only person given any facial features; looking toward us, seen from slightly below and wearing his official IRT cap, he is a familiar presence, not exactly anonymous but not fully human either, someone passengers look at and have an exchange with, but a monetary exchange. The pewlike shapes of the ocher entrances, the crosslike shapes of the turnstiles (which have been rotated upward to face us) and the glowing yellow light inside the booth, all define a municipal order which ironically echoes a sacred one. In fact, framed by the booth's window and surrounded by an old-master brown, the money changer, looking like a painting-within-the-painting, becomes an icon, permanent and disquieting, of the scene of civic order that he presides over.

Working for the WPA

"Here," we might say—as Rothko did of his Center Academy students' work—"is a social art," commenting on urban solitude, impassivity, and confinement. Yet here, too, with its geometry of intersecting rectangles, is an art whose underlying construction is as formal as Mondrian's. Rothko's sketchbook drawings of the subway platforms often omit people and eliminate detail in order to map out the space as a abstract structure of empty rectangular planes, sometimes tilted or pushed together to create a claustrophobic feeling. In this modern urban space, the architectural dominates the human, except for the sensibility of the painter. For both the grim feeling and the formal severity are modified by Rothko's expressive use of color and light, both of which work to brighten and humanize his subway scene.

Colors have not been dictated by the IRT but chosen and applied by the painter. In the upper half of *Subway Scene* pale colors—flat, thinly painted bands of cream, white, and a soft purple—lighten the stark architecture. The contrasting brown of the change booth, which becomes a smoldering orange-brown inside the window, adds drama, depth, and some warmth. The gray cement floor, painted, like the rear gray wall, in rapid, swirling brushstrokes, forms, in the foreground, a dense, cloudy substance on which the blue railing seems gently to sit. As with the floor, the painterliness of the lower green-black halves of the steel girders gives them an almost watery translucence which makes them partly solid, partly not. The railing bars could have suggested imprisonment, particularly if Rothko had painted them black, hard-edged, and in strict geometrical perspective. Instead, they have been rapidly and freely painted, first in gray, then in a fuzzy light blue which sometimes thins into nothingness. These bars soften and brighten the painting, their sky-blue offering its one hint of a natural world that is outside. A mysterious, sourceless light—neither natural nor artificial—has been evenly dispersed through this underground enclosure, giving it a poetic, otherworldly character.

In *Subway Scene,* then, Rothko's ultimate concern is neither social nor formal, but personal and emotional. Whereas his other subway paintings stress the quiet isolation of people who are waiting together, Rothko here stresses movement. At the rear left a stairway steeply rises, while in the center foreground another stair descends; at the front left we see part of a closed green door. Rothko has placed his work in a middle region evoking unseen upper and lower realms. He has placed us in a glowing chamber where strangers enter and leave, go up and down, though we don't know where. The down stairway, in particular, enters a rectangular opening that has been narrowed by the gentle inward slope along its top and filled with a creamy green color, as if the descent were into a mysterious light—or nothingness. As we have seen in *Street Scene*, Rothko was interested in public architecture as symbolic of a social order in which he, as a Russian immigrant and a modernist painter, felt himself to be an alien. *Street Scene* severs the public from the private, the geometrical from the emotional; *Subway Scene* integrates them by taking a blank, impersonal place of public movement and trying to absorb it and make it part of the artist. Without sentimentalizing it, Rothko has domesticated the public order, made himself feel at home there.

• • •

All copied things are worthless. The slightest thing produced which is the result of inner experience, is worth more than the cleverest copying.

Franz Cizek

"Over to Marcus last night his book is coming along fine, sounds pretty good to me," Milton Avery wrote to Louis Kaufman in June of 1936.[40] Several of Rothko's friends from the 1930s remember him reading to them from a book he was then writing, a theoretical treatise on painting which they, unlike Avery, found incomprehensibly abstract and convoluted. After listening to a chapter, Morris Calden, George Okun's replacement as Rothko's spare-room tenant, commented, "Marcus, I've read Kant and I've read Schelling and I've read Hegel. I have at least average adult intelligence and I can't understand it." We don't know when Rothko began writing this book, how much of it he did write, or when he stopped working on it. The manuscript, whether pretty good or pretty obscure, seems to have vanished.

What does survive from Rothko's unpublished writings in the late thirties is mainly "The Scribble Book," a collection of notes and drafts for a kind of manual (both theoretical and practical) on teaching children's art. Rothko's critics, however, have generally viewed "The Scribble Book" as the source of a Center Academy talk given by Rothko in 1938, at the school's tenth anniversary, a speech itself surviving only in a very rough draft.[41] Beginning his talk with a backward look across the last ten years, "Rothkie" pronounces the "progressive art methods" formerly viewed "as a suspicious innovation and experiment" as now firmly established. "Today this method needs no martyrs." He points to "an increased knowledge and appreciation by the public in art in general and contemporary art currents particularly" as well as "a widespread interest in the art of children" by museums, galleries, and other cultural institutions.

Most of the talk, however, restates the leading ideas from Rothko's 1934 "New Training for Future Artists and Art Lovers." Emphasizing "the difference between sheer skill and skill that is linked to spirit, expressiveness and personality" (or between "the painter who paints well and the artist whose works breathe life and imagination"), the self-taught Rothko—whom no one ever accused of living off mere facility—continues to define art as self-expression. Accordingly, children in his classes are not asked to produce "a duplication of methods and examples," a requirement which would mean that "the sum total" of the child's "experience was the sum of the things he learned to imitate." Art is not copying, and Rothko was not trying to create a generation of Lewis Brownes. At Center Academy, "from the very beginning," the child "is encouraged to be an artist, a creator," "to give concrete expression to his imaginings, fancies, proclivities." "The result," Rothko eloquently concludes, "is a constant creative activity in which the child creates an entire child-like cosmology which expresses the infinitely varied and exciting world of a child's fancies and experience."

Yet "The Scribble Book" was not just a prose laboratory for preparing this 1938 Center Academy talk. For one thing, a list Rothko made of his exhibits establishes that parts of "The Scribble Book" were written after late 1939 and thus some time after the talk. For another, Rothko's papers contain a title page, an elaborate three-page outline and about ten pages of drafts for what would become a long essay or short book comparing "the basic plastic elements, styles, and processes common to both the creative paintings of children and traditional art." It was this work, far more ambitious, sophisticated, and systematic than the Center Academy talk, but apparently never completed, for which "The Scribble Book" was preparation.[42]

"The Scribble Book" writings are fragmentary and rough. One page of the book has been ripped out; other pages have been left blank; nineteen pages in, Rothko turned the book upside down and started writing from the back. Of the forty-nine pages of text, many contain struck words, omitted words, misspellings, marginal additions, arrows connecting one entry with another, lists of subjects to be developed later, or brief notations whose import was clear only to Rothko; other entries forcefully state fully articulated positions, like his protest against the Marxist demand that art "fulfill the logic of history." But like a sketchbook, "The Scribble Book" exposes Rothko's mind *in process,* revealing contradictory emphases and directions in his thinking that a more coherent and polished account would have smoothed out.

The notebook, referring to Plato, Kant, and Nietzsche's *The Birth of Tragedy,* reveals Rothko's readings in philosophy as well as his familiarity with such pedagogical texts as Oskar Pfister's *Psycho-analysis in the Service of Education* (1922) and Wilhelm Viola's *Child Art and Franz Cizek* (1936). As in his Center Academy talk, Rothko begins by observing that his progressive art method is "now penetrating degree by degree into the most strongly fortified citadels of conservatism." Rothko's cause here, however, is not merely the educational methods used at a particular Brooklyn school, but the broader advance of the art-education theories developed by Franz Cizek. Cizek, who in the last few years of the nineteenth century had quit painting to open an innovative child's art school in Vienna, abandoned the then standard method of teaching children to draw by having them copy ornamental designs or plaster models.

All children are creative, according to Cizek, who advocated a classroom freedom and spontaneity that would "let children grow, flourish and mature according to their innate laws of development." "The teacher," he warned, "must avoid every form of compulsion." Combining this kind of romantic organicism with a salvationist social program, Cizek proposed not so much to develop great artists as to liberate children from the tendency of "modern civilization" to produce "bored little adults, able only to consume, out of originally creative and gifted children." In a statement with special appeal for Rothko, who believed he had been deprived of a childhood, Cizek declared that "I have extricated children from school in order to make a home for them, where they may really be children."[43]

While his utopian social hopes were never realized, Cizek's art methods flourished. His students' works were exhibited all over the world, traveling throughout the United States between 1924 and 1929. There is no evidence that Rothko read Cizek himself, though he clearly read his disciple, Wilhelm Viola, whose *Child Art and Franz Cizek* includes several pages of quotations from the master. In "The Scribble Book" Rothko transcribed (or in one case mistranscribed) three passages from Viola's text. Viola's "it seemed that all children unconsciously followed eternal laws of form" becomes Rothko's "it seemed that all children unconsciously followed *unconscious* laws of form" (my emphasis). Rothko also recorded Cizek's advice that children who become "too skilled" in one medium and find it "too easy" should "try another which presents more difficulties to them," and he copied down Cizek's Rousseauistic claim that if he could live on a desert island with his students, freeing them from the corrupting distractions of civilization, he could "bring all his children to the purest development of their creative ability." Rothko, then, transcribed passages stressing a universal (or "natural") plastic language residing in the child's unconscious psyche, a language developed in struggle with the artistic medium, a struggle ideally taking place outside of social arrangements and historical pressures, unlike, say, the struggle of a displaced adult to assert his creativity in the compressed cement, iron, and tiled box of a modern subway station.

Many of Rothko's ideas in "The Scribble Book" resemble, and may originate with, Cizek by way of Viola. "Cizek was the first to discover that many children like to begin with colours without having made any previous drawing," Viola writes.[44] Rothko observes, "Tradition of *starting with drawing* an academic notion[.] We may start with color"—an approach to children's art that, several years later, would prove liberating for Rothko himself. But whether Viola's work influenced Rothko or merely confirmed ideas he had already formulated for himself, "The Scribble Book" reveals that Rothko was now striking out on his own. After observing the increasing acceptance of Cizek's program, Rothko remarks that "until now there has been a united front, erasing all differences, in the apostleship for the general cause." While not proposing a schismatic break, he now wishes to "evaluate" results, confront "limitations," elaborate techniques, in short, to assert *his* difference. A few pages in, Rothko declares the painter to be the most effective child's art teacher, because "he has acquired a sensibility." But, Rothko warns, sensibility "is an inconstant factor," "sometimes tainted with prejudices," so "it is desirable to augment this sensibility with knowledge." Despite a temper that Robert Motherwell compared to that of Ivan the Terrible and despite a propensity for rash, dramatic gestures (leaving Yale; marriage after a four-month romance; withdrawing the Four Seasons paintings), Rothko was a ruminator who, like the young man in his pajama tops smoking and silently studying his painting, liked to *consider* his moves. He was both impulsive and deliberate. During the 1930s, reading and writing were two forms of his deliberation, two ways of augmenting his sensibility with knowledge.

"The necessity of an empirical inquiry instead of vague enthusiasms," Rothko wrote in "The Scribble Book." His theorizing there draws on practical knowledge, derived from more than ten years' teaching and fifteen years' painting, in order to substitute a more specific, analytic, and empirically based pedagogy for the vague enthusiasms of Viola. "Cizek teaches no technique," says Viola. "His pupils must work out their technique themselves and make it their own"; this had been Rothko's own position in his 1934 essay on children's art.[45] Cizek's faith in natural growth led him to oppose "skill" or any other sign of will in either teacher or child artist.

In "The Scribble Book," Rothko, though suspicious of *mere* skill, is willing to talk shop. In fact, since his projected work seems to have been a kind of instructor's manual for teachers of children's art, his notes often establish tech-

Chapter Five

nical classifications (e.g., "types of composition") or they organize lists of techniques or effects as a series of oppositions which confront the artist (child or adult) with choices. One notebook page looks like this:

How moderns and old masters   their particular sense of space

New techniques and different techniques for each method

> Absorbent surface
> Non absorbent
> glazing
> opaque
> painting into wet color
> Painting around an object.
> Tonalism
> A-Tonalism

Relationship between medium and technique

As here, the technical sections of "The Scribble Book" are generally spare and very preliminary, as if Rothko's practical, day-to-day familiarity with these issues would later provide him with an abundance of specifics. When he does elaborate, he emphasizes the emotional meanings of technical choices. Scale, for instance, "definitely involves a *space* emotion. A child may limit space arbitrarily and thus heroify his objects. Or he may infinitize space, dwarfing the importance of objects, causing them to merge and become part of the space world." Or, "there may be a perfectly balanced relationship" between objects and space, as in Piero della Francesca, "where both participate equally in an empirical world, one augmenting the dignity of the other, denoting equal veneration for man, the things he has wrought, and his possessions." A feeling for the expressive meaning of scale, Rothko believes, "is inherent in a child." Children, therefore, don't need to be told about choices; only "fallen" adult artists do. Rothko's catalogues of opposites often break down, roughly, into romantic versus classical attitudes, in which freedom *seems* located on the romantic side but is really to be found in a "diversity" that would employ "decorativeness as well as austerity," "lushness vs. acidity," "defined areas, or a merging or a flux," "sharp silhouette or indefinite merging." Freedom, Rothko says, "can be objective and analytic as well as romantic."

In theoretical terms, Rothko is attempting to formulate a tougher, more analytic point of view than Cizek provides with his simplified notion of an originally pure, creative self inevitably corrupted by civilization. Like Cizek, Rothko was concerned with "the proper development of the creative impulse" from childhood, and by separating "the logic of art" from "the logic of history" and insisting that "art is of the spirit" and beyond social "use," Rothko, too, defined that creative self as free, disinterested, and, ideally, outside history. But confronting Cizek's romanticized self generated contradictory lines of thought in Rothko, perhaps one reason he was never able to complete his own account of children's art.

Cizek's self is universal, eternal, ahistorical; so is Rothko's—sometimes. Brooklyn, not even along Eastern Parkway, was no mythical desert kingdom. So at other times Rothko places the self inside history, for example, justifying Cizek's method as one uniquely suited for the predicament of the self in the modern era. "If we had a tradition upon which [we] agreed we could teach it to our children," Rothko says, implying that traditional methods (i.e., copying) were fine for previous times. But liberal "scepticism" and empiricism have undermined faith in collective myths and the traditional means of representing them, so that the modern "artist looked into himself and found himself using his own emphasis (emotional) rather than visual, and using the geometric shape." Without agreed-upon traditions, we are left only with the self, a condition which Rothko experiences partly as liberation, partly as loss.

Rothko admires a "liberalism" which "rejects the unity which it cannot arrive at thru its technic of scepticism. It will not accept a unity from the sheer conviction of the necessity of such acceptance." Yet, even as he heroizes doubt, Rothko affirms the desire to believe. "Human nature," he writes, "is so constituted that it venerates scepticism as well as faith and accords honor to the conqueror and martyr both." Certainly, Rothko's own contradictory nature venerated both skepticism and faith, for just as an inconstant sensibility needs to be augmented by knowledge, so the solitary self needs to be contained within something external.

Rothko thus writes of the freedom which paradoxically "can manifest itself thru tightness as well as exuberance," or of an "action" or "movement" best expressed through "a limited space," as if a subway platform were more likely to generate creativity than the view from the Portland hills. Whereas Cizek idealizes the spontaneous freedom of the child artist, Rothko declares that "the right number of inhibitions or suppressions" is needed "to provide the leaven," the "just right disturbance of equilibrium, to imbue that excitement, that right exhalation of spirit which demonstrates the difference between dynamic organism and static machination"—an instance of *internal* limits generating artistic vitality. The unfriendliness of society or even of one's own psyche are not alien forces to be overcome but the necessary preconditions of a somber creativity.

"The psychoanalyst (Pfister) may find a panorama of confessions of antipathies and obsessions among the expressionists," Rothko observes. But when he quickly retorts that the expressionists "have adopted their tradition in the same way in which the Renaissance painters came by theirs," it sounds as if Rothko is rejecting Pfister's assumption of a driven, irrational self to allow for a self that is at least free enough to choose a style or tradition. But Rothko then concludes: "therefore the same aberrations should be discovered by the sleuth in the work of Titian," as if *all* selves were compelled and *all* art confessional, even if these private "aberrations" are less apparent in traditional work. Rothko's skewed logic here—first attacking, then accepting Pfister's position—reflects his trouble in integrating the impulsive and deliberate sides of his own character.

Throughout "The Scribble Book" Rothko, unlike Cizek, discriminates between children's art and modes of expression that resemble it, e.g., primitivism. "Often child art transforms itself into primitivism which is only the child producing a mimicry of himself," Rothko writes, then concludes epigrammatically: "Primitivism is the exploitation of the picturesque in the charming garb of naiveté." Distinguishing between children's art, psychotic art, and modern art, however, proves to be more complicated. "Is the child mad, the madman childish, and does Picasso try to be a little of both [?]" Rothko asks. "All of them employ the basic elements of [plastic] speech." Children achieve "instinctive representation thru instinctive, primitive, elementary symbols," "the madman by his symbolism."

Painting, then, originates as a symbolic language of the unconscious. Children speak this "plastic tongue" instinctively, the adult artist self-consciously, having "analyzed his problem thru to these basic elements of plastic shapes and emotional symbols." The value of modern art, from this point of view, is that it "has often in the guise of the anthropologist or archeologist ruminated among its own elementary impulses as well as the most archaic forms of man's plastic speech." "In modern art the scaffolding has been left"; its instinctual origins have "not been obscured by style and tradition as that of the old masters."

At one point Rothko transcribes a long passage from Pfister's *Psychoanalysis in the Service of Education*. "The return of the past comes about regularly even in the conscious life," declares Pfister, who goes on to cite the examples of Christ instructing men to become as little children, the Renaissance return to antiquity, Rousseau's projected "return to Nature," and Tolstoy's reversion to the primitive life. "Without such retrogressions no great progressions are possible," Pfister says, "and no fresh creation, however cleverly imagined, has any prospect of a future unless it has borrowed from the past. For it is wrecked on a law of spiritual life—."[46]

One can only be modern, it seems, by way of the archaic. The unconscious may house private "antipathies and obsessions" or it may be the source of a natural and therefore shareable plastic language; Rothko is, again, ambivalent. But art severed from these elementary origins produces "our academy boys with their brown saucy pasts[,] [or] appearing bright hued among our abstractionist shows, [or] emotionally gyrating among the expressionists."

Yet the alternative to the academy is not going native; Rothko, rather, speaks of the modern artist as an "anthropologist or archeologist" who ruminates among the "elementary impulses" of his art without surrendering to them. Accordingly, Rothko now rejects not just its academic derivatives but expressionism itself, which he decribes as "an attempt to recapture the freshness and (naiveté) of childish vision."

. . .

A museum can either be a museum or it can be modern, but it cannot be both.

Gertrude Stein to Alfred Barr

On May 8, 1939, the trustees of the Museum of Modern Art attended a dinner on the penthouse floor of the museum's new 53rd Street building. The occasion was ceremonial, marking the Modern's tenth anniversary, the official opening of the new building, and a changing of the guard: Nelson Rockefeller replacing Conger Goodyear as the museum's president. Dinner was followed by two speeches, then Rockefeller closed the evening by presenting Goodyear with a *trompe l'oeil* painting by William Harnett which, he said, seemed to him "to typify the Museum's interest in American art." The painting, called *Playbill and Dollar Bill,* turned out to be a forgery, but it did prophesy much of the museum's future: money and show business.[47]

Two days later, the public opening of the new building began with a series of forty glamorous dinner parties. One of the more glittering of these events, held by outgoing president Goodyear at a Central Park South hotel, was attended by (among others) Anne Morrow Lindberg (poet and wife of Charles Lindberg), Ruth Vanderbilt Twombly (a wealthy socialite), Salvador Dali, the sculptor Jo Davidson, Alfred Barr (the museum's director), and the actress Lilian Gish.[48] Afterward, the dinner guests joined a crowd of seven thousand at the museum itself, where a show called "Art in Our Time" had been mounted. Later in the evening, Mrs. Barr recalled, "the fashionable crowds" stood "in respectful silence" listening "to a specially arranged radio program" that featured such speakers as Edsel Ford (on "the industrial aspects of modern art"), John Hay Whitney (on the museum's film library), Robert M. Hutchins (on the educative value of the museum) and Walt Disney (on film). At 10:45 P.M. the program shifted to the White House for a fifteen-minute address by Franklin Roosevelt, who climaxed the cultural elite's gala evening by declaring the museum a symbol of democracy.[49]

The cause of modern art in New York had not always been quite so chic. When Rothko came to the city in the mid-twenties, it was an artistically provincial and conservative place, with the provocations of the Armory Show a dim memory. In May 1921 the Metropolitan Museum had made its first and for a long while its only foray into modernity with an exhibit which included Impressionism and Post-Impressionism but stopped short of Cubism; the show nevertheless inspired a widely circulated flyer which equated "this 'Modernistic' degenerate cult" not with democracy but with "the Bolshevik philosophy applied to art."[50] Of course, there were a few private galleries that exhibited such alien modernist work: Alfred Stieglitz's 291, the Montross, Rehn, Valentine-Dudensing, and New Art Circle galleries; A. E. Gallatin's Gallery of Living Art at New York University provided, after 1927, one public collection.

And contemporary European painting was beginning to be collected by a few patrons, one of whom, no bolshevik, was Nelson Rockefeller's mother, Abby Aldrich Rockefeller. Her husband, John D., Jr., stated, "I am interested in beauty and by and large I do not find beauty in modern art. I find instead a desire for self-expression," as if *that* were self-evidently contemptible.[51] Rockefeller himself collected Chinese porcelains and filled the walls of his eight-story brownstone on West 54th Street with Old Masters. But by the early twenties his wife had begun what her family dimly viewed as "an outlandish hobby," namely, collecting modern art. *Her* purchases, which included O'Keeffe, Braque, and Picasso, were hung in a converted playroom on the top floor of the family mansion.[52] In the 1920s, the place of modern art in New York was in the hands of a few wealthy women, who were well-advised to keep it out of sight.

But collecting art is a form of self-expression—and of self-display. Mrs. Rockefeller eventually aspired to a more public space for her private collection. In the winter of 1928–29, as Marcus Rothkowitz was waging his legal battle against Lewis Browne, Abbie Rockefeller travelled to Egypt "to escape the rigors of New York" and met, first, Miss Lizzie P. Bliss and then Mrs. Cornelius J. Sullivan, both of whom were patrons of contemporary painting and both of whom had participated in the Armory Show and then in the 1921 modernism exhibit at the Metropolitan. Together, the three women formulated a plan for a museum of modern art, thus becoming, in the words of the Modern's official historian, "the founding mothers of the Museum, and a formidable trio they were, women of spirit, vigor, adventurousness, and, not unimportantly, of commanding wealth."[53] With the twenty-seven-year-old Alfred Barr as its director, the Museum of Modern Art opened in November of 1929 with a show of van Gogh, Gauguin, Seurat, and Cézanne.

Under Barr's zealous leadership, and backed by "commanding wealth," the museum worked to legitimatize modern art. During the thirties the Modern presented major shows of Matisse (1931), van Gogh (1935), "Cubism and Abstract Art" (1936), "Fantastic Art, Dada, and Surrealism" (1936), and "Picasso: Forty Years of His Art" (1939). The young American painter's initiatory trip to Paris was no longer quite so necessary. New York painters could now view, for a mere 25 cents admission, many of the most advanced works of their European contemporaries. So could an emerging new audience for twentieth-century art.

Not long after the Modern had opened in 1929, Barr epitomized the backward state of New York City's public collections by pointing out that no work by van Gogh was on permanent display in the city; six years later he could still make the same point, in his catalogue for the Modern's exhibit of 127 of van Gogh's paintings. Supported by a publicity campaign which shrewdly capitalized on the melodramatic features of van Gogh's life, the show drew more than 140,000 visitors during its eight weeks in New York, and another 750,000 during its tour of the country. As the museum's publicity director bragged some years later, "we played the van Gogh show like a polo game—dribbled the ball down the field first, and then, bang, right between the goal posts! It was a honey, if I do say so myself." By 1935 modernism—or at least one of its eminent precursors—had progressed from the playrooms of the rich to fashionable shoprooms. "Store windows on Fifth Avenue were filled with ladies' dresses in van Gogh colors, displayed in front of color reproductions of his paintings. His sunflowers bloomed on shower curtains, on scarves, on tablecloths and bathmats and ashtrays."[54]

Again, during the thirties, Rothko remarked (more than once): "I'd like to have money; I'm not crazy like van Gogh." A *Fortune* magazine essay on the Museum of Modern Art, based on interviews with Alfred Barr, formulated the museum's purpose: "If there are any unrecognized van Goghs about in 1938 they should not be forced to starve and commit suicide and the public should not be denied the opportunity of enjoying their work."[55] Like many collectors and curators, Barr thought of himself as on a rescue mission in relation to artists and on an educative mission in relation to the public. In reality, however, the Modern risked converting marginalized painters into commercialized ones. The new museum did make modern work available to painters, like Rothko, who were too young to have seen the Armory Show and who were mainly unimpressed by the work of the American modernists. Along with the WPA, the museum contributed to what Rothko, in his 1938 Center Academy talk, described as the "increased knowledge and appreciation by the public in art in general and contemporary art currents particularly." But the Modern did nothing to better the material well-being of the American artists of Rothko's generation.

When, the month after the museum's tenth anniversary celebration, Alfred Barr visited Gertrude Stein in Paris, she tried to persuade him that a *modern* museum was a contradiction. The new building's rectangular aluminum and glass facade, pointedly juxtaposed with the ornate Victorian brownstones that then lined West 53rd Street, boldly announced its modernity, but modernity at its moment of achieving uptown social prestige and authority. As the museum's official historian puts it, "what had been a missionary church in a Philistine jungle with a small band of passionately devoted young proselytizers dedicated to making converts began to look curiously like, and take on the airs and graces of, a cathedral of the new culture."[56] Originally, the museum was intended to have a shifting collection, with works established as masterpieces moved on to the Metropolitan. In this way the Modern would *be* modern. But bequests from two of the founders helped to undermine that plan. Now, in the museum's growing permanent collection, once-disruptive works were enshrined in a temple of art, one built in the new internationalist style but a temple nonetheless. Thus, in 1961, Mark Rothko would equate a one-man exhibit at the Museum of Modern Art with an invitation to dwell on Mount Parnassus: it made him not modern but eternal.

But the cost of being eternalized is being historicized. On the jacket cover to his "Cubism and Abstract Art" catalogue, Barr diagrammed the genealogical derivations of all the movements in twentieth-century art, tracing them from the present back to the late nineteenth-century masters of the Modern's first exhibit: van Gogh, Gauguin, Seurat, and Cézanne. Cubism was now *placed,* as the logical outcome of earlier developments and as the central, formative moment of contemporary art. With their commanding wealth, the "founding mothers" had provided modernism with an institutional home. In his scholarly catalogue essays, Alfred Barr was providing modernism with its dynastic history. Modern, which means "of the present," now referred not to a continuing evolution but to an historical period which was *over*.

That history, as the "Art in Our Time" exhibit made clear, apotheosized

Parisian modernism, especially Picasso. The "time" of the "Art in Our Time" show was nineteenth-century America or early twentieth-century Paris, not the New York of 1939. As one historian of the museum put it, "in contrast with its well-organized shows of European art, the Museum of Modern Art's exhibitions of American painting and sculpture throughout the Thirties often reeked of provincial pride and pity, with the works carelessly selected and catalogs to match."[57] In the same year that the Modern's new building opened, the Guggenheim collection established quarters just across Fifth Avenue on East 54th Street as the Museum of Non-Objective Art. By the end of the 1930s, then, New York had three museums devoted to twentieth-century art. The spiritual abstractions of Kandinsky had a home at the Guggenheim, American realism and regionalism at the Whitney, and European modernism at the Modern. What the three museums excluded, however, were the young American painters whose work, whether expressionist or geometrical, had connections with Europe.

In fact, from late 1938 Barr had been turning down requests for an exhibit from the American Abstract Artists.[58] In his role as secretary of The Ten, Rothko wrote to Barr sometime in 1939 to announce that "The Ten, a group of modern American painters, would like to submit to your attention examples of their latest work at your earliest convenience." Barr delegated his assistant, Dorothy Miller, to view their paintings, but no purchases or shows resulted.[59] When, in April 1940, the museum opened an exhibit of drawings and cartoons done for the newspaper *PM,* the American Abstract Artists picketed the museum and distributed an Ad Reinhardt broadside. "How Modern Is the Museum of Modern Art?" "Is the MUSEUM A BUSINESS?" Reinhardt asked, and he quoted Nelson Rockefeller's admission that by becoming the museum's president he was "engaging in show-business."[60] *The* institution by means of which the painters of Rothko's generation would be accepted by the country's centers of wealth and cultural power was now in place. But in 1939 "the cathedral," happy to proclaim the canonization of European masters, kept the young American painters outside on the street—displaced, homeless, modern.

. . .

During the late 1930s, Marcus Rothkowitz and Edith Sachar continued their near-annual migrations to new apartments around New York City. Sometime before May 1937, they moved back to Manhattan, at 3 Great Jones Street in Greenwich Village.[61] Since marrying Edith, Rothko had lived near surrogate families, first the Averys, then the Sachars. Now just a few blocks from Washington Square Park, he had access to the coffeehouses, cafeterias, park benches,

Chapter Five

clubs, and bars of New York's version of the Left Bank. In the Village, with its ample opportunities for gossip, the airing of shared gripes, and shoptalk, art was a less lonely thing. At the time, moreover, the art world was still small enough so that everyone *could* know everyone else, but still so marginal and scattered that not everyone *did* know everyone else—as Willem de Kooning found out one evening relaxing on a bench in Washington Square Park when he noticed "a husky man" at the other end of his bench. "We were just sitting there—wasn't a soul around." After a while, the stranger observed that it was "a nice evening"; de Kooning agreed, and the man asked him what he did. "I said, 'I'm a painter'." "He says, 'Oh, you're a painter? I'm a painter, too'. And he said, 'What's your name?' I said, 'I'm Bill de Kooning'. I said, 'Who are you?' He says, 'I'm Rothko'. I said, 'Oh, for God's sake'." The two men laughed, talked for a while, and a few days later Rothko visited de Kooning's studio.[62]

Rothko had not met any of the best minds of his generation in the small park across the street from his Park Place apartment in Brooklyn. The Village, in fact, had begun to attract some of the painters, critics, and curators who would be important in the formation of the New York School. A. E. Gallatin's Gallery of Living Art was located at nearby New York University, while the Whitney Museum was on Eighth Street, then the Village's main boulevard. Hans Hofmann's art school was close to Washington Square; Jackson Pollock, Lee Krasner, Franz Kline, and Arshile Gorky were all then living in the Village, as were Clement Greenberg, Meyer Schapiro, and Dorothy Miller. Barnett Newman had a studio on West 3rd Street. The Village even had community art shows, one of which, "Currents of Life in Greenwich Village, 1900–1938," Rothko participated in.[63]

To a young painter in the 1930s Greenwich Village meant low rents, artistic community, and freedom from bourgeois demands. From adolescence, Rothko and Edith had been drawn to experimental styles of life. Both had quit college; both had then decided to "bum about"; both had chosen the arts. Before marrying, they had lived together; then they eloped; afterward, they had lived the impoverished lives of apprentice artists, in cheap, messy flats. One of their young tenants, Morris Calden, recalled the Park Place apartment as "cluttered; the sink was full of unwashed dishes; books, records, were lying around; clothes were too." Their living room served as painting studio, sculpture studio, and gathering place for sketching classes, for which Edith sometimes posed in the nude.[64] From the perspective, say, of a Portland or a Dvinsk pharmacist, Marcus and Edith looked like wayward bohemians.

But the gaiety, thrills, and extravagance of bohemia attracted Rothko even less than the neatness, comfort, and respectability of bourgeois existence. He would live in the Village for only about three years, before moving to the Lower

East Side.[65] For Rothko, the political liberal and family nonconformist, was also a social conservative who repudiated conventional behavior in order to preserve deeper values he had absorbed from family, class, and ethnic sources. When he had transcribed in "The Scribble Book" Pfister's dictum that "fresh creation" must borrow from "the past," Rothko had found an abstract statement of his own psychological process. He lived with Edith; he eloped with her; but he was also traditionalist enough to marry her. An early riser who often began the day still wearing pajama tops, cigarette in hand, studying one of his paintings, Rothko was no enemy of the Franklinian work ethic. His alternative to middle-class propriety was clutter and material deprivation, not out of bohemian indulgence but because he found in self-denial a harshness that was at once familiar and stimulating.

"Jan. 1937. Just got canned by WPA. Marcus is a very sweet boy. Married four years two months. Still unhappy," reads the final entry in Edith's diary. Does she mean that she is still unhappy or that Marcus is still unhappy? Very likely, she's referring both to herself *and* her husband, as if each of them had married to escape unhappiness and had been disappointed. Marriage had offered Rothko a possible means of separating himself from his family while replicating it in the idealized form he perceived in Milton Avery's domestic life. For a dislocated young man looking for an anchor, marriage might provide the kind of stability that would make an inward "unknown adventure" possible. As Edith's sugary maternal tone ("Marcus is a very sweet boy"—he was then thirty-three) suggests, she was to take care of him, emotionally and even, it turned out, financially. Her self-sacrifices would enable his.

Edith worked for the WPA, probably as a sculptor; she taught crafts part-time at the Center Academy.[66] Sometime in the 1930s her interest in sculpture led her to jewelry and metalwork, which she studied at the New York School of Arts and Trades.[67] She had first invented a children's craft kit—called "Linkatrinket"—consisting of charms, chains, hooks, and tools with which to fashion bracelets and necklaces. But when her efforts to market the game through department stores failed, she started a silver jewelry business of her own, selling her work first through crafts shows, later through distributors to department stores. What Edith had originally wanted to do was to paint, an activity she pursued only after her divorce from Rothko, who "felt that it might conflict with our marriage," that "we might have jealousies" if she painted.[68] So Edith freed her husband for high art by taking on commercial art. Like Jacob Rothkowitz, Marcus was a dreamer who relied on his wife to manage practical matters.

Many years later Edith recalled that "most of their happy life" had occurred on vacations in Croton Falls, about thirty miles north of New York City; she

Chapter Five

also remembered many trips to 57th Street galleries, the Whitney, the Museum of Modern Art, with Picasso, Matisse, and de Chirico as Rothko's chief enthusiasms.[69] "Do you know Marcus you are the only person I have ever felt near to," Edith wrote to her husband. "To be so absolutely without human relationship to people[,] to be so introverted that I could never feel really close to another human—and then to discover you—To love you[.] You must know that it was the very beginning for me of a new life."[70]

Yet when Edith wrote that letter to Rothko, she had separated from him, during the summer of 1937, first working at a children's camp, then living on her own in Woodstock, New York. The separation was intended to be permanent, but her letters to Rothko that summer reveal ambivalence. "I dreamt that we were together and I was very happy—Then suddenly it was all over this happiness and I was miserable," Edith wrote, commenting that in the dream "I was probably thinking that I would like to be with you and then the thought of how miserable we had been together drowned out the possibility of that."[71] She turns away Rothko's offers to visit; she speaks, as she had before their marriage, of her need for freedom and solitude, saying that he "would be too much of an influence on me" were he to visit. She writes of nights spent drinking and dancing at a local bar.

On the other hand, she addresses Rothko as "darling," wishes he were there to watch the sunsets with her, writes of "a depression that is hard to shake," hopes for a letter from him "to drive this melancholy from me."[72] Then, in an undated letter probably written near the end of the summer, as Rothko is about to visit, she blames herself for their troubles. She has been tense, irritable, quick-tempered, and the reason is that she has been hiding something from Rothko—that she's been attracted to another man. "Then," she writes, "the [WPA] project[,] the worry over my job—your job—complications and all that mounted so fast that it seemed we had always quarreled so with each other—[.]" He is the only person she's ever been close to, yet she has tried to "sever" their love. "I think back on our life together," she closes, "and I must say that I think you are so sensitive and beautiful inside and I feel that somehow I have smudged you marred you for myself and you—[.]"[73]

That fall they reconciled. But the "violent arguments" that their roomer, Morris Calden, remembered occurring almost daily in their Park Place apartment soon resumed; and the leading issue, as before, was money. Not that Rothko objected to poverty; he objected to Edith's wish for something more.

"My sister Edith would complain to my mother that they didn't have more material things than they had," Howard Sachar remembered. But "when she did make any money at anything, Marcus would come and complain to my mother, 'What is she doing? Why is she doing it? What's she making money for?'" In her husband's view, Edith was "materialistic." Dorothy Dehner, the first wife of the sculptor David Smith, found Edith "too bourgeois to be an artist's wife." Perhaps she was just too independent to be an artist's wife. But the Rothko who bitterly resented affluence, the Rothko who conceded "I'd like to have money"—unlike that nut van Gogh—this Rothko had his own conflicts about money which in his marriage were expressed as a conflict between him and his wife; *she* was the materialist. Ostensibly a solution to their money problems, Edith's jewelry business, in the words of her younger brother Howard, "drove a wedge between them."

People who knew Edith when she was married to Rothko most often describe her as "chilly." Sally Avery called her "a cold fish" who "had an inflated idea of herself and her work." Assessing Milton Avery's painting, Edith once declared that "I wouldn't hang one in my bathroom," a comment that "mortified" Rothko. Others found Edith reserved and aloof; she did not much impress the staff at Center Academy, one fellow instructor describing her as "limpid—not a vivid person," another as "superannuated, a pale personality."[74] Members of Edith's family, however, stress her determined independence, e.g., Howard Sachar citing Edith's "starting up her own business and being very successful at it. And on her own, completely on her own, with nothing but grumbling from Marcus." Remembering that her sister did not wear a wedding ring and that she kept her maiden name, Lilian Klein called Edith "a modern woman before her time," "very opinionated," "a very strong person" who knew how to manipulate people.

But Marcus, a "sweet boy" known to grumble, had married to be taken care of, not manipulated. "He was a very sloppy sort of person," said Edith, who recalled that Rothko, whose impatience and carelessness made him vulnerable to self-injury, once picked up a razor blade along with the soap to wash his hands and severely cut himself; he was then outraged that the doctor who stitched the wound expected to be paid. Lewis Browne had bristled at Rothko's failure to hang up his coat and vest; at home, Rothko "was a slob—he took his clothes off and he threw them on the floor. He didn't care about his personal appearance in any way. Edith acted as a mother, to make him presentable so she could take him out and not be ashamed of him."[75] Of course, Rothko, who would later be dressed like a workingman to meet the president of Harvard, was *quite* conscious of his appearance; it's just that, as we have seen, he felt embarrassed in the neat, proper bourgeois dress that denied his poor, immigrant origins. Edith discovered, as had Browne, that Rothko would determine for himself in exactly what ways he would be taken care of.

If Edith was often perceived as "chilly," Rothko's "tremendous emotional capacity for despair" often left him gloomily withdrawn. "From the very beginning, according to Edith, he was a very, very moody person; and these moods would be blacker and blacker under certain circumstances. He wasn't really an alcoholic, but when he drank, it didn't make him any more cheerful."[76] When he wasn't brooding (or even when he was), Rothko dominated his wife. "She was kind of in Marcus' shadow at that time," said Howard Sachar. "If there was an area where Marcus did his art work, Edith would have a little corner—very little of the places they had was devoted to what she wanted to do." Socially and intellectually, "Mark tended to put her down." When his painter friends visited, the attitude was: "the little woman—keep her in the back room while we boys talk about what is art and why." "Maybe behind the argument about money," speculated one of their young tenants, "she wanted to be recognized," a desire both Rothko and Edith felt so strongly it drove another wedge between them.[77]

When the back room was converted into a silver jewelry operation and as Edith's business grew, the familial balance of power shifted. "He was unhappy because she made the money," but "the complaints from Marcus were not that he as a man should be doing that, but that she shouldn't really want those things."[78] On the other hand, she was unhappy because he was making very little money. "She was pushing. She wanted to make some money. She was very driving and she wasn't going to hang around with him if he didn't do something." She felt that "he was sponging on her."[79] Unlike Jackson Pollock and Robert Motherwell, both of whom were to marry gifted painters, Rothko lacked the self-confidence to have a second painter around the house. So far as we know, Edith did not protest. But when it came to her business, she not only held her ground against her husband's protests, she eventually began to make her own demands. By 1942 her sales had increased enough for her to rent a loft on East 21st Street where several people helped her produce the jewelry she designed. By this time, she had also succeeded in getting Rothko to work as a salesman in her jewelry business.[80] He *did* protest. "He said he was very upset because he felt like an errand boy," Sally Avery recalled, "and she was sort of lording it over him."[81] Her stubborn insistence, his bitter resentment, generated the crisis that led to their divorce in early 1944.

By the late 1930s, the highly romantic nineteen-year-old girl from Brooklyn with whom Rothko had eloped was a woman with desires and ambitions of her own. Looking for maternal support and consolation, Rothko experienced maternal domination, from a woman whose attention, he felt, was turned away from him. Edith was now aggressively pursuing her business; Rothko was still aggressively pursuing his painting. Both were still unhappy.

• • •

Working for the WPA

During the summer of 1939, Edith and Rothko were living in a brownstone at 313 East 6th Street, near Second Avenue, having moved from the Village in the fall of the previous year. They had been married in what had been the dog kennel in an Upper West Side mansion; now, at the north end of the Lower East Side, they occupied a flat in a brownstone which housed a small synagogue in its basement, and Rothko liked to complain that he had to hide from its members, who wanted to make him a participant.[82]

About to begin his tenth year of teaching at the Center Academy, Rothko would turn thirty-six that September. A determined, ambitious painter closing in on mid-life, he was still struggling in poverty and obscurity, and he was nearing the end of the sixth year of a marriage that was disintegrating—as were other of his external supports. In late October of 1939, The Ten, breaking up under the pressures of individuality, held their last show. On August 17, the WPA had terminated Rothko's appointment.[83] Public events were looking even more grimly chaotic. In April, Franco had marched into Madrid, sealing a fascist victory in the Spanish Civil War; six days after Rothko had been fired from the WPA, on August 23, the German-Soviet pact was signed, one of the two events that, along with the Russian invasion of Finland in November 1939, led to the collapse of the American Artists' Congress.

From a painter's point of view, however, not all consequences of these historical events were disastrous. The war in Spain inspired Picasso's *Guernica,* which was exhibited at the Valentine Gallery in May of 1939. Roberto Matta, the first of the Surrealists exiled by the European war to New York, arrived that fall. In New York, modern art continued to receive more exposure and even legitimacy. During 1939 the Museum of Modern Art presented two important shows: "Cubism and Abstract Art" in the spring and "Picasso: Forty Years of His Art" in the fall. With the opening of the Museum of Non-Objective Art (now the Guggenheim) in June, the city now had a public collection that emphasized not the Cubism of Picasso but painters such as Kandinsky whose abstractions were spiritual and expressionistic. New York was about to become a truly international art center, in ways that would affect Rothko and many other painters of his generation.

For many of these painters, however, the summer of 1939 was, simply, another summer. Jackson Pollock spent it with his brother Sanford in Bucks County, Pennsylvania; Franz Kline, living in Greenwich Village, had a portrait concession at the New York World's Fair; Clyfford Still had the summer off from his teaching duties at Washington State University in Pullman; Robert Motherwell, having recently left Paris in fear of a European war, was living in his family's beach house along the Washington coast; Milton and Sally Avery were in Rawsonville, Vermont; Adolph and Esther Gottlieb in East Gloucester.

Chapter Five

As they had for the last few summers, Rothko and Edith rented an abandoned schoolhouse at Trout Lake, New York, about seven miles north of Hearthstone Point, where they had first met seven years before. Rothko swam, sketched, painted; he held "an informal art class for a group of students who were vacationing in the area."[84] Just "over the hill" was the Bolton Landing farmhouse where David Smith lived with his first wife, Dorothy Dehner. Smith and Rothko had been friendly for several years, though Smith mockingly labelled Rothko "the sad rabbi" and the two men had increasing political differences. In 1940 the radical Smith would stay with the Stalinist American Artists' Congress from which the liberal Rothko would split.

Not long after the signing of the German-Soviet pact in August of 1939, Rothko and Edith came to a lunch at which, Dehner recalled, the two artists "renewed" their political debates. Smith offered the standard American left account of the treaty; the Russians were "buying time." "But Rothko didn't buy that at all." His position focussed on anti-Semitism. "I think he feared the persecution of Jews wherever it might be and I think that was very prominent in his political attitudes, how the Jews were being treated," said Ms. Dehner. The argument effectively ended the Rothko-Smith friendship.

With the signing of the German-Soviet treaty, "almost everyone now took for granted that the upcoming Labor Day weekend would prove the last peacetime vacation for years."[85] For that weekend, Rothko and Edith drove, with Joseph and Milly Liss, to a cottage they had rented on the Housatonic River, near Derby, Connecticut. Rothko had met Liss, a writer then studying with the Theater Collective, in the mid-1930s. The two men, with similar Russian backgrounds and a common interest in literature and the theater, became friends. Rothko, Liss said, "was a very lively conversationalist, very friendly, very outgoing, a big man in many respects, both physically and emotionally. A big eater, a big lover, lover of life. He seemed to worry a great deal about his career, determined some day that he would be a great painter."[86]

Because the Liss's "dilapidated" Model A Ford had "bad brakes, if any," the trip to Derby, normally two hours, took seven. But in this case the sometimes volatile Rothko was "the perfect stoic." Milly Liss had brought along "a generous prime steak," partly to celebrate her husband's birthday, "but mostly to watch Mark eat. He was always a zestful eater." The summer was about to end with something a bit more appetizing than bean soup.

So eager was Rothko for the steak that when he "lumbered into the shadows of first dark to gather fuel" for the grill, he took boards from a collapsed privy and ended up stepping on a nail in one of the "infested privy boards"—another of his careless self-injuries. "A bulk of a man," "he came down hard" and the nail went deep. Liss drove him to town for a tetanus shot.

"Mark had looked forward to a physically active weekend, walking in the woodlands and swimming in the Housatonic. Rothko wasn't much of a nature man, no Thoreau he. But when restrained, by doctor's orders, he longed for action."

All day Saturday Rothko, "his body a boulder in a deck chair," sketched Liss with a pencil on a pad. Rothko, Liss recalled, "seemed to be glowering at me, observing my every movement, frustrated and envious (I presumed) as I swam, walked about, chopped wood, activity unlike his own sedentary and luckless state." Like the figure in his self-portrait, the Rothko of the 1939 Labor Day weekend was a physically powerful man whose injury produced an angry, aggressive looking—which was also creative: several weeks later he presented Liss with an oil portrait based on the sketches.[87]

But the Rothko in the deck chair, unlike the one in the *Self-Portrait,* was located in a specific historical context. On the day he had impaled himself on the privy board, Hitler had invaded Poland. On the following day—which the glowering, immobilized Rothko spent sketching his active friend Liss—the German airforce bombarded several Polish cities. At 6:30 A.M. Sunday morning, England and France declared war on Germany. By September 3, 1939, the thirties were just about over, but the Depression was not; and World War II had begun.

6 "All-Out War"

The heart within them screamed for all-out war. . . .

Aeschylus, *Agamemnon*

"They are all gone," she whispered, "murdered, in cold blood."

Dvinsk, 1941

In his autobiography German field-marshall Eric von Manstein fondly relives one of his *Lost Victories:* "Now, exactly four days and five hours after zero hour, we had actually completed, as the crow flies, a non-stop dash through 200 miles of enemy territory. We had brought it off only because the name of Daugavpils [Dvinsk] had been foremost in the mind of every officer and man. . . . It gave us a tremendous feeling of achievement to drive over the big bridges into the town, despite the fact that the enemy had set most of it on fire before pulling out."[1]

"Zero hour" had been 3:00 A.M., Sunday, June 22, 1940—when a German invasion force of 3 million soldiers began moving across the thousand-mile western border of the Soviet Union. In the north, Field Marshall von Manstein, commanding the 56th Panzer Corps, had been instructed to capture the two bridges crossing the Dvina River to Dvinsk, bridges crucial for the German army's advance on Leningrad. To capture the bridges intact, surprise was necessary, and it was accomplished by combining modern Panzer efficiency with an ancient stratagem, a kind of Trojan lorry maneuver.

As the 56th Panzer's tanks neared Daugavpils early the morning of June 26, they were suddenly pulled over to allow four Russian lorries to pass—vehicles, it turned out, driven by disguised German military intelligence agents whose lorries were hiding, under tarps, twenty-five soldiers. The lorries descended the last slope outside the town. "Across the road bridge in the centre of Daugavpils traffic was flowing as in peacetime. Across the big railway bridge a locomotive chugged amid puffs of steam. The lorries bumped along towards the town. Past the Soviet outposts. The drivers in their Russian uniforms exchanged jokes with the pickets. 'Where are the Germans?' the Russians asked. 'Oh, a long way back!'" Within minutes the lorries had reached the bridges, been discovered and, then, after a brief exchange of gunfire, captured them. At 8:00 A.M. von Manstein was informed: "Surprise of Daugavpils town and bridges successful. Road bridge intact. Railway bridge slightly damaged by demolition charge, but passable." The Germans burned many of the city's stores, and withdrew; the Soviets then bombarded the town.[2]

At first the Germans were greeted as liberators, since Latvia, the year before, had been reabsorbed by the Soviet Union, which then initiated a new Russification program—i.e., mass deportations to Siberia. When, after a six day pause, von Manstein's corps moved on toward Leningrad, they were replaced in Daugavpils, as elsewhere, by the *Einsatzgruppen,* Hitler's killing squads which, with the assistance of local Latvian collaborators (including some police), began implementing a "Germanification" program—i.e., mass murder.[3]

With Nazi occupation, all of the city's synagogues were immediately destroyed. Some of the town's Jewish population had left, fleeing by railroad or on foot into Russia. But the rapid German advance left little time for evacuation; most remained. A Gestapo office was opened. The city's Jews were required to register, to wear cloth Stars of David on the chest, back, and (for men) one knee. Within just a few days, several thousand men and boys were shot outside the Daugavpils prison on Shosseynaya Street.[4] On July 25 the town's Jews were confined to a ghetto in a prison located just across the river from the Fortress.

Here, in the words of one survivor, there were "thousands and thousands of people, with hardly any sanitary facilities, no food; with only one or two taps for water." "The overcrowding was almost unbearable, its horrors augmented by the summer heat wave." In early August the Germans announced that the old and sick would be removed to a more comfortable place; 1,500 of them were taken off and slaughtered. A few days later, parents with small children were offered resettlement. "This time again, the flood of people who wanted to go was enormous." But "in a day or two, strange rumours started to filter through. Someone heard from non-Jews who lived out of town that for a day and a night shooting took place at a certain place where no one was allowed to go. Slowly the picture emerged—there were definitely fresh mass graves!" Eight thousand had been killed; ten days later several thousand more were executed. On November 8 and 9 eleven thousand were killed. Others died of hunger or froze to death during the severe winter of 1941–42. By May 15, 1942—National Unity Day in Latvia—of Daugavpils' thirty thousand Jews, four hundred remained.[5]

Now, throughout the Wood of Mezhiems just outside Daugavpils, there *were* mass graves, from which Rothko's resented "transplantation" had saved him. In Portland, by May 1942, Rothko's sister and brothers—like many Portland Jews of their generation—had moved across the Willamette River to the more residential East Side. Kate Rothkowitz now lived with Sonia, whose husband had died, leaving her with three children and a coffeeshop ("Jack's") to manage. Moise, with two children, was running the Eagle Drug Company, while Albert, with one child, had given up his attempts at running a pharmacy and recently been hired as a Russian translator for the Foreign Broadcast Information Service. One of Rothko's nephews would serve in the army, two in the navy during the Second World War.[6] His Seattle cousin Harold Weinstein, who had been a witness at Rothko's wedding and at one time was "very close to Marcus," volunteered for the service and was assigned as a translator to the OSS (forerunner of the CIA). When his ship was torpedoed off the coast of Sweden, Weinstein was the only man, of the fifty-six on board, who was not rescued. The arbitrary victim of modern mechanized warfare, Harold Weinstein met a fate that struck Rothko as less tragic than ironic. "That was a fitting death for him," Rothko sardonically commented to Edith. "The Rothkos are not heroes."[7]

No hero himself, Mark Rothko was declared 4F, a painter probably saved from the draft by his bad eyesight; throughout the war he remained in New York. In the early 1940s, New York City, as Robert Motherwell recalled, was "a strange mixture of Cole Porter and Stalinism, immigrants and emigrés, establishment and dispossessed, vital and chaotic, innocent and street-wise—in short, a metropolis clouded by the war."[8] For those at home, the war imposed rationing and shortages, say, of automobile tires and nylons, but by transforming America into the "Arsenal of Democracy," the war also stimulated the economy, ending the Depression and giving consumers the money with which to buy such available luxury items as, say, jewelry or (eventually) paintings.[9]

"Most people had never known such prosperity."[10] Edith's business gradually improved and expanded. By early 1941 she and Rothko had moved uptown, to 28th Street near Fifth Avenue, into what Milton Avery called "a nice big apartment," "really quite swell."[11] In a letter to Joseph Liss, Rothko, after complaining about being "very low financially" and requesting $50 Liss owed him for a painting, went on to speak rather grandly of "our magnificent new home."[12] Like many other Americans, Rothko was less impoverished and somewhat more comfortable than he had been, at the same time that he was living in a city clouded by war and a marriage clouded by strife.

• • •

Good God, how can you go on chattering about sculpture and painting when the children of Poland lie slaughtered by Hitler's bombs?

Magazine of Art, 1939

Chapter Six

On October 2, 1941, J. Edgar Hoover wrote to the FBI office in New York to complain that he had received "no information" in response to his ordered investigation of the American Artists' Congress. For the FBI, too, the early 1940s were "boom times," since the Second World War, like the first, generated an aggressive nationalism which made spies, aliens, and political dissenters the objects of popular suspicion, official surveillance, and criminal prosecution. In the case of the Artists' Congress, the FBI was boldly moving in just after the organization's collapse.[13]

The Russian invasion of Finland in November 1939, an extension of the Soviets' seizure of the Baltic states (such as Latvia) produced the *Daily Worker*'s most memorable headline: "Red Army Hurls Back Invading Finnish Troops." The invasion also produced a political crisis in the Artists' Congress that eventually broke the group's left-liberal alliance. At first, the leftist executive committee of the congress ignored the Russian-Finnish war, as well as a request from the Hoover Committee for Finnish Relief. But a liberal group, led by the art historian Meyer Schapiro, pressured the board to adopt a position, demanding that the congress "make clear to the world whether [it] is a remnant of the cultural front of the Communist Party or an independent artists' organization."[14] At a general meeting on April 4, 1940, the spokesman for the left urged a strict neutrality, "even in thought," while Schapiro argued that such a policy would betray the original opposition by the congress to war and fascism. The left won by a vote of 125 to 12. But on April 15, the *New York Times* announced the resignations of Schapiro, Lewis Mumford, Stuart Davis (a former national chairman), William Zorach (the New York chairman) and two members of the executive board, George Biddle and Ralph Pearson. Two days later, the *Times* reported the "secession" of seventeen congress members, among them "M. Rothkowitz."[15]

The resignation was one of a series of individual and group withdrawals from the official left that occurred in the months following the German-Soviet pact. In their public statement, the dissident artists charged that the April 4 congress meeting had "endorsed the Russian invasion of Finland and implicitly defended Hitler's position by assigning the responsibility for the war to England and France"; they criticized the congress for revising "its policy of boycotting Fascist and Nazi exhibitions," for failing to react to the new Nazi-Soviet "esthetic policy of cementing totalitarian relations through exchange exhibitions," and for making "participation in a projected fascist show at Venice" "a matter of individual taste."[16] The adolescent Marcus Rothkowitz and his family "had closely followed and applauded the Russian revolution," but once the progressive Soviets signed their treaty with the German fascists, many American intellectuals and artists, particularly those who were Jewish, found it extremely difficult to support the popular front alliance. Rothko's debate with David Smith over the German-Soviet pact late in the summer of 1939 had anticipated the liberal/radical split which, in the spring of 1940, effectively destroyed the American Artists' Congress.

The liberals' resignation statement closed by calling on fellow-artists to "join us in considering ways and means of furthering mutual interests." By mid-June several of these dissenters—including Meyer Schapiro, Adolph Gottlieb, Louis Harris, Ilya Bolotowsky, and Rothko—were among the founders of the Federation of Modern Painters and Sculptors, a group formed "to promote the welfare of free progressive artists working in America."[17] As the words "welfare" and "free progressive" suggest, these mutual interests were both economic and political. According to the federation's "No Blackout for Art" statement (1942), "The early get-togethers of this new organization were . . . stormy. The world was already badly shaken. Invading forces were trampling the Lowlands; Belgium and Holland collapsed between meetings and France doomed as well. The artists with visions of tomorrow felt the repercussions as strongly as though they were only yards away." At first some members advocated a direct political response, "but eventually another course was taken." "Each and every man was to perform his social obligation to keep and protect freedom. Their Federation was to stand for the kind of artistic independence the world struggle symbolized."[18]

By defining "social obligation" as "artistic independence," the federation repudiated the 1930s faith in collective action and adopted the rhetoric of the war effort ("keep and protect freedom," "independence the world struggle symbolized") to justify a new individualism that would eventually try to separate art from history and politics. But for members of the federation, the immediate problem was to find some way, ideally some nonillustrative way, of registering in their work those historical "repercussions" they felt so intimately.

Within two years, the organization had sixty-eight members and twenty-four sponsors. Like The Ten, the federation was primarily an exhibiting group, less cohesive, but larger, with a more diverse membership, and thus more effective. Just six days after its incorporation, the group's "First Exhibition of Paintings and Sculpture" opened in the rotunda of the American Art Today Building at the New York World's Fair.[19] In March of 1941 a series of annuals began, supplemented by a number of smaller shows at the Smith College Museum of Art, the Yale University Museum, the Wadsworth Atheneum, the Institute of Modern Art (Boston), the Lotus Club, the National Arts Club, and other places. Less than a year after being fired by the WPA and dropped back into the "free market," Rothko helped form an organization which provided him with an important access to an audience.

At early meetings, the membership decided not to protest the role of the reactionary Colonel Sommerville on the art jury for the Federal Art Project or to protest the firings of WPA workers who had "signed various petitions in the past"—the kind of causes that would have been taken up without discussion at an Artists Union or an Artists' Congress meeting.[20] Not politically activist, the federation combined liberal politics with an aesthetic activism. During the war years Rothko, serving on the cultural, membership and exhibition committees, was an engaged, influential member. As the federation's representative to the Artists' Coordinating Committee, an organization of fourteen artists' societies, Rothko—"the earliest anti-Stalinist I knew," according to George Okun—actively participated in the federation's battles with the official left.

In 1936 the Artists' Coordinating Committee had pressured TRAP into taking on more artists (leading to Rothko's appointment), and then in 1937 had persuaded the Federal Art Project to hire artists (like Rothko) who had been terminated by TRAP. By 1941, however, the committee was chaired by Hugo Gellert, a doctrinaire Marxist, author of *Karl Marx's Capital in Lithographs* (1933) and *Comrade Gulliver* (1934), whose "policy," Rothko reported at one federation meeting, "seems to be *not* to notify unsympathetic groups of the meetings (non-communists)." "Mr. Rothko objected to [Gellert's] having chosen three [symposium] speakers where 14 societies were involved. Mr. R[othko] saw to it that representatives from all 14 societies [will] come to next meeting on Monday." "Elections are constantly delayed," Rothko complained. The federation, he contended, had to decide "what to do to counteract Mr. Gellert['s] complete control" and to form "a plan to carry on [the committee's] work if we force a change in control."[21]

At a federation meeting on December 30, 1941—three weeks after Pearl Harbor—one member complained about "too much control so far by 'leftists' in the one group and 'conservatives' in [the] other." The one group was the Artists' Coordinating Committee, the other the Artists for National Defense. After the German invasion of Russia six months before, Stalinists had shifted from neutrality to a prowar policy; with the entry of the United States into the war, the American Artists' Congress participated, along with a dozen artists' societies (including the federation) in starting Artists for National Defense, which urged "the creation of a government bureau whose sole purpose would be to commission art directed toward increasing civilian and military morale." Within a month, Artists for Victory, a larger coalition (also including the federation) was founded "for the single purpose of advancing the war effort with propagandistic art."[22] The political left and the political right had now joined in an aesthetically conservative effort to mobilize the home front and help win the war.

Early federation meetings, debating about the qualifications for membership, reflected some uncertainty about the group's identity. In July 1941—as the Germans were advancing on Leningrad and the *Einsatzgruppen* began implementing the policy of racial extermination—members of the federation, now "one year old," introduced a new and what turned out to be a unifying theme into their discussions: "the importance of Esthetics." And they began to consider practical means of "selling [the] idea of and explaining of Esthetics in order to get our idea across."[23] "Esthetic" suggests a work created for its own sake, rather than, say, to advance the war effort or to advance the career of the painter. But even the idea of the "esthetic," like any paintings it may produce, is an idea that must be *sold*.

Not politically reformist, the federation sought to further the "mutual interests" of its members within the existing institutions for the promotion and sale of art, pursuing educational programs, marketing schemes, publicity campaigns, and written polemics. In connection with its annual exhibit, the federation arranged symposiums, with Rothko speaking on "The Artist's Point of View" (1942) and "The Influence of America on the Artist" (1948). At their second meeting, the federation compiled a list of seven hundred potential patrons to form a "Committee of Sponsors" and sent trial letters to two hundred of them. Later, shrewdly anticipating a new clientele for art, the organization developed a plan to invite businessmen (one of them, Rothko's later friend and adviser, Bernard Reis) to join the Ways and Means Committee as associate members (and $100 contributors), though a later meeting agreed to "concentrate on Patrons now—Businessmen later."[24] In the summer of 1941 the Exhibition Committee proposed holding a show in a large 40' × 80' tent which "should draw great crowds" and "should make money if we charge a small sum as entry fee. Suggested we have lots of publicity (advance) featuring the *Modern* aspect of our particular group," as if its modernity, which marked this particular group as oppositional, also provided it with the polemical edge that outsiders need to draw the attention of critics, viewers, and prospective buyers.[25]

Like The Ten, the federation could more precisely identify its repudiations ("Local Scene-ism and Class Conscious Scene-ism"—i.e., Regionalism and Social Realism) than it could define itself in more positive terms. The organization's "No Blackout for Art" statement, after espousing "artistic independence," quickly turns around to limit that freedom by distinguishing it from an "anything goes" attitude: "instead we bear in mind the noble privilege to create art as art instead of practicing a pictorial form of story telling without aesthetic concept."[26] In Europe, World War I had produced Dada, which was anti-art; in America, World War II now produced the Federation of Modern Painters and Sculptors, which affirmed "art as art."[27] If federation members felt "repercussions" of the war "as strongly as though they were only yards away," they would register those responses in aesthetic objects which transcended the historical realities which provoked them.

Characterizing the war as a struggle between barbarism and civilization, American propaganda legitimatized the creation of art while "the children of Poland lie slaughtered by Hitler's bombs" as part of the effort to preserve democratic civilization: "Each and every man was to perform his social obligation to keep and protect freedom," "No Blackout for Art" urged. The statement thus concluded with a uplifting affirmation, which, rather than separating art from politics, linked them: "The fact remains that true modern art is vigorously alive and has the same great future as democracy." Reflecting a widening mistrust among intellectuals of all political ideologies and a fear of both German and Russian totalitarianism, the federation defined "true" modernism as individualism, emphasized freedom of expression, and identified the fate of modernism with the fate of democracy, i.e., America. This loosely formulated and sometimes conflicting cluster of notions—modernity; the aesthetic; individual freedom—provided the federation with a liberal politics and with an elastic identity that was native but not regionalist, international but not socialist, modern but not European.

The federation was *American* modern, a characteristic that often placed it in vigorous opposition with the Museum of Modern Art, to which the group related like a son angry with a father who is too involved with his own father to pay much attention to the son. As a member of the active Cultural Committee—of which his close friend Adolph Gottlieb was the chairman—Rothko participated in a kind of yearly rite at the federation: dispatching a letter of protest to the Museum of Modern Art, often with copies sent to the local press. In February 1942 the committee accused the museum's "Americans 1942—18 Artists from 9 States" exhibit of reducing "American art to a demonstration of geography" and regretted that the museum, which "has shown a fine sense of discrimination" in selecting "the very best contemporary European artists," "has not extended the same sense of discrimination" toward American art.[28]

The following year the Cultural Committee denounced the Museum's "Realists and Magic Realists."[29] In 1944 the federation's membership, reacting to the museum's "Romantic Painting in America" exhibition, submitted a five-point statement of criticisms and suggestions. They proposed that the museum abandon shows of "works rightly considered academic and out-moded even in the Victorian era" and shows "interesting only on scientific and ethnographical grounds"—to allow "an adequate presentation of all the progressive facets of modern art." Again attacking the Museum of Modern Art "for adopting one set of standards for the European art which it displays and a thoroughly different one for its American selections," the federation deplored the sacrifice of "seriousness of purpose" for "publicity" which has led the museum to emphasize "such ephemeral fads as the output of certain refugee-surrealists and types of American scene-illustration" "out of all proportion to their qualities as art." "Let the museum show its true colors by holding an exhibition of its entire permanent collection," urged the statement, which then closed by calling the museum "an enervating influence rather than a stimulus to the more inventive artists of America."[30]

The "cathedral of the new art" dealt with these schismatic utterances not by issuing a reasoned response but by launching an inquisition. In 1942 Alfred Barr asked the federation to supply him with the names of the members of the Cultural Committee.[31] In 1944, James T. Soby, the museum's director, sent a letter to selected members of the federation, to ask whether or not they had voted for the statement. The tactic reminded Clement Greenberg in the *Nation* of "the Stalinist telephone-pressure campaigns of a few years ago," and Greenberg went on to lament the control at the museum by the aesthetically conservative rich who will end, he predicted, "by making the Museum of Modern Art an educational annex to the Stork Club."[32]

• • •

New Times! New Ideas! New Methods!

Mark Rothko

New Year's Eve, 1941: Rothko and Edith had arranged, with two friends, the writer H. R. Hays and his wife, Juliette, to go out to dinner and then to a party in Greenwich Village. Since it was New Year's Eve and Manhattan, the Hayses were "all dressed up" but just as they were ready to leave "Marcus called" to say he and Edith were "too broke" to go. The Hayses offered to pay, and took their friends not to the Stork Club but to the Hotel Pierre, hoping to "get them in a good mood." Only a few days before, the Hayses had seen a painting of Rothko's which had "quite astonished" them because of its "drastic change" from his earlier work. Over New Year's Eve dinner, they announced they wanted to buy the new picture. "Of course, he was pleased on the one hand, but on the other hand he was not feeling too sure about whether or not he should let the painting go," Juliette Hays recalled. "He wasn't quite sure about the direction his painting had taken."

The painting, which the Hayses eventually bought, was *The Last Supper*, one in a series of new mythological works which typically dealt with Christian or classical subjects by rendering hybrid figures—part god, part human, part animal—in a flat, relief-like space which, divided into rectangular horizontal compartments, at once flattened and severed the bodies of these grotesque creatures. It is not clear exactly when Rothko started producing these works. He once claimed that in 1940 he had stopped painting for a year to study myth, a characteristically hyperbolic statement that may even be true.[33] It was probably at this time that he read Freud's *Interpretation of Dreams* and that he read (or reread) Frazer's *The Golden Bough* and Nietzsche's *The Birth of Tragedy*; he may have read Jung, with whose theories of the collective unconscious Rothko's close friend Adolph Gottlieb was familiar.[34] By January 1942, Rothko probably had been involved in his myth project for about two years; but he had yet to exhibit any of these new paintings.

"We are very well, except for the grip and that we are very low financially," Rothko wrote to Joseph Liss in February of 1941. "I have been peddling my pictures again," Rothko went on, as if he now felt like the boy who had sold newspapers on Portland street corners, "and there is the possibility of a good exhibition later this season." "I think you will be surprised to see my new pictures. There has been another transition with some excellent results. More emphasis on the objects themselves, and the pattern simpler and less important as such."[35] Still financially low and now nervous "about the direction his painting had taken," Rothko, on New Year's Eve, 1941, was just five days away from the first public showing of work that was more ambitious, and more violent in its distortions, than anything he had exhibited before.

On Sunday, January 4, 1942, the *New York Times* printed an announcement by the Macy Galleries of an exhibit and sale of "Contemporary American Paintings"—"many well-known artists! some brilliant discoveries!"—ranging in price "from $24.97 to $249 framed." On the eighth floor of the department store, among the "179 canvases by 72 important Americans" were Rothko's *Antigone* and *Oedipus*. "Choose the picture that speaks to you; be assured that any one you choose will possess real merit. All are priced with great modesty."[36] In the 1930s the Artists Union had called for an expansion "within the art movement itself toward the entire people"; now R. H. Macy, the same kind of store that sold Edith's jewelry, was directing the sale of paintings not toward wealthy patrons, or even toward affluent businessmen, but toward middle-class buyers. The show had been selected by Samuel Kootz, a public-relations man in the film industry who had provoked a major controversy the previous August with a letter to the *Times* which had denounced American artists who, although now "hermetically sealed by war against Parisian sponsorship," have failed "to experiment, to realize a new method of painting." After all, observed Kootz, soon to open his own gallery, "Money can be heard crinkling throughout the land."[37]

Coinciding with the irrational violence of the war and with the home-front prosperity created by the war, rendering brutal images of archaic, hybrid creatures, Rothko's myth pictures were undertaken with considerable self-doubt. But he was not alone. He was working, in a kind of collaborative venture, with Adolph Gottlieb, with whom he was then "very very close."[38] Rothko had met Gottlieb in 1929, at the Opportunity Gallery, where both men had also met Milton Avery.[39] Born like Rothko in 1903, Gottlieb had grown up in Manhattan and the Bronx, not Dvinsk and Portland; his parents, both Jewish immigrants from what later became Czechoslovakia, made a comfortable living from a family stationery business.[40] At twenty, Rothko quit college; at sixteen, Gottlieb quit high school. After working for his father "for about a year," Gottlieb decided that business "was not for me." "I wasn't interested primarily in making money. I rather despised people who were primarily interested in making money." While in high school, Gottlieb had taken Saturday classes at the Art Students League and "found that I was good at art." In the next few years Gottlieb studied life drawing at Parson's School of Design, design at Cooper Union, attended lectures by Robert Henri at the Art Students League, took an illustration course from John Sloan.

Gottlieb's family "deplored [his] being absorbed in art." In 1921–22, while Rothko was still a student at Yale, the eighteen-year-old Gottlieb (without telling his family) hired on with a passenger ship, which he then jumped (without a passport) when it arrived in France. He spent the next year and a half studying art in Germany, Austria, and (mostly) in Paris. "The only good art school is a museum," he concluded, having familiarized himself with the old masters in the Louvre and the modern masters (Picasso, Matisse, Léger) in the Parisian galleries. Now primarily interested in making paintings, Gottlieb returned to New York, completed high school at night, took a teacher-training certificate at Parsons, studied in John Sloan's painting class at the Art Students League, visited the Metropolitan Museum of Art and the New York galleries. His experience in Europe, however, had persuaded Gottlieb "that art had to be international." As one of the Ashcan school, John Sloan "believed in going, directly, so called, to life"; but Gottlieb was attracted by "what the Cubists were doing with studio painting, and what Cézanne was doing with still life." The young Gottlieb was, in theory at least, already a modern.

When Rothko and Gottlieb met in 1929, both were beginning painters who had rebelled against the expectations of their Jewish immigrant families. Both were intelligent, articulate, and ambitious young men with a range of literary and philosophical interests; both were inward, melancholy painters who first worked in a somber expressionist style. Being Jewish though not religious, both were internationalists, in art rather than in politics. In 1932 both men married, as had Milton Avery, women who would sacrifice their own artistic interests in order to support their husbands.[41] But Gottlieb, not having suffered the dislocations, losses, and poverty of Rothko's childhood, was less angry and aggressive, more reserved and quiet, less given to despair. Sharing much with Rothko, Gottlieb offered an important difference: a kind of personal solidity.

Soon after they met, the two men were drawn to Milton Avery as a personal and artistic mentor. As Sally Avery recalled, Rothko and Gottlieb "used to come around our house almost every day to see what Milton had done that day and that stimulated their own painting."[42] Rothko and Gottlieb were part of the Averys' social circle, attended the sketching classes and literary readings at his home, and along with Barnett Newman, whom Gottlieb had met in 1922, often spent summer vacations with the Averys during the 1930s and 1940s. Expressionists in painting and liberals in politics, Rothko and Gottlieb were both members of The Ten and, later, the Federation of Modern Painters and Sculptors, where they served together on the Cultural Committee. In June 1943 the two painters collaborated, along with Newman, in writing a letter to the *New York Times* art critic Edward Alden Jewell, a statement which formulated many of their shared assumptions—as did their joint statement "The Portrait and the Modern Artist," broadcast on Radio WNYC in October of 1943.

"Milton taught not by what he said but by what he did," Sally Avery said. At the end of each day on their summer vacations the productive Avery showed the younger artists what he had done. Lengthy discussions would follow. But one summer in the late 30s, Sally Avery recalled, "Milton decided these boys were getting a little too dependent on him, so he decided not to show them anything." "At the end of the summer he showed them all his work but it wasn't this day-to-day thing that he had been doing." Less rebellious with their mentor than with their parents, Rothko and Gottlieb were "very upset" by Avery's gentle nudge toward independence, "but it was really very good for them because it forced them to delve into their own beings for their own ideas."[43] Gottlieb later remarked of this period, "I think I lost myself in Avery."[44] Moving to Tucson, Arizona, during the winter and spring of 1937–38 because of his wife's arthritis, Gottlieb found the geographical distance artistically liberating.

In Tucson, Gottlieb, separated from his mentor, his friends, and the art market, felt freer to take his time in working out "some problem (simple as it may be) to its logical conclusion" without feeling "too anxious to arrive at the final result." "Perhaps having someone else comment on your work every other day tends to sidetrack one, and also having a sympathetic commentator close at hand may be a form of self-indulgence," Gottlieb observed in a letter to a friend.[45] Even a supportive community can distract the painter from himself and provide a false comfort. Living at the edge of the arid expanses of the Arizona desert, Gottlieb began to render, he said, "real shapes, real objects" (sometimes taken from the desert) in a radically flattened space so that "they became transformed and didn't look like real things."[46] Gottlieb was now exploring Surrealism, which Avery deplored.

When Gottlieb returned to New York in June of 1938, he felt uncertain about his new work and for a few months didn't show it to anyone. When, that fall, he showed it to The Ten, their response was "completely negative." Disenchanted with The Ten, less reliant on Avery, Gottlieb did grow closer to one sympathetic colleague—Rothko. In the early 1940s, according to Edith Sachar, her husband, Gottlieb, Newman (and others), held many "philosophical" discussions on a crisis of subject matter.[47] "We felt the moral crisis of a world in shambles, a world devastated by a great depression and a fierce World War," Newman later recalled. "It was impossible at that time to paint the kind of painting that we were doing—flowers, reclining nudes, and people playing the cello." "Painting is finished," Newman declared. "We should give it up," as he himself did from 1940 to 1944.[48]

Like Newman, both Gottlieb and Rothko felt an impasse in American painting; but, unlike him, they felt challenged and even liberated by their situation. "Due to [the] provincial position in which the American artist was pushed," Rothko later stated, "he had nothing to lose and everything, a world, to gain." Or, in Gottlieb's words, "the situation was very desperate and everything seemed hopeless and we had nothing to lose, so that in a sense we were like people condemned to life imprisonment who make a dash for freedom."[49]

During 1940 Rothko and Edith separated temporarily and he lived alone in a Brooklyn Heights apartment. He and Gottlieb, who lived nearby, saw each other almost daily.[50] As a result of their conversations, Gottlieb recalled, "Rothko and I temporarily came to an agreement on the question of subject matter.... Around 1942, we embarked on a series of paintings that attempted to use mythological subject matter, preferably from Greek mythology."[51] Beyond any desire to make the next innovative move in art after Benton or Gropper or even Picasso, their turn to archaic myth derived from contemporary political reality, specifically the war. As Rothko said in "The Portrait and the Modern Artist," "those who think that the world of today is more gentle and graceful than the primeval and predatory passions from which these myths spring, are either not aware of reality or do not wish to see it in art."

Seeking the impact of a *movement*, Rothko and Gottlieb tried, unsuccess-

Chapter Six

fully, to involve other painters in their mythical explorations.[52] Now, rather than riding along in Avery's wake, Rothko and Gottlieb became two not quite solitary figures working against the stream, trying to realize a new method of painting.

• • •

> It is strange, altho' no longer new that art should persist in evolving these chimeras, these unreasonable distortions, this outward savagery and apparent ugliness and brutality.
>
> Mark Rothko

On December 7, 1942—exactly one year after Pearl Harbor—"Artists for Victory" opened a show of 1,418 works by contemporary American artists at New York's Metropolitan Museum of Art.[53] With many of its masterpieces in protective storage for the duration of the war, the museum, never very keen on art that was contemporary or American (much less both), had donated twenty-eight rooms and $51,000 in purchase awards for the exhibit. John Hay Whitney, a trustee at the Museum of Modern Art, had asked in mid-1940, "Does it seem strange to you to think of a museum as a weapon in national defense?" By late 1942 it would not have seemed strange at all, the Modern having exhibited "U.S. Army Illustrators," "Art in War," "Wartime Housing," "Road to Victory," "Camouflage for Civilian Defense," "The Museum and the War," "Art from Fighting China," and "National War Poster Competition." "Artists for Victory" contained only three works dealing explicitly with the war, but as "Jock" Whitney went on to say, a museum could "educate, inspire, and strengthen the hearts and wills of free men in the defense of their own freedom."[54] To such ends the Artists for Victory jury selected *Wisconsin Landscape* by the American regionalist John Stuart Curry for the first prize in painting. Isolationist nationalism, although politically defunct, retained cultural authority.

But "Artists for Victory" did generate two protest exhibits; Rothko participated in both, as did Gottlieb and several other members of the federation. For "American Modern Artists," at the Riverside Museum, January 17 to February 27, 1943, Barnett Newman's catalogue essay, complaining that "isolationist art still dominates the American Scene," introduced "a body of art that will adequately reflect the new America" which, he predicted, will "become the cultural center of the world"—as if regionalist nationalism were about to be replaced by a higher (i.e., modernist) nationalism. The catalogue for "New

York Artist-Painters," February 13 to February 27, 1943, pointedly cited "large exhibitions of reactionary painting" as proof of the persistence of cultural isolationism.[55] After seeing the show, Joseph Solman observed in a letter to Jacob Kainen that "Marcus [was] going to myths and ghostliness."[56] For "American Modern Artists" Rothko had stuck to his expressionist work; but in "New York Artist-Painters" he exhibited, for the first time in more than a year, his myth pictures: *A Last Supper, The Eagle and the Hare, Iphigenia and the Sea,* and *The Omen of the Eagle* (color plate 9).[57]

Like many of Rothko's myth paintings of the early 1940s, this one is severed into four horizontal tiers. At the top, a row of thinly painted sun-yellow faces—two kissing (on the left), two kissing (on the right), one gloomily defeated, one sleeping, one smiling broadly, one angrily staring off, all flat and masklike—provides us with shifting, partial views of several Greek deities, or multiple angles of vision on one, but in either case a god (or gods) stonily removed and inaccessible. Possibly male, possibly female, the heads sit above two flesh-colored pear-shaped forms (with small white circles inside), which resemble breasts and which have been placed on a blood-red and purple rib cage which, down the center, has been cracked open. But the pearlike shapes may also be heads—the heads of two blank-eyed bald eagles, one in profile, the other in three-quarter view—with the rows of red and purple "ribs" now resembling stylized feathers and wings.

The eagles, in turn, sit on a receding series of structures that alternate bulb-shaped solids with bulb-shaped openings. At once architectural and strangely organic, these structures create a labyrinthine space that is open and empty, yet mysterious and hidden. Here, access is invited, and then obstructed. Looking into the large curved opening at the front right discloses a pale yellow slab or wall, with its own rectangular opening, inside of which a brown talon or hook ominously hangs down. Occupying the part of Rothko's hybrid figure associated with procreation, this space is abstract, constructed, man-made, looking as though nothing organic could ever emerge from it. This chimera is sterile.

With its friezelike row of heads, its construction of a rib cage (or the feathered bodies of two eagles) out of what resemble thick wooden slats, and its architectural rows of columns, the painting's only natural forms are, at the bottom, the painfully twisted human feet, animal claws, and (on the right) a cloven hoof which, despite their confused jumble, constitute a carefully balanced pedestal on which Rothko's cold, sculptural, and monumental creature grimly stands. Surrounded by a sea-green ground, this archaic figure fills the space of the canvas, along the left even extending beyond the edge. The three top horizontal tiers, moreover, form a single, large vertical rectangle—

anticipating Rothko's signature format. But here, instead of freeing his rectangles to "float" back and forth, Rothko locks them to the edge and secures them on a stand. Like many of his female figures from the 1930s, Rothko's mythical being, seen from very close up, needs to be distanced and held in—held off, as if it represented something *inside* him he needed to place *outside*.

"The theme here is derived from the Agamemnon Trilogy of Aeschylus," Rothko commented when *The Omen of the Eagle* was reproduced in Sidney Janis's *Abstract and Surrealist Art in America* (1944). "The picture deals not with the particular anecdote, but rather with the Spirit of Myth, which is generic to all myths at all times. It involves a pantheism in which man, bird, beast and tree—the Known as well as the Knowable—merge into a single tragic idea."[58] Yet the painting's title does allude to a particular anecdote at the beginning of the *Agamemnon,* where the chorus recalls an omen—two eagles devouring a pregnant hare—revealed to the Greeks as they impatiently wait to sail for Troy to avenge the abduction of Helen. As interpreted by the Greek prophet Calchas, the eagles represent Agamemnon and Menelaus, "two eagle-kings" whose predatory violence against the hare and its unborn offspring foretells an eventual Greek victory entailing the destruction of Troy and its innocent citizens. More immediately, the omen summons Agamemnon to sacrifice his daughter Iphigenia (to allow the Greeks to sail for Troy), a murder that in turn provokes Clytemnestra, after the war, to kill her triumphant husband, Agamemnon. Three Rothko pictures—*The Eagle and the Hare, Iphigenia and the Sea,* and *The Omen of the Eagle*—deal with this anecdote; all, shown at "New York Artist-Painters," were very likely painted in 1942.

In 1942, the eagle was the national emblem of both Germany *and* the United States.[59] In America, the war was propagandized as a conflict between barbarism and civilization. In *The Omen of the Eagle,* Rothko conflated the two sides into a single barbaric figure, at once violent and damaged. Discussing his work in 1943, Rothko observed "the potentiality for carnage which we know so well today," and he ironically dismissed "those who think that the world of today is more gentle and graceful than the primeval and predatory passions from which these myths spring."[60] Aeschylus' "anecdote" prompted Rothko's archetypal image, which alluded to the war not as a specific historical event but as the expression of a primeval aggression, eternal and instinctual, directed (like the eagle's assault on the pregnant hare) against the very sources of life.

Treated indirectly, universalized, the war offered a subject matter that, unlike "flowers, reclining nudes and people playing the cello," was "tragic and timeless."[61] And so in 1942, a year when Germany controlled most of Europe, and Japan controlled most of the western Pacific, when American industry, operating twenty-four hours a day, seven days a week, was producing 125,000 planes, 75,000 tanks, and 10,000,000 tons of merchant shipping, and German U-boats were sinking two ships a day off the Atlantic and Gulf coasts, Mark Rothko, who had once aspired to be an actor, pondered the tragic drama of Aeschylus, a skeptic whose irony exposed his characters' lofty, logical arguments for violent retribution as justifying a savagery which merely generated further bloodshed.[62] Rothko, familiar with official terror from his Russian boyhood and doubtful about political solutions to it since the 1920s, was no Artist for Victory.

Commenting on *The Omen of the Eagle,* Rothko equated mythological consciousness with a pantheistic unity merging man, bird, and beast. The painting itself, however, divides and then abruptly juxtaposes its antagonistic parts; god, man, and bird—like male and female—are forcibly joined, forcibly disjoined, as if unity and dismemberment were equally violent. Obliquely criticizing the war, Rothko does not split his world into sadistic eagles and blameless hares, but creates a single tragic figure, at once predator and victim, who literally embodies the conflict. Rothko, in fact, structures his painting in part by moving from head to breast to pelvis to feet. Yet he also fragments the figurative by severing it into an abstract pattern of horizontal rectangles. Compositional order, here, is created out of an antagonism between the natural and the geometrical.

Rothko, then, does not exempt himself from the violence he depicts. As his paintings explore an instinctual, prerational self very different, say, from the original innocence postulated by Franz Cizek, their aesthetic designs become rigid and gridlike, as did those of Adolph Gottlieb, whose contributions to the myth project (his early "Pictographs") construct elaborate flattened grids which "balance the irrational images of his unconscious with a clear formal structure."[63] In Rothko's paintings, however, irrational images and formal structure oppose each other. For this progressive member of the Federation of Modern Painters and Sculptors, it is as if the self can be controlled only by an externally imposed, arbitrary order that is itself violent. A few years later, Rothko would be referring, jokingly, to these paintings as his "trunk murders."[64]

Wallace Putnam recalled a conversation "one evening during the late thirties," when Rothko "expatiated on the idea—the myth is dead: the old stories having lost appeal, credibility, there are no loved, widely known themes for the painter today (one cause for abstractions)."[65] In "The Scribble Book," Rothko had remarked that after the erosion of collective myths by liberal skepticism, "the artist looked into himself" and, like an "anthropologist or archeologist," "ruminated among [his] own elementary impulses as well as the most archaic forms of man's plastic speech." Adolph Gottlieb similarly believed that at this time "one had to dig into one's self, excavate whatever one could."[66] The painter was now an archaeologist of the unconscious; myth was alive, buried within the self. Made not less but more inward by the political crises of the late thirties and early forties, Rothko ruminated among his own most elementary feelings of aggression and hurt as he read the Greek tragedians.

"The Rothkos are not heroes." But for a painter excavating the psychic depths, myth offered one way to articulate the irrational, to understand the private as public, and to achieve heroic scale. What Rothko said of Clyfford Still in 1946 was true of his own work in 1942: "He is creating new counterparts to replace the old mythological hybrids who have lost their pertinence in the intervening centuries."[67] Yet Rothko was really looking for something beyond mere myths, which are, after all, narratives bound by the historical and cultural circumstances in which they originate. Narratives can only be illustrated; and cultures can only change. Rothko, rather, was trying to find images for what he called the "Spirit of Myth"—not the Greek or Christian story but its transcultural emotional origin or core. In the 1930s Rothko's melancholy urban and domestic scenes had dramatized a "human incommunicability" which his expressionist sincerity struggled to make communicable. In the early 1940s Rothko's mythological visions dramatized a division so basic to human nature that they would transcend division and speak directly—i.e., subliminally—to a viewer. Myth, as Rothko insisted, expresses "something real and existing *in ourselves*" (my emphasis).[68]

Yet the very fact that Rothko would spend a year studying myth (or say that he did) reveals that, socially, "the myth *is* dead." *The Omen of the Eagle*, rather than drawing on widely known stories as the tragedies of Aeschylus did, combatively confronts its viewers with something real and *repressed* in themselves. Rothko's tragic image aims not at communal catharsis but at disturbing the individual psyche. So while criticizing the war as primal irrationality, *The Omen of the Eagle* itself seeks an irrational communicative power directed at the unconscious. Yet, even as he seeks the elemental and universal, Rothko remains a social outsider and modernist painter whose plastic language self-consciously alludes to Greek friezes and cubist multiple perspectives, Native American totem poles and classical architecture. Rothko's image of the archaic reflects a modernist cultural eclecticism which juxtaposes stylistic fragments. The painting's enigmatic title adds another kind of allusion, this one to an ancient text most of his viewers won't remember in the unlikely event they have read it. A viewer must struggle to 'make sense' of the painting's citations and its disturbing stylizations; direct emotional apprehension is not in the offing. Constructed out of cultural fragments, this "mythological hybrid" has been excavated from the private consciousness of Mark Rothko.

• • •

Marriage is an impossible situation for an artist to engage in.

Mark Rothko

A Threesome. Because they are handsome, because they are handmade, because they are sterling silver, you will want these for your very own.

Order them by mail from Edith Sachar, 29 East Twenty-Eighth Street. The curling leaf pin, $4.50; the graceful ear-clips, $3.75 a pair (plus 10% tax).

Vogue

Endorsed by *Vogue* magazine,[69] Edith's earrings, pins, bracelets, and necklaces, unlike her husband's paintings, were selling. At the beginning of their marriage, the couple had lived like virtual paupers. Now, while not always able to afford a night out on New Year's Eve, they were living like virtual members of the lower middle-class. Yet, as Juliette Hays put it, "tremendous conflict started taking place when Edith's jewelry was catching on." As she began to make money, Edith demanded that Rothko help in her business. He did, Milton Avery writing to Louis and Annette Kaufman, in September of 1941, that "Marcus . . . has eased up on his book and been acting as salesman for Edith his wife's efforts in jewelry designing."[70] According to friends, Edith became "officious" in manner; she appointed herself Rothko's "manager," and she appointed him her salesman, forcing Rothko, who was still teaching part-time at Center Academy, to ease up on his book, not to mention his art.[71] Barnett Newman liked to joke, "well, fellas we're going to have to gird up our loins and send our wives out to work."[72] Yet in Rothko's case, this fantasy of female acquiescence collapsed; his wife started a business, girded up *her* loins, and sent her husband out to work—for her.

Sometime in 1940 Edith and Rothko had temporarily separated, not because Rothko, feeling imprisoned, made a dash for freedom, but because Edith told him to leave. Once again, Rothko had been "transplanted," this time by his wife. "He loved her very much, but finally she threw him out, and he took to his bed," recalled their boarder, Morris Calden. Rothko "really absolutely collapsed," said Calden. "He wasn't sick; he just was in bed. He couldn't get over the fact that she had thrown him out, and just took to his bed and he'd lay in his bed week after week and I used to come and visit him and he'd just lie there" and deliver "soliloquies" in which "all he talked about was Edith," alternately warning that "she'll never get someone else like me; she'll regret it" and complaining that she had "humiliated" him by tossing him out.

When Rothko emerged from this "breakdown," Calden said, he "started the myth paintings."[73] After the couple reconciled, Rothko was working for his wife and producing his new paintings, in a studio loft he shared with Edith. "I had the front part of the loft as a workshop making this hand-made jewelry. I had several people working for me," one of them being Rothko, who was also "working in the back on his own paintings."[74] "She didn't want him to paint because he didn't sell anything," Sally Avery recalled. Edith felt freer to make demands, and to have doubts. Buffie Johnson thought Edith had begun to question her husband's talent; Juliette Hays, that Edith had begun to wonder whether his talent would ever be accepted. Either way, Rothko had too many doubts of his own to tolerate any from his wife. And he had too many ambitions of his own to tolerate putting in time persuading department-store buyers to purchase his wife's silver jewelry. Yet Rothko remained vulnerable to Edith: "he loved her very much" and "he wanted her approval." At first he resisted selling and complained; then he complied and complained. Rothko "felt like an errand boy," as if he were once again working for a Weinstein uncle or Lewis Browne. Selling for Edith tied Rothko down in soulless commercial activity. "He was very unhappy; he couldn't see his way out." Their "nice big apartment" on 28th Street might look "swell," but the familial balance of power had shifted. Rothko, Sally Avery said, felt "mortified."[75]

In the early summer of 1943, Rothko and Edith found that marriage was an impossible situation for either an artist or a jewelry designer to engage in; they separated, this time permanently. The first full year of World War II for the United States, 1942 was also the last year of Rothko's marriage, a "home front" characterized by frequent "very violent arguments."[76] Rothko's paintings registered the repercussions of these battles as strongly as though they were only yards away. So did his reading. Aeschylus' trilogy, after all, views the Trojan War by way of the home front and domestic strife; and *Agamemnon,* the source for *The Omen of the Eagle,* narrates the murder of a Greek king by his ambitious and angry wife. In Rothko's painting, the two pairs of heads at either end of the top rectangle are kissing—or, more accurately, their shut lips coldly touch; and the mythic creature's "heart" has cracked.

So *The Omen of the Eagle* critiques the irrationality of World War II; but the painting is also a kind of surrealist self-portrait, universalizing through myth the deep psyche of a man at war with his wife, and with himself. Possessing beak-like breasts, drooping, chalk-white testicles, and a hooked, labyrinthine structure for a womb, Rothko's figure mixes male and female. Not that he has invented a mythic model of androgynous unity; rather, the angry, mortified artist has created a compelling image of merged antagonists. In *Sculptress* Rothko's expressionistic distortions dramatized the tension between his desire for closeness with and his need for distance from his wife; in *The Omen of the Eagle* male and female fuse. "He couldn't see his way out."

Rothko angrily related to Robert Motherwell that as an infant he had been bound tightly in swaddling clothes—a story that, true or not, articulates the persistent feeling in Rothko's paintings of being enclosed and hemmed in.[77] An ink drawing from a sketchbook of the early 1940s (fig. 24) shows parent and child, side by side, squeezed into a cramped, box-shaped space and literally *locked* in an embrace by five pairs of rigid, boardlike arms that cover bodies which seem to be fused from neck to knee.[78] Below, the child, who seems to be wearing billowing, Russian-style pants and small boots, has been lifted from the floor and twisted around to face the parent. At the top, their heads, like the classical heads in Rothko's frieze paintings, can be read as either facing us or in profile. The adult, with heavily lined brow and widely separated eyes, splits into woeful and angry selves; the imprisoned child, stiffly submitting, looks worried, dazed. As they turn toward each other in profile, their heads joined by the lines sketching-in their hair, the parent's blank eye looks sadly away and inward. This is a self-preoccupied parent who won't let go.

By the early 1940s Rothko was using his sketchbook not as a way of recording impressions of the female body or the local subway station, but as a place to engage in a kind of visual free association. In this drawing he generated an image that suggests the emotional origins of his frieze paintings which, both artistically and psychologically, engage the issues of boundary-marking and boundary-breaking. In "The Scribble Book" Rothko had copied out Pfister's dictum that without "retrogressions no great progressions are possible." His marital battles had pushed Rothko to ruminate among his own most archaic fears and desires.

"I belong to a generation that was preoccupied with the human figure and I studied it. It was with utmost reluctance that I found that it did not meet my needs," Rothko later commented. "Whoever used it mutilated it."[79] In the myth paintings of 1942 Rothko was discovering, perhaps not as reluctantly as he later liked to think, that he could find a language for the deep psyche only by mutilating the human form he had been drawing and painting for nearly two decades. Another sketchbook drawing (fig. 25) creates a composite figure— either one person split, or two or more fused—whose flesh and muscle have been stripped away from the front of the torso and from one arm and one leg.⁸⁰ Here, instead of being boarded up, the body has been torn open, exposing a thin, fragile skeletal structure and lots of empty space beneath.

Untitled (c. 1940; color plate 10) similarly depicts a squat, muscular, wall-eyed creature, part male, part female, who stares blankly off to the right and, in a smaller, more shadowed, and more feminine profile, grimly gazes toward the left at a painting in progress. The figure's contorted body, too, has been twisted to face several directions simultaneously. At the front, the trunk has been pulled open, revealing, toward the bottom, the spinal column and rear rib cage, and above, inside the chest, a long, twisting, rose-red, snakelike tube, whose small triangular "head" sits in the position of the heart. Where chest and pelvis meet, a small wedged-shaped black area first invites, and then blocks, an effort to look further inside. The profile facing to our right stares unheedingly into the distance, while holding, in a chalky white hand, what looks like a small human head bent backward and squeezed tightly between "her" breasts. That head sits loosely on what looks like a narrow column attached, in turn, by a joint to a lower leg and foot which seem to belong to the head but which, since the foot is so large and points to the right, may also belong to the "main" composite figure. In these paintings of the early 1940s, bodies—sometimes bulky, gray-fleshed solids, sometimes bony hollows, sometimes limp and boneless—these bodies contort, split, merge.

Despite its geometrical simplicity, the painting-within-the-painting, a vertical light blue rectangle held within a white border outlined in dark blue, similarly refuses to remain a separate, integral object: its white border blends with the white wall. At the same time, this work refuses to stay *on* the wall: the dark blue lines defining the top and right edges of the painting cross in *front* of one painting hand and, below, a left foot. The bottom edge of the painting-in-progress, instead of receding diagonally backward along the wall, has been rotated forward and downward, opening the work at its bottom, where the grotesque painter's feet—one solid, the other a fleshless X-ray image of a foot—enter his work. On the one hand, this painting appears to be immaterial, since the artist's hands and feet enter it. On the other hand, the painting, at its bottom edge, expands into three dimensions, again incorporating parts of the artist's body. In either case, a work of art, even a geometric abstraction, cannot entirely be separated either from its environment or its creator.

In this painting, Rothko looks inward to uncover an elementary self that is brutish and delicate, tortured and commanding, open and hidden: a contradictory, elusive, and multiple being who even paints with two arms, one thin and feminine, the other muscular and masculine. He confronts his viewers, be they Macy's shoppers or uptown gallery patrons, with a threatening, primitive reality ("existing in ourselves") where persons and objects are no longer separate, simply bounded, and easily identifiable. In paintings like *The Omen of the Eagle* such fluidity has been bound, formally, by Rothko's pattern of horizontal rectangles. But to explore the psychic depths, the artist must painfully open himself, as if it were his tragic fate to be a hybrid—part rapacious eagle, part pregnant hare—as if his artistic creation violated the very core of human life.

• • •

Where is now the mythopoeic spirit?

Nietzsche, *The Birth of Tragedy*

In the early 1950s, a college student, broke and temporarily given a bedroom in Rothko's flat, remembered that "in the evenings he would lie on the couch for hours saying nothing, just contemplating or looking at one of his pictures that was hanging up and listening to music." One morning she got up very early to go hiking, and walked out into the living room to find Rothko stretched out on the couch, looking out a window and watching the sun rise. A relative recalled how Rothko, during visits, "could spend very happy hours, flat on his back on the couch, listening to Mozart." Herbert Ferber remembered Rothko "lying on the grass in Vermont listening with total attention to the whole of *Don Giovanni*," while Carlo Battaglia, Rothko's host during a 1966 visit to Rome described him "stretched out on a leather couch in Rome, windows open wide above the Renaissance plaza," again listening to *Don Giovanni*. Rothko loved to lie down; he loved to be horizontal.

Yet, at other times, talking with friends or relatives, Rothko couldn't sit still, speaking as he paced the floor with his hands clasped behind his back. "Rothko was a nervous and often impatient man," writes Dore Ashton. "Sometimes at dinner in my home, he would get up and wander between courses, cigarette in hand."[82] Like any other claustrophobic, Rothko was restless. But with his large, barrel-chested body stretched out on a couch, watching the sun rise along 52nd Street or listening to Mozart above a Roman plaza, Rothko was not painting, eating dinner, taking a walk, selling his wife's jewelry, teaching schoolchildren to paint, or riding the subway. He was not striving to impress, control, or even to communicate with the world. He was relaxed. Not aggressive, not completely passive either, he was open and receptive, yet alert and attentive. He was alone, withdrawn into a solitary inner space, yet given over to a pleasurable flow of sensations, as if he had recovered the core emotional self he sometimes believed he had lost in childhood. To be horizontal is to be at rest, to be comfortable; to be horizontal and listening to music—something Rothko loved to do—is to be enveloped with affecting sound, as if the listener were temporarily freed from the struggles, superficialities, and limits of an adult personality.

"I became a painter," Rothko said, "because I wanted to raise painting to the level of poignancy of music and poetry." Of course, Rothko also claimed that he had become a painter after he saw a nude model at the Art Students League. One story associates the origin of his work with erotic pleasure, the other associates it with an expressiveness that is so keenly affecting it is poignant, i.e., painful. Both stories sound like later, retrospective attempts by Rothko to explain, as much to himself as to anyone else, his passionate engagement with a medium for which he at first showed less native gift than he felt he had for music or writing. Very likely, his ambition to "raise" painting—as if it had hitherto been mere craft and copying—to the expressive power of music and poetry was shaped by a book that Rothko told many people had been important to him, Nietzsche's *The Birth of Tragedy*.

As late as 1960, Rothko "loved the terms Dionysian and Apollonian," using them to categorize fellow painters.[83] Rothko's familiarity with *The Birth of Tragedy* went back *many* years, "long before I had made the acquaintance of either Freud, or the Surrealists [or the] Cubists," he later recalled.[84] Possibly, Rothko had first heard of Nietzsche in Portland, where one of Emma Goldman's 1915 lectures had dealt with "Nietzsche and War."[85] A sardonic comment in the *Saturday Evening Pest*—"once we had occasion to mention the name of Neitche [sic] and our friends asked us whether he was a Russian Bolshevik"—suggests that Rothko may have read Nietzsche by the time he was at Yale.[86] If he knew *The Birth of Tragedy* prior to reading Freud, and prior to learning of the Cubists and the Surrealists, he would have read the text by the time he left Yale or shortly thereafter. While "the ideas" of Freud and the "actual images" of the Cubists and Surrealists were "concrete" in relation to his painting, he later wrote, "I can more closely identify my own feelings with" Nietzsche's essay, "for it provides the concrete moral objectives, which may be overlooked in the works themselves." So "I have returned to [*The Birth of Tragedy*] on a number of occasions."[87] A notation in "The Scribble Book," "Nietzsche & Greek tragedy" suggests that the late 1930s, as he was beginning to explore mythic subjects for his art, constituted one of those occasions.

"Without monsters and gods, art cannot enact our drama," Rothko wrote in "The Romantics Were Prompted." "When they were abandoned as untenable superstitions, art sank into melancholy." Modernism entails loss—the loss of collective myth, social community, religious tradition, transcendent meaning, heroic action. "Doesn't it make you feel lonesome?" Losing faith in a father who had left him first in Dvinsk and then in Portland, Rothko emancipated himself from a religion with which he had been intensely involved, and sank into melancholy. As in figure 24, the nine-year-old Russian "infant prodigy" had been left *locked* in the arms of a mother whom he perceived as preoccupied with her own melancholy. Just as art was left trapped in the "probable and familiar" (i.e., realism) with the death of the gods, so the disillusioned young Rothko had been left trapped in a modern, secular world, purely physical and material, longing angrily for transcendence.

"Man today," writes Nietzsche, "stripped of myth, stands famished among all his pasts and must dig frantically for roots, be it among the most remote antiquities"—an apt account of the multicultural allusiveness of *The Omen of the Eagle*. *The Birth of Tragedy,* itself a myth about the loss of myth, relates the reconciliation of Dionysus and Apollo in the tragedies of Aeschylus, followed by the usurpation of tragic myth in the "scientific optimism" of "theoretical man"—i.e., Socrates. In Nietzsche's text, Dionysus is the god of intoxication, transport, and fusion, Apollo the god of dream, illusion, and individuation. Dionysian wisdom proceeds from an ecstatic self-transcendence, a "dismemberment" or "unselving" which reveals "the maternal womb of being," "the original Oneness" which, having named it as one, Nietzsche instantly divides: "the ground of Being, ever-suffering and contradictory." Later, Nietzsche identifies man as "the incarnation of dissonance" and writes of "the contrariety at the heart of the universe." Like Rothko, Nietzsche was a dualist who yearned for a unity he associated with maternal origins.

The contrariety of being, in *The Birth of Tragedy,* derives from its merging of transience and permanence. Dionysian art "makes us realize that everything that is generated must be prepared to face its painful dissolution." Immersion in the oneness of being confronts us, then, with the annihilation of the self, with death, which Rothko had sternly pronounced "the only serious thing; nothing else is to be taken seriously." Yet, as we fuse with "the primal Being," "we experience its insatiable hunger for existence" and grasp the "eternal life continuing beyond all appearance and in spite of destruction," as if death, like Greek tragedy, issued in a rebirth. Loss is not absolute. Tragic art, combining melancholy with exhilaration, conveys "a metaphysical solace"—like one of Rothko's mature paintings.

Dionysus, moreover, is the god of music, Apollo the god of the plastic arts. In Nietzsche's account, the orgiastic music of Dionysus, a universal symbolic language prior to and beyond image or concept, represents not appearances but being itself—the "Original Mother," eternally creating and destroying. An expression of our most archaic experience, such music gives "birth to myth," "above all, to the tragic myth, which is a parable of Dionysian knowledge." In the beginning was dithyrambic music, out of which arose the individuated characters and events of classical tragedy. Apollo, god of boundaries and restraint, shapes Dionysian knowledge into particular, material images to render it bearable. "Tragedy is an Apollonian embodiment of Dionysian insights and powers." Yet the spirit of Apollo, who is also the god of dreams, so constructs the "delightful illusion" on the stage that the spectator knows it to be an illusion. Tragic myth, then, creates a "veil" through which the spectator, his vision "spiritualized" by the music that accompanied the Greek, penetrates to the Dionysian wisdom within.

Nietzsche's view of music as the primordial language of feeling; his heroization of Aeschylus; his "longing for a metaphysical world"; his impatience with the realm of physical appearances; his celebration of a tragic myth that aroused both elation and melancholy—all of these resonated in Rothko at levels so deep he was unable to get some of them into his painting until the 1950s. Nietzsche's orphic, dithyrambic prose makes reading him like stretching out on the couch and listening to a Wagnerian opera.

Yet Rothko did not read *The Birth of Tragedy* passively, like a *cheder* student studying a Talmudic text. Rothko, who classified himself as Apollonian, was too reserved, murky, and deliberate a personality to follow Nietzsche's advocacy of the Dionysian mysteries—or, in the early years of World War II, his strenuous German nationalism. Nor could Rothko accept *Birth*'s theory of myth or its limited notion of painting. Aligning myth with Apollo, Nietzsche viewed it as a narrative imitation of the phenomenal world, and he could only imagine a visual art that was similarly mimetic. But Rothko wanted a return to the "*Spirit of Myth*," a prenarrative core, common to all myths, which Nietzsche associated with music. To raise painting to the emotional immediacy of music, Rothko would have to complete the dismemberment of the human figure he began in the early 1940s, and become an abstract painter. In this way, he would invent a modern art, without monsters or gods, which *could* enact his inner drama.

7

"'Globalism' Pops Into View"

I quarrel with surrealist and abstract art only as one quarrels with his father and mother, recognizing the inevitability and function of my roots, but insistent on my dissension: I, being both they, and an integral completely independent of them.

Mark Rothko

The vital task was a wedding of abstraction and surrealism. Out of these opposites something new could emerge. . . .

Adolph Gottlieb

At 8 P.M. on October 20, 1942, Peggy Guggenheim's Art of This Century Gallery opened on the two top floors, formerly tailor shops, of 30 West 57th Street. Admission was $1.00, with proceeds contributed to the American Red Cross. "Opening this gallery and its collection to the public during a time when people are fighting for their lives and freedom is a responsibility of which I am fully conscious," she said.[1] At Guadalcanal, U.S. army, navy and marine planes were bombing Japanese troop concentrations; in Stalingrad, the Russian garrison was defending against a German tank attack; along the eastern coast of England, German planes bombed villages and small towns, killing twenty people.[2] In New York, hundreds—among them Mark Rothko—attended the reception for Art of This Century, to view Peggy Guggenheim's collection of modernist art and to see the exhibition space designed by the Surrealist architect Frederick Kiesler.[3]

Peggy Guggenheim's mother had come from one of the oldest and wealthiest German-Jewish families in New York City; her father merely came from one of the wealthiest, but he unwisely sold his share of the family mining business, condemning his daughter to think of herself as a "poor relation" and the "enfant terrible" among Guggenheims. Compared to a Rothkowitz or even a Weinstein, however, she was far from poor. When she was ten, she began her art education with a private tutor who came to the family's town house at Fifth Avenue and 72nd Street. Growing up, Peggy Guggenheim was never much interested in white-gloved tea dances at the Plaza; as a young woman, she worked as a clerk in a bookstore, became involved with New York avant-garde literary circles. In 1920, at twenty-two, she sailed for bohemian Paris. As an expatriate, she soon married, became unhappy, had numerous affairs. She began to collect pictures. By the late 1930s, when she had moved to London, taken on Marcel Duchamp as her main advisor and opened an art gallery ("Guggenheim Jeune"), some of the men in her life, and many of the pictures in her collection, were Surrealist.⁴

In early 1941 she was living in the unoccupied south of France with Max Ernst. At first, the Second World War had inspired her to put herself on a regime of buying one work of art a day from painters and dealers fearing a German invasion. "The day Hitler walked into Norway, I walked into Léger's studio and bought a wonderful 1919 painting from him for one thousand dollars. He never got over the fact that I should be buying paintings on such a day."⁵ But Ernst was a German whose art had been declared "degenerate" by Adolph Hitler; Peggy Guggenheim was Jewish. Europe was too dangerous; the two flew to New York City in July 1941.

Peggy Guggenheim's extensive collection of modern art had been shipped to America as household goods. She decided to open a museum to display her goods; her friend Bernard Reis persuaded her to include a commercial gallery.⁶ In Kiesler's design for Art of This Century, the space for the temporary exhibitions (the "Daylight Gallery"), with white painted walls and natural light from large windows overlooking 57th Street, was the most traditional, though the room also held a painting library where visitors, seated on wood-and-blue-canvas folding chairs, could view works stacked in storage bins. To exhibit the Guggenheim collection, Kiesler designed three innovative environments, an "Automatic Gallery," a "Surrealist Gallery," and an "Abstract Gallery."

In the Surrealist gallery, two concave wooden walls and a suspended wooden ceiling formed a long tunnel-shaped room; unframed paintings, attached to the walls by sawed-off baseball bats and to the bats by flexible mounts, could be adjusted to suit the viewer's height or pleasure. The lights illuminated one wall for two minutes, shut off for three and a half seconds, then illuminated the opposite wall; every two minutes the sounds of a railroad train filled the room. In the Abstract gallery, the walls were created by a gently curving ultramarine curtain suspended between the floor and ceiling by rope lacing; the floor was painted turquoise. As in the Surrealist gallery, paintings— again unframed—came off the wall, in this case floating at eye level from transparent, triangular columns shaped from rope or cloth tape tautly suspended between ceiling and floor. Many years later Robert Motherwell, after drawing a diagram of the gallery, commented, "The first time I saw the two wings, I realized the two directions abstraction and surrealism had to be joined."⁷

At her Art of This Century opening, Peggy Guggenheim herself had worn one earring ("a tiny oval painting of a bone-strewn pink desert") by Yves Tanguy and one ("a wire and metal mobile") by Alexander Calder in order, she said, "to show my imparfiality between Surrealist and Abstract art."⁸ But however evenhanded, or even-eared, Peggy Guggenheim tried to appear, she mainly exhibited Surrealists in the first two years of Art of This Century, she mainly collected Surrealists, and she was even married to one. As Max's son, Jimmy Ernst, recalled, "The potent voices with access to Peggy's ear on aesthetic questions were largely the Surrealists."[9]

In New York, 1942, the first year of the war and the last of Rothko's marriage, was also the year of the Surrealists. During the 1930s their work was known in this country through exhibits at the Julian Levy and Pierre Matisse galleries, the "Cubism and Abstract Art" show at the Museum of Modern Art (1936), and, especially, that museum's "Fantastic Art, Dada and Surrealism" exhibit later that year. Reproductions of Surrealist work were available in the group's magazine *Minotaure* and, later, *View*. With the war, many Surrealists were "transplanted" to New York, Wolfgang Paalen, Kurt Seligman, Roberto Matta, and Yves Tanguy arriving in 1939, followed by Gordon Onslow-Ford in 1940 and André Masson, André Breton, and Max Ernst in 1941. The year 1942 began with concurrent shows of Salvador Dali and Joan Miró at the Museum of Modern Art, included an "Artists in Exile" show at Pierre Matisse, one-man exhibits of Masson, Ernst, Matta, Tanguy at New York galleries, the founding of the Surrealist magazine *VVV*, the arrival of Marcel Duchamp in June, and, in October, "The First Papers of Surrealism," where Duchamp created a dense web out of two miles of white string he crisscrossed among the walls, ceiling, and partitions of the exhibition room at the Whitelaw-Reid mansion on Madison Avenue.[10] When Art of This Century opened less than a week later, it culminated the American arrival of this French movement. The war, which also brought Marc Chagall, Fernand Léger, Jacques Lipchitz, and Piet Mondrian to this country, had forced the provincial New York art scene toward internationalism.

Art of This Century provided a gathering place for emigré artists, as did Peggy Guggenheim's 51st Street town house. The impact of her collection went deeper. "A relief from the past decade's WPA murals, Left Wing 'realism,' and war agency posters, Peggy Guggenheim's war-time gallery was both old-fashioned and 'advanced'. It echoed the heroic days of Paris vanguardism of the twenties, and it evoked the tradition of individual experiment in twentieth century art."[11] Art of This Century encouraged further experiment by giving one-man shows to such younger American painters as William Baziotes, Robert Motherwell, Jackson Pollock, Clyfford Still, and Mark Rothko. If, in the minds of painters like Rothko and Gottlieb, the American wedding of Surrealist and abstract art produced abstract expressionism, then Peggy Guggenheim was the rich Jewish aunt who paid for the reception.

But Peggy Guggenheim's was not the only New York salon for Surrealists.

When the members of the Federation of Modern Painters and Sculptors had compiled their list of potential patrons, one name they included was that of Bernard Reis, a lawyer-accountant in his late forties, who had been buying art for about twenty years.[12] Reis, in fact, was precisely one of the new businessmen-collectors the federation had been looking for. In France, Max Ernst had feared the French authorities who twice interred him as an alien and might have deported him to Germany; in the United States, Ernst was feared as a possible German spy. While on Cape Cod in the summer of 1942, Ernst was brought in and questioned for several hours by the FBI, chiefly about Matta, whom they suspected of being an even bigger spy. To intercede for Ernst with the Bureau of Enemy Aliens, Peggy Guggenheim turned to Reis, who was already known as someone able to help artists in financial or legal difficulty.[13] As his wife Rebecca put it, "he knew the law and had the ingenuity to get them out of any jam that did arise."

A native New Yorker born in 1895, Reis had worked his way through New York University, getting a B.A. in commercial science, then attended NYU's law school at night while working days as a legal secretary. In 1921, he was certified as a public accountant and passed the bar exam. Unable to do the required year as a law clerk because he had to support his parents, Reis started his own accounting firm. After their marriage in 1920, Bernard and Rebecca Reis began to travel and to buy art, beginning with Chinese ceramics and textiles, moving on to primitive and twentieth-century art. Having assisted Felix Frankfurter with a book on public utilities, Reis also became involved with the consumer's movement, being a founder, director, and treasurer of Consumer's Research in 1932, a director and treasurer of the Consumer's Union in 1934, and the author in 1937 of *False Security,* an angry, well-researched exposé of the deceits and manipulations to which inexperienced, middle-class investors in the stock market are vulnerable. Legislators, judges, accountants, and bankers—those responsible for protecting the consumer— don't, according to Reis, who offers no Marxist dismantling of the capitalist system but a New-Deal-style reform: members of this interest group should organize and appoint agents they *can* trust.[14] Three years later, Reis heard the call and chose himself, helping to found the American Investors Union.

"My husband, Bernard, growing up a poor boy himself, realized that the artist is the most unprotected creature in the world," said Rebecca Reis. Bernard "acted as a very knowledgeable friend who understood the artist's career—how to further it where possible, what kind of arrangement to make with his dealer," all very important services since the artist is "a helpless man in matters of practicality" and needs "a guiding spirit and a loveable one." For consumers, Reis proposed organization, with investors turning their interests over to trustworthy authorities such as himself. For painters, too, Reis offered himself as trustworthy friend and authority, on whom creators were encouraged to remain passively dependent. As it later turned out in the lawsuit over Rothko's estate, Reis himself offered *False Security*.

After helping Max Ernst, Reis became friend and business advisor to Peggy Guggenheim; Rebecca Reis sometimes took over at the door of Art of This Century, collecting the quarters that Guggenheim insisted on charging as admission. The Reises bought paintings from the gallery, and, already, Reis was accepting works from artist-clients unable to pay him. By the early 1940s, the Reis apartment on lower Fifth Avenue held an extensive art collection and had become "a sort of meeting place" for the exiled Surrealists to assemble "maybe once or twice a week."[15] The Reises had a French cook, good wine, and a twenty-year-old daughter, Barbara, a painter who spoke rapid, colloquial French; the couple helped finance the Surrealist journal *VVV,* for which Reis served as treasurer. For the French emigrés, the Reis home offered, Robert Motherwell said, "one of the few moments that they felt expansive, taken care of, secure, respected, well-fed, well-dined. After all, they were political exiles and I imagine in many ways were quite frightened."[16]

Peggy Guggenheim remembered that Rebecca Reis "loved to fill her home with Surrealists and then give them a free hand to do what they liked."[17] Breton liked to preside over *Cadavre Exquis,* in which one person wrote a noun on a piece of paper, folded the paper over so that the word could not be seen and then passed the paper to the next person, who supplied a verb—and so on until a complete sentence had been constructed. Breton's "favorite game," however, was *Le jeu de la verité,* the aim of which was "to dig out people's most intimate sexual feelings and expose them." If Breton judged that a participant had lied, he extracted a "forfeit": "You were punished by being brought blindfolded into a room on all fours and forced to guess who kissed you."[18] Given a free meal and a free hand in their benefactors' apartment, the Surrealists converted their faith in unconscious creation into psychoanalytic parlor games, performing like so many amusing, indulged, and sometimes cruel children. Anaïs Nin noted in her *Diary* "the highly artificial evenings at the Bernard Reises, for all the famous artists."[19] To a young New York painter, the salon could feel decadent, or even threatening. Robert Motherwell, for one, warned William Baziotes to "stay away" from the artistically deadening influence of the "Reis-Surrealist milieu."[20]

Taken up by affluent patrons, uptown dealers, and the Museum of Modern Art staff, the expatriated Surrealists were concerned with their own economic survival, their occasional legal troubles, their frequent doctrinal infighting, and the making and promoting of their own work. Displaced, they didn't like New

York any more, say, than Rothko had liked Portland. Café life didn't exist; the weather was bad; the pace was too fast. Breton, a literary-political revolutionary who thought that "everything not French is imbecile," refused to learn English, which others in the group only spoke haltingly. The Surrealists, in Hedda Sterne's view, "preferred to have others take the trouble to understand them—they had an arrogance." Jimmy Ernst, for whom this issue also had a familial twist, complained that the Surrealist painters judged "my American friends" "almost entirely" by their "compliance" to Surrealist doctrine.[21] Max Ernst and Mark Rothko had accidentally met on the ferry from Ellis Island, when Rothko was returning to the city with a friend he had picked up and Ernst was returning with his son. But a few years later when Jimmy Ernst gave a party for his father, then visiting New York from Arizona, Max Ernst pretended not to know Bradley Walker Tomlin and Mark Rothko. The Europeans considered the Americans "beneath their dignity."[22]

Of course, Jimmy Ernst's American friends had a nervous arrogance and an evolving point of view of their own which made them both intimidated by and resentful toward these "highly cultivated, highly sophisticated" expatriates. After all, the Surrealists were (mostly) French, often (after Dada) anti-art and (in theory) politically left; the New York painters were looking to replace Parisian with American internationalism, asserting the importance of the "esthetic" and developing a liberal politics. Many Surrealist painters, while politically radical, remained conservatively illusionistic, prompting Gottlieb in his "The Portrait and the Modern Artist" statement with Rothko to comment that "it is not enough to illustrate dreams." The individualistic Americans were also alienated by the Surrealists' college of cardinals organization, with Breton possessing papal powers of excommunication. As Robert Motherwell remarked, "it's inconceivable that, let's say, Rothko would—as Max Ernst, for example, would say—yes, there is an intellectual leader that I believe in."[23] Besides, Surrealism was now nearly twenty years old, making it, by modern standards for vanguard programs, nearly geriatric.

To the less well-fed, well-dined Americans, the Europeans, treated like imported celebrities, occupied gallery space, critical interest, and collectors' money rightfully belonging to the native artists. The new businessmen-collectors, like Bernard Reis, bought Europeans. "If you look at [Reis's] collection," Motherwell noted, "it's predominantly European. The best pictures are European. The only money was spent on Europeans. . . . He was very conservative and snobbish that way without really knowing it." Excluded, embittered, and poor, the Americans adopted "a very stand-off relation with the Europeans." A few painters, such as Motherwell and Baziotes, had access to the Surrealists, and were included in their "First Papers of Surrealism" exhibit. But generally the Frenchmen were too aloof and exclusive, the Americans too suspicious and insecure, for there to arise anything like a relaxed exchange of ideas between the two groups. In fact, the Old World and New World artists, according to Motherwell, "really didn't intermingle at all."[24]

Rothko did know Roberto Matta, and he knew Max Ernst, who sometimes knew him.[25] Yet, in spite of any envious ranklings or social snubs, "Mark was very interested in psychic automatism," Motherwell said. "He was one of the few American painters who really liked Surrealist painting, went to Surrealist shows, and understood" what they were up to. Rothko also told Motherwell that "there was always automatic drawing under those larger forms" in his signature paintings.[26] But even before the Surrealist presence in New York, the poetic silence, the enclosing geometries, and the suggestions of classical architecture in Rothko works like *Street Scene* and *Subway Scene* reveal his debt to the proto-Surrealist de Chirico; and in his frieze paintings of the early 1940s, Rothko's fantastic, sexually ambiguous creatures, his severings of the human body, and his whole engagement with classical myth are indebted to Surrealism.[27] "The surrealist has uncovered the glossary of the myth," Rothko later wrote. Herbert Ferber said that "Rothko has often mentioned that Surrealism was one of the strongest and most fruitful influences in his work." But psychic automatism offered, in Motherwell's words, "*a creative principle* that was *not a style,*" and thus Rothko, rather than deriving subject, image, or gloss, could now adopt—while remaining "an integral completely independent of them"—the Surrealist method of generating new subjects and images.[28]

As the movement's founding principle, psychic automatism had been defined by André Breton in the *First Manifesto of Surrealism* (1924) as submission by the artist to "thought's dictation, in the absence of all control exercised by the reason and outside all aesthetic or moral preoccupations."[29] Like a psychoanalytic patient on the couch, but without the hovering attention of a doctor who might interrupt with a disturbing comment, the Surrealist invited himself to free-associate. So an artist might doodle with pen or pencil, or let the brush wander across a canvas, or cover a canvas with a wash, which he or she then randomly rubs with a rag, or simply pour paint onto the canvas. "Rather than setting out to paint something," Joan Miró said, "I begin painting and as I paint the picture begins to assert itself, or suggest itself under my brush."[30] Line and color are freed from any mimetic obligations, or from describing that material world into which, in Rothko's account, painting had sunk, melancholy, with the death of the gods. Yet Rothko, who abandoned the human figure only with "utmost reluctance," did not seek to liberate his medium from representation only to lose it in purist abstraction. "One does not paint for design students or historians but for human beings," he said, "and the reaction in human terms is the only thing that is really satisfactory to the artist."³¹ With automatism, shapes emerge from the unconscious, like primitive life-forms crawling up out of the sea, and so, while suggestive rather than literal, they evoke human associations and feelings.

To Rothko, as to many painters of his generation, psychic automatism thus opened a humanistic alternative to both the formalism of the American Abstract Artists and to the idealized figurations of the American regionalists. Heretofore, Rothko—the Rothko, say, who sat in the morning, his pajama tops still on, smoking a cigarette and contemplating his latest work—had been a very deliberate painter. As Bonnie Clearwater points out, he "planned his myth paintings carefully and relied heavily on drawings and preparatory sketches," some done with pencil or pen, others with watercolors. In the 1930s, too, oil paintings had begun as sketches from life, then grew out of a process often involving as many as twenty preparatory studies.³² When he was painting, Marcus Rothkowitz was no slacker.

So far, the further inward Rothko went, the more structure he felt he needed, so that in *The Omen of the Eagle* instinctual feeling is represented by a grotesque, threatening chimera which is stabilized by being placed atop a "stand," locked to the painting's left edge, severed into four horizontal tiers, and structured *both* geometrically (as stacked rectangles) and organically (based on the human body). Even as they express a buried inner life, paintings distance, control, and hold it in. It's as if Rothko's painstaking process of creation replicated that inhibited, withdrawn quality of life that his paintings so often critiqued. Psychic automatism offered Rothko a liberating way to begin to free his most elementary impulses and led him to initiate a series of stylistic experiments that would occupy him for the next several years. Once again, Rothko was *choosing* insecurity, this time as a creative principle.

• • •

Our thinking in the future must be world-wide.

Wendell Willkie, *One World* (1943)

Now that America is recognized as the center where art and artists of all the world meet, it is time for us to accept cultural values on a truly global plane.

The Federation of Modern Painters and Sculptors, 1943

When the federation's third annual exhibition opened at 4 P.M., June 2, 1943, at Wildenstein's on 64th Street, the show had already received a mainly negative review from Edward Alden Jewell in that morning's *Times*. "You will have to make of Marcus Rothko's 'The Syrian Bull' what you can," Jewell wrote. "Nor is this department prepared to shed the slightest enlightenment when it comes to Adolph Gottlieb's 'Rape of Persephone'."[33]

Four days later Jewell professed a similar skepticism about the brochure that accompanied the catalogue for the show.[34] The federation's statement had characteristically called for an end of artistic nationalism, even as it asserted a new form of American artistic nationalism. Drawing on the popular appeal of Henry Luce's prophetic vision of "The American Century" (1941), the federation observed that "today America is faced with the responsibility either to salvage and develop, or to frustrate Western creative capacity," a responsibility that "may be largely ours for a good part of the century to come." During the war, the country "has been greatly enriched, both by the recent influx of many great European artists" and "by the growing vitality of our native talent." In the future, America will be judged as a civilization: "did it nourish or starve this concentration of talent?"

From the simultaneously long-range and provincial perspective of the federation, the American crisis of mid-1943 was not a military or political but a cultural crisis—one that Jewell, among many others, would fail. "As a nation we are being forced to outgrow our narrow political isolationism," the federation statement continued. American power established America, or at least New York, as *the* international art "center" and thus required both the end of narrow artistic nationalism, which is to say, American regionalism, and the acceptance of "cultural values on a truly global plane," which is to say, the invention of an American-based version of international modernism.[35] Jewell, after quoting generously from the statement, still "wasn't so sure, looking around Mr. Wildenstein's nice and graciously provided galleries, that anything globally halcyon had as yet materialized."

Placing "cultural values on a truly global plane" expresses an oddly contradictory ambition, since cultures are local and specific; but the phrase does articulate the desire, felt by Gottlieb, Rothko, and others, to create a new plastic language that was universal, or broadly human. Rothko's title, *The Syrian Bull* (1943; color plate 11), suggests that he did have a fairly extensive knowledge of myth, since it refers to a very obscure story mentioned only briefly, for example, in the omnivorous *Golden Bough*. The legend survives mainly in reliefs depicting Mithra, an ancient Persian deity whose worship spread throughout the Mediterranean (and beyond) and lasted into third-century Rome.[36] By slaying a bull, Mithra, the god of celestial light, creates the world. In the reliefs, the god, wearing a cape with many folds, sits astride the bull (which faces the viewer's right) and with his left hand grasps the animal by the mouth to pull its head back, while his right arm plunges a dagger into its shoulder. Mithra faces us, often with a sad look, as if reluctant to kill the bull. A dog (or sometimes a snake) attacks the open wound; a scorpion threatens the bull's genitals, as if to drain the life out of the animal. But the bull's tail typically ends in three ears of corn—a new life that issues out of the bloodletting. According to the myth, the bull's blood metamorphoses into wine, his spinal cord into wheat.

The mythical bull symbolizes male strength and tranformative power, generated through violent sacrifice. In Rothko's work, the heavy, wounded bull has been transformed into a flat, thinly painted, sun-yellow abstract shape, with three round holes in it—a shape which floats against a blue sky filled with smokey gray clouds and which is gently held down to a chalky pink ground by eight skinny legs, each ending in a black, flamelike hoof. In the year since *The Omen of the Eagle* Rothko's composition and drawing have loosened up considerably. While set within a traditional earth/sky division, his shapes here have not been severed into geometric compartments or stabilized on a pedestal; they are less representational, at once more abstract and (generally) more organic.

At the right, a large, yellow, bulbous form drifts upward—an inversion of the two white, wooden, drooping testicle shapes in *The Omen of the Eagle*. At the left, a yellow disc tilts forward from the top of a yellow cone, as if the bull's tail ended not in three ears of corn but in the fructifying presence of the sun itself. Just to the right, a yellow rectangle holds a brown rib cage or spine, schematic remains of the animal's bone structure. Warm, bulging upward, and fertile, weightless and filled with sunlight, floating yet secured by its four rear legs to the horizon line, Rothko's bull has been transcendentalized, beautifully fusing body and spirit.

Mithra, source and protector of life, is the creator. In *The Syrian Bull,* a yellow area in the upper center suggests the blond hair of this eternally young and virile god, the folds of whose cape have been transformed into gray, feathered, winglike shapes. What looks like a thick brown board, with white sides, covers the god's face and extends downward into two sharp points; just to the left are two red "boards"—one a triangle pointed downward, the other a rectangle whose upper edge either locks into the brown board or is covered by it and whose lower edge softly replicates the two points at the bottom of the brown rectangle. The two red shapes are held in place by two blue double chevrons which, in turn, cover parts of the wings. Below, the brown reappears as a bird's leg and claw, whose elongated nails have broken off as they plunge into the yellow "body" where they begin metamorphosing into feathers. The creator-god's arm is an eagle's claw, at once violating his subject and being absorbed *by* it. Occurring in many of Rothko's drawings and paintings from this period, the eagle emblematizes a predatory violence associated in part with the "carnage" of the Second World War. *The Syrian Bull,* in fact, was painted as the war, with Allied victories at Stalingrad and Guadalcanal, was beginning to turn in the Allies' favor; and it was painted in the final few months of Rothko's first marriage. Would new life issue from either of these bloodlettings?

In the shallow, low-ceilinged spaces of Rothko's rooms and subway stations of the 1930s, the inhabitants look walled-in, as if Rothko felt trapped in the self he was trying to express. In *The Syrian Bull,* the space of Rothko's mythical landscape is still shallow, yet the flattened, sunlit, feathered, floating shape— partly geometric, mostly organic—conveys sensual pleasure and spiritual freedom, as if Rothko were now trying to get *out* of himself by expressing himself. By emancipating his art from the melancholy imitation of any familiar external reality—by a violent sacrifice of the shared social, historical, and natural worlds—Rothko can create new forms capable of subtly expressing his inner life. Such liberation demands power, just as abstraction requires an imposition of the internal onto the external world. Like the young god with his sad look, Rothko violates physical reality "with utmost reluctance."

Yet in *The Syrian Bull* we cannot see the face, or the body, of the creator— they have been covered by the three areas in the painting that are the most resolutely artificial and man-made. Resembling wooden boards that have been cut into angular, pointed shapes, with similarly sharp, geometric patterns scratched onto their tops, probably with the tip of the painter's brush, they associate Mithra with *artistic* creation, and they point downward, anticipating the bird's claw and connoting a creativity that must *make* art happen rather than *let* it happen. When, in "The Romantics Were Prompted," Rothko identified his pictures as "dramas," with his shapes as the "performers," he went on to say that "they have been created from the need for a group of actors who are able to move dramatically without embarrassment and execute gestures without shame." Here the painter is no longer the archaeologist of his private psyche; Rothko, who as a young man had tried acting, now imagines himself as a writer-director who, by concealing himself behind, *and within,* the public drama he has created, is now looking for a way to express himself "without embarrassment."

But *The Syrian Bull* associates exposure with danger and art with hiding. On the one hand, Rothko, covering over the specific physical being of the creator-god, has diffused his presence into expressive color, light, and shape of the bull—as if, again, painting provided a way to get free of and beyond the self. The bull's body contains three round openings (absences which echo, negatively, the sun); part of the animal's spine/rib cage is visible; and the two white polyps (partly stained with a watery red) midway along the right edge may also suggest mysterious inner organs externalized. So, too, Rothko has opened himself and exposed his "insides."

Yet, on the other hand, Rothko needs to cover and conceal, as if he were unable to display his most intimate feelings "without shame." Shame differs from guilt, which has to do with specific actions; shame is a state of being, the feeling of being *seen through*—the self is experienced as transparent and exposed as lacking. In his self-portrait Rothko had depicted himself wearing dark glasses; in his frieze paintings of the early forties, a row of fused heads had given the self an elusive multiplicity. In his lecture at Pratt, Rothko would characterize his paintings as "facades," not insisting on telling "all like at a confessional," but preferring "to tell little." In *The Syrian Bull*, when we look at the row of legs, arranged in near and far pairs, the animal seems to have the bulk we associate with bulls; but the legs can also be seen as simply longer and shorter, attached to what the three circular holes reveal to be a flat surface, except for the large yellow bulb on the right. The bull is mainly represented *as* his covering—his hide; except for the leg/claw, Mithra is represented as golden hair, voluptuous feathers, two blue double chevrons, one brown and two red "boards"—as a *series* of coverings. Like the eyes in Rothko's *Self-Portrait*, the face of Mithra has been aggressively painted over, with the sharp-edged brown board looking as though it had been *thrust* into place. Art exposes; art conceals—and it does both violently.

A warrior/hunter especially venerated by Roman military officers, Mithra, however reluctantly, assaulted the bull to produce new life, just as in North Africa soldiers of the U.S. Army were killing Italians, however reluctantly, to produce a "new America." *The Syrian Bull* continues Rothko's critique of the war's violence; but his painting also reflects Rothko's search for a creativity that was neither a mere imposition upon nor a romantic blending with his subject. Rothko had never been the kind of artist who wrestled with something outside of himself and pinned it down in order to produce a beautiful object. Even when he was drawing the female nude or painting an IRT subway station, Rothko was always struggling to look inside.

In *The Syrian Bull* he struggles to merge with his creative core, here represented as a massive, fertile, floating body, filled with light. To do that he needs, simultaneously, to impose and to eliminate the self—slay the bull and cover the face of the creator. But the self can only be hidden, not eliminated, and so in *The Syrian Bull* god, bird, and beast are not fused but verge on dissolving into each other, as if Rothko needed to hold back as much as he needed to probe more deeply. Even as he revealed himself, Rothko wished to remain opaque, enigmatic, and hidden. And even as he reached out to communicate with an audience, he feared that it contained at least a few scorpions.

. . .

Edward Alden Jewell, of course, had been the first to step forward and attach himself to Rothko's bull. In his June 6 critique of the federation statement, the *Times* critic reported that one of the group's artists had "phoned in and promised a statement that might help disperse my confessed befuddlement" over the Gottlieb and Rothko pictures. Gottlieb had made the phone call, and Jewell's feigned confusion, plus his own interest in generating a controversy, gave the two painters a polemical opening as well as a public forum in the *Times*. Very likely it was as a result of the ensuing publicity that the two were invited to speak on "The Portrait and the Modern Artist" on New York's WNYC radio station the following October.

On Sunday, June 13, under a large headline, "The Realm of Art: A New Platform and 'Globalism' Pops Into View," Jewell printed a letter signed by Rothko and Gottlieb, along with photographs of *The Syrian Bull* and *The Rape of Persephone*. But rather than simply turn his column over to the voices of the two artists, Jewell introduced their response, mockingly named their new movement "Globalism," interrupted their statement with his own ironic comments and then closed by professing to find their text just as obscure as the paintings.

Not exactly rhetorical innocents themselves, Rothko and Gottlieb begin their manifesto not with bohemian flamboyance or angry nihilism but in a tone of wry graciousness:

> To the artist, the workings of the critical mind is one of life's mysteries. That is why, we suppose, the artist's complaint that he is misunderstood, especially by the critic, has become a noisy commonplace. It is therefore, an event when the worm turns and the critic of the TIMES quietly yet publicly confesses his "befuddlement," that he is "non-plussed" before our pictures at the Federation Show. We salute this honest, we might say cordial reaction towards our "obscure" paintings, for in other critical quarters we seem to have created a bedlam of hysteria. And we appreciate the gracious opportunity that is being offered us to present our views.

Yet Rothko and Gottlieb firmly refuse to help the critic by tacking explanatory notes to their paintings.

Chapter Seven

> We do not intend to defend our pictures. They make their own defense. We consider them clear statements. Your failure to dismiss or disparage them is prima facie evidence that they carry some communicative power.

The painters don't want to violate the self-sufficient integrity of their work. Yet, seeking "communicative power" with an audience, they don't want to be trapped in avant-garde purism either. So even as they refuse specific comments, they slip some helpful suggestions in; and pointing out how "easy" such interpretation is, they make Jewell look dumb. "We refuse to defend them not because we cannot," the statement continues.

> It is an easy matter to explain to the befuddled that "The Rape of Persephone" is a poetic expression of the essence of the myth; the presentation of the concept of seed and its earth with all its brutal implications; the impact of elemental truth. Would you have us present this abstract concept with all its complicated feelings by means of a boy and a girl lightly tripping?
>
> It is just as easy to explain "The Syrian Bull," as a new interpretation of an archaic image, involving unprecedented distortions. Since art is timeless, the significant rendition of a symbol, no matter how archaic, has as full validity today as the archaic symbol had then. Or is the one 3000 years old truer?

In their nondefense of their pictures, Rothko and Gottlieb suggest some of the artistic aims informing their myth paintings; they also reveal some crucial problems raised by their project. Looking for an expression that is "poetic" rather than literal, Rothko and Gottlieb want to convey not the *story* of Persephone's abduction by Pluto but the "essence" (or what Rothko called the "Spirit") of the myth. It is as if the two painters wished to reduce mythic narratives to their core moment—the way Rothko had "essentialized" the story of his early family life or the story of his emigration in the frozen, symbolic moments of *The Rothkowitz Family* and *Street Scene*. Those paintings had evoked archaic private experience; now, Rothko and Gottlieb seek the *racially* archaic, what is therefore "elemental" and "timeless." And just as Rothko's constructions of his personal past hinted at parental dominance and coercion, so the essentially human, during these years of World War II, remains the "brutal" truth of Persephone's rape or the sacrificial slaying of the Syrian bull.

So, on the one hand, Rothko and Gottlieb search for an elemental plastic expression that is pre-narrative, pre-civilization, pre-conscious, even pre-verbal—beyond explanation or defense. Yet, the language of the primal in human experience is an *abstract* language, of a "concept," an "abstract concept," providing "a new *interpretation* of an archaic image," as if modern consciousness were fated to be always at one remove from its primal origins. Similarly, under modern conditions the archaic image must be *newly* interpreted, suffer "unprecedented distortions," as if the "timeless" *were* historical. After all, primitive artists did not engage in polemical debates in the daily newspaper.

After Rothko and Gottlieb question whether the 3,000-year-old image might be "truer," Jewell breaks in: "Well, up to this point it seemed as if we might be going to get somewhere on a concrete basis." But as if they sensed themselves about to lapse into just the kind of explanation Jewell wants, the two painters sternly pull back.

> But these easy program notes can help only the simple-minded. No possible set of notes can explain our paintings. Their explanation must come out of a consummated experience between picture and onlooker. The appreciation of art is a true marriage of minds. And in art, as in marriage, lack of consumation is ground for annulment.

So viewing pictures constitutes a physical, even erotic experience, and only someone who has surrendered to the painting can talk about it with authority. Still,

> the point at issue, it seems to us, is not an "explanation" of the paintings, but whether the intrinsic ideas carried within the frames of these pictures have significance.
>
> We feel that our pictures demonstrate our aesthetic beliefs, some of which we, therefore, list:
>
> 1. To us art is an adventure into an unknown world, which can be explored only by those willing to take the risks.
>
> 2. This world of the imagination is fancy-free and violently opposed to common sense.
>
> 3. It is our function as artists to make the spectator see the world our way—not his way.
>
> 4. We favor the simple expression of the complex thought. We are for the large shape because it has the impact of the unequivocal. We wish to reassert the picture plane. We are for flat forms because they destroy illusion and reveal truth.
>
> 5. It is a widely accepted notion among painters that it does not matter what one paints as long as it is well painted. This is the essence of academicism. There is no such thing as good painting about nothing. We assert that the subject is crucial and only that subject-matter is valid

which is tragic and timeless. That is why we profess spiritual kinship with primitive and archaic art.

Withholding program notes, Rothko and Gottlieb are still willing to articulate the enabling assumptions behind their paintings. The first two of these—that "art is an adventure into an unknown world" and that "the imagination is fancy-free"—derive from Surrealism's identification of the artist as risk-taking genius, freed from mimesis of external reality, from social and aesthetic conventions, from audience expectations.

Yet in a way characteristic at least of Rothko, having separated the painter and his audience, the statement reconnects them, though in a relation that is more antagonistic than erotic, more coercive than seductive. Not absolutely "free," the imagination is "violently *opposed* to common sense"; the artist forces "the spectator [to] see the world *our* way—not his way." In this "consummated experience," the artist is an aggressor who remains on top. Freeing the viewer, controlling the viewer: this ambivalence will shape Rothko's approaches to his audience for many years to come. Here, as if communicative power could be achieved only by the most basic of means, he and Gottlieb favor simplicity, the "unequivocal" "impact" of the "large shape."

If they first align themselves with Surrealism, however, the two men then associate themselves with the modern abstract tradition that had begun with Cubism: "We are for flat forms because they destroy illusion and reveal truth," an allegiance realized in the grids of Gottlieb and the rectangular compartments of Rothko, both of which flattened the painting's space. Like many New York artists of their generation, Rothko and Gottlieb wanted to wed Surrealism with abstraction, in order to legitimatize themselves as the new and independent American offspring of these European opposites. So, as soon as they acknowledge their roots in modern abstraction, they insist upon their dissension—by differentiating themselves from academicism and modern formalism, both of which value accomplished technique over subject-matter. "We assert that the subject is crucial and only that subject matter is valid which is tragic and timeless." Rothko and Gottlieb had begun by ebulliently affirming art as "an adventure into an unknown world" that is "fancy-free." But they close with a somber assertion that art confronts us, directly and unequivocally, with the brutal and basic human truths of pain and aggression that are the "essence" of myth.

"Consequently," the statement concludes,

> if our work embodies these beliefs, it must insult anyone who is spiritually attuned to interior decoration; pictures for the home; pictures for over the mantle; pictures of the American scene; social pictures; purity in art;

prize-winning potboilers; the National Academy, the Whitney Academy, the Corn Belt Academy; buckeyes; trite tripe; etc.[37]

Professing "spiritual kinship with primitive and archaic art," Rothko and Gottlieb "insult" not just such targets as the American Regionalists and the Social Realists, but just about anyone then in New York who might buy, sell, review, show, or make a painting—except, that is, for the members of what Rothko would call, a few years later, "the small band of Myth Makers who have emerged here during the war."[38]

In the history of avant-garde manifestos, the Rothko-Gottlieb letter to Jewell hardly emerges as the most radical or destructive. Yet Jewell's response reveals how conservative and provincial an art center New York was in 1943. Treating their statement as a time bomb too intricate to be dismantled, Jewell warned his readers that the letter "had best not be picked to pieces, especially by the simple-minded, for it might explode." Two weeks later, he was still kicking sand over the bomb, printing letters supporting his contention that paintings and manifesto alike were unintelligible. Rothko and Gottlieb were discovering that readers, like viewers, were not easily compelled to view things *our* way.

Still, however Jewell might try to contain their provocations, Rothko and Gottlieb had finally succeeded in stirring a public controversy. By no means stand-offish with artists' organizations, both men, former members of The Ten, belonged in 1943 to American Modern Artists, New York Artist-Painters, and the Federation of Modern Painters and Sculptors, where both, as members of the Cultural Committee, had been major participants in the group's active campaign of protest letters. With the letter to Jewell, they transformed an attack on their work into an occasion for theory and promotion—for theory *as* promotion—and they did so not in the back pages of a little magazine like *VVV* but by gaining half the space on the Sunday art page of the *Times*. Unlike "The Ten: Whitney Dissenters," the "globalism" debate drew significant public attention to two forty-year-old, unknown painters, whose new work risked alienating them even further from an audience they did not yet have.

· · ·

When Rothko spoke in 1946 of his "small band of Myth Makers," he was referring, in addition to himself and Adolph Gottlieb, to William Baziotes, Jackson Pollock, Richard Pousette-Dart, Theodoros Stamos, Clyfford Still, and Barnett Newman. Newman in fact had been a silent collaborator on the letter to the *Times,* silent because his own work had not been attacked, but a collaborator because he was a skillful polemicist who was now a close friend of both Gottlieb and Rothko. Gottlieb had met Newman in 1922, when Newman was a high school senior taking courses at the Art Students League and Gottlieb was (in Newman's words) a "romantic figure . . . already a dedicated artist" who had just returned from his European trip.[39] Rothko did not meet Newman until 1936, at a wedding breakfast given by Gottlieb for Newman and his new wife, Annalee.[40]

Two years younger than Rothko and Gottlieb, Newman, whose parents had emigrated from Lomza, Poland, soon after their marriage, had grown up rather comfortably in a northern section of the Bronx that, in his boyhood, was still rural.[41] Newman's father, after starting out by selling sewing machines to garment district workers, had built a lucrative business manufacturing men's clothing; Newman's mother, the daughter of an affluent, cultivated family, "enjoyed music, literature and the arts."[42] As a boy, Newman enjoyed sports, symphonies, opera; he studied piano. But from the time he could grasp a pencil, Newman most enjoyed drawing. Later, as a student at De Witt Clinton High School, "I consistently played hookey from school to spend my days" at the Metropolitan Museum of Art.[43] He decided to become a painter and took a drawing class at the Art Students League. But when Newman announced his preference for art school over college, his father, "a strong, self-reliant man with a military bearing," resisted, citing the economic uncertainties of art. At a similar turning point, Gottlieb had quit high school, Rothko had quit Yale; Newman went to City College.[44]

Beginning there in 1923, Newman during the next four years developed a range of literary, philosophical, and political interests. Like the young Rothko in Portland, Newman became (and remained) a political anarchist, believing anarchism "the only criticism of society which is not a technique for the seizure and transfer of power by one group against another."[45] During his freshman year at CCNY, Newman also studied at the Art Students League, and throughout his undergraduate years he continued to visit the Metropolitan Museum and the New York galleries, often with Gottlieb. While taking a philosophy class, he organized a class trip to visit the Barnes collection near Philadelphia, only to discover that admission was limited to students at the Barnes school. "He was astounded to find that he and the class were refused permission to see the famous Renoirs, Cézannes, Picassos and Matisses. A rich man claimed them as private property and denied access to them." Angry, Newman wrote a polemic—which led him to discover, he later said, "what a painting is . . . that it's something more than an object."[46]

At graduation from CCNY, Newman was seemingly free to pursue painting, except that his father now insisted that he accumulate some capital by working as a partner in the family business for two years. But just before those two years ended, the stock market collapsed, as did the family business. Men's clothing, it turned out, provided little more economic security than painting. When his father refused to declare bankruptcy, Newman ran the business until his father's heart attack in 1937 finally forced its liquidation. Rothko had been outraged by his brief stints in the Weinstein clothing enterprises; Newman—perforce "an expert in materials, cutting, fitting, marketing"—managed such a business for eight years.[47] But since the firm was no longer very profitable, and since he refused the WPA as a dole—like his father refusing to declare bankruptcy—Newman also worked during the thirties as a substitute art teacher in the public school system.

Newman did, however, combine his business responsibilities with some bohemian flamboyance. "What is particular about Anarchism," he held, "is not its criticism of society but the creative way of life it offers that makes all programmatic doctrine impossible."[48] In 1933 he ran against Fiorello La Guardia for mayor of New York City, issuing a manifesto "On the Need for Political Action by Men of Culture," which urged the creation of city departments of clean air and water, the closing of all parks to cars, free music and art schools, a municipal opera, a municipal art gallery, shutting down some streets to allow for open-air cafés, etc.[49] Newman's "men of culture," unlike those at the Barnes Foundation, embodied a utopian vision imagining the integration of the arts with a humanized urban environment. Somehow, Newman did find time to paint during the thirties; and he participated in the evening sketch classes that Rothko and Gottlieb attended at Milton Avery's apartment. But as soon as Newman completed a painting, he destroyed it, as if his fierce artistic conscience, when not combating enemies with manifestos, mercilessly turned against Newman himself. It was around 1940 that he told Adolph Gottlieb that "painting is finished; we should give it up," and then gave it up himself—for about four years.

Theoretically at least, modernism had freed art from moral or, in some versions, *any* content. But "there is no such thing as good painting about nothing." Newman spoke not of an aesthetic but of a "moral crisis," just as Rothko later insisted that, in his ostensibly empty canvases, "my preoccupations are primarily moral."[50] During the Second World War, Newman felt obliged to decide not *how* to paint—i.e., figurative or abstract—but *what* to paint, if a painting were to be something more than an aesthetic object. Until he could solve that problem, Newman, an anarchist in politics whose artistic conscience was absolutist, refused to paint anything.

Around 1940–41 Rothko may have stopped painting to investigate myth. At just that time, Newman turned from painting to natural science, studying botany, geology, and, especially, ornithology. He took courses at the Brooklyn Botanical Garden, spent his 1940 vacation at the Audubon Nature Camp in Maine, and took Cornell summer-session courses in botany and ornithology. With his wife, Annalee, Newman became a enthusiastic bird-watcher, an activity with which it is *very* difficult to associate the restless, chain-smoking Rothko. Refusing romantic enjoyment of nature as a world of physical sensation, Newman closely scrutinized the natural world, "to investigate the beginnings of life, how it emerged, how its orders developed,"—and that was an activity with which it would become increasingly possible to associate Rothko and Gottlieb's explorations of archaic myth.[51] By the early 1940s, as Rothko was writing his treatise on the teaching of children's art, Newman was publishing polemical essays and writing equally polemical unpublished "monologues," as if conducting an underground military campaign on behalf of a kind of painting he himself could not yet begin to produce. Combining his own moral fervor with the political rhetoric of the home front in "What About Isolationist Art?" Newman annihilated American regionalism by identifying it with isolationism, which, "we have learned by now, is Hitlerism."[52]

But Newman was even more disturbed by a European cultivation which he believed had betrayed painting for the Beautiful. In "The Plasmic Image," Newman writes like an austere New England preacher warning a slipping congregation against the "sensuous," yea, even "voluptuous art" of the Continent. American art is a kind of paternal business enterprise; European art, a beautiful and cultivated but corrupting woman. Not limiting himself to provincial attacks on the provincialism of the regionalists, Newman assessed Mondrian, then living and widely admired in New York, as if this unknown and not even practicing New York painter and the European master were on equal footing. "In his fanatic purism," his insistence "that subject matter must be eliminated," Mondrian has reduced painting to the "decorative," the beautiful object, Newman asserts.[53]

At the same time that the Federation of Modern Painters and Sculptors was formulating a theory of the aesthetic, Newman, like Rothko, was trying to formulate a theory for something *beyond* the aesthetic. "It was the Greeks who invented the idea of beauty," Newman contends in "The New Sense of Fate," widening his campaign beyond modern geometric abstraction to include the entire Western art tradition. Yet Newman must begin as a self-conscious, twentieth-century cultural relativist: "we now know because of our wider knowledge of comparative art forms that the notion of beauty is a fiction." Clearly a reader of *The Birth of Tragedy*, like his friend Rothko, Newman in "The New Sense of Fate" transforms Nietzsche's Apollo/Dionysus dialectic into a hierarchical opposition between an effete Greek visual art and a more vigorous primitive tradition. Before the Greeks, a work of art "was a visible symbol of hieratic thought. Art was an attempt to evoke the metaphysical experience."[54]

The Greeks admired and sought such an art, but their "pride of civilization" (the Greeks too were nationalists) "prevented them from understanding the barbarian's totemic fanaticism." Whereas the Egyptian gods symbolized the "abstract mysteries involved, for example, in their attempt to comprehend death," the Greek gods "had to be not only mysterious forces but also ideal sensations," "objects of beauty," "things to admire rather than objects of worship." Limited to the concrete, Greek art degenerated into an art of "the pure shape," as if the Greeks were already Mondrian. So the Greeks understood tragedy as showing man's inability to predict or control the social consequences of his acts, contrasting with the "Egyptian notion that each man is his own tragic entity and that the nature of his being is in inevitable death."[55] In Egypt, tragedy was ontological; in Greece, it was social.

But now hieratic thinking and metaphysical evocations are returning in the work of a new movement, a loose cluster of New York painters in whom "the break with Western European traditions is complete." Acknowledging the new painters' debt to abstract and surrealist art, Newman still insists on their independence from these movements, with which they might be—and were being—confused. For the new painters cannot accept either the dream world of Surrealism or the geometric forms of pure abstraction. They exemplify what Newman calls "subjective abstraction," distinguishing it from the exploration of private feeling in Expressionism. "Subjective abstraction" is concerned not with "personality," but "with the penetration into the world mystery."[56] Art is a romantic quest, and a uniquely male quest, as if Newman were saying to his contemporaries, "well, fellas, we're going to have to gird up our loins, send our wives out to work, and penetrate the world mystery."

Lest this quest sound *too* romantic and pleasurable, Newman warns that the new art "is a religious art which through symbols will catch the basic truth of life which is its sense of tragedy." The new American art, moreover, is "creating forms which by their abstract nature carry some abstract intellectual content." "Art is an expression of the mind first," Newman asserts, "and whatever sensuous elements are involved are incidental to that expression." Newman was announcing a painting, like his own future work, that would seek to "transcend the plastic elements in art."[57]

Here, Newman and Rothko parted company, since Rothko, whose future paintings *would* be beautiful, sometimes voluptuously so, sought to balance the sensuous and the metaphysical. But in composing their letter to the *Times* Rothko and Gottlieb were thus working with an old and like-minded friend who was a skillful polemicist then formulating for himself a mythicized history of a painting movement just beginning to evolve. The collaboration has generated some territorial disputes about who contributed what to the final text. Mrs. Newman believes her husband was the primary author, pointing out that Rothko and Gottlieb, grateful for Newman's help, gave him the two works—*The Syrian Bull* and *The Rape of Persephone*—that Jewell had attacked.[58] Gottlieb, saying that Rothko supplied only the point advocating a "tragic and timeless" subject matter for art, claimed to have written the rest of the letter.[59] Rothko stated that "neither he nor Gottlieb wrote" the letter, implying that Newman did.[60] Yet the surviving drafts in Rothko's handwriting reveal his significant role in the evolution of the document.[61]

• • •

"I am neither the first nor the last compelled irretrievably with the chimeras that seem the most profound message of our time," Rothko declares in one of several draft pages written in the first person, suggesting that at first he and Gottlieb were responding separately to Jewell.[62] In this somewhat theatrical and inflated style, Rothko's letter mounts a theoretical defense of those modern painters who "have distorted the present to conform with the forms of Niveneh, the Nile or the Mesopotamian plane [sic]." Like Newman, Rothko acknowledges a remote, anonymous primitive ancestry, in order to play down his dependence on the European tradition while also reinventing the primitive in his own image. With an implied dig at Picasso, Rothko points out that it is not merely the "formal aspects of archaic art" which engage the contemporary artist, who, rather, feels "a spiritual kinship with the emotions which these archaic forms imprison and the myths which they represent." "Too unremunerative to be an affectation," modern distortion, in one of Rothko's drafts, "jolts, moves, instigates to new discoveries," as if violation of nature were needed to affect a dulled modern audience. In another draft, the artist distorts his "models" until he awakens "the traces of their archaic prototypes," as if violation of nature were a means of conjuring archetypes.

Either way, the artist does not choose, but is *fated*, to distort. In a painting like *The Omen of the Eagle* Rothko explores his own aggressive impulses. But in his letter to Jewell, filled with words like "inevitably," "unavoidably," "necessary," and "compelled irretrievably," aggression derives from historical necessity, with the artist burdened to expose "the unpredictability which lay under man's seemingly ascending reason," "the potentiality for carnage which we know too well today." Curiously, Rothko's determinism affects only "the most gifted painters," since there are still artists who "confound sunset and long shadows, and the melancholy aspects of the times of day" with "the tragic."

The viewing public, denouncing the work of the gifted few as "ugly, savage, and unreal," has understandably "resented this spiritual mirroring of itself." Yet condemning this art as "illogical and unreasonable is about as effective as railing at the complete materialism of our every day life," a remark which reveals how much of Rothko's notion of the tragic has absorbed his political disillusionment. Indeed, it is the artist's tragic fate—dramatized in Rothko's grandiloquent language—to reflect modernity in those "ugly," "barbaric," and "unremunerative" works to which the public reacts "so violently."

At some point Rothko and Gottlieb decided on a joint response in which they would declare their "aesthetic beliefs" in a list of brief, challenging statements. The three surviving pages of Rothko's drafts for this document show him trying out assertions, characteristically veering back and forth between more daring and safer positions. At one point he boldly asserts: "We deny that the world has any objective appearance. The world is what the artist makes it." But then he qualifies the first of these two sentences with an insertion: "we deny that *for the world of art* the world has any objective appearance," and then, as if recoiling from his own caution, he defiantly shifts into hyperbole: "we deny that for art the world of objective appearance has any precedence over the world of hallucinations."

As in *The Syrian Bull,* Rothko wants to assert the artist as a transcendental subjectivity whose visions have priority over "objective appearance." On one of the draft pages, he begins to formulate his own list of shared aesthetic principles with a series of stern negations aimed at freeing the painter from external physical or social constraints:

1. We deny that the world has any objective appearance, the world is what the artist makes it.
2. And in this world the eye [is only an element of the totality of experience] has no precedence over feelings and thoughts.
3. And reason has no precedence over unreason, the paradox, hyperbole, hallucination, etc.[63]

After leaving a large blank space, Rothko adds another negation, no. 6: "A picture is not its color, its form, or its anecdote, but an intent entity idea whose implications transcend any of these parts"—the side of Rothko which shared Newman's desire to create "forms which by their abstract nature carry some abstract intellectual content." Both artists, impatient with mediation, are looking for a painting that goes beyond painting, toward speculative thought.

On another page, Rothko supplies the missing entries in his list and adds one more:

4. We liked the virulence of the reaction, whether in praise or disdain, because to us it was a proof that the picture struck home.

5. It does not displease us if these pillars of culture to whom only the familiar is acceptable are repelled by our works. Art is justified by its adventuring into unknown lands which can be transversed only by those who are willing to take the risks.

7. All of these are [stem from] false values (whose resemblance to art is solely coincidental which never have nor ever can produce art) and which serve only those who would confuse art with popular art.

As it turns out, even for artists whose inner visions transcend both external reality and common sense, painting is a social act, like writing a joint letter to the art critic of the *New York Times*. The letter, in fact, attempts to create a favorable social context for the reception of experimental art. Rothko's own letter had stressed his "spiritual kinship" with primitive art in order to convey his own vision of the gifted artist as tragic victim. In Rothko's later drafts for the collaborative letter, primitive art drops out and he appeals to a notion of the artist as romantic genius whose "adventuring into unknown lands" provokes a revulsion from the pillars of bourgeois culture which the artist sardonically rises above by assuring himself that his picture has "struck home." Rothko's own letter turns fatalistic in relating art to the "carnage" of the war, whereas his list of aesthetic principles emphasizes individual freedom in art's eternal battle with "false values." By 1943, avant-garde rhetoric of emancipation had become sufficiently familiar—and useful in shaming philistines—to be chosen as the most effective means toward gaining social acceptance for advanced art in the Sunday *Times*.

Never a cohesive movement, Abstract Expressionism existed in the mid-1940s as several small clusters of painters, one of which consisted of Rothko, Gottlieb, and Newman, all of whom were products of the Jewish immigrant experience in America. None of them was particularly religious. All three were secular, urban, emancipated American Jews whose lives radically differed from those led, say, by their European grandfathers. All three chose culture over business, in spite of family pressures toward middle-class security. All three also combined a strong sense of social injustice with a skepticism about political change and ideological solutions. All three chose art, then a particularly insecure profession in America and one in which they, as Jews, were "aliens." Being painters marked them as social outsiders in America; and being Jewish marked them as social outsiders in painting—one reason they looked to primitive art as an alternative to the Western tradition. All three—smart, verbal, socially gregarious, with broad intellectual interests—were "men of culture" who were very actively involved in the business of promoting their work. Art offered them an alternative to traditional Jewish piety, to Jewish dissident politics, and to American materialism; art meant freedom.

Yet, though they sometimes made statements that sounded like endorsements of the modernist belief in the autonomy of art, they viewed austerely, with great suspicion, the merely aesthetic or the merely sensual, as if freedom were a condition not to be enjoyed but to be suffered. To their scrupulous consciences, art had to be something more than a beautiful object. Locating its origins in ritual, myth, and religion, they wanted an art that was "tragic and timeless." Art meant freedom; art meant pain, as if for these Jewish-American painters the very means of emancipation from their ethnic origins had to reflect the tragic suffering of the Jewish past—and, in 1943, the Jewish present.

. . .

Jews have hurt me the most.

Mark Rothko

Mark Rothko told Bernard Malamud, among many others, his version of the end of his first marriage: "One night he told us how he had left his first wife. He had gone off for an army physical during World War II and they had turned him down. When he arrived home and told his wife he was 4-F he didn't like the look that flitted across her face. The next day he went to see his lawyer about a divorce."[64] In this narrative, Rothko, chagrined at Edith's affront to his manhood, divorced her. Like many of Rothko's stories, this one, literally false, contains a kernel of emotional truth: in his divorce, as in his marriage, Rothko felt that his manhood was at issue.

On October 4, 1943, his old friend Lou Harris served a legal complaint on Rothko, then sharing a flat with the painter Boris Margo at 22 West 52nd Street.[65] Edith had filed for divorce, charging that Rothko, the month before, while living in a Washington Place rooming house, had committed adultery. Edith herself was now living at 71 Washington Square, her business located at 36 East 21st Street.[66]

The "Action for Absolute Divorce" was heard on January 3, 1944, before a referee at Manhattan's County Court house. Edith testified only briefly, revealing that she and Rothko had been separated since June of 1943. She was followed by Lou Harris and a book dealer named Benjamin Shaw. According to Harris, he was having a drink with Rothko in his room on September 12 when Rothko asked him to leave because he was expecting someone; Harris left, then called Edith, who had asked him to look out for possible infidelities by her husband, and related what had happened. The referee took a dim view of Harris's actions, and even his profession:

Referee: Were you with him when he picked up the girl, or what?
Witness: No, I was at his room, and he suggested that I leave, that he expected some one.
Referee: Then you, a friend, go and tell his wife—is that part of your profession as an artist to do such things?
Witness: You see, sir—
Referee: As an artist you are not much of a gentleman.
Witness: I thought I was being a gentleman.
Referee: You did—to testify against your friend—I don't know what code or country you found out that was being a gentleman.
Witness: It was this way—
Referee: Are you getting paid for it by any chance?

Harris went on to testify that after he met Edith and Shaw in a Village cafeteria, the three of them proceeded to Rothko's room, knocked on the door and were told Rothko was too "busy" to let them in. When Shaw announced "Well, it is urgent, I want to see you about something," Rothko opened the door slightly and all three pushed their way in to discover Rothko in a bathrobe and a woman, undressed, in his bed. Shaw's testimony supported Harris's story. Rothko, not contesting the divorce, did not appear in court, and the divorce was granted on February 1, 1944.

Rothko created one fiction about his divorce; the legal system created another, as the referee, asking Harris if he had been paid for his testimony, rightly suspected. Harris and Shaw were telling the narrative of adultery one had to tell, in New York City in the 1940s, to be divorced. If, as some of his early forties paintings imply, Rothko felt that living with Edith created an uncomfortable fusion of male and female, then splitting with her was a painful process which tore him apart. To Hedda Sterne, Rothko compared separating from Edith with pulling the skin from his cheek: "it was so painful." Rothko, given to hypochondriacal imaginings—in the 1930s, according to Sally Avery, "he thought he had cancer and signed himself into a hospital for three weeks for tests"—now checked himself into a Manhattan hospital where Adolph Gottlieb and Howard Baumbach visited him. In Baumbach's view, Rothko experienced a "serious breakdown" at the end of his marriage.[67]

For a brief period after the breakup, Rothko stayed with Jack Kufeld, a friend from The Ten, with whom he shared an hotel apartment on West 74th Street.[68] Then Rothko characteristically responded to injury by withdrawal: he left New York and went home, first visiting his family in Portland, then traveling to the Bay Area where, in Berkeley, he met Clyfford Still, and then to Los Angeles, where he saw his cousin Arthur Gage and where he also visited Louis Kaufman, the Portlander who had introduced him to Milton Avery.[69] The Kaufmans took Rothko to visit Walter Arensberg's well-known collection of modern art. In early October Avery wrote Kaufman that "Marcus reported very extensively about his visit to you. Did he say anything about his break up with Edith? . . . She has a divorce and he has taken a place on 52nd Street." In fact, Rothko had brought up his divorce, about which he was "bitter": "he felt that Edith was interested in money and said that he was a failure. I think that really galled him," Annette Kaufman recalled. By November Avery was reporting to Kaufman that "Marcus seems to be bearing up very well."[70] Still, Rothko complained to Sally Avery that being married to Edith had been "like living with a refrigerator," as if the divorce had freed him to express his own dissatisfactions with the marriage.

Sometime after his return to New York that fall, Edith visited Rothko in his 52nd Street apartment, "looked around and said, 'This is the kind of thing I took you out of.' That hurt him deeply."[71] Rothko—"the loneliest man I ever knew"—was once again on his own, sharing a small midtown flat with another painter, supporting himself with his small salary from Center Academy and by the very occasional sale of a painting. It was as if he had been "transplanted" back to the late 1920s and were starting all over again.

Yet around this time Rothko wrote to his sister Sonia that "my new household is about complete. I have managed by going to auctions to equip myself nicely with little money, and all in all I have the best home for my needs I have ever had. It is handsome, comfortable, and above all I like to spend my time in it." As a new bachelor "my social life is quite heavy, and during this period of readjustment, I consider it very good, tho' a pitiful waste of time. I am working again and leading a fairly normal life." Rothko goes on to report that "things between Edith and me are completely cleaned up. The financial settlement has been completed and divorce proceedings started. The whole process was very messy, but it was lucky that it was so, for it has made it certain that we will not get together again." Rothko had been "transplanted" into a kind of painful freedom.

"And so," he concludes, "here at the age of 40 I am on the brink of a new life. It is both exciting and sad, but I regret nothing about it. The last thing in the world I would wish would be to return to the old one."[72]

8 "A New Life"

There is a moment of blinding light. There is a moment that seems like death, a paralysis. Then a new man, Paul, emerges from the experience. Rothko, the most famous example, changed his name, his wife and his style in a few months of profound self-questioning.

Thomas Hess

So goes the myth of a "complete break."

Rothko's own way of narrating his life, as a series of dramatic moments of self-transformation, both shaped and reflected what became the "official" biographical account of him and his generation.[1]

In reality, Rothko changed his name in 1940, was divorced by his first wife in 1944, married his second wife in the spring of 1945, and he altered his style slowly, rather cautiously, in the ten years between 1939 and 1949.

. . .

This new year of 1945 can be the greatest year in human history.
Franklin D. Roosevelt, State of the Union Message, 1945

While in Los Angeles during the summer of 1943, Rothko visited his cousin Arthur Gage, a Hollywood agent then married to Sophie Rosenstein, a Hollywood drama coach. For many years after his own venture into acting, Rothko enjoyed being with people in the theater, and he was "very friendly" with Sophie Rosenstein, whose students included the actress Ruth Ford. That summer, Buffie Johnson, a young American painter whom the war had forced back to the United States from Paris, was visiting Ruth Ford. Sophie Rosenstein "asked Ruth if she could bring over her nephew, Mark Rothko."[2]

Buffie Johnson was "sick of meeting people's nephews that paint" so she arranged to have her hair done during Rothko's visit. But he was still there when she returned. "Well, in a few minutes of talking with him, I realized he was a very interesting man, with an excellent mind." She asked Rothko what sort of work he did. "From his shirt pocket—he'd taken off his jacket—he took out a little spiral notebook, just the size of a vest pocket, and began showing me these watercolors." "I've been visiting up and down the coast with my relatives," he said. "I did these things on my travels." The small watercolors, "surrealist" in style, impressed Buffie Johnson with their "originality" and their "beautiful color."

Did Rothko have a gallery? she wanted to know. He did not. "The only place I feel these really belong is Peggy Guggenheim's gallery," said Buffie Johnson, who had known Guggenheim in Paris. When Johnson and Rothko were both back in New York, she arranged for him to meet Peggy Guggenheim's advisor, Howard Putzel. During its first year, Art of This Century had mainly shown European Surrealists. But after Peggy Guggenheim separated from Max Ernst and Putzel replaced Duchamp as her advisor, the gallery turned to young Americans, beginning with Jackson Pollock's show in November of 1943. Art of This Century was now providing what the Museum of Modern Art did not: a prestigious avant-garde museum-gallery willing to show unrecognized American painters.

Putzel admired Rothko's work; Rothko admired Putzel, believing "that while Peggy Guggenheim had her interests scattered in many directions, none of them particularly intense, Putzel's commitment to his [Rothko's] work was so serious that it got a great deal of his time and attention." In fact, Peggy Guggenheim had to be tricked into giving some time and attention to Rothko's painting. "I don't know who this man is; I never heard of him. I really don't have time" to look at his pictures, she said. But Putzel "was convinced that she would accept" Rothko's work "if she saw it. He therefore gave a party and hung Rothko's paintings on the walls. Guggenheim came to the party, saw the paintings, and accepted Rothko into her gallery."[3] In the spring of 1944 Rothko participated in "First Exhibition in America of Twenty Paintings," one of three young Americans (along with Pollock and Motherwell) shown alongside such European masters as Picasso, Braque, Léger, Mondrian, and Miró. From January 9 to February 4, 1945, Rothko held his first one-man exhibit at Art of This Century, showing fifteen oil paintings and some gouaches.

"Marcus is getting in the swim. He is having a show at the Guggenheim next season and he seems to be happy," Milton Avery had written to Louis Kaufman in June 1944.[4] As the exhibit neared, Rothko was putting pressure on himself. "My exhibition opens on January 9th," Rothko wrote to Sonia that November, "and I am painting feverishly not because I need the pictures but because I hope by miracles to outdo myself (as if one can). In addition, I am framing my own pictures, seeing loads of people, going miserably into debt, because it takes money to put up a show right. I hope to sell enough to cover that expense. Such is my life." To his sister, Rothko presents himself as hard-working, hard-pressed, yet ambitious and firmly optimistic: "I have however made powerful friends for my work in the last year"—presumably Putzel and Guggenheim—"and my chances are good for finding an important place for myself in the art-life of our times."[5]

By the beginning of 1945 eventual Allied victory in the Second World War was certain. As Franklin Roosevelt said in his State of the Union message, "We have no question of the ultimate victory. We have no question of the cost. Our losses will be heavy." Everyone's losses would be heavy, as its final eight months proved the most savage in this "total war." German V1 and V2 rocket attacks on Britain continued. In February, American and British planes firebombed Dresden. That month American carpet bombing of Tokyo and other Japanese cities began, as did the battles of Corregidor and Iwo Jima. On Easter, April 1, the 82-day battle of Okinawa began, to end in the deaths of 70,000 Japanese, 10,000 Americans and 80,000 Okinawans. Japanese kamikaze attacks intensified, now supplemented by a new weapon, a piloted bomb. In Europe, as the Allied lines advanced toward and into Germany, many thousands of Jews and other prisoners, already weak and sick, were evacuated from the Nazi slave-labor camps by the SS and forced onto what became death marches. That April, firsthand reports of the Holocaust began to reach the United States. In May, Germany surrendered, as did Japan in August, after American atomic bombs were dropped on Hiroshima and Nagasaki. Such was the greatest year in human history.

For Mark Rothko in New York, however, the winter and spring of 1945 were a professional and personal high point. In addition to his Art of This Century exhibit, Rothko participated in two controversial shows; and on March 31, in Linden, New Jersey, he married Mary Alice ("Mell") Beistle. Both "A Painting Prophecy—1950," at the David Porter Gallery in Washington, D.C., in February, and "A Problem for Critics," at Howard Putzel's 67 Gallery in June–July, asserted the existence of a new movement, synthesizing abstraction and surrealism, among younger American painters, and challenged critics to "name" this new venture. That Porter and Putzel, both dealers, were quite eager to "discover" and label a *movement* suggests that gallery operators, like art historians but for different reasons, have a vested interest in establishing brand names for their products. Porter, describing the new work as "a unique blending of Romantic and Abstract painting," offered no name, but Putzel, proposing a solution to the "problem for critics" he had invented, offered "metamorphism," stressing the importance of Picasso, Arp, and Miró—given their own wall in his show—as "forerunners."[6]

"I believe we see real American painting beginning now," Putzel declared.[7] At the Museum of Modern Art, European modernism dominated. At Art of This Century, the three permanent galleries exhibited European moderns. And even at the 67 Gallery of Howard Putzel, the Americans were legitimatized as the descendants of Picasso, Miró, and Arp. No longer grateful just to be invited in out of the cold, or elated just to be hung alongside an acknowledged master like Picasso, the Americans were now beginning to assert their independence, the more so because of their real debts to European modernism.

Rothko's "Personal Statement" for the David Porter exhibit opened by announcing, "I adhere to the material reality of the world and the substance of things." Adopting a different position from his drafts for the Jewell letter, Rothko now grants "equal existence" to mental and physical worlds. "If I have faltered in the use of familiar objects," he writes, "it is because I refuse to mutilate their appearance for the sake of an action which they are too old to serve; or, for which, perhaps, they had never been intended." His tone defensive, as if responding to accusations (or self-accusations) of a removal from reality in his work, Rothko asserts his faith in an external world as precisely what differentiates him from those surrealist and abstract artists who, like parents, provided the "roots" from which he has now grown "completely independent."[8]

In the Sunday *Times* for July 1, Edward Alden Jewell, again trying to stir up controversy, took up Putzel's "problem for critics," printing Putzel's brochure for the exhibition, photographs of two works in the exhibit (a painting by Picasso and a watercolor by Rothko), plus a supplementary statement by Putzel which argued that, whereas the Cubists worked from reality toward abstraction, the new American painters start with "a kind of automatism" and work toward reality. Jewell wondered—rightly—how anyone looking at a picture could tell whether the artist had worked toward or away from reality, and commented that "it would be very interesting to learn just what the artists concerned have to say about all this."[9] The following Sunday, one of the concerned artists did respond—Mark Rothko, who converted his refutation of Putzel into another occasion for declaring his independence from European modernism.

Resemblance to "natural appearance"—an issue in Cubist painting and purist abstraction—is *not* a problem that engages Rothko and his contemporaries, who "are in a sense mythmakers and as such have no prejudices either for or against reality." Stressing modern European "forerunners," Putzel played down the new painting's relation to "totemic images, earliest Mediterranean art and other archaic material." In both their letter to Jewell and their WNYC radio dialogue, Rothko and Gottlieb emphasized their "spiritual kinship" with primitive art, art that gave their work a legitimating authority that was outside of and prior to the *entire* Western art tradition, not just modernism.

"If there are resemblances between archaic forms and our own symbols,"

Rothko argues in his letter to the *Times*, "it is not because we are consciously derived from them but rather because we are concerned with similar states of consciousness and relationship to the world." Such resemblances result not from influence but from the "parallel condition" in which the primitive and the modern American create, a condition which, for Rothko, combines freedom with terror and drives the artist inward. So, Rothko, in closing his letter, now separates himself from modernist abstraction not by way of his adherence to "material reality" but by way of his adherence to subjective reality: "If previous abstractions paralleled the scientific and objective preoccupations of our times, ours are finding a pictorial equivalent for man's new knowledge and consciousness of his more complex inner self."[10]

Rothko customarily greeted friends with the question, "How's business?" He had rejected business and the professions as a young man; his later paintings would lean toward atmospheric spaces, spiritual transcendence, and monastic solitude. Yet Rothko's attachment to material reality was strong enough to engage him with advancing his career: "I'm not crazy like van Gogh." When Rothko spotted Emily Genauer of the *New York World Telegram* at his Art of This Century show, he wrote to her that he "was keenly disappointed not to read your opinion of it on Saturday." "Should you be able to find the space for it on some subsequent Saturday, it would make me very happy."[11] All during the 1940s, through his work with the Cultural Committee of the federation, his collaborations with Gottlieb, and his own writings, Rothko sought to draw favorable publicity and sympathetic attention to his work, the better to find an important place for himself in the art-life of our times. If in 1959 he would refuse the hanging of his murals in the Four Seasons restaurant, in the mid-1940s he was happy to have a painting hung for a week in a window at the Bonwit-Teller store.[12]

"I am sending you the copies of the Times you must have missed," Rothko wrote to Barnett Newman shortly after the "Problem for Critics" episode. "As you will see, the corpse was never much alive and is quite laid out by now."[13] Professionally, the high point for Rothko in the first half of 1945 was his show at Art of This Century. At his first solo exhibit in more than a dozen years, Rothko, hanging pictures, from *The Sacrifice of Iphigenia* (1942) to *Slow Swirl at the Edge of the Sea* (1944), provided a brief review of his recent experiments in mythmaking.[14] The show, widely and quite favorably reviewed, did not have the critical impact of Pollock's November 1943 exhibit at the gallery, but it did establish Rothko's place as an important figure in his generation of painters. In fact, Rothko the outsider had now entered a privileged inner circle from which others were being excluded. "During the time when Mark was with Peggy, that group that was with Peggy felt superior to everybody else," Esther

Gottlieb remembered.[15] In immediate material terms, however, the Art of This Century show was no success. Having gone "miserably into debt" hoping that sales would cover his expenses, Rothko sold only three works, valued at $265. Peggy Guggenheim, who bought one work from each of her one-man exhibits, purchased one of the three, *Slow Swirl at the Edge of the Sea*.[16]

Approximately 6' high and 7' wide, *Slow Swirl* (color plate 12) was the largest, most ambitious, and in Rothko's view the "most important" work he had so far attempted.[17] It is also his most festive. Against a softly luminous, pale tan atmosphere, two large, not quite fully evolved human figures slowly swirl upward from a brownish sea, toward a rosy dawn sky. The imprisoning walls of Rothko's rooms and subway stations, the oppressive weight of his blocky nudes—these constitute later social and physical stages of human development which isolate and frustrate. In this painting, human and animal, male and female, inside and outside—before at odds in Rothko's work—coexist in a buoyant rhythm of blending and separating.

At first, the green figure on the left—more distinct and further evolved, the object of the gaze of the more primitive figure on the right—holds our attention, its three-cornered hat, spinning necklace, busty upper body giving this faceless creature a female, perhaps a bridal, look. A white/pink/black/blue shape at the breast could be a decorative pattern on a fancy dress—or it could be an inner organ, her intricate, solid, and self-enclosed core. But whether clothing or skin, her very thin covering is transparent, as if her body, not yet fully incarnate, existed as a rising, weightless, hour-glass shape. Below, two green legs merge into a single tiny green foot, which, repeated in blue, then white, passes beneath the low horizon line and becomes a bony, primeval paw.

To the left of her necklace two green lines begin to curve downward. One fades into the tan/white background; the other echoes the contours of the body, then thins out. At the lower thigh a new line splits off, slopes down, forming a wide tan leg. Along the other side of the figure, a dark green area, lightly painted over, extends down to the right, creating the shadowy hint of another leg. Which of these lines defines the boundaries of this elusive figure? Along her left shoulder the light green paint passes across the contour line and continues outside the body. In this emergent world, where colors are sometimes contained by shapes and sometimes not, drawing and painting can exist independently of each other. At her squeezed-in waist, two thick green lines curve in, then out—then stop, leaving the upper body's form open at the bottom. Throughout the painting, contour lines are multiple, broken, discontinuous; the body has not been *torn* open, as in *Untitled* (c. 1940), but, still in the process of assuming form, remains partially, and happily, merged with sea and air. As human life swirls up from its watery origins, boundaries, marking the difference between the human and the natural, figure and ground, inside and outside, have yet to be sharply defined.

Gazing toward the bosom of the female figure, out of two large blank eyes in a skull-like head, the figure on the right, with enormous, bulging shoulders, suggests a grinning prehistoric muscle-man on the beach. Yet his skull is transparent, as are his shoulders, which float weightlessly, while the remainder of his body consists of a series of hovering circular, sometimes saclike shapes, culminating not in legs and feet but in the tail of a sea animal. With parts that are even less clearly distinguished from the surrounding elements and less securely attached to each other, this expansive, loosely unified figure seems a still earlier form of humanity than its more socialized partner.

So far, I have been referring to the figure on the left as female, the one on the right as male. But Anna Chave in her *Mark Rothko, Subjects in Abstraction* reads the left figure as a leaping male dancer in "extravagant costume" and the right one as a female with "oversized," "pendulant breasts bouncing away" from her sides.[18] Certainly, in this painting about birth (or rebirth) the bulbous form at the waist of this figure, containing swirling blue water, suggests a womb, in which the primal sea has been absorbed into the human body and preserved as its creative source. Possibly, the left figure is male, the right female. Possibly, both are female. Possibly, the left is female, the right an admiring, wide-eyed, young man. Yet the point is finally that these open-formed, transparent figures, both of whom strongly resemble prehistoric animals below the waist, and neither of whom possesses specifically sexual organs, are too elusive to fix with *any* sexual identity, as if something had enabled Rothko to reach back to an early stage of psychic life that preceded sexual difference.

During the thirties and early forties, Rothko, despite his expressionist sincerities, conceived of art as a kind of mastery. The painter aggressively looks inside, fixes the essence of his subject and renders it through distortions of natural appearance. When he looked, what Rothko often found was the separation that prompted his aggression, and he painted symbolic family scenes or urban tableaux which exposed the emotional distance within the physical proximity of domestic or city life. Obsessively, the unhappily married Rothko gazed at the female body, often drawing or painting thick, heavy-set nudes whose bodies more resembled that of his mother than that of his trim wife. More oppressive than erotic, certainly not idealized, these removed, melancholy women are subjects which Rothko seeks to master in his work, as if their bulky bodies held the secrets to union and creativity. Yet the secret, for Rothko, lay within the "complex inner self," to which automatism was now giving the painter more and more access.

In *Slow Swirl,* it is not just that the two main forms are incomplete. All through this work, thin layers of paint allow earlier shapes and colors to show through, Rothko letting us look inside his painting of emergence to see its errors and corrections, its own slow process of creation. Painting is no longer about fixing the essence of a person—say, a *Sculptress*—in some suggestively arrested moment. In fact, one reading of *Slow Swirl*—as representing a muscle-bound youth gazing, wide-eyed and clownishly, at the breasts of a faceless, glamorously dressed woman whose hour-glass figure is just as exaggerated as his muscles—playfully mocks the appropriative male gaze. And that is only one out of a multiplicity of possible readings of the painting; for both selves and paintings now *are* fields of possibility—an effect conveyed not by a Cubist technique of rendering several views of one head, as in *The Omen of the Eagle* and *Untitled* (c. 1940), but by the creation of protean, indeterminate shapes whose multiplicity is let be. Creating a field in which forms can emerge from and commingle with a warm, luminous environment, painting moves away from mastery.

"I have created a new type of unity; a new method of achieving unity," Rothko would claim in 1953.[19] In *The Omen of the Eagle* unity had been thrust upon Rothko's grotesque mythical beast in the form of four strict rectangular compartments. In *Slow Swirl at the Edge of the Sea,* a ghostly, partial version of such a grid persists, mostly in the middle left of the painting. In the 1930s, a more deliberate Rothko had used such grids to "scale up" (or enlarge) drawings into paintings. In the early 1940s, his rectangular compartments rigidly contained dangerous imaginary beasts. But by *Slow Swirl,* the archaic was no longer felt as instinctual aggression, though the painting does contain its own suggestions of danger, especially in the animal-like lower sections of the two main figures. In *The Syrian Bull,* violence generated new life; here, the generation of new life holds a potential violence. Yet Rothko's need to hold off, and hold in, by strict geometric means, has relaxed even as his forms grow fluid and indeterminate.

Geometrical pattern still exerts a presence in *Slow Swirl,* as, for example, the fullness of the green figure is squeezed in just where the ruled, hard-edged lines of the grid meet it at the neck and the waist. It is as if the shape of this emergent human body conformed as much to abstract geometrical patterns as to the laws of nature—and as if the artist needed at least the fragment of an abstract structure to contain his gyrating human figures. Yet the grid *is* incomplete, a scaffolding fading into the background, and it does not—like the rectangles in Rothko's frieze paintings—sever the figures. *Slow Swirl* is filled with incomplete circles, triangles, rectangles, many of which serve no referential function. Other shapes suggest human forms less evolved than the two dominant figures. But rather than creating a tension between abstract form and natural instinct, as he had in *The Omen of the Eagle,* Rothko here allows geometric and organic to commingle in a new and fertile unity.

Imposing in size, frontal in presentation, elated in feeling, *Slow Swirl* creates a sense of mobility within a shallow space, flattened by the partial grid. Both of the human figures enter the brown rectangle beneath the low horizon line as if rooted there. Yet bony clubfeet and spiny tail are not secured to the horizon, as are the rear hoofs of the Syrian bull; the sea, though painted in earth tones, offers not a ground in which to root but a flowing, supportive medium, from which human forms buoyantly emerge. Rothko's watercolor beach scenes of the early thirties had been inhabited by lonely spectators, passive and dreamy. Now, once again at the edge of the sea, Rothko paints two figures, not yet quite people, who happily gyrate. In this painting, Rothko evokes an existence prior to the physical and emotional damage, the self-division and unease he represented in his *Self-Portrait,* and that existence has everything to do with *movement*—which is to say, freedom. Rothko's shifting, ambiguous contours, the concentric circles at the waists of the two main figures, the whirling necklace, the floating body parts—all convey a world in process. Beginning his search for a "new type of unity," Rothko has made this, his largest canvas to date, into a field within which his fluid, open forms—rather than being locked to an edge or stabilized on a pedestal—have been freed to evolve in a watery world that is hospitable to them and from which they derive.

In June 1946, Peggy Guggenheim, having loaned *Slow Swirl at the Edge of the Sea* to the San Francisco Museum of Modern Art several months before, gave the painting to the museum. In the fall of 1962 Rothko exchanged a much more valuable painting, *Untitled* (1960), for *Slow Swirl,* which he then gave to his wife, Mell, and which thereafter hung in their living room, playfully referred to as "Mell Ecstatic."[20] "She watched him paint it and she sort of felt that it was dedicated to her, whatever the figures were supposed to represent," Kate Rothko said. "It was the first painting she felt she had participated in." To Rothko in the early 1960s, by then living comfortably but not blissfully in his 95th Street town house, *Slow Swirl* evoked the ebullient early days of his courtship.

Often, during this time, Rothko would suddenly exclaim in the middle of a conversation, "Isn't she the most marvelous thing you ever looked at?"[21] Botticelli's *The Birth of Venus* had been exhibited in a controversial show of "Italian Masters" at the Museum of Modern Art in 1940.[22] *Slow Swirl,* too, depicts the birth of Venus, but not by showing the nude, fleshy goddess of beauty standing on a seashell, blown to the shore by wind gods and greeted

Chapter Eight

by a cloak-bearing nymph. Instead, Rothko has gone back to beauty's *birth,* her slow evolutionary ascent from the primal flux, through animal existence, toward a gaily dressed, physically ample yet ethereal life.

. . .

I was a foreigner and she made an American out of me.

Mark Rothko

I think Mark thought Mell was his Venus.

Juliette Hays

Venus sprang, miraculously, from the sea-foam near Cyprus; Mary Alice ("Mell") Beistle had been born, from Aldarilla Beistle, on January 3, 1922, in Cleveland, Ohio. Mell's mother, formerly Aldarilla Shipley, descended from an English family that had emigrated to Baltimore before 1700, then moved westward first to Pennsylvania and then to Ohio; her father had worked in the insurance business.[23] Mell's father, Morton James Beistle, descended from German farmers who had emigrated to the United States in the 1830s, started west, but settled in northeastern Ohio when their covered wagon broke down; his father served in the Civil War. As an adolescent, Morton Beistle left the family farm for Cleveland, went to high school at night and worked during the day. Aldarilla Shipley wanted to be a writer and, after graduating from high school, lived in New York City for a year. Morton Beistle was poor, rural, uneducated; Aldarilla Shipley was affluent, urban, literary.

The two met in 1915, fell in love, were separated during the four years Morton Beistle served in the Army Corps of Engineers in World War I, and were married, after his discharge, in July 1919. After the war, Morton Beistle started what grew into a successful business, a road construction company, Allied Products Corporation. By family rumor he was remotely related to Abraham Lincoln; Aldarilla Shipley descended from Lord Baltimore. Unlike Edith Sachar, and Mark Rothko, Mary Alice Beistle—WASP, midwestern, and middle-class—was solidly American.

Her brother, Robert Morton, had been born in 1920 and her two younger sisters, Barbara and Shirley, were born in 1924 and 1928. The family lived a pleasant, upper-middle-class life in suburban Cleveland Heights, where Mell Beistle attended Fairfax Elementary School, Rocksboro Junior High School, and Cleveland Heights High School. Aldarilla Beistle, who "had always wanted to write," had lived a year in New York, but "New York was a pretty wild and wicked place as far as families in Ohio were concerned in 1914," so her family persuaded her to return to the tranquilities of Cleveland. Once her four children reached school age, however, she began writing and adapting works for children's productions done, first, by Players on Wheels and, later, the Cleveland Public Playhouse; she also had a children's program on a local radio station. Mell Beistle had been interested in art "right from the beginning." Unlike her mother, "she was encouraged," especially *by* her mother, and she took classes at the Cleveland Art Institute. As a prize for an elementary-school art contest, she won a copy of *The Graphic Bible,* with drawings by Marcus Rothkowitz.

Like her mother, Mell was interested in writing and the theater. At Cleveland Heights High School, she helped found and became editor of the school literary magazine, *Crest;* she also belonged to the Literary, Art, and Motion Picture Appreciation Clubs.[24] When she was a junior, sixteen years old, she and her mother produced the first of five collaborative children's books, with texts by Aldarilla and illustrations by Mell Beistle. "My mother wrote the books strictly in cooperation with Mell so the two of them could work together," Mell's sister Shirley recalled. The first, *Mr. Heinie,* published by David McKay in 1938, tells of Mell's dachshund who, though small and suburban, caught grasshoppers and butterflies and thought himself a mighty hunter—until he was stung by a bee; this cautionary tale urges domesticity, the path chosen by Aldarilla Beistle and later by her oldest daughter. These books, all skillfully illustrated, continued to appear through Mell's years in college.[25]

Mell Beistle wanted to attend the Cleveland Institute of Art. Her father, a "very conservative and very rigid" man who "had very set ideas on where it was proper for women to go to school," wanted her to attend college. "Mell had a very close relation with her mother, a very difficult relation with her father—resentful of him because of his insisting that she go to college," according to one friend. Morton Beistle prevailed and his oldest daughter went to Skidmore, a small women's college in Saratoga Springs, an upstate New York town twenty miles south of the Lake George camping ground where Rothko had met Edith Sachar.

In September 1939, as the Second World War was beginning, Mary Alice Beistle entered college. "*Day One:* We were snatched away from the station, piled three deep in taxis, and deposited green and wondering into our Advisor's hands who initiated us into the minor mysteries of dorms and dinner."[26]

No socialist experiment like Commonwealth College, the Skidmore of the early 1940s was affluent and highly social, with freshman hazing and dorm parties, dances and dates, cokes and burgers at the local pharmacy, Christmas

Vespers and ski weekends, bike rides and tennis games, tea with the president, picnics at the Spa.

But freed to pursue interests like her mother's by going to the kind of college chosen by her father, Mell Beistle, in the words of her classmate, "blossomed." Having chosen Skidmore because of its well-known art department, Mell worked at oil painting, watercolors, and clay sculpture; to help support herself, she worked for the art department, matting and framing work for student shows. She majored in fine and applied arts.

Her friend Ruth Moran remembered that Mell's next interest, after art, was men. Though they were scarce during the war, Mell had "lots of boyfriends," including an affair with a professor who taught her sculpture class. During her junior year, she was engaged to Vernon Trevor Patey, a member of the Royal Canadian Air Force who, Mell learned during her last year, was shot down and killed in the war. As a junior, Mell had been elected president of her class. As a senior, she was a member of the executive board, the judicial board and the honor board; she was art editor of the school literary magazine, *Profile*; and she was president of student government. A full-page picture in her senior yearbook identifies her as one of the "Big Three" in her graduating class.[27] The young Mary Alice Beistle was neither social outsider nor alienated artist.

In June 1943, as Mark Rothko and Edith Sachar were finally separating and Rothko exhibiting his *Syrian Bull*, Mell Beistle graduated from Skidmore and returned to Cleveland, because her father had died, suddenly, that April. Wanting "to be home until she saw how mother and everyone was doing," she worked as a draftsman at the Parker Appliance Company for about nine months. "She just detested it," her sister Shirley recalled. Having already spent one high-school and one or two college summers in New York living with the family of her publisher's printer, Mell now "desperately wanted to go to New York because that's where the action was." Her mother encouraged her to leave. In the spring of 1944 Mell Beistle moved to New York, living alone in a one-room apartment at 21 Jones Street in Greenwich Village.[28] She cooked on a hotplate behind a screen, washed her dishes in the bathroom sink, and dried them in the tub. As one of her sisters observed, "I think my mother probably looked at Mell and thought, 'Oh, you are doing what I always wanted to do'."

During the war, jobs illustrating children's books were hard to find. Instead, Mell worked for McFadden Publications, which did pulp magazines such as *True Confessions* and *True Stories*. She produced sketches, which were used to pose models who were then photographed to illustrate the stories. "I don't think she particularly liked it," said her sister Shirley. "I think it was a good job. She still had that job when she met Mark." Instead of acting out her mother's unfulfilled ambitions, or her own, Mell Beistle continued this commercial work and followed her mother into marriage. "My mother," said Kate Rothko, "used to go around saying that she had decided by college that she was going to move to New York and marry an artist." She moved quickly. Home for Christmas of 1944, Mell told Shirley that she had "met this marvelous Russian." The two had met at an artists' party to which Mell had been brought by the photographer Aaron Siskind, with whom she worked.[29] The following spring, at noon on March 31, Mary Alice Beistle, wearing a gray hat and a gray silk suit with violets pinned to it, married Mark Rothko in the chambers of a Judge Schwartz in Linden, New Jersey.[30]

"Marriage is an impossible situation for an artist to engage in," Rothko had pronounced at the end of his first marriage, telling one friend he was "through with it."[31] Yet for this artist, who remarried just six months after his divorce became final, marriage was an impossible situation *not* to engage in. "The life of a bachelor is not nearly as ordered as that of a married man," Rothko complained in a letter to his mother early in 1944. "There are many more demands on you socially. You are called constantly to go here and there," he says, as if invitations could not be turned down; or, as if, speaking to his mother, he preferred to think of himself as a victim of social pressures rather than as a forty-one-year-old bachelor enjoying a new social (and sexual) freedom that was enabling him to have concurrent relationships with three or four women.[32] But "I suppose I shall tire of that soon," he adds to his mother, speaking of his social comings and goings with a weary (and affected) self-detachment.

Several months later, writing to his sister, Rothko notes that until "several months ago" his personal life had been "quite shifting and I took care to keep it so." Recently, "I have more or less settled to a more normal life with a very young woman who has meant a good deal to me, but not enough I believe to build the rest of my life on." So he will "have to move on—a thought which makes me sad." His new life, he tells Sonia, "has been very good for me. My world has become infinitely enlarged, and I do not believe that many of the things which have happened would have been possible had I not kept myself free to move about wherever I wished." Marriage offers regularity; freedom offers a stimulating mobility. "For the security of my former life, I paid with a certain dulling of the senses and energies; for what I have now I pay with a sense of insecurity." The "solution," he concludes, "is to find a mate who can provide the security and also keep your sensations and movement alive, for which I hope and look for very hard, believe me."[33] This avant-garde artist, ideally, would rely on the security of a middle-class marriage to launch his imaginative ventures into unknown worlds.

"He was very happy in those early days when he married Mell. She was a young attractive woman and that of course fed his ego."[34] Rothko had been nine years older than Edith; he was nineteen years older than Mell. Or: Mell was just four years older than Edith had been when she married Rothko, as if his "new life" required obliterating his old one, so that he could relive it, this time right—and, since "Jews have hurt me the most," this time *goy*. Like Edith, Mell was young and beautiful; and like Edith, she worked as a commercial artist. But rather than making demands on his time, Mell helped to free Rothko from obligations. By June of 1946, he was able to leave the part-time job at Center Academy he had held since 1929.[35] Ideally, wives were young, marvelous to look at, supported the family, managed the household, and adulated their husband, the Artist.

Edith is remembered as "chilly." "Mell was warm—she was the opposite of Edith that way."[36] Edith tired of bean soup and wished for a more bourgeois life. One of the women Rothko pursued after his divorce commented, "I'd just come back from Europe and a very glamorous year, and I certainly wasn't interested in a railroad flat with a starving artist."[37] Mell had grown up in a comfortably middle-class home, but willingly adjusted to a frugal style of life. "And she did have confidence in what he was doing and was ready to adapt to the circumstances as they were. She had a flair about her—handsome and also she would make places where they lived very attractive and evidently sustained him very much."[38] During their courtship, Rothko had given Mell a copy of Kafka's *The Trial*, as if to say, "Whatever romantic ideas you may have about my Russianness, or my Jewishness, or the life of an artist, this novel will tell you what my life has *really* been like."[39]

Mell's brother had died in a trucking accident while working for his father's firm; her father died of a heart attack; and her fiancé was killed in the war: all died suddenly during the time she was in college. Mell confided to Ruth Moran that she had a terror of going to sleep and not waking up again because of these sudden deaths. "It was a real obsession that loomed over her terribly." Her losses, her apprehensions, her insomnia—all of these connected the outwardly cheerful and hard-working Mell Rothko with a husband who liked to think of himself as a "supreme pessimist."[40] Rothko differed from Mell's earlier boyfriends: they were younger and better-looking. She told Ruth Moran that she was not romantically enthralled with Rothko, but because he took such pleasure in their relationship, it gave her a vicarious pleasure. Besides, she believed "he was a genius."

Rothko's first wife hurt him very much; his second sustained him very much. Still a bit green and wondering—"a country bumpkin," according to some of Rothko's more hard-eyed New York friends—"she looked up to him."[41] All through their marriage, Mell always called her husband "Rothko," as if she had married a myth, not a man. According to her friend Elizabeth Morrow, "Mell almost hero-worshipped him." According to his friend Stanley Kunitz, "Mark was a kind of divinity to her." A few days after they met, Rothko called to ask for a date and was told she already had one. "He was so angry and so upset about it. He said, 'Oh no, you are not going on any date'."[42] His young, beautiful, innocent bride from the midwest would provide the material security and emotional warmth that enabled her somber, touchy, Russian-Jewish husband to feel more at home in America, while keeping his "sensations and movement alive."

In his new marriage, Rothko was the dominant figure, and having attained a kind of mastery in his personal life, Rothko was now freer to explore ways of surrendering it in his work.

• • •

Clyfford Still's vision liberated him.

Hedda Sterne

We were complete opposites. He was a big man. He would sit like a Buddha, chain-smoking. We came from different sides of the world. He was thoroughly immersed in Jewish culture. But we had grown up only a few hundred miles apart. We had read many of the same things. And we could walk through the park together and talk about anything.

Clyfford Still

While on the west coast in the summer of 1943, Rothko had met Clyfford Still at the home, in Berkeley, California, of Earle Blew, a musicologist. They had a drink, spoke just briefly, and did not discuss painting.[43] "When, two years later, he heard I was in New York, Rothko insisted on seeing some of my paintings," Still wrote. "I continued postponing an invitation for him to visit me. One evening he came to my studio uninvited. After seeing some of the canvases I had stretched, he became visibly excited and asked permission to tell Peggy Guggenheim about them."[44] Still's narrative depicts Rothko as a kind of eager, almost pushy admirer with strong involvements in the art market, while Still himself remains an unmoved mover, aloof both from admiration and self-advancement. The events he describes are not related, as they could have been, to suggest Rothko's generosity; nor does Still anywhere suggest that Rothko had any effect on *him*. But Still was writing many years after he had judged Rothko too "practical" in his dealings with the market and, with Jehovah-like finality, had terminated their friendship.[45]

A full depiction of their relationship must wait until their correspondence and Still's diary are made available, something that won't happen, according to Mrs. Still, "for many years."[46] All of our present knowledge of Still's life relies either on interviews with him or on chronologies in art catalogues that were assembled by Still himself, whose struggle to control his artistic fate led him to operate not only as his own curator but also as his own biographer. Like Rothko, Still mythologized his life; but whereas Rothko viewed his life as a series of cruel impositions that provoked dramatic acts of rebellion, Still related his past as if he had always held the ethic of absolute self-reliance that he arrived at in the early 1940s. In this verbal self-portrait, Clyfford Still emerges as a craggy pioneer and solitary Old Testament prophet seeking individual freedom in a modern world of Kafkaesque threat and intrigue. His widow has perpetuated her husband's mythologizing by refusing access to his papers. Yet the myth *is* revelatory, since it rewrites Still's life into an idealized form in which the man perfectly coheres with his mature works. Many of Still's letters, moreover, are in public collections; several of his friends and students have been willing to talk; and they provide some supplement to Still's own accounts.

Rothko "needed companionship desperately," according to Stanley Kunitz. "He needed comfort, encouragement, consolation all the time." Still was no comforter or consoler, but he did offer Rothko needed encouragement, and during the late 1940s the two men were, in the words of Ernest Briggs, one of their former students, "very tight and a tremendous stimulus to each other."[47] As a result of Rothko's intervention with Peggy Guggenheim, Still was given a one-man exhibit at Art of This Century in February of 1946, for which Rothko wrote the catalogue essay, praising Still's "unprecedented forms and completely personal methods."[48] By the time of his show, however, Still was living in Alberta, Canada; that fall he began four years of teaching at the California School of Fine Arts in San Francisco. About Rothko's summer 1946 exhibit at the San Francisco Museum of Art, Still wrote to Betty Parsons, "By the way, Mark Rothko's show went over in the strongest way out here. It was without question the best show I have ever seen in the gallery for years and it commanded the highest respect from those out here who know good work when they see it."[49]

Rothko visited San Francisco on a west coast trip that fall, and again when he himself taught at the California School of Fine Arts in the summers of 1947 and 1949. Of Still's 1947 show at the California Palace of the Legion of Honor, Rothko raved to Parsons that "Still's show has left us breathless both my students and everyone else I have met."⁵⁰ That September, at the Federation of Modern Painters and Sculptors annual exhibit, each member presented a work by a nonmember. Rothko presented Still's *Apostate*.⁵¹ Still spent the summer of 1948 in New York, involved with Rothko, Robert Motherwell, David Hare, and William Baziotes in forming an art school to be called "The Subjects of the Artist," a project from which Still withdrew to return to the California School of Fine Arts, from which, in turn, he withdrew in 1950 to return to New York City. During Rothko's 1949 visit to San Francisco, Still loaned Rothko his *1948–49-W No. 1*—a 92″ × 71″ black painting that hung in Rothko's bedroom, like a massive, tough, grim conscience, for the next six years, until Still demanded it back.⁵²

Having seen Rothko's "Recent Paintings" at Betty Parsons in April 1951, Still declared them "the work of a very great man and I do not use the term with abandon. I consider myself one of the specially favored to know and to perceive this power and to have seen and I think understood its genesis and development." Still also felt obliged, however, to distinguish himself from Rothko's "more vocal admirers and incorporators." "To stand beside and work with real greatness is not a common privilege," he pronounced. "To try to own it, kill it by explanation or analysis, is the most common of pastimes."⁵³ In his self-congratulatory way, Still viewed himself and Rothko as embattled geniuses involved in a life-and-death struggle with painting, yet freely standing beside each other as supportive equals rather than trying, like the "common" lot, to "own" or appropriate the other.

In the long run Rothko proved to be a little *too* other. But between 1947 and 1950, as Rothko, a cautious and self-doubting painter, entered a period of sustained and bold experimentation, Still, whose painting had already advanced into abstraction and whose character was, in the words of Earle Blew, "supremely confident," provided the stimulation and encouragement that Rothko needed.⁵⁴ Rothko "told me that Clyff had been a tremendous influence in his thinking and in giving him courage," said Katharine Kuh. "He gave Mark the freedom to be himself or to be something even better than himself."⁵⁵

"Rothko was far more personable and outgoingly warm toward others," said their mutual friend Clay Spohn. "But at the same time there was a feeling of futility in his thinking. He used to speak of life as a tragic comedy." "Still had a contempt for the general run of people, since he felt most of them were stupid fools," whereas Rothko "desired respect and recognition of the fact that he was a loveable guy. Still only loved his ideals and his objective."⁵⁶ According to Ernest Briggs, a student at the California School of Fine Arts, Rothko "could talk endlessly and very brilliantly and poetically and metaphorically and mysteriously." He was "the epitome of the New York Jewish intellectual artist/painter

Chapter Eight

and exuded an entirely different kind of energy, urbane, deep intent, quintessential New Yorker" as opposed to Still's "austere puritan almost Calvinist manner."[57] Indeed, so different were the two in personality and background that it seems less surprising that their relationship eventually broke off than that it grew so close to begin with.

Still had been born November 30, 1904, not in a Latvian railroad junction like Dvinsk or even a midwestern city like Cleveland, but in the northern American plains, in Grandin, North Dakota. When he was still an infant, his family moved to Spokane, Washington, where his father worked as an accountant. But in 1910—the year Jacob Rothkowitz came to the United States—Still's father moved to southern Alberta, Canada, to homestead, and Still grew up moving back and forth between this subsistence prairie farm and the home his family had kept in Spokane. "My arms have been bloody to the elbows shucking wheat," Still bragged.[58] Rothko narrated his childhood with images of Jewish victimization, Cossacks lashing him with whips; Still related his childhood with images of pioneer hardship. And if Rothko loved to be horizontal, Still asserted a rugged verticality: "when there were snowstorms, you either stood up and lived or laid down and died."[59] When, instead of snowstorms, Still later grappled with old masters, modern masters, museum bureaucracies, greedy dealers—the social and cultural institutions surrounding art—he sternly called for "the vertical rather than the horizontal; the single projection, instead of polarities; the thrust of the flame instead of the oscillation of the wave."[60] Verticality pushed upward from the flatland of common pastimes toward a triumphant freedom, or absolute mastery.

Still wished to give painting "the kind of vastness and depth of a Beethoven sonata or a Sophocles drama—the possibilities of humanity, of aspiration and joy and tragedy that they represent"; this was his version of Rothko's desire to "raise painting to the level of poignancy of music and poetry."[61] Like Rothko, Newman, and Gottlieb, Still pursued broad cultural and intellectual concerns in music (Beethoven), literature (Blake), and philosophy (Hume, Nietzsche, Hegel, Kant). Among painters, he early admired Rembrandt and Turner. Yet Still was a cultivated man whose fierce self-reliance eventually moved him to perceive the entire European tradition as "death itself."[62]

In the fall of 1925, when Rothko was studying the still life with Max Weber, Still visited New York for three months, signed up for one class at the Art Students League and left after forty-five minutes. In the west he had learned about painting through kitsch texts like *Masters Everyone Should Know* (found in the local "preacher's library") or by riding five miles on horseback to look at art magazines. But when he visited the Metropolitan Museum in New York— with whose collections Rothko, Newman, and Gottlieb were then becoming familiar—Still was repelled by the museum's use of paintings to illustrate schools, its display of objects used "to glorify popes and kings or decorate the walls of rich men."[63] As the Barnes Foundation had for Newman, the Metropolitan revealed to Still the dangers of appropriation. Rather than write a polemic, Still chose provincial solitude in the American west and returned to Spokane.

"You become accustomed to being alone," Still said, "without the feeling of loneliness," a discipline that the restlessly gregarious Rothko would never learn. After attending Spokane University for one year, Still went to Alberta, Canada, for the next four years, working alone. He returned to Spokane University in 1931, graduating in 1933. From 1933 to 1941 he taught art at Washington State College in Pullman, continuing to paint. "For me all *places* are temporary," Still later declared. "I've created a world of emancipation for myself."[64] He often called his painting an "instrument," metaphorizing it as a knife. So Still, who later applied his paints with a palette knife, spoke of "the blade of my identity" or of "cutting through all cultural opiates, past and present, so that a direct, immediate, and truly free vision could be achieved."[65] For Still, as for Rothko, painting, no mere aesthetic activity, became a human "instrument" aggressively clearing a space for personal emancipation.

"Turner painted the sea, but the prairie to me was just as grand," Still said.[66] Clyfford Still began, in the late 1920s and early 1930s, not as an artistic outsider but as an American regionalist. *Row of Elevators* (1928–29) suggests that by Still's time the western plain, supporting shacks, fences, telephone lines, wagons, trucks, railroad cars, grain elevators, and a few small, anonymous human figures, had been reduced to scrubby yellow fields, shallow, muddy ponds, and devastated tree stumps.[67]

Still had not crossed Turner with Benton to produce a nostalgic celebration of the vast grandeur of the prairie. Yet, viewed from a vantage point very close to the ground, set dramatically against a thickly painted, heavily clouded white sky, the looming vertical presences of the elevators, five flat monumental slabs, assert a kind of lonely and primordial grandeur that Still would later find not in industry but in the psyche. During the summers of 1934 and 1935 he painted at Yaddo, a colony for writers, musicians, and artists in Saratoga Springs, New York. He there decided, "more or less deliberately, to begin again."[68]

Still was required not just to abandon American-Scene painting, but to make a completely fresh start: "I realized I would have to paint my way out of the classical European heritage." In relation to the tyrannical decadence of Europe, Clyfford Still was Barnett Newman in extremis. "I have not 'worked over' the imagery or gimmicks of the past, whether Realist, Surrealist, Expressionist, Bauhaus, Impressionist, or what you choose," Still asserted. "I went back to my own idioms, envisioned, created and thought through."⁶⁹ Clyfford Still was self-created.

Yet, in 1935 Still received a Master of Fine Arts degree from Washington State. According to the "Biographical Chronology" in *Clyfford Still*, "A master's degree in 1935 was a required concomitant of the hours spent in the school: he did not work for the degree."⁷⁰ Yet Still did manage to write an M.A. thesis, "Cézanne, A Study in Evaluation." Its thirty-four densely argued pages do not so much show Still rejecting the authority of Europe as creating a Cézanne with whom he can strongly identify and yet can finally exceed. "In his every move," Still writes, "we see the maladjustment of the crude, groping Provincial brought face to face with facile and urbane gentlemen," as if Cézanne were a North Dakotan confronting New York City's 57th Street. Still himself had moved back and forth between cosmopolitan centers (New York, San Francisco) and provincial retreats (Spokane, Alberta, Pullman); Cézanne retired to his estate in the south of France and there, "avoiding and avoided by painters and townspeople alike, he pursued the lonely and isolated way."⁷¹

"Cézanne has been called the father of modern art," Still writes, doubting "that the master would claim or even recognize his offspring." "Cubists, Vorticists, Chromists, Surrealists," Still says, all "emphasize technical factors" and are thus "derivations, not continuations" of Cézanne. But Still himself attends to technical issues, stressing the way "Cézanne's grim, almost brutal earthiness demanded a strong structural base for his work." That base Cézanne found in his effort "to express form by means of color." "So did he try to realize form in color rather than make color look like form," Still writes, praising Cézanne's gift "for rhythmically synchronizing rugged volumes." With remarkable prescience, Still has separated Cézanne from his modernist offspring in order to make him the father of Still's later earthy, rugged development of color as form.⁷²

While Still was living in New York during the summer of 1945, among the paintings he showed Rothko were *1944-G* and *1945-H*, both of which establish that, at this time, Still's work was more advanced than Rothko's, as well as that of Rothko's closest artist friends, Gottlieb and Newman. Still had moved beyond Surrealism. Both of these Still paintings are large-scale works, completely nonfigurative, composed of immense, raw areas of dull somber colors, through which thin, jagged, lighter forms seem to crack.⁷³ At one time he called these shapes "life-lines"; at another, he stated that his "fluid, often flame-like vertical shapes have been influenced by the flatness of the Dakota plains; they are living forms springing from the ground."⁷⁴ Close up, these canvases, thickly and ruggedly painted, marked with the short, rapid strokes of Still's palette knife, push the viewer back, to a vantage point from which they expand into a lonely, cosmic boundlessness. With such work, "space and figure in my canvases had been resolved into a total psychic entity." "My feeling of freedom was now absolute and infinitely exhilarating." The surrealist idea of art as "an adventure into an unknown world" associated painting with imaginative freedom; but Still was pointing Rothko toward a new, and toward an American, conception of painting as a means (or "instrument") toward personal and social freedom, a space in which "the totality of my being can stand stripped of its cultural camouflage."[75] Painting, now a moral, psychic, and even metaphysical enterprise, expressed, or invented, a core being outside history and society.

Clyfford Still was American, Calvinist, western; Mark Rothko was Russian, Jewish, New York. Still, a sophisticated painter, sought provincial isolation; Rothko, another sophisticated painter, fled it. With most people, Still was contemptuous or at best aloof, Rothko warm and gregarious. Both artists had messianic ambitions for their work, though Rothko was more vulnerable to self-doubt. Both found ways of painting that went around their limitations as draftsmen, but Rothko's surfaces are seductive, translucent, atmospheric, thinly painted and sensitively edged, while Still's are hard, opaque, earthy, thickly painted and roughly edged. In the words of Elmer Bischoff, who knew both men at the California School of Fine Arts, Rothko "voiced the hope of breaking through solitude," whereas Still emphasized "the valiant and solitary stand the artist must take for the sake of his own integrity."[76] Rothko's paintings come out toward a viewer, Still's simply stand there, waiting to be taken on their own rigorous terms. Yet such differences in temperament and style freed these two men to affect each other's work in the mid to late forties, especially for the supremely confident Still to affect the more hesitant Rothko.

Some writers have seen specific shapes in Rothko works of the late 1940s that resemble shapes in Still.[77] Even more important, in the long term, Still encouraged Rothko to enlarge the scale of his work and to express form in large areas of color. While Rothko was teaching in San Francisco during the summer of 1947, Still's show at the California Palace of the Legion of Honor— the one that left Rothko and his students "breathless"—was negatively reviewed in the *San Francisco Chronicle,* and, in response, Rothko gathered some students and, Ernest Briggs recalled, "we had lunch together and he was agitated." Urging the students to write a letter of protest, Rothko talked "at length in a very passionate manner about how he thought we should be supportive of Still, and take a position and write a letter. And in that long two hour conversation, he indicated his debt and his great respect and his profound kind of feeling for Clyfford and his accomplishments." Rothko revealed "that he wouldn't have clarified his own ideas without their association," "that there was a direct influence on his attitudes" as his painting evolved, "and he was well aware that there was an inspiration from Still's big attitude of what painting can be" that gave Rothko "not his start, but gave him his confidence, perhaps his heart to put into it."[78]

"I await your arrival to announce the magnificent evil which our work must be to those who would suppress us," Still, in San Francisco, wrote to Rothko in April 1949.[79] Bonded in their freedom, and in their rage, these two demonic rebels imagined their works as weapons in a social struggle, aimed not at collective man but at the private psyches of individual viewers. Since for both Rothko and Still painting offered a means of personal emancipation, they closely identified with their works and became advocates of freedom who insisted on a great deal of personal control over the sale and exhibition of their work. Thus both men, according to Clay Spohn, were involved with "the politics of art, or how to beat the game, or who has control . . . in the presentation and marketing of one's art." Still referred to such activities as "guerrilla warfare."[80] So Still and Rothko ended up as two guerrillas who wished to convince the enemy to buy their weapons and hang them as wall decorations, and it was their differing ways of resolving this paradox—or Still's intolerance for Rothko's resolution—that eventually drove them to conduct their battles in different parts of the jungle, with Still occasionally sniping at his old cohort.

9 "An Art That Lives and Breathes"

I will say without reservations that from my view there can be no abstractions. Any shape or area which has not the pulsating concreteness of real flesh and bones, its vulnerability to pleasure or pain, is nothing at all. Any picture which does not provide the environment in which the breath of life can be drawn does not interest me.

Mark Rothko

At the end of the spring 1947 season, Art of This Century closed, Kiesler's avant-garde furniture was sold off, and, writes Peggy Guggenheim, "I left my collection in storage and flew to Europe with my two dogs," eventually settling herself, her collection, and her dogs in a palazzo along Venice's Grand Canal. Some of Guggenheim's artists, among them Rothko, had grown dissatisfied, perhaps because of slow sales, perhaps because of Guggenheim's inclusion of her daughter Pegeen, her ex-husband Lawrence Vail, her sister Hazel, and her friend Gypsy Rose Lee in Art of This Century shows. "The gallery became a plaything," said Ethel Baziotes. "The artists were uneasy."[1] Yet however uneasy they were with Peggy Guggenheim, her young American painters might well be uneasy without her. Art of This Century had made available to young painters an extensive collection of modern art, provided a social meeting ground, conferred prestige on young, unknown artists, and drew the attention of critics and museum officials, if not buyers.

Even before Peggy Guggenheim's departure, Rothko had hoped to join Howard Putzel's 67 Gallery, but Putzel died in the summer of 1945, "much to the regret of Adolph Gottlieb and Rothko," Milton Avery wrote, "as Putzel was pushing them and they expected to have 2 shows this coming season." But Rothko and his friends had not exactly been left out in the cold. True, the older uptown dealers who had taken up the European Surrealists—Pierre Matisse, Curt Valentin—backed off from the young Americans. "I must be going blind," Curt Valentin said. "I can't see them at all." Some of Peggy Guggenheim's painters, knowing her intention to return to Europe after the war, had already moved—as had Robert Motherwell and William Baziotes—to Samuel Kootz's new gallery. In 1944 Peggy Guggenheim had introduced Rothko to Betty Parsons; Barnett Newman, having met Parsons at about the same time at an Adolph and Esther Gottlieb dinner party, became her close friend and advisor. When Rothko, Newman, and Still decided they wished to go as a group, they signed on with Betty Parsons, whose gallery had opened at 15 East 57th Street in the fall of 1946. Parsons named these three painters, along with Jackson Pollock, her "Four Horsemen of the Apocalypse."[2]

In March 1947, Rothko held his first one-man exhibit at the Parsons Gallery. That November he signed a contract granting Parsons 33 percent of all sales through the gallery and 15 percent of any studio sales, making her responsible "for the promotion of the artist" and requiring him to obtain written permission for any exhibits outside her gallery. At forty-four, Rothko, painting for more than twenty years, had his first dealer. Parsons, who had done Rothko's watercolor show at Mortimer Brandt in the spring of 1946, gave him five annual one-man exhibits between 1947 and 1951, plus including him in "The Ideographic Picture" show curated by Barnett Newman in 1947.[3] In addition, Rothko, the former "Whitney Dissenter" who later refused to participate in the Whitney's 1952 Annual, declaring the museum a "junkshop," showed work in seven Whitney exhibits between 1945 and 1950.[4] And late in the summer of 1946 Rothko held his first one-man museum exhibit, at the San Francisco Museum of Modern Art, since the small showing of his and his students' works on paper at the Portland Museum of Art in 1933.[5]

So far as any viewer of Rothko's exhibitions between 1946 and 1948 could tell, he was still a Surrealist. In his March 1948, show at Betty Parsons Rothko presented *Phalanx of the Mind, Beginnings, Intimations of Chaos, Sacred Vessel, Dream Memory, Ceremonial Vessel, Aeolian Harp, Vernal Memory, Geologic Memory, Poised Elements, Gethsemane, Agitation of the Archaic, Dance,* and *Companionship and Solitude.* Some of these fourteen paintings *may* have been recent, but ten of them had been shown before, some having been done a couple of years earlier, with one—*Poised Elements*—being about four years old, having appeared in Rothko's Art of This Century show.[6] With his prices rising and his reputation growing, Rothko, in his painting, appeared to be treading water.[7]

Yet beginning in 1946, Rothko produced new paintings—they have become known as "Multiforms"—in which he attempted a series of bold and severe repudiations, seeking to purge from his work myth, symbol, landscape, figure, drawing of any kind, in order to paint in patches of hazy, luminous color.[8] "I have assumed for myself the problem of further concretizing my symbols," Rothko had written to Barnett Newman in the summer of 1945, a process, he added, that gives "me many headaches" but it also makes "work rather exhilarating. Unfortunately one can't think these things out with finality, but must endure a series of stumblings toward a clearer issue."[9] In the closing years of the 1940s, Rothko entered a period of intense, painful, yet exhilarated search, no longer trying to concretize his symbols but trying to concretize his *work* by eliminating symbols and realizing form through thinly painted areas of color that seemed to pulse with an inner life of their own.

"I am beginning to hate the life of a painter," Rothko dramatically announced in a letter to Clay Spohn in May 1948—not the first or the last such complaint from a man with a love/hate relation to his vocation. "One begins by sparring with his insides with one leg still in the normal world," he went on. "Then you are caught up in a frenzy that brings you to the edge of madness, as far as you can go without ever coming back. The return is a series of dazed weeks during which you are only half alive." Such has been the "history" of his past year, Rothko says. But "I am beginning to feel that one must break this cycle somewhere. For the rest you spend your strength resisting the suction of the shopkeeping mentalities for whom, ostensibly, one goes through this hell."[10]

With his painting now freed from representation not just of the familiar human world but even its watery primeval origins, strife, inner splitting, and acts of resistance become integral to Rothko's creative act. The artist begins by *sparring* with his insides, as if his interior were a separate being, an old and elusive boxing partner with whom he jabs and feints, but lands no heavy blows. Somehow, this bout in the gym yields a kind of creative "frenzy," as if the sparring partners had melted into a Dionysiac fusion. Yet like Nietzsche's tragic artist, Rothko remains self-conscious and split, experiencing a frenzy to which he must surrender (passing out of the "normal world"), but which he must also resist (or face "madness"). Even afterwards, the exhausted painter must battle the annihilating power of normality, in the form of the 57th Street "shopkeepers."

At the time he was painting them, Rothko exhibited only a few of his multiforms, and that was at his Parsons show in the spring of 1949, where he mostly showed paintings consisting of several stacked horizontal rectangles— just one step away from his mature format.[11] As he had with his myth paintings in 1940–41, Rothko, doubtful of his new "stumblings" and mistrustful of his viewers, withheld the multiforms from public view for at least a couple of years. In fact, it was at this time that he formulated his well-known statement about the dangers of exhibiting pictures.

> A picture lives by companionship, expanding and quickening in the eyes of the sensitive observer. It dies by the same token. It is therefore a risky and unfeeling act to send it out into the world. How often it must be permanently impaired by the eyes of the vulgar and the cruelty of the impotent who would extend their affliction universally![12]

Rothko "needed companionship desperately," Stanley Kunitz said. So, Rothko felt, did his pictures. He felt relaxed and expansive, powerful and alive, in the presence of a warmly admiring friend (or wife). As he had imagined himself in his *Self-Portrait,* Rothko here imagines his pictures as powerful, yet vulnerable, easily damaged by the cruelty of shopkeepers, collectors, critics, not to mention mere strangers who, "impotent" themselves, vengefully seek to impose their lack on others. So Rothko splits viewing into an intimate, loving, quickening gaze that comes close to fusing with its object and a cold, unconsciously hostile look that kills. He has now begun to think of the shapes in his work as living "organisms," yet to quicken into life they relied upon a not particularly reliable class of people—those who attend gallery shows and museums. The life-versus-death rhetoric of Rothko's statement resembles that of Clyfford Still; its emphasis on the "risky and unfeeling act" of sending pictures out into the world reveals a Rothko who, in the late 1940s, was beginning to feel very protective toward creations with which, since they had evolved from such a torturous, intimate, creative struggle, he very closely identified.

Between his two marriages Rothko had, in a letter to his sister, weighed the advantages of bachelorhood (mobility) against those of marriage (security) and envisioned a solution in "a mate who can provide this security and also keep your sensations and movement alive."[13] With his beautiful new wife and the reassuring friendship of a more advanced artist like Still, Rothko's life had circled back to the early 1930s, the time of his marriage to Edith Sachar and his friendship with Milton Avery. "On the brink of a new life," Rothko had written to his sister, "the last thing in the world I would wish would be to return to the old one." But now, more securely anchored, he could repeat the past by transforming it into a "new life."

Mary Alice Beistle provided the companionship, comfort, consolation, and even adulation Rothko needed from a wife. Clyfford Still provided the unbending strength and admiration that Rothko needed in a mentor. More ambitious and more aggressive than Avery, Still had completely broken with figuration and advanced a sense of color *as* form that allowed Rothko to draw and expand upon what had learned about color from Avery. Rothko, moreover, needed a wife the way a swimmer needs the concrete side of a pool, as a solidity from which to push off and to which he could return. Edith had not wished to remain the stable foundation for her husband's "fancy-free" imagination. In fact, by dispatching Rothko to Macy's to peddle her jewelry, she set the suction force of the shopkeeping mentality going *within* the home. His second marriage allowed Rothko, who felt adrift when alone, to place one foot firmly in normality—a security which enabled him, creatively, to stretch out, to keep his sensations and movement alive, and to transform his art into "an unknown adventure in an unknown space."[14]

For the most part, the multiforms do not look as if they emerged from a torturous creative process. Their warm, intense colors, their fertile variety of shape and hue, their ebullient sense of freedom and creative search—all these suggest a man who, while he may protest that he hates the life of a painter, is working in a state of infatuation with his medium, as if he had just discovered it. Before, Rothko's somber colors and grotesque distortions affronted his viewer, as if to jolt an admirer, say, of Renoir with a shock of grim reality. Now, as he works toward the more radical end of eliminating recognizable forms altogether, Rothko's paintings grow beautiful, reaching out to a viewer with their sensuous color, as if on this physical yet subliminal level he could break through solitude and communicate with those viewers he at once needed and suspected.

Untitled (1948; color plate 13) is built up of a multiplicity of glowing, brightly colored, softly edged, translucent, predominantly horizontal, two-dimensional forms.[15] Some are circular; others, ovals or rectangles; but even these geometrical forms, bulging and contracting irregularly, have been organicized, and most of the painting's shapes are unique and amorphous, impossible either to identify or to name, as if the painter were seeking to induce a state of consciousness prior to, and more fluid than, the comforts of recognition. Lacking solidity and weight as well as sharp definition, many of these diaphanous color patches—the white, yellow, blue/gray and red/orange ones above and below the painting's center—appear to float, ethereal and unattached, on the picture plane. Their fuzzy edges make it look as though these areas are expanding outward, as if they were living organisms. Shapes secured to the edges—the thin gray strip on the right, the red/orange patch at mid-left—suggest that the painting depicts a universe that continues beyond its edges; but these forms, along with others attached to the sides, top, and bottom, push inward, working toward containment.

No subway-station rectilinear architecture, no strata of horizontal rectangles, not even a dissolving grid provide the artist with a compositional scaffolding. Rothko's colored forms have been freed both from representation and from predetermined structure. Without such external supports, Rothko's new freedom, presenting agonizing problems of weight, proportion, and placement, requires a willingness to flounder around, to cut one's self adrift, to let things happen. In the multiforms, composition must be improvised, a unique and delicate balancing act. While not precisely or (as in *Slow Swirl*) ambiguously contoured, many of Rothko's shapes are contained, differentiated from the fleshy pink ground. They are also typically placed very close to each other, some gently touching, with one sometimes supporting another. Often, adjacent areas have interlocking shapes, as if they had been, or could be, joined. Yet the space is not cramped. Unlike Rothko's physically close yet emotionally distant figures of the 1930s, his shapes here—separate, yet proximate to and even intimate with each other—have plenty of breathing room. Energetic yet stable, they neither push closer together nor press further apart. Instead, as if held together by the invisible pressures of a magnetic field, they exist as independent presences comfortably suspended in a shallow, fluctuating space. Rothko has created a freedom-within-stability, a dynamic stasis, or what he later called a "live unity."[16]

With its oval shapes and openings, the glowing horizontal sun-yellow form that floats across the lower part of this painting resembles, and transforms, the carved wooden slab that crosses the beast's pelvis in *The Omen of the Eagle*. That hybrid, whether male, female, or both, looks sterile and empty, and Rothko's title alludes to a chorus in the *Agamemnon* which describes two male eagles devouring a pregnant hare, violating the life process at its reproductive core. Other Rothko paintings from this period show an eaglelike bird, along with a rabbit whose body contains a large hole where the stomach/womb should be.[17] In these works, Rothko probes the instinctual violence of the war; he also probes his own creative instincts, which had always produced distortions of the human figure. Rothko, who preferred to think of himself as victim rather than as aggressor, was made uneasy by his violations of nature. After 1950 he condemned them as sadistic. Now, instead of bending the external to express his vision, Rothko lets his inner vision emerge on the canvas, materializing it not in symbolic forms but in expansive patches of color, as if paint itself could speak, could provide a language of the deep psyche.

Yet figuration proved a language hard for Rothko to repudiate. After all, his passion for painting had begun, in his own account, with his response to the female body. An outsider partly by ethnic fate and partly by professional choice, Rothko, for all his lack of trust and faith in people, for all his reticence and reserve, possessed a warmth and gregariousness, and a need for companionship, which led him to paint in "the hope of breaking through solitude." Rothko's notion of painting as a language as natural as speech or song; his conception of children's art as a shared expressive speech; his idea of myth as an archaic, universal language; his explorations of automatism as the utterance of a common unconscious—all these were the efforts of a withdrawn, solitary man to convince himself that his medium *could* overcome the isolation and silence he had so often used it to represent. Nonfigurative painting, then, was dangerous, threatening to dissolve that conventional world the artist shared with a viewer and thus to thwart the very human need that vitalized the activity of painting for Rothko.

"From the time he began to leave the surrealist phase," said Herbert Ferber, "he did what he once described to me as avoiding subject matter to the extent that if he saw something in one of his paintings that resembled an object, he would change the shape."[18] Or, Rothko would turn the canvas on its side or top: "drips of paint meandering in several directions indicate that he turned these canvases as he worked," Bonnie Clearwater writes—"a method probably intended to suppress the unconscious creation of recognizable forms."[19] Ironically, not just private, invented forms, but recognizable forms inhabit the unconscious. Creation, then, involves not just a spontaneous release—as the Surrealists held—but a complex series of negotiations between the will and the unconscious, each of which is itself divided. So, like some repressed unconscious memory, figuration kept returning in the multiforms of 1946–49, as if these works issued from a contest, or a sparring match, between an avant-garde painter moving into abstraction and a conservative humanist who feared losing his foothold in normality.

In *Untitled* (1948; color plate 13), the two large red circular splotches above the center resemble eyes, the horizontal red smear below them a mouth, the white above hair, the white below a nose, and the yellow oval to the right an ear. Below, on the right, a pink shoulder curves down into a pink and red/orange arm that, bent at the elbow, has been folded back across the front of the figure, while on the left—though less distinctly—a pink shoulder leads down to an arm that is similarly folded back across the figure. So some, though by no means all, of Rothko's colored shapes generate a form: a blank-eyed, down-at-the-mouth, yet warm and glowing, expansive and barrel-chested human figure, whose arms are folded across the front of the body. The untitled painting of 1948, in fact, transforms—by transcendentalizing—Rothko's *Self-Portrait* of the mid-1930s.

That painting emphasized Rothko's physical bulk. In this one, imposing size is suggested, but the body looks weightless and buoyant—on the *verge* of disembodiment. The pink areas within and around the body may be a kind of luminous flesh or they may be a ground color, in front of which features such as the eyes and mouth hover. The body's boundaries are thus indeterminate, and its solidity doubtful, for it can be seen either as covered with a veil of pink flesh or as open—not torn open like the painter's body in *Untitled* (c. 1940)—but containing empty spaces that invite us to look inside. Looking, we don't see anything as bony, hard, sterile, and identifiable as that triple-headed painter's spinal column and rib cage. Instead, in *Untitled* (1948) a boneless "figure" is composed of soft, rounded, warm, sensuous shapes that occupy a mysterious, shifting space.

Within this figure's "breast," a blue oval glows from inside a larger gray one, from which a smaller gray oval, with smudges of blue inside, has emerged (or broken off), but which remains connected to and supported by its source. Inside, this figure is not hollow, violated, but has rich, generative (egg-shaped) depths. There are no wounds displayed here, as in the earlier self-portrait; nor is the body contorted, as in *Untitled* (1940). But two hollow red eyes, the left one grotesquely enlarged, and the smeared red downturned mouth give the face a pained expression. Before, multiple, merged heads (or bodies) conveyed an agonized self-division; now, multiple colored shapes with open spaces between them allow differing sides, independent parts of the self, to coexist in a "live unity." The *self* is a "multiform."

Stable yet precarious, *Untitled* (1948) does not delineate a human figure or anything else substantial, but evokes a kind of spiritualized human presence which looks as though it has either just come together or is about to come apart. Technically, too, Rothko was spiraling forward by drawing from the past. "Tradition of *starting with drawing* an academic notion," Rothko asserted in "The Scribble Book." "We may start with color." In his *Self-Portrait,* as in many paintings of the 1930s, Rothko had worked not, say, by drawing his face, but by building it up out of small areas of color. The difference between the self-portrait and *Untitled* (1948), then, is that he is no longer seeking anything like a recognizable image, and that his thin color splotches have consequently been detached from each other, neither fused nor completely isolated. As a result, the human drama, in a painting which seems to have abstracted *from* the human, deals with the issues of separation and merging. Its indeterminate figure-ground relations dramatize a primary struggle to form a self out of surroundings which nevertheless remain part of the self.

Not all shapes in this painting, however, have figurative associations. Just to the left of the "face" and descending into the "shoulder/chest" of the "figure," a vertical rectangular form, with white, pink, gray, yellow, orange, and burnt sienna areas, stubbornly resists such a reading. More broken and indeterminate, more intensely worked, more brushy and gestural and yet more thinly painted and transparent, this space lets us look inside the painting itself. Throughout *Untitled* (1948) Rothko's flat shapes cover but, being translucent, do not completely conceal the colors beneath them. Colors break through, glow through, slip around the edges or, like the ghostly gray shapes within the rosy pink in the upper right corner, they persist as shadowy presences. The picture has a literal depth—layers of paint. So far I have been referring to the fleshy pink as the ground color, but at some points white or gray or yellow becomes visible behind the pink, leaving the painting without the stability of a certain ground.

Yet in the area where we can look inside the painting, we discover a burnt sienna which has persisted as a kind of negative space created by the encroachment of the surrounding white, pink, orange, and yellow colors upon the underlying burnt sienna. Pushed back, and held back, by a horizontal orange bar, this shape's hard opacity toughens an otherwise buoyant, luminous work and creates a kind of ironic self-reflection within the work. If the burnt sienna is the ground, then the painting's colorful surface may be viewed as a construction, one which covers but does not entirely conceal something distant and impenetrable, something resistant to transcendent longings, something that just is—like solitude or death.

. . .

In the winter of 1947–48, *Possibilities* published Mark Rothko's "The Romantics Were Prompted":

> The romantics were prompted to seek exotic subjects and to travel to far off places. They failed to realize that, though the transcendental must involve the strange and unfamiliar, not everything strange or unfamiliar is transcendental.
>
> The unfriendliness of society to his activity is difficult for the artist to accept. Yet this very hostility can act as a lever for true liberation. Freed from a false sense of security and community, the artist can abandon his plastic bank-book, just as he has abandoned other forms of security. Both the sense of community and of security depend on the familiar. Free of them, transcendental experiences become possible.
>
> I think of my pictures as dramas; the shapes in the pictures are the performers. They have been created from the need for a group of actors who are able to move dramatically without embarrassment and execute gestures without shame.
>
> Neither the action nor the actors can be anticipated, or described in advance. They begin as an unknown adventure in an unknown space. It is at the moment of completion that in a flash of recognition, they are seen to have the quantity and function which was intended. Ideas and plans that existed in the mind at the start were simply the doorway through which one left the world in which they occur.
>
> The great cubist pictures thus transcend and belie the implications of the cubist program.

Chapter Nine

The most important tool the artist fashions through constant practice is faith in his ability to produce miracles when they are needed. Pictures must be miraculous: the instant one is completed, the intimacy between the creation and the creator is ended. He is an outsider. The picture must be for him, as for anyone experiencing it later, a revelation, an unexpected and unprecedented resolution of an eternally familiar need.

On shapes:
They are unique elements in a unique situation.
They are organisms with volition and a passion for self-assertion.
They move with internal freedom, and without need to conform with or to violate what is probable in the familiar world.
They have no direct association with any particular visible experience, but in them one recognizes the principle and passion of organisms.

The presentation of this drama in the familiar world was never possible, unless everyday acts belonged to a ritual accepted as referring to a transcendent realm.

Even the archaic artist, who had an uncanny virtuosity, found it necessary to create a group of intermediaries, monsters, hybrids, gods and demigods. The difference is that, since the archaic artist was living in a more practical society than ours, the urgency for transcendent experience was understood, and given an official status. As a consequence, the human figure and other elements from the familiar world could be combined with, or participate as a whole in the enactment of the excesses which characterize this improbable hierarchy. With us the disguise must be complete. The familiar identity of things has to be pulverized in order to destroy the finite associations with which our society increasingly enshrouds every aspect of our environment.

Without monsters and gods, art cannot enact our drama: art's most profound moments express this frustration. When they were abandoned as untenable superstitions, art sank into melancholy. It became fond of the dark, and enveloped its objects in the nostalgic intimations of a half-lit world. For me the great achievements of the centuries in which the artist accepted the probable and familiar as his subjects were the pictures of the single human figure—alone in a moment of utter immobility.

But the solitary figure could not raise its limbs in a single gesture that might indicate its concern with the fact of mortality and an insatiable appetite for ubiquitous experience in face of this fact. Nor could the solitude be overcome. It could gather on beaches and streets and in parks only through coincidence, and, with its companions, for a *tableau vivant* of human incommunicability.

I do not believe that there was ever a question of being abstract or representational. It is really a matter of ending this silence and solitude, of breathing and stretching one's arms again.[20]

When, in the summer of 1950, Rothko was asked to write statements for *Tiger's Eye* and the *Magazine of Art,* he refused, because "I have nothing to say in words which I would stand for. I am heartily ashamed of the things I have written in the past. This self-statement business has become a fad this season."[21] As Rothko eliminated recognizable forms from his painting, he grew more reluctant to talk, publicly, about his work, abandoning even titles, as if *any* words would distract viewers from a necessarily uneasy confrontation with his work's mysterious simplicity. "The Romantics Were Prompted" constitutes the first, and only, extended published statement about his work that Rothko ever made on his own. Culminating several years of activism on behalf of his art that began with his exertions for the Cultural Committee of the Federation of Modern Painters and Sculptors, the essay, abjuring the polemics of the letter to Jewell, reflects the confidence of Rothko's new position in the art world at the same time that it tries to prepare an audience for works—i.e., the multiforms—which their self-doubting creator had yet to show publicly.

"The Romantics Were Prompted" justifies—perhaps as much to its author as to any reader—Rothko's abandonment of *any* kind of figuration, and it does so by constructing, in broad, global terms, a mythicized account of the historical place of the modern American artist. Earlier, Rothko had stressed the "spiritual kinship" between modern and archaic art, though such works as *The Omen of the Eagle* and *The Syrian Bull* dramatized the contemporary fragmentation of ancient wholeness. "The Romantics Were Prompted" assumes the *difference* between modern and archaic; it also assumes that reality—physical, social, historical, daily reality—is insufficient, lacking.

"I adhere to the material reality of the world and the substance of things," Rothko had announced in his "Personal Statement" of 1945. But material reality now requires something else, something beyond. In archaic societies, "where the urgency for transcendent experience" was "given an official status," the familiar and the transcendent had been linked, through ritual, in a hierarchical unity. This sounds like an idealized reconstruction of primitive society, and it is; but Rothko, whose father had imposed the rigors of orthodox Judaism on him as a boy, had once lived in a world so conceived, observing the body of Jewish law known as *Halacha,* which not only codifies morality but "invests the texture of daily life with more than practical significance by weaving into it the ritualized repetition of acts and words which relate that texture both directly and indirectly to the divine."[22]

But Rothko quit the temple, he was transplanted from Dvinsk to Portland, his father died—a series of liberations that imposed loss. Just so, when the "monsters and gods" who acted as "intermediaries" between human and divine "were abandoned as untenable superstitions, art sank into melancholy." Modern skepticism split the human from the transcendent. Limiting itself to "the probable and familiar"—i.e., to realism—art could movingly express only the frustration and solitude entailed by its own limits, in "pictures of the single human figure—alone in a moment of utter immobility." Only an art of transcendence, abandoning the human figure as untenable, Rothko implies, opens a way out of such melancholy solitude.

Yet a *modern* transcendence—one not tied to any particular theology, not even to the romantic theology of Nature—can be found only within the "unknown space" of the private self. At the same time, Rothko identifies his pictures as "dramas," as if withdrawing into the self could create a public art-form. Unlike the plays of Aeschylus, Rothko's modern dramas can draw upon no shared mythology—another loss that turns out to be liberating. For, freed from the constraints of any ideology or artistic "program," Rothko's new art necessarily proceeds as an open-ended process, an act of discovery, an "unknown adventure." Such pictures are less the product of craft than they are "miracles," and, no longer confined to the probable and familiar, they can yield an "unexpected and unprecedented" "revelation." Some of Rothko's language here ("miracles," "revelation") has religious associations; some of his language derives from avant-garde rhetoric ("unexpected and unprecedented"). By expressing his transcendental longings, Rothko's paintings will also meet avant-garde imperatives for artistic novelty.

Modern society, says Rothko, "increasingly enshrouds every aspect of our environment" with "finite associations." Real objects—finite, familiar, and thus affectless—feel dead to Rothko; he needs to get beyond them. Real objects, after all, are other—not-him; the "unique" shapes in his painting are *his own creations*. So he speaks of them as living "organisms," independent of him once the intimate process of creation has ended and he takes his seat as just another "outsider" in the audience. Like actors, Rothko's colored shapes are on display, being looked at, but they "have been created," he writes, "from the need for a group of actors who are able to move dramatically without embarrassment and execute gestures without shame."

Many of the same relatives and friends who describe Rothko as warm and gregarious also describe him as reticent, reserved, secretive. It is this Rothko, the one who here assumes that, normally, to be seen, to exhibit one's self on stage, is to be ashamed and embarrassed; the one who, at his 1961 Museum of Modern Art opening, felt that "he was on display as much as his paintings," "began the evening in an agony of stage fright" and ended it convinced that his works were "nothing," as if the lack was not in reality but in *him*. But beginning with the multiforms and for about the next ten years Rothko's pictures will be shamelessly sensual and seductive, eager to be looked at and to give pleasure. His new paintings were "dramas," beautiful constructions evolved from him yet independent of him, by means of which shame could be transcended and the self transformed into a commanding presence "with volition and a passion for self-assertion."

The shapes in the multiforms do not "need to conform with or to violate what is probable in the familiar world." "They have no direct association with any particular visible experience." Rothko, Hedda Sterne said, liked to brag, "I'm not visual." "He claimed that he didn't look at things. He only had to use inner vision"—one reason he typically painted himself with blanked-out eyes.[23] Rather than referring to an external and familiar visual reality, Rothko's autonomous shapes *are* realities or, more exactly, they behave *as if* real, moving with "the principle and passion of organisms." As such, they are "unique," opaque and mysterious, rich with suggestion rather than enshrouded with "finite associations." So these shapes *are,* but they are also "*actors,*" in "disguise," performing in a public space, theatrical and constructed, a drama imagined by an alien artist in an alien environment, the drama of his "internal freedom." In the heady optimism of Rothko's "new life" and his new creative search, the "tragic," so prominent in his thinking during the war, never enters "The Romantics Were Prompted." Loss does, not as a personal experience but as a generalized modern condition, the death of the gods; but that loss, like shame, can be transformed into freedom.

Yet Rothko is characteristically ambivalent about the nature and origins of this freedom. On the one hand, he imagines freedom as a romantic quest for sensation, as if he were a kind of Jewish Rimbaud. In those pictures from the Western tradition that do move Rothko, the "single figure" cannot "raise its limbs in a single gesture that might indicate its concern with the fact of mortality and an insatiable appetite for ubiquitous experience in face of this fact." What might animate that immobile figure are the realities of death, ephemerality, oblivion—an awareness of which activates a desire to consume all of experience.[24] A sense of mortality can free us from moral and social and familial constraints, as the death of Rothko's father had in certain ways freed him. Yet it is also as if the thought of death, of nothingness, makes Rothko feel restless and empty, hungry for new sensations that can never quite fulfill him ("insatiable").

Chapter Nine

On the other hand, the Rothko who quit Yale to "starve for art" in New York City imagines liberation as issuing from sacrificial pain. Isolated and deprived, lacking community or bank account, the artist is depicted as the victim of society's "unfriendliness" or its active "hostility." But Rothko also describes the artist's position ("just as he has abandoned other forms of security") as chosen, as an act of *self*-sacrifice. In this essay Rothko does not dwell, as he often did, on his injuries. Whether imposed or elected, hostility and insecurity lift ("act as a lever") the painter toward freedom, torment him into transcendence. Of course, by 1947, Rothko had just enough security—from his second marriage; from sales and recognition; from his wife's job; from his friendships with Gottlieb, Newman, and Still—to allow him the freedom to romanticize insecurity *as* freedom. It was only after he felt somewhat more at home in *this* world that he began to speak of, and to paint, "transcendental experiences."

"Art is of the Spirit," Rothko had written in "The Scribble Book." The young Rothko had been a romantic idealist; his favorite teacher, Max Weber, had praised the power of art to make "dead or indifferent matter the very *abode* of spirit"; Sally Avery recalled Rothko "discussing and discussing Plato" well into the 1930s; and Rothko's discussions of children's art emphasize an inner core of creative spirit usually lost through social conditioning. Occasionally in the thirties, a blank pink wall or a mysterious doorway will suggest a way out, figures on a beach will gaze off toward the horizon, but generally Rothko's melancholy people, whether bulky nudes or attenuated subway passengers, are trapped in matter. In the early forties the hybrid in *The Omen of the Eagle* has a pelvis which makes the creature look as though it might, like the rabbits in some of Rothko's paintings and drawings of that period, be hollow at the core.

But in just a few years, spirituality, or a yearning for it—so long held in—begins to emerge, associated with the air, soon to replace water in Rothko's work as the element of liberation. The figures in *Slow Swirl* gyrate upward from sea to air. Two or three horizontal bands forming the ground in many works of the mid-forties often suggest earth/sky or sea/earth/sky divisions; and diaphanous abstract shapes floating in the sky—in paintings like *Primeval Landscape* (1945) and *Gethsemane* (1945)—imply a purified release from the agonies of the flesh depicted in the lower registers. *Gethsemane* represents Christ as a bird, and birds in paintings done around this time often evoke, not the heavy, rapacious eagles of a few years before, but spiritual flight and renewal. The thin, weightless, sun-yellow body of *The Syrian Bull* similarly hints at transcendence. In these years, exploring the "complex inner self" increasingly involved reaching back to recover a core of spiritual/creative life that, through the

Plate 1. *Street Scene*, 1936
(National Gallery)

Plate 2. *Portrait of Rothko's Mother*, n.d. (Rothko Estate)

Plate 3. *The Rothkowitz Family*, c. 1936
(National Gallery)

Plate 4. *Untitled*, early 1930s
(National Gallery)

Plate 5. *Untitled*, early 1930s
(National Gallery)

Plate 6. *Sculptress*, early 1930s
(National Gallery)

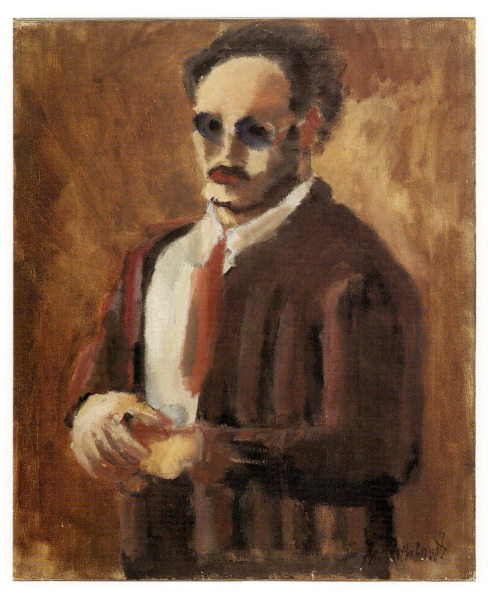

Plate 7. *Self-Portrait*, 1936
(Rothko Estate)

Plate 8. *Subway Scene*, c. 1938
(Rothko Estate)

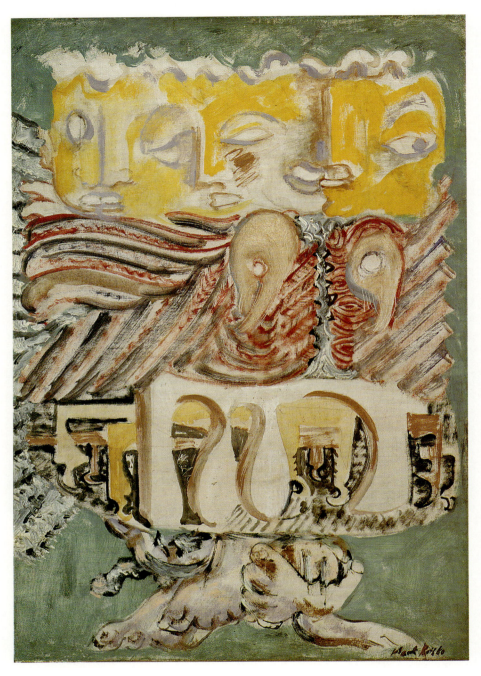

Plate 9. *The Omen of the Eagle*, 1942
(National Gallery)

Plate 10. *Untitled,* c. 1940
(Rothko Estate)

Plate 11. *The Syrian Bull*, 1943 (Annalee Newman)

Plate 12. *Slow Swirl at the Edge of the Sea*, 1944 (Museum of Modern Art)

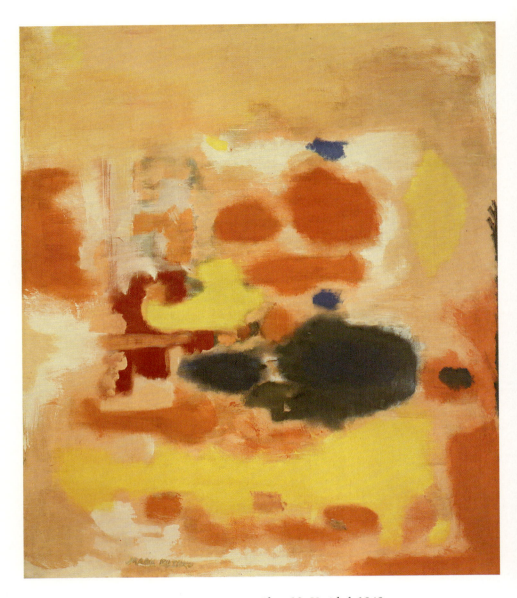

Plate 13. *Untitled*, 1948
(Rothko Estate)

Plate 14. *Number 10, 1950*
(Museum of Modern Art)

Plate 15. *Number 12, 1951* (Rothko Estate)

Plate 16. *Red, Brown and Black*, 1958
(Museum of Modern Art)

Plate 17. *Red on Maroon*, 1959
(Tate Gallery)

Plate 18. Harvard Murals, Panel Four, 1962—damaged (Harvard University)

Plate 19. Houston Murals, east triptych, 1964–67 (Menil Collection, Houston)

Plate 20. *Untitled*, 1967
(National Gallery)

Plate 21. *Black on Grey*, 1969
(Rothko Estate)

injuries of socialization, Rothko felt he had lost. As Oskar Pfister had declared in a passage that Rothko copied into his "Scribble Book," "without such retrogressions no great progressions are possible, and no fresh creation, however cleverly imagined, has any prospect of a future unless it has borrowed from the past."

In 1949 Rothko would arrive at his classic simplified format of two or three stacked rectangles which seem to locate a viewer at a "doorway" between the physical and transcendent worlds. For Rothko's shapes to feel alive, they had to be independent, free of reference to the ordinary visual world. "They move with internal freedom, and without need to conform with or to violate what is probable in the familiar world." Yet, just a few sentences later, Rothko strongly asserts their need to violate: "the familiar identity of things has to be pulverized in order to destroy the finite associations with which our society increasingly enshrouds every aspect of our environment." To "pulverize" is to "crush, grind, into a powder or dust," an activity familiar to Rothko, who in the late forties was grinding his own pigments with a mortar and pestle. "He spent hours at it," George Okun recalled. This way, he could save money; he could create his own colors; and he could engage in an activity familiar to him from his boyhood in a turn-of-the-century Russian pharmacy where Jacob Rothkowitz ground his prescriptions in a mortar and pestle.

Now Rothko does not wish to withdraw from the sensible world or to swallow it up, but to crush it into tiny particles, bringing it to the edge either of dissolution or a new beginning. Loss merges with liberation, in nonfigurative paintings which, by pulverizing the "familiar identity of things," construct a transcendent beauty which consoles us for their loss. Yet Rothko's imagined destructiveness, apocalyptically dissolving all that is self-contained and separate, fills a human need. His work, he carefully states, offers "an unexpected and unprecedented resolution" not of a painting problem or of a private conflict but "of an eternally familiar need." The languages of religious revelation and avant-garde manifesto are resolved in the language of a universal humanism, the one form of familiarity that survives Rothko's pulverizing skepticism. "I do not believe that there was ever a question of being abstract or representational," Rothko writes, dismissing the difference of means as trivial. "It is really a matter of ending this silence and solitude, of breathing and stretching one's arms again." In his new paintings Rothko will construct a space which, permitting such elementary human activities as breathing, aspiring, will provide a public stage on which the human and the transcendent can be rejoined.

· · ·

Chapter Nine

Art's "Street" is Manhattan's Fifty-seventh Street, the most imposing and seemingly dignified of the city's cross-town thoroughfares. Here are the heart, brain, and nervous system of the art business of America.

Fortune, 1946

Fifty-seventh street is a stinking mess.

Mark Rothko, 1948

On March 28, 1949, Rothko opened the third of his annual exhibits at the Betty Parsons Gallery, 15 East 57th Street. He showed eleven paintings. All were new; all were abstract; all were designated by number and year—e.g., *Number 1, 1949*—rather than by a descriptive (or portentous mythic) title.[25] Many of the paintings were quite large; *Number 1, 1949* measured approximately 5½' × 4½'. A few of these paintings contained a myriad of colored shapes, like *Untitled* (1948). But some of Rothko's work in the last three years had consisted (or come close to consisting) of several brightly colored, delicately edged, stacked rectangles. Now that image was the predominant one. The grid, its geometry simplified and its borders fuzzy and humanized, had returned to Rothko's painting. From our position, looking backward across his career, Rothko is now just a step away from resolving his search. But to anyone familiar with the Surrealist calligraphy of Rothko's two previous Parsons shows, these new pared-down, nonfigurative works marked a dramatic and perhaps disturbing break.

"The progression of a painter's work, as it travels in time from point to point, will be toward clarity," Rothko asserted in a statement published later in 1949 (along with reproductions of five multiforms) in *Tiger's Eye*; "toward the elimination of all obstacles between the painter and the idea, and between the idea and the observer. As examples of such obstacles, I give (among others) memory, history or geometry, which are swamps of generalization from which one might pull out parodies of ideas (which are ghosts) but never an idea in itself. To achieve this clarity is, inevitably, to be understood."[26] To readers of *Tiger's Eye*, who, having seen several of Rothko's Surrealist works reproduced in two earlier issues, might view his work as proceeding toward greater obscurity, he provocatively declares his aim to be "clarity." Here, eliminating objects, people, symbols—even titles—is not about pulverizing the material world, not about "internal freedom," "transcendental experiences," or avant-garde purification of the medium. Rothko's reductions are about removing the "obstacles" between painter and work, between work and viewer; they are about ending separation, removing the "obstacles" to more immediate communication, about being "understood."

Yet even with such clarifications, understanding does not "inevitably" follow. The two art-journal reviews of Rothko's 1949 Parsons exhibit focused on composition, as if formal unity were the central issue. "The unfortunate aspect of the whole showing is that these paintings contain no suggestions of form or design," Margaret Breuning judged in *Art Digest,* while in *Art News* Thomas Hess, after first noting the "strength of composition" supporting Rothko's emotionality, went on to criticize "his insistence on making the grand gesture, on building in a huge scale." "The very ambition which went into covering such immense surfaces, the very refusal to exploit the full resources of the oil medium, has resulted in the ambiguity of the decoration which cannot be decorative." A third review, written by Paul Mocsanyi for United Press, praised Rothko as a "neo-mystic" whose "feelings are expressed in an interplay of color that does not want to be anything else than color."[27] With Rothko just about to achieve his final clarifications, ways of misapprehending his work—containing it within the narrow terms of a critical formalism or fixing it with names like decoration or mysticism—were already forming ranks.

Rothko wanted to be understood; he wanted to be *recognized,* to be *seen,* in the deepest sense. Yet recognition entailed its own dangers: if he *were* understood, then he was no longer an outsider—he lost his edge. For the next twenty years, as his reputation grew and he became an internationally celebrated artist, he continued to insist that he was misunderstood. If someone praised the sensual beauty of his paintings, Rothko pointed to their spirituality; but if someone else hinted at spiritual properties, he defined himself as an earthy materialist. It is as if almost *any* verbal response, any *naming* of his work, made Rothko uneasy. He wished the self displayed in his works to remain elusive, free, hard to fix; and he wanted to feel that he was still, despite success, "resisting the suction of the shopkeeping mentalities," not to mention the critical, curatorial, and art historical mentalities. Wronged and deprived, he still needed consolation, comfort, encouragement. Embattled, fighting the absorptive power of the marketplace, he stayed angry. The "unfriendliness of society"—sometimes real, sometimes imagined—acted as a necessary lever toward creativity.

In the spring of 1949 Rothko could have comforted himself by considering that now at least there *were* reviews to wring his hands over. Or by reading the shrewd, sympathetic essay on his work that Douglas MacAgy—the first journal essay on Rothko's work—had published in the January issue of the *Magazine of Art.*[28] Beginning with Rothko's own remark that "a painter commits

Chapter Nine

himself by the nature of the space he uses," MacAgy distinguishes between a (Renaissance) space where "things may exist separately without necessity of interrelationship and the areas between things are defined as absences of contact" and a (Rothko) space where "objects and their environment seem to give way to each other so that dramatic emphasis cannot be fixed in a permanent unity." "Identities are elusive and roles enter a shifting relationship." Rather than trying to fix Rothko, MacAgy asserted his elusiveness, portraying him as an ambitious innovator.

Rothko damned the "shopkeeping mentalities." He railed against the "stinking mess" on 57th Street. Part purist, Rothko wished to protect his paintings from the mire of the marketplace. But Rothko needed money; he sought communication; he enjoyed self-display; he liked recognition. Part pragmatist, he shrewdly managed his career. For the early part of the summer of 1948 Rothko and his wife had rented a small house in East Hampton, Long Island. Rothko worked prolifically. At the end of the visit he invited several people—among them the critic Harold Rosenberg—to view the work, and, Rosenberg recalled, "he trotted out about, oh maybe fifty paintings he had done that summer."[29] "And I thought they were marvelous, it was just one of the most exciting visits to an artist's studio that I have ever had. He took out one painting after another and set them down. They were just absolutely terrific." Rothko was bringing out paintings he had yet to exhibit publicly—the multiforms. But when Rosenberg visited Rothko's 1949 Parsons exhibit, "I found it very disappointing because all of those terrific paintings he had done in the summer weren't in the show. He went back to New York and painted a whole show," and the new paintings "didn't have any of the variety and surprise" of the ones he'd seen the summer before. "They were simplified versions of those paintings. Having done those paintings, he then studied them and made up a format based on them."

When Rothko called the day after the opening of his Parsons Gallery show to ask about Rosenberg's reaction, the critic bluntly told him, "I thought it was lousy." "What the hell happened to all those terrific paintings you did at Louse Point?" Rothko answered that "he had talked to a friend and they had decided there was too much variety and that he should do something more identifiable." The same Rothko who was trying to eliminate recognizable shapes from his painting "wanted a recognizable image."[30] Before the end of 1949, after one final act of simplification—reducing the number of his rectangles to two or three and expanding their size—Rothko found in his empty, fluctuating rectangles an image that created the elusive yet recognizable presence he was after.

Speaking with his students at Brooklyn College, a few years later, Rothko stressed "somebody getting territory, this is your territory, you develop something and it's yours, it's your territory. Once a territory is taken, there's no reason for somebody else to take that territory. And to emulate one by imitation would be ridiculous."[31] In the last few years of the 1940s Rothko, Jackson Pollock, Willem de Kooning, Franz Kline, Robert Motherwell, Barnett Newman, and Adolph Gottlieb were all evolving "signature styles," unique expressions marking the individuality of the painter, yet characteristic expressions marking that individual as recognizable—as *familiar*. Soon, it will make sense to speak of "a Rothko," a form of recognition with its own set of dangers. Like so many white settlers, the painters could turn unexplored inner territory into stylistic private property. Meanwhile, for Rothko, creating an image so identifiable that he didn't need to sign the painting—his identity being dispersed throughout the canvas—fulfilled not only personal but also marketing imperatives: a recognizable object, a "name" brand, a known value, can more easily be sold.

Rothko's dealer, Betty Parsons, was, for better *and* for worse, no shopkeeper. Born Betty Pierson in 1900 at 17 West 49th Street (the present site of Rockefeller Plaza), she spent her summers at Newport and her winters in Palm Beach, was educated at the Chaps School and Miss Randall Keever's Finishing School.[32] Her father's family was old New York, wealthy and conservative; her mother's family was Southern and French, more lively and intellectual, though not artistic. Art was not much in evidence around the West 49th Street house, or the ones in Newport and Palm Beach. It was the Armory Show, in 1913, that awakened Betty Pierson to the possibility of art, "but my family disapproved highly of this."[33] Her family also opposed college for women. Instead, after the revelations of the Armory Show, she was permitted to study sculpture with Gutzon Borglum, who gave us Mount Rushmore. At nineteen, however, Betty Pierson married Schuyler Livingston Parsons and seemed destined to become a Long Island socialite. Three years later, having determined that Parsons drank too much, she went to Paris for a divorce, then stayed for eleven years, living on the Left Bank, studying art (mostly sculpture), getting to know Alexander Calder and Man Ray, Hart Crane and Max Jacob, Gertrude Stein and Tristan Tzara, as if destined to become an expatriate artist.

But in 1933, left broke by the Depression, she returned to the United States, living first in Hollywood (where she got to know Marlene Dietrich and Greta Garbo) and then in Santa Barbara. Continuing to study sculpture, she supported herself by giving art lessons, painting portraits, and working in a liquor store. "I always wanted to get back to New York, though."[34] After six years on the west coast, she sold the expensive engagement ring her husband had given her and used the money to return to New York. As a result of a successful showing of her work at the Midtown Gallery, she was asked to work for the gallery as a salesperson. She then worked, for a while, at a gallery owned by Mary Sullivan who, along with Abby Rockefeller and Lizzie Bliss, had been one of the three founders of the Museum of Modern Art. In early 1940, Betty Parsons started a gallery in the basement of the Wakefield Bookshop on East 55th Street, where she showed Joseph Cornell, Saul Steinberg, Hedda Sterne, Theodoros Stamos, and Adolph Gottlieb. Betty Parsons was adventurous.

When, in 1944, the Wakefield Bookshop moved, the Wakefield Gallery closed. Mortimer Brandt, until now a dealer in Old Masters, decided to try a modern section, which he hired Betty Parsons to run. Through Peggy Guggenheim, Parsons met Mark Rothko around this time, and she arranged an exhibit of his watercolors in the spring of 1946. Rothko called this "my most successful show," saying that he had sold enough to quit teaching at Center Academy and that "one person invested more than $1000 in the stuff. So maybe there is hope."[35] But when Brandt examined the books after the 1946 season, he concluded that the cause of modern art was hopeless, moved to a new location, and left his space at 15 East 57th Street for Betty Parsons to use. She raised $5,000—$1,000 of her own and $1,000 each from four friends—and opened the Betty Parsons Gallery in the fall of 1946.

Provocatively, the gallery opened with an exhibit of Northwest Coast Indian art, curated by Barnett Newman, now a close friend and advisor of Parsons. Newman extolled the aesthetic value of the tribal objects he had assembled, but his catalogue essay mainly appealed to the authority of the primitive in order to justify the contemporary vanguard. "The dominant aesthetic tradition" of these Native Americans "was abstract," Newman writes. "Does not this work," he then asks, "rather illuminate the work of those of our modern American abstract artists who, working with the pure plastic language we call abstract, are infusing it with intellectual and emotional content, and who, without any imitation of primitive symbols, are creating a living myth for us in our own time?"[36] The essay establishes the intellectual closeness between Newman and Rothko in the mid-1940s; it also revealed the direction of the new Betty Parsons Gallery which, among "our modern American abstract artists," would soon acquire Jackson Pollock, Mark Rothko, Clyfford Still, Barnett Newman, Ad Reinhardt, and Theodoros Stamos.

"I realized that they were saying something that no European could say," Betty Parsons later remarked. "Europe is a walled city—at least, it's always seemed that way to me. Everything is within walls. Picasso could never have done what Pollock did."[37] Too patrician to be a mere shopkeeper, too engaged with art to make her gallery a mere "plaything," and too adventurous to play it safe, Betty Parsons soon moved into and improved upon the space vacated by Art of This Century. Samuel Kootz's gallery showed young Americans (William

Baziotes, Robert Motherwell, Adolph Gottlieb); so did Charles Egan (Willem de Kooning, Franz Kline). But from 1947 to 1951, Betty Parsons ran *the* vanguard gallery. She *was* old New York Society, and that could create uneasiness with her proletarian painters. But as an artist herself turning to abstraction at this time and a collector who often bought the work of her artists, Parsons realized a painter's utopian fantasy of the humane dealer. Her gallery became a place for painters to meet, talk, hang each other's shows. "On Saturday afternoons, a dozen or more artists might gather in the back room and stay several hours, and then go out to dinner together."[38] One painter described the gallery as more like an "artists' cooperative" than a business. Clement Greenberg found it "a place where art goes on and is not just shown and sold."[39]

"I give them walls," she said. "They do the rest."[40] In 1946, the decor of a 57th Street gallery, with lush wall-to-wall carpeting, potted plants, long elegant couches, ornamental molding, and walls (in one case) of *boiserie* and velour, denied its commercial character and reduced art to one among many luxuries in an opulent Victorian parlor. At Betty Parsons', the walls of her two gallery rooms were white, empty of decoration; the floors were plain, wooden. Parsons had invented the physical space of the modern avant-garde gallery, which denies commercial reality by seeming to focus solely and reverentially on Art. "It was the ideal environment for the big, single-image, visionary painting of the New York School." The more so, since Parsons *did* let the artists do the rest—select and hang their own shows, enlarge the size of their paintings without griping about the difficulty of selling such works. "Once Rothko wanted to hang more pictures than the walls would accommodate; he got Tony Smith and his other artist friends together the afternoon before the opening, and they stayed in the gallery overnight building a freestanding wall and installing the rest of the show."[41]

Betty Parsons gave her artists walls and she gave them unusual freedom in filling them. But she didn't give them many sales. "Since 1940, Fifty-seventh Street has had an unprecedented boom," *Fortune* reported in 1946, just as the boom was about to expire, and just as Parsons was about to open.[42] Due to a war-induced prosperity that made money available for "luxuries" such as works of art, sales by 57th Street galleries had increased by 300 percent between 1940 and 1946.[43] The growth of the art market entailed, moreover, a shift in the social and economic identity of its clientele. A survey done by *Art News* in 1944 reported that one-third of the paintings sold the previous year had been bought by people purchasing their first painting. Collecting was no longer the prerogative of the tycoon (or his wife or heir). The "new collector," according to *Art News,* was under forty-five, upper-middle-class, a businessman, professional, or actor, and was inclined to buy Americans. "American paintings are cheaper; they are more plentiful; it is easier to find good ones; it is considered 'patriotic' to help by supporting American artists; there is a feeling, as one dealer put it, 'of getting in on the ground floor'."[44]

Yet of the $6 million spent on art in 1945, only 15 percent went to Americans; in a market still dominated by the French, many American ground floors remained deserted.[45] Certainly, for many years this "boom" did not benefit Mark Rothko, who, for instance, had sold only three paintings (for $265) through his 1945 Art of This Century exhibit. But Rothko did gradually increase his prices, so that *Gethsemane*, priced at $550 at Art of This Century in 1945, cost $750 in 1948 at Parsons, and his 1946 watercolor exhibit at Mortimer Brandt did generate substantial sales, including his first museum purchase, *Tentacles of Memory*, to the San Francisco Museum of Modern Art.[46] Two works exhibited in this show, *Entombment I* and *Vessels of Magic*, were acquired the following year by the Whitney and Brooklyn museums. Among established collectors, Peggy Guggenheim bought *Immolation*.[47]

But for the most part Rothko was selling to the "new collectors," for whom an inexpensive watercolor by a relatively unknown contemporary showing at an "old" 57th Street firm might make an ideal purchase. Of course, new collectors, like old ones, might be looking to establish an image of cultivation for themselves; they might be playing the art market as if it were the stock market. Or they might actually enjoy art, as seems to have been the case with Edward Wales Root, an upstate New Yorker, the son of Elihu Root, Theodore Roosevelt's secretary of state and himself a painter. Though he had started collecting many years earlier, E. W. Root concentrated on young American abstract artists after 1944, buying works by William Baziotes, Theodoros Stamos, Robert Motherwell, and Willem de Kooning. In the late 1940s Root bought two Rothko oil paintings.[48]

Rothko's success at the Mortimer Brandt show may have persuaded him to sign on with Betty Parsons, who had arranged the exhibit; it certainly encouraged him to quit his teaching job at Center Academy. Ironically, Rothko was acquiring a dealer, beginning to develop a reputation, and becoming more dependent on the art market for income just as the postwar art boom was ending. There was a national recession in 1948–49, and between 1947 and 1950 the art market was depressed, an economic reality that may have added to Rothko's reluctance to exhibit his new, more abstract multiforms.[49] If so, sticking with his surrealist canvases did not prove an effective marketing strategy. From his March 1947 exhibit at Parsons, Rothko sold one painting: *Omens of Gods and Birds* to E. W. Root for $400. From his March 1948 show, he sold none.[50] From the March 1949 show, where he first exhibited the purely abstract works, Rothko sold two oils, for $100 and $600, the latter to the architect/sculptor Tony Smith, a friend. "So maybe there is no hope," he might have concluded. For he was now contending with several negative forces. Not only was the market bad; he was showing oil paintings, not the less expensive watercolors; and his dealer, however humane and committed to his work, did not vigorously promote her artists.

The entrepreneurial Sam Kootz, whose *New Frontiers in American Painting* (1943) had prophesied the American vanguard that was now emerging, had opened his own gallery in 1945. Instead of selling paintings for a commission, Kootz paid his artists a $200 monthly stipend in exchange for a yearly quota of seventy-five paintings. "It was very demanding because he had so few artists that each of us had to have many shows," Robert Motherwell recalled. "It was really bad for a young artist such as myself to be committed to so much work. He was always desperate for money and drove himself and us very hard."[51]

A former advertising executive, Kootz perceived that changes in the market required bold changes in marketing, i.e., strenuous use of advertising in the media to reach a more dispersed and less visible clientele. He directed publicity campaigns at the "new collectors" with a shameless flamboyance that, along 57th Street, must have caused both the old guard dealers and his own new guard artists to wince. Parsons showed "Northwest Coast Indian Art" and "The Ideographic Picture"; Kootz did "Modern Paintings for a Country Estate" and "Building a Modern Collection." He arranged "theme" shows—on paintings of "The Birds and The Beasts," on "Big Top" paintings:

> GAYEST SHOW OF THE YEAR—COLOSSAL, TERRIFIC
> PAINTINGS OF THE CIRCUS.
> HURRY, HURRY, HURRY
> SEE CLOWNS, TUMBLERS, ACROBATS—
> Admission absolutely free.[52]

Yet Kootz also arranged to become Picasso's American dealer, a coup that elevated him "to a respected position within the market" and "acted as a tremendous draw to collectors." "Hopefully, they would come in for a Picasso and go out with a Baziotes or a Motherwell."[53]

Betty Parsons, on the other hand, managed her new, vanguard gallery with the reserved discretion of an established dealer in Old Masters whose customers came to *her*. "Most artists don't think I'm tough enough," she said. "That I don't go out and solicit, call up people all the time. I don't. I know how people hate that sort of thing, because I hate it myself, so I don't do it," as if, for Parsons, *any* aggressive promotion were vulgar and suspect.[54] Her artists liked the freedom and control she gave them; but they also needed to pay the rent and at least one of them was looking to find "an important place" for himself "in the art-life of our times." For these reasons, in 1951, her "four horsemen" left the premises in search of a more profitable barn.

One of the paintings in Rothko's 1949 Parsons exhibit, however, had been sold four months before the show opened—in what had been his most important sale to date. Purchases by the Brooklyn, Whitney, and San Francisco museums—along with his one-man show at the San Francisco Museum of Modern Art—provided the first official art-world certifications for this artist in his middle forties. Purchases by the "new collectors" *might* provide some needed income, and they *might* provide the kind of loving companionship that Rothko sought for his pictures. But these museums did not include *the* authority, the Museum of Modern Art, and the new, upper-middle-class collections did not possess the prestige attached to the old, "aristocratic" (i.e., robber baron) collections of a J. P. Morgan or a John D. Rockefeller.

In the winter of 1948–49 Philip Johnson, building a guest house on East 52nd Street for John D. Rockefeller III, was advising Mrs. Rockefeller on buying works of art for the house. Johnson, who had been associated with the Museum of Modern Art since the early 1930s and was about to become director of its architecture and design department, brought Mrs. Rockefeller to Rothko's apartment with Dorothy Miller and Alfred Barr. Since the summer of 1945 Rothko had been living at 1288 Sixth Avenue, between 51st and 52nd streets.[55] A short walk from the Museum of Modern Art, a block down the street from Radio City Music Hall, this small, second-floor flat, above a seafood restaurant, was often filled with the smells of cooking fish. What had been the living room of the apartment now served as Rothko's studio.[56] "It is amazing that he could paint in such a limited space," Dorothy Miller recalled, "and he had such difficulty showing us the paintings"—a difficulty compounded by the size of Rothko's works.[57] Mrs. Rockefeller selected *Number 1, 1949,* for which she paid $1,000.

In thirty years, modern art had moved from the upstairs playroom in the mansion of John D. Rockefeller, Jr., to the 52nd Street guest house of John D. Rockefeller III. Yet it is a "risky act" to send paintings to such a place, where "transcendental experiences" could function as bold, chic wall-decorations for the rich. Ironically, as the size of Rothko's canvases expanded and his reputation grew, he necessarily relied more and more on patrons (and institutions) with sufficient wall space, and money, for his pictures. More immediately, the Rockefeller sale encouraged Rothko to raise his prices substantially, as he did for his 1950 Parsons show; and it certainly didn't damage either his self-esteem or his reputation in the family.[58] After all, in a transaction authorized by three representatives of the Museum of Modern Art, Marcus Rothkowitz, a poor despised Jew from the Settlement of Pale, had sold a painting to a family that stood as the very symbol of American capitalism; and in a society where painters lack "official" status, the power to confer legitimacy is held by museum directors and plutocrats.

• • •

> Due to [the] provincial position in which the American artist was pushed, he had nothing to lose and everything, a world, to gain.
>
> Mark Rothko

When the art historian Milton Brown returned to New York in 1946 after serving three years in Italy with the U.S. Army, he recalled that when he had left "the major trend in America was social art." Then he had assumed that the "struggle for supremacy" would be waged between "American scene and social realism." Instead "I have returned to find with some surprise that in the interim the dark horse of abstraction has swept into the lead."[59] Between 1947 and 1950 many artists of Rothko's generation, having crossed the frontier into abstraction, were in the process of getting territory. Jackson Pollock began to pour paint onto his canvases in the summer of 1947; Barnett Newman's *Onement I* (1948) marked the first of his "zip" paintings; in 1949 Robert Motherwell made the first of the paintings in his "Elegy for the Spanish Republic" series; Willem de Kooning moved as far away from recognizable imagery as he would ever get in works like *Ashville* and *Attic* (both 1949). Rothko was by no means alone in abandoning figuration.

"In any case the fate of American art does not depend on the encouragement bestowed or withheld by 57th Street and the Museum of Modern Art," Clement Greenberg pronounced in 1947, separating art from its institutional context. "The fate of American art is being decided," he continued, "by young people, few of them over forty, who live in cold-water flats and exist from hand to mouth. Now they all paint in the abstract vein, show rarely on 57th Street, and have no reputations that extend beyond a small circle of fanatics, art-fixated misfits who are as isolated in the United States as if they were living in Paleolithic Europe." The isolation of the artists, Greenberg concluded, "is inconceivable, crushing, unbroken, damning."[60] Yet it was this very isolation that had led them to abstract art.

Most of the painters who later became identified as "Abstract Expressionists" had gradually been moving away from figuration for some years. By 1947, the Surrealists had returned to Paris. Their presence in New York had helped to demystify these mythic Continental figures: "we were able to see them in the flesh," Adolph Gottlieb said, "and see that they were just ordinary people such as we were."[61] If European masters could be ordinary people, then Adolph Gottlieb and his friends might be, well, American masters. Abstraction offered an alternative to the forms of "social art" that predominated both before and during the war; an expressive or subjective abstraction more ambitiously offered a way to assimilate and surpass Cubism and Surrealism—European modernism. The new mode did not impose a style, like Cubism, or prescribe a creative process, like Surrealism; it opened a vast expanse of new creative territory within which a range of individual styles could—and did—develop. In postwar America, abstraction already had a thirty-year history, already, at the Museum of Modern Art, *was* history; yet many dealers and buyers, like Curt Valentin, couldn't see it, while the public found it fraudulent and foreign. In postwar America, abstraction possessed the power of both authority and insurgency.

The painters drawn to it, moreover, shared a past that included World War I, the Depression, the WPA, World War II, Auschwitz, and Hiroshima. Isolating themselves from American middle-class life—or, in Rothko's more romantic terms, "freed from a false sense of security and community"—these artists found bohemian freedom complicated by economic misery, urban anonymity, world cataclysm, and the pressures of political ideology. After the war, in an act of both social aggression *and* withdrawal, they sought freedom from historical constraints in the domain of an abstract art which could express feelings independently of any social or natural origin for them. Psyche is severed—isolated—from external reality, an antihistorical premise that derived from a generational history. For the "complex inner self" now seemed to provide the only remaining space for personal (i.e., "internal") freedom.[62] In the case of Rothko, whose notions of tragic myth and eternal human needs entailed a fatalism about history and society, exploration of the individual self provided the only means toward transcending the limits of a rigidly bounded self.

At first confident that there was plenty of open territory around to be shared, the painters worked their new field independently, each occupying his own stretch and developing it without worrying too much about trespassers or thieves. The Abstract Expressionists did not collaborate, like Picasso and Braque; nor did they join in a unified movement, like the Surrealists. When Sam Kootz opened his 1949 season with "The Intrasubjectives" (including Baziotes, de Kooning, Gottlieb, Motherwell, Pollock, Reinhardt, Rothko, and Tomlin), the show represented yet another try by a dealer to affirm, name, and market the new painting as a movement. Yet the artists refused to formulate a program, resisted efforts at organization, and opposed attempts at naming.

Rothko, a busy joiner and polemicist before, now stayed apart from formal group activities, wrote "The Romantics Were Prompted" (viewing the act of painting as a process of discovery transcending any program), then attempted to withdraw altogether from public statements. In the early 1940s, Rothko and Gottlieb had tried to form a movement based on ancient myth; later, when asked about the phrase "Abstract Expressionism," Rothko insisted that both the "label" and "the whole notion of [a] movement" had been "imposed from outside": "never thought of myself as either abstract or expressionist." "It is more of a question of specific painters whose paintings are very much alive."[63]

"It is disastrous to name ourselves," warned de Kooning.[64] But de Kooning was speaking at a three-day symposium on the "Modern Artist in America," an event to which not all the artists in New York had been invited and at which the participants continually spoke of a "we," just as Rothko alludes to "us" and de Kooning to "ourselves," as if a group identity *did* exist. But with the ideological struggles of the thirties and the governmental propaganda efforts of the war behind them, these artists were now more concerned to preserve their personal and artistic freedom than to gain the benefits of collective action. Talking about the invention of Cubism, Braque compared himself and Picasso to two mountain climbers linked by a safety rope; Rothko and his contemporaries resembled a dozen well-spaced rock climbers, all scaling the same sheer cliff, but independently, on their own.

By the late 1940s, however, all of these artists knew each other, viewed each other's work and formed a social network that incorporated close friendships, bitter rivalries, shifting alliances, common grievances, gossip, intrigue, and a shared past. By this time, too, there was an "uptown" versus "downtown" distinction. The downtown artists—de Kooning, Kline, Pollock—met in studios and bars, most often the Cedar Bar in Greenwich Village. The uptown artists—Ferber, Gottlieb, Motherwell, Newman, Rothko—met in studios and each other's homes, most often that of Ferber, who earned enough money from his dental practice to be able to afford good food, drink, and a penthouse apartment along Riverside Drive. Robert Motherwell described himself and his friends as "waifs who came to dinner at Ferber's, and he would cheer us up and the whole atmosphere became benign and secure." The evenings would begin at 8:30 or 9:00 and, according to Ferber, they would "sit around until the earlier morning hours talking, talking, talking about each other's work, about European art, about ideas, about books, about everything. It was a free-wheeling, open forum."[65]

Condemning "ambitious egotists out for grabs," Rothko claimed that "it's this kind of egotist who frequents the clubs and by the way the Cedar Street Bar is nothing but a club." And he added loftily: "I avoid clubs; I prefer solitude."[66] Yet the tense, restless Rothko did not always prefer solitude; he found the evenings at Ferber's quite congenial. There, the group was predominantly Jewish. Downtown the atmosphere was more wild, bohemian, sometimes violent; uptown the atmosphere was more conservative, meditative, sometimes boisterous. At the Cedar Bar, where the standard dress was paint-spattered jeans and T-shirt, Pollock might get drunk and start a fight. At an uptown dinner party, where all the men wore suits, Rothko might get drunk and start singing along with a recording of *Don Giovanni*.[67] To some degree, these differences in social style reflected aesthetic differences as well, since the uptown artists tended to distill their painting to a single, vibrant, iconic image while the downtown artists leaned toward the violence, speed, and brio of "gestural" painting. The downtown temperament was expressionist, uptown more meditative.

Yet it is not as if *no* tensions developed within these groups (by the mid-fifties Newman would not be speaking to either Rothko or Ferber), or as if the borders dividing the groups had been shut down. Newman, Motherwell, and Rothko occasionally drank at the Cedar Bar. Newman, a close friend of Rothko's, was also close to Pollock. During the late forties, in the absence of sales and critical recognition, this loose field of social relations, with artists attending each other's shows, engaging in conversations, spending Saturday afternoons at a gallery like Parsons' or Saturday evenings in an apartment like Ferber's—all these provided a stimulating, supportive context for innovation as well as relief from "crushing" isolation.

• • •

Writing to Clay Spohn in February 1948, after speaking sternly of "men like us who seem to fester with indignation," Rothko expressed "nostalgia" for his previous summer teaching at the California School of Fine Arts (CSFA), in San Francisco. Particularly in contrast to the "stinking mess" on 57th Street, "last summer" now "seems to have been so magical": "As I remember there were a lot of pulls and twists which made me at that time wish it were over. Yet you, Clyff, Doug, etc. set up tensions which made us exist, I believe, on a very desirable plane, and I miss it."[68] During the two summers that Rothko taught at the school (1947 and 1949), the faculty included Elmer Bischoff, Edward Corbett, David Park, Hassel Smith, Clay Spohn, and Clyfford Still; Richard Diebenkorn, a graduate student, taught at night; Douglas MacAgy was the director. Socially and intellectually, a community created out of the "tensions" Rothko mentions could form a *live* community.

Conducting a studio class for advanced students three mornings a week, and giving a one-hour lecture one afternoon a week, Rothko's teaching obligations, in both summers he visited, were fairly minimal.[69] Yet Rothko, the autodidact and Yale dropout, was now teaching adults for the first time; the experience yielded mixed results. The presence of a number of GI-bill students at the school created a division between more and less advanced students, a problem that was exacerbated in the summer session, where "you will have some people who don't know anything about anything," one of Rothko's students recalled. But Rothko made a "valiant try." He pushed for "trying to find something unknown, something new, something different; the word was 'unknown,' and working on a painting if you associate to something in the painting or if you recognize something in the painting, take it out." Even some advanced students had trouble with Rothko's critiques; the less advanced ones "just didn't get the point and they went on painting barns and cows or whatever."[70]

Hassel Smith, a faculty member whose Marxist conception of art often placed him at odds with Still and Rothko, recalled that sometimes when students asked Rothko questions "his response was, 'Why should I tell you? You're going to become a competitor. So why should I let you in on my secrets?' Some people thought it was very funny but others didn't think it was a bit funny." Yet some of Rothko's more advanced students, like John Hultberg and Ernest Briggs, found him supportive. Hultberg's surrealist paintings had been criticized by his teachers for violating the picture plane. Rothko urged him, "Go ahead. Do what you want to do. Don't change your style." "He encouraged me," Hultberg said. "I felt very good when I studied with him." Rothko also warned Hultberg against "French style abstraction, to abstract from a model." "He said it was much better to start from the other end. He said, 'I'd rather paint eyes on a rock, put a couple of eyes on a rock, than take a human figure and make it mechanical the way Picasso does. Or Léger'."[71]

For these students Rothko also offered an alternative to Still, who, regarding teaching "as an economic expedient to be given as little time as possible," managed to become an influential force at the school without spending too much time in the classroom. But "from time to time," Still "would enter the classroom and begin to expound about the 'revolution' which was going on in painting, insinuating that the center of it was precisely in the room where we all were at the moment, and that we were engaged in some conspiratorial movement together, subverting the values of Western art." Rothko, on the other hand, "went from person to person," Ernest Briggs recalled, and "was much more directly involved in the individual and had something to say." If Still declaimed like a Calvinist preacher, Rothko, seeming to muse aloud, "could talk endlessly and very brilliantly and poetically and metaphorically and mysteriously." A "half-understood Still influence" had generated "dark earth colors, blacks and umbers, muddy dark colors." Rothko's presence "created an instantaneous release of pink and blue and reds and soft edges." "Rothko presented another personality and another possibility," said Briggs.[72]

His once-a-week lectures made Rothko anxious; but instead of preparing organized talks, he improvised, as he was doing in his painting, looking for a more organic way to convey the freedom and experiment of the art. "I have had enough nerve to go into these sessions completely unprepared," he wrote Newman, "and just ramble along and perhaps have conveyed many of our mutual ideas with a vividness which would not have been equalled had I tried to organize the material into some sort of system."[73] Clay Spohn brought a carefully prepared, sometimes naively earnest set of questions to one of these sessions, and then transcribed Rothko's responses:

Spohn: What is your personal view toward Picasso?
Rothko: Picasso is certainly not a mystic, nor much of a poet, nor does he express having any very deep or esoteric philosophy. His work is based purely upon a physical plane, a plane of exciting sensuous color, form, and design, but it does not go very far beyond this.
Spohn: Do you believe that the act of painting is, or can be, a means, or method, of philosophic and scientific thought?
Rothko: If painting is based upon the expression of thought rather than mere visual reactions, or sensations, then it can be simultaneous with philosophic thought, it can also be the source of the creation of philosophic decisions, it can be a philosophic expression.
Spohn: After all painting is a form of thinking (or a means of thinking) is it not?
Rothko: Painting certainly is a result of thinking. It causes thinking. It therefore can certainly be a form, or means, of thinking, a means of philosophic thought.
Spohn: If in your opinion there is a possibility of producing paintings that are more in advance than say Picasso, or any other top-ranking painter of today, or masters of the past—what direction do you think those paintings will take, or might possibly take?
Rothko: Toward esoteric reasoning; expressing qualities of, or the essence of, universal elements; expressing basic truths.
Spohn: That is, what can the young artist of today look forward to, in order that he may have some idea of how to prepare himself for the future?
Rothko: By learning the physical elements of painting, their use and con-

trol, and by formulating some personal philosophy of painting. By getting some general understanding of psychology, philosophy, physics, literature, the other arts, and writings of the mystics, etc.
Spohn: Can a painting give one a hint as to the meaning of, or solution of, the absolute, or the universal design of things?
Rothko: Yes, there are many examples among primitive creations, such as examples of mysticism, or esotericism, expressed in idols, fetishes, and various religious objects. In the symbolism of the field fetishes, dance wands, breath feathers, religious ceremonies, etc. of the South West Indians.
Spohn: Or, do you think it more important that the artist only be concerned with his compulsions, and not be concerned with what he thinks is the best way to paint, or what he should or should not do?
Rothko: The most interesting painting is one that expresses more of what one thinks than of what one sees. Philosophic or esoteric thought, for example.[74]

An urbane, sophisticated, cosmopolitan painter from New York, Rothko, himself once a naive young man from Oregon, was now bringing word of the east-coast revolution to the western provinces. Even by the time of his 1947 visit, he was already known in the Bay area because of his one-man show at the San Francisco Museum of Modern Art the previous summer, and particularly because of the museum's hanging of *Slow Swirl By the Edge of the Sea,* which, he wrote to Betty Parsons, "has a beautiful hanging in the rotunda of the Museum." Prior to Rothko's second visit, Still, who had influenced Rothko's appointment, had read from Rothko's letters to his classes and he had shown students the color reproductions of Rothko's work in *Tiger's Eye*.[75] In this period Rothko was eager to meet young artists, and they were eager to meet him, though perhaps not for the same reasons. "I cannot describe the adulation I have received from the artists in S.F.," he confided to Parsons.[76]

Both summers the Rothkos lived in a wooden Victorian on Russian Hill, a short walk from the school. "Our house is exquisite with a view of the bay on one side and Coit Tower on Telegraph Hill on the other. We are living in one of the Howard's houses, with a Hayter, Gorky, and Chas. Howard on our walls and a refrigerator in the kitchen," Rothko wrote Newman. "Besides, MacAgy has given me a little studio in the school and my canvas is prepared, my paper stretched and all I need is a blow on the head. Mell is deliriously delighted with the idea of being mistress of such a house, the attention and the beauty of the place, etc."[77] For his two San Francisco summers Mark Rothko was not living and painting amid the cooking smells from a seafood restaurant.

He had his own studio, assistants, contact with Clyfford Still, a lively community of artists, some income, an opportunity to travel, a comfortable home, and the "adulation" of local painters.

When Mark and Mell Rothko arrived in San Francisco in 1947—by ferry, after a train ride—they were met by his nephew, Julian Roth, and his wife, Dorothy. Wearing an old overcoat and a straw hat torn all around the rim, Rothko was carrying a broken-down brown suitcase tied with rope, and a basket. Mell, her hair in a long braid wrapped around her head, was also dressed shabbily. "They looked like they had just come from the Pale," Roth recalled. Of course, when Rothko had actually arrived from the Pale, he had felt humiliated dressed up in a Dvinsk version of a Buster Brown suit, as if disgraced by bourgeois respectability. In 1947 Rothko was enjoying his first real recognition and success, but not so much as to feel contaminated, threatened, or exposed. Still an impoverished artist whose income in the next two years would diminish, due to a depressed art market, Rothko alludes to "a kitchen with a refrigerator in it," as if to something strange and exotic. He can still speak, proudly, of himself as a man festering with indignation. He can still feel, and look, like a poor immigrant boy from the Pale.

. . .

There is no such thing as good painting about nothing. You have nothing—but content.

Mark Rothko

While Rothko was teaching in San Francisco in the summer of 1947, he and Clyfford Still discussed an idea that Still had first proposed to Rothko during a New York visit the previous April: the formation of their own "school." By January of 1948 Robert Motherwell had been involved in their discussions, for Still wrote to Motherwell that "the problem confronting us reduces to the very small minimum of setting down our work under circumstances conducive to the best possible results." Yet Still could not yet satisfy himself with this pared-down hope for individual salvation in the studio, and so he goes on to imagine an "us" with a kind of social power of their own: "And collecting around us a gradually enlarging group with the ability and integrity and insight to see the implications and worth of their thinking." "Certainly," he adds, "somewhere can be found someone, or means, uncorrupted by political ends or social needs to make such a plan possible."[78]

After resigning from CSFA in the spring of 1948, Still moved to New York; discussion of the proposed school continued, with William Baziotes and David Hare now proposed by Motherwell to join the staff. "The idea of creating a center of free activity for imaginative effort," Still noted in his diary after one meeting at Rothko's. "A group of painters, each visiting the center one afternoon a week, each an entity different from the others, each free to teach in whatever way he chose or free to stay away, every student free to work or remain away, attend every teacher's meetings or none."[79] Still imagined an anti-institutional institution, small, with no administration, run by artists and granting complete individual freedom to both faculty and students. But Still's standards for what might qualify as "uncorrupted by political ends or social needs" were *very* severe. By the end of the summer he had quit, returned to San Francisco and was teaching again at the CSFA.

Rothko, Motherwell, Baziotes, and Hare carried on with the project. They rented a cluttered Greenwich Village loft at 35 East 8th Street, and spent a lot of time cleaning it out.[80] It was at this time that Mark Rothko met Bernard Reis, when he accompanied Robert Motherwell to Reis's office to ask Reis for $500 to buy stoves to heat the loft. The school's first ten-week session began in October 1948; its second, with Barnett Newman added to the staff, began in January 1949. With the spring term, to introduce "the students to as wide an experience as possible," a series of twelve Friday evening seminars, "each to be conducted by an advanced artist or intellectual," was instituted, with Motherwell serving as a kind of master of ceremonies.[81]

Joseph Cornell presented three programs of rare films; John Cage spoke on Indian sand painting, Richard Huelsenbeck on "Dada Days," Julian Levy on Surrealism, Jean Arp on his work, Willem de Kooning on "A Desperate View," Adolph Gottlieb on the "Abstract Image," Ad Reinhardt on "Abstraction." With the public invited, attendance averaged 150. When the school closed after the spring session, the Friday seminars continued as "Studio 35," with Rothko speaking on "My Point of View" in November of 1949.[82] The series closed in April 1950, with the three-day symposium later published as *Modern Artists in America*. What had begun as a small, idealistic alternative art school ended as a lively and wide-ranging forum for debate, self-justification, and even a bit of publicity for the artists.

When the school had opened, its name—"The Subjects of the Artist School"—suggested a more specific agenda than Still's original conception of a free space for creativity. "The title was Barney's," Motherwell said, "and I remember we all agreed that it was right because it made the point that our works did have subjects." The school's printed announcement defined the curriculum "as a spontaneous investigation into the subjects of the modern artist—what his subjects are, how they are arrived at, methods of inspiration and transformation, moral attitudes, possibilities for further explorations, what is being done now and what might be done, and so on."[83] When Newman had spoken of a crisis of subject matter in the early 1940s, he had been asking *what* to paint. Almost ten years later, the painters knew what they wanted to paint—Newman himself, having returned to painting around 1945, produced the first of his "zip" paintings in 1948; Rothko was painting his multiforms—the issue now was to establish *that* there was a subject. The school's title, according to Motherwell, "was meant to emphasize that our painting was not abstract, that it was full of subject matter."[84]

"We assert that the subject is crucial and only that subject-matter is valid which is tragic and timeless," Rothko, Gottlieb [and Newman] had written in the letter to Jewell. And in his radio talk on "The Portrait and the Modern Artist," Rothko had claimed that his pictures "depart from natural representation only to intensify the expression of the subject." By "subject" (or "content") Rothko does not mean any suggested resemblance(s) between the painting and external visual reality; he means—meaning. Rothko's language in the CSFA talk transcribed by Clay Spohn hints at a *kind* of meaning—philosophic, esoteric, mystical, poetic; and he gives more stress to "formulating some personal philosophy of painting" than to mastery of technique. Douglas MacAgy recalled Rothko at the CSFA endlessly smoking cigarettes, "the curling smoke almost a symbol of how he talked: very elusive talk."[85] It was easier to assert the presence of a subject matter than to define it; that was partly because Rothko's subject matter *was* elusiveness.

When asked, in 1954, for a statement on his work by Katharine Kuh, about to exhibit his pictures at the Art Institute of Chicago, Rothko replied: "from the moment that I began to collect my ideas it became clear that here was not a problem of what *ought* to be said, but what it is that I *can* say."[86] In the end he found he could say—nothing, and refused to supply any rationale for his work. Yet Rothko and his colleagues did want to distinguish their work from purist abstraction; it wasn't easy to sit by and wait for critics and viewers to perceive the human content in work that *had* been purified of recognizable forms. The Subjects of the Artist School provided one platform from which these painters tried to extend their influence and even shape their reception.

At the same time, the school reveals a group confidence felt by the artists, now willing to compete both with more conventional institutions, like the Art Students League, and an older alternative school, like Hans Hofmann's. "The artists who have formed the school believe that receiving instruction in regularly scheduled courses from a single teacher is not necessarily the best spirit to advance creative work," reads the school's catalogue—with a sardonic glance aimed two blocks down 8th Street toward the single-teacher, single-theory art school run by Hofmann.[87] There, plastic means and the autonomy of art were dogmatically propounded. At The Subjects of the Artist School, where there were no technical requirements for admission, about fifteen students freely circulated among the five artist-teachers; authority was dispersed, and students were encouraged to discover their own subjects. "The painters walked around us as we worked and made remarks to individuals, often contradictory," recalled Florence Weinstein. "The idea was that you didn't get influenced by one artist." Like the lecture series, conversations, during and outside of class, engaged the kind of "general understanding" of psychology, philosophy, literature that Rothko had advocated for young artists at the CSFA. Yvonne Thomas remembered that "Rothko was more interested in talking about life in a way than in criticizing paintings."[88]

Yet Thomas also recalled that as the fall session went on Rothko became quiet and withdrawn. Rothko wrote to Still that he had experienced a "minor breakdown; that he had completely retired from participation in the school." Still attributed Rothko's troubles to the school, Rothko having written to him of his own concern that activities like the lectures and seminars being pushed by Newman "would obscure the enterprise as it was conceived."[89] Robert Motherwell recalled that Rothko was "clinically depressed" in late 1948, for reasons that had nothing to do with the school. Rothko, according to his first wife, had "a tremendous emotional capacity for despair." Many of Rothko's current friends knew that, in Herbert Ferber's words, "he had periods of severe depression." Some of them sensed that, in Robert Motherwell's words, Rothko was in a particularly "troubled psychological state."

• • •

You know it's not the critics, in the end it's our family we care about.

Mark Rothko

On October 10, 1948, Kate Rothkowitz died in Portland. She was seventy-eight. Rothko had visited Portland in the summer of 1946, probably to introduce Mell to his family, and at both the beginning and end of his San Francisco trip the following summer. By October of 1948 Kate Rothkowitz's death, coming after a "long, painful illness," had been expected for some time. "The death of his mother is the only personal thing he talked to me about at length," Robert Motherwell remembered. "He became obsessed over whether or not to go back to Portland."[90] It was during the time his mother was dying that

Chapter Nine

Rothko told Motherwell that it was not the approval of the critics, but "our family we care about." Rothko did not make the trip.

One afternoon in the late 1940s, Rothko, spending the summer in East Hampton, embarked on an ill-fated fishing trip off the Long Island shore, near Louse Point, with Harold Rosenberg and Jackson Pollock and a fourth man. The boat was leaky, it began to take on water and eventually to sink. The three other men jumped and swam for shore, but Rothko, though a strong swimmer, hung onto the side of the sinking boat until the last possible moment, then swam in. When Lee Krasner, who had been sitting with Clement Greenberg on the beach, asked Rothko what had happened, he said "that, as the boat went down, and he stayed there unable to plunge into the water and start swimming, he was thinking of his mother," as if he associated his mother, remembered in the family as forceful and determined, with passivity and despair.[91]

When his mother died, Rothko had just turned forty-five. He told the painter Ben Dienes, after *his* mother's death, that "he knew how I felt because when his mother died he stopped painting, and he wrote a novel. He didn't paint, he said, for a year or more." Rothko similarly told Alfred Jensen, a friend who had stopped painting to start an autobiographical novel, that after his mother's death, he "wrote a book which took him two years to complete." "He thinks I am doing the right thing to get myself down on paper," Jensen wrote. "That is the first step toward enabling one to think clearly and vigorously, to express one's direct sensations with violence and conviction."[92] Rothko produced many paintings in the year following his mother's death, so that if he did stop painting, it was not for very long. Nor does any evidence for his writing a book in this period survive. Whether or not he did quit painting or did write a book, his later statements—like his claim that he stopped painting to study myth in the early 1940s—sound characteristically dramatic, as if he felt only such a statement could convey his feeling of loss with proper violence and conviction.

Too much domesticity, too much family, made Rothko bored and restless. Visiting his family in Portland, Rothko would go out for long walks. When he visited his mother-in-law in Cleveland, he liked to do two things: "he could spend very happy hours flat on his back listening to Mozart" or he would leave the apartment and ride around in streetcars. "He was particularly fascinated with the route that went past all the funeral homes. He felt that Cleveland was a city fascinated with death."[93] It wasn't Cleveland. "The only serious thing is death," Rothko had declared during the 1930s. "Nothing else is to be taken seriously."

At mid-life himself, struggling to remove "history" and "memory" from his paintings, Rothko was pushed back into his own past and into himself by the death of his remaining parent. Only ten when Jacob Rothkowitz had died, Rothko had been left with an outraged sense of injustice: life had not given him his due. He might triumphantly assert that the world's unfriendliness really freed him; but he also festered with indignation. His mother's death drew Rothko back to even earlier losses. He once said that he turned to large canvases "because I wanted to paint my own size. I wanted to recognize myself in my work." Another time he acknowledged that "when I recognize myself in a work, then I realize it's completed."[94] Recognition was a charged, complex issue for Rothko, an eternally familiar need. His early portrait of his mother viewed her close up, but as removed, hard, absorbed in her own melancholy, inaccessible—looking away, like the mother in *The Rothkowitz Family*. The son of a mother he perceived as a more powerful than loving presence, Rothko lacked recognition from very early.

"I do think there was a great vacuum at the center of his being," said Stanley Kunitz. Rothko, "the only important artist that I ever met wholly indifferent to objects," as Robert Motherwell recalled, did not attempt to fill himself with material objects and possessions. Someone who often nervously paced with his hands clasped behind his back when visiting friends or who liked to walk the neighborhood streets at night, Rothko was physically restless, as if agitated by some lack. He looked for companionship from men, consolation from women, and adulation from both, as if to comfort him for some loss. Rothko could never quite get enough. He had a "ravenous appetite"; he smoked endless cigarettes; he drank. As his doctor later said, "his greatest sources of consolation were calories and alcohol." In reality, however, his greatest sources of consolation were his paintings which now, by abstracting from physical and social surfaces and looking deeply inside, created an image of himself that he could recognize. As Rothko said of Arshile Gorky, "I wonder if perhaps his love for art furnished him with his single greatest source of happiness. I believe it did."[95]

In the year following the death of his mother, Rothko, now distilling his paintings down to two or three large and empty rectangles, began to paint his deprivation, as if that absence constituted a self he *could* recognize; and he painted his deprivation as *full*—of colored light, sensual pleasure, fluctuating movement, charged feeling. By expanding the size of his paintings and detaching their blocks of color from the edges, Rothko made his shapes advance toward and envelope a viewer, at least one with a "quickening" gaze. Sometimes softly enfolding, sometimes threatening to consume, always awesome and commanding, these paintings enact the most archaic human drama: the difficult boundary negotiations worked out by a child who desires love, fears possession, and needs autonomy.

As in the description of his creative process in a letter to Clay Spohn, or in his *Untitled* (1948), Rothko sought to construct a "live unity" out of such primordial human tensions. After mid-1949, Rothko's paintings confront, and then transcend, loss—by universalizing it in an abstract painting language that can express "one's direct sensations with violence and conviction" by freeing those feelings from their specific occasions in the external world.

Rothko's new paintings grieve; they portend; they exalt; they release. They transform hollowness and despair into transcendence and nurturing beauty. These empty canvases are full. The death of Kate Rothkowitz, thrusting her son backward psychologically, helped push his work one last step toward a "new life."

10 Rothko's New Vision

> My work has the power to convey a new vision. Its message becomes visible in a new structural language. . . .
>
> Mark Rothko

At the end of Studio 35's three-day symposium on "Modern Artists in America," Adolph Gottlieb proposed that the participants protest the conservative bias of the juries selected for the Metropolitan Museum of Art's national contemporary art competition. What in 1935 would have produced a mass picketing of the museum, in 1950 produced an "open letter" which confidently asserted that "for roughly a hundred years, only advanced art has made any consequential contribution to civilization," declared that "the choice of jurors" warrants no "hope that a just proportion of advanced art will be included," and announced the artists' refusal to submit any of their work. Written mainly by Adolph Gottlieb, the letter was signed by fourteen of the painters at the symposium (including Willem de Kooning, Robert Motherwell, Barnett Newman, Ad Reinhardt, Hedda Sterne, and Theodoros Stamos), plus four additional painters (including Jackson Pollock and Mark Rothko).[1]

In the cultural politics of 1950, "advanced" artists were still outsiders. Francis Henry Taylor, the outspoken director of the Metropolitan, viewed modern art as a reflection of the disintegration of Western civilization; he called the Museum of Modern Art "that whorehouse on 53rd Street."[2] The Metropolitan's Hearn Fund, intended for the purchase of living American work, had long gone unused. Yet these advanced artists had by now accumulated sufficient collective authority for their letter to merit a front-page article in the *New York Times*, something the active Cultural Committee of the Federation of Modern Painters and Sculptors had never been able to accomplish. "18 Painters Boycott Metropolitan; / Charge 'Hostility To Advanced Art'," read the headline on the May 22 story. The following day, an editorial in the *New York Herald Tribune* attacked "The Irascible Eighteen" for "distortion of fact." Articles in *The Nation*, *Art News*, *Art Digest*, and *Time* expanded media coverage, the sardonic *Time* piece closing with a crushing judgment from Taylor: "the contemporary artist has been reduced to the status of a flat-chested pelican, strutting upon the intellectual wastelands and beaches, content to take whatever nourishment he can from his own too meager breast."³

Life decided to do a photo story, timed to appear with the Metropolitan's December announcement of the competition's winners. Some of the artists hesitated about cooperating, among them Rothko, on the grounds that *Life* "epitomized mass culture."⁴ Others feared being made to look foolish, and with good reason. At first, the magazine wanted to photograph the artists on the steps of the Metropolitan, each holding one of his or her paintings. The artists refused, in Gottlieb's words, "because that would look as if we were trying to get into the Metropolitan and we were being turned down on the steps." This protest against the Metropolitan did not, like the "Whitney Dissenters," seek to dramatize the artists' exclusion; nor did it challenge the jury system as an institution. The artists, rather than questioning the structure of authority, wished to expose its conservative bias, both to publicize their rejection (official rejection being a mark of greatness for the modern artist) and to assert their own growing cultural power. Even their refusal to pose on the museum steps worked; *Life* backed down—"they were very surprised at this, because nobody refuses anything to *Life* magazine," said Gottlieb—and the magazine's art editor arranged for Nina Leen to photograph the group in a West 44th Street studio.⁵ Even the scrupulous Clyfford Still agreed to participate. On November 24, twelve pictures were taken, and a photo-essay, "IRASCIBLE GROUP OF ADVANCED ARTISTS LED FIGHT AGAINST SHOW," appeared in the *Life* for January 15, 1951 (fig. 32).

This self-selected, ad-hoc group of avant-garde artists thus succeeded in controlling the image projected of them in a mass-circulation magazine—a visual representation which, as Irving Sandler points out, "has become *the* image whereby we envision the artists who achieved the triumph of American painting." Socially, the 1950s were dominated by middle-class values and mores, which *Life* both reflected and promulgated. Before the picture-taking session, Barnett Newman had "kept insisting that the group be photographed *like bankers*," as if advanced artists were obliged to establish a more-middle-class-than-thou respectability.⁶

Though working-class in income, these neatly dressed painters don't look poor or proletarian; nor do they present themselves as angry rebels eager to batter down the cultural gates. There are no bohemian flourishes. Except perhaps for Ad Reinhardt, they don't much resemble people who run a bank, but they do look like people you might meet *in* the bank, making a modest deposit or withdrawal. Both uptown and downtown painters wear a shirt, tie, and suit or sport jacket (or, in the case of Hedda Sterne, a dress). "Each artist occupies his or her own space and emerges as an individual," Irving Sandler writes of the photograph. Too respectable to be threateningly avant-garde, too grim and intense to be merely bourgeois, the artists project an image of respectable individuality which allows them to enter both the middle-class and the mass media without being absorbed by them.

On the whole, the protestors look more grave than irascible—except for Pollock and Rothko. Pollock, looking accustomed to having his picture taken, leans forward, left elbow resting on his leg, cigarette in hand, glowering at the camera as if across a barroom at a patron who has just insulted him. Nina Leen had let the artists decide where to position themselves; Rothko placed himself in a prominent front position, at the right corner of a triangle formed by himself, Newman, and Stamos, as if, having put aside all his doubts about the *Life* photo, he were now eager to display himself. Yet Rothko, looking unaccustomed to having his picture taken—cameras, after all, don't offer quickening looks—sits on a stool, stiff and uncomfortable in a rumpled jacket at least two sizes too large for his bulky upper body (and which seems to hold a heavy object in its bulging left pocket). The way his jacket has been pulled too far forward on the left and too far back on the right, the way his body turns away from the camera while his head turns back toward it, the way his right hand (holding one of his endless cigarettes) covers his left—all are reminiscent of the uneasy, self-conscious pose of his *Self-Portrait,* his ambivalence about being looked at. Here, Rothko glares at the camera, through his thick-lensed glasses, in an expression that combines apprehension with belligerence. It's as if when Rothko looks out at the world, or when the world directs its attention toward him, he begins to wonder, "What are they going to do to me *now*?" and he tries to ward off the danger with a killing look.

. . .

When Rothko sat for the *Life* photo session in the West 44th Street studio, on the day after Thanksgiving in 1950, he was forty-seven years old. He'd been married for five years to Mell, who was now eight months pregnant. He was a self-employed "advanced" artist who, two days before the birth of his daughter Kate on December 30, received a statement from Betty Parsons revealing that during the year he had sold six pictures, earning him $3,279.69 for 1950.[7] At the time of the *Life* photo, Mell either had already or would soon leave her job with McFadden Publications, and Rothko was looking for a teaching position. Again just before Kate's birth, Rothko learned that, as of the first of February, he had been appointed an assistant professor in the Department of Design at Brooklyn College.[8]

"I don't express myself in my painting," Rothko later said, trying to shake free of the label "Abstract Expressionism." "I express my not-self."[9] In 1950, to look at Rothko and then to look at a painting like *Number 10, 1950*, or *Number 12, 1951* (color plates 14 & 15), is to be impressed with the *difference* between the look of the man and the look of his work. Rothko's new paintings may hint at cosmic expanses and spiritual illumination (*Number 10, 1950*) or they may revel in a joyful carnality (*Number 12, 1951*), but in either case the works possess a delicate and even elegant beauty. Yet Rothko himself, with his heavy, fleshy build and his plain, often rumpled clothing, never resembled anybody's idea of the refined, sensitive artist. Rothko often marveled at the beauty of Edith and later of Mell, as if amazed that an attractive woman would have anything to do with *him*. He himself had a sensuous, "feminine" mouth, but his eyes were slightly too far apart and slightly bulging, his nose large and wide, his jaw slack. By 1950 his brown hair had thinned, receded, and started to gray. Myopic, a painter with blurred vision, Rothko looked (or glared) out at the world through thick lenses held in plain, clear plastic frames; his large, square hands, with long, thick fingers, seemed more like those of a workingman than an artist. At 5'11", big-boned and thick-chested, Rothko possessed a bulky muscularity, but he was no athlete. Famous among friends and family for his clumsiness, Rothko often moved as if distracted, as if his heavy, awkward body were a bit beyond his control.

A classic 1950 photograph of Jackson Pollock shows him working over a large area of canvas that he has rolled out (but not yet cut) from a bolt on the floor of the East Hampton barn he had converted into a studio (fig. 33). Dressed in a black T-shirt, black jeans, and black shoes, his right leg twisted, his tense body leaning forward, with his left foot *on* the work, Pollock holds a can of black paint in his left hand, applying it by rapidly swinging his brush about two feet above the canvas. A classic photograph of Mark Rothko shows him sitting in a green wooden deck chair, his back to the camera, cigarette in hand, contemplating one of his paintings in an East Hampton garage he had temporarily converted into a studio (fig. 34). Both artists are presented as immersed in their work, as if we have been granted a privileged look into the privacy of their studios. In one of a series of pictures that publicized his innovative painting methods, Pollock displays a figure of intense "masculine" energy and dynamism. Very secretive about his working procedures, Rothko did not like to have people watch, much less photograph, him while painting. Yet even in his more relaxed attitude, he, too, is at work—weighing, feeling, measuring, *judging* his painting.

The difference is that Pollock's body dominates the picture, his lithe black form twisted and bent forward, straining toward and actually stepping onto the white canvas he has marked with blots and swirling lines of black paint.

Rothko, casually dressed in slacks and a striped shirt, an uptown painter on vacation, has finished painting, washed up, changed his clothes, taken a seat, lit a cigarette, and begun to *look*. Pollock *acts;* Rothko *meditates.* Placed in the center foreground with his back to us, his body mostly hidden by the chair, Rothko has drawn back from his painting in order to take it all in, unlike Pollock, who is too far inside his painting to see all of it.

In reality, both artists alternated rapid application of paint—Rothko's thin glazes were applied very quickly—with longer, more deliberate periods of rumination and study. Yet these two images, though clearly constructed by a professional photographer, probably with promotional ends in mind, evoke an important difference between the two artists. Pollock struggles for bodily presence, something that prompted him, in *Number 1, 1948,* for instance, to dip his right hand into a can of paint and then to impress several blackish-red handprints across the top and down the left side of the canvas. Ironically, Pollock's desire to make the painting record his physical movements also distanced him from the canvas, so that he no longer *touched* it with a brush, but tossed his paint onto it. In *Number 1, 1948,* he momentarily discards brush or stick, literally takes his paint in hand to apply it to the canvas. Yet the indistinctness of several of the handprints exposes Pollock's body as a *fading* image whose mark must be made again and again in a desperate, sometimes "bloody" struggle for presence.

It is impossible to imagine Mark Rothko placing his handprint on one of his paintings. He once said that paint should be "breathed" onto the canvas, as if it could be applied without the contaminating labor of the body. Yet his work does not exactly struggle for bodily absence—it is too sensuous for that—but for transcendence of that *specific,* defined, bounded physical existence with which he felt so ill at ease. Tall, husky, middle-aged, balding, claustrophobic, restless, clumsy, hypochondriacal, given to self-inflicted injuries, Rothko painted to diffuse and transcend his physical self. Protective of his own autonomy, eager to find a unique "recognizable image" for his work, Rothko insisted on an individuality he wanted to get beyond. Here at rest in a deck chair, physically removed from his painting but absorbed by it, Rothko contemplates a large, black rectangular void placed on a bright red ground— one version of his "not-self."

• • •

> *Rothko said he wanted a presence, so when you turned your back to the painting, you would feel that presence the way you feel the sun on your back.*
>
> Murray Israel

Chapter Ten

"Beware of a too vague, too abstract, too symbolic concept," Rothko warned Alfred Jensen. "When a person is a mystic he must always strive to make everything concrete."[10] Rothko often maintained that he was a "materialist" whose "new areas of color are things," not symbols. "Mondrian divides a canvas; I put things on it." Diminishing his Dutch modernist predecessor to a mere formalist, Rothko imagines himself as the creator not just of material but of living presences. "My art is not abstract; it lives and breathes," he said, just as in "The Romantics Were Prompted," he had characterized his shapes as "organisms with volition and a passion for self-assertion."[11]

Anthropomorphizing his works, Rothko often spoke of them in the life-versus-death rhetoric he shared with Clyfford Still. Looks can quicken; looks can kill—especially historicizing looks. By absorbing particular works into evolutionary narratives, art historians achieve "a unity of death," Rothko claimed, whereas "what we want is a live unity." In fact, any kind of writing about his work—by critics, by curators, or even by Rothko himself—fixes the artist in a "premature entombment."[12] Living presences, as powerful, warm, and life-sustaining and *silent* as the sun, Rothko's new paintings were at once independent of, and yet closely identified with, their passionately self-assertive creator.

It was not just, as Rothko said at Pratt, that a time came when "whoever used" the human figure "mutilated it." He had *never* really—until around the time he met his second wife—been able to represent the human form without violating it. He had subjected the body to expressionist distortions, imagined grotesque creatures, half-human, half-animal, which he then severed into rectangular compartments or whose flesh he had torn open (the self turned inside out) to expose an empty and sterile interior. Bulky domestic figures were squeezed into cramped, bare rooms or attenuated urban travelers were trapped within the stony, rectilinear architecture of subway platforms, as if either private or public space subjected these depressed and defeated figures to a "premature entombment." Life in the flesh, life in *his* bulky, awkward frame and vulnerable flesh, left Rothko uneasy, restless, lacking, embarrassed. When he had studied acting, he was trying to learn to express emotion *by means of* his body. When he arrived at his classic format around 1950, Rothko, as if feeling an inner spirit not fully incarnated in his body, began to create paintings which no longer represented the body (or any other identifiable objects) because they were themselves organisms, idealized bodies which could—"without embarrassment"—incarnate his living spirit.

In paintings like *Number 10, 1950* (color plate 14), Rothko creates not just a recognizable image but a personal icon, "a new structural language" flexible and rich enough to engage—or obsess—him for the next fifteen years. Approximately 7½′ × 4¾′, *Number 10, 1950,* much higher than it is wide, asserts a large, imposing, vertical presence, composed of colored horizontal blocks and bars of white, yellow, gray set on a violet-blue ground. Consisting of just a few simple, vacant, elemental shapes, paintings like this one can easily be dismissed as merely simple, merely decorative, or merely static. Certainly, in my own experience, standing, say, in a room filled with five such paintings at the National Gallery, many museum visitors still mock them as too easy and quickly pass through, satisfied with having identified the works as "Rothkos." Such treatment constitutes a premature entombment, for a painting like *Number 10, 1950,* "lives by companionship, expanding and quickening in the eyes" of an observer willing to yield to its commanding simplicity, let time slow down, and relax into an alert contemplativeness. It is as if the painting *were* static, or dead—until brought to life by the physical presence of a viewer whose look quickens because it is prolonged.

What *happens* when we look at this painting? At first we are drawn to the dramatic yellow rectangle—by its intense, glowing color, its greater size, its dominant position. The rectangle contains—nothing—and so, weightless, it rises and floats out from the picture plane *toward* the viewer. Yet its golden surface is also translucent and we look *into* this spacious rectangle—like looking into the sun, except that this sun will not blind or burn; it is a humanized sun, powerful, yet warm and embracing. Filled with a deep yellow light, the surface of this rectangle constantly fluctuates as varying densities of paint change the hue from golden to a dark orange where a brownish-red area beneath, still visible as a fringe around the yellow, pushes through to create mysterious shadowy presences that form and dissolve as our eye, with nothing definite to arrest it, keeps moving around inside this inviting shape.

If we look downward, seeking some relief from the pulsing intensity of the yellow, the gray rectangle below may at first suggest a pedestal, on which the yellow is being displayed, as if *it* were the subject of the painting. Yet the yellow no more rests on the gray than the gray rests on the bottom edge of the painting. In the mid-1940s, Rothko had typically divided his canvas (or paper) into two or three horizontal tiers which formed a ground. In the 1950s and 1960s, he released these rectangular areas from the edges and from each other; he made them autonomous. In *Number 10, 1950,* both the yellow and gray shapes, fuzzy-edged, detached, and independent, hang suspended, or float, as if they were "*things,*" but *immaterial* things. Thinly painted, looking more like gauze than marble, the gray area lacks the solidity to support any weight. Semitransparent, the gray contains two vertical white columns which emphasize the yellow by pointing toward it, but which also suggest, together with a white horizontal band joining them and two darker thin horizontal lines above, a classical architectural structure seen through a gray veil.

Looking at *Number 10, 1950,* we enter a pictorial space whose properties—its colors, shapes, weights, spatial relationships—keep shifting, keep *moving.* Rothko's empty canvases are filled with ceaseless movement, a perceptual abundance. What seems at first to be a simple, absolute geometry turns out to be equivocal, as a gray shape, for example, can be perceived as one or two or three rectangles. Above the yellow block appears a strip, brownish-red thinly painted over with gray, a narrow rectangle which echoes the white bar at the top of the painting and the gray one just below the yellow. This dark red strip continues the fringe along the sides of the yellow, now perceived as sitting inside and partially covering an earlier, larger rectangle, whose dried-blood color often pushes through to create the evanescent dark orange shapes within the yellow square. Patches along the top and sides of the yellow reveal yet another rectangle, this one white, between the red and yellow ones. So the yellow rectangle recedes into luminous golden depths; but the yellow rectangle is also a flat surface, with some of Rothko's watery-thin yellow paint dripping down (on the left) into the gray. Just so, the violet blue band, resembling a midnight sky, suggests a cosmic boundlessness, while wisps of smokey gray, lightly painted on top of the blue, bring it back to the surface, as does the boardlike, yet vigorously brushed white bar near the top of the painting. The opposition between flatness and depth, like that between substance and void, collapses in an ambiguous space where shapes cannot be firmly bound, easily located, or securely identified.

The painting's elusive mobility constitutes what Rothko might have called a "tragic" freedom. Its white, yellow, and gray bands have all been placed close to the edges of a tall, narrow canvas whose edges seem to push in, seem to have *already* pushed in. Rothko's rectangles, though they float, look hemmed in. Yet, as if this pressure acted as a lever for true liberation, their softened, delicate edges make their sides seem to expand and push outward. It is really a matter "of breathing and stretching one's arms again," Rothko had written in "The Romantics Were Prompted." *Number 10, 1950,* dramatizes the effort to move and breathe in a compressed space, as if one of the solid, blank walls in a Rothko domestic interior of the 1930s had gently metamorphosized into a colorful curtain, admitting air and light to a cramped, suffocating room. "The problem with living in this world," Rothko pronounced to William Seitz, "is to keep from being smothered."[13] The story Rothko related, with "rage," to Robert Motherwell, of being bound in swaddling clothes as an infant gives a characteristically intense expression to feelings of constriction. Large-boned, bulky, powerfully built, Rothko, who was also soft-edged and sensitive, constantly felt the imminent danger of being "smothered" by encroaching physical, social, or domestic circumstances. His new paintings created breathing space.

Yet these paintings do not seek simply to "transcend" the walls of an unalterable external reality by soaring upward into either an untrammeled freedom or a vaporous mysticism. Rather, by (in Rothko's word) pulverizing the familiar world of recognizable, stable objects—by grinding them to the verge of dissolution—his works free us from the weight, solidity, and definition of a material existence, *whose constricting pressures we still feel*. Rothko combines freedom with constraint, and if these paintings create "dramas," with the shapes as the "performers," they stage a *struggle* to be free.

The rectangular shapes in Rothko's new paintings are autonomous in the sense that, though they stimulate multiple associations and provisional identifications, they elude the obligation to represent any fixed external reality. Yet to be autonomous is to be rigidly bounded, self-enclosed, apart; in short, to suffer that very rootless solitude which Rothko's works now seek to remedy. In *Number 10, 1950,* yellow paint drips down into the gray on the left; flecks of the gray drift up into the yellow on the right. Yellow covers but still reveals a dark red beneath; the upper half of the grey covers a purple band, left exposed along the right, where it bulges inward. The cool blue intensifies the yellow, which deepens the blue. In Rothko's "new vision," autonomy coexists with mutual interaction and dependence. Rothko's actors, in fact, perform only *in* relation, not just to each other but also to their audience. Silent and empty, Rothko's works urgently communicate a desire to communicate. Sensuous and inviting, they convey an eagerness to be liked and admired. Requiring a kind of empathetic looking to activate their movements, they *need* to be looked at. Advancing toward and receding from a viewer, they embody their creator's ambivalent play of reticence and gregariousness.

Evolved during the year following the death of Kate Rothkowitz, the classic format of Rothko strives to recover not so much a lost object as a lost relationship. An illusionistic painting which divides its space into human figure/natural ground assumes a world of detached, bounded, separate objects, a world that Rothko could experience only as one of paralyzing solitude: "for me the great achievements of the centuries in which the artist accepted the probable and familiar as his subjects were the pictures of the single human figure—alone in a moment of utter immobility." Alone in his studio, Rothko could shut the world out and paint, while filling the room with music, ideally Mozart. "He wanted that music," said Stanley Kunitz, "to saturate the room, to diffuse it in the same way that his paintings were diffused through a room."[14] Raised to the level of poignancy of music, painting could fill an empty room, or self.

Rothko painted lack, he painted the "great vacuum at the center of his being," he painted nothing—as a luminous, sensuous, fluctuating, diffused space large and mobile enough to surround and envelope a viewer. His new works travel back psychologically, to recover subjectivity in the *process* of forming, prior to language, prior to the immobilizing melancholy of hard boundaries, sharp definition—individuation. Going several steps further than he had been willing to go with the emergent figures of works like *Slow Swirl,* Rothko was now painting his "*not-yet*-me."

Unlike Clyfford Still's jagged assertions of embattled masculinity, Rothko's canvases communicate a maternal feeling, as if Rothko were imagining his way back to a warmer, more nurturing presence which had preceded, and perhaps remained hidden inside, the hard, removed, and melancholy Kate Rothkowitz he had painted in the late 1920s. Rothko no longer represents the literal mother; nor does he mourn her specific loss. Instead, abstracting from discrete people, objects, and events, he produces a kind of painting that will, through its interactions with the viewer, recreate the reciprocities and tensions of that early mother/child relationship; and it is Rothko's capacity to draw on such buried psychic experience that provides his abstract and vacant works with the core of human content (or subject matter) that he insisted on. By dissolving the familiar physical, social worlds and confronting us with a void, Rothko's paintings also convey a melancholy sense of loss, what he called their "intimations of mortality." Even more, these works disturb viewers—not just those viewers of 1950 who expected *some* sort of mimesis, and not just those viewers, then and now, who find the paintings too easy, but even those sympathetic viewers who, offering the prolonged ruminative gaze Rothko sought, are made anxious by the picture's enveloping power, like a small child too close to a powerful and seductive mother.

Commenting in May, 1951, on the size of his pictures, Rothko pointed out that while "historically the function of painting large pictures is something very grandiose and pompous," his own were intended "to be very intimate and human." "To paint a small picture is to place yourself outside your experience, to look upon experience as a stereopticon view or with a reducing glass. However you paint the larger picture, you are in it. It isn't something you command."[15] Small pictures place us back in the world of separate objects and distanced relations. Large pictures sweep us up and place us *inside* a fluid space of shifting, indefinite boundaries. Commanding and aggressive as well as inviting and intimate, they emanate a larger than human force—perhaps liberating, perhaps overpowering, but in either case not something we can control. So Rothko's viewers, too, can begin to feel hemmed in, threatened by fusion, by an absorptive, smothering unity.

"What we want is a live unity." For Rothko that meant *tension,* created out of unresolved oppositions, say, between freedom and coercion, expansion and contraction. As William Seitz concluded after several conversations with Rothko: "antitheses, Rothko feels, are neither synthesized nor neutralized in his work, but held in a confronted unity which is a momentary stasis."[16] He delivers the viewer from the solidities and divisions of ordinary physical and social realities; he confronts this viewer with loss and the anxieties aroused by the absence of defined boundaries; and he offers this viewer the protections of boundaries that are still in the process of being formed. The advancing movements of Rothko's large pictures can make them feel intrusive; their diffusion and brooding emptiness can arouse uneasiness. We crave limits, and so the endless oscillations of his paintings *are* contained by the edges of the canvas, just as the diffusions of his colored areas are held in by the rectangles, in turn held in by the border of ground color. In his 1958 lecture at the Pratt Institute, Rothko spoke of the "tension" in his work as a "curbed desire," as, say, the desire for freedom might be curbed in the very act of expressing it. He no longer wanted his pictures enclosed by frames, which sharply divide the inside of the work from the outside; his rectangles are not hard-edged and geometrical, but soft-edged and blurred. Freedom, then, is a *controlled* movement, but a *gently* controlled movement, this tension making it an intimate, human, and "tragic" freedom.

Once asked how close a spectator should stand to one of his paintings, Rothko, in his provocateur mode, answered "eighteen inches."[17] Yet in my observations, viewers of a Rothko painting will typically place themselves at the middle of the canvas, several feet back, at a point where the work fills their peripheral vision—but they will then alternate this position with a series of much closer ones. The activation of the work depends not just on the quickening gaze of a disembodied eye but also on the *bodily* movements of a spectator who enacts a process of closeness and distance, being drawn in and pulling back. The closest anyone can come to being "in" the painting is the artist as he creates it, and even for him "the instant one is completed, the intimacy between creation and the creator is ended. He is an outsider," a spectator, like the Rothko seated before his painting in a deck chair in East Hampton, trying to feel his way back into the work.

The completed painting may not be something a spectator can command; but neither is it something that simply commands the spectator. Wary of people in general, particularly suspicious of the kinds of people most likely to show up in a museum or gallery—collectors, critics, curators—Rothko found it necessary to use dramatic means—large pictures, absence of identifiable content, warm, glowing colors—to grasp and to hold the attention of a visitor.

Yet his empty, richly evocative canvases allow considerable latitude of association—not an infinite but a gently controlled freedom. Incomplete (or entombed) until looked at, a painting like *Number 10, 1950,* needs a viewer, whose needs for freedom and limitation, distance and intimacy, sensual pleasure and spiritual sustenance, are, in turn, fed by the painting.

Yet, if Rothko maintained that his works were living organisms, he also called them " 'portraits' of states of the soul," and it does feel as though these paintings offer us an intimate look inside the artist, as if opening a window on his inner spirit. But these windows obscure as much as they reveal, and the Rothko who spoke of his paintings as spiritual self-portraits or as physical presences also called them "facades," a word that suggests an imposing and artificial exterior behind which something remains concealed.[18] "For all his gregariousness," and for all his eagerness to communicate, Rothko "was shy," a reserved and even secretive person who kept large areas of his life and himself hidden, though in ways that both aroused and blocked curiosity. In conversation, he liked to debate, he liked to pronounce, he liked to stretch out on a couch and ponder aloud; but he found intimate talk more difficult. He had clusters of friends who not only never met each other but never knew of each other's existence. He was very secretive about his working methods; he did not like to be watched painting; and once he could afford to do so, he worked in studios outside his home, where he said he felt under "surveillance."

A painting like *Number 10, 1950,* persistently implies the presence of something behind the surface, whether an earlier layer of paint, a dimly perceived shape, or a hidden source of light. "Some artists want to tell all like at a confessional," Rothko said in his lecture at Pratt. "I as a craftsman prefer to tell little. My pictures are indeed facades (as they have been called)." The faces in Rothko's early work had often resembled dramatic masks, just as his urban scenes often resembled stage sets. Now, in Elaine de Kooning's acute formulation, "the painting is a hiding place," itself a mask, a window with the curtains drawn. Rothko holds back, remains outside, tells little and in this sense too paints his "not-self," our desire to look inside him curbed at the very moment it occurs, as if full exposure *would* prove embarrassing. Protective facades, theatrical, Rothko's living "organisms" are also constructions, fabrications, within and behind which their shrewd creator remains a dispersed, elusive, and absent presence.

· · ·

I never realized how really new our world is until I came here.

Mark Rothko, in France, 1950

> *When I went to Europe and saw the old masters, I was involved with the credibility of the drama. Would Christ on the cross if he opened his eyes believe the spectators?*
>
> Mark Rothko, 1958

Stanley Kunitz, who met Rothko in the early 1950s, recalled the painter's "vehemence about the European scene, about the whole tradition of European painting beginning with the Renaissance, and his flat rejection of it—his saying, 'We have wiped the slate clean. We start anew. A new land. We've got to forget what the Old Masters did'."[19] In 1945, Rothko had been willing to identify himself as the offspring of surrealist and abstract art; now, empowered by the resolution of his own painting and his sense of participating in a collective impetus ("we"), Rothko, whose paintings reveal a sensitively edged self in the process of taking on form, speaks as a self-generated master, claiming a well-bounded autonomy purified of any invasive influence of the past.

Of course in New York, Old Masters were not the looming presences that they were in Paris, Florence, or Rome. But beginning in the mid-1920s, Rothko had spent many hours with the collections at the Metropolitan, particularly admiring Rembrandt. He was also familiar with the collections of the new Old Masters at the Museum of Modern Art, particularly admiring Matisse, having "spent hours and hours before *The Red Studio* once it was permanently installed in 1949." "When you looked at that painting," he said, "you became that color, you became totally saturated with it," as if it were music.[20] Rothko also knew the Surrealists and Surrealism, particularly admiring Miró who, in his view, was the artist who had broken with the Renaissance, rather than Cézanne or Picasso.[21] Rothko had come to art fairly late, he came to it in what was then an artistically provincial city, and as an American and a Jew he came to Western painting as an outsider, its tradition yet another place where this transplanted Russian never felt entirely at home. Still, his engagements with artists and works in that tradition, and the awarenesses they brought, could not be repressed, or even forgotten.

On March 29, 1950, this middle-aged American painter, convinced that he and his cohorts had wiped the slate clean, sailed on the *Queen Elizabeth* for a five-month trip to Europe, funded by a small inheritance from Mell's mother, who had died just four months after Rothko's.[22] Rothko was not traveling as an American immigrant looking to return to his origins; in none of the three trips he made to Europe during his lifetime did he visit Russia. On this visit, he and Mell stayed in Paris (three weeks), Cagnes-sur-Mer (near Nice, three weeks), Venice (eight or nine days), Florence, Arezzo, Siena, Rome (four weeks), back to Paris (two weeks) and then to London (three or four weeks): an itinerary that was shaped, except for the three weeks on the French Riviera, around viewing Old Masters. But Rothko was no passionate pilgrim out of Henry James; nor was he a beginning painter, like Adolph Gottlieb in 1921, open, curious, eager to absorb. Already formed, having only recently reached what he called his "delayed maturity," Rothko viewed Europe, especially New York's rival, Paris, in a mood less eager to receive fresh impressions than to confirm settled judgments.[23]

Shortly after arriving in Paris, writing to Barnett Newman, Rothko complained that he and Mell had head colds from visiting "damp and cold" cathedrals in the "abominable" Parisian weather, and then assured his friend that not even "all the differences that we had postulated between our state of minds and that of Paris ever approached even a fraction of the actuality." "Never did I conceive," Rothko writes, "that the civilization here would seem so alien and so unapproachable as the actuality . . . appears to me." Perhaps echoing the response of a Russian boy arriving in Portland, Oregon, from the Settlement of Pale, or the response of a provincial young man from the west coast arriving in New York, Rothko feels shut out. But he then goes on to deliver a critique of postwar Paris which sounds like that of an aloof American tourist of the 1950s convinced of the moral superiority of his own more vital civilization.

> The city is extremely engaging to the eye in 2 respects because of the grandeur, largeness and abundance of monuments which are the more impressive because of their ugliness—and then the many streets and alleys in which crumbling plaster and dangling window shutters form a continuous pastiche of textures. A street of buildings in good repair is unendurable. But morally one abominates a devotion to such decay and to the monuments which commemorate nearly everything which I, and France, too, must abhor.

The exterior of Chartres, Rothko concludes, is "truly wild—really like N.Y. where the impulse to pile on more stones is never resisted. Nevertheless Paris seems to me no less medieval than Chartres."[24]

From this premodern civilization of ugly monuments and social decay, an American avant-garde painter has little to learn. About three weeks later, Rothko wrote from Cagnes-sur-Mer to the sculptor Richard Lippold that traveling around France, "I feel about as if I were in the theatre"—the same unreal feeling, based on his city scenes of the 1930s, he had once experienced wandering around New York. "What is attractive here is the crumbling, monstrous and picturesque. I am still looking for the fabulous which they say I will find in Italy." But instead of continuing to travel, Rothko feels "like staying put here somewhere for a month or two and making again those things which I am sure few here could have a feeling for." A restless person made uneasy by his "wandering" after just a few weeks of it, Rothko wants to give up the pleasures of the French Riviera and Italy in order to do some work, as if the lack of "feeling" for it he anticipates in this alien environment, driving him inward, acted as a lever toward creativity.[25]

Instead, Rothko left "medieval" France for Italy, where he found something like the "fabulous" in some of its early Renaissance art. Rothko visited Arezzo, whose principal attraction is Piero della Francesca's major work, a cycle of twenty murals, *The Legend of the True Cross*, which fills the walls of the choir in the church of San Francesco. Rothko liked to think of himself as a Renaissance man, not a narrowly professional artist but a broadly cultivated man with interests in music, literature, and philosophy as well as art. And he liked "the idea of the Renaissance man who identified the 'I' with the universe. He himself was the center and from him everything expanded outward into the cosmos"—Renaissance man reconceived in the image of romanticism. But Rothko did not much admire Renaissance art. "I travelled all over Europe and looked at hundreds of madonnas but all I saw was the symbol, never the concrete expression of motherhood," he complained a few years later.[26] Rothko also criticized the "cruelty" of Renaissance painting: "the paintings of stigmata and Judith and Holofernes and the beheadings—all of that bothered him."[27]

But when Rothko visited Florence, he discovered the frescos done by Fra Angelico for the cells in the convent at the Church of San Marco. "He loved Fra Angelico's bright tempera painting," Robert Motherwell recalled.[28] Moved by the Dominican monk's sourceless, evenly dispersed light and his meditative serenity, Rothko was also stimulated by the physical and social circumstances of the paintings. "As an artist you have to be a thief and steal a place for yourself on the rich man's wall," Rothko declared.[29] In Fra Angelico's world, art, "given an official status," occupied a legitimate human place. Large works usually placed on the wall across from the door in small monastic cells, Fra Angelico's paintings were not valued as prize "possessions" or as beautiful decorations but, ideally at least, as emanations of the sacred, contemplative objects integral with the daily life of the resident monk, whose beliefs, shared with the painter, allowed a "feeling" for the art.

"I'm of the generation that has nothing to conceal from itself," Rothko, rather pompously, declared to Alfred Jensen. "Our forebears had a kind of humanity influenced by religion, property, morality, and above all by illusions, and they used all this paraphernalia to conceal from themselves the tragic situation that each of us must ultimately face in our own solitude." The modern end-point of that liberal skepticism Rothko had praised in "The Scribble Book,"

Rothko's art, purged of illusions (and the paraphernalia of illusionism), exposes tragic solitude, surrounding the viewer with a beautiful void. "Despair," Rothko adds, "is the only way in which one can expose one's inner self with honesty."[30] Modern art is thus produced in monkish solitude by a painter who can only create honestly after he has despaired of recognition; and once complete, his work leaves the artist's "cell" to enter the world of property and prestige values. There, "you spend your strength resisting the suction of the shopkeeping mentalities" while also plotting "to steal a place for yourself on the rich man's wall," a place some of your closest friends may also wish to occupy.

Around 1950, the severities of creation, along with the intricacies of distribution, proved exhausting for Rothko, who had traveled to Europe partly to recover from what Annalee Newman described as his "breakdown" of 1949. Mrs. Newman thought Rothko's collapse occurred because her husband's Betty Parsons exhibit in January/February of 1950 established that "he had found what he was looking for but Rothko had not." Actually, Rothko had found what he was looking for and had exhibited sixteen of his new paintings at Parsons in the show immediately preceding Newman's. Rothko's depression had more to do with the death of his mother than the progress of Newman's art.

But it is quite possible Rothko was disturbed by the first public showing of Newman's "zip" paintings, since Newman, hitherto the polemical spokesman for his painter-friends, had suddenly emerged as their equal and rival. Still, the five letters Rothko wrote to the Newmans from Europe sound friendly enough, and Rothko's depression before leaving—also recalled by Robert Motherwell—likely resulted from a variety of personal and social tensions that came with his new importance in the art world. From London, shortly before sailing back to New York, Rothko urged Newman that "we must find a way of living and working without the involvements that seem to have been destroying us one after another. I doubt whether any of us can bear much more of that kind of strain. I think this must be a problem of our delayed maturity that we must solve immediately without fail."[31] Insistent, almost desperate in his desire to assert some kind of control and avoid destructive strain, Rothko is exhorting himself as well as Newman. In just a few years, however, Rothko and Newman, like Rothko and Still, would no longer be speaking.

When Rothko returned from Europe in late August, he "came back a transformed man," Robert Motherwell said. At forty-six, two years after the death of his mother, Rothko was an expectant father, Mell now five months pregnant with a daughter to be named "Kathy Lynn," but called "Kate" after Kate Rothkowitz.[32] Rothko told friends that the child had been conceived on their first night aboard the *Queen Elizabeth,* and Kate Rothko *was* born on

December 30, 1950, almost exactly nine months after their March 29 departure. The pregnancy was confirmed in Rome on the first of June. "We are happy about it," Rothko wrote to the Newmans, "so happy, that we are leaving the practical considerations until we reach home."[33] Herbert Ferber remembered that Rothko was "very happy" about the pregnancy, adding "he thought of it as a sign of his virility, his sexual prowess which he was always mentioning." Edith had undermined his masculinity, but Mell enhanced it, looking up to, adulating, and providing for the man she called "Rothko." In Rothko's myth paintings of the early 1940s, male and female at once battled and fused in his sexually ambiguous hybrids, Rothko identifying both with eagle-aggressor and its (pregnant) hare-victim. In Rothko's automatist works of the mid-1940s, male and female separate yet gravitate toward each other, as "identity" dissolves into a creative fluidity that precedes sexual difference. The muscular, "male" figure, on the right, in *Slow Swirl* contains a uterus filled with swirling blue waters. In 1950, fathering his first child and making innovative paintings with a secret process he had invented—"maternal" paintings that enveloped, sustained, and nurtured a viewer—Rothko could feel creative *and* powerful in his delayed maturity.

. . .

If I were working with garbage men or waiters, they would not have treated me as my friends did at Brooklyn College.

Mark Rothko

"Our money is getting low," Rothko wrote to the Newmans about his reasons for returning from Europe to New York, "and I want to look for a job." In fact, he had started his job search shortly after arriving in Europe, his letter to Richard Lippold having inquired about "an opening in your school" in Trenton, New Jersey. "Certain developments in our circumstances," Rothko went on, awkwardly alluding to Mell's pregnancy, have made it necessary for him to teach, though "I have long thought it the best solution for the artist."[34] It was not a solution easily obtained, however, and by the end of October Rothko still had not found work. Not until late December was he offered an assistant professorship in the Department of Design at Brooklyn College.[35]

By providing the security of a regular income, teaching art *might* solve the problem of the artist's financial dependence on an unstable market, and it certainly beat selling jewelry. "Now I can support them," Rothko proudly said, as if supporting his family, like Mell's pregnancy, made him feel more manly.[36] "Working at Brooklyn College was a bonanza," said Regina Bogat. "He needed that job desperately. After all there was Mell and the baby. And it gave him stature; it gave him position." And it lifted a man who had never graduated from college into a professorship. Yet, adds Stanley Kunitz, "Mark always gave the impression that wherever he worked for a salary he was an unwilling slave," perhaps the more so in the case of Brooklyn College since, for the past five years, Rothko, treated like an Old World Talmudic scholar whose wife protected him from mundane domestic obligations, had (mainly) been supported by Mell's commercial art—an arrangement that had helped him through the period when he most boldly advanced and finally resolved his painting. For *this* artist, girding up his loins and sending his wife out to work offered an ideal solution. Teaching, on the other hand, imposed many obligations on his time and energy, a new involvement that placed further strains on this artist in his delayed maturity.

Rothko's professorship, moreover, provided a very ambiguous sense of "position." The *Broeklundian,* the Brooklyn College yearbook, for 1953 prints a photograph of eleven members of the design department's faculty, most of them seated on high stools around worktables covered with jars of paint, brushes, cloths, drawings. Alone in the center foreground sits Robert Jay Wolff, the department's chairman and only tenured professor; on his right sits Milton Brown and on his left Martin James, both art historians. Three men, one of them Ad Reinhardt, stand at the rear. On the right, his body again turned away from the camera and his head turned back toward it, sits Mark Rothko, again glaring, but now seated in the rear on a chair so low that only his head is visible above the top of one of the worktables. In *Life* magazine, Rothko had occupied a prominent foreground position among his irascible contemporaries. Among his academic colleagues, Rothko appears isolated, diminished, pushed to the rear and squeezed out, someone who stands out because he doesn't fit in.[37]

Rothko had returned to the United States only to find himself, soon after, working in a European enclave, a kind of Bauhaus in Brooklyn. In 1942, Serge Chermayeff, an architect close to Bauhaus founder Walter Gropius, had been hired to build an art department at Brooklyn College. In 1946, when Chermayeff left, Robert Wolff, then running the painting and sculpture program at the Chicago Institute of Design (originally the New Bauhaus), was hired to replace him and remained chairman for the next seventeen years. Rothko was teaching not in an *art* department but a department of *design,* where, in the yearbook description, "no artificial distinctions are made between fine and applied arts." Rothko had now grounded his painting in a state of consciousness that was presocial; his new department, with its functionalist aesthetic, wished to combine beauty with social use. In painting, the department under Wolff's direction leaned toward the American Abstract Artists, members on the faculty including Burgoyne Diller, Harry Holtzman, Carl Holty, Ad Reinhardt, and Wolff himself.[38] This commitment to neo-plastic principles was not monolithic: Wolff did hire Rothko. Of course, in the spring of 1954, he also led the movement to fire him.

Summers at the California School of Fine Arts, Rothko had taught one studio class and given one improvised lecture a week. At the Subjects of the Artist school, Rothko had taught a studio class one day a week. At Brooklyn College, the pay was better—in one year he made $5,190—but he taught four courses, having to commute forty-five minutes (each way) on the subway two or three days a week; and not all of his teaching consisted of studio courses.[39]

At this time the design department had no graduate program; most of its undergraduate students were either prospective elementary school teachers required to take one art course or prospective high school teachers majoring in art. Primarily, design, in keeping with its professed functionalism, worked as a service department, less engaged with nurturing young artists than with certifying teachers. In keeping with its Bauhaus principles, moreover, the department offered courses in "Advertising Design," "Interior Design," "Mechanical Drawing," "Mechanical Drawing for Engineers," and "Workshop for Pre-Dental Students." As a result, assignments teaching, say, the "Workshop in Creative Painting" were hard to come by, and faculty members, having been liberated from artificial distinctions between fine and applied arts, were expected to teach a range of courses.[40]

When Rothko began teaching at Brooklyn College in the first week of February, 1951, one of his courses was "Graphic Workshop," studying the techniques of "etching, engraving, and block printing" and the "development of drawing skills through these processes."[41] Rothko had attempted some etchings in the mid-1930s, and, according to Stanley William Hayter, Rothko made some prints at Hayter's Atelier 17 in the mid-1940s.[42] Both times, Rothko's involvement seems to have been fairly transient; graphic arts were hardly a strong point. So in order to give the graphic workshop class, Rothko the teacher was forced to become a student again, returning to the Art Students League for one week to study etching and lithograph techniques in a course offered by Will Barnet.[43] At Brooklyn College, Rothko, who claimed not to believe in art history and was now refusing to theorize in public about his work, taught "Contemporary Art" and "Theory of Art." An artist who had renounced line in his own painting, he was assigned "Elements of Drawing." A masterful colorist, he was assigned "Color," which he transformed into a painting workshop.[44] In his seven semesters at the college, Rothko, already recognized as one of the leading painters of his generation, was never given a painting studio to teach.

The beloved "Rothkie" of Center Academy, having moved a few miles south across Brooklyn and several steps up in the world, was now Mark Rothko, whom many of his not-so-advanced students found intimidating or just bewildering.[45] "Mark thought of himself as a great artist, and the students can either take it or they don't," said Milton Brown, who found Rothko's attitude "arrogant." Students, whether superficial or serious, knew that painters like Diller, Reinhardt, and Rothko were primarily involved with their own work. "The truth of the matter is," one student admirer of Rothko pointed out, "it was a job for them where they made a living." Sometimes, instructors did not show up for class. Sometimes, at the 4:00 o'clock break in a 2:00 to 6:00 class, Rothko and a few students left for Luigi's Bar and Grill, at the nearby junction of Nostrand and Flatbush Avenues, where they often met Reinhardt and some of his students, and did not return to class.[46] Gone was the commitment and egalitarian idealism of Rothko's earlier belief, in the 1930s, that "painting is just as natural a language as singing or speaking," an idiom that anyone can speak. For elementary school children painting *may* be a language as "natural" as song or speech, but for college students, especially those fulfilling a requirement, the issue is a bit more complex, and Rothko, Celina Trief recalled, "got absolutely furious about the people who were not taking what they were doing very seriously." With one student he agreed to pass her only "if she swore never to take another art course again as long as she lived."

Rothko's new paintings, while large and mural-scale, do not address a large, collective audience. "When a crowd of people looks at a painting, I think of blasphemy," he said. "I believe that a painting can only communicate directly to a rare individual who happens to be in tune with it and the artist." Similarly, it was a private exchange between like-minded but not exactly equal individuals that Rothko sought with those students who *were* seriously committed to art. Or, as Rothko himself bluntly put it: "a man learns by conversing with men of consequence."[47] (It is not clear how women learn.) But students such as Murray Israel, Celina Trief, and Cecile Abish found Rothko a "warm," "permissive and delightful," "encouraging" presence. "Rothko was a very human person," said Israel. "The sense of humanity. And I think that's what he really exuded, a certain warmth, responsiveness, intelligence. He had all of my regard."

On the opening day of his graphic workshop course, Murray Israel remembered, Rothko began by frankly admitting that he "had no experience, or almost none," so that the course became "purely exploratory." "He allowed you to do what you wanted, then he'd discuss what you did with you. It was a very very rich and generative experience." Technical shortcomings bothered Rothko less than others, since one principle which had informed the teaching of this self-taught artist from the start, was that the classroom was not a place to impart skills but to release creativity.

"He spoke about art with such love during the whole Contemporary Art class that I'll never forget sitting there with the feeling this is the way art is—and suddenly you can paint past a kind of technical kind of thing," Celina Trief recalled. For these students (and a Brooklyn College student in the early 1950s could be as provincial, say, as a young man from Portland in the early 1920s), Rothko provided a model who made real the life of an artist ("I saw another world," Israel said), who gave access to an ongoing revolutionary movement in art, who provided recognition simply by taking their work seriously, and who was friendly and open enough to invite them along for drinks, have them to his studio, and offer paternal advice on personal problems.[48] When asked by Murray Israel and his girlfriend whether they should marry, Rothko told the woman not to marry the artist, then told Israel, humorously but seriously, that "it was a very good idea for an artist to get married because you didn't have to go running around, you couldn't spend all your time running around, you really had to get down to work." When Cecile Abish was broke, the Rothkos gave her room and board for six months in their small Sixth Avenue flat in exchange for baby-sitting duties. "It was a tremendous act of kindness," she recalled.

In the classroom, Rothko worked from a kind of abstract expressionist pedagogy, stressing process, teaching the student to teach him or herself. In "Contemporary Art," which Rothko provocatively began with Rembrandt—"he felt that Rembrandt represented the first time an artist painted whatever he felt like doing"—he "was always talking about the artist in the act of making art as completing and fulfilling himself." In studio classes like "The Elements of Drawing" he emphasized that "*you* had to take responsibility of doing it. And he would be there to advise and to talk about what you did. But he would impose himself on what you were doing."[49] Or, he did impose himself (and his own history) indirectly by requiring students to search on their own. "All of those men felt the process, and they were process painters, was one of discovery, of finding, to find out who you are and what you have to say in the process," said Israel. "We didn't know what we were supposed to find. We had to find it, then we would know. They could point out where they'd been and what they'd found and oh, wonderful, but that's their territory, you can't do that, so what do you do? And we all struggled like hell."

Rothko had been given a three-year contract; so had Jimmy Ernst, who had been hired around the same time as Rothko. When their contracts and that of one other assistant professor expired in the spring of 1954, only one tenure-line position could be kept. The department's personnel and budget committee, chaired by Wolff and including Ad Reinhardt, was forced to choose among the three painters; they voted unanimously not to renew Rothko's contract.[50] So on March 16, 1954, Rothko received a letter from New York City's Board of Education, officially notifying him that he would not be reappointed to his position at Brooklyn College.[51]

Two years later, in February of 1956, Rothko confided to Alfred Jensen, "I'm in terrible circumstances at present. I could kick myself for having messed up my teaching job at Brooklyn College, but how could I have done otherwise?"[52] When relating the story of his being fired, Rothko was usually less self-accusing and regretful and more the outraged victim. He was given a copy of Robert Wolff's letter to the dean recommending his termination, so Rothko composed his own letter to the dean. Characterizing Wolff's presentation of the design department's curriculum as "mechanical and statistical," Rothko predicted that if the college accepts such values, "the department is doomed to retrogress to a place a half a century removed from living forces instead of only being a decade behind." Institutions can progress only by the "circumvention of such obstacles," he insists, "just as it is only by the circumvention of the real intent of the Bauhaus ideology of the courses in Basic Design, Drawing, Color 1 & 2 that I have been able to lay before my students what really I felt had to be said."

Confronted, as he thought he had been as a student at Yale, with a functional view of education, Rothko appeals to the loftier ideals of liberal education, just as he had done at Yale. He realizes that "the college is not an art school, and that we are not involved in making artists." What makes Wolff think "that artists can be made anyway?" But Rothko does insist that an artist's "relentless," "demonic" passion gives him "the one thing which a school of liberal arts must impart above all"—"and I insist that I am singularly equipped to convey this" and "that no iota of what is here meant can be conveyed by the study of advertising design." When can young people obtain this kind of experience if not "during their adolescence before they are catapulted into the confusion of their complex civilization." Instead, Wolff's letter "is permeated with a vocational outlook" which favors "the applied arts" and "makes the art in my sense" into "a poor and unwanted relation." That position, dramatized by his literal place in his department's yearbook photograph, was very familiar to Rothko.[53]

He appealed the committee's decision, was given a hearing, and was refused again, after which, festering with indignation, he transcribed part of the conversation. The official letter from the college president, Harry Gideonse, informing Rothko of his termination, is stamped with the gray imprint of his right shoe.[54] At fifty, with a three-year-old child and wife to support, feeling betrayed, Rothko was again solely dependent on the marketplace.

As in the Lewis Browne trial, Rothko at Brooklyn College was partly asserting himself against what he perceived as a narrow and rigid authority and partly setting himself up, an Isaac who stretches himself out on the altar and dares Abraham to plunge in his knife. Robert Jay Wolff—already the chairman for seven years and, again, the only tenured professor in the department—"was always looking for acceptance" by Rothko, whose work Wolff "admired," but he only got "equivocal answers." Nor had Rothko made any secret of his contempt for Wolff's Bauhaus principles. At the time of his review, moreover, Rothko, who in his letter to the dean openly stated that he taught to circumvent those principles, announced he would no longer teach anything but painting courses.[55] No one could accuse him of bootlicking.

"We knew that Mark was a more important artist than Jimmy," said Milton Brown. "But Jimmy was much more versatile, and of course younger, and willing, and Jimmy was willing to teach advertising, he was willing to teach anything." With his demand, Rothko also "ran up against his best friends. And I think at that period Ad Reinhardt was probably as close to him as anybody, and it was Ad especially who couldn't take it because Ad wanted to teach painting," of which there were not many sections to go around. "Rothko was insisting that he was first among equals," Brown said. Rothko's colleagues found him "arrogant" or "egocentric."[56] His chairman, a few years later, bitterly recalled Rothko's "grandstand play against the department on the grounds of freedom, flexibility and the sanctity of the individual," and went on to assure his college dean that "I don't think we have any reason to worry about anyone in the department as it stands because, since Rothko is gone, we have no one there who does not understand and accept the fact that he is there because he is a teacher and not as a great painter or great what-not. Rothko could not take this. . . ."[57]

Wolff wished to subordinate the artist to the teacher; Rothko wished to subordinate the teacher to the artist—an irreconcilable conflict, dramatized in Rothko's reconstruction of his appeal hearing:

Q: You are not flexible enough. Could you teach advertising?
Rothko: In an extreme emergency, I may use advertising as a lever for my point of view, but there is no reason for the necessity to arise.
Q: Why are you willing to work in a department devoted to an antagonistic philosophy?
Rothko: That is the history of every artist's life. If we awaited for sympa-

thetic environments, our visions which are new would never have to be invented and our convictions never spoken. . . . Harmony based on substantial agreement with the Bauhaus philosophy would be a perversion. . . .

Q: A department is like a team. One assigns bases and duties must be carried out for it to run smoothly.

Rothko: What kind of a team? My idea of a school is Plato's academy, where a man learns by conversing with men of consequence.

Q: Have you been able to continue your professional activities, paint and have exhibitions since you have taught here?

Rothko: Yes, it is a matter of public record.

Q: If you obtain tenure, would you remain teaching?

Rothko: But I have been able to teach and work all of my life. One cannot make prophecies forever. However should I find that I cannot do both I would have to stop teaching. . . . I insist that precisely that knowledge is what makes me valuable to the school. Of what value would I be . . . if I were willing to sacrifice my work for teaching? It is the opposite which guarantees my unremitting concern and involves me in the subject which I teach. I was not brought into this department because I am primarily a teacher or an advertising man or a textile man. I was asked to join the department because I am Mark Rothko and the lifelong integrity and intensity which my work represents.[58]

The committee conceived of teaching as a social activity taking place within an organizational context requiring collaboration and compromise. Rothko asserted the autonomy, and authority, of the gifted individual. He refused to yield; the committee denied his appeal.

How could he, or they, have done otherwise?

11 Recognitions

I guess Mark Rothko left me because I just couldn't sell him.

Betty Parsons

Sometime during the 1951–52 art season Betty Parsons met for dinner in her fifth-floor studio apartment on East 40th Street with a small group of her artists that included Barnett Newman, Jackson Pollock, Mark Rothko, and Clyfford Still. "They sat on the sofa in front of me, like the Four Horsemen of the Apocalypse, and suggested that I drop everyone else in the gallery, and they would make me the most famous dealer in the world."[1] When Betty Parsons had taken on these men, they were unknown. Personally involved with her artists, allowing them complete freedom in selecting and hanging their shows, preferring progressive art to sure profits, creating an ideal gallery space in which to exhibit their abstract works, Betty Parsons, protecting her artists from the bruisings of an impersonal marketplace, made a perfect dealer—as long as her painters did not *expect* to sell.

At that point her human virtues translated into professional defects: she wasn't discriminating enough in selecting artists for the gallery; she did not market aggressively; she kept books sloppily; she was too poor to produce catalogues. She didn't promote; she didn't sell. Now, made confident by their growing reputations, her leading painters ate her dinner, sat on her sofa, and made a power play. Long embittered by exclusions, these men now maneuvered to exclude others (many of them women and old friends of Parsons'), proposing that the dealer abandon the rest of her artists, concentrate her energies and resources on a self-selected few, who would pull her along with them up the road to Mount Parnassus and international fame. "But I didn't want to do a thing like that. I told them that, with my nature, I liked a bigger garden."

By May 1952, Jackson Pollock had angrily quit Parsons and moved across the hall at 15 East 57th Street to the Sidney Janis Gallery.[2] Worried, Betty Parsons spent a $5,000 gift from an old friend buying three works by Still and three by Rothko, hoping to hold on to these artists.[3] But Still, who had not made his dealer's job any easier by announcing, in September 1951, that he would no longer exhibit his paintings, had, by December of 1953, signed with Sidney Janis without bothering to inform Parsons.[4] Newman, more upset with his reception than with his dealer, left, on friendly terms, after his April 1951 exhibit. Rothko, the last to depart, also left amicably: "I'm doing you no good. You're doing me no good," he told Parsons.[5] In February of 1954 Rothko and his family, the last tenants left in their condemned Sixth Avenue building, were desperately looking for a new place to live. Rothko was teaching his last term at Brooklyn College; Mell had (briefly) returned to work, free-lancing. That spring Rothko, too, left Parsons, eventually making the walk across the hall to join Sidney Janis.[6]

By that time Rothko's relation with the art world had taken a peculiar and ultimately frustrating turn. His paintings, while still new enough to shock, were steadily gaining acceptance. When Alfred Barr wanted to obtain *Number 10, 1950,* for the Museum of Modern Art, he knew the board of trustees would not approve the purchase, so he persuaded Philip Johnson to buy the painting and then give it to the museum. "Alfred Barr did not believe the trustees would dare reject it if I gave it," according to Johnson. Barr was correct, though A. Conger Goodyear, who had helped found the museum, resigned from the board in protest.[7] With this purchase, Rothko had been admitted to the canon of modern art; that he had to be let in through a side door only proved that in this life few things come pure. So, too, with the reviews of his two one-man shows at Parsons in 1950 and 1951. "This talented New Yorker's most brilliant show to date," wrote Thomas Hess in *Art News,* calling Rothko "one of the most gifted manipulators of color at work today." Most of the seven reviews of these two exhibits were less enthusiastic, viewing Rothko as primarily engaged with "exploration of color relationships," comparing him to Mondrian, and complaining about the limits of a formalism the critics themselves had imposed upon him. Rothko was discovering that he could be publicly seen, without being recognized.[8]

Yet for accrediting an American painter, exhibits—the number of exhibits, the prestige of the gallery or museum—pull much more weight than reviews. In addition to his two one-man shows at Betty Parsons, Rothko, in the early 1950s, participated in two Whitney Annuals, "Seventeen Modern American Painters" (organized by Robert Motherwell) at the Frank Perls Gallery in Beverly Hills, the Los Angeles County Museum's 1951 Annual ("Contemporary Painting in the United States"), an annual at the California Palace of the Legion of Honor (San Francisco), two group shows at the Sidney Janis Gallery, group exhibits at Yale, Harvard, Wesleyan, and the Universities of Illinois, Indiana, Minnesota, and Nebraska. Internationally, Rothko's work was seen in Tokyo, Berlin, Amsterdam, and São Paulo. Rothko's *Number 14, 1949,* his first picture exhibited at the Museum of Modern Art, was included in the museum's survey of "Abstract Painting and Sculpture in America" in early 1951, with his work also appearing in "Selections from Five New York Collections" that summer.

The Modern's sporadic series of shows of living American painters concentrated on "a limited number of artists, devoting considerable space" to each—in pointed contrast to the one-picture-per-artist annuals organized by museums like the Whitney. In the spring of 1952, Rothko was selected by Dorothy Miller for the important "Fifteen Americans" exhibit, which also included William Baziotes, Herbert Ferber, Jackson Pollock, Clyfford Still, and Bradley Walker Tomlin. The first in the series since 1946, the show certified the abstract art of Rothko and his colleagues as "the dominant trend in mid-century American painting," and it elated Rothko, who showed eight pictures in a gallery of his own.[9] Two months after "Fifteen Americans" closed, he wrote to Herbert Ferber, having just visited the museum, that "*my room* is now inhabited by Marin and O'Keefe [sic]. I must admit that the afterglow remaining from my own stuff made these quite invisible to me at least."[10]

Yet Rothko was still worried about money. "I don't know how I'm going to feed my family this winter," Rothko told Yvonne Thomas. In 1947, at Rothko's first Parsons show, his prices for oil paintings had generally been in the $300–$500 range. In 1951, at his last Parsons show, his prices ranged from $500 to $3,000. Of the ten large oils he showed, two cost $3,000, four $1,500, one $1,200, two $900 and one $800.[11] A rising reputation justified—in fact, demanded—a corresponding rise in prices; so did the expanding size of his pictures. But Rothko could not have been elated when, in the early 1950s, he read his statements from Parsons. The asking price for *Number 10, 1950,* had been $1,500, but Philip Johnson (or the museum) was given a 25 percent discount, so the selling price was $1,250; Rothko's share was about $830. But *Number 10, 1950,* was the *only* painting Rothko sold in 1951. In 1953 he sold one—*Number 18, 1953*—and made $900. His $3,279.69 in 1950 would be his largest income from painting until 1955, when he cleared $5,471 in his first year at Janis, roughly the salary he had been drawing at Brooklyn College.

Having helped Rothko create a reputation, Betty Parsons was not helping to create a demand for his work. Yet it is also true that Rothko's sales in the early 1950s reflected changing economic conditions. The boom of 1950 marked the peak of recovery from the 1948–49 recession, but the start of the Korean War in June of 1950 began a period of economic uncertainty and instability which culminated in the recession of 1953–54 and coincided with the decline of Rothko's sales. Such a decline might not hurt, might even help, the sale of a solid Old Master investment, but paintings by contemporary Americans, being more speculative, were more vulnerable. Both Rothko and Parsons suffered from market forces beyond their control. But Sidney Janis was able to sustain Rothko's sales during the recession of 1958. If he were to enjoy the material as well as the symbolic fruits of his labor, Rothko, once he lost his job at Brooklyn College, needed a more aggressive dealer. Man cannot live on afterglow alone.

• • •

On June 17, 1953, Rothko met with his friend Alfred Jensen, who transcribed their conversation.

> Again I had a long conversation with Rothko. We gradually discovered that Michel Sonnabend's visit to Rothko's studio had been instrumental in affecting both of our attitudes toward art. Finally we began to compare notes on the validity of Sonnabend's reactions.
>
> Rothko felt that M.S. is too much a connoisseur and is too much in love with too many facets of creative expression. I told Rothko about Sonnabend's criticism of his work. He felt that Rothko's paintings failed to satisfy universal standards, that they lacked touch with the life patterns of generalized experience. These lacks explained S's preference for Tomlin's paintings which he found had more universal content. He granted that his own evaluation was highbrow and, though he admired Rothko's work, it was Tomlin's that he felt had broader meaning.
>
> Rothko replied, "Michel Sonnabend in the first place is not a highbrow even though he claims to be. And I cannot agree with the idea that a painter must step down to the public's level and deal with familiar generalities in order to become universal. Tomlin dealt with the more traditional patterns of picture-making; therefore his work is perhaps better liked than mine. However, from my own experience with people's reactions to my work the fact is that my paintings are *there;* they *are;* they exist for themselves. People who are able to understand Rothko's work can later understand Tomlin's, but when you reverse the process it does not work. Knowing Tomlin's paintings first does not result in liking or understanding Rothko's."
>
> He went on to say that the preference for Tomlin's canvases is caused by *a priori* judgments. For the public to accept Rothko first would demand a new vision on its part. The fact that people prefer Tomlin on first sight only demonstrates their own state of imprisonment; their bondage to traditional practices. "I know my own paintings have universal appeal," he said. "If this were not true why do people from all over the world visit my studio? The reactions that I myself get from the Japanese,

the Germans, the French, etc., is they are all agreed my work has the power to convey a new vision. Its message becomes visible in a new structural language never before experienced by them. In my work one therefore finds the direct awareness of an essential humanness. Monet had this quality and that's why I prefer Monet to Cézanne. Cézanne was torn within himself by complex and personal conflicts; his battle was visible and very disturbing. The quality of one's feelings on seeing his work is mitigated by conflicting elements. Despite the general claim that Cézanne had created a new vision and that he is the father of modern painting, I myself prefer Monet. Monet was for me the greater artist of the two. I do not myself agree with present public opinion about the colorists and their art though it may be right to a certain degree, for color per se can belong to the more sensual side of art. Nevertheless I feel we must always be open to all kinds of art be it purely sensual or otherwise as long as it is an authentic human expression. I have always told my students that Mondrian was capable of constant caressing attention to a white surface and that with certain paintings he could continue this process for a whole year. To my way of thinking Mondrian was one of the greatest sensualists who ever lived. And this sensual quality as projected by him shows itself despite his not being a colorist. When people find similarities in my paintings with the works of others, it only proves that my work is taking its rightful place in the development of art history.

"I feel that in American art today a valid sense of scale has returned. In Greek painting of the great period two kinds of specialists were known —the vase painters and the mural painters. They really monopolized the field. The vase painter was dealing with a relatively small three-dimensional object in a decorative vein. The other was working on a large two-dimensional surface, creating a new reality. Maybe you have noticed two characteristics exist in my paintings; either their surfaces are expansive and push outward in all directions, or their surfaces contract and rush inward in all directions. Between these two poles you can find everything I want to say.

"When I talk to you, Jensen, about art I find reassuring your intense and passionate participation. I find that you are digging for the same truths I am after. It makes our conversations together very refreshing experiences for me. I myself dislike the glib and clever intellectual who in detached conversation conveys the mentality that one encounters all too frequently here in New York."

With this compliment Rothko finished his talk with me. He has been suffering from an attack of gout for the last couple of weeks but now he is again back at work and has recommenced a large fifteen-foot canvas, the one I described to you last year.¹² It is a red picture with a sense of inward suction rushing into a blue rectangular shape, a shape that exists within the red surface of the entire picture. After a year's rest from working on this large painting Rothko said, "I can't recognize myself any longer in this particular painting, and therefore I must take it up again. I am forced to continue working on it. In many of my older works I continue to recognize myself and so do not need to repaint them. When I recognize myself in a work, then I realize it's completed."

• • •

We shouldn't be accepted by the public. As soon as we are accepted, we are no longer artists but decorators.

David Hare

In its April 15, 1950, issue *Vogue* magazine invited its readers to contemplate the differing charms of the "many-picture wall" and the "one-picture wall." A photograph of the apartment of a wealthy New Yorker showed a "dark painted wall arranged in an abstract pattern of Piranesi prints, Michelangelo drawings, a bust of Hermes, a *collage* of stones, old English prints and prints of sea captains, Greek medallions, and random paintings." Such an arrangement creates "a composite still-life," absorbing individual works into a socially functional unity and making the collector (or decorator) the artist. "The artfully cluttered wall gives the effect of intimacy, of a group of compatible guests, of gaiety and spontaneity." Artfully constructed spontaneity was an effect familiar enough to readers of *Vogue,* which went on, however, to propose the advantages of the one-picture wall, illustrated by a full-page photograph of Rothko's *Number 8, 1949.* Rothko's work "not only dominates the wall (it is eight feet high by five feet wide), but animates the whole room with a glowing sense of space and light and liberated shapes." His painting evokes not a gay, intimate dinner party but a more formal and formidable event—perhaps a visit from the Prince of Wales. "The boldly sparse wall suggests a single guest of honor, serenity, undefined vistas, and an intangible excitement."¹³

"Mark always gave the impression that wherever he worked for a salary he was an unwilling slave." But was the Rothko of 1950 painting in the studio of his Sixth Avenue flat the unwilling slave (making about $550 a work) of rich patrons seeking to add some undefined vistas and intangible excitement to their living rooms? Rothko variously identified his paintings as spiritual emanations, material things, portraits of the soul, facades. But he was quite consistent about what he was *not* doing: he was not a formalist; he was not a colorist; and, most emphatically, his paintings were not decorations—all rejections he needed to insist upon because these ways of receiving his works either reduced them to familiar art historical terms or to socially acceptable wall hangings for, say, a millionaire's guest house. Thus historicized or domesticated, his commanding works lost "presence," i.e., power; they were emasculated. "It is therefore a risky act to send [a picture] out into the world. How often it must be permanently impaired by the eyes of the vulgar and the cruelty of the impotent who would extend their affliction universally."

Rothko often complained to Milton Avery, "you're not selective enough. You let your paintings be hung anywhere," and Avery would reply, "What do I care? Once I've painted them, I'm not interested."[14] For Rothko, however, hanging the painting—determining the physical context in which it would be seen—was an extension of the creative process, something he became vitally interested in during the early 1950s as his pictures were being more widely exhibited. Dorothy Miller recalled that the Rothko she knew—she could not have known him very well—was "always sweetness and sunshine"—until the "Fifteen Americans" show. She selected paintings for the exhibit at Rothko's studio, but when "the Museum's truck brought the paintings in he had changed my selection and added a number of other pictures which I had no room for. I had considerable difficulty with Rothko since he did not wish to allow me to arrange his gallery. He wanted to have the four walls of the gallery completely covered with paintings touching one another, and he did not wish to accept the Museum's gallery lighting proposing instead to have blazing lights in the center of the ceiling." Rothko, who would quickly reverse field on the "blazing lights" issue, wanted to surround and saturate viewers with his large, vibrant paintings, as if to give museum visitors no choice but to look at them. But Miller, believing that to make "his gallery so different from the others would be very destructive to the show as a whole," argued with Rothko; Alfred Barr argued with Rothko; finally René d'Harnoncourt, the museum's director, persuaded Rothko to accept Miller's hanging.[15]

It was in this period that Rothko began to speak of "controlling the situation."[16] Near the end of 1952, Rothko, having first declined to participate in that year's Whitney Annual, and then to submit two pictures to the museum's purchasing committee, wrote to the Whitney's director, Lloyd Goodrich:

> My reluctance to participate [in the Annual], then, was based on the conviction that the real and specific meaning of the pictures was lost and distorted in these exhibitions. It would be an act of self-deception for me

to try to convince myself that the situation would be sufficiently different, in view of a possible purchase, if these pictures appeared in your permanent collection. Since I have a deep sense of responsibility for the life my pictures will lead out in the world, I will with gratitude accept any form of their exposition in which their life and meaning can be maintained, and avoid all occasions where I think that this cannot be done.

I know the likelihood of this being viewed as arrogance. But I assure you that nothing could be further from my mood which is one of great sadness about this situation: for, unfortunately, there are few existing alternatives for the kind of activity which your museum represents. Nevertheless, in my own life at least, there must be some congruity between convictions and actions if I am to continue to function and work.[17]

Turning down a museum purchase in 1952 was a bold act for a man who was not selling many paintings at the time, a stand made possible partly by his salary from Brooklyn College. Rothko, in actuality, had exhibited in every Whitney Annual between 1945 and 1951, and the museum had purchased a watercolor, *Entombment I,* in 1947. But what about all those years before 1945, when this museum of American art, which had accepted many mediocrities, excluded him and his friends when they desperately needed recognition and support? In 1952, at the Whitney, with a regular income from teaching and a growing reputation to back him up, Rothko felt free both to strike back for earlier neglects—by refusing the Whitney—and to protect the "real and specific meaning" of his pictures.

From this time on, Rothko grew more and more reluctant to participate in group shows. Beyond any arrogance or vengefulness or desire for special treatment, Rothko, according to Herbert Ferber, "felt that the sensitive quality of his work, the kind of evanescent feeling in his work, would be drowned out by bad lighting or by the proximity of paintings that were in a different vein," and in group shows "he couldn't limit the people on either side of him." Rothko worried, according to Robert Motherwell, that in group shows the presence of others' paintings could "hurt" his own. Commanding presences, Rothko's paintings created effects so delicate they could be "hurt" by improper lighting or a nearby work. Or, as Stanley Kunitz put it, "he wanted that room, that atmosphere, that environment, all to be his own. . . . If you have a different set of vibrations challenging his own, something has gone awry with the work."[18] The problem of exhibiting, as with living in this world, is to keep from being smothered.

Yet in his struggle to protect his works, Rothko was engaging a complex web of issues for modern painters who, unlike poets or composers, invest themselves in unique physical objects which are intended to be sold and therefore lost. One sunny afternoon in the early summer of 1954, two young painters, Ben Dienes and William Scharf, met Rothko carrying a large painting up 53rd Street. "This doesn't belong to me. I only painted it," Rothko joked, explaining that he was carrying it from the home of a collector to be restored.[19] Once it leaves the studio, a painting, even one inducing presocial states of consciousness, acquires a social identity and life of its own, being priced, bought, sold, loaned, shipped, stored, exhibited, evaluated, restored—an independent object, a possession now belonging to someone else, a commodity which can belong to anyone. "A picture lives by companionship," said Rothko, but "transplanted" from its home environment in the studio, the painting enters an alien and impersonal place (or series of places) where it does not quite belong—a living "organism," now displaced, rootless, lost in the crowd, unprotected.

Anthropomorphizing his works, Rothko closely identified with them, blurring the boundaries between the artist and his creation, as if the artist never were fully "outside" his works even after their completion, or as if they were never really complete without him to protect their "life and meaning." Living presences, surrogate bodies, these paintings were also surrogate children, "for as he explained they were his—his children—and not some objects in which he ever abandoned involvement."[20] Not an uncaring father who deserted his offspring, Rothko was their over-solicitous, possessive, and self-sacrificing Jewish mother. According to Herbert Ferber, Rothko had "an umbilical attachment" to his work, as if he were mother to these "children."[21]

Rothko liked to hang around during his own exhibits, and he told Budd Hopkins of an incident that occurred during the "Fifteen Americans" show. As Rothko was looking at his paintings, a man approached him and said, "You look like a sensible human being. How can anybody get away with this? Look at this. There's nothing. How can anybody get away with this? It's just . . . it's a disgrace." Rothko asked why it upset him so, "and the man started to sputter and carry on, but he couldn't really articulate what he objected to. It just wasn't enough, there on the wall." After letting the man "go on a little bit," Rothko finally said, "well, you know I painted these paintings," something he had to prove by pulling out his driver's license. "And he said the man was totally flabbergasted." Rothko invited him to come to the museum's coffee shop and talk; a few weeks later, the man called asking to visit Rothko's studio, see his work, and talk again. "He ended up buying a painting." In fact, Rothko added, "I have an appointment with him now at 2 o'clock. He owns three works of mine." This story—with the artist as missionary converting the heathen—sounds apocryphal, the more so as Rothko seems to get carried away in telling

Chapter Eleven

it, ending by claiming to be on the way to confer with the man. Nor are there any sales records to substantiate the anecdote. But whether fact, fiction, or mixture of both, the story reveals Rothko's wish both to create and to vanquish shocked resistance and to make a sale a *personal* transaction, so that his painting finds a *home* where it will be cared for.

Paintings are "skins that are shed and hung on a wall," Rothko told one friend.[22] Pieces of his life, they could not be exchanged and simply forgotten, as if they were mere "objects" or commodities. As another friend observed, "My feeling is that essentially he never felt he sold a painting."[23] A sale or gift entailed an act of trust that was violated if the "owner" decided to resell. As Donald Blinken, a collector who purchased his first Rothko in 1956, observed, "The one thing Rothko could not tolerate was what he viewed as infidelity to his art. If you bought something, you could take your time, you didn't have to make quick decisions, but once you had it, he was very unhappy if you decided in six months really you didn't want it, or you sold it to someone else for something else or traded it in. He felt that was a kind of betrayal, because what you were acquiring from him was, yes, oil on canvas, but it was also a part of his psyche and his feeling about the world, and if you suddenly changed your mind about that, you were not only rejecting the picture, you were rejecting a piece of him."[24] Sometime during the 1950s Rothko gave a painting to a dealer who had let him use some space as a studio in an empty building he owned, "and then subsequently Rothko heard that this fellow wanted to sell his painting, and he walked into the man's home and slashed the painting."[25]

• • •

> *I have foolishly engaged myself to write something in relation to my Chicago show. So I have dusted off my machine and am going thru the fires of hell, having walked the plank for the last few weeks between my typewriter and my brush.*
>
> Mark Rothko
>
> *Silence is so accurate.*
>
> Mark Rothko

Just before returning from Europe, Rothko wrote to Barnett Newman to explain his refusal of a request from the little magazine *Tiger's Eye* for an essay/statement. In the first place there was some unspecified danger of offending Robert Motherwell; in the second, if Rothko agreed to write for *Tiger's Eye*, he would also have to agree to a similar request from the *Magazine of Art*, and "I simply cannot see myself proclaiming a series of nonsensical statements, making each vary from the other and which ultimately have no meaning whatsoever." But "the real reason," he tells Newman, "is that at least at this time I have nothing to say in words which I would stand for. I am heartily ashamed of the things I have written in the past. This self-statement business has become a fad this season, and I cannot see myself just spreading myself with a bunch of statements, everywhere, I do not wish to make."[26]

Whether paintings or statements, Rothko will only produce *living* creations, ones he can stand behind; either they reflect *him* or he will feel not guilty but "ashamed," with the hollowness of his words or his marks publicly exposed. For Rothko, talking publicly about his art involved not just the issue of translating a visual into a verbal expression, or even the issue of explaining a visual expression that was abstract and vacant. The real issue was that Rothko's paintings pull us back into state of consciousness that is preverbal; they communicate *through* silence. Yet he wanted so intensely for them to communicate on these terms that it was hard *not* to discuss them, help them along in an alien world, anxiously control their reception. Rothko felt as ambivalent about public discussion of his paintings as he did about selling them.

Sometime early in the spring of 1954 Katharine Kuh, an art critic and a curator at the Art Institute of Chicago, began a long friendship with Rothko when she visited his studio, looked at paintings, and spent some time talking with him. Soon after, she wrote to propose that he become the first in a series of one-man shows she would arrange at the institute. The show, Rothko's first one-man exhibit at a major American museum and his first one-man exhibit since his 1951 show at Betty Parsons, would open on October 15, lasting six weeks. "I would like in each case," she added, "to publish a very modest and small pamphlet called *An Interview with Mark Rothko, An Interview with Mark Tobey*, etc." Rothko, who was in the midst of moving out of his Sixth Avenue apartment when the letter arrived, who had recently lost his position at Brooklyn College, who had sold very few paintings in the last four years, and who had not had a one-man exhibit since 1951, was happy to participate.[27]

Their subsequent correspondence, particularly as it circles around the issue of Rothko providing some kind of statement for the exhibit, dramatizes Rothko's conflict about such statements. At first, he was eager, wishing to formulate a statement, telling Kuh that their conversation had stimulated "a process of speculation about ideas and work, in which I have not engaged for some years, and which I find valuable and enlivening." He promised to "carry" the process "to some conclusion" and then to forward the results to her. His statement never materialized; but that was all right, because Kuh herself preferred a dialogue, a pamphlet in the form of *An Interview with Mark Rothko*.[28]

Very quickly, however, the interview was reconceived: no longer a conversational exchange, it would be an exchange of letters—a kind of correspondence-within-their-correspondence: "Meanwhile," Kuh wrote in early June, "within the next few weeks I will start our correspondence which, as you recall, we planned to print in a little brochure which will accompany the exhibition." On July 8, lying in the sun on a Cape Cod beach, she started: "what I really want to know and what I really want to print is information about what you are after, how you work and why you have chosen the particular form you have . . . how you got started in the direction you are following." Her letter, he replied, "has had the effect of starting me in the attempt to collect my thoughts and setting them down," but he made clear that his response did not yet constitute part of the Official Correspondence: "I hope that soon I will be able to send you something that at least from this side will seem right."[29]

Even in the privacy of a letter, Rothko remained guarded and scrupulous, though one way he could talk about his work was by talking about how to talk about it. So Rothko had plenty to say, not in answer to Kuh's questions, nor in questioning her particular questions, but in questioning the "usefulness for us of the question and answer method" itself. He urged that "we abandon any preconceived notions of what ought to be said and printed" lest "it bind us to a course that will inevitably lead to the meaningless banality of forewords and interviews."

"Rather than create the pretense of answers to questions which either should not be answered or which are essentially unanswerable," Rothko went on, "I would like to find a way of indicating the real involvements in my life out of which my pictures flow and into which they must return." He identified those involvements as "primarily moral" rather than aesthetic, historical, or technical. But then, instead of elaborating on what he meant by moral, Rothko turned the interview format around on Kuh, asking her to indicate "the real nature of your own involvements in the world of art and ideas, which, if I am at all a good judge, are very intense and human." Before disclosing his own "real involvements," Rothko needed to reassure himself his new friend was someone who shared his assumptions, was someone he could trust.

Rothko then went on with his "misgivings," warning against creating in their correspondence "an instrument . . . which will tell the public how the pictures should be looked at and what to look for." Such a move, while seeming "an obliging and helpful thing to do," would result in "the paralysis of the mind and the imagination (and for the artist a premature entombment). Hence my abhorrence for forewords and explanatory data." Rothko's open, empty canvases invite—in fact, they rely upon—a kind of associative freedom on the part of the viewer. Since that freedom provides part of the paintings' "moral" content, it would hardly do to bind or paralyze viewers with preconceived notions. "If I must place my trust somewhere," Rothko concludes, sounding a little unhappy to have to place it anywhere, "I would invest it in the psyche of the sensitive observer who is free of these conventions of understanding. I would have no apprehensions about the use he would make of these pictures for the needs of his own spirit. For if there is both need and spirit there is bound to be a real transaction."[30] But like good men, real transactions are hard to find.

In this letter to Katharine Kuh, Rothko imagines his ideal viewer: "a sensitive observer who is free of these conventions of understanding" found in forewords and other explanatory data. Rothko did not like to think of himself as a formalist speaking to art professionals. Self-taught, a man who typically expressed his approval of others by saying "he's a mensch," Rothko wanted "real"—which is to say, human—"transactions."[31] His avant-garde pictures were thus painted for what turn out to be old-fashioned humanistic reasons: they spoke to, and from, "need and spirit," "real involvements," not aesthetic sensibilities. As Rothko insisted to Selden Rodman, after he praised Rothko as "a master of color harmonies and relationships on a monumental scale": "I'm interested only in expressing basic human emotions—tragedy, ecstacy, doom, and so on—and the fact that lots of people break down and cry when confronted with my pictures shows that I *communicate* those basic human emotions."[32] The ideal viewer, then, responds out of a basic—which is to say, a universal—humanity.

It sounds as though Rothko, the son of a poor immigrant Jewish family, an impoverished artist who for many years felt neglected by museums and collectors, wants to imagine a viewer whose "ordinary" humanity transcends professional expertise, social privilege, cultural limits. And Rothko imagines himself as a kind of modern Sophocles or Shakespeare, whose "dramas"—"tragedy, ecstacy, doom"—affect the groundlings as well as the aristocrats. But as just a short time spent in any museum gallery displaying Rothko's work will reveal, many "ordinary" Americans cherish very conservative notions about art which lead them to ignore or mock his art. Rothko himself specifies an observer who, like his paintings, like Rothko himself, is "sensitive," and he can write, loftily, of his pictures being "permanently impaired by the eyes of the vulgar." Like his model of education—"a man learns by conversing with men of consequence"—Rothko's model of viewing is hierarchical, a transaction between single, gifted individuals.

Katharine Kuh, an art critic for the middle-brow *Saturday Review of Literature* and a curator, was a professional viewer, but one whose involvements with art Rothko sensed to be "intense and human." His letters to her, as he continually talked himself in and out of his promised statement, constitute an elaborate testing of her loyalty. As he writes to her in July, her letters are "invaluable." Not only do "they help sharpen issues and my ideas about them," they also "make of you a concrete audience to whom I am addressing my thoughts, whose warmth and understanding make me want to be truthful and clear." Fearing the "cruelty" *and* the anonymity of the marketplace, Rothko wished for "a *concrete* audience," as if he could make his relation with his viewers a personal one, though one in which he remained the dominant figure. Viewers, like his wife, could call him "Rothko." In fact, Rothko's *perfect* viewer would be an admiring young woman, an idealized maternal figure whose "warmth and understanding" would reassure and inspire him.

Yet when, at the end of his letter, Rothko assures Katharine Kuh that her questions stimulate his thinking, he has already made clear his belief that *no* words can catch his elusive meaning. He has now abandoned the question-and-answer method "for the question imposes its own rhetoric and syntax upon the answer regardless of whether this rhetoric can serve the truth, whereas I have had to set for myself the problem of finding the most exact rhetoric for these specific pictures." Viewers should not be imposed upon with answers; artists should not be imposed upon with questions. So Rothko, having created his pictures, wishes to create "the most *exact* rhetoric" for them. Dialogue, whether in interview or in correspondence, will not serve, for "try as I will, I cannot directly answer the questions posed in your letters without distorting my meaning." Rothko has decided to return to the original idea of writing a statement of his own. But even as he announces this new project he already suspects that the "battle" is "futile." For what he has realized, Rothko writes, is "that here was not a problem of what *ought* to be said, but what it is that I *can* say."

As an example, he cites the word "space." To discuss this concept,

> I would first have to disabuse the word from its current meanings in books on art, astrology, atomicism and multidimensionality; and then I would have to redefine and distort it beyond all recognition in order to attain a common meeting ground for discussion.
>
> [It] is a dangerous and futile battle. The strategy may be brilliant but the soldier is [not].

In "The Romantics Were Prompted," Rothko had urged that "the familiar identity of things has to be pulverized in order to destroy the finite associations with which our society increasingly enshrouds every aspect of our environment"—a method he here suggests needs to be applied to ordinary language, perhaps futilely, since this foot soldier is not all that confident with words. Yet, the actual fact is that I do not think in terms of space in painting my pictures, and it is better to let myself find my own words at the right time, and I will come closer to the feelings about my pictures which you have so vividly described, and which I think I understand, and respect.[33]

But in the end he could not find the right words of his own. No statement, no interview, appeared, though Kuh did quote two passages from one of Rothko's letters in her brief essay about the exhibit.[34]

Silence is so accurate; but silence is so absolute, too severe a discipline for someone so eager to communicate. Rothko could talk about the difficulty of talking about his work; and he was quite willing to talk about how his work should be hung, as he did in a letter to Kuh in late September.

> Although I have studied the blue prints carefully, I realize that it is impossible for me to visualize the real feeling of the room and what the hanging problem will be. I thought that it may be useful to tell you, here, about several general ideas which I have arrived at in the course of my own experience in hanging the pictures.

Confronted with a concrete practical task, Rothko could freely discuss some of his intentions for his work, while also revealing how those intentions were formed partly out of his concerns about whether or not his observers would be truly "sensitive" to his intentions. "Since my pictures are large, colorful and unframed, and since museum walls are usually immense and formidable, there is the danger that the pictures relate themselves as decorative areas to the walls," he warned. "This would be a distortion of their meaning, since the pictures are intimate and intense, and are the opposite of what is decorative; and have been painted in a scale of normal living rather than an institutional scale." Rothko advises Kuh to avoid the decorative effect "by tending to crowd the show rather than making it spare." "By saturating the room with the feeling of the work, the walls are defeated and the poignancy of each single work" becomes "more visible."

So the physical reality of the gallery space must be "defeated," just as the viewer must be gently universalized into a "sensitive observer." "I also hang the largest pictures so that they must be first encountered at close quarters, so that the first experience is to be within the picture," Rothko continues. "This may well give the key to the observer of the ideal relationship between himself and the rest of the pictures." Pictures, particularly the largest ones, should be hung "low," "often as close to the floor as is feasible," and some of them, he concludes, "do very well in a confined space." The "ideal relationship" Rothko speaks of is intimate, intense, human-scale; yet Rothko's desire to *saturate* the room with the feeling of the work, to have viewers encounter large canvases (hung low) at *close quarters,* perhaps within a *confined* space—all suggest an effort to place the viewer *within the picture,* where cold, detached, killing looks are impossible. Just as Rothko's delicately edged rectangles gently contain the fluctuating forms and the diffused colored light within them, so Rothko needs, gently—by hanging, not talking—to control those viewers he seeks to free.

At the end of his letter about hanging the show, Rothko says that he "would like to entertain" Kuh's idea of his giving a lecture, so that he could see the exhibit.[35] A few days before the show opened, she wrote that she could cover Rothko's expenses for a brief trip to Chicago if in return he could "talk in the gallery where your paintings are installed to a group of our painting students and to some of us on the staff." "Perhaps," she added, "after you have spoken about your own work, you would be willing to answer some of the questions the students might bring up."[36] But Rothko finally declined the invitation: "I find that I have not the stomach for the role of apologist for the pictures in such proximity to the exhibition, both as to time and place."[37]

"There is more power in telling little than in telling all," Rothko believed.[38] To lecture on these reticent paintings, and in such proximity to them would be, in effect, to place a human figure in the foreground, and to relegate the paintings to the background, paintings in which Rothko had dissolved the figure/ground division. Surrounded by eight of his "facades," the real artist would step forward, like Shakespeare suddenly walking onstage in the middle of Act III to deliver a lecture on *Hamlet.*[39] Such an act would be *too* aggressive, *too* concrete, *too* personal, revealing the pictures to be the creations of a specific historical individual, the biographical "me" they were striving both to express and transcend. Bits of his flesh and "transcendental experiences," Rothko's paintings are both personal and anonymous. "It is a disturbing thing to have the pictures hung at such a distance," Rothko wrote to Kuh, asking her to send him details of the show's reception to "make the exhibition much more real to me."[40] But for Mark Rothko to impose his physical presence and his words on a gallery filled with "Rothkos" would be for him to resolve their contradictions and snap the tension that gives them life. Closely identified with his creations, he still had to remain a mysterious presence hovering behind and dispersed throughout his canvases, if "real transactions" were to take place.

• • •

Sometime in April 1954, Rothko and his family moved from their condemned Sixth Avenue building to a slightly larger, slightly less run-down flat, at 102 West 54th Street, between Sixth and Seventh Avenues, on the present site of the Hilton Hotel.⁴¹ In fact, as the hotel was being built in 1963, Rothko grumbled to a friend who worked for the construction firm, "If this were in Europe they would make a little gold plate on the place where the [flat] was and mention who had [lived] there." A few months later a public relations man from the construction company called Rothko and suggested he come over, select "a few bricks—and objects," and build a collage of them which would be placed in one of the Hilton's walls while photographers recorded the event. He "couldn't understand" why Rothko was not interested in "this chance for publicity."⁴²

To move the two and a half blocks up Sixth Avenue, Rothko and his friend William Scharf simply carried the Rothkos' worldly possessions through the midtown streets. The new flat—a third floor, seven room walk-up rented at $60 a week—was decorated with black linoleum pulled up from the floor of the old flat ("he wanted a shiny black floor and white walls") and furnished with oak pieces from the Salvation Army that Mell had scrubbed and refinished; "and then on the walls were all these magnificent paintings." Rothko's new apartment, moreover, was just around the corner from a studio at 106 West 53rd that he had occupied since early 1952.⁴³

"Our age is an age of assault," Rothko one day announced to Alfred Jensen. Rothko was not talking about the holocaust or Hiroshima or the Korean War or the lynching of a black man in the south or a Cossack lashing at the face of a Jewish boy in the Pale. He was talking about a young, half-drunk painter who had recently come up to him in a bar and declared, "You have said something in your work which I admire, Rothko; however I want to go beyond what you have said because I need to sell and that's something you haven't done too well." At least by the time this insult had been transformed into a "story," Rothko was trying to rise above the situation by labeling it "tragicomic." Since the art market in America will not "improve for generations," the young painter will eventually find himself "in the same tragic situation that I am," and he must face this "tragic" reality "before he can be an artist." "He knows this at heart, therefore his need to assault me." Instead of viewing the exchange as one in which he was hurt or angered, Rothko abstracts from the specific, adopts a position of lofty moral superiority (the young man evades the reality facing him), and views both himself and the young painter as archetypal figures, fated players in a "tragic" generational drama.

It's a risky act to send the self out into an impersonal and sometimes cruel public world. At social gatherings, where people draw together "to evade solitude," says Rothko, one also meets "the ambitious egotists out for grabs." "It's this kind of egotist who frequents the clubs and by the way the Cedar Street Bar is nothing but a club." "I avoid clubs," Rothko sternly concludes. "I prefer solitude." Social encounters can be dangerous; but social encounters are also futile. As Rothko puts it in a later conversation with Jensen: "cliques are only stupid and reactionary clubs. It is the artist's lot to remain in solitude. Do you actually think that Pollock or Kline or de Kooning would go to the Cedar Bar if they did not suffer from solitude? It is because I suffer from solitude that I do not go to the Cedar Bar. If I went everything would be just the same; the artist is by his very nature doomed to solitude."[44] To the dangers and distractions of the social encounter, Rothko prefers the monkish solitude of the studio.

Something he was able to afford on his Brooklyn College salary, Rothko's 53rd Street studio was his first outside the home—and the first of five such work spaces he would occupy over the rest of his life. Rothko's large paintings, "painted in a scale of normal living rather than an institutional scale," did "very well in a confined space," he told Katharine Kuh. Between 1949 and early 1952, paintings like *Number 10, 1950,* had been created and hung in a place of normal living, the small, confined rooms of Rothko's Sixth Avenue walk-up. Such spaces can more easily be "saturated" with Rothko's large paintings and the literal walls "defeated" by their living presences. But it is also as if Rothko needed and wanted the confining pressure of walls like those in the claustrophobic rooms in his paintings of the 1930s, as if physical constriction, like social hostility, could "act as a lever for true liberation."

True liberation, however, is experienced not in visionary flight but in a state of tension between constraint and freedom, just as Rothko's paintings alternately squeeze and expand, push forward into the room, recede back into the wall. As he stressed to William Seitz, one can be a Seventh Day Adventist—i.e., separate one's self from the world—but this is "not true of me. I live on Sixth Avenue, paint on 53rd Street, am affected by television, etc." His life has a diverse particularity. "My paintings are part of that life."[45] Conveying sensations from that life, but detached from their literal referents, these paintings are at once abstract and human. They would be most at home in a kind of small domestic space where, nowadays, they are least likely to be found. Seeking to direct the hanging of his "Fifteen Americans" and Art Institute of Chicago exhibits, Rothko wished, by defeating the institutional scale of the museum, to transform its gallery into something like the space in which his paintings had originated, one where they *belonged*.

Rothko's new studio separated art from the household, a separation he felt necessary with a two-year-old in the house. The studio also provided him with a private space where he could shut out the loud world, work, saturate the room with music, and be alone with his creations. Rothko sought forms of stability in his life that, like the rectangles in his paintings, instituted a flexible order. Not only did he want the regularity of marriage, he liked regular working hours as well, telling one of his Brooklyn College students that "he liked the idea of going off to his studio as if he were going to a job," getting dressed for work, walking around the corner, "and working a full day there." Rothko's nine-to-five workday struck Dan Rice, his assistant in the late 1950s, as "amusing because I was part of the downtown crowd in which it was very acceptable behavior to paint through the night or paint only at night or even to paint anytime. And the idea of a painter leaving the house and going to the studio and returning for dinner was totally new to me."[46]

Rothko may have come and gone with the regularity of a banker, but once inside the studio, insulated from domestic obligations, social slights, and commercial realities, he could feel autonomous, creative, and full, in control of a place that was *his*. A long, narrow room, with a ten-foot-high unfinished ceiling, the 53rd Street studio had two small windows at the rear and large floor-to-ceiling windows, facing north, along the front. The back was used for storing completed works and prepared canvases; the front, heated by a Franklin stove, was furnished with a couch, rocker, some other wooden chairs and two small tables. The middle area, containing a homemade wooden worktable, served as Rothko's place to produce paintings and, with a small wooden bench, for him and others to sit and view them.[47]

Painting is a *physical* activity, involving manual skill not just in the application of oil paint to the canvas but, for an artist unable to afford an assistant, in building stretchers, stretching the canvas, preparing the canvas, mixing paints. Rothko was not much of a carpenter. When he did hire Dan Rice to assist him with the Seagram mural project, Rice mentioned the job to Franz Kline, who commented, "Gee what a relief to be able to look at the back of a Rothko and not think of a chicken coop." Part of the problem was Rothko's use of cheap materials. "He would use the worst kind of stretchers, packing cases, boards, put them together with staples, and very indifferent about it," said Sidney Janis. "I was guilt ridden that we would sell a picture like that and deliver it to a client and have him hang it on his wall in the company of great antiques in a duplex apartment on Fifth Avenue."[48] So in some literal sense Rothko's elegant paintings stretched on "chicken coop" supports *were* "facades." Given Rothko's sales record in the early and mid-1950s, it is not surprising he would economize on stretchers; but this frugality continued even after he was well-off, as if he still felt poor.[49] Yet another part of the problem was Rothko's incompetence. "He just *whacked* something together," Rice recalled. "He was very impatient working with his hands." In his *Self-Portrait* of the 1930s, Rothko represented his hands as damaged, his vision as impaired. In this artist who could barely see without his glasses and had large bony hands with thick fingers, hand-eye coordination was never a strong point.

Yet in his paintings of the 1950s and 1960s Rothko's touch is often light, feathery. He imagined himself "breathing paint on the canvas," achieving a kind of spiritual application of paint. Despite being largely self-taught, Rothko, as Dana Cranmer points out, worked "as a relatively conventional technician." When compared with such innovative contemporaries as Jackson Pollock and Franz Kline, Rothko—who "stretched canvas on wooden stretchers or strainers," "applied paint using standard brushes," "worked standing up before the canvas," "appears almost academic." Or, beginning with the multiforms of the late 1940s, his working methods characteristically combined the conservative with the experimental. His explorations, however, "were focused not on methods but on the physical components and quality of the paint film itself and the variety of effects possible in the manipulation of the medium."[50] Not much of a carpenter, Rothko was involved with the kitchen activities around painting, using old recipes, inventing his own, to concoct the colors that gave substance to his simplified forms. He used lots of eggs in his work, "like his mother would bake bread," he said.[51] No mere colorist or decorator, Rothko liked to think of himself as feeding, sustaining his viewers, addressing their most basic human needs.

By 1950 Rothko had evolved a set of working procedures that served him for most of the rest of his life. He began with raw, unprimed canvas, to which he applied a glue size mixed with powdered pigments, "so that," in Dan Rice's words, "even the glue would go on in a color." Rothko then covered this ground with an approximation of that color in oil, the ground color usually going 'around the corner' at top, bottom and both edges, to cover the tacking margins of paintings which Rothko insisted on keeping unframed—a procedure that at once asserted the painting's physical existence as a three-dimensional object and left it open, rather than enclosed and sharply divided from its surroundings. On top of the ground color Rothko created his fields of color with glazes of paint mixtures, to which, in the 1950s, he began adding "unbound powdered pigments and whole eggs," often diluting "the paint film with a solvent" like turpentine. The Rothko who had started out applying dark paints in the thickly impastoed manner of Max Weber was now applying very thin washes of transparent color in the manner of Mark Rothko. Rothko thinned his paints to the point that "pigment particles were almost dissociated from the paint film, barely clinging to the surface," Dana Cranmer writes. As a result, "light penetrated the attenuated paint film, striking the individual pigment particles and bouncing back to suffuse the surface and engulf the viewer in an aura of color." In other words, by diluting the paint to the verge of disintegration, Rothko created his unique inner luminosity.

According to Dan Rice, Rothko's glazes were "very lightly brushed, with dotted as well as full sweeps of the brush." "The physical movement," he adds, "was very active and very graphic." Sometimes to keep his layers of paint from mixing, Rothko would cover a layer with an egg mix, into which he sometimes placed powdered pigment.

> When he worked out closer to the edges or where he wanted thin spots for the ground to come through, he'd become more or less actively engaged with the surface that he was painting over; he would necessarily slow up a little, so the paint wouldn't go on either as thickly or as quickly. Often, just the very tip of the brush, a big 5″ housepainting brush, would just sort of flicker over the surface, so the area was not covered as rapidly.

Then Rothko "would sit and look for long periods, sometimes for hours, sometimes for days, considering the next color, considering expanding an area." This process led him to work on more than one painting at a time, "so if he felt himself hung up in these long periods of thought about the possibilities of one painting, he could turn to another painting to release some of that energy."

Rothko's veils of color were applied quickly and spontaneously; he once told Robert Motherwell that "there was always automatic drawing under those larger forms."[52] His large paintings were not to be "something you command." Yet Rothko sometimes called himself Apollonian, and most of the time in his 53rd Street studio was spent sitting silently on his bench and looking, contemplating changes of size, color, and the like.[53] A later assistant compared Rothko to "a Bavarian clockmaker—very careful and slow and precise."[54] Rothko's "organisms" were *deliberately* constructed.

After Rothko hired an assistant in the late 1960s, the young man was told: "I'm a secretive person and whatever you see, it's private."[55] He was referring to business transactions, personal affairs, and especially to painting techniques. Perhaps Rothko's guardedness came partly from a sense of painting as transgression, violating both the Second Commandment and his family's expectations for him. But his secretiveness about his working methods was one he let people know about. He thereby aroused curiosity while keeping himself a veiled presence behind his work, surrounding both the paintings and the painter with an aura of mystery. Rothko's works—"*his* children"—emerged from a process as hidden and creative as the one which, inside Mell, during 1950, had produced Kate. No longer doing plein-air watercolors of the Lake George or Portland landscape; no longer sketching subway or urban scenes, Rothko was now a painter of the studio, private and withdrawn from the world. The womb in which his art was conceived, the studio emblematized a core self immune to violation—or assaults—from the outside. Being alone there with his creations furnished this melancholy Russian Jew with his single greatest source of happiness, a feeling reflected in his elated paintings of the early 1950s.

But Rothko did not paint in a converted barn behind a house in rural upstate New York, as an artist who unequivocally preferred solitude might do; he worked in a second-floor urban loft, in mid-Manhattan, less than a block away from the Museum of Modern Art and just a few blocks further away from the "suction of the shopkeeping mentalities" on 57th Street. The studio was quickly equipped with a telephone that Rothko found it hard *not* to answer. He preferred an isolation in tension with and struggling against the interruptions and corruptions of the outside—as if only when he felt squeezed-in was he moved to expand.

Located above a glass-manufacturing shop, Rothko's studio had a wooden floor containing four large rectangular sections of glass placed right in front of the wall space where he painted, and viewed, his work. "Light came up from the store below," one visitor recalled, "and his paintings, which by today's standards are not enormous, really filled that room. And when you walked into that room, with this light coming from below, it was like a chapel in there." Sacred space tucked away in a large modern city, the studio also provided a place to show paintings to family, friends, fellow artists, curators, dealers, critics, art historians, collectors. The studio was a private space, but, as Stanley Kunitz remarked, "Mark loved an audience. And though he did not actually paint while you were in his studio, he wanted you to be part of the scenery, and to admire what he was doing. He would watch you like a hawk to be sure that you weren't concealing any emotions about what you saw."[56]

Many studio transactions were professional or commercial ones. Dorothy Miller and Katharine Kuh visited to select paintings for exhibitions; William Seitz and Elaine de Kooning visited to look at paintings and interview Rothko; collectors visited to look, to buy, or not to buy. But no one came who was not admitted by Rothko; and curatorial decisions could be unilaterally overruled by the painter, as happened with "Fifteen Americans." The studio, then, made an ideal gallery space, in which the artist could function as his own curator and dealer. Viewed by a select few, Rothko's creations remained under his protective control.

• • •

It must have highly disturbed Mark Rothko how much to project into the world and how much to recede.

Ethel Baziotes

Moving from Sixth Avenue between 51st and 52nd to 54th near Sixth, Rothko was choosing to stay in the part of town he had lived in for seven years, the longest he had lived anywhere since leaving Portland. It was not just his proximity to the Museum of Modern Art and the 57th Street galleries; he liked the feeling of this neighborhood before construction of skyscrapers like the Hilton and the Sperry building (on the site of his Sixth Avenue flat) transformed it. Rothko "was so impatient," Stanley Kunitz recalled. "He was the most impatient man I think I ever saw. He couldn't sit. He always had to be moving. And he was so restless in spirit. He was never quite satisfied. Things were never quite right." Rothko's restlessness explains his wish for regularity in his life. "His meditation," Kunitz adds, "I think was largely when he was working, when he would put on his Mozart and play it [as] background music."[57]

Yet even the insulation of a studio filled with his own tranquil paintings did not fully satisfy Rothko. "Mark was a very restless man who had to get out of the studio as much as possible," Sally Scharf commented. An insomniac, Rothko would often "be out prowling around at one o'clock, two o'clock in the morning—not sleeping or not wanting to sleep. I always thought his death would be to be hit by a car just wandering across the street without paying attention." In the evening the Scharfs—he a painter, she an actress—spent time at Jerry's Bar, at the corner of Sixth and 54th, "and Mark would walk down at night, and Kate would go to bed and Mell would be reading, to look for us and join us" and the young actors and actresses who gathered in the bar/restaurant. "When Mark came in wearing his big long overcoat—with a cigarette dangling from his lips—he moved like a ferryboat bumping from side to side into port."[58]

Daytimes, Sally Scharf recalled, Rothko liked Baby's, "a wonderful, old-fashioned New York drugstore with a counter for eating." He sometimes ate breakfast there. He sometimes ate lunch there, occasionally bringing along his young daughter, and he would "want to linger and talk over coffee and cigarettes—he was a chain smoker, one cigarette after another—and Kate would spread out on the floor and have a beautiful tantrum and Mark would just stay and try to talk above her." And sometimes Rothko came to Baby's in the late afternoon "and he'd always have a glass of tea," said Celina Trief. "He insisted they put it in a glass. The old Russian, the Russian in him. He really did love that drugstore. They knew him very well." If he often ate lunch at Valmor's, where he knew he'd meet Alfred Barr and Dorothy Miller, the restless Rothko sought more casual talk at the local drugstore. "He really took great pleasure in talking to the people behind the counter." It *was* the old Russian in him, the Russian boy who had grown up in pharmacies, drinking a glass of tea and talking with his father or older brothers.

Chapter Eleven

Stanley Kunitz once called Rothko "the last rabbi of western art." "When I said that to him once, he enjoyed it; it made him feel very good. I meant that there was in him a rather magisterial authority . . . a feeling in him that he belonged to the line of prophets rather than to the line of great craftsmen."[59] Rothko associated his childhood with persecution from Czarist authority and oppression from orthodox Jewish authority. Emigration meant modernization, emancipation—freedom. By 1950 Rothko, now living in New York for almost thirty years, had changed his citizenship, changed his name, married a *goy* from Cleveland and, officially at least, named his daughter "Kathy Lynn," as if he and his wife were Scarsdale WASPs. Traveling to the prewar center of European art, Rothko disdained the cultural and social "decay" in Paris, and back in New York he was proclaiming that he and his generation of American painters had "wiped the slate clean. We start anew. A new land," a rhetoric as conventionally American as it was modern. The embarrassed Dvinsk boy, stiffly dressed in his Dvinsk version of a Buster Brown suit, had been Americanized. In fact, like his polemical friends Newman and Still, he had grown into something of a cultural chauvinist.

Yet one problem of living in this country, a problem especially acute in the 1950s, is to keep from being smothered by middle-class values. Rothko's social identity, especially his Jewishness, gave him an edge of resistance and difference. Whether Rothko vowed never to enter a synagogue again after his father left Dvinsk or after his father died, he kept the vow; he was not a religious Jew. Nor was he, like Marc Chagall, interested in pictorial preservation of his Russian-Jewish heritage. Rothko the modernist, speaking out of his "tremendous emotional capacity for despair," judged religion to be one of those illusions that conceal man's tragic solitude. "Modernization is a trauma," James Murray Cuddihy writes in his study of the strains of Jewish acculturation, *The Ordeal of Civility*.[60] But when Rothko had stepped off the SS *Czar* in the summer of 1913 and entered his new land, consciousness had not been magically, or even traumatically, wiped clean. On the few occasions when he spoke of that moment, he remembered feeling humiliated by the way his fancy dress seemed both to expose and to deny his origins. Resented as "transplantation to a land where he never felt entirely at home," emigration meant an *imposed* freedom, and one based on another item in Rothko's list of "illusions": property. In fact, compared with the impersonal and cruel marketplace of capitalism, Dvinsk's Jewish community, in hazy retrospect, offered a unified, organic culture, the possibility of social warmth, common understanding, higher moral values: real transactions. Rothko longed for the forms of a collective life within which he thought he would feel less "lonesome"; and he searched for the mythic (or "fabulous"), yearning for a traditional religious framework, the loss of which had left him "melancholy." Rothko's new vision, expressed in solitary paintings emptied of social and natural forms, yet filled with a colored light whose source remains hidden within or behind the paintings, embodies both his despair and his spiritual longings.

Rather than being fixed, Rothko's social identity moved in a fluid space "between"—between his Americanness and his Jewishness. In the 1950s, as Rothko began to achieve and even to enjoy recognition, "there was a kind of affluence about his being," Kunitz said. "There was a great capacity for pure affection. There was a sense of embracing warmth in Mark's presence at his best. He was a lovely person to be with. He was responsive, charming in his address. You had the feeling when you were with Mark this was truly somebody who cared about you in a deep way." Kunitz, a close friend until Rothko's death, was Russian-Jewish and a creative person, but a poet, not a painter, not a rival. "He was so wary of friendship among his peers. You always felt that he preferred another kind of social life that wasn't involved with the art world," Kunitz observed.[61] Still, at least during the early fifties, Rothko remained close to the "uptown" painters, especially Ferber, Gottlieb, and Newman, all of them, like Kunitz, Jewish.

But his growing reputation expanded Rothko's social life, and with people he knew less well he could be charming, even courtly, "all sweetness and light." Elaine de Kooning remembered the early 1950s as "a great period for parties. Really scintillating, sparkling parties when the conversation was just wonderful" at, say, the Village apartment of Jeanne Reynal (a mosaic artist who owned a Rothko) or the Park Avenue apartment of Yvonne Thomas (a former Rothko student from The Subjects of the Artist School). "Mark Rothko was very social, very smooth socially," de Kooning said. "He had kind of an aloof manner. He would stand up very straight with his head tilted back looking down and with a little archaic Greek smile on his face and make these dry little wisecracks. And I found him very witty and also a very attractive man."[62] Rothko's manner could be civil, urbane.

"To make oneself accountable for one's appearances before strangers is the first step to social modernization," Cuddihy writes.[63] Rothko remembered his arrival in this country as an experience of being looked at—and through—by strangers: it is a risky and unfeeling act to send one's child into such a world. From Rothko's point of view, a too-respectable social appearance signified cultural shame. Rothko did like wide-brimmed, flamboyant hats, but being Jewish, he did not need to advertise his marginality with odd clothing, flowing beard, or long hair.[64] Besides, bohemian styles of dress might set him *too* far apart from that middle-class regularity with which he had ambivalent relations. Like other "uptown" painters he generally wore suits, not jeans and T-shirt, though Rothko's clothes were typically ill-fitting, cheap, slightly disheveled, as if he insisted on looking slightly different. Getting Rothko dressed for a formal occasion was always an adventure, and even after he got there, proper behavior wasn't guaranteed. No Jackson Pollock, Rothko didn't start fistfights or piss out of his host's bedroom window; but touchy and suspicious, Rothko could be "difficult," combative, explode with anger, affront with deliberate vulgarity, "make a scene," threaten to sue, slash a painting. Sometime in the late 1950s, Rothko, in the lobby of the Whitney, became so angry he put his fist through a plate glass window.[65] "He was a volcano," remarked Robert Motherwell, "a primitive Ivan the Terrible."[66] In his own description, Rothko festered with indignation, and his angry sense of rejection and exclusion was part personal, part collective and ethnic. To be moderate and polite, to be merely civil, meant surrender to American Protestant social codes, the creation of a decorous "not-me" that *was* empty.

Rothko's social behavior, of course, varied according to the particular circumstances. Alone with a favorite nephew and his wife, Rothko might stretch out on his living-room couch and discourse at length on world politics, art-world politics, Nietzsche, Shakespeare, or Mozart. In larger gatherings, with people he knew less well or was less sure of, Rothko, in David Hare's words, "wasn't somebody who walked into a room and took over, it wasn't somebody dominant, it was somebody who kept to himself," as if Rothko had built "a fence" around himself "and it wasn't that you didn't communicate; it was that you waited there." Asked to summarize her sense of Rothko, Elaine de Kooning remembered "a dignified man standing off in the distance, aloof"—"and vulnerable, on guard, extremely sensitive, complex, witty, trenchant." The actress Jane Lawrence, Tony Smith's wife, recalled that Rothko had "sort of a mysterious aura about him; it wasn't as though he was just totally straight, direct, back and forth like a tennis game. There were just certain things going on that you couldn't quite pin down. I always felt his mind was constantly acting, that there was a space that didn't relate to our conversation."[67] Or, as Cecile Abish, the Brooklyn College student who briefly lived with the Rothkos, put it, "He always had, if he didn't have his eyeglasses on or even with his eyeglasses on, it was like there was something between him and you. It wasn't a wall. It was sort of a mist. It wasn't dreamy. It was contemplative."

Socially, Rothko placed himself not outside but slightly apart from and above the company. His large frame and bulky muscularity gave him an imposing physical presence observed by just about everyone who knew him. He spoke, according to Robert Motherwell, with "a very deep voice, with all the words clearly articulated—very resonant," and his lofty manner of speech was captured by Alfred Jensen in his transcriptions of their conversations. Partly

Rothko was animated by nineteenth-century ideas of greatness: romantic genius. But Rothko, who looked neither the bohemian nor the refined artist, was more accurately the painter as Jewish immigrant and patriarch. After "removed" and "self-absorbed," the word "dignified" most often occurs in descriptions of Rothko. "He had a great deal of dignity, and he had dignity that comes from a very serious, long, religious background," commented Louise Bourgeois. Stanley Kunitz was not alone in perceiving Rothko as rabbi or Jewish prophet. Rothko and Newman struck Jane Lawrence as "sort of Old Testament, like patriarchs and prophets and judges." According to Louise Bourgeois, "He always sounded like a religious official. His demeanor was that of a prophet. He talked that way. He never talked about himself. He was not at all intimate—very lofty—I wouldn't say pretentious or condescending." Donald Blinken described Rothko as "avuncular and prophetic, with gravitas."[68] Commenting that "every painter is a painter centrally and marginally something else, a decorator, an illustrator, an architect, a sensualist," Budd Hopkins concluded: "Rothko was a rabbi." Jewishness set him apart. His experience as a Jew—in Dvinsk, in Portland, in New Haven, in New York—impressed upon him the insecurities of human existence, creating not just resentment but a moral seriousness that gave his social manner its grave, lofty (or "magisterial") style of authority.

One day, talking with the painter Ben Dienes, Rothko suddenly declared, "'Ben, it is not painting.' Mark started getting excited. He says, 'It's beyond painting.' He says, 'The struggle is beyond painting, not with painting.'" Or, as Budd Hopkins observed: "Painting was less the central thing for him than for other painters. He was much more interested in the iconic force that these works could have in the world at large rather than what other painters thought about them. Painting was the channel by which he got at something at the center of his life. You look at the painting and you're seeing through it into something else, which is the fuel of the painting, the source of the meaning"—the "content" or "subject" hidden, like the light source, within or beyond the painting. "I always had the impression that he had some sort of message to give to the world, and painting was his form of expression," Donald Blinken said.

Rothko was not just embarked on a "search for a style." He was animated by a mission, one that redeemed, even glorified, his years of poverty, suffering, and rejection. As Elaine de Kooning pointed out, Rothko played only one role, and it was a role that went beyond mere rabbi or prophet: "the role was that of the Messiah—I have come; I have the word. I mean Rothko had a very healthy self-worship and he did feel that he had discovered some great secret."[69] Quiet, aloof, dignified, speaking slowly and deliberately in articulate, well-formed sentences, wearing a rumpled, oversized suit with wrinkled shirt and tie askew, staring intently through his thick lenses, making wisecracks or making grim pronouncements, Rothko came bearing a "new vision." Beyond language, beyond painting, Rothko's art would emotionally nurture, spiritually feed, and finally *save* its viewers.

Social occasions might be sought to avoid man's "tragic solitude" or to find some reassurance, warmth, and understanding; they pose their own dangers, but they also make possible self-display, and "Mark loved an audience." He enjoyed self-display. Herbert Ferber noted that Rothko "wanted to be an actor at one time, and he remained an actor all his life. I mean all of his acting in relation to other people was a kind of dramatization of himself. . . . I wouldn't say that he was acting a part which he didn't believe in. But he was very conscious of the fact that an artist is different from other people. He consciously tried to create an image of himself which he thought would fit the picture of an artist. His conversation, his dress, his opinions were to some people outrageous; so that he thought of himself as presenting ideas that would jolt people. And he really did work at creating an image." Elaine de Kooning believed that "Rothko became totally involved in his own mythology, more than anyone I know except Barney Newman. They were both tremendously involved with their self-image."[70]

Touchy and adversarial, or dignified and rabbinical, Rothko could also be the dissident modern artist who likes to "jolt people." During the 1950s, Rothko, self-consciously presenting himself as a social outsider, was drawing on a familiar (or "recognizable") "image" of the artist, just as he had done to present himself in his *Self-Portrait*. Like that painting, Rothko's social interactions combined self-expression ("I wouldn't say that he was acting a part which he didn't believe in") with theatricality, as if only by thinking of social encounters as "dramas" and himself as a "performer" could Rothko express himself freely and "without embarrassment."

Many of Rothko's friends mention their difficulty in deciding how seriously to take his more outrageous statements, or how fully to believe his stories. As his nephew Kenneth Rabin stated, "he could be hyperbolic . . . he could be jocular." Rothko's self-presentation was *manifestly* theatrical, so that, rather than standing behind his words, he often seemed to be disengaging himself from them even as he uttered them. So Rothko fabricated a "recognizable image," behind which part of him remained concealed, split. Activating the literal space between painting and viewer, filling it with the advancing/retreating movements of the painting and the "quickening" gaze of the viewer, Rothko's art develops a tension between autonomy and intimate relation. Socially, Rothko dramatized himself, played roles that came across as roles, keeping his listeners off-balance, so that he could feel free while in relation. Rothko put a "fence" or "mist" or "facade" between himself and others, evoking a part of him that was turned inward, recessed, abstracted, sealed off. By remaining slightly apart—not fully present—he avoided full exposure and preserved a fluid social identity.

One afternoon Budd Hopkins met Rothko at Baby's Drugstore. As the two men sat on adjacent counter stools eating sandwiches, Hopkins told Rothko about something that had happened that morning in a class he was taking from Meyer Schapiro at Columbia. Schapiro was talking "about Soutine and the Jewish culture he had come from," drawing on a study he had read comparing Jewish gestures with Italian gestures, and illustrating the study with funny examples. "And in the middle of the lecture, just as he's like bowling along, he said, you know that of course this culture has been wiped out totally by the Nazis and by pogroms in Russia and the Stalinist purges and it is now almost totally non-existent. And Schapiro suddenly stopped and started to sob, in front of a class of fifty people." Schapiro had also mentioned that Rothko had come from a similar part of Russia, but when Hopkins reached the point in the story "where suddenly Schapiro started to cry, and his shoulders shook, he lowered his head, and of course it was a reference to the Holocaust, absolutely," Rothko—whom Hopkins thought would be touched by the story—instead became very angry and said, "He's so sentimental. I can't stand it. He's so sentimental," and then "tore out" of the drugstore.

Rothko wasn't necessarily opposed to open displays of emotion. "The people who weep before my pictures are having the same religious experience I had when I painted them," he said, and he enjoyed reporting sightings of museum visitors weeping before his works. One reason he was so fond of Theodoros Stamos, he said, was that Stamos had wept at the death of a close friend; and Rothko himself wept when he heard of the death of Matisse, when he learned of the assassination of John F. Kennedy.[71] In the mid-1960s, Albert Grokest, Rothko's physician and friend, while waiting in the studio, overheard a conversation between Rothko and a much older man from Dvinsk; the two men spoke of pogroms, they drank, and they wept.

Why, then, was Meyer Schapiro so outrageously sentimental? Schapiro was not speaking in a private conversation with a *landsman,* where warmth, understanding, and thus real transactions are possible. Speaking in an American university classroom, Schapiro exposed private emotion before an audience of strangers, many of them detached and Gentile. Weeping at the extermination of Eastern European Jewish culture—rather than, say, being angry about it—Schapiro made Jews look weak, like figures of pathos, "sentimental"—an embarrassment.

Rothko, of course, had his own stories of Jewish victimization, notably the one he told to his close friend Al Jensen and worth repeating here: "it was a childhood memory of his family and relatives talking about a Czarist pogrom. The Cossacks took the Jews from the village to the woods and made them dig a large grave. Rothko said he pictured that square grave in the woods so vividly that he wasn't sure the massacre hadn't happened in his lifetime. He said he'd always been haunted by the image of that grave, and that in some profound way it was locked into his painting." Some of Rothko's narrower horizontal rectangles pull us into a dark, choking, gravelike space. But the shapes in other of his paintings suggest windows or doors or empty stages or tombstones or landscapes or geometricized human figures, as many viewers have testified. The story of the mass grave does suggest that Rothko, with the guilt of a survivor, did want to associate his work with the dangers (pogroms; the Holocaust) he had escaped. The story does not provide an "origin" for Rothko's painting, but it does reveal that Rothko's creations—stories or paintings—cannot be severed from his Jewishness.

As Rothko told William Seitz, his paintings grew out of his daily life, out of his accumulated life-experience, and he wasn't being flippant when, asked during the hanging of his Museum of Modern Art retrospective how long he had spent on a large painting, he replied: "I'm 57 years old, and it took me all that time to paint this picture."[72] Among the least diaristic or autobiographical of painters, Rothko did not represent particular persons or places, specific historical events like the Holocaust or more private events like his emigration or the death of his mother. Even his expressionist works of the 1930s reveal Rothko as a rather removed and impersonal painter, representing the "human drama" through distorted, immobilized figures suspended in symbolic moments, wrenched out of time. About representing the Holocaust Rothko told Peter Selz, "Well, you know, this kind of disfiguration and this kind of thing you cannot touch, but it is, you know, part of what you feel and part of what you express about the tragedy of it all." Kate Rothko recalled that while the Holocaust was never discussed at home, it was "always there in the background." In Rothko's paintings, too, his Jewishness was always there in the background—as a given. Abstracting from the particulars of his experience, Rothko sought to represent that experience in an impersonal art of tragic dignity, not pathos.

Rothko's diffused, shifting fields of color obliterate the social, historical "me." Yet his very effort to create this *kind* of art derives in part from a crucial moment in his social history, when he literally crossed boundaries: his emigration from Jewish Dvinsk to American Portland. Rothko's passage saved him from the perils epitomized by the mass-grave story. In this literal sense his migration gave him "a new life," a kind of rebirth, an exhilarating sense of release that later led him to imagine art as a migration, a going beyond, a crossing over, a "*trans*cendental" experience, "an unknown adventure in an unknown space." But Rothko's crossing on the SS *Czar* imposed separation and entailed the loss not just of particular people, places, things but of a whole way of feeling about himself and being in the world. It was as if Dvinsk had died, or only remained alive inside him, as a private store of memory and self that, sealed up and withheld, kept him apart, saved him from being absorbed (or "smothered") by his new culture.

Rothko lost his home, he lost his father, he lost his "stability." Crossing borders was, as he wrote to Sonia of his "new life" after his separation from Edith, both "exciting and sad."[73] After 1949, his paintings, combining elation with melancholy, create a fluid space that is *between*—between the familiar, seemingly secure world of bounded objects, now left behind, and a mysterious new realm, ominously empty yet luminous. "The struggle is beyond painting, not with painting," Rothko declared. But he didn't paint the beyond; he painted the struggle—as a difficult crossing into an unknown space where life appears on the verge either of a new start or disintegration.

12 The Dark Paintings

I can only say that the dark pictures began in 1957 and have persisted almost compulsively to this day.

Mark Rothko, 1960

A self-consciously modern artist—Pablo Picasso in painting, James Joyce or Ezra Pound in literature—builds a career out of discontinuities, constantly dismantling his own achievements. As if style, rather than the authentic expression of a core self, were the chosen fabrication of a protean self, the modern artist invents a multiplicity of manners, discarding each as it becomes familiar, socially acceptable, ossified, no longer *modern*. The Abstract Expressionists, individualists who operated in a market where the artist's "name" is promoted, tended to develop "signature styles"; and Rothko—a *conservative* avant-gardist—was more single-minded than most. When he met Hedda Sterne at a Isamu Noguchi show, Rothko's judgment was: "too many images." "You see," Sterne said, "typical. The strength of being totally obsessed in one sentence. That's a great strength to be that biased." Having invented his iconic image in 1949, Rothko committed himself to exploring its expressive possibilities for the next fifteen years. As he told one friend, "If a thing is worth doing once, it is worth doing over and over again—exploring it, probing it, demanding by this repetition that the public look at it."[1]

Rothko also liked to think of his image as a kind of absolute invention, without any debt to the past, including his own past work. At his Museum of Modern Art retrospective in 1961, he tried to institutionalize this view by refusing to show any work prior to 1945. When William Seitz, then writing a Princeton Ph.D. thesis, "Abstract Expressionist Painting in America," visited Rothko's studio in January of 1952, Rothko turned the occasion into a lively debate about the art-historical premises of his interviewer.[2] Seitz's notes reveal Rothko as not unfriendly, but as blunt and aggressive in argument, quick in delivering definitive pronouncements:

"The past is simple; the present is complex; the future is even simpler."

"The problem of living in this world is to keep from being smothered."

"Today things are institutionalized before they are dry." Pausing to ask

Seitz if he liked paintings ("I said yes"), Rothko dramatically announced "I do not like paintings," a statement he was to make to *many* other people.

"I never was interested in cubism."

"Abstract art never interested me; I always painted realistically. My present paintings are realistic."

"I am not a formalist." "I have never had an interest in Mondrian." "My paintings do not deal in space." "Mondrian divides a canvas; I put things on it."

"Intuition is the height of rationality. Not opposed. Intuition is the opposite of formulation. Of dead knowledge."[3]

At the very start of their conversation, Rothko assumed the initiative, the humanist painter confronting the art professional, directing Seitz to write down, "as a direct quote": "one does not paint for design students or historians but for human beings, and the reaction in human terms is the only thing that is really satisfactory to the artist." Rothko went on to denounce "emphasis on craftsmanship" along with the Bauhaus, and then recalled a lunch with the president of Brooklyn College, Harry Gideonse, "who suggested that divergent tendencies" in the design department "would come to a common meeting" ground. Rothko's response: "I do not want unity." Rothko then declared to Seitz that "my own work has a unity like nothing (I do not mind saying even if I appear immodest) the world has ever seen." "Historians' unity is a unity of death. What we want is a live unity."

As Seitz calmly observed in his notes, "my conversation tended to be an argument for historicity as a contributory value to the richer understanding of the artist, while his was an attack at its value, at my position in a tradition which he regarded as a dead hand and a straitjacket. Which killed things by formulation." At some points Rothko opposes not just professional but *any* writing about art: "as soon as you write it down, as soon as you formulate it, it is dead." Or, more radically, he opposes any writing about life: "we are here drinking wine . . . write it down and it is gone [i.e., quality of experience]." At other times he calls for a new kind of art criticism: "the kind of writing we need today is for people to write their responses to painting," "to verbalize what . . . as humans, the paintings really mean to them." Later, Rothko inquires about Seitz's reaction to his paintings. "I told him I reacted in terms of space, etc. 'But what do they *mean* to you? Just because an area [is] like undulating silk, is this important? Lots of people can make like undulating silk. Writing should look into the writer and find what the painting really means.'" Painters, too, narrow and professionalize their responses: "I do not like to talk to painters. They go to an exhibition, and remark on design, color, etc. Not pure

The Dark Paintings

human reactions. I want pure response in terms of human need. Does the painting satisfy some human need?"

At the end of the interview, as the two men walked out onto the street, Seitz commented, "I want to keep self out of this," to which Rothko, who sometimes claimed to have removed self from his painting, replied: "I want to put you back in." Exactly what kind of art writing is Rothko calling for? He was understandably disgruntled with a reception that, in the critical language of the 1950s, either praised or denounced him as "formalist," "colorist," "abstractionist." Yet it is very unlikely that by urging Seitz to talk about what, as a human, the paintings really meant to him, he was inviting critics to record their subjective musings before a painting. The two later essays about his work that Rothko most admired—by Robert Goldwater and David Sylvester—were both written by professionals, speaking well within the conventional bounds of art discourse; their responses were "pure" only in the sense that they wrote about Rothko's work with a thoughtful sensitivity to his intentions.[4] When, working with Katharine Kuh in 1954, Rothko himself had tried to invent a language for talking about his painting, he finally gave up. His goal seems to have been an unreachable ideal that rendered just about any actual response inadequate. "He was never quite satisfied." Yet Rothko's exchange with Seitz poignantly reveals his own human need: to believe that, through works he intended to be alien and disturbing, he was still addressing himself to an essential humanity, a subjective consciousness outside history, beyond culture, "pure," uncorrupted by professional or other forms of social conditioning.

So what Rothko most vehemently opposes, in talking with Seitz, is the imprisoning of his creations in the language and narrative of the art historian. He refuses a request for "evolutionary" photographs of his work. Seitz notes: "Trying to bring him out on the development of his work, I remarked that the thing that tied his early figure things, his symbolic things, and his late things together was the backgrounds. That it was as if he had removed the figure for swirling calligraphy, symbols, etc. and simplified the three-toned backgrounds." Rothko dismisses this account as "silly," exposing "the error in the evolutionary approach." "It was not, he said, that the figure had been *removed*, not that the figures had been swept away, but that the symbols for the figures, and in turn the shapes in the later canvases were new *substitutes* for the figures." "My new areas have nothing whatever to do with the three tier backgrounds in the symbolic style. . . . My new areas of color are things. I put them on the surface. They do not run to the edge, they stop before the edge."

Seitz, like many writers after him, observed the haunting presence of the rectangle throughout Rothko's work, in the box-like rooms, subway architecture, rectangular compartments, and horizontal bands of the paintings of the 1930s and 1940s. The paintings of the 1950s thus, in this account, evolved from Rothko's removal of the foreground—human figure, symbolic form, Surrealist drawing—to discover, in the background, the form that had preoccupied him all along. So Rothko's art advanced by a series of subtractions, or renunciations—a view supported by Rothko's own 1949 statement (which Seitz brings up in their conversation) that "the progression of a painter's work" moves "toward the elimination of all obstacles between the painter and the idea, and between the idea and the observer," toward the ideal elimination of all cultural mediation so that the painting confronts the viewer as an immediate "presence." Yet Rothko rightly objects to Seitz's simplified evolution, to emphasize the impact of detaching his rectangles from the edges of the canvas. In many of Rothko's paintings prior to 1943, these geometric shapes, far from being mere backgrounds, actively oppose and distort—squeezing, bending, or severing—the figurative content. In *The Omen of the Eagle,* for example, an instinctual (or bestial) violence is held in, and held off, by the rigid rectangular divisions, whose formal severity, cutting the hybrid's body into sections, achieves stability through violence.

Rothko's mature format, with two or three stacked rectangles, offered an image that was simple, symmetrical, frontal, and (given large size) monumental. Soft-edged and horizontal, the rectangles work to *contain* diffused expanses of colored light and to provide a reassuring *stability* for the amorphousness of inner life. Detached from the edges of the canvas, the rectangles themselves are free to move, to participate in the flux which they contain. Yet, as Rothko said, these shapes are "new *substitutes* for the figures." Themselves held by the border of ground color, they expand or contract—"push outward" or "rush inward"—in a drama recalling the tension between architecture and figure in the 1930s, except that now the substitution for the figure, rather than being trapped and immobilized, moves and breathes. In these paintings, container and contained, no longer fighting each other, merge, forming geometric shapes which act and feel like living organisms.

Repeating this format over a long period of time established a "recognizable image" which eventually helped dealers market Rothko's work. More important, his chosen format also gave the restless Rothko a desired regularity, a scaffolding (to use a metaphor of his in "The Scribble Book") which relieved him from having to invent composition all over again with each painting, as he had with the multiforms. Some people have compared Rothko's form with the sonnet, to suggest its variety-within-stability. But the external shape of a sonnet is strict, always prearranged. Rothko's flexible format more closely resembles a loose musical form, like the sonata, which stretches, bends, tightens as it interacts with specific content. Rothko sought limits, as long as they felt self-imposed and nonconfining; and within his format, he could vary the size and shape of the canvas, the width and color of the border, the number, size, and color of the interior rectangles (as well as their proportions), color harmonies between or among the rectangles and between individual rectangles and the border, the relative opacity or transparency of his colors, the closeness or distance between two adjacent shapes, the softness or hardness of the edges, and his touch (from brushy to feathery). Working with a repeated form, in fact, enabled Rothko to call attention to the way subtle variations affect feeling. Rothko's scaffolding, readjusted as each new work evolved, was elastic.

From 1949 to 1956 Rothko worked almost exclusively with oils on canvases that tended to be vertical and big, usually at least 6' high and 4' wide, sometimes as large as 9½' × 8½'. Sometimes Rothko employed cool blues and greens or even earth colors, as in *Earth and Green* (1955) or *Green, Red, Blue* (1955). But mostly Rothko creates "things" which, pulsing with "hot" yellows, oranges, reds and glowing with an intense brilliance, convey an ecstatic sense of pleasure and release. It was in this period that Rothko, in argument with Robert Motherwell, insisted that "ecstacy alone was it; art is ecstatic or it's nothing." Ominous shadows, vacant expanses, frayed or torn edges, narrow bars holding two larger shapes apart, stern blacks, all dramatize loss and separation, creating a melancholy undertone that saves these paintings from lapsing into cheerful decoration. Yet an elated joy predominates in the works of the early and mid-1950s, which seem to celebrate their own discovery, as if, after his twenty-year search, Rothko were now exulting, "I've *found* it!" Or, as if his new ebullient shapes were substitutions not for the solitary human figures in his early work but for those "monsters and gods" with whose demise "art sank into melancholy." Rothko's "new structural language" enabled him to confront, embody, and transcend loss.

But beginning in 1957 his paintings grew darker, a trend that would continue, though with many exceptions, until his death. Now, as in *Red, Brown and Black* (1958; color plate 16), the veil of warm, inviting celestial light is stripped away, replaced here by stark black, fiery red, and earthy brown (with green and ocher inside) on a light plum ground. Less seductive, less gregarious, less eager to be liked and admired, this painting silently smolders. A narrow black rectangle, dramatically stretched across the top of a painting 117" wide (and 107" high), first grasps our attention; inside, a thin internal border, darker and more opaque, frames and pulls us into its murky interior depths, a choking darkness. The red and brown shapes below are larger and lighter, as if they might offer some relief; but the orange-red, which keeps fading back into the plum ground, seems thin and ephemeral, and the brown, which, like the black, has *some* depth, is filled with a thick, oppressive greenish smoke.

All three rectangles are hard to move around in; the observer strains, struggling to make things out. Viewing one of Rothko's mature works had always involved a prolonged process which alternated between looking inside the rectangles, looking back and forth between or among them (comparing size, color, weight, texture, placement), and taking in the whole painting as a unified image. In *Red, Brown and Black* the black rectangle's internal border contains it; the red rectangle has "arms" at either side that both make its width ambiguous and hold it in; and while the red and brown have been placed close together, they never touch, remain firmly divided. Self-contained, all three shapes engage our attention separately and, given their murkiness, for a long time; integrating Rothko's simplified compositions has been made more difficult. In 1957, his pictures grew darker—more somber, more inward and self-absorbed, more difficult, and more demanding.

• • •

> *Rothko was a rather secret person you know, and a very difficult person, difficult on himself and difficult on everyone else around him. That difficulty magnified as he became more recognized.*
>
> Sidney Janis

During 1957 Rothko's income from his painting tripled.

In 1955, the year of his first show at Sidney Janis, Rothko sold six paintings for $5,471; in 1956 he sold eight for $6,805. But during 1957 Rothko sold seventeen paintings for $19,133, and in 1958 thirteen for $20,666. In 1959 his income again tripled, as he sold seventeen works for $61,130.[5] Betty Parsons may have *discovered* Rothko; but Sidney Janis *sold* him.

Rothko had first met Janis in 1943, as Janis was visiting the studios of New York artists to compile his book *Abstract and Surrealist Art in America*. Janis asked Rothko whether he wished to be included in the abstract or the surrealist section, and Rothko, less suspicious of critical labels then than later, replied, "Oh, by all means the surrealist." "I was struck by Rothko's confidence in himself," Janis recalled. Rothko did not convey that he was struggling to move beyond surrealism, but "what he showed me he was quite confident that this was what he wanted to do." At the time Rothko "liked Miró very much," and he continued to do so: around 1949 Janis had hung "a large Miró monochrome, brown background painting on the wall in my office. He used to come in specifically to look at that Miró."[6]

Betty Parsons came to sell art by way of her involvements with creating it. Sidney Janis, in 1943 a businessman turned Museum of Modern Art advisor and art writer, came to sell art by way of his involvements with collecting it.[7] Born in Buffalo, New York, in 1896, Janis attended public schools there, briefly pursued a career as a vaudeville dancer, served in the navy during World War I, then returned to Buffalo, working for a brother who owned a chain of shoe stores. In 1925, Janis, striking out on his own, moved to New York City, married, started the M'Lord Shirts Company, and started an art collection by purchasing a Whistler. "The Janises led a modest suburban existence, first in Sunnyside, Queens, and then in Mamaroneck, putting most of the M'Lord profits into art rather than into more conventional investments."[8] The shirt manufacturer from Buffalo met Arshile Gorky, who became a friend, guide, and advisor. "We used to hit the Fifty-seventh Street galleries and the museums, and used even to travel out of town together. Gorky was terrifically verbal and terrifically informed."[9] Mostly, Janis, who used his Whistler to buy a Matisse and the Matisse to buy Picasso's *The Painter and His Model,* bought Parisian moderns.

During the Depression M'Lord shirts continued to sell well, so well that Janis could afford to spend more of his time and more of his profits on his art collection. The year following the stock market crash, he bought three Klees from a Museum of Modern Art exhibition. In 1933—now living in an apartment at 25 Central Park West—Janis paid $33,000 for Henri Rousseau's *The Dream.* That year he was appointed to the advisory board at the Modern, and two years later the museum exhibited his collection, which now included, in addition to the Klees and the Rousseau, six Picassos, two Légers, a Matisse, a Gris, a de Chirico, a Dali, a Mondrian, and a Gorky. By 1939 Janis was able to close down his business and devote all of his time and energy to art—curating, lecturing, writing, collecting. In addition to *Abstract and Surrealist Art in America* (1944), Janis wrote *They Taught Themselves* (1942)—on American "primitives"—and *Picasso: The Recent Years* (1946)—on Picasso during the Nazi occupation of France.

By 1948, however—the profits from books being less than from shirts—Janis felt he needed to generate some income. "I had been writing for nine years when I decided that I had to go back into business and I wasn't going into anything that I didn't love, so I opened an art gallery."[10] When Sam Kootz decided to move his business from his gallery to his apartment, Janis bought Kootz's lease and moved into the fifth-floor space at 15 East 57th Street, across the hall from Betty Parsons. Eventually, after a fierce legal fight, Janis took over the entire floor, just as he would take over many of Parsons' artists.[11] At first Janis showed, as he had collected, Parisian moderns, but during the 1948–49 recession not many people were buying any kind of art. From the gallery's opening show of Léger, only two works were sold, and those after the exhibit had closed.[12] During the next few years Janis mounted several "idea exhibitions"—e.g., works all done in 1913, or a show pairing works by young American and French painters—but these events generated more publicity than sales.[13] Not until a 1950 exhibit of French Fauves did the gallery begin to make a profit. But "before long, Janis found himself a consistently successful dealer in French modern masters."[14]

In signing on artists, Betty Parsons was adventuresome, Sidney Janis more prudent. "As a dealer, he has always shown a preference for moving in on an established talent rather than risking his money or reputation on a new one."[15] A businessman and entrepreneur, Janis specialized in converting the symbolic capital of artistic reputation into real capital; yet his long involvement with art as a collector, curator, and writer certified that he was no *mere* businessman, no crass Frank Lloyd, who would later warn his employees at the Marlborough Gallery: "Remember, I don't collect pictures; I collect money."[16] Yet twenty years of activity in the New York art-world, particularly his relation with the Museum of Modern Art, had given Janis many associations with the people who buy and evaluate art, and he felt none of Betty Parsons' Old New York inhibitions about aggressively pursuing them. Though sometimes inclined to long-winded, pedantic lectures about work he liked, Janis was a shrewd, experienced salesman. When, in 1952, Betty Parsons' "Four Horsemen of the Apocalypse" decided to seek greener pastures, Janis offered just the combination of seriousness, respectability, and successful promotion that they were looking for in a dealer. They, in turn, offered him the challenge of converting recognition, or in Pollock's case notoriety, into real—in this case, cash—transactions.

Pollock signed with Janis during 1952, and Rothko in 1954, after he had lost his position at Brooklyn College. In 1953 Willem de Kooning had joined the gallery, as did Clyfford Still.[17] By 1960, William Baziotes, Arshile Gorky's estate, Adolph Gottlieb, Philip Guston, Franz Kline, Robert Motherwell were exhibiting with Janis. Rothko, who had not held a one-man exhibit at a New York gallery since his 1951 show at Betty Parsons (his Brooklyn College job temporarily freed him from the market demand for annual exhibits), held his first show at Sidney Janis in April/May, 1955, his second (and last) in January/February, 1958. Between 1954 and 1964, he participated in the gallery's annual group exhibits every year except 1955. In the fall of 1962, protesting Janis's "The New Realism," which included many of the new Pop artists, Rothko—

along with Adolph Gottlieb, Philip Guston, and Robert Motherwell—resigned from the gallery.[18]

One day in the mid-1950s Budd Hopkins visited the Janis gallery and Janis came out to talk to the young artist, who asked what the next show was. Janis told him Mark Rothko, and "I said, 'Oh, terrific,' and he said, 'well, you know, Mark has some very big paintings, it's going to be very exciting, he has some very big paintings, and we have to have them brought into the gallery rolled, and we have to stretch them in the gallery because they won't fit in the elevator and you can't get them upstairs'." Later, as Hopkins left the building and walked out onto 57th Street, he met Rothko and told him that Janis had just mentioned his upcoming show. Rothko—"with this anxiety all over his face"—asked, "what did he say?" Hopkins reported that Janis said he was looking forward to the show, that Rothko's paintings were very large, that they would have to be rolled. "Was he upset about that?" Rothko nervously questioned. The incident impressed Hopkins with "how really insecure everybody then was emotionally, financially, in terms of the art world itself." Rothko, out on the street, worried whether his dealer up on the fifth floor had been aggravated by his large paintings, the established artist fretting like an anxious dependent.

Ideally, the relation between artist and dealer might work as a collaboration in which both the producer and the distributor share a common interest: selling paintings. In reality, however, the relation is often experienced as a parent/child relation, in which the dealer "takes care of" the artist, emotionally like Betty Parsons or financially like Sidney Janis. Both parties, moreover, are moved by private interests: the dealer also needs to take care of his clients, his gallery, himself, while the artist needs to take care of his paintings, his reputation, himself. The parent/child relation thus operates in a commercial arena which intensifies, and multiplies, conflict—the more so, ironically, for the successful artist who, wishing to feel morally pure and "above" economic motives, projects all such motives onto the dealer. In the charged dealer-artist relationship, issues of dependence and autonomy (touchy ones for Rothko) are engaged, disappointments felt, scapegoats designated, and power struggles develop, as when Betty Parsons' leading artists tried to take over her gallery.

"When Mark Rothko came with us, he was a very modest guy," Janis said, implying that Rothko did not stay modest. "I need only so much to live on," he told Janis, who assured him: "if you can't make four times what you need to live on in the first year you're with us, we don't want you." Like Parsons, Janis let Rothko select and hang his own shows. "When we did the first show, he did every lick of work. He wouldn't let our staff do a thing." In one small gallery, Rothko hung "four huge pictures," two of them covering the wall from floor to ceiling. "It was a terrific experience to walk into that room. It was just floating in luminosity—very breath-taking." As in the past, Rothko placed works close together; and if, as happened in one case, a canvas extended beyond its wall and into a doorway, that didn't bother him.[19] He wished, as he had written Katharine Kuh, to "defeat" the actual physical space of a room.

As Janis realized, Rothko "created an ambience that way. He knew very well how his paintings worked, probably better than . . . any other of the artists of his generation." Rothko also used lighting to create an ambience, not the bright light he had sought for his "Fifteen Americans" room at MOMA, but a very dim light, an obscurity from which the paintings—soon themselves to grow dark—only slowly emerged. This insistence caused some trouble for Janis, who didn't want his commercial space looking like a cave. "No matter how low it was, he would reduce it," Janis complained. "It made the gallery so dismal, but he wanted some kind of mystery attached to his painting." Philip Guston recalled coming with Rothko to visit one of his Janis shows: "they strolled into the gallery and Mark, without a word, switched off half the lights." When Janis came out from his office, the three men "chatted a bit and, in a pause in the conversation, Janis slid off and turned all the lights back on. Rothko didn't say anything." Janis returned to his office. As the two painters were leaving, just before they entered the elevator, "Rothko turned half the lights back off again."[20]

Yet Rothko treated his paintings with a peculiar, and characteristic, combination of solicitude and carelessness. Exacting about their hanging and lighting, Rothko stretched his paintings in a slipshod way, using cheap materials; and this practice really disturbed, or in his word "depressed," Janis, perhaps the more so as Rothko's prices rose and Janis's clients might expect something better than packing case boards supporting a $5,000 painting. But while the artist might inwardly agonize about what his dealer *really* thought, the dealer—as in their silent cat-and-mouse game with the lights—approached his volatile artist warily. "He was a complex mixed-up guy emotionally, and I didn't want to cross swords with him. I took the line of least resistance."[21] In his first year at the gallery Rothko did not earn four times what he needed to live; but by his third year Rothko's sales generated four times what he had been making at Brooklyn College.

"The art industry is a million dollar one; 25,000 people, museums, galleries, etc. etc. are supported by it: everyone gets money out of it except the artist," Rothko bitterly complained to a studio visitor in early 1955. "I can exhibit my paintings in a 100 different exhibitions. But I do not get any money. I can lecture. But they do not pay for lectures. I am written about, shown everywhere but do not get even $1300 a year."[22] By 1959, however, Rothko had completed an economic migration in which he travelled from the edge of poverty (after losing his Brooklyn College job) to the comfortable affluence of the upper middle-class. Yet, as with earlier migrations, Rothko's success left him feeling less rather than more free, secure, or satisfied. This new life, too, entailed loss.

As practically everyone who knew him testifies, Rothko disdained the kinds of material objects—clothes, cars, furnishings, houses—he could now afford. "Indeed," Robert Motherwell observed, "he hated objects, as he did so much else."[23] As far as Sidney Janis could tell, financial success only burdened Rothko, making this originally "modest" painter more "difficult," less happy. "It was a tragedy that he couldn't enjoy it," as, say, Janis himself had enjoyed his income from M'Lord. "He was a poor boy all his life; he was a poor boy and he just couldn't get used to riches. That money problem was an albatross around his neck, like the ancient Chinese, the wealthy, who would carry these big stone pieces of money around their necks. It weighed him down. It weighed him down. It depressed him."[24]

Material success did not reveal the emptiness of desires that Rothko never had. Rather, worldly goods (or money) constituted part of that heavy and oppressive realm of dead matter that Rothko was seeking not just to transcend but to pulverize in his paintings. Besides, Rothko, whose experience had impressed him with the capriciousness of human life in general and the art market in particular, remained convinced that, due to fate or fashion, he could stop making money just as quickly as he started making it. "Today my price is six thousand or better," Rothko said. "Tomorrow it may be six hundred."[25] "Mark was intractable that recognition can explode in your face at any moment," said Motherwell. Still, Rothko did desire, even at times demand, the assurance of praise, and so he relied on sales as a symbolic form of recognition and commitment, thus implicating the autonomous artist in a network of professional institutions, social relations, and economic transactions that weighed him down.

"He had tremendous doubts and tremendous ego," Hedda Sterne recalled. Success fed both. "Rembrandt and Rothko," Rothko would say to a friend; then pause, smile, and say, "Rothko and Rembrandt."[26] "He liked one to treat him as a genius," Robert Motherwell said, describing a visit to Rothko's studio as an "audience." "He was very conscious of needing approbation all the time," Sally Avery commented. "He wanted to be treated like a genius or a great man. I remember once Harold Diamond [a dealer] meeting him on the street," and saying "Hi." Rothko was offended, "Don't talk to me like that. Treat me with respect." "He was very, very unhappy at being sort of just hailed like an ordinary person."[27] Yet when his works began to sell and his prices to rise,

Rothko began to question himself. If rich collectors were hanging his paintings in Park Avenue apartments, did that mean they *were* decorative? Once his paintings became socially acceptable, then he could no longer speak of "the unfriendliness of society," or think of himself as an alien. What *were* his paintings? Who was *he*?

Writing to Motherwell of Herbert Ferber's recovery from surgery, Rothko said, "he had many apprehensions about the operation, and the recovery had just enough complications, minor to be true, to have reaffirmed in him a respect for human foreboding and tragic intuition which are so precious to the artist." Rothko usually had little problem sustaining his sense of "human foreboding." "During the last 18 months or so I have been able to live by my work for the first time in my 53 years of life," he wrote to Clay Spohn in September 1957. "I really have little faith that it can continue. But that kind of security I am well used to." In 1957, with Janis selling twice as many paintings as he had the previous year, Rothko began producing dark pictures "almost obsessively," as if to make sure that an overly friendly society could not appropriate *these* works as decorations, as if to impose a more demanding and difficult experience on his viewers—as if to bring forward a more melancholy (or "tragic") inner world existing behind his now recognizable public image. Janis believed that these new pictures would prove "tough to sell," though he didn't mention that to Rothko, who "would pick up the least adverse nuance and make a whole thing of it." Rothko, feeling that his brighter pictures "had an audience and didn't need his support," "was defensive about his dark pictures because they weren't readily acceptable."[28] Yet these were the pictures Janis was selling in 1958 and 1959, when Rothko's income jumped (roughly) from $20,000 to $60,000, as if his sales were now driven by forces outside of his, or his dealer's, control.

They were. Mark Rothko was not the only painter, or the only American, to reach affluence in the 1950s. The "art market is boiling with an activity never known before," *Fortune* magazine excitedly announced in the first of a two-part essay on "The Great International Art Market" which appeared in the winter of 1955–56.[29] Enticing its readers with anecdotes of paintings bought cheap and sold for fortunes, statistics documenting feverish market activity and dramatically rising prices, the essay aimed to lure new investors into the art market and to increase the demand for art it documented. "To the wealthy man, the ownership of art offers a unique combination of financial attractions," *Fortune* advised, citing art as "a hedge against inflation," a flexible "investment medium," "a route to legitimate income-tax reduction," a way to lighten "the burden of inheritance taxes." Art historians map their territory by style or school; *Fortune* maps the same territory according to investment risk, dividing

Fig. 26. Mell Beistle at Skidmore, 1940 (Elizabeth Schoenfeld).

Fig. 27. 1945–46 (Kate Rothko Prizel and Christopher Rothko).

Fig. 28. Yorktown Heights, c. 1949 (Kate Rothko Prizel and Christopher Rothko).

Fig. 29. With Mell Rothko and Clyfford Still, San Francisco, 1947 (Kate Rothko Prizel and Christopher Rothko).

Fig. 30. With Mell Rothko, East Cleveland, Ohio, train station, summer 1949 (Kate Rothko Prizel and Christopher Rothko).

Fig. 31. Mark Rothko at Betty Parson's (Aaron Siskind Foundation courtesy the Robert Mann Gallery).

Fig. 32. "The Irascibles," 1950. Bottom row (l. to r.): Theodoros Stamos, Jimmy Ernst, Barnett Newman, James Brooks, Mark Rothko; middle row: Richard Pousette-Dart, William Baziotes, Jackson Pollock, Clyfford Still, Robert Motherwell, Bradley Walker Tomlin; back row: Willem de Kooning, Adolph Gottlieb, Ad Reinhardt, Hedda Sterne (Nina Leen, *Life* Magazine, January 15, 1951).

Fig. 33. Jackson Pollock, 1950 (Hans Namuth).

Fig. 34. Mark Rothko, East Hampton, 1964 (Hans Namuth).

Fig. 35. Mell and Mark Rothko, early 1950s (Kate Rothko Prizel and Christopher Rothko).

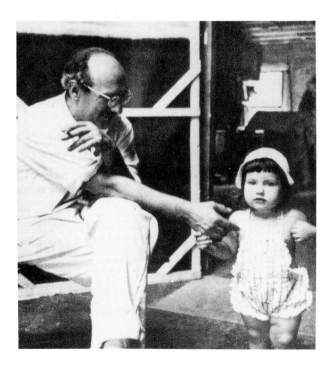

Fig. 36. With his daughter Kate, early 1950s (Kate Rothko Prizel and Christopher Rothko).

Fig. 37. 53rd Street Studio, early 1950s (Kate Rothko Prizel and Christopher Rothko).

Fig. 38. Mid-1950s (Rudy Burkhardt).

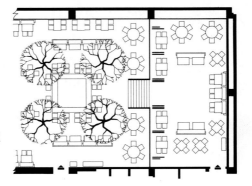

Fig. 39. Partial floor plan, Four Seasons Restaurant, designed by Philip Johnson (Philip Johnson).

Fig. 40. 1960, at 222 Bowery (Regina Bogat).

Fig. 41. 1960, at 222 Bowery (Regina Bogat).

Fig. 42. 118 East 95th Street (Author photo).

Fig. 43. With son Christopher, summer, 1964 (Hans Namuth).

Fig. 44. Exterior, 69th Street Studio (author photo).

Fig. 45. Houston Chapel project, 69th Street Studio 1965–66 (Hans Namuth).

Fig. 46. Houston Chapel paintings, 1965 (Alexander Liberman).

Fig. 47. Exterior of Houston Chapel, 1971 (Hickey and Robertson, Houston, Texas).

Fig. 48. Houston Chapel, interior with original skylight, 1971 (Hickey and Robertson, Houston, Texas).

Fig. 49. In the garden of Dimitri Hadzi's studio, Rome, summer 1966 (Peter Selz).

Fig. 50. Living area, 69th Street studio, 1969 (Morton Levine).

Fig. 51. Black on Grey paintings, 1969 (Morton Levine).

Fig. 52. 1969 (Morton Levine).

art into "*the gilt-edged security*" (Old Masters), "*the blue-chip stock*" (Impressionists; Post-Impressionists; Picasso) and "*the speculative or 'growth' issues*" (contemporaries; one of those named: Mark Rothko).[30] As an investor's tip sheet, *Fortune* offered sound advice: a Rothko purchased for $1,250 in 1955 would be worth $5–6,000 by 1960, $25–30,000 by 1965.

"The international art market is boiling today because of an incendiary supply of money," *Fortune* declared. In the United States, while recessions in 1953–54 (after the Korean War) and in 1957–58 temporarily slowed down the economy, the 1950s constituted a period of increasing prosperity for those in the middle and upper classes, earning for the country in that decade John Kenneth Galbraith's wry designation, *The Affluent Society*.[31] As *Fortune* pointed out, there was now "for the wealthy and well-to-do, a semi-satiety of tangible luxury goods: art stands out as one of the most attractive remaining targets for excess cash."[32] Rothko imagined himself as a premodern, humanist painter addressing real human needs; *Fortune* addressed the "need" of the modern wealthy or well-to-do to use "excess cash" to generate—still more excess cash. Old Masters were already scarce; Impressionists, Post-Impressionists, Fauves soon would be. "There is no other direction for an American collector to go now but America," said Edith Halpert of the Downtown Gallery.[33] But one further step was required before the "incendiary money supply" could heat up the market for Rothko and his contemporaries.

Around the time of the *Fortune* articles, Sidney Janis had offered Jackson Pollock's *Autumn Rhythm* to the Museum of Modern Art for $8,000. But Alfred Barr could not find the money. When Pollock ran his car into a tree during the summer of 1956, his death illustrated the British critic Herbert Read's axiom, quoted by *Fortune*: "death is the greatest thing that can happen to an artist"; the number of the painter's works now being finite, his prices rise.[34] Soon after Pollock's death, Barr called Janis and asked, "How about that picture?" Janis said he would have to confer with Lee Krasner, Pollock's widow. "When I got back to Alfred I told him Lee's price was $30,000." "So shocked" was Barr that he never answered Janis's letter. "We sold *Autumn Rhythm* almost immediately to the Metropolitan Museum for $30,000," Janis recalled.[35] One of "The Irascibles"—the dead one—entered the collection of a museum traditionally indifferent and sometimes hostile to American art.

As the *Fortune* essay pointed out, "the worth of paintings on the market is ultimately established" by "the great museums," "be their names the Louvre, the Prado, the National Gallery, or the Metropolitan Museum of Art." Such institutions, because they were (in theory) "outside" the marketplace, could confer value and establish place *in* the marketplace. The Pollock sale "served as an important validation of Abstract Expressionism," Deirdre Robson writes,

Chapter Twelve

"for it was the first time that a major museum had bought a painting in this style for a price commensurate with what it might pay for a work by a major European artist." Or, in the metaphor of the founder of M'Lord Shirt Company: "I think the artists sort of, if you'll accept the homely expression, rode in on the shirttails of dead Pollock."[36]

The year after the Metropolitan's purchase of *Autumn Rhythm*, Rothko's prices rose somewhat, from about $1,300 to about $1,700, but his sales increased dramatically, from eight paintings (1956) to seventeen (1957).

. . .

It all went from love to hate in four years.

Betty Parsons

Here [in New York] is where the showdown fight really goes on—It's bloody and real. No illusions about social morality high or low. The artist is his brother's enemy like nowhere else....

San Francisco offered hope—but didn't fool us. New York offers a slash across the belly. You know your friend has a knife and will use it on you.

Clyfford Still

On February 15 and 16, 1956, a libel suit initiated by Barnett Newman against Ad Reinhardt was tried before Justice S. Samuel Di Falco of the State of New York's Supreme Court. In an essay called "The Artist in Search of an Academy," published in the *College Art Journal*, Reinhardt, who for years had been ridiculing his fellow artists both in cartoons and essays, described the two rising trends in painting. One, "a contribution of the forties, is the cafe-and-club-primitive and neo-Zen-bohemian, the Vogue-magazine-cold-water-flat-fauve and Harpers-Bazaar-bum, the Eighth-street-existentialist and Easthampton-aesthete, the Modern-Museum-pauper and international-set-sufferer, the abstract-'Hesspressionist' and Kootzenjammer-Kid-Jungian, the Romantic-ham-'action'-actor," one of whom Reinhardt identified as Mark Rothko.

The other, "the latest up-to-date popular image of the early fifties," was "the artist-professor and traveling-design-salesman, the Art-Digest-philosopher-poet and Bauhaus-exerciser, the avant-garde-huckster-handicraftsman and educational-shop-keeper, the holy-roller-explainer-entertainer-in-residence," one of whom Reinhardt identified as Barnett Newman. Newman alleged libel, malice, and injury in the pursuit of his profession as an artist; Reinhardt denied the charges and after two days of testimony by Barnett and Annalee Newman, the case was dismissed; a subsequent appeal was rejected.[37]

Discussing this suit with Alfred Jensen, Rothko claimed that Reinhardt "has appropriated many of my esthetic concepts and he's also taken a lot from Barney Newman. Newman fathered Ad for years when Ad was literally a nursling of Papa Newman. The thanks we get for all this is a vituperous attack from Ad's vicious pen." Reinhardt's satire simply confirmed that our age is an age of assault, particularly of assault by the ungrateful young on their elders. "The father role is like King Lear; today one hasn't any assurance of respect from the young because the father authority is nil," Rothko commented, sounding less like a modernist than a sorrowful traditionalist. "No matter what we older ones have done the youth of today disregards us; no reverence is due us. We are used up, discarded, and despair is our outlook"—the more so if, as it turned out with Rothko, that this King Lear also has some aggrieved brothers eager for assault.[38]

About a year before Newman's suit, responding to an invitation to the opening for Rothko's first, April 1955, show at Sidney Janis, Clyfford Still wrote Janis a letter that makes Reinhardt's put-downs sound tame. Portraying himself as a high-minded idealist who had been much too trusting of Rothko, Still writes: "I remained oblivious to, or disregarded . . . many of his acts which pointed to expediency, hypocrisy, or worse. For these were, Rothko assured me, but of his needs, or the idiosyncrasies of one who felt himself a 'foreigner'."

> But for several years now I have been unable to avoid the morbid implications of Rothko's works, and the shrewd ambivalence of his verbalisms and acts. His need for sycophants and flattery, and his resentment of everyone, or every truth, that might stand in his path to bourgeois success, could no longer be ignored. In fact he was compelled to remind me of it one day when he grinned and announced that he "never had any illusions that we ever had anything in common." Be assured that it gave no pleasure, that afternoon three years ago, to be told that what I had considered to be gestures of concurrences were merely intended to conceal the claw of exploitation.

Still denounced Rothko's "record of duplicity and appropriation," from "his skillful use" of the foreword he wrote for Still's Art of This Century exhibit, through his "debauching of my plan for liberation into an incestuous mockery for publicity called The Subjects of the Artist," down to "more recent times when I had to turn my back in disgust and walk away from the patent farce he enacted in Brooklyn College." But Still saves his most scorching rhetoric for an assault on Rothko's work:

> Insomuch as the "form" of this painting and the man who makes it are one, Rothko requires that his paintings be read as an exercise in Authoritarian imagery. When they are hung in tight phalanx, as he would have them hung, and flooded with the light he demands that they receive, the tyranny of his ambition to suffocate or crush all who stand in his way becomes fully manifest. This is the way he would have his work seen, and act, in the Modern Museum show of the "15." This, he has stated, is his highest ambition. It is not without significance, therefore, that the surfaces of these paintings reveal the gestures of negation, and that their means are the devices of seduction and assault. Not I, but himself, has made it clear that his work is of frustration, resentment and aggression. And that it is the brightness of death that veils their bloodless febrility and clinical evacuations.[39]

As an interpreter of Rothko's work, Still does apprehend its aggression—which he then isolates and exaggerates into a violent rage-to-dominate more characteristic of Still himself.

Most narratives of the social history of the Abstract Expressionist painters have this group bonding in rejection and poverty in the 1930s and 1940s, then splitting apart once they arrived at success in the 1950s. Yet the notion of an original closeness among these gifted, ambitious, and ego-strong painters amounts to a myth, one first spread by the artists themselves, nostalgically recalling a youthful feeling of community, forever lost. James Brooks has spoken of the "comradeship of poverty" felt by his generation, and it is true that a shared sense of exclusion muted individual differences and created a very loose social cohesion.[40] But even in the early years, the social relations among the artists of Rothko's generation took various, shifting forms, some of them organized and professional (The Ten; the Federation of Modern Painters and Sculptors), some of them professional but not organized (the Rothko/Gottlieb myth project), some of them professional and institutional (the painters associated with a particular gallery like Art of This Century or Betty Parsons), some of them spontaneous and social (the group around Milton Avery; the "uptown" and "downtown" groups). But these clusters were not only fluid; they contained personal jealousies and aesthetic differences, and individual friendships (Newman and Pollock) sometimes cut across their fluctuating borders.

"There was a sense of exaltation among the artists in the late 1940s and early 1950s," Thomas Hess writes, "the shuddering heightening of spirit that comes from realizing that a risk has been taken, that one has come through, and that another danger lies just ahead. It created a camaraderie among artists."[41] Yet both the loose alliances and some of the strong friendships among these artists first begin to crack in the early 1950s, well before any of these painters reached financial success, and well before any of them, except Jackson Pollock, had attained significant public reputation. "We must find a way of living and working without the involvements that seem to have been destroying us one after another," Rothko had written to Newman in 1950. Rothko did not provide a casualty list, but his own 1950 trip to Europe had been planned partly to help him recover from the depression that had coincided with the death of his mother and his involvement with The Subjects of the Artist School, and he is surely speaking of himself when he adds to Newman, "I doubt whether any of us can bear much more of that kind of strain."[42] But worse strains would follow.

Clyfford Still felt it would compromise his integrity to attend Rothko's opening at Sidney Janis; so did Barnett Newman, who, like Still, felt compelled to elevate his absence into a public issue by writing a letter to Janis, who must have begun to wonder just who *would* show up for the opening.[43] "I am frankly bored with the uninspired, or to put it more accurately, I am bored with the too easily inspired," Newman began, in a tone of lofty disdain. Reporting Rothko's comment that "it does not matter that an artist 'looks' at other painters" since "it is not what he 'sees' but what he 'does' with what he 'sees' that counts," Newman goes on to deride this view as "the credo of a virtuoso, of the salon painter, of the social and public man." "This easy ability to be inspired not only reduces the concepts that form his sources, not only distorts the act of painting itself, but it is so at variance with my own point of view that I can only reject everything it involves."

One of those sources, Newman believes, is Newman's work. "It was Rothko who in 1950 said to me that he could not look at his work because it reminded him of death." "Why," Newman asks, "should I look at his death image? I am involved in life, in the joy of the spirit." Rothko's "death image," moreover, appropriated Newman's joy of life. "When Rothko returned from Europe, it is obvious that he 'saw' enough of this sense of life in my work to 'see' how he could subjugate it, just as previously he had 'looked' at the work of other artists for the same purposes." Now that some of them were gaining acceptance, Abstract Expressionists began to dispute the issue of priority, one charging the other with trespassing on territory he had taken, with backdating paintings to cover the violation. Each fought to preserve the integrity of an *absolute* autonomy.

Like Still, Newman also accused Rothko of a contaminating desire for bourgeois success, a peculiar charge to make in a letter to the man who, after all, was Rothko's dealer. "Rothko talks the fighter. He fights, however, to submit to the philistine world," Newman writes. "The same virtuosity that begs in the work for public approval has been the means whereby moral issues against the philistine world could be juggled." Still judged Rothko an authoritarian bully; Newman regarded him as a virtuoso charmer. Each isolated a real element in an opposition that creates a tension in Rothko's work—his aggression; his eagerness to be admired—then identified that element as the *essence* of a painter whom they now deemed to be a fraud and pariah. "I must unequivocally separate myself from Rothko because he has publicly identified himself with me so that the expression of my own personal integrity becomes for him a shield whereby he can achieve perpetual surrender," Newman declares, recovering his integrity with a gesture that sounds egocentric and spiteful.

Ill-feeling had been building between Rothko and Newman at least since 1952. "Barney has remained invisible," Rothko commented to Herbert Ferber in the same August 1952 letter in which he spoke of visiting his room—now hung with Marin and O'Keeffe—from the "Fifteen Americans" exhibit at the Museum of Modern Art.[44] According to Annalee Newman, Rothko and her husband "drifted apart" after Rothko and Still, included in "Fifteen Americans," did not push for Newman's inclusion. Clyfford Still told Newman that Rothko had actively sought to "keep him out." Newman was already embittered by his fellow-artists' cool, sometimes hostile reception to the 1950 and 1951 Betty Parsons exhibits at which he first showed his "zip" paintings. In these years, Newman "was attacked from most—then, from all—quarters, and there was no defending thunder from Motherwell or Still, no open letters circulated by Reinhardt or Rothko." His friends, happy to let Newman fulfill his destiny as their polemical spokesman, did not consider Newman a painter; in fact, according to Sally Avery, "they thought it a little presumptuous on his part to start painting," and they accused him of appropriating the fruits of their many years of laborious struggle. Among artists disdainful of bourgeois values, painting ideas were viewed as private property. Rothko began telling people, "I taught Barney how to paint." All this made Barney feel "betrayed," and, withdrawing his paintings from Parsons' gallery, he became professionally invisible, refusing to show again in New York until 1959. On the invitations to the opening reception for this show sent to Rothko and Still, Newman wrote, "You are not invited to the opening."[45]

As Rothko and Newman were splitting, Clyfford Still, never reluctant to cross swords or wield a knife, was adding both men to his long list of traitors to the cause. As Still was preparing to switch from Betty Parsons to Sidney Janis, without informing Parsons, he was wondering "whether to withdraw totally, or go in and spend another chunk of life slugging it out with Newman,

Reinhardt, and Rothko and show them up for the Bauhaus bullies they are. They have really put over a terrific fraud; Rothko even naming the time, five years, that it would take them to achieve their notoriety."[46] Not long after the *Fortune* essay endorsed Rothko as a growth issue, Still demanded the return of the painting he had loaned Rothko. "Still warned Rothko of the presence of a new kind of crass young collector-on-the-make bent on exploiting their creations. He had come to the point, he wrote, where he felt like arming himself with brass knuckles each time he came across any art world type."[47] After this letter, written several months before Still's tirade to Janis, the friendship ended. Still began claiming he had taught Rothko how to paint.

Ad Reinhardt's public ridiculing of Rothko, Newman (and others, including de Kooning, Gottlieb, Pollock, Still) appeared in the summer of 1954; that spring Reinhardt had voted against Rothko for tenure at Brooklyn College, leaving the two painters estranged for several years. With two of Rothko's oldest artist-friends, Adolph Gottlieb and Milton Avery, no dramatic break occurred. Rothko remained friendly with both men, but saw much less of them, something that either caused or reflected personal strains. When Milton Avery suffered a heart attack in 1949, "Rothko said he couldn't be around sick people because he would begin to attach the illness to himself," Sally Avery recalled. Rothko's fear of his own hypochondria did not endear him to the Averys. According to Harold Baumbach, a close friend of Gottlieb's, "Adolph had reached a point of success before Rothko. Then Rothko overshadowed him. Gottlieb always resented the fact that Mark had gotten ahead of him."

But it was his rifts with Newman and Still that disturbed, and hurt, Rothko the most; his friendships with these two men, coinciding with the early years of his marriage, had given the more hesitant Rothko two supportive and self-confident allies during the period of his boldest production. During the 1950s, as Rothko achieved first reputation and then financial success, both Newman and Still withdrew from exhibiting their work, publicly separating themselves from the commercial entanglements of art, though they continued to sell work from their studios. In the words of Ben Heller, one of the young collectors of the 1950s, "Mark, with all his moaning and groaning about not showing and sending these sensitive, delicate, tender little things out into the big bad hard world, played their game." Newman and Still remained uncompromising, independent; Still in particular Rothko projected as his artistic conscience. "Rothko adored Still to his dying day. He never repudiated Clyff, never. However, Clyff repudiated Rothko," said Katharine Kuh. After Still left New York City for rural Maryland in 1961, "Mark would always ask me, 'When are you going to see Clyff again?' Always. Clyff was on his mind all the time." "Mark would say, 'Remember me to Clyff.' And then when I'd come back, he'd say, 'What did he say about me?' like a little boy"—or like the Rothko on 57th Street worrying about what Sidney Janis thought of him. After one of her visits with Still, Katharine Kuh finally told Rothko, "Well, he said that you're living an evil, an untrue life."[48]

Breaking with the purists Still and Newman made Rothko fear that maybe he *was* being corrupted; he also longed to return to their old intimacy. In the late 1940s and early 1950s, once Rothko had finished painting for the day, he would call up Newman "and talk his heart out and get out all of his angst." As a friend, according to Annalee Newman, Rothko "always needed someone to lean on. He hated to be alone." After his rupture with Newman, Rothko would complain, "How I miss Barney."[49] Rothko also "yearned" to renew his relationship with Still, Katharine Kuh believed, but Still refused. After Rothko's aneurysm in 1968, she told Still how depressed Rothko had become, and how important their friendship was to him, but Still was not impressed.[50] By the mid-1950s, Rothko was drifting away from old friends like Avery and Gottlieb; two of his closest friends had declared themselves enemies. And this was a man who, in Stanley Kunitz's words, "needed companionship desperately."

. . .

We spend our time here in search of a human being. In the course of our being entertained here not too infrequently, there was no trace of one. Our desperation forces us to hold on to hope.

Mark Rothko

In 1952, two days before the opening of "Fifteen Americans," Rothko received an invitation to teach in the eight-week summer session at Black Mountain College, a small, experimental school in the western hills of North Carolina, near Ashville, where people such as John Cage, Merce Cunningham, Charles Olson, Joseph Albers, Willem and Elaine de Kooning, and Franz Kline either had taught or were still teaching. A kind of Commonwealth College devoted to art rather than politics, Black Mountain offered a freewheeling alternative to the Bauhaus orders of Brooklyn College; but it only offered $160 pay for the summer, a $100 travel allowance, plus free room and board for the artist and his family.[51] Rothko refused, perhaps because of the low pay, perhaps because of the difficulties of traveling with an eighteen-month-old child, perhaps because he thought he could get more work done where he was.

So Rothko spent the summer of 1952 in New York, freed of the obligations

The Dark Paintings

of any kind of teaching, but a bit gloomy and lethargic. "The town here has been inordinately quiet," he wrote to Herbert Ferber that August, "and we shuffle lazily between park, studio & home." Rothko sounds not relaxed, but bored, unengaged, going through the motions, as if the usual strains of art-world activity were not destructive only, but somehow energizing. There have been domestic obligations, painting his flat and laying down linoleum. Ferber's vacation place sounds "like God's Country" and will no doubt prove restorative. "We ourselves are getting a little restless and there is a strong impulse to hit the road." "Fifteen Americans" has come down, and Rothko is left only with its "afterglow." During his visit to the Modern, "I met and had a long talk with [Abraham] Walkowitz whose glaucoma has made him almost blind. Still he haunts the museum daily. I have always had the highest respect for him. And so it goes. Barney has remained invisible." Apologetic about his "gloomy" musings, Rothko makes a self-conscious effort to close more cheerfully: "the weather here is heavenly and one walks about in the sun and the breeze really feeling like a million bucks. You up there should feel like two million."[52]

A few days later Rothko and his family did hit the road, traveling to East Hampton to visit Robert Motherwell and his family, whereupon the two men left almost immediately to attend a two-day conference on "Aesthetics and the Artist" at Woodstock, the art colony about eighty miles north of New York City.[53] The conference produced what has become Newman's best-known epigram: "esthetics is for artists as ornithology is for the birds."[54] Robert Motherwell recalled that his own paper was badly received, and that, having been given "the cold shoulder" at the conference, particularly by the Marxists, he and Rothko went their separate drinking ways at the end of the first day. The next morning Rothko woke Motherwell to announce they now had a series of meetings for the day. Having explained to the other participants that he and Motherwell were not making any money from their work, Rothko established them as noncorrupt and earned them social acceptance. To Motherwell, the incident demonstrated Rothko's "street wisdom."

To Rothko, the upstate conference proved just as wearying as the city. When he returned to New York, he again wrote to Ferber, congratulating him for "having the best and wisest summer I have ever heard of—doing nothing, which to do with relish is the highest wisdom of all according to Nerothustra [*sic*; Rothko presumably means Nietzsche's Zarathustra]." Rothko could *paint* nothing with relish, but he could not *do* it, one reason he didn't enjoy family vacations. "Our own trip brought us home thrice exhausted," he wrote. "Kate in contrast [to Ferber] insists on doing everything, which produces the opposite of the well-being that you are experiencing. I went off with Bob for the weekend, leaving Mell alas with Kate in the country, to Woodstock, where the perfect weather plus copious drinks and food did much to drown the banal words which were even more copious."[55]

A few months after being fired by the design department at Brooklyn College, Rothko was offered a temporary position at the University of New Mexico; he declined, expressing interest in a summer-session job which did not work out.[56] As with Rothko's two summers at the California School of Fine Arts in 1947 and 1949, these visiting artist positions offered a restless artist one reason to hit the road, make a little money, receive a little adulation in the hinterlands, have a working vacation without too many formal obligations to work.

So for eight weeks in the summer of 1955, Rothko taught at the University of Colorado, in Boulder, receiving $1,800. When Rothko and his family reached Boulder, he bought a used car, "from a dealer," he wrote in a joint letter to the Motherwells and Ferbers, "recommended for having a reliability to be found only West of the middle west. The car was guaranteed to take us enthusiastically to every point of wonder in the vicinity. It was eight miles up Boulder Canyon that our radiator gave out. We were waving our arms frantically for help and who stopped to help us? Gerry Levine, Mr. and Mrs. Byrnes, Inez Johnson and one dog. It was wonderful to see them, for the smell of their contact with you and of that Paradise, N.Y. still lingered about their clothes."[57]

Then director of the Colorado Springs Fine Arts Center, James Byrnes, who had first met Rothko in 1951, had driven to Boulder on the chance of finding Rothko at home, instead finding him "a few miles from their home [when] we saw an old car with its hood erupting in a cloud of steam." After helping Rothko cool the radiator down, Byrnes learned that "it hadn't occurred to him that the car needed more than gas and oil to keep it going. He confessed that he had no interest in things mechanical and he would probably have abandoned the car had we not come along." As alien from the mechanical as from the natural, Rothko, relating to a car in the same distracted way he related to his body, was always banging into things, nearly banging into things, getting lost, having breakdowns.[58]

While the Rothkos were visiting the Byrneses the following weekend in Colorado Springs, Byrnes "was musing about the wonderful period my wife and I spent in Italy and mentioned that if I were forced to make a change I'd love to return to Rome and open an art gallery on the Spanish Steps where I'd represent artists of the New York School whose work I believed the Europeans were ready to collect." In reply Rothko alluded to "his need to earn five thousand dollars a year to take care of his family and to paint," then "abruptly ended the conversation with, 'You ought to get out of here—it's for the Greeks'." Byrnes interpreted Rothko's enigmatic remark "as meaning that I give up the 'corrupting facade of security' to be free to return to the Eternal City," just as Rothko, the year before, had provoked himself out of his secure, $5,000-a-year job at Brooklyn College.⁵⁹

Writing to the Motherwells and Ferbers, Rothko praised the Byrneses as "excellent hosts, and let me say that their devotion to you is of an intensity and wholeheartedness that occurs only in the undevout." But speaking privately to his New York artist friends, Rothko revealed another reason for urging Byrnes to get out: "I would say that for that [i.e., their devotion] I forgive the real shoddiness of their enterprise and that of the world in which it operates." Woodstock was banal; Colorado Springs, like Boulder, shoddy. From eighteen hundred miles across the country, New York now looked like "that Paradise," and Rothko, not the emerging artist in San Francisco but the eminent artist in Boulder, wrote to his sophisticated friends about western provinciality with a wry, sometimes patronizing irony.

"Let me tell you one East, West incident which may amuse you," he wrote.

> Buying a car found me in a series of transactions in which it was known that I was from New York. First the dealer hinted he couldn't understand how anyone could live in N.Y.; the license plate man said he had been there once, had enjoyed the noise (how can one stand it), but once was enough; the clerk who gave me the eye test hinted at the corruption of large centers, etc. etc. Finally we left the station, the dealer renewed the chant. In a moment of folly, I stopped him and passionately described for him the great cities of the world, Paris, Rome, London (and threw in Berlin and Oslo for local ethnic reasons). And, I added, of all these wonders, New York was the greatest wonder of all.
>
> He smiled his slow Rocky Mountain smile. "I wouldn't go to one of them places either" was what he said.⁶⁰

Complacent Western biases render the cosmopolitan New Yorker's passionate endorsement futile.

With some self-irony, Rothko tells, in a subsequent letter to the Ferbers, of "three pressures which are being exerted against me here":

> 1—All our local acquaintances want us to climb mountains; 2—Mell wants to get me on a horse; 3—My students want me to teach them how to paint abstract expressionism.

But Rothko refuses to "submit." The natives are insular, his students naive, and his chairman an exiled, New England WASP. "My boss here is Boston, Harvard, and alas a poor cousin of the Fricks. To him I am Yale, Oregon and a cousin of the rabbi of Lodz." But it is the self-conscious cousin of the rabbi who

Chapter Twelve

condescends to the cousin of the Fricks, still attached to the symbols of East-Coast academic prestige and now dependent on the kindness of local matrons. The Rothkos and the Frick relation "are going next week to Denver where we will lunch at the Harvard Club and then if we are through in time at Montgomery Wards, have cocktails at the Yale Club. We attend parties filled with old dowagers to whom we are polite in the hope of bequests."[61]

While in Boulder, the Rothkos lived in a faculty development "which is devoted to breeding wholeheartedly and as a result there are many friends for Kate and we have periods of relief from her which we need so badly." But living there also gave Rothko a satiric vision of present-day and future academic life.

> The Geographic situation makes it microscopically vivid. The University itself is on the hill. At its base are the faculty apartments which are shells around appliances facing a court into which the children are emptied. Two hundred yards away is Vetsville, in which the present faculty itself had lived only four or five years ago when they were preparing to be faculty. Vetsville itself is occupied by graduates from army headquarters, already married and breeding who will be faculty in faculty quarters three or four years hence. They breed furiously guaranteeing the expansion which will perpetuate the process into the future.
>
> The faculty itself is allowed to stay here only 2 years whereupon they must assume mortgages in similar housing slum developments where thereafter they must repair their own cracks and sprinkle their grass....
>
> Here is a self-perpetuating peonage, schooled in mass communal living, which will become a formidable sixth estate within a decade. It will have a cast of features, a shape of head, and a dialect as yet unknown, and will propagate a culture so distorted and removed from its origins, that its image is unpredictable.[62]

Routinized and anonymous, domesticated and middle-class, a servile "peonage" yet a potent emerging "sixth estate," this shoddy new academic caste, breeding "furiously," rising through the ranks yet getting nowhere, constitutes a social machine which will obliterate all individuality and distinction.

"Two of my paintings hang here for the last 3 weeks," Rothko wrote the Ferbers. But if he had gone west looking for admiration or even understanding, he was disappointed, though in a way that left him curiously satisfied, as if rejection felt more real to him. "The silence is thick," he went on. "Not a word or look from faculty, students, or the Fricks. One of them, on my first visit I found was hung horizontally. I phoned the hanger about his error. 'Oh, it was no error,' he said. 'I thought it filled the space better.' I swear by the bones of Titian that this is true."[63]

Two years later, in February–March 1957, the Rothkos traveled to New Orleans, where Rothko had been appointed Visiting Artist at the Newcomb Art School, Tulane University.[64] As a letter to the Ferbers shows, distance, once again, had idealized New York, though Rothko also alludes to the friendships lost back there: "one needs a glimpse of elsewhere and others; to know how blessed it is to be set in New York, and how tailor made and unique are the few friendships that have percolated down in the passing years." He has been living "in a suburb called Metairie, which is an exact equivalent of plush Westchester."[65] Instead of a walk-up on 54th Street (or an apartment in a faculty development), "we have a house, a garden of proportions, manicured lawns and manicured neighbors. Symbolic of our style is our shower stall which has seven powerful needle sprays and which we have named the 'Iron Maiden'." According to Pat Trivigno, the faculty member who had invited Rothko to Tulane, Rothko was "very offended by his upper-middle-class neighborhood." His letter to the Ferbers maintains a cheerfully ironic distance from all this suburban affluence, until Rothko elaborates a vision of suburbia as dominated by restless, needy women: "we are being dined and wined by these same neighbors whose wives have the restless itch and have glued their souls to the University Art department. I weep for us and their husbands more. If there were any doubts, we can say firmly now that these represent the lowest point of civilization anywhere and anytime, and here lie the poisons by which empires destroy themselves."

Why is Rothko so vehement here? Why does he at once become severely moral and yet cruel, taking pleasure in his demeaning representation of these women? After all, he is only talking about people who, as *he* characterizes *them*, are sexually restless and who adulate artists—hardly the stuff on which empires (or even suburbs) founder. If in Boulder he had envisioned a form of "mass communal living" that would efface all distinction, in Metairie he imagined manicured suburban wives out of control and impossible to get rid of, betraying their husbands and gluing themselves to the art department—threats to *male* power and distinction.

Then Rothko, in his letter to the Ferbers, abruptly switches from anxious male, prophesying doom, to upbeat tourist, reporting the weather: "there have been a number of benign days of early summer, sun, warmth and lush growth. In March this alone justifies our venture, as well as the fact that distance has lulled all problems and irritations, as if they were not to reappear in full force in three weeks from now. In great measure we are even enjoying the tearing about socially." He even chastises himself for his cruelty to suburban females:

Chapter Twelve

his tearing about "is new, revealing, [and] rather sad in relation to the people whom we judge so harshly."

> We got to the French Quarter which is in part like a miniature of a section of Paris with its intense charm of scale and affords all the pleasure of walking and browsing around in. We have also had a glimpse of the plantation country.

The Rothkos went to the Mardi Gras, which they timed their visit to see; and Trivigno recalled a boat trip up the Mississippi and the two families spending a long enjoyable afternoon flying kites along the New Orleans levee. He perceived Rothko as a "kindly family man."

On the whole, however, travel, particularly excursions into the American interior, did not strike Rothko as an exciting opportunity to "adventure" in an "unknown" territory. Hardly a sensitive observer of either social reality or the landscape, Rothko wasn't looking for novel sensations, seeking unexpected encounters, or exploring new possibilities. Vague about his pleasures, turning standard 1950s perceptions about mass culture and suburban living into apocalyptic prophecies, Rothko saw much that distressed and little that surprised or puzzled him. It wasn't just that he was a myopic New Yorker. To this Russian emigré, "paradise" always seemed the place, though a sometimes melancholy place, he had left behind him, as if travel suggested displacement, or transplantation, and new locales made him want at least to *appear* distant, alien, ironic.

While at Tulane, Rothko "did not teach specific classes but gave a series of talks and critiques."[66] According to Trivigno, Rothko "would just talk, rarely about art, usually about music or literature," comparing Tolstoy and Dostoevsky, for example, contending that whereas Tolstoy created a panoramic overview Dostoevsky explored the human soul, as Rothko himself wished to. Some students complained that Rothko wasn't telling them more about their work; others were more responsive to his indirect approach, but, said Trivigno, "everyone felt a presence in the department, someone with an important and valid expression." The school had arranged for four or five of Rothko's paintings to be shipped to New Orleans, and he hung a show in a small room in the school's art gallery. But Rothko insisted that the door to the room be kept closed, because he "wanted to control who would enter. He wanted to talk to the people to see if they were sympathetic and sensitive to his work." "He was obviously," Trivigno commented, "carrying around a lot of hurts from earlier shows."

Talking with Trivigno while in New Orleans, Rothko, "very self-conscious about content in his paintings," would identify the subject matter in his paintings as "my wife," "your wife," "you," as if the paintings were "elusive, but very strong metaphors for his deeper feelings about the 'subject'." Living in a house vacated by the death of a faculty member's mother, Rothko used the garage as a studio, bought paints at a local hardware store, had students stretch some canvases for him, and produced two paintings—*White and Greens in Blue* and *Red, White and Brown*—which he then and later claimed to be "important 'breakthrough' paintings."[67] "The canvases [now] grew larger, the edges of his forms less shadowy and the colors less transparent, with an overall somber mood."[68]

Painting in a garage in the plush New Orleans suburb of Metairie during February and March of 1957, Rothko, "able to live by my work for the first time in my 53 years of life," yet filled with forebodings that such success could not last very long, drew into himself and painted the first of his "dark pictures."

. . .

I would like to say to those who think of my pictures as serene, whether on friendship or mere observation, that I have imprisoned the most utter violence in every inch of their surface.

Mark Rothko

Rothko's two one-man shows at Sidney Janis had been received by reviewers with the respectful enthusiasm due a major artist. True, Emily Genauer complained in the *Herald Tribune,* of the 1955 exhibit, that "Rothko's pictures get bigger and bigger and say less and less," but hers was a lone dissent. "The first impact of the 12 gigantic canvases on view is startling in its breadth, simplicity and the beauty of color dealt with on such a vast and subtly modulated scale," wrote the *Arts Digest* reviewer, who went on to praise the show as "an ensemble of serenity and stability," and in *Art News* Thomas Hess called the show "one of the most enjoyable" in several years, declared that it established "the international importance of Rothko as a leader of postwar modern art," and commended his creation of an "elementary serenity of symmetry in a way that avoids the paralyzing boredom perfect symmetry aspires to."[69] No longer mainly perceived as a modern formalist producing blurry versions of Mondrian, Rothko was now in danger of being understood as diverting modern viewers with voluptuous images of romantic serenity.

At Rothko's second Janis exhibit in 1958, reviewers were no more disturbed than buyers by Rothko's turn to less accessible and more somber paintings. "The new Rothkos are darker, composed of the rich reds, browns and blacks we associate with the numinous, the royal and the religious," E. C. Goossen wrote in *Art International*; he judged the Janis "a handsome, major show." Writing in *Arts and Architecture,* Dore Ashton speculated that Rothko has "struck out with exasperation at the general misinterpretation of his earlier work—especially the effusive yellow, orange and pinks of three years back. He seems to be saying in these new foreboding works that he was never painting *luxe, calme,* and *volupté.*" Praising his "deeply developed sense of the tragic," Ashton declared that Rothko "stands alone," "the most constructively disturbing" among his generation of New York vanguard painters.[70]

Since 1949, except for a brief comment on his desire to make his large pictures "intimate and human," delivered during "A Symposium on How to Combine Architecture, Painting and Sculpture" (1951), Rothko had offered no public statements about his work—or anybody else's work, for that matter.[71] Not that he was entirely happy to leave discussion of his work to others: "he has threatened to sue if anyone wrote about his paintings," Herbert Crehan reported.[72] In fact, Crehan, a former Clyfford Still disciple from the California School of Fine Arts, was himself boldly violating that taboo by writing the first essay ("Rothko's Wall of Light") on the artist's classic paintings. Occasioned by Rothko's 1954 Art Institute of Chicago exhibit, Crehan's article shrewdly urged the achievement of a *modern* spiritual vision. "The beauty of Rothko's painting is its evocation of the idea and the feeling that it is still possible for us to discover serenity in the midst of turbulence and that by accepting the contradictions of our transitional times and the complexity of our desires, it is possible to create an abstract form of poise." But Crehan—unlike a couple of the reviewers of Rothko's 1955 Sidney Janis exhibit—did not stop with Rothko's "serenity." Comparing the "immanent radiance" of his work with the light released by a nuclear explosion—"a light softer, more pacifying than the hues of the rainbow and yet detonated from some wrathful and diabolical depth"—Crehan saw the "tension of the color-relationships" in certain Rothko paintings "raised to such a shrill pitch that one begins to feel in them a fission might happen, that they also might detonate."[73] Crehan sensed a powerful rage, barely held in.

Discussing this essay with a friend just a few days after its appearance, Rothko found its prose "possibly a little too purple" and he "resented" Crehan's account of his dealings with museums as "none of the public's business." But Rothko declared Crehan's insights "acute," particularly valuing "Crehan's noting the 'violence' in his paintings." Rothko complained that "people mistakenly speak only" of his "serenity," when "a more accurate description" was "serenity about to explode."[74] If they were merely serene, then Rothko's paintings were removed from the constrictions and pressures of modern life; they were pleasurable diversions, hollow, as he sometimes, in his despairing moments, feared them to be. Such a reading, another way of calling his work decorative, would deny the aggressive power of the paintings.

Having read *The Birth of Tragedy* early, Rothko said, he returned to that text "on a number of occasions," one of them around this time, as he attempted to compose an essay or talk on his debt to Nietzsche.[75] From the beginning, Rothko writes, "I found in this fable the poetic reinforcement for what I inevitably knew was my inevitable course: that the poignancy of art in my life lay in its Dionysian content, and that the nobility, the largeness and exaltation are hollow pillars, not to be trusted, unless they have as their core, unless they are filled to the point of bulging by the wild."[76] On this occasion, Nietzsche's opposition between Dionysus and Apollo offered Rothko a language in which to formulate the "intensity," or fullness, he wished to claim for his work. "I have one ambition for all my pictures," he writes, "that their intensity be felt unequivocally and immediately."

According to Rothko, Nietzsche's Dionysus signifies "the raw experience, the thing in itself," not an external object but an unmediated inner state, instinctual or "wild." This god "has the secret of direct access to the wild terror and suffering and the blind drives and aspirations which lay at the bottom of human existence and which relentlessly assault our ordered lives never thoroughly allayed or intimidated by our catalogues and categories."[77] "In speaking of the 'thing itself'," Rothko writes in another draft, "I am speaking of the boundless aspirations and terrors, the welter of restlessness, the senselessness, the desires[,] the alterations of hope and despair[,] out of context and out of reason[,] on which is constructed the shaky security of our ordered life." As in "The Romantics Were Prompted," any sense of security is deemed a "false sense," here vulnerable not so much to "the unfriendliness of society" as to an "assault" from within, from turbulent feelings, arising from no apparent "context," out of all "reason," in a kind of encapsulated consciousness.

Apollo, on the other hand, signifies that raw experience "sublimated to the level of nobility and contemplative exaltation"—the thing in itself "filtered and made endurable by presenting itself thru a series of reflections, reflection being meant in both ways." Robert Motherwell recalled that in the 1950s, Rothko's "constant term was 'to endure'. A work was fully realized if he could 'endure' it, if it were not a lie."[78] At several points in these drafts Rothko asserts that the function of the Apollonian is to render the painful chaos of interior life "endurable." As Rothko wrote to Clay Spohn in 1948, creativity induces a "frenzy that brings you to the edge of madness."[79] Apollo, reflecting that frenzy in an image, reflecting *on* that frenzy, keeps you from going over the edge.

The artist, Rothko says, "must find the extroverted image of the raw experience," an image rendering that experience "endurable and more socially consumable." The "question of form," then, "while it involves the image shape," resolves itself into "the question of measure" (another favorite term of Rothko's)—i.e., "of how much can be revealed before the reality becomes unendurable." Yet the artist must also avoid so distancing, taming, subduing, or domesticating this "reality" that the work is left "a hollow shell." To this end, the artist must keep "the interval of time between the experience and its expression . . . so short" that, like a "shriek or spasm," "it constitutes a reflex, and therefore a completion of the experience of which the pain was the inception." The work, therefore, will be "a segment of the experience itself rather than a contemplated reflection about it."[80]

So "to those who think of my pictures as serene," Rothko asserts, "I have imprisoned the most utter violence in every square inch of their surface." Reacting against the reduction of his paintings to the all-too-bearable, Rothko's polemic exaggerates both their violence and constraint. But he does anticipate that people will "ask why I have adopted a form which might to some be deceptive, why I have not used the physical means of agitation[,] of speed[,] of fast motion." In other words, why, if you believe as you say, are you not Jackson Pollock or Willem de Kooning? To such inquiries, "I can only answer that this was the way in which I could achieve the greatest intensity of the tragic irreconcilability of the basic violence which lies at the bottom of human existence and the daily life which must deal with it." His art opens a window on a Dionysian violence which, in the confinements, distractions, and hypocrisies of daily life, necessarily stays firmly shut, with the blinds drawn.

"That such violence remains endurable" in a work of art, Rothko says, "can be compared to the ritual celebrating the power of a God whose potential is destruction, who must be propitiated by the very image of this potential if one is not himself to be destroyed." In this account, art functions as a ritual in which the power of a fierce god is evoked, acknowledged, and propitiated by creating an image of that god. A destructive/creative force exists prior to, outside of, antagonistic toward, and resisted by shaky social, rational orders; that force is imagined as mythic in part because Rothko experiences it as an alien power at once *in* the self and *beyond* the self ("not-self") and in part because this jumble of bottled-up feelings (existing independently of any present "context" or cause) has its origin in the larger-than-life hopes and terrors, desires and despairs, of childhood. In one of the poems he had written as a young man, Rothko portrayed himself as "bound to the past / By invisible chains," bound to the "primitive barbarous people" of the Old Testament, to a "primitive mother," to "the fierce darkness within her," to "all the primitive fears / Rustling and slipping about me." Then, he had wished to rise above these irrational ties. Now, the adult painter names these forces as a "god" and imagines their expression as a propitiating "ritual," one that transforms his private ordeal into mythic drama, into something "universal," into something he has endured.

Yet it is a universal which, by Rothko's own account, is almost universally obscured, buried, repressed. The reception of his own paintings, categorizing them as formalist experiment or romantic mood ("serene") constitutes one such repression. Rothko declares: "the response of society to protect itself from the truth, . . . the endless layers it has woven to hide it," is "immediate." "All our institutions prepared bulletins in which these [artistic] forays were announced as expeditions to discover new methods[,] new notions of space, new techniques, as anaesthetics to distort the real truth of what was going on, in the overwhelming upsurge of this Dionysian life." Cossacks whip; fathers coerce; societies constrain; critics crush. These defensive forms of violence create a hollow or "shaky security," while artistic violence, filling Apollo's reflections (to the point of bulging) with the "fierce darkness" of Dionysus, creates works that disrupt (or "assault") those shaky orders.

As Rothko points out, Nietzsche believed that Greek social conditions permitted a temporary "reconciliation" of Dionysus and Apollo in the tragic dramas of Aeschylus and Sophocles. The modern artist, however, working on his own, can achieve no such reconciliation. Instead, he can create "the moment of their greatest antagonism when they are constrained by some outward force (the artist) to inhabit together this limited space. And intensity is the resultant[,] the fire of this terrible constraint." Violent emotion, violently held in: Rothko's polemic does not explain or more accurately identify his work. His writing on Nietzsche, rather, expresses some of the same smoldering frustration to be found in the "dark paintings," as if the "new life" he had built up since the time of his divorce were now disintegrating, its shaky order collapsing under the pressure of older, more powerful, and more primitive forces.

. . .

On February 14, 1956, Rothko met with Alfred Jensen:

> Yesterday I again visited Rothko at his studio. I found that he had developed as a painter since I saw his work last spring when I told him he included elements of father, mother and child in his paintings. Now in his present canvases he has united these three distinct elements into a family unit.
>
> "Jensen, what you say pleases me and when I get home I'll tell Mell

Chapter Twelve

about it. I know that it will please her that you have discerned this new expressive element in my recent work. You are the only one to have understood this. I'm always happy to get your response to my work. Others will say this canvas is beautiful, etc., but they do not see the depth and significance of what I'm after. You know that we all as artists share the distinction of being catalytic idealists. This is the turn of mind we labor under. We as artists are strange creatures. Look at de Kooning, look at you, Jensen, look at me, and what does one see? Surely strange lives! I'm in terrible circumstances at present. I could kick myself for having messed up my teaching job at Brooklyn College, but how could I have done otherwise?

"I'm sorry that other painters disapprove so strongly of Philip Guston's show. They accuse him of impotency; they say he can only caress a woman's backside, a pleasant occupation, but they mean that Philip can't go on to take the woman to himself to fuck her. To fuck a picture thirty or forty times a year is quite an order to fulfill. However, I guess that even if a painter fucks a picture to a real climax once a year, it is quite a record. Ten to fifteen times is what the average good artist can accomplish each year.

"Now, Jensen, you maintain that a painter must be concrete, abstract, figurative, or geometric. You maintain that the woman must be seen as an image; the ugly must contrast with the beautiful. Let us take de Kooning's women. Bill de Kooning contrasts the distorted fragments of a woman and fuses them with his sense of the pictorial. Picasso's Grecian nudes that he did in the twenties are extremely sensual works of art, but what Renoir did with his nudes is something that belongs to his epoch. However, today one can't make a figurative painting of a woman without distortions and ugliness. Picasso avoided the ugly by his references to another epoch. While he was doing his women he was inspired by their beauty and so painted them as Greek goddesses.

"Now Milton Avery is the only painter today who can create the concrete image of a woman without having to resort to distortion. Matisse is sensual but distorts his women, while Avery is nonsensual and paints the pure loveliness of womanhood. If I weren't shy about painting the direct image of woman, I would concentrate on her loveliest features. I hate any kind of distorted image in art. There is something about our times that does not allow us as artists to represent woman. Matisse still felt about the woman as one does about a chattel. He used her, he fucked her. He painted her as he lived with her. Today woman has her independence: man looks at her as his equal and something indefinable stands between them. Not as yet to my mind has anyone discovered what this something is. Whatever it is, it blocks the painter from seeing her the way former generations did. Because as an artist today I cannot see her, I paint the abstract image of woman until something happens to show me the way toward a direct representation—a new attitude perhaps toward her.

"It might be true, Jensen, as you claim[,] that comedy, ecstacy and loftiness of spirit are what I actually stand for and that I only exploit talk about tragedy and despair. I'm at present reading Sigmund Freud's letters to a Dr. Fleiss, a nondescript doctor whom no one ever heard of. However, Freud made use of him as a sounding board, and made Fleiss a focal point to whom he addressed some of his most important ideas. Thus an insignificant person like Fleiss can be of great indirect service to mankind. However it is also true as you brought out, Jensen, that both Boswell and Ackerman, even though they seemingly played minor roles in the lives of their friends Johnson and Goethe, still in their own right remained important, and besides also benefitted mankind by their published conversations.

"You, Jensen, might not be recognized this year by the art world, and I am; yet ten years from now you might be well known and I might be forgotten. It thus is very difficult to judge our contemporaries.

"You say that Lil who was present at our last conversation found that your written report was not exactly what she heard me say, that indeed what you wrote is better than what she remembers that I said. Lil is in love with you and therefore it's no wonder that when she reads your interpretations of my thoughts, she prefers your version. Her response is very womanly.

"By the way, I've begun to hate Negro masks and other Central American pre-Columbian art, and all the other primitive art manifestations. These objects take on a minor role for me, sort of an anthropological phenomenon. I really have begun to deny their value as art. Look at those Picasso pictures, suffering from a cult of ugliness and deriving from primitive sources.

"When young painters come to me and praise my work, I am certain that they are really assaulting me. Beneath their praise I feel their envy and jealousy; they assault me with praise. Nevertheless they assault, by praising me they actually try to destroy my influence over them. It frightens me to accept their praise."

• • •

Chapter Twelve

"Today woman has her independence: man looks at her as his equal and something indefinable stands between them," Rothko told Jensen—a very strange observation to make in the middle of the 1950s, governed by a powerful postwar domestic ideology which subordinated women and relegated them to the home. Perhaps Rothko was thinking about his first marriage. But his remark suggests that, for him, in relations between the sexes, equality produces division and conflict. In painting, sexual equality produces "distortions and ugliness," a violation of the woman, a bending of her to the artist's will which, announces Rothko, he refuses. "I hate any kind of distorted image in art." Instead, he paints "the abstract image of woman," transforming her into a timeless realm of essences, universals.

Yet removing woman from history works simply to return her to her "eternal" place—a violation in itself. It was, moreover, in the surfaces of these same abstract paintings that Rothko, on other occasions, was claiming to "have imprisoned the most utter violence." And it is Rothko who, after some talk with Jensen about one of his paintings as exemplifying domestic unity, imagines the creative act as a kind of hostile sexuality. Before, like many male artists, Rothko had compared the creative process to women's reproductive powers; his paintings were his children. Now, like many more male artists, Rothko compares the creative process to sexual intercourse, itself imagined as an overpowering of the female canvas by the male artist, who keeps score. So, in his own mind at least, Rothko's abstractions work in the service of old-fashioned, patriarchal values; and the balance between the urge to dominate and the wish for intimacy—one of the animating tensions of his work for the last ten years—has begun to break down.

• • •

When you're feeling bad, the thing to do is eat. Otherwise, you're going to feel terrible.

Mark Rothko

The gout has been nibbling at my feet for the best part of the time you have been gone.

Mark Rothko

In the summer of 1956 Rothko had been bedridden for about two months with what had been diagnosed as rheumatoid arthritis; but the pain in his joints was getting worse. Herbert Ferber suggested Rothko consult a young physician named Albert Grokest. But when Grokest came to Rothko's 54th Street flat, Rothko refused to give him a medical history, refused to let Grokest examine him, and declared that he did not trust doctors. "I said, 'Well, you're incapacitated by this, it's getting worse. Why not give me one whack at it?'" Rothko still refused to allow Grokest even to touch him, much less to take a blood sample, but as the two men talked, the doctor noticed a "lumpy whiteish mass" in Rothko's ears. Rothko agreed to an examination of his ears which led Grokest to conclude that Rothko did not have arthritis; he had gout, which is worsened by bedrest. Grokest prescribed colchine, and within a day or two Rothko's symptoms had quieted down.

Rothko would "bundle up in scarves and hats when the weather became the least bit cool and would worry long and loud about the slightest symptom of illness."[81] Physical health, like material success, could not last long, not in an imagination so given to foreboding. Grokest eventually learned, though he found Rothko very reluctant to talk about either his past or his feelings, that Rothko did not limit his mistrust to physicians. He distrusted lawyers, professors, dealers, curators, critics, collectors, viewers. Grokest commented: "I don't think he trusted anybody. And it went back to his mother and father starting with them. He had zero trust in his parents, and that led to this extended, protracted distrust in the outside world." Though he refused to provide specifics, Rothko did reveal that he was "very much upset" first by his father's departure from Dvinsk and then by his father's death soon after Rothko's arrival in Portland. Rothko's distrust isolated him in a world he experienced as unreliable and unstable, sometimes merely indifferent and sometimes actively cruel toward him.

Nor did Rothko, a hypochondriac, much trust his own body. In fact, he treated his body with the same combination of anxious solicitude and neglect with which he sometimes treated his paintings; and he didn't like either, paintings or body, being scrutinized by the unfeeling eyes of professionals. Rothko's ideal relation, in either case, merged concerned intimacy with mystifying distance. His body was his private property, to be *kept* private, protected, inviolate, as if his physical being constituted another situation, like the exhibition of his paintings or his critical reputation, that he could control by establishing very *firm* boundaries. Yet Rothko's ways of controlling, of insisting on autonomy, were often damaging and self-punishing.

In 1956, "he'd been drinking and living high and getting overweight," said Grokest, adding that Rothko found calories and alcohol "far more consoling than people. You know, he really didn't know how to confide." Like many others, Elaine de Kooning remembered Rothko as "a dignified man, very dignified always—dignified privately and dignified publicly." But, as she discovered visiting Rothko's studio while preparing an essay on him, "he was a secret drinker."

> You know, at parties you didn't feel that Rothko was drinking more than anyone else. He never got drunk, and his secret drinking also did not make him drunk. But he would start at 10:00 in the morning. I discovered this when I went to write the article about him, I think in 1956. He offered me a drink at 10:00 in the morning and I said, "No, I haven't had breakfast yet." And Rothko said that he took one drink an hour all day long.[82]

"I tipple," he told de Kooning.[83] Rothko didn't get drunk. He drank just enough to make life, and work, bearable.

But he was not so measured when it came to food. Many of his friends recall both his voracious appetite—he was particularly fond of Chinese food—and his messy table manners. Grokest, who occasionally had lunch with Rothko, said, "he'd get food all over the table and his face and his shirt," eating as if he were simply too famished to observe 'civilized' decorums of the table. Lofty and rabbinical, exacting in his work, Rothko dressed (still) in ill-fitting, secondhand clothes and he could eat with a sloppy abandon, refusing bourgeois niceties, as if his dignity somehow transcended his physical or social appearance.

Ignoring Grokest's advice about controlling his drinking and eating, Rothko "would continue alcohol, various amounts, and he would eat without discretion," with Grokest finally realizing he would simply have to tolerate his patient's "dependence." The boy who, craving calcium, had eaten the plaster from the walls of the family home in Dvinsk, who had grown up with an intense appetite, the young man who survived the Depression on bean soup, could now at fifty-three afford to eat well, and he did, especially the rich foods that someone with gout should avoid. In the late 1950s, Rothko grew portly. His body seemed unmanageable.

Rothko distrusted doctors. But he also admired, in Grokest's words, "skillful thinking and orderly solutions," so Grokest, a violinist who shared Rothko's love for music, remained Rothko's physician until the end of his life. Late in November 1956, Grokest first saw Rothko in his office, with subsequent visits in February and October 1957, May, November, and December 1958, May and June 1959. In addition to the gout, Rothko "was myopic and had tearing in his eyes," with "shadowy forms" and "persistent blurry vision in his left eye," and he often complained of "how exhausted he was," particularly in 1958–59 when he was "working very hard, very tired." His gout "was relatively easy to manage," except that "when he felt good, he would stop my preventive recommendations," i.e., diet and exercise. Nor was Rothko the kind of patient who regularly visited his doctor. "He would wait until everything was caving in, then he would call on me," Grokest said.

"Life around here proceeds very much as it was. Our child will be seven this winter and the presence of a child alters radically your whole life, which consists of mostly being home bound with regular intervals at the studio which is some ten blocks away," Rothko wrote to Clay Spohn in September of 1956.[84] The need to find playmates for Kate, the difficulty of finding rest with a young child around—these constitute minor refrains in Rothko's correspondence while on the road during the 1950s. Writing to Robert Motherwell of a weekend spent with Theodoros Stamos in East Hampton, Rothko praises his "wonderful hosts," but adds, "the problem however of being an excellent guest with a child is a tense one, and always diminishes the quality of rest and change that you hope for and that you so badly need."[85] The Rothko who had advised one of his Brooklyn College student-artists to marry because "you had to live a regular life to do your work," was now finding the regularity of domestic life constraining. It didn't take much to make him feel that way: as husband and father, Rothko was mainly absent.

Cecile Abish, the student who boarded with the Rothkos for six months in the early 1950s, remembered that "they were very warm, and they were very affectionate to each other and to me," inventing nicknames for her, leaving food for her. In the evenings "he would lie on the couch for hours saying nothing, just contemplating or looking at one of his pictures that was hanging up. Mell would be sitting there, sewing maybe. They'd be listening to music." Rothko loved to be horizontal. "Mell soothed his passage into mid-life, into the new work he was doing then," Abish said. "She was always the first to see the new work at his studio." Kate, at two-and-a-half, was "smart, talkative, *very* bright—a pleasure to be with." Yet, said Abish, Rothko had trouble "with ordinary things, the rituals of living." As a parent, he participated, but he gave the feeling that "he was perhaps just playing a role," that he was more engaged with the idea of being a father than the complex reality. "I think he was thinking about his work. And when he wasn't thinking about his work, he was thinking about how he could get his work out."

Occasionally, Kate Rothko recalled, she visited her father's studio and "he'd set me up in a corner with paints." Rothko in the 1930s had idealistic commitments to the teaching of children's art. Twenty years later, with his daughter, art was a way to occupy her so he could return to his own work. She remembered these visits as "very positive—except that I always had the impression that my father did not like to be watched while he painted. He wouldn't tell me that I couldn't watch him, but he'd always kind of shove me off into a corner and make sure that I had something to do myself, so he wouldn't feel like he was being watched." Mostly, he labored in contemplation of his work, rather than in the physical act of applying paint to canvas. "He spent a lot of time planning what he was going to paint, looking, just sitting and thinking before he started."

In his daughter's memory, Rothko's involvement with his work left little time for his family. He was at the studio all week, went to museums on weekend afternoons. "So even as I grew older I remember him only being at home on Sunday mornings. His devotion of time to me was to take me on Sunday morning to Horn and Hardart and then to Central Park." On those Sunday mornings, Rothko sometimes behaved awkwardly, at a loss about what it was one actually *did* with children. His way of teaching Kate to ride a bike was "to run behind the bike and scream. He was afraid I would fall over, maybe because he didn't know how to ride a bike himself." Kate's father "was definitely the disciplinarian. He had a certain tendency to fly off the handle. If anyone was going to spank me, it was going to be my father," even though "he was not there in any day-to-day sense."

As Kate grew up, "I spent less time with him. I don't even remember having those Sunday outings as I got older." They stopped when she was about eight. Communicating with her father also proved difficult. They never talked about "anything personal," and on loftier subjects he "had very strong feelings that young people needed to be educated; he sort of didn't have respect for their opinions," an attitude that, in his daughter's view, caused "a lot of conflict." "It wasn't that he wasn't loving—he was very loving and concerned with what I was going to do—but he was very difficult to have a conversation with about something, because it was based on the attitude that young people didn't know enough, and rather than sitting down, as some fathers might, and teaching me things so that I would know more, his attitude was I had to learn them first and then we could have a conversation."

Difficult to reach when he was around, Rothko, the family disciplinarian, held his daughter to the kind of high educational standards he himself had first met, then rejected, as a young man. "He was very concerned that I got good grades; there was always a lot of emphasis on that, but I don't think he was very involved. It was always from the outside and expecting me to do things but really knowing very little about what was going on." When Kate gained weight, her father grew very concerned, complaining to her and to his friends, getting exasperated when nothing changed, as if she were the only one in the family with a weight problem. "The father role is like King Lear," at home as in the art world. "No matter what we older ones have done the youth of today disregards us." Rothko himself was not the kind of artist who enjoyed discovering and promoting young talent; nor was he the kind of father who received gratification from teaching his young daughter about the world. More like King Lear than he knew, he disregarded youth, then complained that they disregarded *him*.

With friends and family, Rothko could be tender, warm, and affectionate, and his paintings of the early and mid-1950s envelop viewers with spiritual warmth and emotional sustenance. Yet their emotional generosity functions impersonally: Rothko opens himself to strangers, anonymous viewers whose "needs" and "spirit" make them willing to extend to his works the prolonged, patient, and *respectful* regard he sought. But in person, Rothko was too restless, too moody, too absorbed with his own needs, with getting his work done and with getting his work out, to feel anything but constrained and frustrated by daily domestic life. Removed and controlling, irritable and demanding, Rothko as a parent adopted the very style of authority which he himself most resented being subjected to and which, as paintings like the portrait of his mother and *The Rothkowitz Family* suggest, he associated with his own parents.

The Rothko who was secretive, who objected when Harold Diamond greeted him too familiarly, who didn't want Albert Grokest to examine his body, who impressed friends as dwelling behind a wall or fence or within a mist, could in life wish for and sometimes impose rather strict boundaries. And as Rothko's lament about the decline of "the father authority" suggests, his notions of family unity were at once old-world traditional and in keeping with 1950s American notions of sexual roles. "I find the young eighteen-year-old girls of America ravishing," Rothko told Alfred Jensen in the summer of 1956. "Such beautiful women drive me crazy."[86] He'd even married one. In the early, elated days of their courtship and marriage, the twenty-three-year-old Mell became the forty-two-year-old painter's "Venus." As Anne-Marie Levine observed, "Mark related to women as dolls—to be loved and hugged and played with and not taken seriously." Young, beautiful, and blond, women existed to be looked at; or, married, they existed to stay at home, so a husband could work, visit museums, hang out at drugstores or bars, all the while still feeling vaguely home-bound.

In the summer of 1956, eleven years after her marriage to Rothko, Mell was thirty-four, still attractive, a full-time housewife, the mother of a six-year-old child, attending to all those rituals of daily living which her husband, in his impatience, distraction, and clumsiness, could not manage. That summer, with Rothko abed for two months with misdiagnosed gout, Mell Rothko was taking care of a six-year-old and a fifty-three-year-old, both strong-willed and needy.

Chapter Twelve

Anna Chave has found, in several Rothko pictures of the mid-1940s, traces of the conventional pietà or entombment composition, in which the Virgin mourns her dead son, his body stretched out horizontally across her lap. Observing that these paintings in turn echo certain representations of the Madonna with the infant Christ on her lap, Chave argues for a mythic death/rebirth content in Rothko's pictures.[87] As Stanley Kunitz remarked, Rothko "needed comfort, encouragement, consolation all the time." The paintings Chave refers to were produced after Edith Sachar had divorced Rothko, while he was meeting, falling in love, and starting a new life with Mary Alice Beistle. All of these paintings show a tragic male victim whose sufferings have earned him a maternal solicitude not associated with the hardened, removed images of his mother (in her portrait) or of his first wife (in *Sculptress*). All through his life, Rothko's hypochondriacal fears, his real illnesses, his self-inflicted injuries, his reluctance to seek treatment or, if sought, to follow it—Rothko's bodily afflictions (along with his psychic ones) issued a dramatic call for consolation. The role of "Venus," once she had slowly swirled up from the primal waters, was to support, encourage, and minister to her distressed husband. Domesticated, she could offer some solace against the dangers of physical life, the strains of social life, and the bruisings of the marketplace.

Mell Rothko soothed her husband's passage into and through life. But with the birth of a child, her responsibilities had been enlarged and her attentions divided. On Sixth Avenue and later on 54th Street, the Rothkos lived in a neighborhood with museums, drugstores, bars, and restaurants, but not with many children or places for children to play. Partly for this reason and partly because Kate Rothko was "extremely shy" as a child, she spent most of her time with her mother. "My mother was constantly devoted to entertaining me. I was not the world's most self-entertaining child. She spent a great deal of time with me, doing arts and crafts projects with me and actually playing with me," until Kate started nursery school at the Dalton School when she was three. Had Kate Rothko been a slim, beautiful, quietly deferential—in short, a doll-like—child, Rothko might have been happier. Instead, Kate was bright, strong-willed, demanding, a girl (in one family friend's description) "longing for her father," and one much *like* her father. Rothko had a competitor for Mell's attention.

"Mark not only accepted the patriarchal role," said Dan Rice, "but kind of rejoiced in the responsibility of it. And Mell never made any indication that she felt insulted by it." Mell and Mark Rothko socialized mainly with his friends, many of whom found Mell "naive," "mundane," "a non-stop talker," "trivial," "boring." She sometimes found them boring too. At a dinner attended by the Rothkos, Harold Rosenberg and his wife May, and others, after long

The Dark Paintings

serious conversations about art, Mell suddenly announced, "I'm sick of all this talk, let's go dancing." The story was circulated by May Rosenberg to illustrate Mell's superficiality.[88] More and more, Mell Rothko was isolated, disregarded.

When she first visited Dr. Grokest, sometime during 1957, complaining of a numbness in her fingers that turned out to derive from spinal-disk pressure, she revealed that she was frequently drinking "heavily," and over the next few years she had two serious falls which Grokest attributed to her drinking. Eventually, she stopped seeing Grokest because "she didn't like my emphasis on her substance dependence." Painting, Rothko could take father, mother, and child and join "these three distinct elements in a family unity." But by 1957, the kind of family unity Rothko relied on to produce those paintings was creating tensions and divisions, isolation and neglect, withdrawal into alcohol.

In his writings on Nietzsche, Rothko spoke of the "tragic" "irreconcilability" between the "basic violence which lies at the bottom of human existence and the daily life which must deal with it." Art, allowing a ritualized acknowledgment of that violence, makes it bearable. Daily life, American middle-class daily life, Rothko's daily life, denying that violence, becomes pervaded by it.

13 The Seagram Murals

This building is our greatest piece of advertising and public relations. It establishes us once and for all, right around the world, as people who are solid and care about quality.

> Edgar Bronfman,
> president, Joseph E.
> Seagram and Sons

In July of 1954, Frank R. Schwengel, then president of Joseph E. Seagram, announced that the corporation would build a modern office building at 375 Park Avenue, between 52nd and 53rd streets. "Major depressions are a thing of the past," Schwengel confidently declared. "Despite great maladjustments due to war and continuing political uncertainties, business activity in the United States has remained near its highest levels, except for minor and temporary declines." To be designed by a California architectural firm, Pereira and Luckman, given a $15 million budget, the building would be completed in time for the House of Seagram's 100th anniversary in 1957.[1]

Samuel Bronfman, who had started, built, and still ran the business, sent a copy of the proposed plans for the Seagram Building to his daughter, Phyllis Bronfman Lambert, who was painting and sculpting in a Left Bank atelier in Paris. She responded with a sixteen-page critique of the design. When her father asked her to return to New York and conduct the search for a better architect, she agreed, asked Philip Johnson to assist her, and together they assembled a short list of architects, most of them practitioners of the modern "international style," including Walter Gropius, I. M. Pei, Frank Lloyd Wright, Le Corbusier, and Mies van der Rohe. Phyllis Lambert chose Mies and by November of 1954 he had been contracted to design the building, with Johnson to assist him. "Make this building the crowning glory of your life as well as mine," Sam Bronfman enjoined the sixty-eight-year-old Mies.[2]

Establishing himself as a solid and quality person amounted to an obsession for Bronfman, a Canadian who for many years lived in a turreted mansion he called Belvedere Palace, who named Seagram's Seven *Crown* and sold Chivas *Regal* Scotch, *Lord* Calvert, *Crown Royal* and *Royal* Salute, and whose fondest dream was to be knighted by the British Crown. Born in 1889 aboard the ship on which his parents were emigrating from southwestern Russia to southwestern Saskatchewan, Canada, Bronfman was an ambitious Russian-Jewish immigrant who sought assimilation not into the middle class but into the British aristocracy.

His impoverished family survived life on the Canadian prairies by selling first firewood and frozen whitefish, and then horses—until young Sam, observing that horse deals always closed with drinks in a local bar, pointed out to his father that the bar was probably making more profit than he was, and so "instead of selling horses, we should be selling drinks." They did, raising enough money to buy a hotel/bar, and then a series of such hotels, often along railroad lines in western Canada, where their income came mostly from the sale of alcohol and women. Eventually, Sam started manufacturing and distributing the liquor, but he did not really make his fortune until Prohibition passed in 1919 in the United States. As a smuggler and "business" associate of figures like Meyer Lansky and Charles "Lucky" Luciano, Bronfman ran businesses that had accumulated an estimated $800 million profit by the time Prohibition was repealed in 1934.[3] Sam Bronfman's social ambitions were financed by a career as a bootlegger.

Buying up the old Joseph E. Seagram and Sons firm in 1928 had provided Bronfman with a corporate name change and a respectable past, but he never did attain knighthood. To achieve his crowning glory, he gave Mies van der Rohe complete freedom and an ample budget—about $43 million—to design and erect his first building in New York and his largest structure so far. Combining a restrained, simple rectilinear design with expensive materials, Mies, the former director of the Bauhaus, proceeded to build the most elegant office tower constructed in New York during the postwar skyscraper boom and gave Sam Bronfman the quality facade—of tinted glass and bronze—that he had long been looking for.

"The entire building was designed to provide executive suites for prestige-conscious tenants."[4] Set ninety feet back from Park Avenue, the thirty-nine floor bronze and glass rectangular tower still enters across a spacious, block-wide plaza of pink marble, with symmetrically placed pools on either side (containing rows of softly jetting fountains), the borders of the plaza made of Tinian marble. Separated from the plaza only by a glass wall containing three entrances, the building's foyer has travertine walls, ceilings finished with gray glass mosaic placed in black cement, and granite floors. At the rear of the foyer, behind the elevator banks, a short travertine staircase leads up to a landing, from either side of which a short hallway opens into spacious, high-ceiling areas, the one on the south a bar and grill, the one on the north side the Four Seasons restaurant.

"The mural decorations are an integral part of the space," Phyllis Lambert wrote, "and I bought and commissioned prints, posters, tapestries, paintings, and sculpture for the offices of the Seagram company, the public areas and the restaurant."[5] Phyllis Lambert had known Rothko's work since 1954, purchasing his *Brown and Black in Reds* (1958) for the Seagram collection in 1958. Sometime in the spring of that year, Philip Johnson, who knew both Rothko and his work and who had been told by Alfred Barr that Rothko was "the greatest living painter for this kind of project," approached the artist about producing a series of paintings for the smaller of the two planned dining rooms at the Four Seasons. On June 6, 1958, Sidney Janis wrote a letter to Phyllis Lambert, confirming conversations between Johnson and Rothko in which they had agreed that the artist would provide "500 to 600 square feet of paintings" for $35,000. On June 25, the House of Seagram issued a purchase order for "Building Decorations" to be executed by Rothko for $30,000 to $35,000, with $7,000 furnished "at once for immediate expenses" and the rest to be paid in four annual installments. According to Philip Johnson, Rothko "was given *carte blanche* to design the wall decorations any way he chose."[6]

Not long after this agreement was reached, when Willem de Kooning met Rothko at the Museum of Modern Art, "he was very happy. I had never seen him so happy about his work. It was the time that he took on a commission for the Four Seasons. The reason why he was happy—he made a contract; he was very careful. He made a contract so he could get out of it."[7] Rothko's agreement stipulated that "if for any reason the paintings are to be offered for sale during the payment period, they are first to be offered to the artist at a cost no greater than the sum paid." Rothko had "made a contract so he could get out of it" because he felt ambivalent about the project from the start.

Rothko felt, at best, ambivalent about *any* exhibition of his work. "He was the kind of personality that approached all public displays with great and horrendous turmoil, great anxiety," said Dan Rice. "Before an opening, he would throw up, more like the behavior of an entertaining artist, an actor. He literally had to go to bed as an exhibition approached. He'd be physically ill. I don't mean, come down with a cold or something like that. He'd be throwing up, just completely torn apart, physically as well as mentally." Rothko had not just been posturing when he declared it a "risky" act to send a picture out into the world. During his seven years with Sidney Janis, Rothko agreed to just two one-man shows, in 1955 and 1958. As he would on the night of his 1961 Museum of Modern Art opening, Rothko feared that public display of his works would enable "everyone" to "see what a fraud I am."

"He liked one to treat him as a genius—a visit to his studio was an audience," Robert Motherwell writes, but "in his heart of hearts he also had a deep-rooted ambivalence, a persistent doubt, questioning his intimates as to whether he was a painter at all, that went far beyond an artist's usual doubts at work—an ultimate doubt, so that his patrons, whom he sometimes terrorized or overnight made pay more, were to him possibly out of their minds and he a charlatan conjurer of color."[8] Rothko also distrusted *himself*. Invented out of his "blackest despair" even as they veiled that despair, his paintings, Rothko worried, might be *mere* facades, beautiful decorations lacking human or spiritual sustenance.

"An artist needs a lot of time to be by himself; to contemplate and question his reasons for working," Rothko believed.[9] An artist eager to communicate, and an artist eager to be revered as a genius, Rothko questioned his reasons for working *and* for accommodating himself to the art market. Clyfford Still, Barnett Newman, and Ad Reinhardt were certainly helping that process along. In early 1948, referring disdainfully to "an organized attack on 'unintelligible art'" in the media, Rothko had written to Clay Spohn that "the attack is the greatest signal honor which we have received here in 10 years. To be intelligible to them is dishonorable and suspect."[10] Ten years after *that*, Rothko himself had become an intelligible and respected figure in some of these same media. Did he now judge himself as dishonorable and suspect? Partly a child of a poor Jewish immigrant family from the Portland ghetto, Rothko looked at his paintings as if he were one of his brothers and wondered if his works were just a sham. Partly a high-art purist, Rothko looked at his career as if he were Clyfford Still and wondered if he were corrupt.

In 1952, Rothko, like Clyfford Still, had refused to let his paintings travel to Europe with the rest of the "Fifteen Americans" show, apparently because he could not supervise their installation. That was also the year in which he declined to participate in the Whitney Annual. He refused that museum's invitation to show in its 1954 "The New Decade: 35 American Painters and Sculptors," and he rejected another Whitney invitation in April 1957.[11]

Two months after accepting the Seagram commission, Rothko learned that his *White and Greens in Blue* had been named the national winner in the Guggenheim Museum's International Awards competition, the painting having been submitted to the competition (without Rothko's knowledge) by Sidney Janis. Stating that he looked forward "to the time when honors can be bestowed, simply, for the meaning of a man's life work—without enticing pictures into the competitive arena," Rothko refused the award and returned the museum's $1,000 check.[12] Of course, as soon as Rothko's pictures left his studio and even before, they entered the competitive arena. Sometimes Rothko's standards in negotiating his way around that arena were soft-edged, at others hard-edged. If financial success and becoming a "name" made Rothko feel corrupt, they also gave him the power to refuse and thereby maintain some sense of moral purity.

The Seagram Murals

Why did Rothko, so anguished about showing his work, so fearful it would be reduced to decoration, and so exacting about where and how to exhibit it, so imbued with "human foreboding and tragic intuition," accept the Four Seasons commission?

One difficulty in answering that question arises from the differing accounts of what Rothko was told about the use of the room he was to decorate (fig. 39). Both Philip Johnson and Phyllis Lambert state that, in Johnson's words, "Rothko knew perfectly well it would be an expensive restaurant."[13] Both of them also remember visiting the site with Rothko, as the restaurant was being built, and discussing the project with him. Lambert specifically recalled discussing that "the paintings would be high above the heads of the diners." On the other hand, Rothko's assistant, Dan Rice, stated that Rothko was originally told that the larger of the two rooms on the north side of the Seagram Building would be an employee cafeteria and the smaller one (where Rothko's paintings would hang) a boardroom. Raised by a short stairway from the larger room and separated from it by a wooden wall with a wide door and four wide "windows" in it, Rothko's room, Rice said, "could be seen virtually as a proscenium, or at least one long wall [the far wall] could be seen through the open doors from the cafeteria where the workers of the building ate."[14] Dore Ashton similarly recollects that Rothko's paintings were "to have been seen from an adjoining employee's dining room through large doors."[15]

Dore Ashton was a close friend of Rothko's and Dan Rice worked with him on the project day-to-day. They are very likely remembering what Rothko told them, and perhaps what he had been told. The common element in their two accounts—the visibility of Rothko's paintings from an employees' dining room—does sound like an arrangement with appeal to Rothko's social conscience. "It pleased him greatly that the workers in the building would be looking at one wall of his creation," said Rice. Yet this scheme only raises a new set of questions. It places the "workers" roughly in the position of poor children pressing their noses to the ballroom window to watch the aristocrats inside enjoying themselves. But of course the "workers" in the Seagram Building—"designed to provide executive suites for prestige-conscious tenants"—were hardly proletarians; they were the kind of people who would eat at a restaurant like, well, the Four Seasons. And setting aside the issue of whether the diners in the larger room were to be working people, rich people, or just plain people, how suitable was any dining room (or boardroom) as a place to view Rothko's paintings?

Calling large museums "mausoleums," imagining how he would like his works shown, Rothko once said that "it would be good if little places could be set up all over the country, like a little chapel where the traveler, or wanderer[,] could come for an hour to meditate on a single painting hung in a small room, and by itself." He spoke to Phyllis Lambert "of his ideal as a kind of wayside chapel, not one in the city where you could just drop in, but more out of the way, a *destination,* outside the city." While traveling in England the summer of 1959, Rothko made two visits to an unused chapel at Lelant, St. Ives, and considered buying it as a kind of private museum.[16] The smaller room at the Seagram Building was not all that small, hardly out-of-the-way, and certainly no chapel. It was a dining room where, as a man of "ravenous appetite" would have known, people gathered not for solitary contemplation but to fill their bodies, to impress themselves and others, and to talk.

When, on his first night out sailing from New York to Naples in June 1959, Rothko wandered into the tourist-class bar looking for someone to talk with, he found John Fischer, quickly determined that Fischer was a writer with no connections to the art world, and then opened the conversation by revealing "that he had been commissioned to paint a series of large canvases for the walls of the most exclusive room in a very expensive restaurant in the Seagram building—'a place where the richest bastards in New York will come to feed and show off'." "I accepted this assignment with strictly malicious intentions," Rothko declared. "I hope to ruin the appetite of every son of a bitch who ever eats in that room," and he hoped to do so with paintings that would make the diners "feel that they are trapped in a room where all the doors and windows are bricked up, so that all they can do is butt their heads forever against the wall."[17]

By this time Rothko knew perfectly well where, for whom, and why he was painting. Whatever he had originally been told (or thought he'd been told) had left him doubtful from the start. He resolved the conflict by thinking of his motives as aggressive, imagining his paintings as subversive presences able to get inside the rich and upset *their* digestive tracts. Rather than appropriating or corrupting him, the Seagram commission would then reconfirm his sense of himself as an alien artist producing works that discomforted comfortable people. Some of Rothko's friends, preferring to think of him as a purely contemplative painter, have questioned the reliability of Fischer's memoir of Rothko on the grounds that Rothko never mentioned his malice to them, and that he did not know Fischer all that well.[18] Rothko's dramatic statements to Fischer may have been aimed at impressing a new acquaintance, but the shipboard conversation was not the first time Rothko mentioned anger as a force behind his engagement with the project. In July 1958, just a few weeks after agreeing to do the murals, Rothko had written to Robert Motherwell, "I finally did accept the commission," sounding as if he had deliberated over the decision for some time and still felt uneasy about it. "What I like about the commission," he continued, "is that it has steamed up enough anger in me to imbue the pictures with unbearable bite, I hope."[19] As he began the project, Rothko festered with indignation.

Many forces pulled him toward accepting it. One was the possibility of equalling or even exceeding projects by the two early twentieth-century painters he most respected. Rothko's talk of wayside chapels suggests his awareness of Matisse's work (1948–50), designing murals, stained-glass windows, and liturgical vestments for a small Dominican chapel in Vence, France. Rothko also knew and admired a 38½-foot-long mural executed by Joan Miró (1947) for the penthouse restaurant in the then new and modern Terrace Plaza Hotel in Cincinnati.[20] Matisse had worked with a sacred space, Miró with a commercial one. Rothko's aggression would transform a commercial into a contemplative space.

Three of Rothko's close friends had earlier been involved in creating art for a public space—Herbert Ferber, Adolph Gottlieb, and Robert Motherwell having been asked in 1951 to produce works for the B'nai Israel Synagogue in Millburn, New Jersey. Rothko had not approved. "Mark used to be caustic about those of us who took commissions, did things for synagogues," Gottlieb said. "One day at a party at Bernard Reis's house, he said he'd never do a synagogue, if he did anything it would be for a Catholic church. So I said, 'So Mark, why are you beating your breast?'"[21] Claiming to be "above" accepting a commission from a synagogue, Rothko still reveals the jealous rivalry that Gottlieb's rejoinder exposes.

But his response is not all sour grapes. He wished to be thought of as a religious but not as a specifically Jewish painter; that ruled out synagogues. Catholic churches were safe, since no one was likely to accuse him of being a Catholic painter, but no Catholic offers were forthcoming, at least not until John and Dominique de Menil came along with their Houston chapel a few years later. Accepting a commission to decorate a fashionable, expensive restaurant exposed Rothko to the caustic judgments of his friends, his enemies, his own conscience. Would Clyfford Still have accepted such an offer? Ferber, Gottlieb, and Motherwell had produced *individual* works to decorate a synagogue. By producing an ensemble of paintings, Rothko would not be embellishing a pre-existing space; he would be using individual paintings to go beyond painting, to *create* a space: "I have made a place."

"As soon as the public has caught up with a painter," Rothko said, "it's time for him to take another direction."[22] With the Seagram commission, Rothko would be working for the first time with a *public* space and for a *particular* space. Rothko's long, narrow dining room (approximately 55' × 26' × 15') was not the kind of small, confined space that, hitherto, he preferred (fig. 39).[23] Its interior design, moreover, posed special challenges. The short north wall, of glass, would admit considerable natural light; the window, moreover, would have a "curtain" of metallic chains, looped from mullion to mullion, whose hypnotically rippling movements (caused by movement of the air) would be distracting. The south wall, at its east corner, would contain a door used by waiters.[24] The long east wall, about fifteen feet high, would have plenty of open area for hanging paintings, but the opposite wall, of French walnut, would not. That wall would be broken by a box-shaped doorway that projected into the room—and by a series of four large openings looking out over the main dining room.[25] On this wall, paintings could only be hung very high, in the seven feet remaining above the openings and doorway.[26]

Rothko had always wanted his single paintings hung low, so they would confront and surround a viewer. But throughout the Four Seasons room, his murals would have to hang above the diners' heads, or they would not be seen. Later talking about installing these works at the Whitechapel Gallery in London, he said that they "were painted at a height of 4'6" above the floor. If it is not possible to raise them to that extent, any raising above three feet would contribute to their advantage and original effect."[27] Design features of the specific space he was asked to decorate created pressures which would force Rothko to push his art in a new direction.

"I believe he actually felt that he had gone as far as he could in painting until the proposal for the Seagram Building murals was presented to him," Dan Rice said. "It absolutely supplied him with a whole new dimension." In the past, Rothko had carefully hung one painting in relation to another. He had assembled the nine paintings in his Art Institute of Chicago exhibit as a group, but, as de Kooning pointed out, "this was the first time he was making one painting in relation to another painting." The new project would extend his concern to control the situation of viewing, return him to his preoccupation with the tensions between architectural space and human presence in many of his paintings of the 1930s, and allow him to advance his notion of a live unity into a whole new dimension. No wonder the commission, in Phyllis Lambert's word, "intrigued" him, tempting him to ignore his forebodings about the ambience of the restaurant.[28] Besides, an opportunity to create such an environment might never arise again. Once he started work, in the late summer or early fall of 1958, Rothko, said Rice, "seized on the project with enthusiasm as though it were a release."

• • •

One must go further, one must go further.

Kierkegaard, *Fear and Trembling*

When Rothko finally accepted the Seagram commission, he had already left New York City, to spend the summer in a small house he and his wife had just purchased at 250 Bradford Street, Provincetown, Massachusetts. "As for ourselves here, we really like our little house, and just yesterday we called a halt to all improvements for the present season," Rothko wrote to Motherwell. "Fortunately or otherwise, the weather has been so miserable that the [unintelligible word] labor in setting up a house has not caused a sense of having squandered a summer." At fifty-eight, Marcus Rothkowitz had become a property owner.[29]

Since his marriage to Mell, Rothko had mainly spent summer vacations in East Hampton and in Provincetown, the Avery-Gottlieb-Newman-Rothko trips having gradually ceased. As a boy, Rothko had enjoyed climbing the Portland hills to look out over the city and the Willamette Valley. As a young man, he had camped in the Portland hills and in the Adirondack mountains, sketching, making watercolors. He liked to swim, spent the summer months at Croton Falls, New York, and Gloucester, Massachusetts, where he sketched, produced watercolors. In the early 1930s, Rothko did watercolor beach scenes. A claustrophobic who wrote eloquently of "breathing and stretching one's arms again" might well be drawn to the open air, the panoramic views from the Portland hills, the flat, expansive vistas along east coast beaches. But as Joseph Liss had observed, "Rothko wasn't much of a nature man, no Thoreau he."

Did Rothko buy a house on Cape Cod so he could get away from the city, relax, and enjoy himself gardening, swimming, boating, sunbathing, walking along the ocean, idling on the beach, playing with his daughter in the sand? Rothko did go for an occasional swim, but he no longer took hikes and couldn't sail a boat. On vacations, Kate Rothko said, "he didn't do anything except go to the beach. And my father didn't like the beach either. He'd go dressed to the beach; he sunburned very badly. He didn't like outdoor activities at all." Esther Gottlieb remembered sitting on a beach with Rothko—a line of insects approached, and Rothko left for the day. Rothko's physical pleasures—eating, smoking, drinking—were consoling rather than invigorating, and natural objects engaged him no more than material or mechanical ones did. Telling Clay Spohn that he had never met the surrealist painter Gordon Onslow Ford, Rothko added that he did know "a pal of his, [Wolfgang] Paalen; who seems to have joined him in [an] excavating, shoveling, back to the land movement, back to everything including nature. Sum total: Rot."[30]

It wasn't just that Rothko would proudly refuse to climb a mountain or mount a horse on a visit to Colorado. "He didn't want to be associated with nature," Stanley Kunitz said. "In fact, one of his statements that shocked me most was saying that he really hated nature, that he felt uncomfortable in the natural world." When Rothko bought his house on East 95th Street, he treated the backyard garden by ignoring it, a little like the Rothko ready to abandon his car when it broke down near Boulder. One day Rothko asked Kunitz, a gardener, for some ideas for improving the garden and "I suggested a few plants that I thought would brighten up that dreary garden which was in any case ruined because their dog had the run of it." But Rothko answered, "Oh, no, I can't stand flowers. No flowers. No flowers. I just want anything that will grow tall and maybe provide some shade, but I don't really want it to be like a jungle of any kind."[31] A situation he could easily imagine getting out of control, the natural order (even in the domesticated form of a backyard garden) made Rothko feel uncomfortable, but not creatively uncomfortable. He preferred city culture, harsh urban pressures, the unfriendliness of *society,* which pushed him into himself, into a small, sealed-off space, like his studio, which he could, with his paintings, saturate with his own presence. Like his body, nature constituted the kind of limiting and given reality he was struggling to pulverize, go beyond, transcend.

Thinking Provincetown too noisy and crowded a place to vacation, Katharine Kuh suggested an alternative "where they could relax in authentic country surroundings, but Mark was horrified at the idea. He didn't want to commune with nature. He needed people. He didn't want to sit with a book under a tree. He was a city person." Like East Hampton, Provincetown was a summer place for city people, especially creative people, many of whom Rothko knew and could talk and gossip with, as if he had never left Sixth Avenue. "I think my father, if he had a choice, would not have left the city ever," Kate Rothko recalled. "He really didn't enjoy summer vacation very much."

Having converted the second floor of the Bradford Street house into a studio, Rothko worked there or he prowled the town, walking "up and down Commercial Street," said Katharine Kuh, "looking for an occasional acquaintance to chat with, to gossip with." "As you must know, Provincetown is agog with [the] Museum and Art Fair?" Rothko wrote Motherwell. "Do you know that none of this reaches our end of town? In that sense your instinct for this part of town was uncanny." He sought quiet—until he found it; then he wanted some company. "And yet there is the street life, and a ten minute walk brings you face to face with Corbett, or Pace, or Botkin, and when you need a face, what matters whose?"—though Rothko quickly backs away from the blunt truth behind his joke, by adding: "I don't quite mean that."[32]

Later in this letter Rothko describes his life in Provincetown as an "exile." In fact, he had been "shuttling back and forth to New York," looking for a space in which to work on the Seagram project. Having moved his studio from a loft on West 53rd to one on West 61st sometime in 1956, Rothko stayed there until the spring of 1958, when the building was demolished.[33] In July 1958, Rothko rented a large room, approximately 46' × 32' × 23', in a former YMCA building at 222 Bowery, and traveled back to the city "to start shaping it up."[34] He had painted in the living room of his Sixth Avenue walk-up; he had painted in two mid-town lofts; now Rothko was painting in what had been the YMCA's gymnasium. About ten feet out from the room's west wall, he built an eighteen-foot high plasterboard partition, behind which he stored paintings. All of the walls were brick, so in order to work on and view paintings, he continued the plasterboard along the south and back up the east wall until, near its north end, that wall is broken by the entrance and a sink. The partition having reduced the width of the room to about twenty-two feet, Rothko then constructed a movable wooden "fourth" (north) wall and installed a pulley system which allowed him to adjust the heights of his paintings. The plasterboard partition blocked the light from four windows along the west wall and from the lower halves of two windows in the south wall, leaving only two small, high north-wall windows to admit natural light, and very little of that. By all accounts, Rothko kept the room "very very dark" when exhibiting work to friends.[35] Working with a space about nine feet shorter, two feet wider, and eight feet higher than the small dining room at the Four Seasons, Rothko began to paint murals for the luxurious restaurant in an oppressive, dimly lit Bowery gymnasium.[36]

When he returned from Provincetown to New York, Rothko began work on the project. By the time he stopped, he had produced what he later described as "three sets of panels," about forty mural-size canvases, along with a number of individual works, which he turned to when stymied in his progress on the murals.[37] Having started by falling off a ladder and banging up his neck while preparing the studio, Rothko worked intensely for the next several months, complaining to Dr. Grokest during this time of "how exhausted he was, working very hard, very tired."

When Rothko reached the studio, usually by cab between 8:30 and 9:00 A.M. every morning, he didn't look much like a banker, or like one of the "bums" on the Bowery. He dressed in the drab, cheap, conservative clothes that a lower-middle-class accountant, not a master colorist, might wear, though Rothko added a few bohemian flourishes—a large-brimmed, floppy hat and, during cold weather, a long, moth-eaten overcoat that came down to his ankles. Once at the studio, Dan Rice said, "Mark would change into his painting clothes which pretty well stood by themselves they were so encrusted with glue and paint."

Chapter Thirteen

Hired during the summer of 1958, Dan Rice had helped Rothko to renovate the studio. Then he built wooden stretchers and stretched canvas which Rothko had bought from a tent and awning shop. Rice also assisted Rothko in applying the ground color, a mixture of rabbit-skin glue and colored pigment. "Glue would just cool too fast on a big painting," said Rice, "so often he would work on a ladder and I would work underneath until I was dripping with this stuff," then they would trade places and Rothko would be covered with the glue. After the ground, all layers were applied by Rothko himself, working rapidly, using big five-inch housepainter's brushes. Then the often restless Rothko "would sit and consider the painting for long long periods of time, sometimes hours, sometimes days." Messy in appearance, clumsy in his movements, Rothko was "extraordinarily meticulous over his work," said Rice. "I've never seen anyone agonize quite as much over the placement of a painting." Once a painting was finished, Rothko struggled to determine its place in the ensemble, its place on the wall. In particular, he constantly adjusted the height, considering, reconsidering, asking Rice for his opinion. He was "very unsure" of the height, Rice recalled.[38]

Previously Rothko, while producing works as large as 9½′ × 8½′, had insisted that he "painted in a scale of normal living." When showing a group of his works in a museum or gallery, he sought to transform the institutional into a human space, crowding the walls with his large paintings, hanging them low, surrounding the onlooker, as if intimacy needed to be forced on people. On the Seagram project, he was working with a large, impersonal and rather cold commercial dining room where his paintings would be hung at least 4½ feet high and his viewers would be seated. Whatever the ambience of the restaurant, whatever the social status of the diners, the scale was decidedly not that of normal living and Rothko's paintings could no longer confront the viewer as enveloping "presences." As Michael Compton points out, "they would be rather high up, be seen from a variety of angles and would be scanned as a group by eyes moving predominantly in a horizontal plane, that is, they would be seen as architecture."[39]

At first, Rothko responded to this challenge by producing horizontal panels—say, 8½′ × 15′—which contained his characteristic horizontal bands of color. But this first set, he told Fischer, "didn't turn out right, so I sold the panels separately as individual paintings."[40] Then, Rothko made a simple, but generative, move: he "turned the paintings on their side," Rice related. If a work like *Red, Brown and Black* (1958) (color plate 16), for example, is placed on its side, the brown and black rectangles resemble vertical columns, while the red area recedes, as if it were an opening between them. While still predominantly rectangular, this new imagery, suggesting windows, doors, portals, was simple, classical, architectural. Rothko had moved his work into a whole new dimension.

. . .

Accepting the Seagram commission had also advanced Rothko's position as perhaps the major living artist of his generation.

At the time he decided to accept it, ten of the eleven new paintings Rothko had exhibited at Sidney Janis in January-February, 1958, were being shown in the United States Pavilion at the XXIX Venice Biennale, organized by the International Council of the Museum of Modern Art.[41] Rothko was one of just two American painters included. While he worked on the Seagram murals in 1958–59, five of his works were traveling through eight European countries in "The New American Painting," organized by Dorothy Miller for the International Council of the Museum of Modern Art "at the request of European institutions for a show devoted specifically to Abstract Expressionism in America."[42] The Modern's international council had been founded "to let it be known especially in Europe that America was not the cultural backwater that the Russians during that tense period called 'the cold war' were trying to demonstrate that it was," so that by 1959, the "Irascibles" of 1950 were being appropriated as a kind of "official" art, emblematizing individual freedom in the cultural politics of the Cold War.[43]

In New York, Rothko's work was receiving more extensive treatment from more influential critics, one of those being Clement Greenberg, whose influential essay "'American-Type' Painting" appeared in *Partisan Review* in the spring of 1955.[44]

Greenberg had met Rothko sometime in the fall of 1943 when he and a friend had a drink with Rothko at the Murray Hill Hotel. Then thirty-four, Greenberg, having recently served three years as an editor of *Partisan Review,* was now the regular art-critic for *The Nation,* already propounding his judgments in a dogmatic, this-brooks-no-argument style. "We talked," Greenberg recalled, "and I found Rothko sympathetic, but I also found him very square. Later on he got pompous. He always stayed a little square."[45] Rothko's ideas about painting struck Greenberg as "banal," his conversation merely fashioned out of "the commonplaces of art talk." In the late 1940s, when Greenberg was best known for his advocacy of Jackson Pollock, he told Rothko that he liked his most recent show less than the one before it. "He blew up at me. I couldn't get angry at him in return, but I got impatient with him. I hate to use the word hysterical, but. . . ." Many years later, Greenberg summed up Rothko's career:

Chapter Thirteen

"Mark was a great painter in '49 and I think until '55. After '55, he lost his stuff."

In print Greenberg mostly ignored Rothko, until 1955, when "'American-Type' Painting" appeared, just as Rothko was losing his stuff. Greenberg's essay asserted the "centrality" and "resonance" of the Abstract Expressionists, and the essay reveals—importantly, after revisionist narratives like Serge Guilbaut's *How New York Stole the Idea of Modern Art*—how contested an issue this claim remained as late as 1955. "When I say, in addition, that such a galaxy of strong and original talents has not been seen in painting since the days of Cubism," Greenberg concludes, "I shall be accused of chauvinist exaggeration, not to speak of the lack of a sense of proportion." Nevertheless, Greenberg stands his ground, boldly claiming canonical status for his contemporary Americans.[46]

By this time, however, Greenberg's judgments were proceeding from a theory, explicitly set forth at the beginning of "'American-Type' Painting," which conceived the history of modern art as a "process of self-purification," a discarding of "*expendable* conventions"—e.g., figuration—in a quest to reduce painting "to its viable essence."[47] Greenberg could admire the Abstract Expressionists only by appropriating them to this formalist history, an account of their work which has been accepted by more recent leftist critics, who have turned it against the artists.

"The most radical of all the phenomena of 'abstract expressionism'—and the most revolutionary move in painting since Mondrian," Greenberg writes, "consists precisely in an effort to repudiate value contrast as the basis of pictorial design." Pollock had grasped this solution—"he had literally pulverized value contrasts in a vaporous dust of interfused lights and darks in which every suggestion of a sculptural effect was obliterated"—but then Pollock had retreated.[48] Now Greenberg was backing the three men he later nicknamed "the triumvirate" as the most revolutionary move in town.[49] "A new kind of flatness, one that breathes and pulsates, is the product of the darkened, value-muffling warmth of color in the paintings of Newman, Rothko, and Still," he wrote. "Broken by relatively few incidents of drawing or design, their surfaces exhale color with an enveloping effect that is enhanced by size itself. One reacts to an environment as much as to a picture hung on the wall."[50] In painting's search for its pure essence, the triumvirate, though they no longer were speaking to each other, had devised the first major advance since cubism.

Had Rothko lived in dismal flats and eaten bean soup in the 1930s in order to find value contrast an expendable element of pictorial design? Rothko spoke of the struggle to go "beyond painting." Greenberg dwelled on formal solutions, aesthetic objects, the priority of the artistic medium. Greenberg, moreover, clearly identified Clyfford Still as the apex of this color-field triangle and its inventor—news of priority that neither Rothko nor Newman would have been happy to hear.[51] That Rothko's art appears "to be indebted as much to Newman as to Still (Rothko has, in effect, turned the former's vertical line sideways) detracts absolutely nothing from its independence, uniqueness or perfection."[52] So goes the first of several sentences in which Greenberg describes those attributes which fail to detract from Rothko's uniqueness—a series of utterances with which Greenberg first slaps Rothko sharply across the left cheek then, mafioso-style, gently pats him on the right. In 1955, as in 1943, Greenberg was patronizing Rothko.

"I hate and distrust all art historians, experts and critics," Rothko told John Fischer. "They are a bunch of parasites feeding on the body of art. Their work is not only useless, it is misleading. They can say nothing worth listening to about art or the artist, aside from personal gossip—which I grant you can sometimes be interesting."[53] Two critics he especially despised were Emily Genauer of the *New York Herald Tribune* and Harold Rosenberg, whom Rothko called "pompous."[54] "Rosenberg keeps trying to interpret things he can't understand and which can't be interpreted. A painting doesn't need anybody to explain what it is about. If it is any good, it speaks for itself, and a critic who tries to add to that statement is presumptuous."[55] By this account, all critics usurp artists; but Rothko had particular reason to abhor Rosenberg.

"At a certain moment the canvas began to appear to one American painter after another as an arena in which to act—rather than as a space in which to reproduce, re-design, analyze or 'express' an object, actual or imagined. What was to go on the canvas was not a picture but an event," Rosenberg had proclaimed in "The American Action Painters," published in *Art News* in late 1952.[56] Imagining the blank canvas as an empty stage whereon the artist played out the drama of his continual self-creation, Rosenberg spoke not the language of modern formalism but of contemporary French existentialism. After many attempts by critics and dealers to *name* the new American painting, Rosenberg succeeded in inventing a term ("Action Painting"), in propounding a theory (somewhat obscurely), proposing a mythic generational biography (with each artist reborn after a grand crisis), and (with a swipe at Clement Greenberg) calling for a new kind of art criticism that would definitely *not* be formalist. Rosenberg coyly named no artists, but his essay was widely understood as generalizing from the practice of the gestural painters, particularly as their creative process had been represented in the Hans Namuth photographs of Jackson Pollock in *Life* magazine.

"The American Action Painters" conveys, say, the energy and surprise of Pollock's drip paintings, but it does so only by locating meaning in an "event" (the process of creation) which is irrecoverable and from which Rosenberg has eliminated all reflection—his way of patronizing painters. So to name this generation of artists Rosenberg must first reduce the gestural act to pure spontaneity, then he must banish the more obviously deliberate color-field painters. "The most comfortable intercourse with the void is mysticism," he warns. Mysticism relates to authentic risk-taking self-discovery as its hollow, facile, and commercially viable parody, which avoids an open-ended, personal struggle by leaning on the Absolute. "The result," says Rosenberg, "is an apocalyptic wallpaper."[57] With this phrase, Rosenberg may have been condemning Pollock's recent work, but his acerbic descriptions more often suggest he has Still, Newman, or Rothko in mind.[58] "The tremors produced by a few expanses of tone or by the juxtaposition of colors and shapes purposely brought to the verge of bad taste in the manner of Park Avenue shop windows are sufficient cataclysms in many of these happy overthrows of Art," he writes. Earlier in the essay Rosenberg had ironically alluded to "symphonies in blue and red rectangles."[59]

When "Action Painters" appeared, it had provoked "numerous and inflammatory discussions and debates" in the New York art world.[60] Clement Greenberg was urged to respond to an essay that clearly sought to usurp his position as the reigning New York art critic, but he declined. His "'American-Type' Painting," assigning prominence to the color-field rather than to the gestural painters, reversed Rosenberg's preference and made a delayed rejoinder. Still, during the 1950s and well beyond, Rosenberg's theory shaped much of the talk about Abstract Expressionism, including the most important essay written about Rothko during the 1950s, Elaine de Kooning's "Two Americans in Action: Franz Kline and Mark Rothko," published in the *Art News Annual* for 1958.[61]

Elaine de Kooning, painter, regular contributor to *Art News,* wife of Willem de Kooning, was no parasite on the body of art. When she first saw Rothko's floating abstractions at Betty Parsons in the early 1950s, "I was absolutely captured by the magic of the presence of the colors—the fact that they did not inhabit shapes." Rather, "they inhabited areas and the areas were enthralling." She wrote a letter to Rothko explaining her response, and "from the day of that letter forth, we were fast friends." They would meet at openings, or at parties given by Jeanne Reynal or Yvonne Thomas. Elaine de Kooning liked Rothko's "dry little wisecracks," adding that "he had an atmosphere of sensuality that I found very appealing." "He was always very flirtatious with me. And his relation to certain women was one of . . . you know, the kind of flirtation that's not intended to lead anywhere, but up in the air is that sense of wouldn't it have been wonderful."[62]

In 1957, as de Kooning was preparing her essay on Rothko and Franz

Kline, she talked with Rothko in his West 61st Street studio, where he was doing "these huge paintings in what I considered a tiny studio." She said, "Mark, I can't understand how you can work in such a small space," and he replied, "I'm very nearsighted."[63] Rothko didn't paint with his glasses off; but his myopia—particularly since it was probably some time before his family discovered, when he was a boy, that he needed glasses—may have been one reason for his blurred forms and one reason he felt most comfortable working in close physical proximity to his immense, enfolding canvases.

Rothko also told de Kooning that "he was lonely. He enjoyed my coming there and he enjoyed our discussions. He enjoyed talking about art from 10:00 in the morning until 5:00 in the afternoon, which is what we did." "He was very articulate. He spoke slowly and would give anything he said a great deal of thought and spoke in well-rounded sentences." She sensed that formulating his thoughts was important to Rothko in a way that it wasn't to her husband or Franz Kline, and that Rothko took pleasure in the process of thought.[64] Yet, as in his correspondence with Katharine Kuh, Rothko couldn't resist undermining their whole conversation. "Silence is so accurate," he declared.[65] Rothko also fantasized "an ideal life" in which he and Mell and Elaine and Bill de Kooning and perhaps another couple would go off to some "isolated" place, "everyone working on his own, but then have each other to talk to at night"—a communal life modeled on the Avery/Gottlieb/ Rothkowitz vacations of the 1930s.[66]

After completing her essay, Elaine de Kooning showed it to Rothko, who commented, "I like the part about Franz very much, but the part about me I don't agree with." She asked what he objected to and he said, "All of it." Though the article was due the following morning, de Kooning tore it up. After she and Rothko talked for two hours at her studio, he asked if he could wait while she rewrote the piece. She warned him she'd be up all night writing; he stayed anyway. She said, "Well, it's the first time I've ever had anyone sit for an article." He said, "Be my guest." Rothko sat, went out for pastrami sandwiches, read some of her books. As de Kooning finished a page, she passed it to Rothko, he questioned something, they debated it, she would make a change. Rothko asked her, for example, to remove a sentence about Milton Avery's influence on him. Finally, Rothko approved the new essay. "Mark really wanted not only to control his paintings," de Kooning recalled, "but he wanted to control what was said about his paintings."[67]

Rothko and Elaine de Kooning did have their differences about his work. She did not see the "sense of foreboding" he located in the brighter works of the early and mid-1950s. "I felt they were very much involved with comfort and luxury and they looked very natural in Jeanne Reynal's luxurious house, and people looked very well against them. They made a wonderful graceful decor, all of which was anathema to Rothko."[68] In her essay de Kooning tactfully transforms this point about the social import of his paintings into one about their metaphysical power: "His canvases have a curious way of transforming the people standing before them. Their skin, hair, eyes, clothes, size, gesture assume a dreamlike clarity and glow. It is as though the painting emptied the space before it, creating a vacuum in which everything three-dimensional takes on an absolute or ideal existence." Indeed, for much of the essay, her ideas and language, supplemented by quotes from Rothko's writings and conversation, place the writer (as Rothko liked to place a viewer) *close* to her subject.

But not *too* close, as de Kooning herself acutely observed. Rothko has "an excruciating sense of privacy about his work. This sense of privacy, in a profound way, actually reaches into the painting itself. It is no accident that a painting by Rothko is a *facade,* almost as though his art were trying to hide behind itself." Breadth of size and scale, she saw, resulted "from the artist's closeness to his painting—which he regards as a private act for a private view; and they are, at the same time, the means to ensure privacy." Elaine de Kooning also perceived the element of violence in Rothko's work. "These large images are always aggressive: they have to be to enter life. They do not stay on the wall. They invade human affairs," as if, while protecting the privacy of the artist, they violated the privacy of the viewer. "The tension of Rothko's work lies in its ominous, pervasive light—that of the sky before a hurricane. In his imperceptible shifts from one pure color to another, there is a sense of atmospheric pressure. His edgeless shapes loom oppressively in an incandescent void, waiting, breathing, expanding, approaching, threatening," Elaine de Kooning wrote, as if she *had* felt the foreboding in Rothko's work.

Yet, if he did read and accept the final version of her essay, Rothko, proving very hard to please, quickly reversed himself and publicly repudiated it. As her title, "Two Americans in Action," reveals, Elaine de Kooning turned to Harold Rosenberg for an account of contemporary painting that would enable her to link Kline and Rothko, drawing, paraphrasing, quoting from Rosenberg (a close friend of both de Koonings), though not following his dismissal of the "mystical" wing of Abstract Expressionism. "Painting for Americans is no longer the exercise of a talent, the practice of a craft or the satisfaction of a private inclination," she wrote. "It is now a bid for an individual identity."

Angered by de Kooning's attempt to fix him with Rosenberg's term, or with *any* term, Rothko dispatched a letter to the editor of *Art News:* "I reject that aspect of the article which classifies my work as 'Action Painting.' An artist herself, the author must know that to classify is to embalm. Real identity is incompatible with schools and categories, except by mutilation." Real identity is elusive, hidden—unidentifiable—and so disturbing enough to provoke embalming operations and violent assaults. "To allude to my work as Action Painting borders on the fantastic. No matter what modifications and adjustments are made to the meaning of the word action, Action Painting is antithetical to the very look and spirit of my work. The work must be the final arbiter."[69]

. . .

On October 27, 1958—two or three months into his intense labors on the Four Seasons murals—Rothko lectured in an old classroom at Pratt Institute in Brooklyn, his first extended public statement about his work since "The Romantics Were Prompted" (1947) and the last one he would make. His talk, which until now has survived chiefly through the notes taken by Dore Ashton and the art historian Irving Sandler, was taped and later transcribed; preserved among Rothko's papers, it is presented here for the first time.[70]

"The work must be the final arbiter." Well, yes; but Rothko knew that critical languages, like the hanging and lighting of a picture, both reflect and create the contexts (or environments) in which paintings are seen, valued, and in some cases mutilated. In "The Romantics Were Prompted," as he broke with figuration and entered a period of experiment and discovery, Rothko had stressed inwardness and freedom. In the mid-1950s, reacting to the characterization of his paintings as serene, he stressed a Dionysian wildness in his writing about Nietzsche. In 1958 at Pratt, as he worked on paintings intended to dominate a public space and as he sought to disengage his work from the term "action painting," Rothko stressed deliberation and control. Before, he had spoken of art as a romanticized migration, "an unknown adventure in an unknown space." Now, "I speak of art as a trade," he declared at Pratt.

"I began painting rather late in life; therefore my vocabulary was formed a good time before my painting vocabulary was formed, and it still persists in my talking about painting," this gifted talker began, speaking "haltingly," without notes, "in a quiet voice."[71] The Rothko of 1958, rotating 180 degrees from his expressionism of the 1930s, now flatly denies that a painting is an act of *self*-expression. "I have never thought that painting a picture has anything to do with self-expression. It is a communication about the world to someone else," and it is as such an act of communication that a work of art acquires value.

After the world is convinced about this communication it changes. The world was never the same after Picasso or Miró. Theirs was a view of the world which transformed our vision of things. All teaching about self-expression is erroneous in art; it has to do with therapy. Knowing yourself is valuable so that the self can be removed from the process. I emphasize this because there is an idea that the process of self-expression itself has many values. But producing a work of art is another thing and I speak of art as a trade.

For Rothko, then, painting is neither Greenberg's formalist research nor Rosenberg's existentialist bid for an individual identity.

Wryly parodying "How to" books about painting, Rothko goes on to offer "the recipe of a work of art—its ingredients—how to make it—the formula":

1. There must be a clear preoccupation with death—intimations of mortality. . . . Tragic art, romantic art, etc. deals with the knowledge of death.

2. Sensuality. Our basis of being concrete about the world. It is a lustful relationship to things that exist.

3. Tension. Either conflict or curbed desire.

4. Irony. This is a modern ingredient—the self-effacement and examination by which a man for an instant can go on to something else.

5. Wit and Play . . . for the human element.

6. The ephemeral and chance . . . for the human element.

7. Hope. 10% to make the tragic concept more endurable.

"I measure these ingredients very carefully when I paint a picture," Rothko continues. "It is always the form that follows these elements and the picture results from the proportions of these elements."

Rothko's ingredients constitute too generalized a set of attitudes to enable any ambitious young painters to whip up "a Rothko"—or even to let any curious critics or viewers know how he mixed, applied, or selected colors. Rothko was talking not to reveal the secrets of his trade but to position himself *in* the art world by creating a place for himself *outside* of its dominant critical languages. Mixing his ingredients "very carefully," slowly measuring, weighing, and proportioning, tossing in just a few grams of "the ephemeral and chance," Rothko is no action cook.

Omitting any mention of his speedy application of glazes, Rothko focuses on the deliberation of his creative process. He had always emphasized the meditative rather than the physical labor of painting, but his practice now entailed more *pre*-meditation: the murals he was producing for the Seagram Building required more preparation and planning than producing single paintings had. Once he hired Dan Rice to assist him with the Seagram project, Rothko had transformed the monastic solitude of the studio into a kind of social space, and he had acquired an assistant whose efforts he had to direct and to coordinate with his own.

His paintings, moreover, were being produced for a preexisting space, the size and shape of which (especially the high, narrow west wall above the door and "windows" into the Pool Room) imposed external constraints on the artist's imagination. And once he had decided to hang the paintings along the east wall as a continuous frieze—which he apparently did rather early—Rothko committed himself to work within a uniform height for these works.[72] And for the first time in a little less than twenty years Rothko used sketches, some (made with gouache on paper) experimenting with the color and shape of individual paintings, others (created with crayon or tempera on horizontal strips of construction paper) to help him imagine a row of five or six of his paintings, probably before the individual paintings had been produced.[73]

But a notion of the creative process as more controlled than impulsive not only grew out of these recent changes in Rothko's practice; it also reflected the more conservative outlook of a fifty-five-year-old man who had long combined his assertions of dissident modernity ("We start anew. A new land") with old-fashioned talk of "eternal" needs, the "universal," and enduring human values. As Rothko went on to tell his audience at Pratt, he was rejecting self-expression in its violent sense, as "stripping yourself of will, intelligence, civilization." From this traditionalist point of view, art does not transgress, dissolve, or extend social boundaries, but accepts such conventions because they permit communication and contain the dangerous irrationality of the self. In art, desire is *curbed*. In 1952 Rothko had advised William Seitz to put the self back into his work. In 1958, Rothko was urging effacement of the self—reflecting his wish to get beyond his own tumultuous, vulnerable personality, *his* fate, to reach a contemplative calm.

But Rothko's talk of subordinating the self also follows from a desire to preserve that place in the world that he, after long struggle, had only recently gained, which he had little confidence would last and no desire to give up. It wasn't just that the young painters of today disregard older artists like himself; it was that they wished, as Rothko dramatically put it, to destroy them. "The kings die today in just the same way they did in Frazer's *Golden Bough*," Rothko told John Fischer. *The Golden Bough* begins with the priest (or king) of Diana's sacred grove, who prowls about the grove, day and night, with drawn sword, "peering warily about him as if at every instant he expected to be set upon by an enemy," as if the priest/king had grown up in a Settlement of Pale town like Dvinsk. "He was a priest and a murderer," Frazer writes, "and the man for whom he looked was sooner or later to murder him and hold the priesthood in his stead."⁷⁴ Rothko, who has just bragged to Fischer that "we destroyed cubism. Nobody can paint a cubist picture today," claims that if he could identify his own potential usurper, "I would kill him." Fathers kill sons—lest sons kill fathers. Succession, in Rothko's imagination, can only occur violently, enacting the "basic violence which lies at the bottom of human existence."⁷⁵ Ideally, young artists, like wives and children, would subordinate themselves, keep their places and revere their masters. Now an older king warily prowling the painting territory he had taken, Rothko identifies not with rebellious or victimized sons but the "father authority."

After offering his "recipe" for art, Rothko went on: "I want to mention a marvelous book: Kierkegaard's *Fear and Trembling,* which deals with the sacrifice of Isaac by Abraham." The "last rabbi of western art" was turning back to the ancestral founder of Judaism, as reinterpreted by a nineteenth-century Christian philosopher. "Abraham's act was absolutely unique," Rothko says. "There are other examples of sacrifice: in the Greek, the Agamemnon story (state or daughter); also Brutus who had both of his sons put to death. But what Abraham did was un-understandable; there was no universal law that condones such a act as Abraham had to carry out. As soon as an act is made by an individual, it becomes universal. This is like the role of the artist."⁷⁶

Or, as Rothko had told Alfred Jensen in April of 1956: "Last year when I read Kierkegaard, I found that he was writing almost exclusively about that artist who is beyond all others. And as I read him more and more I got so involved with his ideas that I identified completely with the artist he was writing about. I was that artist."⁷⁷ No humanist, Kierkegaard's Abraham commits himself to an incomprehensible act, the killing of his son, an act which isolates him socially, and because it can't be explained, silences him. "Silence is so accurate."

"Another problem of Abraham was whether to tell Sarah," Rothko continues. "This is a problem of reticence. Some artists want to tell all like at a confessional. I as a craftsman prefer to tell little." Then, alluding to Elaine de Kooning's essay, he says,

> My pictures are indeed facades (as they have been called). Sometimes I open one door and one window or two doors and two windows. I do this only through shrewdness. There is more power in telling little than in telling all. Two things that painting is involved with: the uniqueness and clarity of image and how much does one have to tell. Art is a shrewdly contrived article containing seven ingredients combined for the utmost power and concreteness.

Or, as Kierkegaard wrote: "Secrecy and silence really make a man great precisely because they are characteristics of inwardness."[78]

It is easy to see why Rothko read Kierkegaard's Abraham—single-minded and silent, admirable and appalling, renouncing the world, confronting "dread," devoted to a vision he cannot explain—as a prototype of the modern artist. To a man who increasingly felt trapped in his marriage, in bloody contests between and within artistic generations, in the contaminating political maneuverings required to distribute his art, in his fragile and unmanageable body, in his tremendous ego and his tremendous doubts—in short, in him*self*—Kierkegaard's Abraham offered a heroic self-image, at once severe and romanticized.

In reality, when Rothko lectured at Pratt, he was working on a commission for the Bronfman empire, to produce paintings for a building designed by Mies van der Rohe, former director of the hated Bauhaus, to hang in a restaurant designed by Philip Johnson, rumored in New York art circles to have been sympathetic to the Third Reich in the early 1930s.[79] Rather than making a lonely journey to Mount Moriah, Rothko was entering the belly of twentieth-century corruption. Abraham appealed to the part of Rothko that admired, and was intimidated by, Clyfford Still. Identifying with Kierkegaard's hero, Rothko could imagine himself as pure, simply motivated yet beyond understanding, great. "No one is so great as Abraham! Who is capable of understanding him?" Kierkegard writes.[80]

Yet Kierkegaard explicitly distinguishes Abraham from the poet (or artist). A "knight of faith," Abraham merges his will with the will of God. If Abraham is separated from this conception of religious faith, he is, as Kierkegaard often warns, simply a murderer. "Kierkegaard has that passion for the 'I,' for that 'I' experience, like Abraham in his *Fear and Trembling*," Rothko told Jensen. "It is the 'I' that I myself experience every day."[81] Of course, it was Rothko who had the passion for the "I" experience, not Kierkegaard, who held that Abraham achieved uniqueness only through submission to God. Self-expressive as reader, Rothko found an Abraham who would satisfy his own needs—needs that he might have experienced as "eternal" because they went so far back in his own experience.

"By faith Abraham went out from the land of his fathers and became a sojourner in the land of promise," Kierkegaard writes. "By faith he was a stranger in the land of promise, and there was nothing to recall what was dear to him, but by its novelty everything tempted his soul to melancholy yearning."[82] Rothko knew how it felt to be a stranger in the land of promise, and he knew how it felt to be the son of a man who has gone out from the land of his fathers to find the land of promise. When Jacob Rothkowitz had

Chapter Thirteen

departed Dvinsk for Portland, he had left his family in a dangerous environment, an act beyond the understanding of a seven-year-old boy, the more so if the father, like Jacob, was a "quiet" (or reticent) man not given to elaborate justifications of his acts.

Was the father abandoning his family or saving it? Was he enjoying himself in the land of promise or suffering from the loss of his family there? Was he self-indulgent or self-sacrificial? Like Abraham's, Jacob Rothkowitz's action was incomprehensible, inaccessible. Yet, Rothko's own vision of authority—the revered patriarch in lonely pursuit of his vision, beyond family or social obligation, telling little—was enacted in his shrewdly reticent lecture, justified by Kierkegaard, and modeled on Jacob, as if Rothko had kept alive, encrypted in one part of his psyche, a cherished, even idealized image of the father he had lost.

Jacob's story ended differently from Abraham's. Six months after his youngest son arrived in Portland, Jacob died, as if in this narrative Isaac had mysteriously returned alone from Mount Moriah. In the Rothkowitz version of the biblical story, the son, a guilty survivor who holds onto a positive image of his father as a model for his own artistic quest, turns his angry distrust against an external world "where he never felt entirely at home." By the time of the Pratt lecture, in which he listed "a clear preoccupation with death" as the first ingredient of his art, Rothko had just turned fifty-five—the age at which his father had died. An eminent artist who would earn around $20,000 from his painting that year, Rothko had exceeded his father, just as the Abstract Expressionists had surpassed the Cubists. Having climbed this long way, he now peered "warily about him as if at every instant he expected to be set upon by an enemy." And he was painting murals with which he hoped to upset, physically, the power elite who would eat and deal in the private dining room at the Four Seasons. Steamed up with enough anger to imbue his murals with unbearable bite, Rothko was painting to protect and extend his own hard-won authority, and to turn his commission into a transgression against the privileged and wealthy class which had given him the commission, which was now buying his paintings, and into which he himself was gradually moving.

After citing *Fear and Trembling* to endorse artistic reticence, Rothko turns to "the problem of the civilization of the artist." He complains of "an exploitation of primitiveness, the subconscious, the primordial." People ask him if he is a Zen Buddhist. "I am not. I am not interested in any civilization except this one. The whole problem in art is how to establish human values in this specific civilization." Rothko then closed his talk by turning to the old and central issue of subject matter. "I belong to a generation that was preoccupied with the human figure and I studied it," Rothko says. "It was with utmost reluctance that I found that it did not meet my needs."

> Whoever used it mutilated it. No one could paint the figure as it was and feel that he could produce something that could express the world. I refuse to mutilate and had to find another way of expression. I used mythology for a while substituting various creatures who were able to make intense gestures without embarrassment. I began to use morphological forms in order to paint gestures that I could not make people do. But this was unsatisfactory.

His pictures now "are involved with the *scale* of human feelings, the human drama, as much of it as I can express," Rothko concluded.

A question period followed:

> Q: Don't you feel that we have made a new contribution in terms of light and color (ambience)?
> A: I suppose we have made such a contribution in the use of light and color, but I don't understand what ambience means. But these contributions were made in relation to the seven points. I may have used colors and shapes in the way that painters before have not used them, but this was not my purpose. The picture took the shape of what I was involved in. People have asked me if I was involved with color. Yes, that's all there is, but I am not against line. I don't use it because it would have detracted from the clarity of what I had to say. The form follows the necessity of what we have to say. When you have a new view of the world you will have to find new ways to say it.
> Q: How does wit and play enter your work?
> A: In a way my paintings are very exact, but in that exactitude there is a shimmer, a play . . . in weighing the edges to introduce a less rigorous, play element.
> Q: Death?
> A: The tragic notion of the image is always present in my mind when I paint and I know when it is achieved, but I couldn't point it out—show where it is illustrated. There are no skull and bones. (I am an abstract painter.)
> Q: On philosophy?
> A: If you have a philosophic mind you will find that nearly all paintings can be spoken of in philosophic terms.
> Q: Shouldn't the young try to say it all . . . question of control?

A: I don't think the question of control is a matter of youth or age. It is a matter of decision. The question is: is there anything to control. I think that a freer, wilder kind of painting is not more natural with youth than with grey old men. It isn't a question of age; it is a question of choice. This (idea) has to do with fashion. Today, there is an implication that a painter improves if he gets more free. This has to do with fashion.

Q: Self-expression . . . communication vs expression. Cannot they be reconciled? Personal message and self-expression.

A: What a personal message means is that you have been thinking for yourself. It is different from self-expression. You may communicate about yourself; I prefer to communicate a view of the world that is not all of myself. Self-expression is boring. I want to talk of something outside of myself—a great scope of experience.

Q: Can you define Abstract Expressionism?

A: I never read a definition and to this day I don't know what it means. In a recent article I was called an action painter. I don't get it and I don't think my work has anything to do with Expressionism, abstract or any other. I am an anti-expressionist.

Q: Large pictures?

A: Habit or fashion. Many times I see large pictures whose meaning I do not understand. Seeing that I was one of the first criminals, I found this useful. Since I am involved with the human element, I want to create a state of intimacy—an immediate transaction. Large pictures take you into them. Scale is of tremendous importance to me—human scale. Feelings have different weights; I prefer the weight of Mozart to Beethoven because of Mozart's wit and irony and I like his scale. Beethoven has a farmyard wit. How can a man be ponderable without being heroic? This is my problem. My pictures are involved with these human values. This is always what I think about. When I went to Europe and saw the old masters, I was involved with the credibility of the drama. Would Christ on the cross if he opened his eyes believe the spectators[?]. I think that small pictures since the Renaissance are like novels; large pictures are like dramas in which one participates in a direct way. The different subject necessitates different means.

Q: How can you express human values without self-expression?

A: Self-expression often results in inhuman values. It has been confused with feelings of violence. Perhaps the word self-expression is not clear. Anyone who makes a statement about the world must be involved with self-expression but not in stripping yourself of will, intelligence, civilization. My emphasis is upon deliberateness. Truth must strip itself of self which can be very deceptive.

. . .

> A trip to Europe was a great event, not only an event in his life but also seen as an expenditure. He felt slightly curious about it, surprised, one, that he could do it and, two, that he would do it.
>
> Dan Rice

In May of 1959 Mark and Mell Rothko were preparing to leave New York for their second trip to Europe. Rothko was tired from his many months of work on the Four Seasons paintings, and "he was not satisfied with the way the work was going," so he wanted rest and a break. A year before, Rothko—along with Willem de Kooning, Philip Guston, Franz Kline, and Robert Motherwell—had signed an agreement authorizing Bernard Reis to represent them in their negotiations with Sidney Janis. Rothko, who disliked and distrusted both lawyers and art dealers, had now designated a law-school-graduate-turned-accountant to handle his negotiations with his dealer. In connection with obtaining passports for the European trip, Reis assisted Rothko in legally changing his name to Mark Rothko and his daughter's name from Kathy Lynn to Kate.[83]

Rothko, moreover, had never made a will, possibly because he had wanted to avoid dealing with an attorney or because he had only recently accumulated sufficient worldly goods to think of himself as having something as lofty as an "estate."[84] Now he had a nine-year-old child; he was affluent, with an income that would rise from about $21,000 in 1958 to about $61,000 in 1959; he owned a house in Provincetown; and, most important, he owned a lot of his own work, the value of which, like Jackson Pollock's, was likely to rise dramatically after his death. "I am . . . happy that this specific picture has found a place," Rothko wrote to Katharine Kuh after the Art Institute of Chicago purchased one of the paintings from his 1954 exhibit there, "for I wonder, often, how my large and important works can physically survive." Protective about his paintings, Rothko also "worried more about his reputation after his death than any other artist I've ever known," Kuh said. "He felt that he was in competition with every artist who had ever lived and still lived."[85] Stipulating the disposition of his works after his death offered one way to try to control *that* situation.

Chapter Thirteen

Just before they left for Europe, Mark and Mell Rothko, assisted by Reis, wrote their wills. Should both of them die, Herbert and Ilse Ferber would serve as their executors and Kate's guardians, with the Reises named as alternates. If Kate died at the same time as her parents, then the estate would be distributed in seven equal shares among Rothko's two brothers, his sister, Mell's two sisters, Ferber, and Stanley Kunitz.[86] In a separate letter sent to the Ferbers and Reis, the Rothkos dealt with the disposition of his paintings:

> Dear Friends:
> We have just made wills which provide that in case of our death and Kate's, you are to be the Executors. Our estates will be divided as set forth in our wills. The principal item in the estates, of course, is the inventory of paintings, and it is our wish that the pictures should be sold as follows:
> (a) The museum or individual who will acquire the largest number to be held in a single place should be given preference;
> (b) To museums outside of New York City and in Europe which will acquire at least six paintings;
> (c) To museums or individuals who will acquire at least three paintings;
> (d) These conditions for distribution should be adhered to for a period of five years.[87]

At least for the first five years after his death, Rothko wished to keep his paintings in small clusters, limiting sales to those collectors and museums sufficiently committed to his work to buy at least three of his paintings.

On June 15, 1958, Mark, Mell, and Kate Rothko sailed, tourist class, on the USS *Independence,* arriving in Naples seven days later.[88] "After dinner on the first night out of New York," Rothko, with no city streets to prowl, "wandered into the tourist-class bar, looking for someone to talk to" and found John Fischer. "Rothko peered around the room through his thick-lensed glasses, then ambled over to my table with his characteristic elephantine gait," introduced himself and immediately began his disquisition on the "malice" behind the Four Seasons murals. "His verbal ferocity," Fischer writes, "was at first hard to take seriously, because Rothko looked anything but malicious. He was sipping a Scotch and soda with obvious gusto; he had the round, beaming face and comfortably plump body of a man who enjoys his food; and his voice sounded almost cheerful. Never, then or later, did I ever see him display any outward sign of anger. His affection for Mell, his wife, and Katie, their daughter, was touchingly obvious: and with his friends he was more companionable and considerate than most people I have known. Yet somewhere inside he did nurse a small, abiding core of anger, not against anything specific, so far as I could tell, but against the sorry state of the world in general, and the role it now offers to the artist."[89]

If Rothko went to Europe seeking rest from his exertions with the Seagram project, his daughter recalled that "it was a working trip. He went to see art. On the entire trip, we spent three days at the beach and that was all we did that a child might have liked. Not that I disliked everything we did, but I was tired, at the end of two and a half months, of visiting museums." Rothko had not come just to check out his old-world competition, though he did return from Europe, once again, complaining of the mutilations in Renaissance religious painting, as if only an abstract malice were acceptable.[90] But Rothko was also looking for ancestral connections, reflections of his own concerns, within the tradition he liked to think he and his contemporaries had usurped. While in Naples, he visited Pompeii, where, he told Fischer, he sensed "a deep affinity" between his current work and the wall paintings in the House of Mysteries, "the same feeling, the same broad expanses of somber color." When the Rothko and Fischer families made a day-long trip south to see the ruins of Greek temples at Paestum, "we wandered through them all morning; Rothko examined every architectural detail with bemused attention, rarely saying a word." As they ate a picnic lunch inside the shell of the Temple of Hera, two Italian high school boys, acting as guides, asked the Americans who they were and what they did. "I have told them that you are an artist, and they ask whether you came here to paint the temples," reported Fischer's daughter, who was interpreting. "Tell them that I have been painting Greek temples all my life without knowing it," Rothko replied.[91]

From Naples, Mark, Mell, and Kate Rothko traveled north to Rome, to Tarquinia (to see the Etruscan murals there), to Florence and then Venice, where they visited Peggy Guggenheim. By July 15, they had reached Paris, from which they proceeded to Brussels, where Rothko's nephew Kenneth Rabin and his wife, Joy, were living; leaving Kate with the Rabins, Mark and Mell Rothko visited Antwerp. Then all three Rothkos journeyed to Amsterdam and finally to London, sailing for the United States on the *Queen Elizabeth II* on August 20.[92]

While Rothko was staying in Brussels, so were Morton and Anne-Marie Levine, whom Rothko had met during his 1955 summer in Boulder. Rothko and Levine would become quite close, particularly in the last years of Rothko's life, when he named Levine one of the three executors of his will. "His greeting was like an embrace," Levine wrote in a memoir. "The expression on his face and the sonority of his voice endowed a simple handshake with the overwhelming quality of a bear-hug, as Stanley Kunitz said. Sometimes the bear-hug broke a bone or two." Yet when Rothko had first met Levine, an academic sociologist,

Rothko shook his hand and crushed his profession: "Sociology and anthropology deal in averages and don't interest me at all. Even their conception of The Individual is a stereotype. No, what interests me is not The Individual but this individual or that individual." In Brussels, when Anne-Marie Levine introduced Rothko to her father, he told Rothko that "there are some wonderful paintings here," thinking of Rubens, Brueghel. Rothko shrugged and announced he was "not interested in painting."[93] Rothko liked to shock new acquaintances. After all, on this trip he had spent many hours in museums, and while in Florence he had again viewed the Fra Angelico frescos in the monks' cells at the Convent of San Marco and discussed them with Giulio Carlo Argan, whose *Fra Angelico and His Times* had appeared just a few years before.[94] But several of Rothko's friends observed that in Europe he had, in Dan Rice's words, "responded more to architecture and music than to painting."

Rothko's responsiveness to architecture, growing out of his concern with the tension between the human figure and its surrounding spatial environment, had informed many of his paintings of the 1930s. In many works of the early 1940s, Rothko's human/animal/godlike figures have been fragmented, frozen, and absorbed by the relieflike architecture. In 1950, on his first visit to Europe he had responded sardonically to the Gothic excess of Chartres "where the impulse to pile on more stones is never resisted." Rothko preferred the classical simplicity of, say, the Temple of Hera at Paestum.

On this visit, in Florence, he returned to Michelangelo's Medici Library at the cloister of San Lorenzo—or rather to the library's vestibule, a small, almost square room (31' × 33') dominated by a large staircase that sprawls into and across the room, filling most of the floor space, leaving only narrow passageways along its front and sides. As if in release from this cramped space, the walls rise three stories (47') high, and their decorations also exert a strong vertical pull. Along the second story, Michelangelo placed pairs of stone columns recessed into vertical boxes, the columns alternating with rectangular, door-shaped tabernacles framed by pilasters on the sides and a pediment on the top. The third story contains a series of windows, blind on the front and rear walls. Rothko referred to the room as "the somber vault."[95]

During his 1950 trip to Europe Rothko had first visited this room, and on his 1959 voyage, talking with Fischer, he recalled it as an unconscious source for the Seagram murals. "After I had been at work for some time, I realized that I was much influenced subconsciously by Michelangelo's walls in the staircase of the Medicean Library in Florence," Rothko said. "He achieved just the kind of feeling I'm after—he makes the viewers feel that they are trapped in a room where all the doors and windows are bricked up, so that all they can do is butt their heads forever against the wall."[96] Michelangelo's walls, because they are juxtaposed with the recesses holding the columns, push forward into an already compressed space, creating the kind of tension Rothko sought in rooms where he hung ensembles of his paintings. In Michelangelo's vestibule, doorlike shapes suggest a way out, but they don't open; windowlike shapes suggest a view of the outside world, but they are inaccessibly high and half of them are walled-up. The room through which monks needed to pass to enter their library halts and compresses, as if Michelanglo wished to give the monks no choice but to turn inward before entering the library.

From Rothko's perspective, it was as if, in an Italian cloister, he had suddenly felt like one of the trapped, immobilized figures in one of his cramped interiors of the 1930s. Only in 1959 Rothko was creating an interior space—in a luxury restaurant, not a cloister—with which he hoped, maliciously, to put its rich patrons in *his place*.

· · ·

In our inheritance we have space, a box in which things are going on. In my work there is no box; I do not work with space. There is a form without the box and possibly a more convincing kind of form.

Mark Rothko

Sometime in the spring or early fall of 1959, Mark Rothko painted *Red on Maroon* (color plate 17), one of the Seagram murals.[97]

This large canvas, 8¾' high and just short of 8' wide, contains a wine-red, doorlike shape which, due to its formidable size and stately proportions, evokes the monumentality of a portal. A door or gate, usually in a large or magnificent building, a portal marks a place of transition, a crossing (sometimes a ritual crossing) of borders, a site of physical movement and emotional crisis, of coming and going, leaving and returning, loss and reunion—some of the principal themes of Rothko's life and work. Rothko's portal invites entry; to stand before *Red on Maroon* is to feel a powerful pull to enter the picture with one's whole body, to pass through this awesome opening, and to cross over to the smoky maroon, filled with gray light, within and beyond.

But if the painting creates a longing to cross a threshold dividing this familiar, physical world from some mysterious realm beyond it, the painting also curbs that desire by thwarting access. At first, the red portal appears as a separate, solid, and imposing entity, holding back the diffused, murky areas behind it, especially the darker, more turbulent, and ominous area across the bottom. But as you physically approach the painting and see Rothko's brushstrokes and drips, observe the varying densities of his paint, you perceive the smoky, vacant interior as solid and opaque, as if *it* were the wall.

Indeed, the longer you look at the painting, the less certain you are as to what is opening, what is wall. Not attached to a wall or supported by a floor, the door hovers in an indeterminate, otherworldly space, as if weightless, sometimes seeming to advance from the wall and into the room. Patches of dark in the red reveal this massive architectural form to be a thin, filmy surface, incomplete, with its own holes and openings. Bulges—say, along the outside of the right column—suggest that this door frame is stretching outward. Rough edges also suggest expansion, both outward and into the interior opening, while the gray held inside, rather than being passively contained, pushes out, wedging into the four corners. Along the bottom, where the structure should be sturdiest, it thins and merges with the thick, murky black. After a while, the monumental door frame loses its substantial character altogether, becoming an opening *into* the maroon/gray. This portal lacks solidity, or stability. *Red on Maroon* creates a sense of foreboding, a tension between a monumental containing structure and a dense, grim flux which it cannot fully contain.

In Rothko's paintings of the 1930s, public architecture emblematized a powerful social order that felt impersonal and dead, from which anything like Dionysian wildness had been drained. In his paintings of the 1950s, Rothko, focusing on the interaction between the viewer and the painting (rather than conceiving of the painting as a self-contained object), wished the "space" of the painting to extend into the "real space" occupied by the human figure in front of the painting. His obsession with controlling the hanging and lighting of his work derived from this effort to generate, out of the physical presence of the work and the physical presence of the viewer, a spatial environment. With these paintings he was creating alternative public spaces, a *humanized* spatial environment, in which "real transactions" were possible.

Rothko's paintings of the 1950s affirm a human presence that has *endured* the "tragic" history of the twentieth century, *his* history. His mural projects, however, came at a time in Rothko's life when conflict in his marriage, the collapse of old friendships, the pressures of professional success (one of those pressures being *this* commission), when all these combined to make him feel angry, constrained, wary, impatient to "control the situation."

Before, Rothko had wished to create large pictures in "the scale of human feeling." These works, he told Katharine Kuh, were "painted in a scale of normal living rather than an institutional scale."[98] At the Four Seasons, however, the scale was hardly that of normal living. Here, the problem was not (as it had been at the Art Institute of Chicago or in Rothko's Sixth Avenue flat) to crowd a small space, but to fill a large, high-ceilinged, and impersonal space, one dominated by visual distractions: the north wall was all window, and five large openings on the west wall would look over into the main dining room. The paintings, all quite large, some probably to form a continuous frieze along the east wall, and all of them to be hung at least 4½′ high and viewed from a stationary and often distant seated position, look more imposing than intimate; they invite, but they also bear down. Partly they respond to the demands of the room; partly, they extend Rothko's need to dominate. As Dan Rice recalled, "Rothko would be able to place a person in an environment that he totally controlled and therefore this person could not help at least see the message."

Instead of clashing with the room's doors and windows, Rothko's murals were to harmonize with these architectural features, in order to "defeat" them. His paintings contain vertical openings, horizontal openings, or square-shaped openings—all familiar shapes that ask us to think about the meanings of windows, doors, gateways, frames, and the issues of coming and going, of looking and being looked at, that they engage. Rothko's paintings attempted to *deepen* the architecture. *Red on Maroon* (color plate 17), which *probably* would have been hung alone on the south wall, echoes the single door in that wall. Rothko takes a small, functional, stable architectural feature of the room, a doorway for waiters, and he turns this rigid and impersonal geometric shape into a massive one that stretches, compresses, solidifies, dissolves. Yet, unlike Rothko's work of the early and mid-1950s, this painting does not enlarge and free the viewer; its drama of entry and exclusion, expansion and contraction, instead leaves the viewer feeling enclosed and trapped. Offering passage to another world that turns out to be inaccessible, the work reflects the pattern of Rothko's life for the past fifteen years, a migration into a new social reality that was producing more and more frustration.

But *Red on Maroon* is not an independent work, a self-contained *whole*; the painting was designed to be a *part,* in a larger whole. This whole is not just an irrecoverable one, like the room at Harvard University where five Rothko murals once hung; this whole, since Rothko finally refused to install the paintings, never existed.

• • •

> *Here, at Manhattan's heart, the leaders of our creative society, men and women from every frontier of our dynamic culture, gather to dine. Amid grandeur, they shape bold ventures, consider abstractions, decide concretely.*
>
> *At the Four Seasons our guests reflect on the arts, ascertain priori-*

Chapter Thirteen

ties, speak of great expectations, celebrate victories, find solace during stress, rebound from loss, toast the triumphs and bliss of being alive.

One Hundred Seasons

"I'm not comfortable vis-à-vis the Japanese."
"They're up to adding; we're up to dealing."
"I'm old enough to put my spin on your shit."

Conversational Fragments from the Four Seasons

The Four Seasons was no Greek temple. Citing its $4,500,000 cost, its $50,000 annual budget for seasonal planting, its staff of twenty captains and fifty waiters, the *New York Times* declared that the restaurant, to open in July 1959, "will be one of the most opulently decorated dining establishments in the United States." With a stage curtain painted by Picasso for a 1919 Ballet Russe performance already hung, the Four Seasons, the *Times* reported, will eventually contain murals by "Mark Rothko, an abstract expressionist" in its smaller dining room. "Until his work is completed the room will display 'Blue Poles,' a mural by Jackson Pollock."[99]

Sometime after his return from Europe that summer and after the restaurant had opened in late July, Rothko decided that he and Mell should have a meal there.[100] Rothko believed that it was "criminal to spend more than $5 on a meal," but he *did* like to eat; and he could, now that the restaurant was complete, see how and where others would actually see his work.[101] After passing a Miró tapestry hung in the traventine lobby, walking up the short stairs to the smaller lobby where the Picasso stage curtain hung, turning left and walking down the dining room vestibule, past the concierge, past the glassed-in wine cellar, through the French walnut doorway and into the main dining room, Mark and Mell Rothko entered a sumptuous, high-ceilinged room, at the center of which stood a square twenty-foot pool of white marble, with a tall potted fig tree at each of its four corners. Two walls, consisting of floor to ceiling windows, divided into vertical panels by Mies's bronze mullions, offered views of the Seagram plaza and 53rd Street. Over these windows "curtains" of shining metallic chains, looped from mullion to mullion, shimmered. The two interior walls, divided into a grid of vertical panels, were covered with natural rawhide. Beyond the marble pool, nine steps rose to the smaller dining room, where Rothko's murals would be installed and Jackson Pollock's *Blue Poles* now hung.

Entering the restaurant, in the words of one breathless reviewer, was "an exhilarating progression into a kind of gently gilded, half-veiled patio, a sensation resulting partly from the airy height of the spaces, the large plants, the pool in the main dining room, and the outdoor view. It is really not an exceptional view, being close to the street, but the gilded veiling at the windows converts it into a magic vision of metropolis—New York the dynamic, fabled and powerful." Its design "colorless and unobtrusive," the Four Seasons "is not a stage setting," the reviewer went on. "Rather it is a theater that is . . . to focus on a perpetually changing *mis-en-scène,* an endlessly improvised drama—of the four seasons of nature, of the world's greatest metropolis, and of the pleasant rituals of serving and being served, eating, drinking, and conversing."[102]

Seated in "Brno" chairs designed by Mies himself, Mark and Mell Rothko contemplated a menu which offered them a cuisine "derived from many of the cuisines of the world," with several items "original creations" by the restaurant's "Swiss-born executive chef, Albert Stockli, whose imagination is largely unfettered by European tradition." Among the main courses Rothko could have chosen were "farmhouse duckling with fresh sage," "fish flamed with dried fennel," "suckling pig in pastry," "coq au vin with genuine cockerels."

Rothko had hoped to paint something that would ruin the appetite of every son of a bitch who ever ate in that room. Instead, the concrete reality of the restaurant probably ruined *his* appetite, and certainly ruined his project. Any specific environment for an ensemble of his works would have caused Rothko some trouble: any material reality diminished the ideal. "I have made a place," he proclaimed to Dore Ashton. But *this* place had been made by Philip Johnson working in collaboration with an interior designer, industrial designers (for glass, china, and silverware), a uniform designer, landscape architect, graphic artist, lighting consultant, and plant physiologist—plus one sculptor (Richard Lippold) and one painter (Mark Rothko). Through meticulous design and expensive materials Johnson and his cohorts had created a luxurious room in which a safely distanced "nature," its passing seasons reflected in the changing colors of waiters' uniforms, table linens and indoor plants, and a safely distanced city, substituted for the real heat and cold, the real haste, noise, clutter, and dirt of New York City.

When he got home that evening, he called Katharine Kuh "in a state of high emotion" to say he was returning the money he'd received and withdrawing his paintings. "When he was working on the project, his imagination plus a dash of wishful thinking projected an idyllic setting where captivated diners, lost in reverie, communed with the murals. I'm afraid it never entered his head that the works would be forced to compete with a noisy crowd of conspicuous consumers." But "real transactions" were not on the Four Seasons menu. The next morning, arriving at his Bowery studio, "he came through the door like a bull, as only Rothko could, in an absolute rage," said Dan Rice. "He said quite explosively—no good mornings or anything . . . slamming his hat down on the table and pounding, 'Anybody who will eat that kind of food for those kind of prices will never look at a painting of mine'." "He was furious," Stanley Kunitz said. "I've never seen him so angry about anything. He could talk about nothing else for weeks."[103]

Having deluded himself, Rothko felt betrayed, enraged, as if the trap he had fallen into had been set by somebody else.

• • •

"So far I've painted three sets of panels for this Seagram job," Rothko had told John Fischer during their first shipboard conversation. "The first one didn't turn out right, so I sold the panels separately as individual paintings. The second time I got the basic idea, but began to modify it as I went along—because, I guess, I was afraid of being too stark. When I realized my mistake, I started again, and this time I'm holding tight to the original conception. I keep my malice constantly in mind. It is a very strong motivating force. With it pushing me I think I can finish off the job pretty quickly after I get home from this trip."[104]

During his two years working on the project, Rothko had produced approximately forty panels. Catalogue essays by Michael Compton and Thomas Kellein have attempted to identify which of these panels belong in which series, as well as to recover Rothko's final selection of paintings for the restaurant. We *can* say that Rothko *probably* intended to hang seven paintings, three on the east wall, three on the west, one on the south.[105] We can also say that many of the paintings are characterized, in Compton's words, by a "more sombre colouring and by a more opaque pigment and brushwork," and that these paintings, reflecting Rothko's view that in the second series he'd backed off too much, probably belong to the third series.[106]

Yet Dan Rice observed that, in addition to his three sets of panels, Rothko also made "a lot of individual paintings that were done almost in exact terms," Rice commenting that "it would be very difficult to say that one was intended as part of the murals and one was not." It would be even more difficult to say that one painting belonged to the second as opposed to the third series, or that a given work was one Rothko intended to install or where he would have installed it. It's impossible to reconstruct an intention that was never realized. Rothko, who, according to Rice, was constantly "gathering all the paintings together again and jumbling them up," proceeded painstakingly and uncertainly. With his later mural projects for Harvard and for the Houston chapel, he produced extra works, alternates which gave him the freedom to continue

The Seagram Murals

pondering his choices at the actual site. With the Seagram murals, Rothko never reached this point.

"He had refused the commission," Werner Haftmann recalled of a visit to Rothko's Bowery studio, and he "now stood, disappointed, in the middle of his work, the actual realization of which was never to be achieved."[107] The German art historian and curator had come to ask Rothko to participate in a *documenta* exhibit. Rothko replied that "he no longer wanted to participate in large, general survey exhibitions. His pictures were not created for that. They needed a room of their own." When Haftmann said that a room could be arranged, Rothko "still refused, adding however that, as a Jew, he had no intention of exhibiting his works in Germany, a country that had committed so many crimes against Jewry."

As the two men were talking, they stood inside the temporary wooden walls on which Rothko had hung a set of the Seagram murals. "At a certain height, there was a darkly luminous frieze of pictures running round the whole room." In the middle "stood Rothko, agitated and zealous." He complained bitterly against the art world. "He told me that he had regarded this commission as a great and wonderful task that had finally been given him, that he had put everything in his power into its execution, and that here his work had reached a climax. In the zeal of his monologue, he did not hesitate to speak of the 'Sistine Chapel'." Rothko showed Haftmann earlier paintings from the project. "All that had been completely destroyed when he learned that this room was to be used as a restaurant for the most exclusive parties. He had no intention of handing over his pictures as decorations for parties which he deprecated as loathsome and miserable, and against which, in his zealousness, he used strong invectives."

After this "outburst," Rothko became "calmer." "Quiet, discouraged and a little hopeless, he pulled out two chairs. We two men sat alone and looked at his pictures for many hours, talking about them peacefully."

"Here and there, a dark curve indicated a kind of gate," Haftmann recalled of the paintings. "But the gate did not open. It was as though it were caught by a darkening plane of light that again veiled the opening." Haftmann was reminded of "hangings, opaque curtains which veiled something, or of an awning or a screen being gently moved from behind by the thing it veiled." The paintings communicated "a pronounced 'sacred' character. It was easy to understand why Rothko feared profanation and why this fear agitated him so."

Occasionally they talked. "Rothko spoke, as he liked to do, of certain 'transcendental experiences', without defining them more closely. He spoke of 'a sense of community' which always moved him while he worked and which allowed him the measure of security needed to drive his work to such an esoteric point, and hold it there. He defined his painting as something like a 'mythical action' and praised the surrealists for having rediscovered mythical possibilities in everyday life. Once he quoted Kierkegaard and his 'fear of nothingness'. He said this 'nothingness' did not concern him, but that his paintings should cover up something similar to this 'nothingness'."

In Rothko's darkened studio, with the painter and a single visitor surrounded by a "frieze" of mural panels, under these controlled circumstances, "real transactions" could happen, even when that visitor was a German and an art historian.

From Rothko's point of view, the Seagram project had played out a familiar drama of trust and betrayal, of advancing into the world, then withdrawing, angrily, from it. Eventually he placed the paintings in storage.

Yet Rothko's loss, though it infuriated him, was not pure; nor was his acceptance of the commission the kind of self-deluded and self-destructive act that, say, suing Lewis Browne had been. Defeat offered *some* satisfactions. Eating at the Four Seasons confirmed Rothko's enmity toward the rich, and his decision to withhold the paintings confirmed his idea of himself as an artist above corruption and beyond understanding. Indignation toward external foes obliterated self-doubt. Like some of his dramatic acts as a young man, like his refusal to return to synagogue or his later refusal to return to Yale, this incident—news of which quickly circulated around the New York art world—generated a story which cast Rothko in the role of a mistreated victim who, though he submitted for a while, finally asserted himself against powerful authorities—an Isaac who at the last minute refused to yield to Abraham. The Seagram commission had also pushed Rothko's work into a new dimension, as if only a project that "steamed" him up with anger could drive him to make such an advance. If, in the end, he felt outraged, he also had advanced his work into a new set of architectural forms, and he had demonstrated, publicly, that his works were not some objects in which he would abandon his involvement.

• • •

He wanted that room, that atmosphere, that environment, all to be his own.

Stanley Kunitz

During his lifetime, Rothko never sold any of the mural panels from the second or third series.[108] He showed the paintings to visitors in his Bowery studio; he included nine of the paintings in his 1961 retrospective at the Museum of Modern Art; and in 1969, after a prolonged negotiation, he completed a gift of nine of the murals to the Tate Gallery in London.[109]

In 1978 the Pace Gallery exhibited ten of the murals then in Rothko's estate, a group which the gallery identified as from the second series. After receiving a gift from the Mark Rothko Foundation in 1985, the National Gallery created a room with six of the murals, claiming they created "a coherent environment as intended by Rothko."[110] During 1988–89 the Tate Gallery in Liverpool showed the nine Tate paintings, along with three of the Seagram panels in Rothko's estate, the gallery's director claiming that the display "marks the first attempt to create the ambience which would have resulted from the murals had they ever been completed and installed in the Restaurant."[111] In 1989 the Kunsthalle Basel organized an exhibit of thirty of the panels, the catalogue printing Thomas Kellein's essay proposing a theory of Rothko's intended hanging at the Four Seasons.

Today the paintings have been dispersed, displaced. Nine of the panels remain at the Tate in London, seven are now at the Kawamura Museum of Modern Art in Japan, thirteen at the National Gallery of Art in Washington, others remain in the collections of Rothko's children.[112]

14 Rothko's Image

"Rembrandt" has become a noun, a noun that conjures up a particular kind of painting. "Rembrandt" has become an image.

Mark Rothko (1961)

Now the language of images is everywhere.

Daniel Boorstin,
The Image (1961)

Mark Rothko's one-man exhibit at the Museum of Modern Art closed on March 12, 1961.

Rothko had tried, unsuccessfully, to have the show extended, arguing that its most important reviews would not appear until March.[1] Yet, all during the seven-and-a-half weeks of the exhibit, and for weeks before, Rothko had been under intense strain. When he visited Dr. Grokest in February, "he told me that he'd been living on alcohol for six weeks." Rothko was also gaining weight, nearing two hundred pounds, his blood pressure was very high, he "wasn't sleeping," and he was suffering from a vascular problem which caused "blurry vision" and "shadowy forms" in his left eye. Rothko revealed that he was getting sedatives from other physicians. Grokest prescribed Surpicil to lower Rothko's blood pressure, and chlorohydrate, a soporific, to help him sleep.

After closing in New York, Rothko's show then traveled to the Whitechapel Art Gallery, London (October 10–November 12), the Stedelijk Museum, Amsterdam (November 24–December 27), the Palais des Beaux-Arts de Bruxelles (January 6–29, 1962), Kunsthalle Basel (March 3–April 8), Galleria Nazionale d'Arte Moderna, Rome (April 27–May 20), Musée d'Arte Moderne de la Ville de Paris (December 5, 1962–January 13, 1963).

For the installation of the Whitechapel exhibit, Rothko transmitted a set of detailed instructions, which show that his desire to control the conditions of viewing was a considered effort to preserve the subtle and delicate identities of his paintings.

Walls should be painted "considerably off-white with umber and warmed by a little red," Rothko instructed. "If the walls are too white, they are always fighting against the pictures which turn greenish because of the predominance of red in the pictures." About hanging, Rothko advised, "the larger pictures should all be hung as close to the floor as possible," except for the Seagram murals, which should be hung, as he said they had been painted, 4½' from the floor. And with regard to the lighting: "The light, whether natural or artificial, should not be too strong," Rothko warned. "The pictures have their own inner light and if there is too much light, the color in the picture is washed out and a distortion of their look occurs. The ideal situation would be to hang them in a normally lit room—that is the way they were painted. They should not be over-lit or romanticized by spots; this results in a distortion of their meaning. They should either be lighted from a great distance or indirectly by casting lights at the ceiling or the floor. Above all, every picture should be evenly lighted and not strongly."[2]

Rothko, in fact, was involved enough with the Whitechapel exhibition to travel alone, by boat—his claustrophobia ruled out flying—to London, arriving on October 2 and leaving October 12, two days after the show opened. Bryan Robertson, director of the Whitechapel, recalled leaving the gallery with Rothko "late one winter afternoon, when the daylight had practically gone. He asked me to switch all the lights off, everywhere; and suddenly, Rothko's colour made its own light: the effect, once the retina had adjusted itself, was unforgettable, smoldering and blazing and glowing softly from the walls—colour in darkness. We stood there a long time and I wished everyone could have seen the world Rothko had made, in those perfect conditions, radiating its own energy and uncorrupted by artifice or the market place."[3] Pure moments such as this one would prove to be rare in the last ten years of Rothko's life.

• • •

The tragedy is that the moment of freedom is so short-lived.

Mark Rothko

One day while his one-man show was still on in New York, Rothko and James Brooks sat talking on the stairway in the building at 222 Bowery where both men had their studios. Rothko "declared at length," said Brooks, "the reason for his deep melancholy." "His work had reached such an acceptance that it now inhabited the investment world as much as or more than the art world," leaving Rothko "bereft of the only thing that meant anything to him—the love that many people had for his work. Now he no longer felt his work was admired for itself, but that it was a rising commodity quotation on the stock market."[4]

The quotations on this particular commodity were rising *very* rapidly. In 1957, Rothko had sold 17 paintings, at an average price of about $1,700; in 1958, he sold 13, at an average of $2,400; in 1959, 17, at an average of $5,400;

in 1960, 11, at an average of $7,500; in 1961, 8, at an average of $12,000—and in 1962, the year following the Museum of Modern Art show, 7, at an average of $18,000.[5] As Rothko's prices rose, the number of paintings sold each year decreased, but not because his production was decreasing. Between 1949 (when he arrived at his format) and 1969 (the last full year of his life), Rothko—regardless of sales, shows, reviews, depressions, marital troubles, health problems—regularly produced about twenty paintings a year, as if his work provided *the* point of stability in an often turbulent life.[6] By limiting his sales, Rothko, who felt ambivalent about letting go of his works under any circumstances, could keep himself in a lower tax bracket, keep himself scarce and thus desirable, and introduce one element of personal control into a market driven by external forces and managed by a powerful art bureaucracy.[7]

The day of the opening for Rothko's Museum of Modern Art exhibit, Sidney Janis had written René d'Harnoncourt about the Museum's wish for a 10 percent commission for any Rothko paintings sold as a result of the exhibit—a standard arrangement that certainly blurs the distinction between galleries and museums. "We have at present and have had for some time now, a long waiting list for the artist's work," Janis explained. "Since in the past few years we have received for sale only a limited number of his paintings, and insufficient to cover the demand, it would be natural that you, too, would have inquiries even prior to the exhibition opening." None of the paintings on loan from the gallery are for sale, Janis wrote; if or when they are, "they will first be made available to those already on our waiting list."[8]

Many painters, among them the young Rothko, would love to have a waiting list for their work. Yet these potential buyers are not acting out of any involvement with a specific work, or a "real transaction." Perhaps they are looking for a solid investment, perhaps they want "a Rothko" to round out their collection of Abstract Expressionism, perhaps they want a large colorful painting to decorate a living-room wall. In any case, they are looking for a particular *kind* of painting. A few years later, Rothko would be sitting in his living room on a hot summer night and overhear a passerby ask, "I wonder who lives in this house with all the Rothkos?"[9] "Rothko" had become a noun, a noun conjuring up a particular kind of painting. "Rothko" had become an image—reproducible, ephemeral as a fashion.

Rothko paintings might be valued as investments, or they might be valued as the means to enhance the social prestige—i.e., the image—of the collector. Consider the effect of the following sentence, spoken at a hypothetical Park Avenue dinner party: "I own a Rothko." The statement expresses pride in possession, membership in an elite, and marks the speaker as a person of sophistication, taste, and wealth. He or she owns a *name* brand. Have you ever seen a gallery show which presented the best twenty paintings done in the last year by the artists represented by the gallery? Painters and sculptors produce unique objects; but galleries promote and market *artists*. From the viewpoint of the painter, to become a *name* is to be differentiated from the surrounding flood of anonymous artists, to become a unique value, to command a certain price, to occupy a place of honor. From the viewpoint of the collector, a name offers security, confidence, trust that one is purchasing a known entity. One need not look, only listen to the experts and buy.

The trouble with names is that—like images, like nouns—they define, bind, stabilize; they *fix*. Reputation springs a trap, of exactly the sort feared by the part of Rothko that wished to remain elusive, *unknown*, hidden, protected, and so free. Rothko once wrote (in a draft) of a "spirit of life which is never fixed always in a state of flux indeterminate and indeterminable variety"—and of the need to "protect" that "live phenomenon" from "those who either try to sell commodities or sell immortality."[10] Rothko created—"presences." Dealers sold, and collectors bought—images.

A "shrewd" man (his self-description), Rothko had sought to differentiate himself in the market by creating a "recognizable image," as had many of his contemporaries. When, in 1949, he discovered his format, he had found an image rich with associations and possible variations, and one simple enough to work "toward the elimination of all obstacles between the painter and the idea, and between the idea and the observer."[11] Now, twelve years later, with his paintings shown in galleries and museums, discussed and reproduced in *Vogue, Time, Life, Newsweek, House and Garden* and various art journals, Rothko's image was familiar, recognizable, already *known*.[12] Now, an image of his image was imposing an obstacle between the painter and his audience. By 1961 Rothko might be well-known, he might even be well-heeled, but he was not, he felt, well-understood.

His conception of the social role of the artist made it very difficult for Rothko to establish a stable, satisfactory relation to an art marketplace whose expansion and transformation coincided with, even as it caused, his own rising sales and income. Rothko was a Russian-Jewish exile whose social manner was sometimes courtly, sometimes testy, but generally a bit removed; he thought of himself as a Renaissance man whose broad cultivation informed his painting; he thought of himself as an Old Testament prophet whose message met resistance and hostility; he thought of his art as a ritual which disclosed, and rendered bearable, Dionysian terrors; he protected his art from distortion, rejecting exhibits, awards, a lucrative commission for the Four Seasons restaurant. Rothko placed himself apart from and above his social world, as if real identity were incompatible with it, except by mutilation.

Yet while jealously guarding his privacy and asserting his special position, Rothko was pulled toward human community. As a husband and father, as a man with a profession, as the owner of a home on East 95th Street and a cottage on Cape Cod, Rothko had secured himself a place in ordinary American social life: the middle class.[13] "When a person is a mystic he must always strive to make everything concrete," Rothko had warned Alfred Jensen. "Otherwise his viewpoint is speculative, obscure, or extremely subjective."[14] Rothko worried about dissociating himself from the ordinary human world. Rather than being an intransigent outsider or a comfortably bourgeois painter, Rothko remained *between,* fluid, enlivened by tensions and dualities.

His paintings, the presences embodying those tensions, attempted to cross the hollow space separating him from others while concealing him and preserving his own separateness. To a degree not true for most artists, Rothko needed to be understood, to communicate, for he looked to his art not just for recognition and regard, but for contact and even, as he told James Brooks, for love. The ideal circumstance would have been for Rothko to be the official artist in a small, cohesive community which both revered his objects and integrated them into its daily secular and sacred life. But Rothko was working in a modern, capitalist economy, and if modern social experience is about being looked at by strangers, modern economic experience is about trade with strangers. A man enters a gallery, examines the work, and (perhaps after some negotiation) writes a check and makes a purchase—no different from buying a suit. If he does this often enough, he rises to the status of "client," but the exchange, between two parties who freely go their separate ways afterward, remains impersonal. Painter and buyer do not meet, nor perhaps care to.

Always somewhat reluctant to let go of his work, Rothko did not like to think of his works as commodities, as objects circulating, passing from impersonal hand to impersonal hand, endlessly migrating, coming and going like the anonymous, ghostly figures in his *Subway Scene.* His living creations were "his children—and not some objects in which he ever abandoned involvement."[15] From Rothko's perspective, then, buying one of his paintings was not acquiring a mere object, much less an investment, but entering into an emotional relation, forming a bond which imposed obligations of care and fidelity. A sale was a reciprocal act of trust. Rothko, who always instructed that his pictures be hung, as he said they had been painted, "in a scale of normal living," was looking for homes for his creations, and he wanted permanent ones. "My father was always careful where his paintings went," said Kate Rothko. "Before he agreed to sell he would invite the people to his studio to meet them." Sometimes, after a purchase, he visited the buyer to check his painting's hanging, once traveling all the way to Philadelphia for the purpose.[16]

It was as if his "children" were being put out for adoption, and Rothko wanted to operate as his own social worker, assuring himself through interviews and home visits that his works were being placed with people committed to their care. No Jacob Rothkowitz, Mark Rothko took care of his creations.

Call him protective or call him controlling, but just as Rothko wished to move "beyond painting," he wished to move beyond exchange—by personalizing his sales. To the consternation of his dealers, once he had them, Rothko had always sold, and would continue to sell, paintings from the studio: face-to-face transactions. In fact, for about a year, between October 1962 and June 1963, Rothko had no dealer, rejecting the gallery system to sell paintings himself at the studio.[17] As he explained to one young painter, "The dealer gets a third, taxes take another third, and there's only a third left for my family. Why pay a dealer? I can sell four or five paintings a year from the studio and have plenty to live on."[18] Rothko's own motives were mixed—partly practical (he could keep the dealer's third), and partly idealistic (by meeting his buyers, he could determine whether they *really* loved his paintings or just wanted "a Rothko"). But he wanted his buyers to have *pure* motives.

But personal distribution simply created a different set of aggravations—for both seller and buyer. "Visiting Mark Rothko's studio in the 1960s was always a moving experience, artistically, and a prickly one, socially," Max Kozloff writes. "Prickly because of the painter's special pride, which could queer any openness in being with him and make it difficult to speak admiringly or to be casual. His visitors were given to understand that they were in the presence of a supreme master, one who might happen to take ill even the most spontaneous respect." "Underneath the arrogant facade," Rothko was "as suspicious of his own worth as he was hard on others," Kozloff believed, but that did not make visits more relaxed. Kozloff was a professional, an art critic; but even an old and close friend like Stanley Kunitz recalled that "it was to be expected that any day of the week if Mark was working on a painting he would call up and say, 'I want to show you something'. Then he would show you; he would stage it very carefully. The light had to be just right; everything had to be right. And he would watch your face while you looked at it. If your face didn't show exultation or if you didn't say anything, he would get very worried. Sometimes he would get a little angry even saying, 'I guess you don't like it'."[19] Eager to please and easily hurt, Rothko depended on the viewer to complete the "transaction," to make him feel whole, alive, beyond self-doubt.

Carefully staged occasions, the creator anxiously hovering about gauging the reactions of his audience, these visits were as casual as a stroll across a minefield. Imagine, then, how many more mines have been planted when the visitor is not a friend, or even an art critic, but a collector wealthy enough to be weighing the purchase of a $20,000 painting. New people were coming to his studio, Rothko complained to Ben Heller in the early 1960s, "and I don't know whether they want to buy a Rothko or they want to buy the particular painting."[20]

Sometimes, he *could* tell. One day President Kennedy's sister, Jean Kennedy Smith, and her brother-in-law, Sargent Shriver, came to the studio to look at paintings. Mrs. Smith asked if she could take home one or two pictures on approval, as if she were buying a dress. Rothko replied, "Look, I am not sending any pictures home on approval. It is not a case of my pictures fitting in with something else." Another woman bought, then wanted to exchange a dark picture—she said it "depressed" her—for a brighter one. Rothko accepted the dark one back and returned her money.[21] Now producing a desirable commodity, Rothko could reverse the power relation between artist and collector. He was no longer the poor relation. He could refuse to sell, or he could refuse to exchange, or (testing their commitment) he could make people wait.

But Rothko's basic problem lay not just with particular collectors, but with collecting. Collectors, after all, are consumers, not surrogate parents. What they *do* is to purchase, possess, accumulate, and display luxury objects. Together, these objects, valued because of their uniqueness, become parts, are absorbed into a new whole—e.g., the Nelson Rockefeller collection—which, reflecting the buyer's taste, judgment, and wealth, fabricates a prestigious social identity, or *image,* for the collector. Rothko wished to induce, through paintings, a diffused, contemplative state of consciousness freed of objects altogether. But collecting exemplifies the possessive self, a self created through objects, carefully selected, beautifully arranged in a domestic interior, in order to externalize—or to create—the subjective interior of the collector.

Given his different aims, values, and social position, and his economic dependence on them, Rothko had always approached collectors warily. Perhaps, within the actual range of possibilities in the New York art world, men like Donald Blinken and Ben Heller represented the best Rothko could do. Both were prosperous businessmen, both a generation younger than Rothko, both bought their first Rothko paintings fairly early (Heller in 1955 and Blinken in 1956), both continued to buy works by Rothko over the years, and both formed social relationships with him. By the early 1960s, Blinken owned five of Rothko's works, two of which hung in his living room, in an arrangement suggested and installed by Rothko.[22] As a 1962 *House and Garden* article on "How Young Collectors Live With Art" pointed out, "white walls, plain light carpeting and a minimum of furnishings, all contemporary," conspired "to make the art the center of attention" in Blinken's apartment.[23]

When Ben Heller had first seen Rothko's *Yellow Green* (1953) in the winter of 1953–54, he found it so beautiful that he suspected "it couldn't be a good painting because we all know that modern paintings weren't so pretty and beautiful; they had to be kind of disturbing and difficult." Over the next year, Heller looked at the painting some more, continued to think it was beautiful, and finally decided to buy it. Rothko wanted $1,500. Heller had determined to spend no more than $1,000 on contemporary American paintings. Rothko offered him the 10 percent museum discount, bringing the price down to $1,350. They continued to debate the price until Rothko declared, "Look, it's my misery that I have to paint this kind of painting, it's your misery that you have to love it, and the price of the misery is $1,350."[24] Heller bought the painting. In 1969, by which time the price of the misery had risen to $60,000, Heller bought his eighth Rothko.

"The one thing Rothko could not tolerate was what he viewed as infidelity to his art," said Blinken. "If you bought something, you could take your time, you didn't have to make quick decisions, but once you had it, he was very unhappy if you decided in six months really that you didn't want it, or you sold it to someone else for something else or traded it in. He felt that was a kind of betrayal, because what you were acquiring from him was, yes, oil on canvas, but it was also part of his psyche and his feeling about the world, and if you suddenly changed your mind about that, you were not only rejecting the picture, you were rejecting a piece of him." Indeed, Rothko, who once described his paintings as "skins that are shed and hung on a wall," could be very sensitive on this issue.[25] In 1969, he "was desperately anxious" for Heller to buy *White and Black on Wine* (1958), one of the early Seagram panels.[26] But for Heller to afford the painting, he had to pay partly with another Rothko. Heller had bought early and cheap; he bought late and expensive; he bought others—notably Pollock—but he was certainly committed to Rothko. Yet, after the 1969 exchange, Heller said, "Rothko would call up, saying, 'This is Rothko. How many Rothkos do you own today?'"[27]

Yet, for all his uncertainties about buyers, for all his possessiveness about his own work, for all of his efforts to personalize the exchange of art for money, for all of his difficulties with *trust,* Rothko, even after he was well-off and even after he was limiting his sales, continued to sell to many of the same institutions and persons that everyone else was selling to. He sold to museums, both American and European.[28] He sold to socially prestigious, "old" wealth (Nelson Rockefeller in 1958, Mrs. John D. Rockefeller III in 1959, and David Rockefeller in 1960).[29] He sold to socially prominent, "new" wealth (John and Dominique de Menil, and Burton and Emily Tremaine).[30] Certainly, Nelson Rockefeller, for one, had been collecting art since the early 1930s. He believed that "in our mechanized industrial age," "paintings and sculptures, artifacts created by individual hands and conceived by individual spirits, satisfy a craving for personality, for uniqueness. . . . Art has fulfilled that spiritual need for me."[31] Nelson knew the script. Perhaps he soulfully revealed to Rothko his thoughts about the spiritual significance of art. Perhaps Rothko even believed what he heard. But such a dialogue is very difficult to imagine taking place between Rothko and Robert and Ethel Scull.

"I know that I'm 'in'," Robert Scull said in 1965. "But," his wife added, "you might be 'out' tomorrow."[32] Their exchange was reported in *Newsweek*. In the mid-1960s, the Sculls were in *Vogue*, they were in a *New Yorker* profile, they were in a Tom Wolfe essay first published in *New York* magazine and later collected in *The Pump House Gang*, they were in *Time* and *Newsweek*, and even the *Metropolitan Museum Bulletin*.[33] As Jane Kramer wrote in the 1966 *New Yorker* profile, "over the past year, more space in the fashion monthlies, the news weeklies, and the daily gossip columns has been devoted to the social exploits and aesthetic predilections of Robert Scull and his wife, Ethel, than to anybody else on the art scene except Andy Warhol and his rock-'n'-roll band the Velvet Underground."[34]

In 1963, Robert Scull had commissioned Andy Warhol to do his wife's portrait. Warhol arrived one day at the Sculls' Fifth Avenue apartment, artist and subject hailed a cab, taxied to Times Square, went into an arcade where Warhol put Mrs. Scull into an automatic photo machine and began feeding the machine quarters. From the more than one hundred of these mechanically reproduced images, Warhol chose thirty-six, enlarged them, silkscreened them onto canvas, painted the squares bright reds, blues, greens, and yellows.[35] *Ethel Scull Thirty-Six Times* (1963) filled one wall of the library of the Sculls' eleven-room Fifth Avenue apartment. Ethel Scull appeared in an Andy Warhol movie. The Sculls were painted by Alfred Leslie and Robert Rauschenberg; they were cast in plaster by George Segal—an event which was covered by New York gossip columnists.[36] The Sculls were photographed in their apartment alongside Segal's images of them. The Sculls were in the media; they were in works of art; those works of art were reproduced in the media. At the end of the *New Yorker* profile, the Sculls, at their East Hampton summer house, are "planning" a "happening" with Allan Kaprow, their conversations being filmed by a WCBS TV crew making a documentary of the "happening," as well as by a second crew making a documentary of the documentary—and Kaprow would use footage from both documentaries in his happening.[37] The entire scene, of course, was being observed, and recorded, by the *New Yorker* journalist. Conspicuous consumption of art had made the Sculls themselves objects of mass media consumption.

The son of Russian-Jewish immigrants, Robert Scull, then Ruby Sokolnikoff, had been born in 1917 on New York's Lower East Side; his father worked as a tailor in the garment industry.[38] By the time Scull was fifteen, the Depression forced him to leave high school; he restored and resold furniture, sold store signs, manufactured soap, and hustled pool. A grandfather took him to the opera and museums, and stirred an interest in art. Scull took night courses at the Art Students League and Pratt Institute. By day he sold shoes, repaired gas stoves and modeled men's clothing. He worked as a free-lance illustrator. With a partner he started a design firm, producing fashion illustrations, designing radios, pens, clocks. In January 1944, he married Ethel Radner, a student at Parsons School of Design whom he called "Spike" after a truck driver. They moved into a one-room flat with a Murphy bed near the Museum of Modern Art, whose restaurant and sculpture garden Bob and Spike used to entertain their guests.

When, a few years later, Spike's father retired from his taxi business, he transferred it to the husbands of his three daughters. Striking out on his own, Scull gradually built up a fleet of a hundred and thirty cabs. He started a taxi-insurance firm, bought an apartment house, owned garages, warehouses, and factories in the Bronx, while he and his family moved to suburban Great Neck. "About 1952 or '53, I wanted a piece of art in the house," so Scull paid $245 for a Utrillo he knew was a fake. He overheard his neighbors gossiping about his "fantastic Impressionist collection." "He enjoyed being known on the block as a big collector so much that he immediately decided to become one."[39] Scull enjoyed the *image* of being a collector, an image invented with a fake. Then *that* became part of his image.

Scull began to buy Abstract Expressionist paintings—real ones. By the early 1960s, he decorated the walls of his living room with Barnett Newman's *White Fire,* Willem de Kooning's *Spike's Folly II,* Mark Rothko's *Number 16, 1960,* Clyfford Still's *Painting—1951,* and Franz Kline's *Initial.* Scull was appointed to the Museum of Modern Art's international council. When a wealthy industrialist or financier collects art—say a Rockefeller or a Morgan—he's attempting to enhance a public image ("tycoon" or "plutocrat" or "robber baron") he already has. But collecting was Scull's means of *creating* an image and gaining entry to the social world of New York's cultural elite. "To the Robert Sculls art is a happy moveable feast," *Vogue* gushed. "Art nourishes their lives, hangs on their walls, stands on their shelves. Their leisure time is a continuing safari through galleries and artists' studios. Their eyes are knowing, educated, their senses alive, their emotions as responsive as bull whips. . . . At times the Sculls' dining table seems like a news ganglion of the art field with the important nerves connecting there." As Tom Wolfe wrote, "Bob and Spike are the folk heroes of every social climber who ever hit New York."[40] Rudy Sokolnikoff and Ethel Radner had arrived—almost.

Once Bob asked Spike to instruct a reporter to refer to him not as a "taxi tycoon" but as a "collector." A hundred and fifty cabs do not a tycoon make, the term implying princely wealth and power. A small capitalist when compared, say, to Nelson Rockefeller, Scull, in fact, was only known as a "taxi tycoon" because of his reputation as a collector. Around places like the Museum of Modern Art, however, taxi money—as opposed to Rockefeller oil money—seemed a little uncouth, even when the tycoon hires (as Scull did) that arbiter of Protestant social codes, Amy Vanderbilt, "to teach courtesy and gracious manners" to his cab drivers.[41] Wishing to be known as a collector, a man who loves, knows, and can afford to buy art, Scull needed to deny his social and economic origins.

Instead, the Sculls continually committed the social gaffes of the nouveau riche. At a large party in Great Neck which introduced the Scull collection to the art world, Warhol recalled, the wife of the Pop painter James Rosenquist took a carnation from one of Ethel Scull's numerous floral arrangements. "Ethel zeroed in on her and screamed, 'You put that right back! Those are *my* flowers'." At an Andy Warhol Factory party, Warhol watched Scull approach a "major young painter," pull out a fifty-dollar bill and say, "We're about to run out of soda water—go get some." At the Tibor de Nagy Gallery, Scull asked if the $125 price on a Ralph Humphries painting could be reduced. The dealer, John Bernard Myers, proposed to Humphries that, if he would accept $85, Myers would not ask for a commission. When Myers reported to Scull that he had spoken to the painter, Scull offered him a $25 tip. Myers asked Scull to leave the gallery and never return.[42] Treating painters and dealers as if they were waiters, haggling over prices and slow to make his payments, Scull behaved not like a wealthy collector but like a cab driver who had dozed off during his Amy Vanderbilt lessons.

At Jasper Johns' 1959 Leo Castelli exhibit, Scull decided he wanted to buy the entire show. But Castelli told him, "No, no, that's very vulgar. We can't do that."[43] Acceptable collectors engage in a discreet interplay of exposure and concealment of their objects. But Scull was too greedy for pictures, too greedy for publicity—too *vulgar*—to be comfortably assimilated by the Protestant cultural elite. Since the high culture of Abstract Expressionism offered no sure ticket of admission, Scull turned to Pop art. Buying these young, still-unknown artists (in the early 1960s) Scull could identify himself as a cutting-edge collector, obtain works at very low prices, and surround himself with work just as engaged with publicity, celebrity, and fashion as he was.

Chapter Fourteen

In the fall of 1965, Scull auctioned thirteen of his Abstract Expressionist works. Declaring in 1966 that Abstract Expressionism had been dead for five to seven years, he banished it from the living-room walls of his Fifth Avenue apartment, replacing the works by de Kooning, Kline, Newman, Rothko, and Still with pieces by John Chamberlain, Jasper Johns, James Rosenquist, Frank Stella, and Andy Warhol. As Warhol observed, "in the period between '60 and '69, the Sculls more than anyone else came to symbolize success in the art scene at the collecting end."[44] Scull was *in*. He had fabricated his image; he became known as "the pop of Pop."

Robert and Ethel Scull, in short, represented everything about the evolving New York art world of the 1960s, everything about *life,* that Rothko abhorred. Ethel remembered an East Hampton party, where, after being introduced to Rothko, she began the conversation by saying "what a great pleasure it was to meet him."

Rothko: "That's no big deal . . . a lot of people are glad to meet me."
Ethel (to herself): "I own a Rothko and he's so mean to me." She asked if she could come to his studio and see his pictures.
Rothko: "I don't just let anybody up to my loft."
Ethel: "Well, I'm not just anybody. I'm collecting art and I love your work and I would love to see it."
Rothko: "No, you can't come up."[45]

So far so good. But the Sculls bought Rothko's *White Center* (1957) in 1959, *Reds* (1957) in 1960, and *Reds* (1961) in 1962.[46]

In the art market of the early 1960s Rothko confronted a situation he could neither transcend nor control, and his efforts at control, however idealistic, were inconsistent, as if part of him were willing to surrender his works to the market in exchange for its symbolic rewards. As Kunitz said, "He always needed confirmation." Even a dramatic act, such as his withdrawal from the 57th Street gallery scene altogether in 1962–63, did not place him outside the market. Instead, it placed the market *inside* the studio, violating, absorbing the space associated with Rothko's creativity and privacy. The whole process could exasperate him, waste time, and failed to produce guaranteed results. A conversation or two might expose the motives of buyers too complacent to be guarded—e.g., who wanted to take pictures home on approval—but it could not certainly determine which ones really *loved* his paintings.

Rothko, moreover, was moving backward, to personal exchange, at just that historical moment when New York's art market was being transformed by the arrival of its first multinational corporation. In mid-November 1963,

Marlborough Fine Art Ltd., with galleries already in London and Rome, opened its New York branch in a vast 12,000-square-foot space in the Fuller Building at the corner of 57th Street and Madison Avenue.

· · ·

You know it's not the critics, in the end it's our family we care about.
Mark Rothko

Rothko's sister, Sonia, and his brothers, Moise and Albert, had come to New York to see his Museum of Modern Art exhibit. Sonia, whose first husband had died, was remarried and still living in Portland, as was Moise, still a pharmacist. Albert, who during the Second World War had translated Russian into English for the Foreign Broadcast Information Service, now worked in Washington, D.C., translating for the CIA.

Contact between Rothko and his family was sparse. In the words of one nephew, "they were fond of each other, and when they were together, there was a very strong family tie and they picked up as if the conversation had had a brief pause," but, he adds, they weren't together that often. After the death of Kate Rothkowitz in 1948, Rothko visited Portland twice, in 1949 when he and Mell drove from New York with Moise and his wife, Clara, on the way to Rothko's teaching at the California School of Fine Arts, and in the summer of 1967, after Rothko's teaching at the University of California, Berkeley. Occasionally, as in 1961, family members came to New York, or they stayed with Mark, Mell, and Kate Rothko while they were vacationing in their Provincetown cottage. When nephews or nieces visited New York, Rothko treated them generously and kindly, showing them around, taking them to his parties, bringing them to his studio, going to their parties.[47]

Rothko did feel close to Sonia, who, he always insisted, had raised him, and to her son, Kenneth Rabin. Old grievances and disappointments did not estrange Rothko from the rest of his family, nor they from him, but differences in the kinds of lives they had chosen, and now differences of income and status, created an underlying strain between Rothko and his brothers. In Rothko's view, Moise, the older and more successful of the two brothers, should have helped support him more during his early years. Both brothers, Rothko believed, ridiculed his work and undermined his success. "His brothers came to town and immediately they took it for granted that if the Museum of Modern Art showed him, the Museum of Modern Art wasn't much." When I interviewed Moise for this book—he was then ninety-three—he began by saying, "I'm tired of talking about my brother." Yet this rivalry was felt on both sides. Rothko told a story about a visit by one of his brothers, during which Rothko suggested, "Why don't you go to see the Statue of Liberty?" and the brother had replied, "I don't like sculpture."[48] "He *loved* to tell that story," said Kenneth Rabin. With this Rothko ridiculed *them*, exposing his brothers' lack of sophistication.

Whenever the subject of Rothko's work arose, Moise declared, "I never understood it." Kenneth Rabin recalled having the same conversation at least five times with his uncle:

Moise: You know, I just don't understand his paintings.
Kenneth: Well, it's not something you have to understand. You look at them. You react. You like them or you don't like them.
Moise: But I don't understand them.

Rothko believed that his work spoke to a universal humanity; he said that an artist really cared about praise and recognition from family rather than critics, and he wanted his paintings to cross the gap separating him from others, to be *understood*. But he could not break through the cultural differences in his own family, not even after he had made an important name for himself in the art world. Less painful, then, to withdraw, keep apart.

Sometime in 1962 Albert Roth was told that he had an incurable cancer, a cancer of the colon—the same condition that had killed Rothko's father.[49]

Albert later recalled that he had been "sentenced to death in Washington," but Mark "found out, dragged me to New York. He was skeptical of doctors." By this time, Albert was very weak and thin, and could barely walk. Rothko sold two pictures to cover Albert's medical bills, arranged for him to be admitted to Memorial Hospital in New York where he underwent the first of three surgeries he would have during the 1960s.[50] Eventually Albert outlived Mark. In his family, Rothko's success and affluence placed him, the youngest and the least conventional, in the position of patriarchal figure, ordinarily a bit aloof, but involved, willing to take care of others in an emergency.

At the time of Albert's cancer, Rothko, concerned that his brother would die of the same cancer that had killed their father, was experiencing health problems of his own. In April 1962 Rothko told Dr. Grokest "how acutely depressed he was," and that he had returned to taking Surpicil, the medication for his high blood pressure. Grokest warned that the drug "does funny things to your adrenalin, affects concentration and nerve cells, and it accentuates depression." Rothko agreed to stop taking it. The following month, Rothko returned to Grokest's office, this time suffering from shingles, persistent bronchitis, a return of his gout (he'd stopped his medication), an injury from a fall, exhaustion, and depression. In June, Rothko was back with one of the worst staph infections Grokest had ever seen, infecting "literally every hair follicle" of Rothko's face, ears, left shoulder, and left wrist. Rothko "kept telling me how fatigued he was," said Grokest, but "my attempt at that point to tell him again that the bugs take over if you're depleted didn't sink in."

Rothko tried to take care of his paintings; he took care of his brother. But he didn't take care of himself. Using medications he shouldn't, not using ones he should have, ignoring Grokest's advice about diet and exercise, drinking, chain-smoking, chronically fatigued, Rothko neglected and abused his body, as if he could tolerate the comforts of an increasingly affluent life only by a kind of self-punishment, the reality of suffering. Now, with his brother under a death sentence, Rothko's own physical and psychic ills intensified, as if he were identifying with Albert's suffering.

"Tragic art, romantic art, etc. deals with the knowledge of death," Rothko had said at Pratt. Tragic art provides a ritualized confrontation with the diffusion which marks the beginning, and the end, of human life. Disturbing, undermining the illusion of security that enables us to manage daily life, such art also makes the insecurity at the bottom of life humanly bearable. In this way, an abstract art, apparently serene and tranquil, so close to the merely beautiful and decorative, faces the ultimate realities of death, loss, emptiness.

It is one thing to encounter dissolution in art; it is yet another to learn that your brother is dying of the same disease that killed your father. Rothko was jolted into the realization that his oldest and darkest fears were, well, *real*. According to one close friend, Rothko, who was "very very concerned" about his brother, also found the situation "frightening." After all, if Albert could die, so then could Mark. There "was a feeling of *timor mortis* in Rothko suddenly."[51] A frightened boy of ten, Rothko had not been able to save Jacob Rothkowitz; but as an adult, he was able to save Albert Roth, as if death *could* be managed.

Writing in late 1962 to Herbert Ferber (in Paris), Rothko told of New York's "superb" weather, a forthcoming Motherwell opening, "a few new pictures," the continuing "grind." "Harvard is coming to a conclusion favorably," he reported of his second mural project, this one for a private dining room at Harvard University.

But "over all," he added, "hangs the shadow of my brother."[52]

. . .

These young artists are out to murder us.

Mark Rothko

Chapter Fourteen

One Sunday in the early 1960s, Andy Warhol was walking through Greenwich Village with his friend Ruth Kligman. They met Mark Rothko. Kligman said, "Mark, this is Andy Warhol." Rothko "turned and walked away without a word."[53]

Another time Warhol, with Robert Indiana and Marisol, came to a party given by Yvonne Thomas. "When we walked into that room," Warhol recalled, "I looked around and saw that it was chock full of anguished, heavy intellects."

"Suddenly the noise level dropped and everyone turned to look at us." Warhol watched Rothko draw the hostess aside, "and I heard him accuse her of treachery: 'How could you let *them* in?'"[54]

While Rothko had been moving his work out of his Bowery studio in January of 1962—prior to moving his studio uptown—Ray Parker brought around Michael Goldberg, who had just returned to New York and was looking for a studio. Rothko asked Goldberg to pay him $300 for the plasterboard walls, the pulleys hung from the ceiling beams, and what Goldberg regarded as a "flimsy" movable wall—all of which Rothko had built for the Seagram project. Goldberg suggested that perhaps Rothko could just leave the carpentry as a favor to a young painter. Rothko refused. Instead, he said, "Come on," took Goldberg to a nearby Second Avenue Chinese restaurant, where he bought him lunch and a drink, then brought him back to the studio, opened a drawer filled with his watercolors and gave Goldberg one. But he still wanted the $300.

When the young painter Al Held had returned to New York after living in Paris for a while, he looked up Rothko, who "treated me like a prince." "He sat me down, literally pulled out every painting in his studio, showed me all his paintings, was very patient, spent the whole afternoon with me. Then we went down to a bar, he bought me a drink and a sandwich, and we talked for a while." As Held was leaving, he thanked Rothko and said, "Well, Mr. Rothko, in about six months perhaps we could do this again." Rothko repled, "Oh, no, no, no, you shouldn't see me; you should find your own contemporaries and build your own world, your own life like I did with my contemporaries." Held felt "terribly rejected," "absolutely enraged." "It took me years," he said, "to realize what a favor he had done me. Other artists in New York were very, very seducing."[55]

During another of Rothko's studio moves, he asked Jon Schueler to help him carry some big canvases. As the two men worked, Rothko began discoursing about the paintings—"he was terribly interesting at bringing out these things and talking about them"—but as Rothko went on, he began handling the paintings roughly. "Each one was like a killing gesture, terribly destructive." Schueler was appalled, "and I'd keep trying to hold things together and at the same time to listen. And then at that point he looked at me and he pulled out a painting and said, 'My paintings are nothing'." Schueler was intrigued by Rothko's statement. Was he being clever? Or melodramatic? If not, what *was* he saying? When Schueler returned the following day to complete the job, Rothko refused to discuss the issue. The job finished, Rothko and Schueler had a beer in a nearby bar. "The talk had been about such close things, things you wanted to understand, that I was really wide open, vulnerable, and I started talking," Schueler said. "He had been talking for two days; now it's Schueler's turn. I told him that I found myself in the mood to try to feel these things, how I wanted my paintings to go, what painting means to me." But whatever Schueler said, Rothko dismissed or derided it. "Whatever I talked about, he'd turn it upside down. Looking back on it, which I can now do quite without animosity, I can see how cruel it was."

Visiting Jasper Johns' first one-man show at Leo Castelli's Gallery in early 1958, Rothko, after looking around at the targets and flags, commented, "We worked for years to get rid of all that."[56]

In 1953, Robert Rauschenberg was wondering "whether a drawing could be made out of erasing." He tried erasing some of his own drawings, but that didn't satisfy him, because he wanted "to start with something that was a hundred percent art, which mine might not be." So he went to Willem de Kooning's Tenth Street studio, where he spent "quite a while" convincing de Kooning to give him a drawing. One month and forty erasers later, Rauschenberg had produced *Erased de Kooning Drawing* (1953).[57]

In 1957, Leo Castelli, a collector and occasional collaborator with Sidney Janis, opened his own gallery, in the living room of his East 77th Street apartment, selling European moderns and Abstract Expressionists from his own collection.[58]

In January 1958, Jasper Johns' one-man show at Castelli's Gallery "hit the art world like a meteor." Johns' targets and flags included *Target with Four Faces* (1955): above the painted target Johns had placed a row of four plaster-cast heads cut off at mid-nose by the top of the wooden box in which they had been inserted. Before the exhibit opened, *Target with Four Faces* had been reprinted on the cover of *Art News,* and before the show closed all but two of Johns' paintings had been sold, three purchased by Alfred Barr for the Museum of Modern Art.[59]

Two months later, Robert Rauschenberg's one-man exhibit at Castelli's was "a *succès de scandale.*" Rauschenberg's combine-paintings included real, everyday objects, such as buttons, a paint tube, a handkerchief, a mirror, a stuffed eagle, a wood chair, a wood ladder, a tire. In *Bed* (1955), Rauschenberg had stretched an old patchwork quilt, added a sheet and pillow at the top, and vigorously brushed, splattered, and dripped red, yellow, white, blue, brown, green in the space from the bottom half of the pillow to the top half of the quilt. "Almost everyone was offended by the show, and only two works were sold," one of them to Castelli.[60]

Jasper Johns was twenty-eight, Robert Rauschenberg thirty-three.

In December 1959, "Sixteen Americans" opened at the Museum of Modern Art, including nine works by Johns, seven "combine-paintings" by Rauschenberg and four Black paintings by Frank Stella. Stella painted stripes, separated by thin lines of canvas, forming a series of concentric rectangles. His premeditated, geometric canvases purged what he called "the romance of Abstract Expressionism." "I began to feel very strongly about finding a way that wasn't so wrapped up in the hullabaloo . . . something that was stable in a sense, something that wasn't constantly a record of your sensitivity, a record of flux."[61] Alfred Barr purchased Stella's *The Marriage of Reason and Squalor* (1959) for the Museum of Modern Art.

In May-June 1960, Stella held his first one-man exhibition at Leo Castelli.

Frank Stella was twenty-four.

One afternoon in 1960 Leo Castelli's manager, Ivan Karp, visited the studio of Andy Warhol. Warhol had "stashed away out of sight" all his commercial work, showing Karp pictures of advertisements (for Coke, corn pads, Del Monte canned peaches, trusses) and comic strips (Batman, Dick Tracy, Nancy, Popeye, Superman). "I still had the two styles I was working in—the more lyrical painting with gestures and drips, and the hard style without the gestures," Warhol later said. "I liked to show both to people to goad them into commenting on the differences, because I wasn't sure if you could completely remove all the hand gesture from art and become noncommittal, anonymous." Karp told Warhol, "These blunt, straightforward works are the only ones of any consequence. The others are all homage to Abstract Expressionism and are not."[62]

By 1961, Roy Lichtenstein, working independently of Warhol, was painting images from Mickey Mouse, Popeye and Romance comics. He described his work as "anti-contemplative, anti-nuance, anti-getting-away-from-the-tyranny-of-the-rectangle, anti-movement-and-light, anti-mystery, anti-paint-quality, anti-Zen, and anti all of those brilliant ideas of preceding movements which everyone understands so thoroughly."[63]

In *Art as an Investment* (1961)—a guidebook for novice collectors—Richard Rush advised that "while there exists a great demand for Abstract painting and there is little question that this type painting is in vogue in the year 1961, this School may already be over the top in public preference."[64]

On December 1, 1961, Claes Oldenburg opened "The Store" on East 2nd Street in New York's Lower East Side. A rear room functioned as Oldenburg's studio, where he fabricated commercial objects, mostly simulated food and clothing (*Liver Sausage with Slices, Cherry Pastry, Roast Beef, The White Slip, Jacket and Shirt Fragment, Blue Hat,* etc.), usually by soaking fabric in plaster, shaping it on a wire frame, then painting the object in bright, gaudy colors. The art (with prices like $69.95) was then sold, by Oldenburg himself, in the front room of the store. Oldenburg characterized his work as a "realism which copies the posters and the ads instead of the thing itself."[65]

In June 1962, *Life* magazine announced that "Something New Is Cooking" in art, pointing to the "assembly lines of pies and cakes" painted by Wayne Thiebaud, the "gigantic fragments of billboard images" painted by James Rosenquist, the sculptured woman seated "on a real seat at a real table, brooding over a real cup," done by George Segal, and the "giant cartoons" produced by Roy Lichtenstein.[66]

On October 31, 1962, "The New Realists" exhibit, including work from France, England, Italy, Sweden, and the United States, opened at the Sidney Janis Gallery. Among the Americans shown were Jim Dine, Robert Indiana, Roy Lichtenstein, Claes Oldenburg, James Rosenquist, George Segal, and Andy Warhol. The scope and size of the show—which overflowed Janis's galleries and continued in an empty 57th Street store—marked it as an Important Event, as did Janis himself in a catalogue essay. Just "as the Abstract Expressionist became the world-recognized painter of the 50s," he wrote, so the new realist "may already have proved to be the pacemaker of the 60s."[67] The show did not uncover a new avant-garde; it announced the uptown arrival of what came to be known as Pop, in the gallery most closely associated with Abstract Expressionism.

To protest the show, Adolph Gottlieb, Philip Guston, Robert Motherwell, and Mark Rothko all withdrew from the Janis Gallery, asking Janis, in effect: How could you let *them* in?[68]

In March 1963, the expanded and renovated Jewish Museum opened with a retrospective exhibition of the work of Robert Rauschenberg. Rauschenberg was thirty-seven.

Calling Pop art "the biggest fad since art belonged to Dada," *Time* wryly observed in March 1963 that "symposiums discuss it; art magazines debate it; galleries compete for it. Collectors, uncertain of their own taste, find pop art paintings ideal for their chalk-walled, low-ceilinged $125,000 co-op apartments in new buildings on Park Avenue."[69]

"More Buyers Than Ever Sail into a Broadening Market," a September 1963

Chapter Fourteen

issue of *Life* announced. The art market, resurging after a stock-market dip, showed a new "trend toward artists who paint recognizable objects," with Pop art "the newest best-seller."[70]

In February 1964, the Jewish Museum held a retrospective exhibit of the work of Jasper Johns. Johns was thirty-four.

For the 1964 Venice Biennale, the American commissioner, Alan Solomon, director of the Jewish Museum, chose four "germinal" artists (Jasper Johns, Morris Louis, Kenneth Noland, and Robert Rauschenberg) and four "younger" artists (John Chamberlain, Jim Dine, Claes Oldenburg, and Frank Stella)—all post-Abstract Expressionist painters. Rauschenberg became the first American to win the Biennale's International Grand Prize for Painting.

On October 13, 1965, Robert Scull sold thirteen of his Abstract Expressionist paintings at a highly publicized Parke-Bernet auction which, as *Newsweek* pointed out, "was bound to raise the question that the art world had been quietly asking: is abstract expressionism passé?" The results for Rothko were not very encouraging, since his *Number 22 (Reds)* went for $15,000, while de Kooning's *Police Gazette* sold for $37,000 and Still's *Painting—1951* sold for $29,000. Scull was financing his move to Pop art, which he described as "possibly greater than any previous art—yes, *any* previous art."[71]

In the summer of 1965, the Los Angeles County Museum of Art had shown "The New York School: The First Generation, Paintings of the 1940s and 1950s." Citing the curator's decision to include no paintings after 1959, Barnett Newman complained: "It seems to me that the attitude toward the show by those who organized it is as if we were all dead."[72]

In 1965, the painter John-Franklin Koenig, visiting New York from Paris, had dinner with Mark Rothko at the house of Dore Ashton. Rothko "stated that he felt as if he were dead; after having been brought to a pinnacle during the heyday of Abstract Expressionism, he was left in the heights where only museums and large corporations could acquire him. On the other hand he was no longer 'hot': no magazines even mentioned him, no young artists even tried to visit him."[73]

• • •

In America, "one can never become a patriarch, one simply becomes an old man."

Mark Rothko

"Rothko was very much of a Jewish patriarch. He looked like it. He thought like it. He acted like it," recalled Peter Selz. A patriarch is a man of considerable age and dignity, a revered founder, like Abraham, or a wise father, like Jacob Rothkowitz. A patriarch possesses a secure *place,* at the head of a line of succession.

On August 31, 1963, Mell Rothko gave birth to a son, named Christopher, called "Topher." Though the Rothkos had tried for many years to have a second child, the pregnancy had not been expected.[74] Christopher had been conceived during the months when the "shadow" of his brother's cancer hung over Rothko's life. Christopher's mother was forty-one, his father a month short of sixty.

"They were very excited about it," said Kate Rothko. "At least to me it seemed extremely positive." Others recall that Rothko was "delighted" and "overjoyed" at the birth of his son, at the birth of *a* son. And "he was very proud of the fact that he was going to have a baby who was born quite a long time after the first one." But one of Mell's sisters remembered that when Mell called with news of the pregnancy, she said, "Mark is bemused," as if he were slightly removed from and puzzled by his late paternity. To a friend he met at a birthday party for Helen Frankenthaler, Rothko commented, "I'm too old."[75]

Among artists, Rothko "wanted to be an elder statesman, a great leader," said Vita Deming. In the early 1950s, Rothko had told David Hare that he and his friends were "producing an art that would last for a thousand years." "That's not a revolutionary idea," Hare commented, "it's the reaction of a revolutionary to revolution, which is that the revolution is going to be permanent." During the 1950s, Helen Frankenthaler, Michael Goldberg, Al Held, Joan Mitchell, Ray Parker, Jon Schueler (among many others) constituted a second generation of Abstract Expressionists, suggesting that the revolution had *some* staying power. But by 1959 *Art News* was already asking, in a two-part symposium, "Is There a New Academy?"[76] As Helen Frankenthaler pointed out, if you raise the question at all, the answer is yes.

Other young painters found their own contemporaries, and built their own artistic worlds, just as Rothko had done with his contemporaries. Beginning painters of the 1950s were the first generation of American artists to undertake their careers with the burden of a set of powerful and immediate predecessors. By the mid-1960s, however, the Abstract Expressionist generation had been weakened by the deaths of two of its leading figures, Jackson Pollock and Franz Kline, by rivalries and disputes, by the advancing age of the survivors, by their concern with protecting rather than taking territory, and by the need of an expanding art market for the stimulus of new names and styles. A new force,

Chapter Fourteen

moreover, had been added to the old network—artist, dealer, critic, curator, collector—which governed the evaluation and distribution of art: the media. An artist like Andy Warhol could now seek, find, paint, and enjoy celebrity. A new, accelerated pace of change allowed figures like Rauschenberg, Johns, Stella, Oldenburg, Warhol to succeed *rapidly,* allowed Pop to displace Abstract Expressionism as *the* "hot" movement.

Rothko himself became convinced that a preference for the Pop artists had led the Italian collector Count Giuseppe Panza di Biumo to back out of an agreement to purchase five of the Seagram murals. "My visits in your studio was one of the greatest events of my collector life," Count Panza had written to Rothko in October 1960. "I remember, like a dream, the beautiful canvasses that I saw at you." At this time, the Count owned one painting by Rothko. By September of the following year, he owned six, and he was talking about devoting the collection in his Villa Litta (at Varese, north of Milan) "almost exclusively" to Rothko's work. To this end, he wanted to buy four to six additional paintings. During Rothko's London visit for the opening of his Whitechapel exhibit, the two men met and agreed that Rothko would sell the count some paintings, to be selected when he traveled to New York in late October. He selected five of the Seagram murals, at $20,000 each. "I am engaged in grouping together all five of your paintings in a single room," he wrote to Rothko. "You may rest assured you have found a man who will always love them and look after them, as some of the highest expression of human beings."[77]

Two years later, however, Count Panza wrote to Rothko that "the bad business conditions now existing in Italy"—the Italian stock market was slumping—made it impossible for him to continue his monthly payments. Having already paid Rothko about $40,000, he proposed that he receive two individual works instead of the five murals. Over the following several months, as Panza and Rothko determined which two paintings the count would buy, he kept reassuring Rothko that the business situation "*is* the only real cause of my decision and I was forced to do so by the adverse situation against my will." Count Panza, a very active collector during the previous five years, did stop buying between 1962 and 1966, a pause he later attributed to the Italian economic crisis of those years.[78]

Believing that twentieth-century painters experienced short periods of strong creativity, Count Panza liked to acquire several pieces from the high periods of those artists whose work engaged him. He eventually owned at least seven Rothkos (all done between 1953 and 1960).[79] When the count wanted to substitute two individual works for the five murals, he asked Rothko to send him slides of 1952–60 works, and he finally selected two "bright paintings," he said, as "more in balance with the dark ones" already in his collection.[80] This preference for older, brighter canvases would *not* have left Rothko reassured. Even worse, by the time the count backed out of his agreement with Rothko, he had made several purchases at Claes Oldenburg's "The Store," and he had bought works by James Rosenquist and Roy Lichtenstein. Count Panza, Rothko came to believe, had—like Robert Scull—abandoned Abstract Expressionism for Pop.[81]

All through the 1960s, Rothko's work continued to sell, his prices continued to rise. Yet Rothko, as many of his friends attest, felt neglected, alienated, displaced; the issue was his *position*. The caricaturist Al Hirschfeld, a 95th Street neighbor, recalled Rothko "was so depressed because he felt that what was happening in the world of art had passed him by somehow." Hirschfeld told him he had just read a poem "absolutely worshipful" of Rothko's work. "Yes," Rothko replied, "but that's all in the past. That's all finished, that's all gone. The new things I don't understand at all. I'm quite out of it. I don't know what they're doing." Pop was "the coming thing, the tide had passed him by."[82]

Rothko's theme, once again, was loss, partly a loss of power and control; he was like a Jewish patriarch whose son has just announced his refusal ever to attend *cheder* again. Sometimes, as in his conversation with Al Held, Rothko could step back and invite a young man to find his own way, just as Milton Avery had done when he decided he would no longer show Rothko and Gottlieb his work each day. Rothko could be cruel to be kind—or he could be just cruel, as he was with Jon Schueler, when his harshest doubts about his own work (it's "nothing") provoked him to lash out at a vulnerable young painter. But by the early 1960s, toward the most visible and independent of the next generation of painters, Rothko felt resentment, and he especially resented their quick success, as if he wished to impose on subsequent artists the frustrations and sufferings of his own past. Yet, as another 95th Street neighbor, the painter Karl Schrag, pointed out, "the problem was not just being replaced, but *what* was replacing him."[83]

The shift from Abstract Expressionism to Pop involved more than just another of the generational battles that have characterized movements in all the arts for the past two centuries. One boundary that Rothko and his contemporaries drew very firmly was the line separating high art from popular art. Like many modernists, Rothko perceived popular culture as a kind of female danger, threatening to weaken, absorb, smother the struggling heroes of the male avant-garde.

Pop art dissolved that boundary, not just by using comic-strip and advertising images, but (in Warhol's case) by adopting a demystified—i.e., cynical—

relation to the market. "To be successful as an artist," Warhol advised, "you have to have your work shown in a good gallery for the same reason that, say, Dior never sold his originals from a counter in Woolworth's," as if Warhol thought marketing a painting were no different from selling a Dior dress. "If a guy has, say, a few thousand dollars to spend on a painting, he doesn't wander along the street till he sees something lying around that 'amuses' him," Warhol goes on. "He wants to buy something that's going to go up and up in value, and the only way that can happen is with a good gallery," as if collecting art as an investment, relying on brand names (in this case of galleries), were by no means developments to be deplored.[84]

Rather than pondering "The Crisis of Subject Matter," Warhol took suggestions from friends about what he should paint, and one evening after he'd asked several people, a woman responded, "Well, what do you love most?" Warhol produced a silkscreen of *192 One-Dollar-Bills* (1962).[85] With his wry, affectless acceptance of the commercial, his innocent tone itself a calculated provocation, Warhol was commenting on the pretensions of a commercially successful generation which claimed spiritual aims and heroic inwardness for its art.

One of those pretensions was "style." "Style isn't really important," Warhol said. His use of preexisting images and of mechanical techniques of reproduction such as silk-screening did not attempt to develop a new style but to question the very notion of the private self on which the goal of a unique or individual style is based. As Warhol said in *POPism*, "Pop Art took the inside and put it outside, took the outside and put it inside."[86] Jasper Johns had moved away from Abstract Expressionism by painting common, recognizable objects: flags, targets, maps. Robert Rauschenberg incorporated actual, everyday objects into his combine-paintings: a wooden chair, a ladder, a quilt. But instead of pushing toward reality, Warhol made works out of *images*: advertisements, newspaper photographs, brand labels. "Now the language of images is everywhere"—the visual language of a postmodern consumer culture increasingly dominated by the visual media.

"By 'modernity'," Baudelaire had written a century before, at the very beginnings of cultural modernism, "I mean the ephemeral, the fugitive, the contingent, the half of art whose other half is the eternal and the immutable."[87] Abstract Expressionism constituted the last major artistic movement within modernism. Painters like de Kooning, Kline, and Pollock, or Motherwell, Newman, and Rothko, conceived of the artist as an alien figure, able to step outside a repressive social environment to uncover a core human presence which had survived the fragmentation, massive violence, Kafkaesque bureaucracies, crushing trivialities, the restlessness and despair of twentieth-century life. Coming at the end of modernism, these painters could achieve the eternal only by transcending (or in Rothko's word, "pulverizing") the mundane and the ephemeral.

With Warhol, the artist no longer set himself up as an outsider. Now, one can no longer lament the fate of a person being reduced to an image—because one can no longer speak of persons. "Some day everybody will think just what they want to think, and then everybody will be thinking alike; that seems to be what is happening," said Warhol. The human inside has been absorbed by the social outside, just as art has been absorbed by commerce. "Angst," "alienation," "freedom," "tragic art," "human scale," "originality"—the vocabulary of Abstract Expressionism—is now mocked as hollow and obsolete. In Warhol's silk-screened photos of celebrities—*Red Elvis* (1962) copies a publicity photograph of Elvis thirty-six times—human presence has been dispersed into a series of infinitely and mechanically reproducible images.

When Rothko turned away from Andy Warhol that Sunday afternoon in Greenwich Village, one of the last generation of modern painters was—rightly—refusing to greet what was replacing him: postmodernism.

. . .

Remember, I don't collect pictures; I collect money.

Frank Lloyd

In November 1963, the Marlborough-Gerson Gallery opened in New York City. Occupying 12,000 square feet on the sixth floor of the Fuller Building at 57th and Madison, its interior designed by Wilder Green (who had helped Rothko install his Harvard mural project), the gallery was larger, more elegantly appointed, and certainly backed by more capital than many museums. Even so, at one point in the evening, so many of the 2,500 invited guests had actually arrived that firemen ordered the doors shut. While those inside sipped champagne and ate French biscuits, others waited in the elevators. *Time* covered the event, commenting that "gallery openings in Manhattan are beginning to rival the opera in silken elegance and the subway for sheer squeeze."[88] As one ominous hint of Marlborough's future—and of the chicanery behind the silken facade—that evening one of the guests, Larry Rivers, was served a subpoena from the Tibor de Nagy Gallery, for violating his contract with them by joining Marlborough.

Lawsuits and champagne, media coverage and crowds: none of these were much in evidence when Peggy Guggenheim had opened Art of This Century.

Chapter Fourteen

In those days, no corporations, no museums, and only about a dozen individuals were collecting contemporary American avant-garde art.[89] Marlborough's arrival, in fact, culminated twenty years of change in the size, economic growth, sales techniques, and social standing of the New York art world—then helped drive those changes up to yet the next plateau. Previously, New York galleries might be hushed Victorian or white-walled contemporary in style, but they were small operations, run by the owner and a few assistants. The owner might be an artist, like Betty Parsons, or a businessman turned collector and connoisseur, like Sidney Janis.

But Frank Lloyd of Marlborough was simply, and avowedly, a businessman. "I have hired many dilettantes who know art, but who are afraid of soiling their hands by making a sale," he said.[90] To this hard-nosed approach, Lloyd added corporate scale, modern methods of promotion, and a certain crass glamor. When he had been a young man in Vienna, Lloyd recalled, "no one knew me. Today the biggest names call me from all over the world. I'm a worldwide operation. When Marlborough Rome is getting up, Marlborough New York is going to bed."[91] The sun never set on Marlborough, as if it were the British empire.

Like Mark Rothko, Frank Lloyd was Jewish, an exile, once impoverished, now wealthy, a powerful, international "name." Rothko was one of the last generation of painters who could believe that painting could carry the burden of "tragedy, ecstacy, doom," as he once put it. Lloyd was the first man to bring what one former employee called "a 20th century-multinational style" to the sale of art. "If someone's a dealer, he's a dealer," Lloyd said. "Many dealers are hypocrites—they say we're here to educate the public. I don't believe it. For a business, the only success is money."[92] Frank Lloyd mocked the pretensions of traditional dealers just as Andy Warhol mocked the pretensions of Abstract Expressionist painting. Unfortunately, Rothko did not turn on his heel when he met Lloyd.

Born Franz Kurt Levai in Vienna in 1911, Lloyd had grown up in a well-off family, his father dealing in antique furniture, silver and china, and sometimes in art. In 1929, Lloyd graduated from Vienna's Commercial Academy, fell in love with an "older woman," fell out with his father, then struck out on his own. He worked for a coal firm, started his own lubricating-oil business, then raised enough Viennese capital to build and operate several gas stations. Independently, and at a young age, Lloyd had built a successful business "in oil," as he later liked to describe it.[93] He even began to collect modern art, buying works by Picasso and the Fauves. All his efforts, however, were shattered in 1938, when the Nazis arrived in Vienna. To obtain a passport and exit visa, Lloyd bribed an SS officer, offering all of his possessions in exchange for the papers. But Lloyd did manage to conceal a few paintings from the Germans and to smuggle them to Paris. Lloyd himself arrived in Paris not long after.

When the Germans invaded France in May 1940, Lloyd fled to Biarritz, near Spain in southwest France. When the French government decided to detain all German and Austrian nationals, Lloyd was interned in a camp near Bordeaux, from which he escaped during the chaos following the fall of France. He then fled to England on a ship evacuating retreating Polish troops. In England, he was first interned, then freed to join the Pioneer Corps, a labor battalion assigned to dig trenches, clear forests, and erect barbed-wire defenses against German invasion.

While doing KP one day, Lloyd met another Viennese refugee, Harry Fischer, who had sold rare books and held small exhibits of drawings by contemporary artists in one room of his bookshop. "Before long Fischer and Lloyd found rooms in a neighboring town where they could keep their civilian clothes, cook themselves unmilitary meals, play the gramophone, sit in at an occasional poker game, and dream about 'after the war'." To the depressed Fischer, Lloyd would say, "Don't you worry. After the war I'll start a new business and bring you in as a partner."[94]

Meanwhile, Lloyd got himself transferred to the tank corps, trained as a mechanic, put "in charge of a tank and heavy transport repair unit," landed on the beaches of Normandy, served in France, and was finally discharged in 1946. "Life No. 2 began after Hitler," Lloyd said. "I decided for the rest of my life never to do anything that I didn't enjoy." Before the war, the independent son of an antique and art dealer built gas stations. After the war—his parents had been murdered at Auschwitz—Lloyd decided that what he would most enjoy was continuing the family business. Remaining in England, he started a small concern exporting antiques. One day, he accidentally met Harry Fischer on the street. Both men were "practically broke," but together they opened a rare-book shop on the first floor and an art gallery in the basement at 17–18 Old Bond Street.[95] Just before the invasion of Normandy, to protect his relatives from German reprisals, Franz Kurt Levai had changed his name to Francis Kenneth Lloyd, after the bank. When Lloyd opened his London business with Fischer, he named it Marlborough, after the duke.

By 1948, the firm had just about acquired a duke of its own, hiring the twenty-two-year-old David Somerset, in line to become the Duke of Beaufort. "We needed some class, some atmosphere," said Lloyd. "David gave it to us. He also gave us entrée into the British aristocracy, which was selling off many of its masterpieces in those days." Postwar economic austerity and high taxes were forcing the English gentry to unload their ancestral collections. Lloyd travelled Europe gaining entrée to the new aristocracy of industrialists and businessmen that would buy those masterpieces. "We linked the supply to the demand," he said.[96]

But Lloyd foresaw "the prospect of a steadily decreasing supply." "There are only so many old masters," he said, "and once one is sold to a museum, it is off the market for good."[97] Marlborough moved into the market for living British artists, not young, promising, unrecognized artists, but well-known ones, with names. By the end of the 1950s, the gallery, now moved to 39 Old Bond Street (above a branch of Lloyd's Bank), had acquired Lynn Chadwick, Francis Bacon, Henry Moore, Ben Nicholson (among others)—all lured away from the London galleries which had been slowly nurturing their reputations for many years. "To a postwar, London art scene still steeped in the Edwardian era," where advertisement was deemed vulgar, "Lloyd brought big-time promotional techniques." Combining aggressive, corporate methods, with a facade of "aristocratic connotations," Lloyd could become a new kind of dealer, moving into a new market (for living artists) which could provide large, quick profits for the dealer and safe investments for the client (since these were known artists).

With artists he was wooing, Lloyd turned on his Viennese schmooze. He flattered. He promised long-term contracts, international exposure, lavish color catalogues, higher prices, corporate scale, modern business methods. He offered free secretarial help, legal advice, accounting services, real estate and travel aid, estate planning, tax guidance—all perks designed to make his artists feel like important people, well-rewarded and well-taken care of. In exchange, Marlborough received a 50 percent commission, not the traditional one-third. "If they want to ride in a Rolls Royce instead of a Volkswagen, they have to pay for it," said Lloyd. "We are the best service organization around."[98] In 1960, Lloyd, with Carla Panicalli and Bruno Herlitzka as partners, opened the Marlborough Galeria d'Arte in Rome. But "art was moving West," Lloyd said. "So did we." In 1963, Lloyd purchased the Otto Gerson Gallery in New York, with its stock of European moderns. He invested $400,000 in designing and furnishing Marlborough-Gerson's space on the sixth floor of the Fuller Building. He held a dinner at the St. Regis Hotel, to which he invited Bernard Reis and three of his clients: Philip Guston, Willem de Kooning, and Mark Rothko.[99] Guston recalled that the conversation went like this:

Lloyd: We will do anything—just tell me what we can do for you.
de Kooning: Okay, stop people from copying me.
Lloyd (nodding, all smiles): Oh yes, we will do that.
Rothko: Will you give me a one-man show in Dvinsk?
Lloyd (bigger smile): Oh yes, we will do that.

Lloyd showed the painters layouts of his London and Rome galleries, plans for the New York gallery's 170-foot-long hall, its blue-slate floor, its movable partitions. By the end of the dinner, Guston said, Rothko was incoherently drunk.[100]

Frank Lloyd had chosen well when he selected Bernard Reis as his entrée into the sale of Abstract Expressionist painting. By 1963, Reis's accounting firm, with offices on East 40th Street at Fifth Avenue, employed about fifteen accountants. He and his staff were not doing tax returns for the corner druggist. Reis's clientele consisted of wealthy, prominent people in or around the arts, including theater people such as Edward Albee, Joshua Logan, and Clinton Wilder, writers such as Lillian Hellman and Gore Vidal, collectors such as Peggy Guggenheim and Albert and Mary Lasker, and painters such as Willem de Kooning, Adolph Gottlieb, Philip Guston, Herbert Ferber, Helen Frankenthaler, Franz Kline, Robert Motherwell, and Mark Rothko.[101]

Reis had continued to expand the collection he began in the 1920s. He collected "primitive" totems and masks, he collected modern art, and he collected art books, including de luxe editions of prints. Since 1945, he and his wife Rebecca had lived in a narrow (16′ wide), five-story brownstone on East 68th Street. The first three floors, sparely but elegantly furnished, displayed works by Picasso, Braque, Gris, Grosz, Chagall, Miró, Klee, Lipchitz—as well as paintings by de Kooning, Gorky, Guston, Kline, Motherwell, and Rothko.[102] The third-floor library contained Reis's vast collection of art books. In a first-floor dining room that looked out through a glass wall into a terraced garden where rose bushes surrounded a large bronze sculpture by Lipchitz, the Reises held small dinner parties, or at other times they filled the house with cocktail parties for 250.

"A petite lady" who carried "a lorgnette through which she would peer with the amused eyes of a tiny owl," Becky Reis "always wore huge primitive bracelets and necklaces of gold or ivory that she carried with the same panache as her lorgnette." Known as a superb hostess and cook, she wrote *The Unharried Hostess: Thirty Dinners in Thirty Minutes* (1963), containing recipes for dishes such as "Strawberries Romanoff" and "Broiled Lobsters a la Reis." "My husband and I have always looked upon great cooking—accompanied by good wines—as one of the fine arts," she declared, and so "on our frequent trips to Europe and the Far East we have sought it out as one of our two major interests, the other being beautiful works of art and their acquisition."[103] Eating and acquiring, as if great food and beautiful paintings were pretty much identical, the Reises enjoyed a style of tasteful, upper-middle-class pleasures.

At sixty-eight, Bernard Reis was pink-faced, gray-haired, elegantly tailored, cheerful, smoking constantly, his cigarettes held in a plastic holder. Possessing none of the theatricality, or the churlishness, of Rothko or Lloyd, Reis was soft-spoken, confidential, intimate in manner, often standing beside, holding the elbow of, the person with whom he was speaking. He was sophisticated and worldly, a connoisseur of travel, wine, and art. According to one friend, he'd actually read many of the art books in his collection—"he was astonishingly erudite"—and bought the 300 artworks that eventually formed his collection "slowly and shrewdly, rarely making snap decisions or capricious choices."[104] By now quite well-off himself, Reis did not collect money; he collected art—and artists.

Reis in fact liked to take care of artists. Since the 1940s, he'd acted as a kind of patron and benefactor for painters—first for George Grosz and Marc Chagall, then for the Surrealist emigrés during the war, and then, after the war, for the Abstract Expressionists. He bought pictures.[105] He dispensed legal and financial advice. He had generated fund-raising schemes for Surrealist ventures like *VVV* magazine, or contributed money to New York ventures like the Subjects of the Artist school. His artists were European exiles or American social outcasts, in either case poor. Bernard and Becky invited them in, fed them good food and wine, engaged them in lively conversation about art, literature, politics. "The Reises were kind and thoughtful and generous and went out of their way to be so," said one artist, adding: "And, of course, Bernard was always so helpful, taking care of nasty business details no one understood."[106]

"I helped them out, but never charged anything," Reis said. He preferred to offer his professional services as a friendly gift. Sometimes, the artists, accustomed to paying doctor and dentist bills with works, gave Reis a painting. "No artist had been equipped to take care of his financial complications," said Becky Reis. "In Bernard they had a wise, a completely informed and loveable human being who understood the problem of living and loved and understood their talents, their position in life, which of course was not easy at all then—and their ambitions toward continuing their art."[107] Bernard was the wise and loving father, the artists his naive and helpless children. Through their personal relation with Reis, the painters could sustain their belief in a strict boundary between nasty business and high art. Bernard took care of business; they took care of art. But the arrangement defined the artists as dependents.

"He did everyone's income tax, mine included," said Dore Ashton. "Reis was indispensable. He could deal with the real world. They *all* depended on him." Success, supposed to bring about autonomy, actually implicated the artists in elaborate social networks within the art bureaucracy, and left them more rather than less dependent. One way of characterizing the stage of Abstract Expressionism's economic development in the late 1950s would be to say that there was now need for an accountant, though not for more than one: Bernard Reis. In May 1958, Guston, Kline, de Kooning, Motherwell, and Rothko had signed an agreement naming Reis to represent them in their dealings with Sidney Janis.

By the early 1960s, "I advised Mark in all business matters and was his close personal friend," Reis said.[108] He counseled Rothko in his negotiations with Harvard, with the de Menil family, with Count Panza, with Marlborough, with the Tate Gallery in London. In addition to preparing Rothko's taxes, Reis pointed out tax advantages, advised about establishing trusts for Rothko's children, advised on the purchase of Rothko's 95th Street house.[109] He drew up wills for both Mell and Mark Rothko, and he helped form the Mark Rothko Foundation. Along with Theodoros Stamos and Morton Levine, Reis was named one of the three executors of Rothko's estate and one of the six directors of the Rothko Foundation. Although Reis did not charge Rothko for his services, by the time of Rothko's death in 1970 the six paintings in Reis's collection which he had received as gifts from Rothko were worth approximately $215,000.[110]

Rothko didn't trust lawyers any more than he trusted doctors. It wouldn't do to call in an attorney, listen to his advice, consider it, and try to arrive at a decision. Rothko experienced many practical issues not as burdens to be stoically endured, much less as challenges to be mastered, but as tasks impossible to perform. If his car broke down on the highway, his first thought was to abandon it. Home repair or caring for a garden or regulating a thermostat, much less dealing with a governmental bureaucracy—these were tasks beyond or beneath him.[111] As one part of Rothko struggled to "control the situation," another needed, or wished, to be taken care of, especially if the issue were one as charged and intricate as the law or money.

Like Reis but for different reasons, Rothko preferred to humanize professional relationships. Albert Grokest, his doctor, became a friend. Bernard Reis, a friend, became Rothko's accountant and "lawyer." Placing his financial or legal interests was like placing one of his paintings: he wanted to find a warm, familiar habitat, someone trustworthy, loyal, caring. Reis liked to help artists; it made him feel important, powerful, a force in the history of modern art. "The fostering of dependence comes easily to many professionals, including legal advisors," Gustave Harrow warns in his study of "The Matter of Rothko." "In a dependent relationship fewer questions are asked and less time is expended," and more power is felt by the advisor. Artists in particular may "desire or need to avoid the transition from aesthetic involvement to legal practicality," Harrow continues, but responsible advisors do not encourage "ready dependency." They provide information and explanation, "rather than assuming a paternalistic role in which it is implicitly assumed the complexities and ritual of legalities are beyond the artist's comprehension or concern."[112] Instead, Reis gladly assumed the paternalistic role; or, more precisely, he assumed the role of a fatherly older brother who was helpful, warm, encouraging, understanding, protective—everything that, in Rothko's view, Moise and Albert had *not* been. "Bernard has a knack for showing great concern," said one artist, "as if *your* life and fortunes were *his* greatest assets."[113] Such concern should be kept at a distance.

When Lloyd arranged the dinner at the St. Regis, the three artists present—de Kooning, Guston, and Rothko—were all Reis clients and two of them, Guston and Rothko, had recently resigned from the Janis Gallery. Not long after the dinner, Bernard J. Reis, Inc., was hired as the accounting firm for Marlborough-Gerson. By the time the gallery opened in November 1963, Adolph Gottlieb, Philip Guston, Robert Motherwell, Larry Rivers, and Mark Rothko, the estates of William Baziotes and Franz Kline—all Reis clients—had joined Marlborough.

In fact, while looking for a way to humanize relations within an expanding and impersonal marketplace, Rothko found in Bernard Reis precisely the point of intersection between the old, precapitalist gentlemanly style (favors and gifts) and the new, late capitalist corporate style (contracts and tax shelters, image and greed).

The June prior to Marlborough's New York 1963 opening, Rothko had sold fifteen works to Marlborough for just under $148,000, the works to be marked up 40 percent and the payments to be made in four annual installments beginning in January 1965.[114] In a separate contract, Rothko gave the gallery exclusive rights to sell, reproduce, and exhibit his work outside the United States for five years. He also agreed not to take on a U.S. dealer for at least one year, to sell paintings at no less than the Marlborough price for comparable works, and to stipulate that his buyers could not resell outside the U.S. for five years.

Rothko had insisted that his paintings were "his children—not some objects in which he ever abandoned involvement." He hoarded his paintings. He interviewed collectors. He inspected hangings. He disliked and distrusted dealers. Why, then, was he willing to sell fifteen of his works *as a batch,* as if they *were* objects in which he had abandoned involvement? And why would he sell them to the loathsomely commercial Frank Lloyd, who represented those values and qualities that the purist in Rothko most abhorred?

Rothko wasn't immune to glamor, or flattery. "Lloyd could woo anybody," said Donald McKinney, a Marlborough vice-president. "He plied Motherwell with champagne, caviar, and lunches at Le Pavillion." David Smith "was offered fine tools and materials and a tie-in with the Spoleto Festival in Italy." Gottlieb joined Marlborough because Lloyd promised him an immediate exhibit, changing "the gallery's entire schedule to accommodate my show," Gottlieb said.[115] Lloyd told Rothko, "You are the greatest painter in the world," said McKinney. "And Rothko would glow." What made Rothko vulnerable to Lloyd was not any desire for elegant lunches or elegant materials or elegant exhibits, but a kind of innocent grandiosity; Rothko was especially vulnerable to that appeal during the spring following "The New Realists" exhibit, the moment when Janis (along with many others) had abandoned Abstract Expressionism for Pop.[116]

Marlborough also appealed to the side of Rothko, now sixty, that looked for security, even though he had always imagined his own art as generated by *in*security. By selling fifteen of his works to the gallery, Rothko assured himself of a base annual income of about $37,000 from 1965 to 1968. Even after Rothko had named Reis his representative with Janis, arrangements were never formalized in a written contract but were placed on the personal, friendly basis that Rothko preferred, though such informality still left plenty of room for worry and suspicion. When one artist proposed to Lloyd, "Let's have a gentleman's agreement the next time around," Lloyd replied, "That's not possible. I'm no gentleman."[117] In his brash, joking way, Lloyd was warning that artists did need to be protected—from Lloyd himself. To painters dissatisfied with the gentlemanly ways of 57th Street dealers, Lloyd's blunt commercialism might (at first) seem refreshingly honest, his systematic bookeeping and accounting more reassuring.[118] Marlborough, in addition, offered the protection of *long-term* contracts, and Reis, finally, was clearly not advising his clients against joining Marlborough.

When Rothko reached his agreements with the House of Seagram and Harvard University, he had built his ambivalence about the projects into the contracts, reserving the freedom to hold onto his paintings and return his advance. His contract with Marlborough similarly protected his freedom. If Lloyd was riding the flood tide of commercialism then inundating the New York art world, Rothko did not just strip down and leap in. He did not simply join Marlborough; he made the gallery his representative outside the United States. Janis's artists complained that he didn't promote their work in Europe. Now Rothko had a powerful agent to exploit that market. Meanwhile, he could continue to sell works from his studio in New York.

15 The Harvard Murals

On the one side he felt, here's Marcus Rothkowitz dealing with the President of Harvard. On the other, he hated their guts.

Ann-Marie Levine

At 4:30 P.M. on October 24, 1962, Mark Rothko had a meeting with Nathan Pusey, president of Harvard University, at Rothko's studio, now a second-floor loft over a five-and-dime store on First Avenue between 77th and 78th Streets.[1] At the beginning of the year, Rothko had reached an agreement with Harvard whereby he would produce a set of murals for a dining room, this one under construction in the penthouse of the university's Holyoke Center, designed by the architect José Luis Sert. The paintings, valued at $100,000, would go to the university as a gift, in return for which Harvard would pay Rothko $10,000 to cover studio rent, assistance, materials, and travel between New York and Cambridge. The university also retained the right to refuse the paintings, about which some members of the Harvard Corporation remained "skeptical," and they had dispatched Pusey to view the triptych and three single works Rothko had completed to determine if they were "acceptable."[2]

When Pusey arrived at what he recalled as "a rickety old building, on a rickety old street" and rang the bell, he got no response. He turned around to see "a burly fellow dressed like a workingman" hurrying across First Avenue carrying a cardboard ice bucket. For his meeting with the president of Harvard—the modern equivalent of a seventeenth-century artist receiving a cardinal stopping in to assess the work on a commissioned altar painting—Rothko did not dress himself in shirt, tie, and jacket, as he had done for the middle-class readers of *Life*. Rather than looking respectable and prosperous, he choose to dramatize the differences in class and social values between himself and his patron, though his income was now closer to that of a university president than that of an auto mechanic. Yet, if Rothko wanted to shock and if, in theory, he hated the guts of university presidents, "he couldn't have been more cordial," recalled Pusey. In fact, having established their social difference, Rothko was free to be friendly, even to make a sales pitch aimed at an administrator who had been a scholar of religion. Rothko took his guest upstairs to

Chapter Fifteen

the studio, poured two drinks into paint-stained glasses and sat Pusey down before what he later remembered as five "eggplant-colored canvases." After a pause, Rothko asked, "What do you think?" Pusey wasn't sure what he thought, but ventured, "Gee, that's kind of sad." "This was obviously the right thing to say," Pusey recalled, and the two men began a "wonderful talk," during which Rothko offered an interpretation in which his somber triptych evoked Good Friday, and his final pink and white canvas suggested Christ's resurrection on Easter morning. The mythic cycle of death and renewal had long preoccupied Rothko; now he was appealing to it as at least one way of reading a series of mural panels he had painted in the shadow of his brother's cancer—from which Rothko helped to save him.[3]

To others, Rothko also compared these paintings, as he often had the Four Seasons panels, with Michelangelo's walls around the staircase in the Medici Library in Florence, as if his sequence did not evoke death and renewal but imposed frustration and entrapment. Nevertheless, convinced of the works' "metaphysical significance," Nathan Pusey returned to Cambridge and urged the Harvard Corporation to accept the paintings. They voted to do so on November 5.

"Harvard understands that Mr. Rothko's wish is to give a group of paintings which will, when installed, create a room for University use that is itself a work of art," John Coolidge, director of the Fogg Museum, had written to an officer of the Harvard Corporation as the agreement was being negotiated in late 1962.[4] Offered another opportunity to go beyond "pictures," to make a "place," Rothko had undertaken this second mural project with the same mixture of "anguish, frustration, and doubt" with which he undertook all of his projects, and in this case he had some compelling specific reasons to worry.[5] A Yale dropout who had been refused tenure by Brooklyn College, Rothko had long reviled the academic world. And he knew virtually from the start this time that the academic world, like the Bronfman family, was giving him a dining room to work with.

The project had first been suggested to him by Wassily Leontief, winner of a Nobel Prize in economics and president of the Harvard Society of Fellows, whom Rothko knew through Herbert Ferber. Sensing that Rothko felt "stagnant" after his Museum of Modern Art exhibit, Leontief proposed that Rothko produce a set of paintings for a penthouse room which Leontief hoped to obtain as a meeting place for the Society of Fellows. Rothko attended a meeting of the society and while "he felt a little out of sorts around the senior fellows," he remained interested in the project.

But the Society of Fellows could not afford the room, and by December of 1961 Rothko knew that the space would be used as a dining room—not a chic commercial dining room, true, but not exactly a workingman's cafeteria either. "It will, I think, without question be the most distinguished dining room at Harvard University, and your paintings would make it more so," A. D. Trottenberg, assistant dean of the Faculty of Arts and Sciences, wrote to Rothko on December 14. "We would hope to use this room as a meeting and dining room for our senior people. It will be used as a place where our governing Boards, the Corporation and the Board of Overseers, will meet for lunch and dinner when they are in Cambridge." Presumably, these are people who might meet for lunch or dinner at the Four Seasons when they are in New York.

After indicating that the room would also be used "by our many visiting committees, academic staff dinners, distinguished foreign visitors' dinners, and by a variety of special groups," Trottenberg concluded that the room would "imply, both by its quality and its usage, that a luncheon or dinner in these quarters is a quite special thing." Writing at John Coolidge's urging, to reassure a hesitant Rothko, Trottenberg, blithely assuming that the artist shared his fondness for academic elites and his institutional self-satisfaction, offered Rothko a glimpse of his actual audience. In the process, Trottenberg also revealed that the university was less interested in transforming a room into a work of art than in creating an ambience of "quality" which would impress both university officials and their guests with their own importance and thus with the power of Harvard to make them feel that way.

Wilder Green, the designer who assisted Rothko in installing the Harvard paintings, remembered that "Rothko was almost obsessed with the idea that his work would be regarded as decorative," and he sought a "very subdued lighting" for his paintings because "he felt that it would convey a non-decorative and more spiritual mood. He was really very concerned with his works as having a kind of spiritual emanation."[6] With his mural commissions Rothko pursued one way of eliminating the gallery as the means of distributing his work and returned to an earlier system of patronage, except that in this case his patron was not a wealthy individual but a modern corporation, with a diversity of interests, values, and responsibilities, but one where art was not always understood as spiritual emanation and abstract art was not always understood at all.

John Coolidge and José Luis Sert (a dean at Harvard) supported Rothko's aims, and just before Pusey's visit to Rothko's studio, Coolidge, pointing out that the university had done nothing for living American painters, urged acceptance of the murals "because thereby the University would be affirming its interest in the highly influential painting of our time."[7] To persuade his boss, Coolidge had to (or felt he had to) argue that acceptance would attach some of the prestige of the art to the institution and make the university *look* progressive. Universities have images too. Harvard, ironically, was affirming its interest just as, in New York, Abstract Expressionism was being declared dead, a 57th Street phenomenon which gave Rothko one more reason to seek "eternal" sites for his paintings, placing them beyond the fluctuations of the market.

Some Harvard officials, like Trottenberg, made no secret that *their* interest was in obtaining "quality" decorations; others found Rothko's "abstract" style not decorative enough, and began to complain about the costs of remodeling the room. As Coolidge wryly remarked to Pusey, "Some people will grumble about these paintings because they dislike them as paintings. If the room had been hung with the work of Andrew Wyeth, the people who grumble the hardest would not have said a word about costs."[8]

Yet the crucial issue involved not costs or public-relations values but the *place* of art in this small penthouse dining room. Early on, James Reynolds, assistant to the president for development, wrote to Bernard Reis that while Coolidge spoke of a set of murals, "a number of us here have always felt that what is needed is a single, large mural (rather than a series) which would be placed on the wall in the western dining room." Reynolds, looking to decorate a dining room for high-toned social and business exchanges, wanted a mural-scale work that would impress but not dominate. Rothko wanted to push viewers inward and transform the room into a kind of meditative environment. This "adversarial" artist and his institutional patron were, from the start, engaged in a power struggle for *control* of this space.

The physical space itself, no more than a "shell" as Rothko began work on the paintings, turned out to be a long, narrow, rectangular room 48' long and 20' wide, with 33' of its west wall recessed about 6', its east wall broken near the center by two doorways 4' apart, and its north and south walls each containing large horizontal windows, about 4½' high, offering panoramic views of the Harvard campus, Cambridge, the Charles River, and Boston. These windows posed a different set of challenges to Rothko's ambitions: they offered a strong visual alternative to any paintings in the room, they made "subdued" lighting difficult to achieve, and they admitted a strong light that, over the years, would cause major damage to Rothko's vulnerable paintings. In his struggle to dominate this space, the painter had also to contend with *natural* realities.

Rothko imagined his mural rooms as creating a space which freed viewers from the pressures and distractions of modern life—*abstracted* them, in other words, from the burdens of their social, historical contexts. Yet more than most painters Rothko was aware that a viewer's experience of a painting differs depending on whether that painting is hanging in Ben Heller's living room, a gallery at the Museum of Modern Art, a dining room on Park Avenue, or a dining room at Harvard, an experience that would, in each case, be further affected by the presence of other paintings in the room, the color of the walls, the hanging of the painting, and the lighting. Rejecting modernism's notion of the work of art as an autonomous, self-enclosed object, Rothko understood that viewing always takes place in a specific physical *context*.

In response to that knowledge, however, he determined to dissolve the painting/room relationship, just as his paintings had dissolved the figure/ground relationship. But he was not creating rooms out of the primal void. In fact, Rothko's mural projects, while striving to vindicate the power of the autonomous artist, were necessarily collaborative, implicating him in an elaborate complex of people, institutions, and events—assistants, architects, designers, museum directors, university presidents, bureaucrats, budgets, accountants, workmen. Creating a space for solitary contemplation necessarily became a social act, in which power and authority were dispersed. The figure of solitary creative genius dissolved into the shifting grounds of social and historical reality.

While still working on the Four Seasons panels, Rothko had declared to John Fischer, "I'll never take on such a job again."[9] When the annex to the Phillips Collection in Washington had opened in November of 1960, it contained a small room in which three Rothko paintings had been hung, *Green and Maroon* (1953), *Orange and Red on Red* (1957) and *Green and Tangerine on Red* (1956). The paintings preceded the room; but the room had been designed for the paintings. When Rothko came to Washington for the Kennedy inaugural in January 1961, he visited the room, proposed arranging the paintings differently and replacing the chairs in the room with a wooden bench. The bench was brought in, and the paintings were moved—for about a week, until Duncan Phillips visited the room and ordered the paintings returned to their original arrangement.[10] The room at the Phillips was not perfect, but it was close enough to stir Rothko's hopes and desires for creating a room of his own.

So while approaching the Harvard project with "anguish, frustration, doubt," Rothko decided to proceed, remaining cautious enough to retain the right to refuse the paintings, in which case he would have to return the $10,000. "He was very very flattered that Harvard had asked him to have the works there," said Green. And if Rothko disparaged the academic world in general and had unhappy memories of the Ivy League in particular, he was still, just a few years later when his daughter was choosing a college, "really set on my going to Radcliffe," Kate Rothko recalled. "He thought it was the best school in the country and why shouldn't I go there?" So why shouldn't her father make a "place" for himself at Harvard? Ironically, Harvard's invitation

Chapter Fifteen

affected Rothko just as Trottenberg imagined the room would affect a visitor: it made him feel important. Creating such rooms was, moreover, now the activity that most fully engaged Rothko as the way to carry his art another step forward, and a mural project at a prestigious institution would engage him as the way to carry his career the next step upward from the plateau he had reached with his Museum of Modern Art exhibit in early 1961.

But it was not as if Rothko were besieged with mural commissions. As Coolidge wrote to Pusey, "at the moment he is enormously successful but he impresses me as an idealist and the opportunities to decorate large spaces which will be used by institutions he respects are very rare."[11] It might be naive, and in the long run it proved wrong, but in 1961–62 it wasn't completely unreasonable to imagine that a venerable New England academic institution would provide a more suitable, protective, and even permanent setting for his work than a high-society dining room. Rothko grumbled to Regina Bogat that he was "still doing paintings for dining rooms." But, he added, "Harvard was different. It wasn't a commercial dining room, and he wanted to see if he could use the new form he had developed for the Four Seasons."

When Reis conveyed Reynolds' suggestion of a single panel to Rothko, he complained to Coolidge, who immediately wrote to Reynolds: "what really threw him"—i.e., Rothko—was the notion of a single painting. "He is interested not in painting one or more pictures but in creating a room. His work is well known and he feels Harvard should trust him to create a room out of the shell that is the western dining room." Suspicious of the authorities, Rothko demanded that *they* "trust" him, a requirement he justified by appealing to his own authority—his *name,* his reputation—which in turn depended on the authority of a set of exhibiting and marketing institutions which Rothko himself often described as arbitrary and unstable. Playing with the Monopoly money of his reputation as if it were hard cash, Rothko bought his freedom from the Harvard Board of Overseers. "I pointed out to him over the telephone that the architect also had rights," Coolidge wrote. "This he acknowledged but he kept returning to the notion that we should trust him to decide how many paintings there were to be in the room."[12]

A Renaissance patron might stipulate size, subject, and time of completion for a commission. A modern corporation, being impersonal, can be more liberal. Harvard agreed to grant the artist "complete autonomy" in determining the number and nature of the paintings, let him supervise the remodeling of the penthouse dining room at the time of installation, and in the deed of gift gave him significant controls over the subsequent fate of the paintings.[13] Reassured by these arrangements, Rothko could withdraw into the private space of the studio and begin to paint, convinced that he had managed to transcend the elaborate network of social circumstances in which he was now enmeshed.

By March of 1962, having moved his studio uptown to First Avenue because he didn't like the subway but was "too cheap" to take cabs, he was working on the project, using the freedom he had insisted upon not so much as an opportunity to experiment as a chance to consolidate the advances he had made in the Four Seasons paintings.[14] Rothko began with preliminary studies, producing three pen-and-ink drawings on white paper and a series of images created with poster paints applied to a plum-colored construction paper.[15]

For the Harvard commission, Rothko produced twenty-two studies in which two or three vertical rectangles are connected at top and bottom by thin horizontal arms with small rectangles (or nodules) at their centers. He was adding the nodules to the post and lintel shapes he had evolved for the Four Seasons panels. In these studies Rothko contemplated shifts in the color, luminosity, weight, and density of the vertical shapes, he varied their width and thus the size of the opening between them, and he experimented with the arrangement of the images in the triptych. But with the Harvard murals Rothko seems to have known from early on the kind of thing he was after, and he found it in the preliminary studies. Five of them, in fact, have been identified as quite specific sources for the five paintings Rothko installed.[16] Rothko had warned Coolidge that, while he expected to complete the work in a year, he might have to paint "three or four sets" before finding one that was "satisfactory."[17] But Rothko had completed the project by the time of Pusey's visit in late October. The evolution of the Four Seasons murals had occupied Rothko for perhaps as long as twenty months.[18] The Harvard murals took him about nine months, partly because Rothko, rather than breaking new ground, was building on "the new form he had developed for The Four Seasons."[19]

In the sanctuary of the studio Rothko could feel "completely autonomous." There, making his preliminary sketches, painting the canvases for Harvard, viewing them hung on partitions built to recreate the space of the Holyoke Center dining room, Rothko was in complete control. A place of solitude, a workplace, the studio also functioned as a place for exhibiting paintings, a kind of idealized gallery. As work on the Harvard murals proceeded, Rothko showed them to friends, weighing their reactions, as was his custom. But once they were completed, Rothko could no longer control the social life of his paintings. Nathan Pusey's October 24 visit was followed, two days later, by the architect Sert, then by visits from Elizabeth Jones of the Fogg Museum and from Eugene Kraetzer of the Harvard Corporation. Having translated, as he said, his "pictorial concepts into murals which would serve as an image for a

Chapter Fifteen

public space," and having received acceptance from his institutional benefactor, Rothko removed the canvases from their stretchers, rolled them and shipped them to Cambridge, where they arrived on December 27.

Fifteen years before, Rothko had warned that it is "a risky and unfeeling act to send" a picture "out into the world," as if doing so were like removing a living "organism" from the safe and familiar environment where it had been made and transplanting it to an alien place where it did not quite belong. Or, worse, since the picture could now be bought, sold, auctioned, inherited, it would occupy a series of such alien places, rootless and abandoned, as a mere commodity. The picture would be "nowhere." At Harvard, however, Rothko did control the decor of the room, and in early January 1963, he arrived in Cambridge with Wilder Green for the first of several trips to direct installation of the paintings. Of the six panels he had shipped, Rothko hung five, all of them, like the Four Seasons paintings, eight and a half feet high. A triptych, formed of paintings 9¾', 15½' and 8' wide (*Panels One, Two,* and *Three*), filled the recessed section of the west wall, while a 15' and a 9¾' painting (*Panels Four* and *Five*) occupied the east walls on either side of the double doorway.[20] All of the panels had a crimson ground, varying from lighter to darker, with two or three vertical rectangular figures (orange in *Panel One,* black in *Panels Two* and *Four,* brown in *Panel Three,* white in *Panel Five*), which enclosed a vertical rectangular opening, sometimes narrow (*Panels Two* and *Three*), sometimes wide (*Panels Four* and *Five*).

Their grounds painted a color that Rothko connected, in talking to John Coolidge, with Harvard crimson, their shapes reminiscent of classical architecture, Rothko's murals at first look elegant and monumental, combining classical simplicity with religious gravity. At first glance, they also seem static—at least until, like Bishop Berkeley's falling tree in the forest that made no noise until someone was there to hear it, a viewer enters the room, whose relationship to the paintings necessarily becomes a dynamic *physical* process of interaction. Unlike a single Rothko work—say, *Number 10, 1950*—his mural projects cannot be taken in "all at once." The viewer may focus on single canvases, taking them in sequentially, reading first the triptych, placed across the room from its two doors, from left to right, and then turning, to continue the left to right movement to include the two works on the rear (east) wall. But even as a viewer contemplates one, other paintings enter his or her peripheral vision; or the viewer will become aware of, and feel a beckoning pressure from, paintings out of sight, behind his or her back; or the viewer may interrupt the linear sequence (or, having completed it, begin again) by walking around, looking back and forth or diagonally across the room to consider likenesses and differences among five paintings that make variations on a single elementary form.

The Harvard Murals

The room isn't something you command. You are inside it, a *body* moving inside it, lingering, adopting not one but multiple vantage points. Unity is not something accomplished by the artist and then handed over to the viewer, like a tree falling in a forest that makes noise even when no one is there to hear it. Unity is something the viewer struggles to make and, given the impossibility of examining all five paintings at once, never accomplishes. The classical facade of *Street Scene,* with its regular geometric structure and stony impersonality, feels heavy, immovable, inhuman—and dead. In the series of classical architectural shapes he invented for Harvard, Rothko created *openings,* their varying widths contracting and expanding, compressing and releasing. Rothko has taken ancient classical *cultural* forms and turned them into works of art where they breathe, as if they were *natural* forms.

In doing so, he "defeats" Sert's architecture. In the first place, he covers just about all of the wall space with his paintings, which repeat, in order to transform, the two remaining architectural features of the room, its doors and windows. The two glass doors, separated by a wall, along the east side of the room, recur in the two broad crimson portals, separated by a black wall, in *Panel Four* (color plate 18), which hung just to the right of the doors. At either end of the room, the horizontal row of windows has been divided, by wooden bars, into a grid which continued upwards into the transparent glass sections above the windows. Rigid, the geometric order of the grid simply repeats; squeezing in or pushing outward, mutually interacting, the rectangular shapes in Rothko's paintings breathe and reverberate with each other.

A rectangular opening in a wall, a window both separates and joins what's inside and outside. In the Holyoke Center dining room at Harvard, the penthouse windows admit natural light and offer a panoramic view of the Massachusetts sky and the darker shapes of the city below; it is a commanding view—you are safely outside it, as if you were looking at an illusionistic painting. Inside the room, where Rothko encompasses the visitor with his five $8\frac{3}{4}'$ high monumental paintings, boundaries are more ambiguous. What, in the center section of *Panel Four,* looks like a heavy, dense, and impenetrable slab of black wall, does not touch the bottom edge of the canvas, lets some of the crimson ground show through, and so also appears weightless and translucent. The door and windowlike openings in all the panels do not offer grand vistas of heavenly or urban space; they show a murky crimson vacancy that seems either prior to or beyond our familiar world of bounded objects. They draw the viewer toward a realm outside the literal room, at the same time that they push forward and intrude into the room. The space within Sert's box expands and contracts, feels free and confining. Rothko has fabricated a *place* out of simple elementary forms that will not stay *in place*.

When the room was remodeled in early 1963, Rothko had the wooden walls covered with "a medium to dark olive-green fabric," a color he selected only after "he struggled and struggled and struggled," according to Wilder Green. The color was a "strange" choice, but "I think he felt that it was kind of an opposite to the color of at least some of the murals. He wanted to be sure that it was in no way chic. He wanted it to be sort of gritty." Rothko and Green also attempted to control the light in the room by installing fiberglass curtains to filter the natural light and by hanging a strip of lights from the ceiling. During the spring of 1963, as remodeling work continued, the paintings returned to New York, where they were exhibited at the Guggenheim Museum from April 9 to June 2, after which one of the panels went to the Lightolier showroom for study of the lighting. By February of 1964, work on the room was complete, except for a final visit from Rothko for a final adjustment of the lights.

Yet, even at the end of this process, Rothko "was very unsatisfied with the whole thing," Green said. The lighting was impossible to control, the ceiling too low, and the room too "crowded" with furniture. "He would have liked nothing in the room, basically, except a bench where you could go and study the murals." Instead, being a dining room rather than a museum or chapel, the room was furnished with long brown wooden tables and numerous black wooden chairs, each with a Harvard seal on its back, so that, when chairs and tables were in place, a row of Harvard seals was visible along the bottom edges of Rothko's panels. The backs of the chairs, moreover, were lined up quite close to the paintings, making them not only a visual obstacle but a danger every time one of "our senior people" pushed back his chair to rise from the table.[21]

My account of both the paintings and the dining room has, however, necessarily been constructed from photographs and documents. Today, the western dining room in the Holyoke Center penthouse has been converted into offices for the Harvard Real Estate Corporation and the paintings, irreparably damaged, have been placed, permanently, in the basement of the Fogg Museum, in Dark Storage. Nine months after Rothko's death in February of 1970, Bernard Reis, one of the three executors of Rothko's estate, met Agnes Mongan, director of the Fogg Museum, and announced that he was "shocked" at the condition of the Harvard murals. Reis, through his influence with a Harvard chef, had managed to slip into the dining room for a private viewing.[22] "He thinks they have been maltreated and that they are in need of care," Agnes Mongan wrote to Elizabeth Jones. Reis threatened to "remove" the works and asked to have their "care" documented. "He feels a proprietary interest in anything Rothko did."[23] Museum officials, by this time, were well aware of the deterioration of the paintings, John Coolidge having observed to Eugene Kraetzer just three and a half years after their final installation, that the murals were "in appalling shape. They have faded and changed color variably and in some cases extremely." He proposed getting in touch with Rothko to "discuss with him what should be done."[24]

During Rothko's lifetime nobody—not Rothko, not the dispersed structure of authority called "Harvard University"—felt proprietary enough to *do* something about the murals. At some point Elizabeth Jones talked to Rothko, a conversation she did not record until the day after Agnes Mongan warned her of Bernard Reis's concern about the paintings. Rothko reported that he had used "mostly oil, that he had glazed over with egg white areas he decided to repaint (the deterioration of the central panel may be the result of this layering of paint) and that when he ran out of paint he had gone downstairs to the Woolworth's and bought some more paint—he didn't know what kind it was." This five-and-dime paint has become a kind of red (or crimson) herring in the story of the disintegration of these murals; it is a vivid detail that sticks in the mind, fixes blame, and conveniently fixes it on the "irresponsible" artist. Yet all of the mural panels suffered damage wherever they were exposed to sunlight, a result that can hardly be attributed to a substitute can of paint or two. At the time of their conversation, Elizabeth Jones had proposed to Rothko that she give the paintings "a light spray-coating of polyvinyl acetate to protect them. He said he did not want me to do that." Rothko did not want to alter the appearance of his works with a varnish in order to stop the process of alteration that was already going on; he did nothing, as if he had lost interest. "There is really nothing I can do, I'm afraid, about the deterioration of poor paint," Elizabeth Jones wrote.[25] So Harvard did nothing, and blamed the artist.

Among Harvard officials, Bernard Reis's threat to remove the paintings activated suspicions of his motives and defensiveness about their own actions. Wassily Leontief warned Agnes Mongan "to watch out for" someone coming "up quietly to see what state the Rothko paintings are in." "Reis is a very sharp operator." "I know Bernard Reis and I know he is an operator," Agnes Mongan assured Leontief.[26] Yet in spite of the silent-alarm buttons being pushed in Cambridge, in this particular case Reis's dealings turned out to be somewhat less than sharp. Reis was not trying to save the paintings; his motives *were* proprietary. On April 2, 1971, he visited the Holyoke Center dining room with Alan Thielker, a restorer for the Marlborough Galleries, which had paid for their trip, this suggesting that Reis had traveled to Cambridge not on behalf of the Rothko Foundation but on behalf of his employer, Frank Lloyd of Marlborough Galleries.[27] Curiously, Reis asked Agnes Mongan if Harvard wanted to sell the paintings. Given the condition of the works by this time, Reis could

Chapter Fifteen

have invoked the deed of gift and moved for the Rothko Foundation to reclaim the paintings. The offer to buy was refused, after which Reis did nothing, as if *he* had lost interest.

Over the years, people at the Fogg Museum had generated a variety of explanations for the fading color of the murals. John Coolidge pointed to Rothko's technique: "the underpainting is showing through," he wrote to Kraetzer. Elizabeth Jones blamed Rothko's "poor paint." A report done for the museum just before Bernard Reis's visit cited paint without sufficient "binding medium to protect the pigmentation from the light."[28] All of these theories proved incorrect. In painting the crimson backgrounds of all five panels and in the figures of two of them, Rothko had used a Lithol Red paint which, unknown to anyone in 1962, is extremely fugitive—i.e., very sensitive to light.[29] For an artist, "transcendental experiences" can only be achieved through the physical properties of paint, themselves subject to natural forces (such as light) and historical limits (such as ignorance about Lithol Red). No room—not even an exclusive dining room at Harvard University—can be sealed off from the temporal contexts in which it came into being and within which it must continue to exist.

Or, in this case, from the institutional context within which it finally ceased to exist. Not all the faded areas were painted in Lithol Red; and not all the damage to the paintings was caused by sunlight.[30] Four of Rothko's five paintings suffered man-made damage. Because they were owned by the Harvard Corporation rather than the Fogg Museum, responsibility for the paintings shifted elusively around the university bureaucracy, at times attached to the secretary of the corporation, the university's director for development, the manager of the Faculty Club, the university's real estate department, at times attached to some combination of these.[31] It's as if Rothko had saved his works from the anonymity of the marketplace only to lose them to a bureaucracy where art was not even much valued as a commodity. Officials at the Fogg wrote memoranda urging that the curtains be kept closed, that the waitresses be careful, the cleaning men be careful, but without too much effect. Alternative locations for the paintings were sought but none found.[32] In 1973 a seven-inch tear was found in *Panel Four*, which was removed from the room for conservation treatment.[33] By 1979 "the most distinguished dining room at Harvard University" had been democratized into the "Party Function Room," "rented out during the week," scene of banquets, seminars and, in one case, an end-of-the-term disco party.[34] In just the fourteen months between February 1978 and April 1979, a conservation report revealed, the works had suffered a number of scratches and abrasions, one had a two-inch tear, another a dent three inches in diameter, and one ALAN C had scratched his name into the paint of *Panel Three*.[35] Shortly after this report, the paintings—now undeniably the collaborative products of Mark Rothko and Harvard University—were removed to Dark Storage.

It is as if when Rothko's paintings left the protective space of his New York studio, they had emigrated to an environment where they never belonged, where there was no place for them—an environment that, for all its apparent dignity and grandeur turned out to be sometimes cold, blank, and alien, sometimes neglectful, and sometimes abusive. Once they were transplanted, these paintings were abandoned.

16 The Houston Chapel

Troubled by the mid-1960s art market, where the bottom seemed to be dropping out from under high culture, Rothko sought firmer grounds by moving in two, characteristically opposed, directions.

On the one hand, he sought to secure his position as a major figure in the New York art world, attaching himself to the power, prestige, and glitter of Marlborough.

On the other hand, he withdrew.

Rothko's 1961 Museum of Modern Art exhibit was his last one-man show in New York during his lifetime. In these years, Robert Motherwell recalled, Rothko was "afraid to show his work, partly because he was afraid the new generation would find it ridiculous."[1] His work, of course, continued to appear in numerous exhibitions, many of which—e.g., "The Peggy Guggenheim Collection," "The Collection of Mr. and Mrs. Ben Heller," "The Sidney and Harriet Janis Collection"—Rothko had no direct connection with. The only important group shows in which he actively participated during the 1960s were the Los Angeles County Museum's "The New York School: The First Generation" (1965), the Museum of Modern Art's "The New American Painting and Sculpture: The First Generation" (1969), and the Metropolitan Museum's "New York Painting and Sculpture: 1940–1970" (1970).

Rothko continued to paint. He continued to sell paintings from the studio. He sought permanent "homes" for groups of his paintings, eventually placing nine of the Seagram murals in a room at the Tate Gallery, London. And he pursued his ambition to create environments with ensembles of mural panels produced for specific sites. He told Katharine Kuh that "he had lost his zest for easel paintings, finding them inadequate and episodic. All that really mattered now, he said, were public commissions."[2]

In early 1965, Rothko signed a $250,000 contract to produce a set of murals for a chapel to be built by the de Menil family in Houston. The "last

Chapter Sixteen

rabbi of western art" would culminate his career by decorating a Roman Catholic chapel in Texas.

• • •

We went to the Rothkos for lunch. We sat on their porch [in East Hampton], overlooking the bay, little Christopher in his playpen, Mark looking with indescribable warmth at his child, watching lovingly as the baby clapped his hands while the Trout Quintet was played, and enjoying Sasha as she patted the baby, her blue eyes enormous in a tanned face, her pink gingham dress. . . . A lunch of appropriate small talk, then we went to the beach where Mark told me of his new studio, and his commission to do a Catholic chapel for the de Menils. He read, years ago, he said, the Patristic fathers (Origen for instance). He liked the "ballet" of their thoughts, and the way everything went toward ladders, he talked about making east and west merge in an octagonal chapel. . . . It is the truly controlled situation he has always demanded. And doesn't sound so strange at all, now, although ten years ago it might have. He could never have done a synagogue, he said. What is wonderful about Mark is that he aspires, and is still capable of believing that his work can have some purpose—spiritual if you like—that is not sullied by the world.

Dore Ashton, Journal, July 7, 1964[3]

• • •

>The magnitude, on every level of experience and meaning, of the task in which you have involved me, exceeds all my preconceptions. And it is teaching me to extend myself beyond what I thought was possible for me.
>   For this I thank you.
>
>   Mark Rothko to John and Dominique de Menil

Rothko's patrons, John and Dominique de Menil, were French, cultivated, cosmopolitan.[4] His family was military, titled, but poor; hers was quite well-off—one grandfather had been a wealthy textile manufacturer. The family wealth enabled Dominique's father and uncle, Conrad and Marcel Schlumberger, to devote themselves to developing a means of electrical prospecting for both minerals and oil. In 1913—as Marcus Rothkowitz was migrating from Dvinsk to Portland—Conrad Schlumberger was planting electrodes and measuring the soil's resistivity in the Normandy basin in order to trace the path of an underground vein of ore.[5] By the late 1920s, Conrad and Marcel were lowering their instruments on a cable into a bored hole, a method later called electrical logging. The Schlumbergers, whom we would now call geophysicists, were at first perceived as no better than two men with divining rods, but they gradually persuaded oil companies in the U.S. and the government in the U.S.S.R. to adopt their methods, and their business expanded. The de Menil fortune, then, was generated through technological innovation in the exploitation of natural resources. By the mid-1980s, Schlumberger Ltd. was a worldwide multinational with stock worth around $10 billion.[6]

Dominique Schlumberger, born in Paris in 1908, was educated at the University of Paris, where she received a B.A. in 1927 and went on to graduate study in mathematics and physics.[7] John de Menil, born in Paris in 1904, left high school to help support his family by taking a clerical job in a bank, though he later attended the University of Paris at night to receive a B.A. in 1922 and graduate degrees in political science (1925) and law (1935). By 1932, he had risen to the vice-presidency of a French investment bank.[8] The mathematician-physicist and the investment banker met at a party in 1930, and they were married in May of the following year. Soon after, Dominique converted to John's Roman Catholicism. "My father was of Gide's atheist generation," recalled Dominique's younger sister, "and Dominique was very spiritual. She badly needed a religion."[9] In 1938, John de Menil left banking to join the Schlumberger family firm.

World War II, by no means a disaster for anyone in the petroleum business, did force the de Menils to migrate from Paris to Houston, the Schlumberger firm's American headquarters. Conrad Schlumberger, a scientist with leftist political views, disapproved of both religion and art. His daughter Dominique, having trained to follow him into science, and having converted to Roman Catholicism, began to collect art when she arrived in America, beginning under the guidance of Father Marie-Alain Couturier, a Dominican priest and painter active in a then controversial movement to revive sacred art by involving living artists—modern, advanced, secular ones—in the decoration of Catholic churches. Exiled in New York City during the war, a friend of many of the European artist-refugees then in the city and familiar with its museums, galleries, and dealers, Father Couturier, whom the de Menils had known in France before the war, introduced them to art and collecting. "He made us greedy," said Dominique de Menil.[10] So he did: forty years later the de Menils had collected 10,000 objects.

According to Mrs. de Menil, "when you stop buying you are history."[11]

Chapter Sixteen

She and her husband bought African tribal objects, archaic Mediterranean art, modern European (especially Surrealist) work, and (later) contemporary Americans; they hired Philip Johnson to design their house in Houston. The de Menils espoused progressive political causes, like civil rights, that horrified Houston's conservative rich; they espoused vanguard art, joining the city's Contemporary Arts Association and arranging shows of van Gogh, Max Ernst, Joan Miró, and Alexander Calder. But when fellow members of the association's board of trustees complained about the expense of such projects, the de Menils moved to the Museum of Fine Arts, where John de Menil's hand-picked director clashed with the board. The de Menils then moved their energies, their time, and their money to a small Catholic college, St. Thomas University, in the Montrose section of Houston. In 1957, they hired Philip Johnson to design a master plan for the university; they purchased land for the college, gave it art, helped fund teaching and research, and financed the art department, of which Dominique de Menil in 1964 became the chair. But, in the words of the school's president, "it became difficult to operate without stepping on one of their toes. It began to look more like de Menil University than St. Thomas."[12]

When conflict arose between the St. Thomas priests and their patrons, the de Menils moved their art and their art department a few miles south to Rice University. "They buttressed a budding art history department, established an Institute for the Arts that sponsored exhibitions, lectures and events, and created an 'Art Barn' for exhibitions," as well as a media center and film school.[13] As one observer of the de Menils' wanderings across the Houston art scene commented, "when they didn't control things, they stepped aside."[14] In 1987, Dominique de Menil—her husband had died in 1973—found a proper home for her art collection by building a $30 million private museum, one block west of the Rothko Chapel.

The de Menils combined French culture, Texas oil money, and ecumenical Catholicism, none of which ingratiated them with Mark Rothko. Was Rothko, already involved with a multinational art gallery in New York, turning to a multinational patron in Texas? Was the alternative to Robert Scull a family that has sometimes been described as the modern Medici?[15]

The de Menils did have their attractions. They were not proposing any public or private dining rooms; they were offering a religious environment, modeled (quite consciously in their minds) on projects like Matisse's Chapel of the Rosary at Vence. The de Menils, moreover, were no corporation, like Seagram, or academic bureaucracy, like Harvard. They were philanthropists, with a long record of involvement in progressive politics. In the words of one artist, "John and Dominique brought a European sense of the value of talent to New York and Houston. They made one proud to be an artist." They were respected private collectors—who had bought their first Rothko painting in 1957—and they were not embarked, like Robert Scull, on a self-made businessman's quest for cultural respect.[16] They were not hard-nosed textile manufacturers, like Ben Heller. Nor did they collect art for profit. "Why did Rothko have an African statue in the foyer of his studio," Mrs. de Menil asked. "These pieces took them [the artists] out of the banality of everyday life," she said. "They reminded them of something transcendental . . . beyond and above. They introduced an element of spirituality."[17] Dominique de Menil spoke a language that appealed to one side of Rothko.

Best of all, the de Menils were willing to pay Rothko well to do what he had long wanted to do, and they gave him complete freedom in doing what he came to regard as the culmination of his life as a painter.[18] High-toned and Old World, discrete and low-key, the de Menils, in the context of the dissolving high cultural ideals of the mid-1960s, were generous, reassuring presences.

. . .

The focus of every pilgrimage journey is the shrine.
David Freedberg, *The Power of Images*

People come from all over the world to the Rothko Chapel.
"The Rothko Chapel"

Visiting the Rothko Chapel today (1992), you have to get yourself to Houston, take a ten-minute cab ride from downtown to the Montrose district, get out at Montrose Boulevard and Branard Street, turn west, cross the small campus of St. Thomas University, enter a quiet neighborhood of modest one- and two-story clapboard or brick homes (all strangely painted a warm, brownish gray), arrive at the intersection of Branard and Yupon, swing around a high bamboo hedge, and walk past the reflecting pool upon which Barnett Newman's 26'-high steel sculpture, *Broken Obelisk*, has been placed. You are now facing a low, pale-red brick wall, the facade of the Rothko Chapel (fig. 47). You see no steps, no portico, no columns, no crucifixes, no statuary, no spire, no dome, no stained glass, no *windows*—just a low, simple entrance with two black, wood doors. Plain, cheerless, geometric, with an interior sealed off from the pleasant neighborhood and park outside, the building looks more like a tomb than a chapel or one-man museum.

Intended for a different site, to serve different social purposes, the chapel originally had a more imposing design. When Philip Johnson had created the master plan for St. Thomas University in 1957, he envisioned a series of low, modernist brick and steel buildings turned inward, their backs to the city, facing each other across a garden mall. "With all the buildings facing inward to the sheltered walk," Johnson said, "the campus proper will form more of a 'green street' than a typical American campus. The strong sense of community which should result is the same sense of cohesion that a cloister gives a monastery." Dominating "the ensemble by virtue of its height and placement," the chapel would be located at one end of, and overlooking, the oblong-shaped mall.[19] Here, the school's Basilian fathers would say Mass (there would be an altar), hear confessions, hold retreats, perform the rites of the Catholic liturgy.[20] In 1969, when the de Menils shifted from St. Thomas to Rice, the site of the still-unbuilt chapel was moved from the campus community, isolated a few blocks away, and put under the control of Houston's Institute for Religion and Human Development, an ecumenical organization on whose board John de Menil sat.[21]

None of these changes would have disturbed Rothko. Ten years before, he had imagined, dispersed across the country, a series of small one-man or even one-painting museums, wayside chapels that travelers come to visit and contemplate. As an alternative to the large contemporary museum, such a Rothko chapel would save his work from competing with crowds of rivals, from the historical narratives museum installations create, from imposed educational purposes, from art bureaucracy, from those crowds of people looking at paintings which he viewed as "blasphemy."[22]

A chapel like the one in Houston offered an environment in which Rothko's silent, elevated paintings could receive their proper regard (silent contemplation) and their proper recognition (as sacred objects), and without migrating through the hands of a series of collectors, only to end up in an institutional home: a museum.

Rothko did not envision a chapel, say, on the Upper East Side of New York City. He wanted one, rather, "more out of the way, a *destination,* outside the city." He wished to withdraw his works from the marketplace into the chapel; and he wished to withdraw the chapel from the art center in New York, as if his work now belonged in the provinces, safe from the professionals, available to those ordinary viewers he had always imagined as the ideal audience for his paintings. Difficulty of access: that counted as one advantage of the provinces, especially one as geographically and culturally remote as Houston in the mid-1960s. There, in a quiet, middle-class neighborhood, his works would compel—for most of us—a kind of pilgrimage journey, one likely to turn up sympathetic and committed viewers.[23]

Rothko now sought, for his work, a lonely eminence in an obscure but sacred site. Better, then, Houston than New York or even Cambridge, Massachusetts. Better yet to sever connection with a university community, a Catholic community, *any* local community. Ecumenical rhetoric, after all, abstracted the spiritual from any specific religious beliefs, symbols, memories; it resembled Rothko's universalist rhetoric, expressed here in his ambition to make "east and west merge in an octagonal chapel."

Nevertheless, during the three years (1964–67) he worked on the project, Rothko believed his murals would be hung in a *Catholic* chapel.

Creating a chapel to occupy the most prominent position on a small, cloisterlike campus mall, Philip Johnson had started with an ambitious and even grandiloquent design. He first conceived a square floor, the concrete building to be raised by several steps from the mall, placed on a platform, and topped by a high, pyramid-shaped tower, its apex severed in order to admit light through an oculus. Rothko first suggested adding an apse, then proposed transforming the square into the octagonal floor he mentioned to Dore Ashton in the summer of 1964. Rothko had admired the octagonal Byzantine church of S. Maria Assunta on the island of Torcello, near Venice. The octagon, most often used by Christian architects for baptisteries and tombs, structures with a hallowed space at the center, would in Rothko's design, surround, enclose—or perhaps enwomb—the viewer within his paintings.

In October 1964, Johnson, having accepted Rothko's floor plan, began developing a series of new designs for the building, and he would continue to do so over the next three years. He remembered the time, and his relationship with Rothko, as "nothing but bad." A dispute arose between the two men around the issue of the tower which, in some of its versions at least, resembled an Egyptian dunce cap. But Rothko did not object that Johnson's design was ugly or ludicrous. As always, Rothko was anxious about the lighting. Johnson imagined the harsh Texan light filtering down through the pyramid, then being diffused throughout the room. Rothko imagined his paintings displayed in a space as close as possible to the one in which they were being created. He wanted to model the lighting on that in his new, 69th Street studio, where, beneath the large skylight, he had hung a parachute, which he could adjust to control the light.[24] Johnson, moreover, imagined a vertical, visually prominent building, into which Rothko's paintings would have to fit. Rothko wanted a building that would fit his paintings, not usurp them. "Mark was very insistent as he went on that he did not want anything fancy or spectacular," Bernard Reis recalled. "He wanted a very simple envelope, octagonal in shape, something that would display the pictures because he did not want any stunts. . . . He did not want anyone to feel that they would go to the Chapel because it was an architectural wonder."[25]

Johnson wanted a vaulted structure; Rothko wanted something more like a vault. "We might come to an impasse," Rothko had warned, of his conflict with Johnson, as early as October 1964.[26] "Even commissions were unsatisfactory," he told Katharine Kuh, "unless he was in total control of the project."

Eventually, Rothko appealed to the de Menils, who supported him. In 1967 Johnson resigned, and the project was then given to Howard Barnstone and Eugene Aubry, two Houston architects who adopted Rothko's suggestions and produced the present building, whose blank, mute, rectilinear facade echoes Rothko's paintings.

• • •

For the first time he felt he would occupy the whole physical terrain.
You would have to not only see his paintings, you would breathe them.
                                                    Stanley Kunitz

When Rothko signed his contract for the Houston chapel commission in January of 1965, he had already been working on the project, he estimated, for "the past four or five months."[27] He and his family had vacationed the summer before at Amagansett, near East Hampton, Long Island, where Rothko had his conversation with Dore Ashton about the chapel project. William and Sally Scharf lived in the 95th Street house, and William Scharf, a painter who had sometimes assisted Rothko in the past, was preparing Rothko's new, and final, studio, at 157 East 69th Street, between Lexington and Third Avenues. There, in the fall, Rothko began work on the Houston murals.

To produce the panels for the Four Seasons restaurant Rothko worked in a darkened, unheated gymnasium, located amid the poverty and dereliction of the Bowery. The Harvard murals had been created in a loft, over a 5-and-10 store on First Avenue. The chapel paintings were made in an elegant, two-and-a-half-story red brick building, with an ornate, arched entranceway, a nineteenth-century carriage house and private riding rink, located amid the fashionable brownstones and upscale apartment buildings of New York's Upper East Side. Bernard Reis lived two blocks away.

Imagine a 50'-square floor, sever its four corners, push its rear border back 6', and you have a very close approximation of the Houston chapel's octagonal plan.[28] Rothko's studio, the former riding rink in the rear of the 69th Street building, was smaller than the chapel, about 40' square, but with a higher ceiling, its yellow brick walls about 30' high, topped by a sloped, wood-beam ceiling with a skylight at the center. At the front, where two horse-drawn carriages had once been parked, the building had been divided, with plasterboard walls, into two areas, 15' wide and 45' deep. A doorway from the street entered a short hall. On the right side was the studio of Arthur Lidov, a commercial artist who lived in the second-floor apartment with his family.[29] Rothko occupied the left side, itself divided into two rooms, leading back to his studio.

In the last fourteen months of his life, after separating from his wife Mell, Rothko lived alone in the two front rooms of the building. Even then, the interior remained sparsely and shabbily furnished, the living/reception room near the street having some bookshelves, secondhand wooden chairs and a table, and two Salvation Army sofas. The inner room contained a bathroom and kitchen area on the right, racks for storing paintings on the left. Just within the studio area, Rothko placed a bed and his only amenity, a stereo and some records.[30] Rothko was not the kind of artist who filled the walls of his studio with photographs of friends, heroes, or family, with reproductions of works of art, paintings by others. The only work on the premises not by Rothko was a sculpture by Herbert Ferber that stood in the entrance hall. Inside his elegant old carriage house, Rothko—whose 1965 income was just under $69,000—worked, and later lived, frugally.[31]

During the summer and into the fall of 1964, William Scharf prepared the studio, building the storage racks, constructing a three-wall mock-up of the chapel interior, installing a pulley and rope system that allowed Rothko to raise and lower the paintings on the wooden walls, and another pulley and rope system with which Rothko could adjust a parachute below the skylight.[32] During the 1950s, painting in the living room of his Sixth Avenue flat or in either of his two small midtown lofts, Rothko had worked in confined, low-ceilinged spaces, and his works had responded to the physical circumstances of their creation by conveying a sense of confinement and expansion, pressure and release.

Rothko's sensitivity to the force of physical context in viewing a painting had pushed him toward creating ensembles of his paintings for particular sites in the first place. In Houston, where his views finally prevailed over the architect's, he had complete control over the space; and it was when he achieved such freedom that he produced his most vacant, and least accessible, work. His ambitious mural projects, moreover, required larger studios—a Bowery gymnasium, an uptown carriage house—which in turn affected the paintings created for the projects. Now, for Rothko, as Pierre Schneider writes of the late Matisse, the studio "was no longer a space the artist worked in, but a space he worked on."[33] But required now to activate large, institutional-scale spaces,

Rothko's murals grew less intimate, less human, more removed and dominating, than his paintings of the 1950s.

The 69th Street studio had been chosen specifically for work on the chapel murals. But, as Rothko's debate with Philip Johnson about the chapel's lighting suggests, rather than a pyramidal tower, Rothko insisted on a skylight with a "diaper"; he was modeling the chapel on the studio, not the other way around.

Dominique de Menil recalled: "The paintings, he felt, should be seen in the same light in which they had been painted. His love for familiar surroundings was such that he wanted also to have the same cement floor, and the same kind of walls."[34] The place where his works were to be seen should resemble, as closely as possible, the place where his "children" had been slowly nurtured into life. Pulverizing the defining, separating contours of physical objects, withdrawing from natural and social realities, Rothko's vacant canvases were themselves placeless, only really attached to, only belonging and alive in, the place of their origin.

After preparing the studio, Scharf stretched unprimed cotton duck, creating "about seventeen or eighteen" canvases; he also mixed paints and did some underpainting. This, said Scharf, was "a trial, an experimental phase," exploring different colors, different kinds of paint, "even to the point that one day he wanted one canvas painted and scrubbed off to see how it behaved and if it could be used again. He was rather happy with the results." Even with the de Menils paying the bills for his materials, Rothko *enjoyed* frugality.

Because he was working with very large areas, paint, Scharf said, "had to be swiftly applied in order to maintain a uniformity of drying, of surface." So Rothko required assistance, and he worked with Scharf as he had with Dan Rice: one of the men worked rapidly on the top half of the canvas on a ladder, while the other worked below, struggling *with* the ladder. Scharf recalled using housepainter's brushes and a dark palette: "brick reds, deep reds, black mauves."[35] Yet, "as beautifully as we might plan, we never really knew how a surface was going to dry, how it was going to turn out. And if it ever did dry uniform, he might decide he wanted it two colors lighter or two colors darker. It could be a perfectly magnificent black or deep wine surface, but after a few days he might decide, no, it's not right, beautiful as it is." Scharf estimates that some of the canvases produced at this time were built up with "fifteen or twenty layers of paint."

In his January 1965 agreement with the de Menils, Rothko envisioned "ten units—one to each of the sides and three for the apse." By the time he finished, however, the project contained fourteen works, Rothko having decided to place triptychs on each of the two long side walls as well as on the front, apse wall.[36] For these side-wall triptychs, which seem to have caused him most trouble,

Rothko created construction-paper sketches, testing different shapes, sizes, and proportions for the black rectangles he wished to place within these canvases.[37] In addition, Philip Johnson early provided Rothko with a scale model of the chapel, for which he devised small models of his paintings, trying out many different possibilities and combinations.[38]

After completing the chapel panels in 1967, Rothko recalled these first stages of the project not as a time of spontaneous experiment and free discovery but one of frustration and "torment." He told Ulfert Wilke and Ray Parker how he had made his small panels, placed them in Johnson's model, changed "their shapes until he thought of a perfect relationship and then had them enlarged," only to discover that this scaling up of his models didn't work. It took him a year, he had told Wilke a few months before, to decide what he wanted to do for this project, adding that he had then determined "to make something *you don't want to look at.*"[39] Rothko wanted a room that would *disturb*.

Scharf helped Rothko during that first year, "and then he reached a point where he didn't want another painter around." But Rothko, sixty-two years old in the fall of 1965, required assistance not only to paint large surfaces rapidly, but also to hoist these heavy paintings on and off the mock walls and even to maneuver them up or down once they were on the walls. So when Scharf left, Rothko hired Roy Edwards and Ray Kelly, two young men from the Art Students League recommended by Rothko's friend Theodoros Stamos. Yet, even after completing the chapel murals, Rothko continued to employ assistants, Jonathan Ahearn (in the fall of 1968) and Oliver Steindecker (from February, 1969, until Rothko's death a year later).[40]

A painter's studio is, first of all, a workshop, a place of physical and mental *labor*. Since the late 1940s Rothko, building up his canvases with thin glazes of quickly applied paint, had spent more time considering his evolving works than he had in the physical act of producing them. Once, the collector Duncan Phillips had asked Rothko, "Am I right that in your approach to your work, *color* means *more* to you than any other element?" and Rothko had replied, "No, not color but *measures*."[41] Of the Houston murals, Rothko declared, "It is all a study in proportion." The Rothko who had claimed he'd never been interested in Mondrian, who wryly described Mondrian as a sensualist, who called himself a materialist, increasingly portrayed himself as engaged not with sensual values (like color) but with mathematical precisions ("measures") and abstract relations ("proportion").[42]

Rothko talked about "breathing paint on canvas," as if he wished to paint without the contaminating mediation of the awkward, limited body. With his mural projects, Rothko more and more removed himself from the physical labors of producing his "presences." For the chapel in Houston, Edwards and

Chapter Sixteen

Kelly painted the grounds for all fourteen panels—which means, since seven of them are monochromatic, that Rothko's hand did not touch the canvas in half of the works. Working for a patron, designing murals for a chapel, the aging Rothko now operated as a kind of small-scale Renaissance master, controlling, directing, supervising the work of his young assistants.

When Oliver Steindecker started work, the first thing Rothko told him was, "I'm a very secretive person and whatever you see, it's private." More than mere painter's workshop, the studio was a *private* space, emblematic of the core private self (or "not-self"), withdrawn from the distractions and assaults of the outside social world, turned inward on its own painful solitude and emptiness.

Rothko's East Side former carriage house thus marks the opposite end of the social spectrum from Andy Warhol's former hat factory ("The Factory") on East 47th Street. "The moment the Factory opened its doors, it became a cultural mecca, part atelier, part film studio, part experimental theater, part literary workshop, and a Salvation Army for all the artists and would-be artists who couldn't find shelter elsewhere." "There were political people, radicals, people in the arts, disaffected millionaires, collectors, hustlers, hookers. It became a giant theater," said Emilio de Antonio. "I once said to Andy, 'You're making a film of a film, aren't you?' He laughed." In fact, Warhol's assistant, Billy Linich, was filming much of what was happening at the Factory.[43]

But just as not everyone got into the Factory, not everyone was shut out of Rothko's carriage house: it might be difficult, but it wasn't impossible to gain entry—even for professionals. Critics visited to view paintings; curators and collectors came to look, perhaps to buy. Judgments were fixed; selections made; sales negotiated. Photographers—though no filmmakers—were admitted, allowed to capture privileged glimpses of the artist in his studio, images subsequently used for publicity. If Rothko believed, as Dore Ashton said, that his work could serve some purpose that was not sullied by the world, it could only do so by getting out *into* the world. The studio also functioned as part of the social and economic network serving to promote and distribute Rothko's art.

Besides, as Rebecca Reis commented, "It is a beautiful studio but it is damn lonesome."[44] Rothko's refuge from the world was equipped with a telephone, which he often used and which he almost always answered. One day, as Rothko was working on a ladder while Scharf worked below, the phone rang, Scharf (on Rothko's instruction) did not pick it up, but Rothko clambered down the ladder, stepped into a bucket of paint, answered the phone, too late, and became enraged at Scharf.[45] It was as if Rothko needed to toss a rope ladder (or at least a phone line) back across the gulf he also needed to separate himself from the world.

"I never met anybody who was that lonesome, really desperately lonely, and yet so friendly," said Regina Bogat. Working on the Houston murals (and after), Rothko typically arrived at his studio early, perhaps 6 A.M., his assistants arrived at 9, and he worked until 11 A.M. The solitude he sought made him restless. "Rothko had no tolerance for introspection," Dr. Grokest believed. "He did not want to change."[46] Inward, self-immersed yet striving to transcend the self, Rothko brooded, preferring to dwell on rather than to question, examine, or alter his feelings. He hung on to them, like his paintings. He might own a home on East 95th Street, work in a former carriage house, earn almost $70,000 a year, have an international reputation as a painter, belong to New York's cultural elite, but he still *felt* ostracized, unrecognized, susceptible to forces beyond his control, unprotected—as vulnerable as a seven-year-old boy living on Shosseynaya Street in Dvinsk whose father had just left for America. Rothko looked into himself so far, but no further, as if he wished to veil himself from himself, or as if he could only bear to be with himself for so long. He needed the warmth, and the distractions, and the confirmations, of human contact.

This need was especially strong during, and just after completing, the two-year mural project he hoped would be his masterwork. "He was keyed up and nervous about it all the time," said Dore Ashton. "Every day there would be someone coming to the studio to look at the pictures," Rothko's assistant, Roy Edwards, recalled.[47] Rothko would call and invite one or perhaps two visitors, ideally at twilight when the studio was very dim, to an intimate, private viewing. Rothko, author and director of this solemn drama, watched. "He'd be looking for your approbation and he would be testing you at the same time," William Scharf said, "testing your loyalty to him and your sensitivity to his work. He needed affirmation—and re-affirmation." Brian O'Doherty recalled that, once you were there, "Rothko would relapse into staring at his work. Or, like the Wedding Guest, he fixed you with a glittering eye while you inspected his paintings, watching for the flicker of a muscle which he could immediately misinterpret."

To these trying rituals, many were called, and many were chosen. "Rothko's invitations and scrutiny made you feel important and privileged," said O'Doherty, "until gradually it came out that *everyone* had been there—that in fact Rothko's chapel pictures were, during the years of their creation, one of the art world's sights."[48]

Both Rothko's uncertainties and his ambitions involved a man prickly about his autonomy in an elaborate network of dependencies—on art professionals and art patrons, on supportive friends, and on assistants, whose presence made the studio a social space and creation less a solitary "adventure in an unknown space" than a joint enterprise. By the time Roy Edwards started working for Rothko, the experimental stage had ended. Now, "all his movements were like thought-out beforehand. He seemed to know exactly where he was at."[49]

Edwards began work in late 1965, Ray Kelly in January 1966.[50] First Edwards helped Rothko stretch unprimed cotton duck canvas on large wooden stretchers. Rothko might be frugal, testing to see if he could reuse canvases, but he was also meticulous: "if there was a piece that had a welt or something running through it, he would discard it. Even though it was a huge piece of canvas to throw away." The two men would spend one day stretching the canvas, the next day, or sometimes the next two or three days, adjusting the tightness, removing any wrinkles. Next, the paint was mixed, "a long process of boiling rabbit's skin glue and the plastic compound that he used in combination with powdered pigments." Rothko wanted the paint "very thin and watery." "The oil paint had to be very thinned with turpentine. I would stir and stir and stir and stir so that it wasn't lumpy at all, just like soup, you know."

Next, instead of the awkward one-man-on, one-man-below the ladder method he had used with Dan Rice and William Scharf, Rothko had his assistants place a stretched canvas on its side against a wall. Then Kelly and Edwards, dipping "thick," 4" to 6" house-painter brushes into bucketfuls of thin maroon paint, started applying the paint from opposite ends of the canvas, working toward the middle. "We had to do it like very fast. Rothko would be there supervising, giving commands, very nervous, you know, high energy," shouting instructions: "You're slowing down on your corner!" Or "Pick up on this end!"

After Edwards and Kelly completed the paintings, Rothko "put them up against the wall and looked at them for a few days," seeing how they would dry.[51] Now, half of the fourteen canvases—the apse triptych and the four angle-wall paintings—were complete; they constituted a new departure for Rothko, his first monochromatic works. Then, for the remaining canvases—the two side-wall triptychs and the single rear-wall painting—Rothko added black interior rectangles. "He began laying out the actual *form* on the canvas," said Edwards. "This was a large black rectangle running up the height of the canvas, so that the maroon color became its border. This was done in a very precise manner with masking tape." These paintings constituted another departure for Rothko. For the first time in his career, renouncing the delicacy of his borders along with the seductiveness of his color, Rothko was painting severe, straight-edged rectangles. Or: his edges, formerly equivocal, had now hardened into absoluteness.⁵²

After marking the dimensions of the rectangles with masking tape, Rothko had Edwards blacken them in with charcoal. "He wanted to see the pictures sitting in relation to each other. So we did several. And after this was done, the only thing he did for about a month was just look at them." Rothko would ask Edwards to expand or contract the size of the rectangles, sometimes by as little as a quarter-inch, but in general—if we can judge from the traces of earlier tapings visible in the paintings—Rothko slowly, cautiously, enlarged these dark rectangles, until, on the side-wall triptychs, only a few inches of the maroon border remained.⁵³

As Dominique de Menil commented, "at first, the [black] field occupied only the central part—an opening in a wall into the night. Step by step, the field was enlarged, leaving only a narrow margin of color. The night had invaded the wall."⁵⁴ Writing about Nietzsche's *The Birth of Tragedy*, Rothko had declared form a question of "measure, of how much can be revealed before the reality becomes unendurable." Evolving the side-wall and end-wall paintings for the Houston chapel, proceeding carefully and deliberately, Rothko confronted the question of measure: how much of a flat, blank, opaque, and humanity-obliterating black could he let in before the painting became unendurable?

When he finally decided on these dimensions, Edwards said, "a fresh canvas was brought out—one that was already primed. The dimensions were put down with masking tape—and I mixed the black paint and he painted the interior form." Once again, the canvas was laid on its side against a studio wall and "he started at one end and worked across. He did all the black forms himself." Painted a flat, impenetrable black, with little variation or visible brushstrokes, these impersonal forms were the only ones painted personally by Rothko.⁵⁵

Sometime in late 1966 or early 1967, Rothko decided to raise the central panels of the two side-wall triptychs about eight inches above the side panels, a move not likely to have been conceived without the pulley system Rothko had placed on the mock-up walls in his studio.⁵⁶ In April of 1967, Rothko called John de Menil to announce that the paintings were finished.⁵⁷ A few months later, Mrs. de Menil, accompanied by her assistant, Helen Winkler, and one of the architects, Howard Barnstone, came to view the paintings.

That morning, Rothko's studio neighbor, Arthur Lidov, recalled that Rothko was very anxious. "Mark was characteristically nervous as a cat about any deviation from what he had just, for the last length of time, been doing successfully," and he was especially nervous about the innovations—

monochromatic panels, hard-edged rectangles—he had introduced in the Houston panels. Two years of work, and a major project—intended to extend and culminate his career—were at stake. The day of the de Menil visit, said Lidov, "I can only say that Mark was shitting bricks. He wandered in, these people were due to come at 3 in the afternoon, and from about 11 in the morning, he wandered in and out of my studio. He'd come out with these, 'Do you think they're going to like them?' But when they came and they did find it an acceptable approach, he was enormously relieved. He was very elated."

The paintings were kept in the studio, shown perhaps not to "everybody" in the New York art world, but to many people. At the end of 1967, they were placed in storage with Rothko's restorer, Daniel Goldreyer.[58] The project was done. . . it seems.

Yet this project, over which Rothko had been given the complete control he had always sought, was never completed by Rothko himself. As he had at Harvard, Rothko planned to install the paintings himself. He joked with Goldreyer that since he, Rothko, refused to fly, the two men would drive to Houston in a rented limousine, bringing along two cases of scotch and checking into a motel whenever they'd had too much to drink. Rothko estimated the trip would take two weeks. But Rothko was dead by the time the chapel building was finished in 1971.

He never visited the site. He never installed the paintings. When he stored the paintings, he selected eighteen, the fourteen now hung, plus four alternates. He never had the chance to reconsider the alternates.[59] When he was working on the paintings, many people had warned him about the harsh Texas sun. "I do remember distinctly telling him," said Scharf, "that Texas light was going to be frighteningly different from what he was contending with in mid-town Manhattan." Rothko never had the chance to confront the actual lighting conditions in the chapel. Since his studio could hold only three of the chapel walls, he had never been able to see more than five of the paintings together. He never had the opportunity to make any last, on-site adjustments in the hanging.

Instead, measurements provided by Rothko during Mrs. de Menil's June 1967 visit—a few of which were revised by Rothko the following day—were consulted to hang the paintings, lit by a large, low, central skylight. On February 28, 1971—almost exactly a year after Rothko's death—the now-ecumenical chapel was dedicated, in ceremonies presided over by Catholic, Jewish, Buddhist, Muslim, Greek Orthodox, and Protestant religious officials.[60]

• • •

The Houston Chapel

Art sank into melancholy.

Mark Rothko

We cannot do justice to the particular nature of the psyche by linear contours. . . . The diffuse color fields of the modern painters would do better.

Sigmund Freud

You enter the Rothko Chapel through two, large, heavy wooden doors, painted black. They admit you to a foyer, with a desk along the opposite wall, where you can buy postcards, slides, copies of Susan Barnes's *The Rothko Chapel, An Act of Faith,* or, on the way out, you can inscribe your thoughts about the chapel in a guest book. One person works behind the desk, one or two more, acting as ununiformed guards, sit on either side of the foyer, by the doors that lead into the chapel.

When I visited the chapel in January of 1992, I entered through the foyer's right rear door, took several steps into the chapel, then stopped to look at the large dark-maroon triptych that fills the front, north wall in the apse. Rothko's octagonal room comes as close to encircling a visitor as a room can and still have flat walls on which to hang paintings, but the apse, faced as you enter and set back six feet, gives the room a front, and gives this triptych an initial prominence.

Three large, imposing, vertical canvases (about 5′ × 15′), all painted a somber, dark maroon, with the center panel lighter and the sides darker, have been joined in a simple, formal, and symmetrical arrangement.[61] At Harvard, Rothko had similarly hung a triptych on a recessed wall. There, brown, black, and orange door- and window-like shapes sometimes looked like solid figures on a crimson ground, sometimes like openings in a solid crimson wall. At Houston, however, the monochromatic apse triptych holds no forms, no shapes that might be "read" as gate or door or window, or, as with Rothko's earlier work, as abstracted landscape or human figure. Three amorphous fields of color, devoid of any reference to external, remembered reality, lacking any containing borders, these massive, empty paintings are at once self-sufficiently present, and boundless.

Or, more precisely, these three canvases *are* bound, rigidly, by their literal edges, as if their diffused fields of melancholy color could only be held in artificially, arbitrarily, absolutely. Yet these three separate canvases have been *joined*. Movement, drama, interaction do not occur here within a painting,

Chapter Sixteen

between, say, two rectangles of varying color, size, and weight, but between and among three monochromatic paintings. At first, the triptych's center panel—brighter, slightly larger than the side panels, its surface filled with subtle nuances of tone, of lighter and darker tones of maroon—draws and dominates attention, as if the adjacent darker panels served only to enhance the prominence of the center. Yet, I found that if I concentrated on the center panel for a long time, it darkened and merged with the side panels, no longer integral, much less dominant.

Looking at these paintings for several hours a day (with breaks for food and an occasional walk through the neighborhood) over a period of five days, I continually tried to isolate single canvases, as if I were confronting a series of fourteen self-contained objects. I could do this for a while, but even close-up, even if I walked up to within just a few inches of the single painting hung on the rear wall, I could always see at least two other paintings in my peripheral vision. In the Rothko Chapel, seeking to fix on a single painting, one instead finds relation.

At first, as I looked at the front triptych, struggling to separate or to join its three panels, my attention would drift away, laterally, to look at the two adjacent angle-wall canvases. All four of the monochromatic angle-wall paintings possess the same imposing size—about 11′ × 15′, they are the largest canvases in the chapel—and they are hung on, and fill, the short diagonal walls, which seem to push into the room, particularly at the front, where they abut the recessed wall. The angle-wall paintings, too, contend for prominence.

When I finally directed my attention to the one at the front left, I discovered it to be filled with horizontal rows of soft, dark, undulating forms that alternate with lighter areas, the whole resembling an aerial view of a forest, at night, seen through an ultra-red light. I walked forward to view this painting close-up, then backed away to compare it with the lighter center panel and the darker side panels of the front triptych, then turned to compare it with the rear angle-wall painting diagonally across from it, then came back (roughly) to my original position, where I turned to my left to begin looking at the triptych on the west, side wall: a large, raised central panel, flanked by smaller side panels, all three containing black rectangles that have expanded almost to the edges, leaving thin, straight-edged maroon borders.

Particularly at first, these black interior forms seem dull and impenetrable, as if Rothko had painted "something *you don't want to look at*." They are *very* difficult to enter, to become involved with, and I kept looking away from them to the nearby angle-wall paintings, which are more varied, attractive, and "beautiful." I walked to the center of the room, turned around and examined the apparently identical triptych on the east wall (color plate 19). As with the

The Houston Chapel

triptych at the front, on the side walls three separate canvases have been joined in a hierarchical arrangement, in which the center painting—here 2½′ wider and raised about 8″ higher than the sides—predominates. But here, too, I discovered that if I looked for a long time at the center canvas, all the triptych's thin borders dissolved, leaving a diffused and utter blackness.

I then spent some time moving back and forth across the chapel, comparing the two triptychs. When the borders remained intact and solid-looking, the narrower, more vertical side panels resembled doorways; in fact, each of the side triptychs abuts, on either side, small (about 4′ × 8′) doorways, leading to areas originally intended for a sacristy or confessionals, now used as storage space.[62] Visitors to the chapel continually start to enter these doors, or crane their upper bodies around to see what's inside—until a guard warns them away. Doors are hard to resist. Rothko's paintings echo, enlarge—they transcendentalize—these actual architectural features of the room. His triptychs, especially when strong sunlight breaks up the stark interior black, resemble openings, immense and formidable triple gates, inviting entry into a cavernous space, filled with a suffocatingly dense, gray-black smoke.

In the religious context of a chapel, triptychs with raised central panels also suggested to me some traditional representations of the crucifixion—Christ's cross flanked by those of the two thieves or by two mourners (or saints)—perhaps because I knew that others had already made this association. Yet by stripping away the figuration in these Christian triptychs, Rothko asks us to contemplate their basic formal elements: abstract notions of prominence and subordination, joining and separating, diffusion and containment. The raised, larger centers assert dominance; the hard-edged borders assert enclosure; but the flat, black anonymous interiors assert the obliteration of *all* distinction. Seeking to move outside and beyond the contemporary art market, where, as he said, he "felt as if he were dead," Rothko accepted a commission to decorate a chapel, to create a monument that would assure him of a permanent, lasting place in Western art, as if he were already immortal. Yet the works that he produced for this chapel question the very desire for prominence by setting it against a self-obliterating despair.

I finally walked to the center of the room and turned to face the single, vertical painting placed on the rear wall. Like the side-wall triptychs, this canvas holds a straight-edged black rectangle on or within a dark maroon, with narrow borders at the sides and top. The difference is that, at the bottom, the border expands upward about 2½′, occupying about one-fifth of the painting's height. Walking up close to this painting, I noticed that this juncture between the top of the maroon and the bottom of the black was about chest-high. Dramatically isolated on a wall about two and a half times its width—the three triptychs and four angle-wall paintings all crowd their walls—and the only canvas in the chapel whose form is not repeated, this painting asserts singularity. Hung on the rear wall, faced just before a visitor leaves the chapel, more securely holding and distancing its black area than do the side triptychs, this painting offers a possible resolution to the ensemble's tensions between containment and diffusion, prominence and relation.

Yet the very uniqueness of this work is defined only through its relations to, its differences from, the other thirteen paintings, two of which—on the rear angle-walls—always hover in the viewer's peripheral vision. The lighter, more open and various angle-wall canvases dramatize the containment of the rear-wall painting as well as its blank uniformity and opacity of surface. Yet even if temporarily considered in isolation, this simple, static-looking emblem of singularity reveals its own tensions and dualities. Because of its size, the interior black predominates, looking sometimes like a flat, dense, monolithic void, at others like a semitransparent, thin, black veil. At still other times, areas of a shiny greenish-white emerge, breaking up the black, hinting at the ghostly traces of human forms.

The same height as the angle-wall paintings, and hung just as far from the floor, the rear wall canvas, two and a half feet narrower than those paintings, looks more vertical, as if its interior black rectangle had been compressed. Yet the thin maroon borders along the top and sides, as with the side wall triptychs, dissolve after prolonged viewing. The larger maroon area at the bottom, however, cannot simply be subordinated to the role of border; it can be seen as part of a windowlike frame, as a solid obstruction in a doorlike opening, or as a painted area of independent interest, receding into shadowy plum-colored depths. The sharply divided black and maroon, moreover, can't be fully separated, particularly at the bottom horizontal junction, where these two opposed areas are at once divided, held in, joined, and even merged. For in the black just above this line, hints of the border color are visible, suggesting that the border may have once been higher, or that what appears to be border actually forms a field *behind* the black. Either way, an apparently rigorous division wavers into ambiguity.

Unlike the soft edges in Rothko's earlier work, which evoke continuing activity, the straight edges in the chapel murals define a stable, arrested movement. Yet, just inside the top of the black rectangle in the rear-wall painting, the markings of an earlier border, established with masking tape, are visible; the black rectangle has expanded. Similar pentimenti are visible in the side-wall triptychs.[63] Some of the chapel murals show some signs of brushwork, but these marks appear mostly in the monochromatic works, where the hand belonged not to the artist but his assistant. In this project, the chief marks of

Rothko's process are the traces of earlier tapings, suggesting a coming-into-being more contemplative than physical, more deliberate and removed than spontaneous or intimate. If the hard-edged borders imply stability, the pentimenti imply movement—and the borders do, after prolonged gaze at what they contain, dissolve. So the unique form of the rear-wall painting has been achieved, the expansion of its black rectangle has been contained—*temporarily*. This work offers *momentary* resolution.

A central skylight admits sunlight to the chapel—the only way in which the nature that made Rothko uncomfortable enters this sealed-off space—so that the light changes depending on time of day, time of year, weather conditions. On overcast days, the black rectangles, for instance, look hard and opaque, whereas on brighter days the light breaks up the black into lighter and darker areas that recede or push forward. One day during my visit, patches of high, broken clouds pushed by a strong wind made it look as though someone in the chapel were controlling the rapidly changing light with a dimmer. In this space, neither parts nor whole remain fixed, but change subtly, and continually, through time.

Nor does the viewer remain stationary. As my account of visiting the chapel suggests, viewing these fourteen paintings is a *temporal* process, one that unfolds, slowly, through time, and a *physical* process, one that requires considerable bodily movement, there being no fixed, ideal position from which to view the murals. It is not just that your vision is always distracted by nearby paintings. It is that you are aware, no matter where you stand, that some of the paintings are behind you, that the limitations of your body force you to *exclude* some of the works you are trying to unify. You can't isolate individual paintings. You can't grasp the whole. Rothko's murals exceed possession.

"You are in it. It isn't something you command."

The eight walls of the chapel create a large, hollow space, in which you are free to move, surrounded or perhaps dominated by fourteen large, empty canvases. They may not make you not want to look at them, but they don't do much to make you look at them either. They refuse the sensuality and drama, the eagerness to be liked, to draw in and connect that we find in Rothko's earlier work. Yet, you can't not look at these paintings. You can't back away very far. If you turn your back on one painting, you're facing another one, aware of the one behind you. You can't step back, detach yourself, stand outside, achieve "perspective," as you could if you were dealing with a series of fourteen discrete, self-contained paintings hung along a single wall. In the chapel, you have entered a field, a hollow space activated by your own physical movements, your reflective and emotional interactions with these paintings.

Among the comments written in the guest book kept in the chapel's foyer,

Chapter Sixteen

the most frequently used word is "peace." Remarks like "indeed a sacred feeling filled me and inspired peace and awe" or "at a time of turmoil and change a peaceful contemplative respite" are typical. Quiet and self-enclosed, severed from the turmoil and abrasive changes of contemporary urban life, the chapel offers a tranquil retreat. Its murals composed of simple forms, its walls hung with symmetrical paintings symmetrically arranged, the chapel instills a feeling of balanced calm. Even the interior black rectangles, empty of representational incident or gestural vigor, seem calm and quiet.

Yet, the two side-wall triptychs, for instance, are neither symmetrical in themselves nor identical with each other, as they at first appear to be. On the east wall, the black rectangles in the sides panels are slightly off center, 1½" closer to the outside vertical edge than to the edge adjacent to the center panel. In all three panels, the bottom borders are wider than the top ones, but the bottom borders of the sides are ¼" narrower than that of the center.[64] The sizes of the three paintings on the west wall match exactly those on the east: sides, 6' × 11'3"; centers, 8'6" × 11'3"; and here, too, the black rectangles in the side panels are a bit off center. But the side borders of all three west-wall panels are somewhat wider than their east-wall equivalents.[65] The center panel on the west wall, moreover, is hung 1¼" lower than that on the east. The room's symmetry is slightly off, its balanced calm slightly disquieting.

After the Houston panels were complete, two artist-friends of Rothko's—Ulfert Wilke and Ray Parker—visited the 69th Street studio to view the paintings. When Parker asked Rothko if the color were the same in the two triptychs, he responded, "Who can tell?" Rothko repeated his assertion that "once he knew that he wanted to do some panels you don't want to look at he knew what he might do," but then went on to suggest that the paintings would elicit prolonged and careful looking. "It is all a study in proportion," Rothko said, "and one can become quite engulfed in considering . . . the two triptychs and wonder whether their shapes are the same—they appear similar but are not the same, one has vertically wider and horizontally narrower borders than the other—the borders might have sheen and the dark inside [might] not or vice versa." "You can be engaged into the study of proportion or the response of your own meditative moods," Rothko declared. He was still debating whether to put simple benches under the panels. "They will protect the paintings; one can sit on them and they will give the horizontal balance which [is] desireable to Rothko."[66]

"I have made a place," this displaced Russian-Jewish painter had said of his Seagram mural project. In Houston, Rothko made a peaceful religious sanctuary, as well as a permanent home for a set of his creations, but one into which he introduced the subtle disturbances and irresolvable tensions of a "live unity." The chapel's balanced formality is sometimes slightly off. Its dark, melancholy, empty, self-absorbed paintings are not easily accessible. Its ensemble of fourteen paintings can neither be fully grasped nor avoided. Combining contemplative rest with dynamic, almost restless activity, the chapel, experienced slowly and patiently, actually offers not a peaceful environment in which to avoid, but a discomforting place in which to confront, an abstract form of *dis*placement.

During my visits to the chapel, I periodically felt a strong urge to walk over to one of the wooden benches, stretch out, and fall asleep. One day, a young woman came in, sat for about an hour on a bench looking at the east-wall triptych, then swung her feet up onto the bench, lay back, and took a nap. Maybe she was tired. Maybe I was tired. But I think that, after time, these paintings begin to feel oppressive. Close-up, they are not engaging, though they are imposing; lacking the thin layers of translucent color, the feathery or vigorous brushwork, the spontaneous, delicate edges of Rothko's earlier works, the chapel murals lack their intimacy, warmth, and humanity. This environment isn't something you command, because it is something *he* commands, and he is aloof and demanding, withdrawn and grandiose, dominating and despairing.

One afternoon, I spent a long time looking at the rear-wall painting, viewing it from close or distant, straight or diagonal positions, relating it to the lighter, wider monochromatic works on the adjacent angle walls, trying to determine how it balanced (or *if* it balanced) the triptych on the front wall, comparing its interior black rectangle with those in the side-wall triptychs. But mostly I tried to concentrate on the rear-wall canvas, dominated by a black void that occupies most of the upper four-fifths of the painting's surface. Close-up, elevated by the 2½' high maroon border at the bottom, the black rectangle loomed over me, an awesome presence which made me bend my head back to see the top of the painting. From the other side the room, the painting as a whole seemed more "manageable," but its side borders were more likely to dissolve, allowing the black to diffuse. Sometimes—partly depending on the light—the black looks as solid as a stone wall; at others, it resembles a dark translucent veil; at still others, it disperses into a suffocating black smoke. Is the black a larger, perhaps boundless area seen through the frame created by the maroon borders? Or is the black an originally smaller area that has, ominously, swelled and even pushed back the frame?

In the Houston chapel, Rothko culminates the critique of looking as possession which he had begun in the late 1940s, by placing us inside an environment where we cannot define, much less master, either parts or whole. Instead of being a painter who "penetrates" the flux of temporal experience and uncovers its core, or inner form, of eternal meaning—as Rothko himself had done with the frozen moments in his urban scenes of the 1930s (see color plates 1 & 8)—he now creates clear, hard-edged forms (echoing the angularity of the octagonal room) which cannot arrest the substance they contain, as if Rothko now wished to uncover the flux, the stuff, the emptiness behind the realm of forms—a substrate we *don't* want to look at.

Yet the dark rectangle in the rear-wall painting pulled me in, holding my attention for long stretches of time. It's not easy to enter: the large maroon area at the bottom elevates the black rectangle, distancing and protecting the viewer, while also obstructing entry. Access, again, is made difficult. Still, the area *is* quiet and calm and solemn; it fills a large framed vertical opening that invites entry; the black attracts precisely because it can't be possessed, because it pulls toward something beyond personality, something that can't be owned—by Mrs. de Menil or Mark Rothko or us. When the black looks solid, it thwarts entry. When the black dematerializes, it draws the viewer into an amorphous, empty, anonymous, all-absorbing—in fact, annihilating—darkness.

Intended for a Catholic chapel, hung in an ecumenical one, these murals are spiritual only in the sense that they renounce the world—the world of material objects, of historical time and social pressures. Decorating a public, sacred space, they express a private and very human desire: a despairing wish to withdraw *from* the human.

. . .

When Rothko's paintings were installed in 1971, they were illuminated by a central skylight, sometimes supplemented by six floodlights placed around the base of the skylight and a row of floods placed about halfway down the sloped ceiling. But the skylight, which Rothko had insisted upon, created two crucial problems. As Lawrence Alloway complained in 1971, "too much light streams in by day, illuminating the middle of the floor like a skating rink, and pushing the paintings back out of the way."[67] Over time, the natural light—the harsh Texas sun that Rothko had been warned about—damaged the paintings, so that by 1974 a scrim had been installed beneath the skylight, an arrangement that, like the parachute in Rothko's studio, modified and diffused the light. Two years later, the scrim was replaced with a metal baffle that is there today.

Unlike Harvard—where a dispersed and often indifferent authority made care of Rothko's murals very difficult—Mrs. de Menil and her staff have carefully monitored the situation in the chapel and invested considerable time and expense in finding a solution.[68] Yet the baffle is *very* unsatisfactory. Covering almost half the ceiling space, this metal canopy hovers distractingly overhead,

The Houston Chapel

disrupts the simple dignity of the room, and, worst of all, leaves in permanent shadow the lower parts of all the paintings, except the apse triptych (since it's recessed).[69] The paintings seen under these conditions are *not* the ones painted by Rothko.

The first day I visited the chapel eight wooden benches were set in a large circle, at the center of which a small round black pillow sat on a small black mat. Two more of these black mats with black pillows, used for meditation, had been placed at either side of the front apse. On the east and west sides of the circle of benches stood two wooden candelabra on five-foot-high metal stands. The chapel, I learned, had been set up for a secular memorial service that afternoon, such services being, along with weddings (!), the most frequent group activities held in the room. For two days, the benches, mats, pillows, and candelabra remained so situated. When I arrived on the third day, they had been rearranged, this time for a Roman Catholic memorial service. Now three rows of eight benches faced the front, where a lectern and two candelabra had been placed; the room stayed this way until after I left.

In the early Christian era, religious painting had been an extension of church architecture; Rothko fought to make the chapel's architecture an extension of his paintings. Rothko had calculated, and recalculated, the dimensions of his fourteen paintings, the proportions of the dark rectangles in seven of them, the size of the doorways. But in the shifting arrangements of the room today, candelabra sometimes impede your view of the paintings, benches determine where you can sit, where you can stand, or where you can move.

At some, necessarily arbitrary, point in a visit to the chapel, you feel tired or hungry or oppressed or frustrated or even satisfied. Or maybe your back hurts or your legs are tired. You turn, face the rear wall, leave through one of the two rear doors, pass through the foyer, and reenter the "outside" world.

• • •

In May 1969, John and Dominique de Menil donated money toward the purchase of a work of public sculpture for the city of Houston, stipulating that the work be Barnett Newman's *Broken Obelisk*, that it be installed near City Hall, and that it be dedicated to the memory of the civil rights activist, Martin Luther King, Jr. This dedication, however, prompted city officials to refuse the sculpture, and in the fall of 1969 Newman traveled to Houston to discuss a site for the work, which had been temporarily placed in one of the reflecting pools outside the Seagram Building in New York. Newman decided on a pool outside the Rothko Chapel, then under construction. "A house happened to be at this location," Mrs. de Menil recalled. "It was bought and pulled down without a moment's hesitation," as if, for the de Menils, removing a house were equivalent to brushing away a Texas fly that's been hovering, annoyingly, in front of your face.[70]

When you leave the chapel, you are looking toward the pool with Newman's sculpture, situated, along with the chapel, in a city-block-sized park. The adjacent blocks to the east are the site of St. Thomas University, designed by Philip Johnson; the adjacent block to the west has, since 1987, been the site of the Menil Collection, a private museum designed for the de Menils by the Italian architect Renzo Piano: a low, two-story 400'-building, its clapboard exterior painted a plain gray. The surrounding four blocks, a quiet neighborhood filled with brick and wood frame houses all painted the same gray as the museum, are also owned by the de Menils; the buildings are used by the Menil Foundation or rented to people in the arts, or to just plain people. Houston has no zoning laws, so in order to preserve—i.e., control—the character of the neighborhood, the de Menils bought it. Removed from the larger social community west of Montrose Boulevard (mostly working-class and black) the Rothko Chapel today sits, enclosed, in a kind of company town of art.

When Dominique de Menil had sent Rothko his first checks for the project, she called them "history making."

> The great venture you have started will lead to others. But yours will be the first in America. I feel proud to be associated with it, and I know something great will be created. I feel sure that right here is the place where it should be. The spiritual and artistic climate is ripe for it. You will feel it yourself when you come.[71]

When Rothko wasn't urging the religious import of his paintings ("the people who weep before my pictures are having the same religious experience I had when I painted them"), he was denying the religious character imputed to them by others ("He'd always say, 'I'm not a religious man'."). Mrs. de Menil lacked Rothko's ambivalence. "Art is incantation," she has written. "Like Jacob's ladder, it leads to higher realities, to timelessness, to paradise. It is the fusion of the tangible and the intangible; the old hierogamy myth—the marriage of heaven and earth."[72]

At the beginning of the chapel project Rothko had spoken to Dore Ashton of the patristic fathers: "He liked the 'ballet' of their thoughts, and the way everything went toward ladders." Yet Rothko later rejected the vertical aspiration of the pyramid Philip Johnson wished to place atop the chapel. All of Rothko's mural panels are vertical, higher than they are wide, but the disposition of the low, flat-roofed building he insisted upon is lateral, both outside and in. The space Rothko created is horizontal, more a womblike enclosure than the phallic thrust of Johnson's sloped tower. The side-wall triptychs and the rear-wall painting suggest openings which alternately keep you out and invite you to enter a black, pulverizing void, a nether realm of absence formed out of the divorce, not the marriage, of heaven and earth.

The de Menils' spiritual idealism led them, generously enough, to support Rothko's "great venture"; but his did not beget others. The chapel, once it was severed from the Catholic St. Thomas campus, did not reflect the spiritual values of any particular community "right here" in Houston. Rather, the project, commissioned by a wealthy patron and executed by an artist whose work was apt to bewilder or offend many of those most likely to enter a building called a "chapel," was imposed from above, reflecting the values and desires of the patron, and finding its place in a quiet and pleasant and modest "neighborhood," an urban art enclave in gray also contrived by the patron.

If he operated within the art marketplace, Rothko's meaning, his *place,* depended on transactions outside his control. By withdrawing from the market and painting an ensemble of his works for a particular site on commission, Rothko could create a kind of Symbolist poem in space, self-enclosed, autonomous, beyond history, eternal. He could "control the situation," a situation he designed in part to impress his viewers with the futility of control or possession. It is not a lesson the de Menils have absorbed.

In her Foreword to *The Menil Collection,* Mrs. de Menil speaks of a painting "I would love to see in the Collection," *St. John the Baptist in the Desert* by Domenico Veneziano, now at the National Gallery of Art. "I am so fond of this strange and miraculous little painting that I experience it as totally mine when I stand in front of it."[73] Love *is* possession for Dominique de Menil; her style is low-key, modest, but imperial. "When they didn't control things, they stepped aside." At the dedication of the Rothko Chapel, Mrs. de Menil had nicely urged a quiet receptivity to the work: "I think the paintings themselves will tell us what to think of them—if we give them a chance." Yet, she could not resist telling us what to think of them: "Indeed they are intimate and timeless," she continues, a little later in her talk. "They embrace us without enclosing us. Their dark surface[s] do not stop the gaze. A light surface is active—it stops the eye. But we can gaze right through these purplish browns, gaze into the infinite."[74] Over the years, Mrs. de Menil has continued to advance her spiritual reading of Rothko's murals, in interviews, in her own writings, and by commissioning and publishing books like Susan J. Barnes's *The Rothko Chapel, An Act of Faith* and Sheldon Nodelman's *The Rothko Chapel Paintings.*[75] Dominique de Menil has sought not just to commission a project but to control the viewing situation, setting the terms, the language, in which viewers can think and talk about the paintings.

Many visitors to the chapel walk in, sit down on a bench, read the brochure obtained at the desk outside, look around, and leave, like tourists in a museum. Others sit on one of the three black pillows, cross their legs, close their eyes, and meditate, while still others sit on a bench, close their eyes and pray. A student will come in with, say, a copy of Virginia Woolf's *To the Lighthouse,* and read for a while. Occasionally visitors actually spend time with Rothko's work, but neither the tourists nor the devout pay much, if any, attention to the paintings. Nor do those who gather in the chapel for memorial services. Few visitors, in short, spend enough time with the work to be discomforted by it—*lest* they be discomforted by it. As many of the comments in the guest book make clear, they find the peaceful sanctuary they are looking for, and often they express gratitude not to Rothko but to Mrs. de Menil for creating the chapel.

Is the chapel a monument to Mark Rothko, or to the status, taste, and philanthropic largess of the de Menil family?

Rothko liked to praise fellow artists of his generation—David Smith and Herbert Ferber are two—as "survivors."[76] He thought of himself as a survivor. The Houston chapel—a plain, low, flat, windowless, brick building, apparently sealed off from the outside—constitutes a monument to a reclusive interiority that has survived. Yet, like the hard-edged borders in Rothko's mural panels, the division between inside and outside does not hold. Natural light has dulled the surfaces of all the panels; some of them have been restored; the means of lighting the room have changed; the surrounding neighborhood has evolved; critical texts have appeared which alter the context in which the paintings are viewed—all of which testify to the ongoing temporal, the *historical,* existence of Rothko's paintings.

17 Rothko's Aneurysm

He really died when he had that seizure.

Hedda Sterne

On April 20, 1968, Rothko had lunch with an old friend, Ulfert Wilke. Rothko "was in a very cheerful mood," Wilke recalled. "It was a sunny lovely day. I took the top of my little yellow car down and Rothko insisted on going to a flower shop to buy two pots of geraniums for Mell, his wife. Next to my car was a Volkswagen all painted with flowers. 'What do you think of that?' I asked and Rothko"—ordinarily no admirer of hippies—"answered cheerfully, 'All cars should look like that'." Back at Rothko's 95th Street home, Rothko called out to Kate and a boyfriend in the living room, "Are you necking?" then proceeded with Wilke to the backyard, where Mell and Christopher were planting. A student of Wilke's was visiting a neighbor "and we talked over the fence like neighbors in a small town."[1] Rothko repeated the story he had earlier told Wilke of overhearing someone passing the house and asking, "I wonder who lives in this house with all the Rothkos."[2]

That evening the Rothkos went out to dinner. As they were walking home afterward, Rothko suddenly felt severe pain in his lower back and numbness in his legs. They took a cab home, where Mell called Rothko's physician, Dr. Grokest, who—given Rothko's symptoms and his history of high blood pressure—concluded, correctly, that Rothko had an aneurysm. When Dr. Grokest arrived, he wanted to put Rothko in Columbia Presbyterian, the hospital he was affiliated with. But Rothko declared, "I hate Columbia Presbyterian," so Grokest called to see if he could get Rothko admitted to the nearby New York Hospital. While he was still on the phone, an ambulance arrived, and, said Grokest, "I didn't know how the hell that happened. I am not that magical." While Grokest was on his way to 95th Street, Rothko had called Bernard Reis, who had called Dr. Irving Wright, a cardiologist he knew who had arranged for Rothko to be admitted to New York Hospital and had called the ambulance. Reis had displaced Grokest. Reis went off in the ambulance with Rothko and his wife, and "I sat there like a dummy wondering what the hell is going on here? Who is in charge and who would be responsible for him? What kind of a controlling character is this that can supersede me in a medical situation which is acute and dangerous?"

At the hospital's emergency ward, Reis took over, "insisting on signing Rothko in and giving all the personal data to the registrar. Because of Reis's advanced age and his help in the past, Mell and Grokest were reluctant to protest his interference."[3] There, Rothko was treated by a younger associate of Dr. Wright's, Dr. Allen Meade, who continued to treat Rothko during the last two years of his life. An X ray established that Rothko had suffered a "dissecting aortic aneurysm"; an arteriogram revealed arteriosclerosis.[4] Hypertension was cited as the cause of the aneurysm. Given Rothko's general health—his high blood pressure, his abnormal electrocardiogram, his early signs of cirrhosis of the liver—and the large size of aneurysm (and there were three of them, Grokest said), surgery was ruled out. Instead, to lower his blood pressure, Rothko was prescribed a tranquilizer and a diuretic. "Everything quieted down right away," said Dr. Meade. Rothko remained in the hospital for about two weeks, then he was confined to bed at home for another few weeks.[5]

Rothko was almost sixty-five. He had survived anti-Semitism in Dvinsk, migration to Portland, the death of his father, poverty as an art student, poverty as an artist, a Depression, the death of his mother, two marriages, years of gout, years of tippling, periodic depressions, and even success. He had outlived Jackson Pollock (d. 1956), Franz Kline (d. 1962), William Baziotes (d. 1963), Milton Avery (d. 1965), David Smith (d. 1965), and Ad Reinhardt (d. 1967). Now, he had survived an aneurysm, just as his brother Albert had survived a cancer of the colon.

But the aneurysm left Rothko literally incapacitated. He could not paint for several weeks, and even then Dr. Meade instructed him not to work on anything larger than forty inches high.[6] He required the physical help of assistants in the studio. For the rest of his life after the aneurysm, he was sexually impotent.[7] Both Drs. Meade and Grokest prescribed medications for him to take, and instructed him to watch his diet (to lower his cholesterol), and to quit smoking and drinking. He was deprived of the pleasures of painting, sex, food, cigarettes, and alcohol.

"He was enormously resentful of its having happened," recalled Arthur Lidov, Rothko's neighbor at his 69th Street studio. Always anxious, often hypochondriacal, Rothko, as many of those around him attest, was very frightened. "It scared the hell out of him and he was upset about having to live as a less-than-perfect physical specimen," said Dore Ashton. Kate Rothko recalled that her father lived in "daily fear of what was going to happen." No longer a philosophical "preoccupation," death was now an alarming, intimate reality. Rothko had every reason for concern, but Dr. Wright, who, as Dr. Meade said, "could put the fear of God into patients in a hurry," didn't help matters when he told Rothko that 95 percent of people with his condition were dead in five years—a remark that would have spoken only to Rothko's "tremendous emotional capacity for despair."[8] Rothko experienced what Dr. Meade described as a "global depression."

Death is one situation we cannot control—short of suicide. But many of the limited means of control that were recommended to Rothko by his doctors, he refused. He did, for the most part, modify his diet, lowering his cholesterol and losing weight, and he may have stopped smoking and drinking for a while, but only for a while. By July of 1968, Robert Motherwell, spending the summer living a few doors away from the Rothkos in Provincetown, was writing to Herbert Ferber of "the fright, the immobilization, the alcoholism" around the Rothkos. "He has taken a small garage as a water-color studio, and he seems to have a few young artists around for company. But it is anguishing to see his difficulty in simply getting through the day, though I am sure he would vehemently deny this." "The difficulty," Motherwell added, "is that Mark's defense mechanism is so massive and takes the form of rejecting anyone else's judgment, that no one can intervene on the one hand, and on the other as a result he is almost metaphysically lonely, hence the bottle."[9]

When Rothko visited Dr. Grokest that fall, he confided that "he and Mell were so alienated that his marriage was getting worse and that he was impotent. He was considering separating from Mell." He *had* lost considerable weight and his blood pressure *was* down.[10] But when Grokest told Rothko that the enlargement of his liver suggested the danger of cirrhosis, he refused to stop drinking. "And through all this by the way he was smoking," Grokest said. "Killing himself."

Dr. Grokest remembered a stubbornly resistant patient; Dr. Meade remembered "a very docile patient, as so many depressed individuals are. He seemed to focus a great deal into little details of his diet, drug schedule, medication schedule—almost like a little child, child-like in some ways that he'd seem very dependent." But Rothko could be demanding, too. A hypochondriac, "he would worry over a symptom or a perceived symptom and then he just had to see somebody." Arriving at the office without an appointment, Rothko "just could not be convinced" there was nothing wrong. "And you'd finish examining and talking with him, and then he would sort of hang on with this very depressed affect, this sort of waiting for something else, a very morose look. I don't think I ever saw the poor man smile. He was just waiting for you to say

Chapter Seventeen

something further. And there was nothing else to say, and so I would help him on with his coat, and then he would sort of shuffle out like a very depressed individual."

Longing for his doctor to say something that would make him feel better, Rothko still rejected the judgment of his doctors, smoking and drinking heavily, preferring the familiar figure of Reis, who visited him daily at the hospital, bringing him chicken soup and (once) poached salmon, reading to him from the daily newspaper—in short, taking care of him.[11]

That fall—on September 13, 1968—Rothko made a new will, and he turned for counsel to Reis. "Bernie, you know I hate attorneys. I hate going up in elevators. . . . Will you prepare something for me?"[12] In the document prepared by Reis, Rothko left the 95th Street house and all its contents (which, at the time of his death, included forty-four of his paintings), plus $250,000, to Mell or, should she die, to be divided between Kate and Christopher. The remainder—almost eight hundred works, as it turned out—Rothko left to the Mark Rothko Foundation, whose directors were to be Bernard Reis, Theodoros Stamos, Morton Levine, William Rubin (curator of Modern Painting and Sculpture at the Museum of Modern Art), and Robert Goldwater (an art historian and critic).[13] In the event of Mell's death, Anne-Marie and Morton Levine would act as guardians for the children; Levine, Stamos, and Reis were named as executors of the will. The will stated no purpose for the foundation that would receive the bulk of Rothko's estate, an omission that became a key issue in the lawsuit over Rothko's estate.[14]

Rothko's business operations were conducted like an old-fashioned dry goods store in which only the owner knew where all the bolts of cloth were kept and, as he grew older, not even he always knew. Though he thought of his works as organisms dependent for their life on the companionship of viewers, Rothko kept hundreds of paintings in storage, some of them for many years, many of them simply rolled. But protectively sealing them off from the world left them vulnerable to damage. So meticulous in the production of his works, so scrupulous about where and how they were placed, Rothko sometimes alarmed visitors by the careless way he, single-handedly, lugged large paintings around the studio.[15] But an entity like the foundation mentioned in Rothko's will required more orderly bookkeeping, so in late November of 1968, Rothko began an inventory of his "stock," as he liked to call it—a lengthy, tedious, and depressing task undertaken by someone already clinically depressed.[16]

Morton Levine, an amateur photographer, was hired to photograph the work; Dan Rice was brought back because of his experience in cataloguing Franz Kline's estate; and Rothko's two assistants in this period—Jonathan

Ahearn in late 1968 and early 1969, and Oliver Steindecker thereafter—also helped. Works were brought in from storage, unrolled, tacked to a studio wall, assigned a catalogue number, photographed, measured, recorded, and returned to storage. Rothko provided dates for the works, something he did from memory, and not always accurately. Both Rice and Ahearn recall Rothko's distress at this confrontation with his life's work, and his drinking. Sometimes Rothko would "already be drunk or busy about getting drunk" when Rice arrived in the morning. Ahearn remembered frequent trips to a nearby liquor store to replenish Rothko's scotch supply, and cleaning up broken glasses and bottles dropped by Rothko, who had "become very forgetful."

Rothko, Ahearn said, "clearly was preparing for his own death."[17]

• • •

> *One day we'll discuss the tragic air around the Rothkos this summer; dreadful to watch, sad, angry-making—powerful and hopeless all at once, and even contaminating for some of us.*
>
> Helen Frankenthaler

In early July 1968, Mark Rothko rented a limousine, rented a U-Haul which he attached to the back of the limousine, and took himself and his family to Provincetown for the summer.[18] The Rothkos rented a cottage at 621 Commercial Street, at the east end of the town; Rothko rented a double garage a few blocks away, where he began painting again, after the two-and-a-half month layoff forced by his aneurysm. The return to work, the bracing sea air and brilliant sunlight of Cape Cod, a family vacation—all of these might have seemed, back on East 95th Street, an ideal way to revive Rothko's ailing body and shaken spirit. But by all accounts, his summer was miserable.

"He wasn't working very well that summer," Stanley Kunitz recalled. "He was in very bad shape. He was drinking a great deal. He was terribly sloppy personally in his habits, and got fat and confused. And then he had these terrible quarrels with Mell that were ugly in every way. I just had the feeling that he was going completely to seed." Anxious about his health, frustrated by his efforts to work, angry with his wife (and she with him), Rothko, more agitated and restless than ever, drank, talked to friends on the phone, walked the streets of Provincetown, dropping in to visit Robert Motherwell and Helen Frankenthaler, sometimes strolling over to the west end of town, to visit Stanley Kunitz or Jack Tworkov. "You felt that he was lost," Kunitz said. "He exuded no satisfaction . . . no joy."[19]

Looking for friendly contact, or just distraction, Rothko sometimes found what he perceived as rejection. One day, as Rothko was walking up the hill by Kunitz's house, the poet was working in his garden. Rothko waved, Kunitz said hello, but did not invite him in. "My garden is very sacred to me and it's also a meditation, a work period for me. I never ask anybody in when I'm working in it." But the next time Kunitz saw Rothko, "Mark just blew up and said I'd been hostile to him." Afterward, Rothko would say, "That time I came by you didn't ask me into your garden, Stanley, I couldn't forgive you. That was a terrible thing to do."[20] Absorbed with his own needs and unaware of the needs of others, sensitively probing for the smallest signs of disregard, Rothko could easily be hurt.

Robert Motherwell thought it might help if Rothko invited a group of young painters into his garage-studio for critiques of their work. One of them, Jonathan Ahearn, Rothko liked enough to ask to take over as his assistant in the fall. In the critiques, Rothko was generous and positive in his comments, even to the point of hypocrisy, Ahearn thought. But at the second meeting one of the students "lit into Rothko about representing the establishment. The guy got really aggressive . . . it was a major kind of almost physical confrontation, you know, yelling and screaming, and Rothko was screaming back at the guy and finally kicked him out." The critiques ended.

"I hate art," Rothko dramatically announced, that summer, to Jacob Kainen, an old friend from the 1930s. He made similar declarations to others. "He had reached the conclusion that the art world was totally corrupt," Kainen remembered, "that art had been turned into a shallow product by art promoters, critics, curators, museum directors, and the news media. He felt he was working in a moral vacuum, where the money-men infected the artists." Now Rothko was the outsider reviling the art establishment. He had depended on painting—as he had depended on a wife—for emotional consolation, for a kind of awed intimacy and attentiveness that he felt had eluded him. He wished for a "sensitive observer." But instead Rothko found—he told Kainen—"the art industry."[21] For simply by being bought, exchanged, evaluated, displayed in unfamiliar surroundings—simply by being *separate* objects with social lives of their own—Rothko's paintings reproduced the feelings of loss and deprivation they were supposed to fill. Art betrayed him.

"He wasn't working very intensively. Whenever I came to see him, he wasn't working," Kunitz remembered of that summer in Provincetown. Insofar as Rothko was working, he was laboring under restrictions imposed by his recent illness, Dr. Meade having instructed him not to work on anything higher than forty inches. So when he wasn't being angry with art, Rothko was being angry with the physical limitations that kept him from working in his custom-ary way.²² Recovering in Provincetown, forced to work smaller, Rothko turned to acrylics on paper.²³

Such, at least, is the usual story of his change of scale and medium toward the end of his life. But Rothko had actually begun producing these acrylics on paper in 1967, *before* the aneurysm (color plate 20).²⁴ The context from which these works emerged was not Rothko's aneurysm but his completion of the Houston chapel paintings in late 1967.

"He put so much into the chapel," William Scharf said. "He was let down after the chapel was finished."²⁵ For three years, Rothko had worked, single-mindedly, on that project, producing just a few individual paintings in this period.²⁶ Very little of this time, however, had been spent in the act of applying brush to canvas. Particularly once the early experimental phase with Scharf ended, Rothko's labors were more mental than physical, more painstaking and deliberate than free-wheeling and spontaneous. Large murals designed to decorate, dignify, and dominate a public space, the chapel paintings, unlike Rothko's single works, were not human-scale. Hardly the productions of a solitary artist laboring in his studio, these murals imposed collaboration. Conceived by his patrons and probably by the artist himself as culminating his career, the Houston paintings moved Rothko to the furthest limits of his art and ambition, in the fabrication of a set of religious icons, gloomy and solemn, near-monochromatic, black and plum voids.

What next?

"Once he finished the Houston series, he was stymied," said Katharine Kuh. "The future was a question mark. He worked on the chapel paintings with such wonderful purpose that he was virtually burnt out when they were completed. . . . He sent all his energies into the murals and now quite suddenly he seemed to have lost his raison d'être."

Cast adrift by the completion of the chapel paintings, Rothko changed his medium, from large oils on canvas to small acrylics on paper, a medium he continued to use until the end of his life. Working with an assistant while in New York, Rothko cut papers from rolls, dampened and stretched the papers, then attached them—at first with staples, later with masking tape—to the wooden walls that had been built for the chapel murals or to plywood easels (he probably worked on a table in Provincetown).²⁷ In New York, assistants mixed colors in a big white pot and occasionally applied a ground color. Using housepainter's brushes, Rothko built up his shapes—the stacked rectangles of his classic format—generally working on a number of papers at the same time, sometimes fifteen or more, always working "very fast." Quickly made and thus easily disposable, these works on paper encouraged a certain creative freedom: if a painting did not succeed, Rothko did not have to throw away three months' labor, as he might with an oil painting. As Steindecker said, either "it's there or he tears it up."[28]

To an artist who had just spent three years in prolonged and painstaking struggle with fourteen large murals, small works done with fast-drying acrylics allowed for quick results, more immediate gratifications.

But if he was exploring the physical properties of a new medium in order to generate fresh imaginative possibilities, Rothko was characteristically seeking transformation by way of a return: "without such retrogressions no great progressions are possible."[29] During the 1950s and 1960s, Rothko had produced some smaller works on paper, sometimes with oils, sometimes with watercolors; and he had made construction-paper sketches for his mural projects. But mainly Rothko used oils on large canvases. In 1967, working rapidly on paper with a water-based medium, he was turning back to the watercolors done in the mid-1940s, in the prolific experimental period around the end of his first and the beginning of his second marriage.[30]

But in the mid-1940s Rothko had embarked on "an unknown adventure in an unknown space." Twenty years later he had begun to worry, as he admitted to Jack Tworkov, about the criticism "that he was repeating the same form, that there was what seemed like very little development in his work." He told William Scharf he'd like to return to the kind of work he'd done in the 1940s.[31] But it was not as if Rothko had been engaged in a formal investigation—"researches," as they are often called—into the properties of the rectangle. A repeated form gave a restless man with turbulent emotions a pliant stability that freed rather than confined him, and his particular form filled so many of his contradictory needs and desires—to veil and to express his emotions, to be alone and to communicate, to be lofty and intimate, to be sensual and spiritual—that he could not easily abandon or go beyond it. Besides, as Rothko told Tworkov, he remembered "how intense the struggle was to find something of his own he could hang on to," so that "it was difficult for him to give up something that he had so struggled to achieve and to attain."[32]

Of Rothko's late works on paper, some were colorful, some were dark, but at first all kept within—or hung on to—his classic format.[33] The small size, however, alters the impact of the form. "To paint a small picture is to place yourself outside your experience, to look upon an experience as a stereopticon or with a reducing glass," Rothko had said.[34] In this provocative formulation, small pictures, being more distanced and controlled, are less intimate than large ones. However you paint the small picture, you are outside it, and so is the viewer. As Bonnie Clearwater points out, these works on paper, "with their symmetry, tidy execution, and minimal gesture," show a "studied perfection," but "often lack the vitality of the large paintings."[35] Rather than opening sublime vistas or inducing "transcendental experiences," these small works are beautiful objects. Viewing them, I alternately admire Rothko's sure mastery and wonder if he isn't operating on automatic pilot, adopting a new acrylic medium whose speed can produce a lack of commitment and whose flatness and opacity can produce an emotional hardness and removal.

The aneurysm forced Rothko to stop all work for several weeks in the late spring and early summer. When, in the summer of 1968, he was able to return to work, small size was no longer a matter of artistic choice but of doctor's orders; rapid execution was no longer a relief from the long absorption of the Houston murals but a fitting process for an artist anxious and agitated, impatient and easily frustrated. A sense of impending doom had given an edge and emotional depth to the "serene" works of the 1950s. But now, aware that at any moment any one of three bubbles on a valve into his heart could break off and produce instantaneous death—and this in a hypochondriac who had always worried about his body failing him—now doom was no longer romantic and cosmological, but immediate and personal. In two series of paintings he created in the last year of his life—"Brown on Grey" acrylics on paper and "Black on Grey" acrylics on canvas—Rothko's confrontation with death would return struggle and emotional depth to his work, and produce a final artistic advance.

• • •

Marriage is an impossible situation for an artist to engage in.
                                                                Mark Rothko

"I remember taking comfort in the Rothko family, in their apparent stability," Musa Mayer writes in her memoir of her father, Philip Guston. "Their daughter Kate was too young to be a playmate for me, but they were still a family, a real family." "At Christmas, the Rothkos' East Side town house seemed like an island of domesticity, full of good food and cheer, a sort of haven for people who missed their own families." She recalls the Rothkos' 1963 Christmas party, with Christopher still an infant. "They seemed to have everything," she thought. "Having a baby late in life seemed so romantic, so ultimately domestic and cozy."[36]

But by 1968 Rothko's marriage, like his health, was disintegrating.

Rothko looked outside himself—to friends, to his family—for reassurance and stability. Soon after his first marriage had ended, Rothko wrote to his sister, Sonia, that he was hoping to find "a mate who can provide the security and also keep [my] sensations and movement alive." He soon found one, and in the early, happy years of his second marriage, he found his repeated form.

Jack Tworkov recalled Rothko's standard answer, when asked how his work was going: "Well, I'm just bored."[37] One danger of the repeated form, artistic or social, is boredom, and in his later years Rothko complained to some of his friends of being trapped within the format he had invented, as if he felt it could no longer keep his sensations and movement alive.[38] Of course, another danger of such repeated orders, when they are human and social, is collapse—by pressures from within or without—as Rothko well knew from long experience: his father's departure from Dvinsk, his father's subsequent death in Portland, the disintegration of his own first marriage, the collapse of some of his closest friendships.

During the 1960s Rothko remained estranged from Clyfford Still and Barnett Newman. By this time Still had withdrawn to a small town in rural Maryland; Newman's work, on the other hand, was being taken up by some of the younger, Minimalist artists in New York. Rothko "really distrusted the young and didn't get along with them," Stanley Kunitz recalled, "and he felt they were worshipping false gods, namely Barney Newman."[39] Clyfford Still disturbed the purist in Rothko who wanted to withdraw from the marketplace; Newman disturbed the usurper in Rothko who wanted to dominate the marketplace. He lost both friends.

In the mid-1960s, moreover, Rothko fell out with Herbert Ferber, who had probably been his closest friend for fifteen years, and was named with his wife, Ilse, to be a guardian of the Rothkos' children and an executor of their estate in their 1959 wills. "What cemented our friendship," Ferber recalled, "was our common ethnic background, Jewish ethnic background, the fact that we had both come out of very poor families, that we thought in liberal terms about politics and social problems."[40] Born in New York City in 1906, Ferber, since the early 1930s, had managed to combine an active career as an artist (mainly in sculpture) with a dental practice. Like Rothko, he was an early member of the Federation of Modern Painters and Sculptors, but the two men did not get to know each other well until the late 1940s, when both joined the Betty Parsons Gallery.[41]

"He supported my work, I supported his. In domestic questions, we talked them over very confidentially, seriously, with each other. Financial questions we discussed. He came to visit us—I had a little farm up in Vermont. He would come up there in the summer and spend a week or ten days. He was my best friend at the time." Yet while professional conflicts had split Rothko from Still and Newman, a domestic question divided him and Ferber: Rothko disapproved of Ferber's divorce, his treatment of Ilse, and of Ferber's new and much younger third wife.[42]

The Ferbers separated, then Ferber had his wife declared mentally incompetent and hospitalized. She called the Reises for help; they believed that Ferber was harassing her, so he could divorce her and marry a young woman who worked for him in his dentist's office.[43] Robert Motherwell, who sided with Ferber, believed Ilse Ferber was crazy: "she would buy two hundred purses at a time." Rothko sided with Ilse Ferber and the Reises.

Herbert and Ilse Ferber were eventually divorced, and Ferber married Edith Popiel in 1967. The affair showed that "Herbert is absolutely ruthless and his ambitions are limitless," Rothko commented. After all, "it was first Ilse who was the artist not Herbert. She was the art historian with a Ph.D. and he was the dentist and only gradually Herbert became the artist and Ilse moved into the background." Now "Herbert feels like a young man with this young woman."[44] Condemning Ferber as selfish and disloyal, Rothko, who in early 1969 would separate from his wife and soon after begin a love affair with a younger woman—Ad Reinhardt's widow, Rita—this Rothko judged his old friend Ferber with rabbinical severity. This break, unlike those with Still and Newman, was only temporary, but it left an uneasy distance between Rothko and Ferber, so that when Rothko rewrote his will in 1968, Ferber was named neither an executor nor a guardian.[45] Thus, in the last few years of his life, when Rothko most relied on others for stability and support, his two closest male friends were Bernard Reis and Theodoros Stamos, both of whom would, in 1975, be found guilty of "a breach of duty of loyalty"—i.e., conflicts of interest—in their roles as executors of Rothko's estate.[46]

When he had tried to write something about Nietzsche's *The Birth of Tragedy,* the book he said came closest to articulating his feelings about life, Rothko had spoken of a turbulent, chaotic inner existence—charged with "the boundless aspirations and terrors, the welter of restlessness, the senselessness, the desires, the alterations of hope and despair out of context and out of reason"—which constantly assaults "the shaky security of our ordered life." Dionysian tumult and Apollonian order contend in a "perpetual strife" relieved only by brief, temporary reconciliations. "The dramas of Aeschylus and Sophocles," Rothko wrote, "represent a moment of reconciliation when Apollo and Dionysus establish on this stage a moment of domestic bliss in which they wait for each other to speak . . . in spite of their irreconcilable strife at all other moments involving alternate triumphs and defeats for one at the expense of the other."[47] In the perpetual power struggle between the sexes, male and female can only be reconciled in "a *moment* of domestic bliss," before the "shaky" domestic order collapses.

Chapter Seventeen

In art, Rothko writes, "it is the function of the Apollonian" to render Dionysian torment "endurable." In marriage, it is the function of the wife to render her artist-husband's torment endurable.

As a young woman, Mary Alice Beistle had shown considerable confidence, self-assertion, and even boldness. "She was always sort of the radical of the family," said Christopher Rothko, who heard stories of his mother from her two sisters. "She was the one who was always having horrible fights with her brother, and she was the one who was always being sent away from the table at dinner, always being punished for something, and always going her own direction."[48] Mell's closest friends at Skidmore recall a poised, smart young woman, successful both socially and academically. Her illustrations for children's books had been, and continued to be, published. She scandalized her friends by having an affair with a faculty member.[49] Having spent some summers in New York City while in high school, she returned to live there, on her own, not long after graduating from college. Her choice of a husband—nineteen years older, Jewish, an impoverished, little-known artist—was not the conventional choice of Skidmore graduates in the mid-1940s, or the kind of man her parents would have chosen.

She liked to tell people—though the story sounds apocryphal—that she went to New York looking for an artist to marry and she found Rothko. She told one of her Skidmore friends that she married Rothko less out of romantic or sexual attraction than out of her belief that "he was a genius," and because he took so much pleasure in her that it gave her a vicarious pleasure.[50] At least when others were around, she called her husband "Rothko."

Mark was the genius, Mell the erotic object—*and* the maternal wife. His primary concern was producing his work, then getting it out into the world; her primary concern was—him. Rothko could be warm, embracing, tender, funny, lively, provocative; he could also be self-absorbed, depressive, melodramatic, obsessed, enraged—and demanding. Mell Rothko loved, admired, reassured, consoled, nurtured, and, for the first five years of their marriage, financially supported her husband. When Mary Alice Beistle married Mark Rothko, choosing to have a vicarious career in art, she was trading self-assertion for self-sacrifice.

"Mell was younger, had no illusions about the sort of deal that she made," said David Todd, a 95th Street neighbor. "She was going to wait on him and she was going to do a lot of the dirty work—she would be out shoveling the snow—she had great respect for him and for his integrity and his art; she always referred to him as 'Rothko'—somewhat dispassionately." But as Rothko's income and public recognition increased, his need for her lessened, and he turned to others for reassurance and support. "Mell said that trouble began when he became successful," Anne-Marie Levine remembered, "then he didn't need her any more." By the late 1950s, Kate attended school most of the day, Rothko worked at his studio most of the day, and, though he now earned a substantial income from his paintings, he didn't want his wife to return to work. "You know, there's nothing for me to do," she said.[51] Mell felt useless and deserted.

In the early 1960s, particularly after Rothko's one-man retrospective at the Museum of Modern Art, the Rothkos' social life intensified. So did their conflicts. Though he might mutter darkly of "assaults," Rothko enjoyed or at least sought social life, the drama of seeing and being seen. "He used to enjoy being the center of things," Kate Rothko said. Aware that their hosts were involved with her husband and not her, Mell preferred to stay home. "I know she was not happy with their social life in the 60s, and I think that was a major source of conflict between them," said Kate. "She did not like some of his new social connections," well-to-do, sophisticated, haughty, and often condescending to her. At the same time, Mell Rothko, no experienced, confident hostess like Rebecca Reis, felt "very uncomfortable entertaining," Kate said. "It was a major ordeal for her to have people over," so "it was something they didn't do very often," holding perhaps three large parties a year, one of them at Christmas. Rothko complained about his wife not inviting people over and often went out by himself; his wife complained that he went out too often. "My mother would have liked to have spent a lot more time with my father." Mell's drinking intensified.

An experienced drinker with a bulky build, Rothko could "hold" his liquor. Mell could not, so in Rothko's view, she was the alcoholic, and he the victim of her drinking. He complained that Mell was drinking "around the clock." Invited to dinner by his neighbor Georgio Cavallon, Rothko warned his host, "Don't give her anything to drink because she's a drunk," but when he issued this warning, Rothko himself was already drunk. Moreover, when Mell Rothko drank, she often grew, in her daughter's word, "vituperative." She drank to release anger. The couple had fierce, bitter fights, "horrendous arguments, with language like in *Who's Afraid of Virginia Woolf?*"[52]

According to Anne-Marie Levine, Mell stopped drinking, in 1963, when she was pregnant with Christopher. But she resumed drinking after the scare of Rothko's aneurysm. He told one friend that the night he came home from the hospital, she was so furious with him she started beating him around the head.[53] Originally, marriage had given Rothko something to hang on to; his wife helped make life endurable. But devoted to serving *his* needs for many years, receiving less and less in return as time went on, Mell Rothko (at the time of Rothko's aneurysm, she was forty-six) increasingly felt constrained, disregarded, betrayed, furious. It was as if, in the Rothkos' Upper East Side townhouse, Mell had become one of those solitary, depressive women Rothko had painted in the 1930s, trapped within and distorted by, a domestic interior, except that Mell, more and more, exploded in anger. Offering only a "shaky security" against the violence churning just below the surface of daily life, domesticity began in bliss but, in Rothko's second marriage as in his first, crumbled into irreconcilable strife. Structured to make life endurable for Rothko, the marriage itself became *un*endurable.

Yet it was difficult for Rothko to give up something that he had so struggled to achieve and to attain.

When he suffered the aneurysm, Rothko, five months short of sixty-five, was the father of a seventeen-year-old daughter and a five-year-old son. To say, as Stanley Kunitz does, that Rothko "was deeply troubled as a parent" is to put the matter kindly.

Rothko imagined the proper relation between a viewer and his work as modeled on an idealized relation between child and parent. A viewer looks lovingly and respectfully at a large, awesome presence, like a small child gazing at a revered parent. Such an idealized relation is difficult enough to attain in art, the Houston chapel representing Rothko's most ambitious effort to design an environment that would, in theory, coerce such looking, though the chapel murals despair of their own longing for prominence.

In modern family life (as opposed to the sealed off space of a small octagonal chapel) such mirroring looks, such reverence for patriarchal authority (or need), are even harder to come by. "The father authority is nil," Rothko lamented. Rather than devoting themselves to reflecting back a parent's sense of self or power, children grow, change, develop their own preoccupations and problems, and they may even—as Rothko himself had—rebel. In short, they turn out to be *separate*. Rothko had always been somewhat awkward and aloof as a parent, usually absent, sometimes intrusive and critical. Now he had an adolescent daughter who, like him, was strong-willed and rebellious.

When Rothko and his family traveled to the west coast in the summer of 1967—he had been appointed a University Professor at the University of California, Berkeley, for a month—they went by train, because of Rothko's fears about flying. Kate Rothko thought the trip would afford an "ideal" opportunity to sit down and talk with her father. She tried to draw him out on family history. "It was awkward," she said. "I do remember trying to ask him things about the family, but it was a fairly awkward three days. Not unpleasant but awkward." Easy-going intimacy was not Rothko's style. Besides, he and his daughter had a history of conflict and were, during the summer of 1967, in the middle of a contest over Kate's decision to leave high school one year early and begin college at the University of Chicago that fall.

Since kindergarten, Kate had been attending Dalton, a private school for girls just a short walk from the Rothkos' 95th Street house. As a teenager, she found the all-girl social world of the school too confining. At home, she was living with her parents' drinking and their ongoing battles. Kate decided she wanted to skip her last year at Dalton and go directly to college, and she chose the University of Chicago, one of the few institutions that accepted such early admissions. "My major motivation for going to Chicago," she recalled, "was to get out of the house because I wasn't finding it a very pleasant place to live." Rothko, however, wanted his daughter to live at home for another year, and he wanted her to go to Radcliffe, which did not admit high school juniors. He was "set" on Radcliffe, it being "the best": an Ivy League education. Nevertheless, she went to the University of Chicago, felt lonely and miserable and, after one quarter, returned to New York. Then she decided she wanted to attend Brooklyn College—hardly, after its design department's refusal of tenure, one of her father's favorite institutions of higher learning. He insisted that Brooklyn College was not good enough. "He was absolutely set that I should go to Barnard." Some friends, notably the art historian Barbara Novak, convinced Rothko "that it wasn't the end of the world if I went to Brooklyn College," and Kate enrolled there in the spring of 1968, living in a nearby $90-a-month Flatbush apartment by the time of her father's aneurysm.[54]

In some respects, Kate, an only child for thirteen years, was treated like a firstborn son. She was smart, and her father encouraged—in fact, expected—her to get good grades all through school, and she did. "He was always very happy that I got good grades, but I don't think he was very involved. It was always from the outside and expecting me to do things but really knowing very little about what was going on." Like her choice of college, Kate's choice of career was, in Rothko's view, her father's decision. "I'd be happy if Kate went into medicine," he once remarked, desiring for his offspring the kind of professional career he himself had spurned.[55] Sometimes, however, the father authority *does* carry weight: today Kate Rothko Prizel is an academic physician teaching and specializing in pathology and transfusion medicine.

But Rothko also wanted Kate to be attractive and popular, or thought he did. Kate was still overweight. An alcoholic who reproached his wife for her drinking, Rothko was also a prodigal eater who criticized his daughter's overeating. "He was very concerned about my social life," Kate Rothko recalled—i.e., concerned that her weight would keep her from having one. Kate should be smart *and* trim. Yet, with a daughter, as with a painting, Rothko felt it was "a risky and unfeeling act to send" one "out into the world." Going to an all-girl school, Kate could meet boys only at dances. When she did, her father "waited up for four hours and then would immediately pounce on me when I walked in to ask who I met." With his daughter, Rothko combined removal with an anxious protectiveness.

With his son, he combined removal with indulgence. "I'm too old," Rothko had commented at Christopher's birth.[56] He was old enough to be his son's grandfather. Never that involved day-to-day as parent, Rothko was now distracted by his own and Mell's drinking, their ongoing strife, his own depression and anger, in addition to his usual preoccupations with his work and its place in the art world. The Rothkos, moreover, could now afford to have a small bedroom and bathroom installed on the fourth floor of the 95th Street house, rooms that were used for a series of live-in babysitters. In the last fourteen months of his life Rothko was literally separated from his son when he moved into his studio, though he arranged to see Christopher often.

Christopher, just six when his father died, recalled a couple of these visits to Rothko's studio, and of all the people who were around the studio that year, he's the only one who doesn't remember a depressed person. "Both of them are memories of him in very cheerful spirits. I remember my father angry in a couple of cases, but generally I remember him as being very jovial. I remember walking down the street with him near his studio. I think we'd been out to a deli to get some food, and I remember him laughing with me and talking to me. And I remember I had just been learning to read at that point, and I was asking him what his favorite letters were. He said 'T' for 'Topher,' which was my nickname at that time." Christopher recollects playing with a basketball hoop Rothko had put up in the studio, "and I remember him taking a couple of shots and generally just seeming to be in pretty good spirits." "And," Christopher adds, "there was always a record on the phonograph." His son shared Rothko's passion for music. At that time Schubert's *Trout* Quintet "was my very favorite piece in the world," and another favorite was a record of Mozart piano trios, and I think it made him very happy that I liked that. He loved Mozart. I remember often listening to *Don Giovanni* with him and I had my favorite sections and he had his favorite sections. I remember arguing about which record to put on."

"You know he was on the portly side, and although not a big-limbed man, he was sizeable and he had what seemed like very big hands to me. But always very gentle. He seemed always like a grandfather would seem to one, largely because of his age, but I think in some way I was almost like his grandchild or he treated me with the same sort of excitement." Rothko had always wanted a son. "Kate was about six or seven years in the works and I was thirteen years in the works, so I think in some sense I was sort of his plaything, and as a result I was horribly spoiled. I don't think I ever really saw, not the harshness of a father, but the strictness of a father," as Kate did. "I guess in a word I have this memory of a big teddybear." Christopher's description of his father calls up the bear-like "Rothkie" fondly remembered by Center Academy students.

Rothko often remarked on the fact that the thirteen-year age difference between Christopher and Kate was identical to the age difference between him and his sister, Sonia.[57] Rothko identified with his son, offered him his best self, and indulged him. "He was enormously attached to that little boy," Karl Schrag observed. Yet, others point out that his aneurysm, making it physically as well as emotionally difficult for Rothko to be involved, created a distance between him and his son.[58] As Stanley Kunitz commented, "Mark was moving out of the world in general. He became solely self-preoccupied. That was one of the after-effects of the aneurysm, and I think he was rejecting family, Mell and the children and everything except art."

At the end of 1968 the Rothkos held their annual Christmas cocktail party. "Mell, as usual, wore a bright red dress and had decorated the house with evergreens and holly. Rothko had given her some expensive pre-Columbian jewelry like Becky Reis's, which she had refused to wear. She and Rothko were barely civil to each other."[59]

The family celebrated Kate's eighteenth birthday on December 30th.

On January 1, 1969—eight months after his aneurysm and fourteen months before his suicide—Rothko separated from Mell, moving into his 69th Street studio. Once again, marriage had proved an impossible situation for this artist to engage in.

. . .

On February 21, 1969, Mark Rothko signed a second contract with the Marlborough Gallery, making it his exclusive agent for the next eight years and selling eighty-seven of his works (twenty-six on canvas, sixty-one on paper) for $1,050,000, to be paid over ten years (later extended to fourteen). A supplementary agreement permitted Rothko to sell four additional paintings a year to Marlborough for 90 percent of their market value.[60] Rothko called Anne-Marie Levine and happily announced, "I have just signed a contract for a million dollars." He described the agreement to Stanley Kunitz as "the greatest contract ever signed by a living artist." Rothko was elated.

The symbolic meaning of the contract—the prestige attached to a lucrative arrangement with the most powerful gallery in New York—pleased him. Yet, from almost any other point of view, the agreement was highly questionable.

Simply put, the contract was a bad deal. By deferring the payments over fourteen years, Rothko was keeping his taxes down and assuring himself of a substantial annual income.[61] But by agreeing to accept those long-term payments interest-free, Rothko was actually selling eighty-seven of his works for around $680,000.[62] Rothko had been using this method of deferred payments for at least several years, largely because he seems to have been obsessed with paying as little in taxes as possible. Yet, by selling just a few paintings outright each year, he would pay no more in taxes, lose fewer paintings, hold on to more paintings, take advantage himself of the likely increase in his prices (instead of letting his dealer do it), and end up with more paintings in his estate. Such a course of action, in fact, was pointed out to Rothko by Ben Heller.[63]

The previous summer in Provincetown, after his first Marlborough agreement had already expired, Rothko had announced to a group of fellow artists: "I'm not going to be part of this commercial racket anymore. It's too demeaning. No more dealers, no more shows. I can live well enough by selling a few paintings a year."[64] Instead, he choose to abandon not just fifteen (as he had in 1963) but *eighty-seven* of his works to the uncaring transactions and endless circulations of a worldwide market. Granted, he would eventually receive over $1 million in exchange, but Rothko was not pressed for money.

During the 1960s, income from his painting had slowly and for the most part steadily increased—from $76,200 in 1961 to $119,990 in 1967.[65] The Rothkos' net worth that year was estimated at $207,538, and from deferred payments on the sale of his paintings Rothko was then owed a total of $415,256 over the next seven years.[66] Independently of shifts in art-world fashion or dips in the stock market, Rothko's prices had continued to rise, increasing at an accelerating pace in the late 1960s. In 1961, Sidney Janis had sold *Yellow Band* (1956; 86" × 80") for $12,000.[67] A picture of similar size, *Number 2, 1962* (81" × 76") sold the following year for $15,000; another—*Green, Red, Blue* (1955; 82" × 78")—for $22,400 in 1963; another—*Number 3, 1967* (76" × 81")—for $26,000 in early 1968; and a last—*Untitled* (1962; 76" × 81")—for $40,000 in mid-1969.[68] In eight years, Rothko's price for this (for him) mid-sized canvas had more than tripled.[69]

During the 1960s, moreover, Rothko's expenditures increased with his income—but not as much as his income. Leaving an expensive French restaurant outside Greenwich, Connecticut, after a 1969 dinner, Rothko, drunk and flushed with anger, turned to Robert Motherwell and muttered, "It's obscene to spend more than $5 on a meal." Rothko was not interested in elegant clothes, fancy cars, beautiful furniture, lavish entertainments, or extravagant restaurants. It is not that he was cheap—he could be quite generous—but, as the child of a poor family and a product of the Depression, he *was* frugal.[70] Material objects offered no consolations, or even distractions, to a man whose empty works sought to transcend them. Travel, consisting of three excursions to Europe over twenty years, was as close as Rothko came to permitting himself a luxury.[71] As a result, Rothko and his family consistently spent a lot less than their income, so that in 1967, for example, family income exceeded expenses by $51,535.[72]

This surplus income Rothko, who had earlier derided the "false sense of security" to be gained from a "plastic bank-book," mainly deposited in solid, old-fashioned savings accounts.[73] "My concept of my father and business was that he put his money in a 5% savings account, and that was about as far as it went," Kate Rothko said. Her memory is quite correct. As if it were still 1932 and he needed to protect himself from bank failures, Rothko dispersed his savings among several banks. By the end of 1967, he had stashed $132,364 in accounts at nine different institutions.[74] The advantage of this reliance on savings accounts was its simplicity: Rothko needn't deal with any investment counselors, stockbrokers, or portfolio analyses.[75] *He* could control the situation. And by refusing to do anything more with the money, to be more *involved* with it, Rothko avoided the reality of his wealth—a reality that might embarrass him or actually give him the sense that he was well-heeled, comfortably placed, financially secure at last.

Yet secure was not how he *felt,* particularly in February of 1969, two months after he had separated from his wife, ten months after his aneurysm. At this time, as his life seemed to be disintegrating, as—according to many friends—Rothko felt frightened, indecisive, and suspicious to the point of paranoia, he came more and more to rely on Bernard Reis, whom he saw almost daily once he moved into his 69th Street studio. Other artists, such as Willem de Kooning, Herbert Ferber, and Robert Motherwell, had left Reis, finding him controlling and his advice debatable. Ferber, for one, objected to Reis's "annoyance at having his advice questioned and his insistence on complete control."[76]

Reis's willingness to take care of artists extended beyond the financial and legal into more personal issues. "He liked to tell you what to do, including your private life," said Anne-Marie Levine. Reis had taken over the night of Rothko's aneurysm; he encouraged Rothko to leave Mell; he encouraged Rothko to end his relationship with Rita Reinhardt; he provided Rothko with a psychiatrist.[77] "You had to give Mark a certain amount of surveillance to have him do the things that were good for him," Rebecca Reis declared.[78] "Reis took charge," said Sally Scharf. "He smothered people." Aware of the defections of other artists, of the perception of Reis as an opportunist, and of gossip about his

Chapter Seventeen

relation to Marlborough, Rothko still often defended Reis. When Dr. Grokest suggested to Rothko that Reis was manipulating him, Rothko replied: "He is the best in the business and he's my friend. I leave everything to him." As Ben Heller observed, "Bernard represented a supposed rock of mature stability in a sea of uncertainty."[79]

When his 1963 contract with the Marlborough Gallery had expired in June of 1968, Rothko apparently did not immediately move to renew it. The gallery was unhappy with him; he was unhappy with the gallery.[80] "He never missed an opportunity of flaying that establishment," said Katharine Kuh.[81] In spite of Frank Lloyd's crass commercialism, his adoption of contemporary sales techniques, corporate size, and organization, he had not done much to promote Rothko's work in the European market.[82] During the five years of Rothko's first Marlborough contract, the gallery had given him a one-man show, exhibiting eight oil paintings on canvas and five works on paper at its small New London Gallery.[83] During those five years, Lloyd had sold nine of the seventeen works purchased from Rothko in 1963—not exactly an amazing record, especially since, according to the Swiss dealer Ernest Beyeler, an "enormous demand for Rothkos" had existed in Europe since 1960.[84] Nor was Marlborough carefully building Rothko's European reputation by placing his work in museums. All nine of these works were sold to private collectors. The real problem, however, was that Rothko suspected that the gallery, in violation of his contract, was selling his work in New York, and he was right.[85] Only two of the nine sales were made by Marlborough London; the other seven were sold to American collectors by Marlborough New York.[86]

Other artists, disillusioned with Lloyd, severed their connection. "The degree of sadism at the gallery was unbelievable even for a big corporation," Robert Motherwell said. "They were catty, bitchy, humiliating, and treated you like a schoolboy standing in a corner." When Motherwell asked Lloyd for a loan, the conversation ended with the dealer shouting at the artist: "Young man, you will never be rich until you are dead." Rothko, too, intensely disliked and distrusted Frank Lloyd.[87] One day Rothko came into the gallery, examined some cards listing his prices, discovered that they were not the prices he and Lloyd had agreed upon, and became infuriated.[88] Donald McKinney, the Marlborough vice-president with whom Rothko worked, recalled that Lloyd and Rothko did not get along, a situation which often forced him to act as their intermediary.

"Rothko would agitate Lloyd just for the sake of agitating him," McKinney said. On the day they were to select the paintings to be purchased with Rothko's February 1969 contract, McKinney and Lloyd came to the 69th Street studio. Refusing to let Lloyd enter the storage space and studio proper, Rothko forced

Lloyd to wait with him in the living/reception area. "Rothko just sat there and looked at us and glared and drank." When Rothko would get up to get some ice or scotch, Lloyd whispered instructions to McKinney, usually directing him to pick more of the more colorful (and more marketable) paintings of the 1950s. Afterward, the three men went to lunch at a nearby Chinese restaurant. Rothko ordered a bass "that was really black and charcoaled, and he picked up the whole fish in his hands and just ate it. The food and his mouth and his face were all covered with this charcoal and blackness and the fish was falling to pieces." Lloyd was aghast. It was as if Rothko felt he had been forced into the 1969 agreement and his only remaining alternatives were symbolic power plays (refusing to let Lloyd into the studio) or symbolic humiliations (aggressive sloppiness at lunch).

Yet, when Rothko signed his second contract with Marlborough, he did have an available alternative, in fact a clearly preferable alternative. Rothko had been discussing a possible sale with Arnold Glimcher of the Pace Gallery since the fall of 1968. "Mark didn't like associating with the Marlborough Gallery anymore," Glimcher recalled. In addition, he told Glimcher, "he needed to raise $500,000 in cash."[89] It is not clear why Rothko, with his multiple savings accounts and several years of deferred income, thought he needed such a large amount, though the financial consequences of a possible divorce may have alarmed him. To help raise the cash, Glimcher brought in the respected Swiss dealer Ernest Beyeler. Beyeler flew to New York, and Glimcher brought him to Rothko's studio, "and we spent a terrific afternoon with Mark." By the end of the conversation, the three had agreed that Beyeler would represent Rothko in Europe—he wanted no exhibitions in New York where, said Glimcher, he felt "very alienated"—and Rothko would receive $500,000 for about eighteen paintings, an average price of about $28,000 each.

It was late, and so Glimcher asked, "Shall we pick out the paintings now," but Rothko replied, "No, come back tomorrow." Rothko needed to confer with Bernard Reis. But when Glimcher and Beyeler returned the next day, "Mark answered the door and said he couldn't sell us the pictures. It was out of his control. He was very sorry. And he began to cry." After a third conversation with Rothko on the following day, "Beyeler left wondering what sort of hold Rothko's accountant had over him."[90]

"It was out of his control." Since the spring of 1968, Rothko had experienced a series of losses. A frightening aneurysm produced a loss of potency, and not just sexual potency, in a self-assertive and aggressive man. He was separated from his wife of twenty-three years, from his six-year-old son, from his nineteen-year-old daughter, now living on her own in Brooklyn. He had left his home on 95th Street. He had lost his place at the cutting edge of the

Chapter Seventeen

art world, usurped by younger artists. He felt helpless, drifting. Rothko turned to Bernard Reis, a rock of paternal stability and loyalty in a sea of loss, confusion, and alcohol.

Many years before, in his 1937 book *False Security*, Reis had warned middle-class American investors against their naive trust in bankers, in boards of directors, in certified public accountants. A banker, Reis pointed out, can loan money to a corporation, then sell the loan to the public in the form of bonds. Those purchasing the bonds assume the banker will manage the loan wisely, but the banker may serve on the board of a corporation whose securities he is selling. "Because of his financial connection with the corporation," Reis writes, "his interest is divided, and he is the servant of two masters."[91] From 1963, Reis had been advising his artist clients in their negotiations with another of his clients, Marlborough. In 1970, after Rothko's death, Reis was appointed an officer at the Marlborough Gallery, at the same time that he was an executor of Rothko's estate. In 1975, Judge Millard L. Midonick, of the New York State Surrogate's Court, concluded that Reis, working as both an executor of Rothko's estate *and* as a director, secretary, and treasurer of Marlborough, was guilty of a conflict of interest (the equivalent of self-dealing) in the sale of estate paintings to Marlborough.

The American public, Reis complained in *False Security*, possesses an "abiding faith in the godhead of American Business." Could the national subconscious be uncovered, we would confront our image of "this god": "a tall, gray-haired gentleman in the late forties or early fifties, active, alert, of distinguished bearing, well tailored, immaculate in his linens, well spoken, well mannered and, above all, a college graduate," a philanthropist contributing "toward the support of the poor and the sick," backing the "opera or a symphony orchestra," or donating "a collection of the finest paintings" to the local museum. By the early 1960s, Reis himself had become a gray-haired, distinguished, well-tailored, well-spoken, well-mannered philanthropist and patron of the arts, the better to elicit an unquestioning trust from his clients. But in his dealings with Rothko, Reis, serving two masters, was dispensing *false security*.

Seeming to protect, Reis encouraged childlike dependence and exercised control.

Looking for stability, Rothko was left dependent, helpless, trapped.

• • •

He was tormented and in such a state of agitation as I've rarely seen.

Stanley Kunitz

Rothko's Aneurysm

On February 26, 1969, Dore Ashton visited Rothko's studio for the first time since the artist's hospitalization in the spring of 1968. He told Ashton he was feeling groggy, having awoke at 4 A.M., worked, slept for another hour, then gotten up again at 8. "He was wearing slippers and he shuffled, with a vagueness to his gait that I attributed to drinking, or long drinking, continuous drinking, but perhaps it was more inspired by the profound emotional difficulties he is clearly having. His face, thin now, is deeply disturbed, the eyes joyless. He wanders. He is restless (he always was, but now it is frantic), he keeps picking up a cigarette, trying to light the wrong end. At one point, after he had said to me that he was never really connected with painting, since he started painting only late, but that literature and music were his base, and that his 'inner life' is his material, his 'inner experience,' he was about to put on a record (Mozart?) and couldn't find the outlet, his hands strayed with agitation, but I felt he was not really looking. He is malhabile, cannot manage life, probably never could."

Rothko began to show her the works on paper he had done during the previous summer. "He named the exact number with pride, as though to say, 'with all my trouble I was able to do this'. Many are very haunting. Some directly expressive of a sinking heart. Many blacks over purple, or blacks over brown with a more decisive, almost *incisive* line dividing the weights. He sees them as very different and asked if they surprised me. I see them as consequent to the murals."

"He says he is a Renaissance painter, has nothing to do with painting today. I think he feels this keenly, and it is perhaps one of his sorrows. He says he has only left home—he uses that phrase, leaving home—seven weeks ago, and he had to because Mell had become so hostile that the night he came home from the hospital she was physically beating him about the head. He did it, he says, to save his life.

"But it is clear he has no life, that he is frantic, that even the interest of women—there are several in love with him he told me, taking little pleasure or pride in it—has not entered his soul as a satisfactory pastime, or pleasure.

"He gave me a little painting, which he said was more in the time that I was related to his work. An older painting. I didn't protest, how could I? I am glad enough to have it. Very glad. I haven't studied it yet, but I think we'll like it. I don't know if it gave him pleasure to give it. Hard to tell. When he tried to wrap it he was hurried, inaccurate, utterly incapable of such a simple series of movements. As we talked he asked me to stay. I had the feeling he both wants and doesn't want company. What his real preoccupations are (fame? the meaning of life? producing?) I cannot in any way fathom. He is still a very shielded man to me."[92]

18 The Gift to the Tate

It seems to me that the heart of the matter, at least for the present, is how to give this space you propose the greatest eloquence and poignancy of which my pictures are capable.

Mark Rothko

In October 1965, Norman Reid, director of the Tate Gallery in London, had visited Rothko's studio. The gallery had purchased Rothko's *Light Red over Black* (1957) in 1959, and Reid had come to explore the possibility of adding to Rothko's representation at the Tate. "He responded warmly to the possibility of his work being in the same building as Turner's paintings and before long the idea had grown into a group and a separate space."[1] "You must understand," Rothko wrote to Reid shortly afterward, "that the whole idea sprang newly born as we sat facing each other. Since then, the idea has seemed better and better."[2]

The idea would have appealed to Rothko for several reasons. The Tate, granted, *was* a museum, and thus activated all of Rothko's suspicion and animosity toward such institutions. And while he would not be creating works for a specific site, as he had for the Seagram and Harvard projects and as he was then doing for the Houston chapel, he was being offered "a separate space" for a selection of already existing paintings, and that space was *not* a dining room. A room of his own at the Tate would place him as an equal of Picasso, Matisse, and Giacometti, the only other artists with rooms there. It would keep a number of his pictures together; and the gift would even provide a tax benefit. "So let us both think about it," Rothko concluded his letter to Reid, "and I think for the present we should keep these ideas to ourselves."

Rothko's own thinking grew ambitious. During their talk, Reid had mentioned a possible selection from the Seagram panels, eight of which had been shown at Rothko's Whitechapel exhibit. But in December of 1965 Rothko wrote to Reid that "I have kept the entire exhibition which took place at the Whitechapel intact"—Rothko later told Reid "he had offered the whole" of this exhibit to New York's Museum of Modern Art, "who declined it"—and it was left to the Tate to decide how much space "it could afford" and therefore

Chapter Eighteen

how much of this exhibit it could use. Seagram panels, of course, were also available.[3]

But there was no need to hurry into a decision because Rothko could not receive any tax benefit from this gift until 1967, when his four years of deductions for the Harvard murals expired.[4] As Reid soon discovered, negotiating with Rothko, who approached decisions slowly, painstakingly, warily under any circumstances, could be very tricky. When Rothko visited London at the end of his 1966 trip to Europe, he had come, he later wrote Reid, for one reason: "to discuss with you in detail, and on location, the disposition and conditions of the gift of some of my pictures to the Tate." Reid "well understood" this purpose from their previous conversations and letters. Yet Rothko felt he had been slighted, disregarded.

"Your complete personal neglect of my presence in London," he wrote, "and your failure to provide adequate opportunities for these discussions, poses for me the following question: was this simply a typical demonstration of English hospitality, or was it your way of indicating to me that you were no longer interested in these negotiations? I would really like to know." While still in London, Rothko had written to the Reises, complaining that "London has been rainy and my impression of the Tate dubious. It has become a junk yard like our own MOMA. It is something I want to talk to you about."[5] Rothko's lofty judgment of the Tate's collection suggests he was already considering withdrawal from the project, because he feared that Reid was withdrawing.

But Rothko had appeared at the gallery unannounced, at lunch time, on the day of a board of trustees meeting. Reid introduced him to the board members, showed Rothko the room which the museum was offering for his work, but "I did not press him to make a final decision as I thought it wiser to leave him to decide in his own time."[6] During his earlier discussions with Reid, Rothko had "several times expressed doubts about the reception of the paintings in London." Having come to be courted and reassured, Rothko mistook English reserve for indifference. In fact, just a few days after Rothko's visit to the Tate, but before receiving his angry letter, Reid had written to Rothko that after thinking more about the gift and discussing it with colleagues, "especially those who are painters," he was now convinced "that we should encourage you to present the whole of the Whitechapel Group of pictures which was your first idea. It would be a princely gesture." There would be an opening exhibit, a monograph with many color reproductions, and then a changing selection from the gift to be permanently exhibited in a Rothko room.[7]

When he did receive Rothko's letter, Reid quickly responded, explaining that he'd been out of town during most of Rothko's visit, pointing out that

Rothko himself had canceled their one scheduled meeting, apologizing for not pressing Rothko more, reassuring, soothing, extolling. "Our shortcomings as hosts," Reid wrote, "must not cloud the fact that we all here put you in the top rank as an artist and we regard the gift you have in mind as one of the most splendid benefactions the British nation could receive."[8] The Jewish boy from Dvinsk, the poor relation from Portland and New Haven, had now risen to the position of the benefactor of a nation—and one whose distrust could act as a lever to pry loose declarations of praise. The project went forward.

But not smoothly. At a February 27, 1967, meeting in New York, Rothko, Bernard Reis, and Reid agreed that within the next two years Rothko would donate "a group of between 6 to 8 pictures[,] followed later by a bequest of a further group of pictures bringing the total up to something like 30 works." In a follow-up letter stating the terms of the gift, the board of trustees agreed, moreover, to keep at least eight of the pictures permanently on display, and stated its awareness "that the group of pictures shown requires to be seen as a separate entity." Rumors of the gift were circulating in both New York and London, and on April 11, 1967, the *New York Times,* in a story citing Reid as its source, reported that Rothko was "considering donating about 20 of his pictures to the Tate Gallery."[9]

Rothko was upset just by the appearance of the story. He had wished to keep the negotiations "to ourselves." He wanted secrecy. He didn't want to be pestered with other curators seeking gifts. And Reid later observed that the reason Rothko "was unhappy when rumors of his intended gift leaked out was mainly because he wanted to feel uncommitted—he found it very difficult to make decisions."[10] Rothko's classic paintings create an ambiguous, fluctuating, and diffused state of consciousness, a contemplative reverie abstracted from action and decision. Actions bind, define, limit, like words. Uncommitted in his dealings with the Tate, Rothko could feel free, and be the more powerful party in the negotiation.

When he saw the *Times* story, Rothko dispatched another angry letter to Reid, who, in turn, dispatched another mollifying letter to Rothko.[11] Buffeted by a misunderstanding, temporarily foundered on a press leak, the project nevertheless lurched forward.

Later that month—April 1967—the Tate board wrote to thank Rothko for his promised gift: "Among our contemporaries there is no other painter whom we value more: consequently we feel that we shall be most fortunate to find the Tate Gallery in possession of so magnificent and representative a group of your pictures." Rothko responded: "I want to thank the board of trustees for their generous letter. It was indeed very touching to receive it. I also received your letter this morning, and I do not see why our discussions should not proceed as they have." Reid answered that he was "glad that you are unperturbed by the irritating interest of the Press and I am delighted that you are now considering everything in detail."[12] What Reid meant by detail was, of course, the (to Rothko) crucial and agonizing process of selecting and installing an ensemble of his paintings.

Just before the end of 1967, Rothko gave one of the Seagram panels, *Sketch for Mural No. 6* (1958), to the Tate.

The following spring, of 1968, Rothko's aneurysm interrupted the progress of negotiations. That summer, Rothko wrote to Reid that "I have been seriously ill and so have had to neglect many things close to my desires. However I have improved at a very rapid rate. I still hold the room at the Tate as part of my dreams," and he wondered whether Reid planned to be in New York that fall or winter, "when we can really set up the nature of the room and provide for the prodigious physical effort, to put it into effect."[13] When Reid replied that he'd be in New York during March of 1969, Rothko asked if he could arrive earlier, in the coming fall, when all Rothko's work would be inventoried and catalogued. "At that time I would like to select finally the pictures for the Tate, give them to you, get them out of my life & warehouses and make the entire agreement final. We could arrange to send them to you at once."[14] Rothko now sounds not just eager to decide, but impatient to be rid of the paintings.

Reid did not travel to New York that fall, but he did write Rothko to advance two ideas. He first suggested that they assemble one group, of which the *Sketch for Mural No. 6* would form a part—clearly a selection from the Seagram panels; then Reid went on to propose a second group of paintings "in a somewhat different register, so that we should have, so to speak, contralto as well as bass."[15] It was important, he urged, to represent "the various aspects of your work." Reid, ominously sounding like Rothko's idea of a museum official, was backing away from the severities of a single group of the Seagram paintings and inching toward the more colorful works of the 1950s. Nothing further happened with the project until the spring of 1969.

By that time Rothko was feeling well enough to be planning a summer trip to England, during which he promised to make his final selections and install the paintings. But he was still fretting over the conditions of the gift, in particular his desire that his work be placed on *permanent* display. Rothko was thinking about eternity, which is what museums seem to offer, at least until you ask for it. The board of trustees could not guarantee to exhibit Rothko's work "in perpetuity." Realistically, they could only promise that they "hope and intend to keep whatever works you may present to the Tate in the same gallery, undisturbed, probably for a number of years, and maybe for a very considerable time."[16]

The Gift to the Tate

With Rothko's expectations scaled down, the project slowly moved forward. Reid sent Rothko a space plan for the room (Gallery 18) in which his paintings were to be hung; then, at Rothko's request, he sent a cardboard model of the room.[17] On August 1, 1969, Reid spent four hours at Rothko's studio, having come expecting to reach a final decision on the gift. Instead, "I was extremely disappointed to find that his studio was completely disorganized by a programme of making photographs of all the works in his possession, many of which had been stored in warehouses for a long time." Rothko struck Reid as "much changed since his serious illness," though he had "produced a series of 40 or 50 paintings on paper, many of which are very beautiful." Rothko told Reid that his illness and talks with friends had led him "to change his views about giving pictures to galleries," and he set forth five points, recorded by Reid in a subsequent memorandum:

(1) His pictures would be on permanent loan to the Tate for as long as the trustees wished to keep them, then they would return to the Mark Rothko Foundation, which had been set up that June.

(2) Rothko was prepared to select a group for Gallery 18. "He is not willing to select a varied group of pictures to show his work over a period of time but intends that it shall be a group which shall establish a mood." Rothko would offer a group of earlier pictures if the trustees provided a separate room for them. "He is clearly not prepared to give pictures which may remain in the basement for even part of the time."

(3) One or two paintings being considered by Rothko needed conservation treatment, to be done by Rothko's restorer at the Tate's expense.

(4) Rothko wanted to ship a larger group of paintings than would fill the space, so final selections could be made in London. The Tate would pay for shipment.

(5) The purpose of his Foundation, Rothko said, is "to help artists over 55 who may not have met with great commercial success."

Reid concluded—correctly, as it turned out—that the Tate would not receive any pictures beyond the first group.[18]

The U.S. tax laws, which had first encouraged the gift, now pushed the project toward resolution, because after January 1, 1970, the allowable deduction for such gifts would be based not on the market value of the work but on the cost of materials.[19]

On November 3, 1969, Reid returned to spend five hours at Rothko's studio, viewing ten of the Seagram panels. Bernard Reis had warned him that Rothko "was in a very depressed state of mind about his work, so that a lot of the time was spent reassuring him that the Tate did want to have the paintings, and in this I appear to have been successful." Reid did reject two paintings which he thought required formidable restoration work.[20] Using the cardboard model and Rothko's miniature versions of the murals, the two men explored "various arrangements," although Reid himself believed that "one cannot make more than a rough shot at an arrangement in this miniature form."[21] Perhaps Rothko should travel to London to preside over the installation himself, Reid suggested. But he "was rather relieved when Rothko said that he thought it unlikely that he would be able to leave America at the moment as his doctor was very insistent that he look after himself well."[22]

Four days later, Reid returned to the studio and Rothko signed the agreement "on the lunchtable in that fish restaurant not far from his studio."[23]

Sometime in late 1969 or early 1970, the eight murals were packed, then shipped to London.

The paintings arrived on the morning of February 25, 1970, the morning that Rothko's body was found in his 69th Street studio. Rothko had killed himself.

19 Rothko's Suicide

Mine is a bitter old age.

Mark Rothko

"Dying is an art," Sylvia Plath wrote. Suicide is a *real* act, performed *theatrically*—performed, that is, before an unwilling and helpless audience composed of parents, spouses, ex-spouses, lovers, ex-lovers, children, friends, in-laws, enemies, strangers, the living, the dead, and even the unborn. Yet this staged quality suggests that suicide involves an internal splitting—into a public self tragically displayed at its chosen moment of self-extinction and a private self hidden behind and directing the public "act." Of her second suicide attempt, Sylvia Plath wrote, "I rocked shut // As a seashell."[1] Along with a theatrical visibility, suicides also want privacy, concealment, and silence—to be closed off and left alone. Suicide is thus at once an angry imposition, *and* an angry withdrawal, of the self.

• • •

Who was this man Mark Rothko who killed my friend?

Hedda Sterne

We were surprised to learn that his suicide was so ritualistic.

Robert Motherwell

Mark Rothko took his life sometime during the early morning of February 25, 1970. Shortly after 9 A.M. that morning, Rothko's assistant, Oliver Steindecker, arrived at the 69th Street studio for work. He entered the living area from the hall, called out hello, but got no answer. Steindecker walked toward the rear, to the small kitchen/bath space, where he found Rothko, face up, lying on the floor. Steindecker ran back through the studio, across the hall and pounded on the door of Rothko's neighbor, Arthur Lidov. "Come quickly, I think Mr.

Chapter Nineteen

Rothko is very sick," Steindecker told Lidov's assistant, Frank Ventgen. Ventgen called Lidov, who went over to Rothko's studio and immediately saw that he was dead.[2]

At 9:35 the police and an ambulance were called. An intern from nearby Lenox Hill Hospital officially declared Rothko dead. Two policemen tentatively concluded suicide, but decided to defer to higher authority in the detective division.[3] That day, a New York City detective, Patrick ("Paddy") Lappin, and his partner, Thomas Mulligan, were being accompanied on their daily tour by a reporter, Paul Wilkes, who was gathering material for a *New York Times Magazine* article called "Why So Many Real-Life Detective Stories End With A Rubber Stamp."[4]

Detective Lappin's thirty-hour day was to include three hours of courtroom waiting, a half hour for a western omelet at "the Greek's" on Madison Avenue, a fight between two drunks, an extortion case involving heroin and several more hours of waiting to see a district attorney. Just before going for his omelet, Paddy Lappin, Brooklyn-born Irish cop, thirty-six, suburban father of three, conservative Republican, drummer with the policemen's Emerald Society Pipers, and currently reading Mario Puzo's *The Godfather,* had been called to the studio of Mark Rothko, Russian-born Jewish painter, sixty-six, wealthy, internationally known, liberal Democrat, longtime reader of Nietzsche's *The Birth of Tragedy,* currently living apart from his wife and son.

In Paul Wilkes's "real-life" narrative, Rothko's death is related by the journalist relying, in turn, upon the confident voice and eyes of a cop.

The body is lying in a pool of blood in the kitchen and the water in the sink is still running. Lappin glances quickly around the room and sees that the double-edged razor blade that apparently inflicted the deep gashes has a piece of Kleenex on one side. "Suicides are amazingly careful not to cut their fingers as they slash their forearms," says Lappin. The artist's trousers are folded neatly over the back of a nearby chair. "Didn't want to get blood on them. And the water in the faucet was on because he didn't want to leave a mess for somebody. He did himself in at the sink and fell to the floor when his blood level got too low. And he has hesitation marks on the forearms—little cuts to test the blade while he thought about it." Rothko's wallet is intact and there is no sign of rifling in the studio, which contains scores of the artist's works, worth hundreds of thousands of dollars.

A call to the artist's doctor reveals that Rothko had been despondent after a recent operation and that his health generally had not been good. "An open-and-shut suicide," says Lappin. Although he has never heard of Rothko and has no idea what the artist's works are worth, he takes no chances; he arranges for the police to guard the studio 24 hours a day.[5]

The scene of Rothko's suicide offers a series of clues which, for the experienced Detective Lappin, are about as difficult to read as a page of *The Godfather*. He swiftly arrives at a definitive conclusion: "An open-and-shut suicide."

Yet, despite Lappin's assurance, his narrative contains some errors, e.g., Rothko had not had a "recent operation," there was only one "hesitation" cut on his arm.[6] The terse police account is also quite selective, very spare on circumstantial detail; it is also incomplete. Where, for example, had Rothko cut his arms? What was the position of his body? Were Rothko's wounds in fact the cause of his death?

Such questions appear even more pressing when we discover, as I did after writing the above account, that Wilkes's "Real-Life Detective Stories" article is actually a journalistic fiction. Wilkes accompanied Lappin and Mulligan for about two weeks, a period he condensed in the essay into a single day. On the morning of Rothko's suicide he was *not* with the two officers. He returned to the studio with them either at the end of the day or the following morning; Lappin's narrative of the suicide took place, in Wilkes' words, "in the absence of the body."[7] Wilkes's fiction, of course, then became historical, affecting the grief of those of Rothko's friends who read it: "We were surprised to learn that his suicide was so ritualistic," said Robert Motherwell. "We had been mourning him and then we happened to see that article a few months later and the pain was revived."[8]

The morning of Rothko's death, Theodoros Stamos was the first of Rothko's friends to arrive at the studio. He and Steindecker began to call Rothko's friends and family. Anne-Marie and later Morton Levine came to the studio; later, Anne-Marie Levine and Steindecker brought Mell Rothko to the studio by cab.[9]

Around 12:30 P.M., about three hours after Rothko's body had been discovered, Dr. Helen Strega, of the medical examiner's office arrived, examined Rothko, looked over the premises, talked with Mell Rothko, tried (unsuccessfully) to call Rothko's psychiatrist, Dr. Nathan Kline, and wrote a report speculating that Rothko had also taken an overdose of barbiturates. Much earlier, Rothko's cardiologist, Dr. Mead, had arrived at the studio. He examined Rothko, measured the pool of blood around the body, discovered two empty medicine bottles of chloral hydrate (a sedative) and judged that Rothko had been dead at least six to eight hours.[10]

The following day an autopsy performed by Dr. Judith Lehotay, of the New York City medical examiner's office, discovered that Rothko, with "marked senile emphysema" and advanced heart disease, had not had long to live.[11] In relation to his death, the autopsy revealed one cut 2½" long and ½" deep on Rothko's left arm and another one 2" long and 1" deep on the right—deep enough to cut into and almost sever the brachial artery. Both cuts were made just below the crook of the elbow.[12] Dr. Lehotay also found "a very severe acute gastritis" in Rothko's stomach, which led her to confirm Dr. Strega's suspicion of a drug overdose.[13] Her conclusion:

SELF-INFLICTED INCISED WOUNDS OF THE ANTECUBITAL
FOSSAE WITH EXSANGUINATION
ACUTE BARBITURATE POISONING
SUICIDAL

With his name misspelled as "Rothknow" and the tape recording of his autopsy never transcribed, Rothko became case #1867 in the files of the medical examiner's office.[14] Officer Lappin had relied on the street wisdom of the experienced cop; the medical perspective provides fuller detail. Together, police and medical authorities, searching through Rothko's studio, his clothing, his wallet, his body, his internal organs, produced the official judgment: death by suicide.[15]

From these accounts, we can construct the following narrative of Rothko's death. At some point early in the morning of February 25, 1970, Rothko had taken a large amount of the drug Sinequan, an antidepressant prescribed by his psychiatrist, Dr. Klein. At some point he removed his shoes and outer clothing and placed his pants over the back of a chair, leaving him dressed in an undershirt, long johns, and long black socks. At some point he removed his glasses. Drugged in order to numb the pain, Rothko took a double-edged razor blade, wrapped a Kleenex over one side of it, took it in his right hand and made the cut in his left arm, switched the blade to his left hand and made the deeper cut in his right arm. When his body was discovered, he was lying, face-up, in a 6′ × 8′ pool of congealed blood, with his arms "outstretched."[16]

"If I choose to commit suicide," Rothko had told his assistant Jonathan Ahearn, "everyone will be sure of it. There will be no doubts about that." Rothko went on to mention the "accidental" deaths of Jackson Pollock and David Smith, both of whom had died in automobile crashes after drinking. By continuing to drink and smoke after his aneurysm, Rothko, too, had been acting out a "slow suicide"—"killing himself," as Dr. Grokest commented. But now, taking an overdose of drugs; cutting into an artery at the elbow (rather than the smaller veins at the wrist); ending his life with a kind of ritualistic blood letting—Rothko acted unequivocally, even methodically, with the deliberation of a man who had spent hours contemplating the violence he saw in his own paintings.

A little more than twenty years before, in "The Romantics Were Prompted," Rothko had written that the paintings which moved him most in the Western tradition were "the pictures of a single human figure—alone in a moment of utter immobility." In taking his own life, however, Rothko left us with the image of a single human figure, alone in a moment of utter silence and immobility, with his arms outstretched in an attitude of Christ-like defeat and victimization.

...

The dark is always at the top.

Mark Rothko

"I was never in my life anywhere at so desolate a party," Rebecca Reis said. She was remembering a party given by Rothko in his studio in December 1969, "when," in Brian O'Doherty's words, "Rothko invited an elite collection of educated eyes to look at the dark works lining the walls. . . . The incongruity of that occasion remains fresh: the small talk and banter under the high ceiling of the old [carriage house] on 69th Street while the works around the walls contracted to windows into some original darkness."[17] Yet, as Robert Motherwell recalled, Rothko remained "surrounded" by these dark paintings, hovering inside the space created by his works as if they were "shields," "as though they would protect him from any outside influence or danger."[18]

So different were these stark new paintings from his previous work that Rothko wondered aloud before friends whether he was "making a Rothko painting by taking the color out," or whether, indeed, he was making paintings at all. When Bernard Reis brought Thomas Messer of the Guggenheim to see these paintings, Messer said he would like to do a show of them, but he needed museum approval and would call. "I doubt very much whether Messer meant what he said," Rothko commented. "He was just trying to be nice to me." But when, just a few days before Rothko's death, Messer returned to the studio to arrange the exhibit, Rothko commented, "I don't know whether I ought to show them or not."[19] "He was a man of tremendous ego and tremendous doubt," said Hedda Sterne, and the doubts extended to himself as well as others.

His December studio party allowed Rothko, however, to present his new work in a one-man, one-evening exhibit, with his own hanging and lighting and with a small, select guest list. Viewing conditions were carefully controlled. Throughout 1969 Rothko complained to many people, among them his daughter, Kate, that he was having difficulty working. Yet, according to his assistant, Oliver Steindecker, Rothko worked regularly that year, keeping the schedule he'd followed for several years. When Steindecker arrived around 9 in the morning, Rothko had usually been painting for a few hours. "He *worked*, while I was there," Steindecker said. "It seemed like he was working every day, always did a lot," and Steindecker recalled Rothko's *physical* involvement with his labors: "he worked with large brushes, like paint brushes from house painters—they might be 6 or 7" wide—really heavy-duty brushes and he really got into his painting, his whole body would go up, down with the sweep of the brush on canvas; it was like he was really into it rather than just moving his arm. His whole body moved up and down with each stroke." As he had in recent years, Rothko generally stopped working about 11 A.M.—then had to confront filling the rest of the day.[20] But despite depression and heavy drinking, despite fears about his health, despite separating from his wife and son, despite anxieties about his position in the art world, Rothko remained engaged with his work, as if painting itself—though he sometimes declared his hatred for it—gave him his most reliable form of stability.

During 1969, Rothko continued to work with acrylics, sometimes combining them with ink.[21] By the end of 1968, he was able to work on papers of some size—e.g., approximately 60″ × 42″—and through 1969 he gradually enlarged the scale of his papers, so that by the end of the year he was working on sheets about 72″ × 48″—the dimensions of a mid-size Rothko oil on canvas.[22] He continued to produce a variety of colorful works on paper, but he also began to create the dark paintings he exhibited at his December studio party. He painted a series of about thirteen "Brown on Grey" works on paper, and he returned to canvas for a series of eighteen "Black on Grey" works.[23]

Neither the titles ("Brown on Grey," "Black on Grey") nor the concept of a "series" came from Rothko, who left these works untitled. So they do not constitute a formal, self-conscious (and numbered) series in the way that Robert Motherwell's *Elegies for the Spanish Republic* or Willem de Kooning's *Women* do. If one side of Rothko felt "bored" or worried that he was repeating himself, another grandly asserted the value of repetition. "If a thing is worth doing once, it is worth doing over and over again—exploring it, probing it, demanding by this repetition that the public look at it."[24] In this sense, *all* of Rothko's "individual" works constitute a series, each reinforcing the seriousness of the others by its similarity to them, each commenting on the others by its subtle difference. That is one reason Rothko wanted his works shown in groups. To call, say, the "Black on Grey" paintings a "series," then, is to emphasize that Rothko is once again exploring, probing, struggling with emotions, demanding our attention to nuances of difference.

But when he showed a group of these dark paintings to the artist Maurice Sievan, Rothko's old friend commented that "they didn't look like Rothkos."[25] They don't. In the "Black on Grey" works the canvas has typically been divided into two rectangular areas, the upper one a flat, opaque, and impersonally brushed black, the lower one gray or blue, usually mixed with greens, browns, yellows, or ochers, and often painted with broad, vigorous, sometimes turbulent strokes. It is not just that Rothko has now renounced warm, vibrant colors, a project he had been engaged in for several years and which had culminated in the vast and solemn black rectangles for the Houston chapel. Beyond that, he is now refusing the glamor and luminosity of oils altogether, using acrylics which, since they do not reflect light as oils do, appear flat and impenetrable.

It is as if all the elation, all the engagement with the juxtapositions of color, all the urgent desire to communicate not by making the picture "talk" but making it silently envelope the spectator—as if all the sensual *pleasure* and seductive *command*—had gone out of Rothko's painting. But deprivations, like losses, could be generative for Rothko, *if* they were self-imposed. No longer beguiling, now bleak and ascetic, Rothko's "Black on Grey" works now sternly declare that there is no way but his way: inward.

Since the 1950s, Rothko had used a ground color—a glue size containing powdered pigments—to prime his canvases. The "Black on Grey" works, however, were primed with gesso, the edges of the canvas then covered with masking tape during painting, the tape later removed to create a narrow (usually ½" to ¾") white border. One of the crucial moments in Rothko's development had come when he detached the stacked rectangles which, in his paintings of the early 1940s, had been locked securely to the edge, and suspended these forms not on but *in* the ground color, freeing them simultaneously to advance toward and recede from a viewer. But with the "Black on Grey" paintings, the rectangles are once again fixed to the edge, held firmly in place. You are always outside them.

After Rothko began working with acrylics on paper during 1967, his practice was to send completed works to his restorer, Daniel Goldreyer, who mounted the papers on Masonite, wrapping the white borders around the sides, which he then painted in the color of Rothko's ground.[26] At some point the possibility of preserving these dramatic white borders occurred to Rothko, an idea he adopted only after considerable hesitation and debate. But, as Donald McKinney has written, "it was from his observation of this classic 'studio accident' that he conceived doing the last major series of paintings—the Black and Grey acrylics on canvas."[27] In addition to stabilizing the rectangles, these white margins also *frame* the image, in the work of a painter who had once equated frames with coffins. Before, Rothko had left his canvases unframed, blurring the boundary between the work and its surrounding environment. Now, stark white borders sever the space of the work from the "actual" space around it. Less a physical "presence," the painting—despite its considerable size—is more a self-contained object, its space boxed-in.

At Rothko's December studio party, Adolph Gottlieb had leaned over to Ray Parker and commented on the placement of the divisions between the black and gray: "these paintings of Mark's, it all depends on how far you pull up the shade in the window or how far down." These junctures, usually placed in the lower half of the painting, also resemble horizon lines, defining a space that pushes back, into the wall. "He accepted the mention of such [landscape] associations," Robert Goldwater writes, "and it was clear that their exact control was part of his purpose."[28] The white borders remind the viewer that he or she is contemplating a two-dimensional surface. The juncture can't be a horizon; the painting flattens. So, rather than enfolding a spectator, the "Black on Grey" paintings create a space which simultaneously draws away and thwarts entrance; they don't look, or *act,* like Rothkos.

A painter's work progresses, as Rothko had written in 1949, "toward the elimination of all obstacles between the painter and the idea, and between the idea and the observer."[29] The "Black on Grey" paintings are faithful to this ethic of subtraction, but Rothko's last and most severe renunciations were made not to remove obstacles between the observer and the idea but in a gesture of personal *withdrawal.* The white margins, along with the austere, somber colors, the opacity of the acrylic paints and the ominous, self-absorbed feeling of the whole, locate the viewer, and the artist, *outside* a bleak, self-enclosed space. It is as if one side of Rothko wished to recoil into himself while another stood back, detached, contemplating, and painting that desire.

"The dark is always at the top," Rothko noted.[30] Since dark areas look heavy, the black presses down on the gray or blue, creating a sense of quiet foreboding. Some of these paintings resemble a stark lunar landscape seen against the black void of outer space. Or they suggest a gray cliff that falls off into a black abyss. In *Black on Grey* (1969; color plate 21) a dense, smoldering brown contains hints of underlying red and purple, but these colors never break through the impenetrable surface. Our gaze is forced *down,* into the lower rectangle, painted an oceanic blue, on which yellow-green, organic-looking shapes have been placed with light, feathery brushstrokes. The space, filled with a diffused, sourceless light, has a submarine character reminiscent of the watery zones in many of Rothko's paintings of the mid-1940s. Because this area is lighter and more varied, has optical depth and contains gracefully curving shapes, it offers an interior space that is cool and somber yet soothing and restful—and rigidly sealed off from the outside. It is as if this space suggests a beauty, fluidity, and capacity for change that, weighed down upon by a vast darkness, is no longer accessible to Rothko. No more a matter of breathing and stretching one's arms again, painting has now become a movement *toward* silence, solitude, and self-enclosure.

Donald McKinney recalled that Rothko "was impatient that so many people, on coming to his studio, would be drawn immediately to his brighter canvases—the ones he referred to as 'easier to understand' and they did not feel the same affinity for his darker 'more difficult' canvases."[31] Of course, one of those people was Rothko's own dealer, and McKinney's boss, Frank Lloyd.[32] Rothko had always insisted he was not a "colorist" or "decorative" painter. With the "Black on Grey" paintings, Anne-Marie Levine said, "he tried, consciously, to create works that were equal in meaning but with as little color as possible . . . so that no one who had not the interest or the courage to face the 'subject' would be tempted to look at or buy the painting." Reducing his format to two rectangles, darkening his palette so that he almost eliminated color, Rothko eluded his "image," tested his audience, and gave his work the edge of risk and difficulty, "as though to say 'with all my trouble I was able to do *this*'." Being an outsider was acceptable, even desirable, for Rothko, as long he chose that position, as long as he was not being thrust aside by ambitious young painters or fashion-bound dealers.

"*I* should have painted them," Rothko once said to Rita Reinhardt, referring to the black paintings of her late husband, Ad.[33] From 1960 until his death in 1967, Reinhardt had limited himself to a single size (a 60″ square), a single color (black), a single format: a straight-edged cruciform shape that slowly emerged from the black, the whole always painted with a flat, anonymous surface. Reinhardt had found something worth doing over and over, demanding by that repetition that the public look at it. Always impressed, and threatened, by such purism, Rothko, in the "Black on Grey" paintings, moved into the territory taken by a younger rival—and beginning in the spring of 1969 he would be involved in a love affair with Reinhardt's widow—in order to claim it as his own. He then worried if he were equal to the task. "He wondered whether his paintings were as good as Ad Reinhardt's," said Stanley Kunitz, and "he thought maybe they weren't." "The difference between me and Reinhardt is that he's a mystic," Rothko asserted in one of his more confident moods. "By that I mean that his paintings are immaterial. Mine are *here*. Materially. The surfaces, the work of the brush and so on. His are untouchable."[34] Rothko distinguishes himself from Reinhardt as more physical and human. Yet "Black on Grey" works like color plate 21 show the weight of an impenetrable black on a more luminous, varied, inviting—a more physical and human—space, now placed under heavy pressure, and sealed off.

Chapter Nineteen

The "Black on Grey" paintings are not simply avant-garde efforts to thwart the expectations of an art market perfectly capable of absorbing any and all gestures of resistance. They are not mere formalist experiments, designed to test how much Rothko could subtract and still have a painting. Nor are they just maneuvers designed to usurp a rival, though they involve all these things. As distanced and controlled as they are, the "Black on Grey" paintings are still strongly emotional: they quite *openly* express the urge to withdraw, to retreat, to 'rock shut as a seashell.' It is not just that these paintings comment on Rothko's death; his suicide commented on these paintings: these feelings, Rothko was asserting, are *real*.

. . .

As if fate had conspired to involve him more and more with some of those very professionals he most mistrusted, Rothko, during the last fourteen months of his life, developed complex, ambivalent relations with his physicians, desperately seeking their help, consulting Dr. Grokest about five times a month, arriving at Dr. Meade's office without an appointment when Dr. Grokest had left on vacation, alluding to terrible pressures on him but refusing to reveal them, becoming obsessive over the details of his diet, alarmed at his inability to stop drinking and smoking, refusing to stop drinking and smoking, hoping for good news, refusing to believe good news, one time morose and docile, the next agitated and resistant.[35]

He did (mostly) adhere to his diet, and he continued to lose weight. By January of 1970, his blood pressure was normal. In other ways, however, Rothko's health continued to deteriorate. Dr. Grokest had warned him in January of 1969 that an enlarged liver presaged cirrhosis, a consequence of Rothko's drinking; and later, in October of that year, Dr. Lawson E. Miller diagnosed "bilateral emphysema," a consequence of his smoking. In the fall of 1968, Dr. Grokest had discovered a hernia, for which Rothko refused surgery.[36] Worst of all, Rothko was suffering, in Dr. Meade's phrase, from a "global depression."

"Depression," William Styron writes in *Darkness Visible,* is "a noun with a bland tonality and lacking any magisterial presence, used indifferently to describe an economic decline or a rut in the ground, a true wimp of a word for such a major illness."[37] What does it *feel* like to experience this dreadful illness? To be depressed is to lose all pleasure, all interest, in people, work, conversation—in life itself; to feel lethargic yet restless, vulnerable to waves of anxiety or panic, unable to concentrate, confused, forgetful, distracted, and worthless, burdened with the weight of sorrow. In September of 1968, Dr. Grokest had referred Rothko to a psychiatrist, Dr. Bernard Schoenberg, "who reported that

Rothko's depression was of such magnitude he should begin therapy immediately." Rothko refused.[38]

Since the early 1950s, Rothko had been a friend of Bruce and Dorothy Ruddick. Sometime after his aneurysm, he asked Ruddick, a psychiatrist, if he could see him in his office on a Saturday. "He came and confessed to me that he was heartbroken. I didn't know what about. He was terribly sad. He was depressed. He had had the aneurysm, which was a terrible blow to his sense of physical self-esteem. He was living on the brink—on the threat of imminent destruction by this dreadful disease." Rothko asked Ruddick if he would treat him; Ruddick replied that, as a friend, he could not. Instead, Rothko visited Ruddick's office on Saturdays, just to talk.[39]

> One thing was his alarm at his own drinking. He was quite upset by the amount of drinking he and Mell were doing. He didn't condemn Mell, but he said, "we drink too much," and he felt it was devastating their lives, and he expressed a serious concern that in some way this might harm his children, especially the little boy. He was dreadfully fond of that child.
>
> He talked about fame and a public role being thrust on him, his loss of any sense of privacy.
>
> He also mentioned that he had pain and that it didn't seem to be measurable or register much. His doctors treated the pain as if it were inexplicable and imaginary.
>
> Getting older and feeling threatened and depressed, perhaps what he wanted to come to me for was somebody who in some way would empathize with and sympathize with his pain. I don't think many people did—because if you could think of a man in such incandescent power, in such a position of public approbation, of acceptance, he was a man in tremendous power and the pain he had seemed almost inappropriate to most people.
>
> I think Mark was talking not only about the real pain in his chest from the aneurysm, which was dreadful at times, but he was told by his doctor that he was perfectly fine, that there was no reason for the pain. It was the psychic pain that he suffered—a terrible one that I'm sure the essential people in his life could not enter into and reduce the pressure.
>
> He felt that the depth of suffering he was going through was debilitating to him as a creative person. He didn't say it stopped him, but it was draining him. He did not feel he had the elan, the vitality and the energy, that he wanted. He also felt that his own anodyne, his own antidepressant, alcohol, was not helping.

He knew he was destroying himself drinking. And he was concerned about Mell's drinking. Separating from Mell, *that's* his heartbreak. He loved Mell, but I think he was probably enraged because he felt she abandoned him in her own way.

When he talked to me there was no anticipating happiness—except for the moments when he talked about doing the de Menil chapel; *that* was happy and it was there. The rest of the time it was not lugubrious but *sad*—not hopelessness expressed but an absence of hopeful anticipation. It wasn't mean depression; it wasn't accusing; it wasn't what we call a claiming depression, and it wasn't a whining insistence that things should be better for him because he deserved more of this and that. It was a desolate outlook on life.

He expressed just his own feeling of despair, these terrible intimations of mortality—plus one fact: his mother's death weighed heavily on him. He spoke of her. He mentioned that it had been a terrible blow. He mentioned it almost as if—and this is an analytic speculation—as if he anticipated some kind of fusion, return, in his own dying.

On Rothko's last visit, Dr. Ruddick offered to find him a therapist, but Rothko said, "No," and "he was a little angry." "Perhaps he sensed not a deep friendship between us but a kind of mutual affection we had for each other as a bridge on which that pain might be shared." Rothko had found a *personal* relation with a therapist, but as soon as Dr. Ruddick wanted to direct him toward a professional, Rothko withdrew. As he left the office that Saturday, Rothko hugged Ruddick and kissed him on both cheeks.

Bernard Reis had a professional to recommend, too: Dr. Nathan Kline, director of the New York State Research Center at Rockland State Hospital, a man who had received grants from the Albert and Mary Lasker Foundation, on which Reis served as director.[40]

Nathan Kline was a psychiatrist who took a dim view of conventional psychiatric practice. "Psychiatry has labored too long," he complained, "under the delusion that every emotional malfunction requires an endless talking out of everything the patient ever experienced."[41] Emancipated from such delusions, Dr. Kline himself promised a quick, inexpensive treatment; he offered drugs.[42]

Nowadays, drugs provide one conventional and often effective way to treat many forms of depression. A pioneer in the field, Nathan Kline believed that depression is almost always "triggered by some disarray in the biochemical tides that sweep back and forth within the body." He sought to calm the biochemical waters with biochemical means, providing symptomatic relief in short-term therapy (three or four months), offered in fifteen-minute sessions.[43] Popularizing his methods with articles in *Vogue* magazine and books like *From Sad to Glad*, Kline impatiently dismissed alternative approaches and critics.[44]

One Kline patient, suffering from a year-long depression, recalled her first visit: "Here I was, all dressed up, holding myself together, with my sympathetic husband at my side. And there he was: Dr. Kline, sitting in a black leather chair, surrounded by marvelous African art and two gray phones that lit up with emergency calls. Dr. Kline was wearing a gray-plaid, beautifully tailored suit. His smile was reassuring in a well-tanned face, capped by startling silver hair."[45]

Practicing psychopharmacology out of a fashionable brownstone on East 69th Street, just two blocks west of Rothko's studio, Dr. Kline cheerfully treated depression. "In many instances," he wrote, "one can recognize depressives on sight. The inner anguish that afflicts them is signaled in many ways by small outward signs such as dress, posture, gait, and manner." Dr. Kline looked at externals—clothes, body movements—and saw within. And wherever he looked, he saw depression. By 1974, he had treated 5,000 depressives, with about 85 percent of them, he claimed, moved from sad to glad. "The locked cells and straitjackets of the past have been largely replaced by the gentle restraints of tranquilizing medication," Dr. Kline declared.[46] As a social utopian he foresaw the tortures of the snake pit replaced by the day of the living dead.

Rothko showed some reluctance about seeing Dr. Kline. As Rebecca Reis said, "you had to give Mark a certain amount of surveillance to have him do the things that were good for him."[47] In this case, a certain amount of active management was called for. On December 9, 1968—three weeks before Rothko moved into his studio—Bernard Reis arranged an appointment for Rothko with Dr. Kline, in the evening when no other patients would be in the office, "so Mark would feel perfectly at ease"—i.e., by keeping *secret* an appointment he felt uneasy about.[48] The Reises suspected Rothko would not show up for the appointment on his own, so Bernard Reis came to the studio and escorted him to Kline's office.[49]

"It is not unusual for a person to be going to more than one physician, but make certain," Kline instructs depressives in *From Sad to Glad*, "that each one knows what the other is doing by having one get in touch with the other if necessary."[50] But for Rothko, Kline prescribed Sinequan, an antidepressant, and Valium, a tranquilizer, without consulting either Dr. Grokest or Dr. Meade. Once again, a physician chosen by Reis had displaced Grokest.

In August of 1969, when both Kline and Grokest were away from the city on vacation, Rothko consulted Dr. Arnold L. Lision, who diagnosed hypertension and prescribed an antidepressant.[51] A few days later, Rothko appeared, without an appointment, at the office of Dr. Meade, whom he had not seen in over a year and who observed that Rothko appeared "totally disoriented, disturbed and dazed." Though he'd had little experience with the new antidepressants Rothko was taking, Dr. Meade was aware that Sinequan could cause changes in heart rhythm, so that "it would not be your first line of thought" with a heart patient like Rothko.[52] He also decided that Rothko was overmedicated: "No question in my mind that he was *way* overmedicated." Subsequently, he noticed that "right after Rothko would start with a new dose of Sinequan, he would become much more depressed and more irritable." Meade would lower Rothko's dosage, leave a message for Kline—whom he could not reach by phone—then "every time I would cut down a medication or change it or stop something, Rothko would check with him [Kline] and then it would be changed back very shortly."

Among colleagues, Kline was thought to be "fairly imperious, charismatic and brilliant and high-handed—an egotistical sort of guy, who might be insensitive" in his dealings with fellow physicians. So he was in his relations with Dr. Grokest. A few days after his first visit to Dr. Kline, Rothko saw Dr. Grokest. The Sinequan frightened him, Rothko said.[53] What should he do? Grokest, who, like Meade, viewed Sinequan as a less than ideal choice for someone with heart disease, told Rothko not to take the medication. Grokest was also disturbed because Kline had prescribed the Sinequan without consulting him about Rothko's medical history, drugs he was currently taking, and so on. "No consultants unless I can talk to them," he told Rothko. A few days later Kline called Grokest, accusing him of interfering with his treatment of Rothko. The two doctors had an angry exchange. When Kline called again, Grokest refused to speak to him. Kline sent Grokest a registered letter, saying Rothko was depressed and suicidal.

Despite Grokest's warnings, Rothko continued to see Kline and to take Sinequan (as well as Valium), just as in the past he had turned to other physicians when Grokest refused to write him sleeping pill prescriptions. When Bernard Malamud visited Rothko's studio sometime in 1969—the two men had first met when they and their wives rode on the same bus (marked "Cultural Leaders") to a Lyndon Johnson inaugural party—Rothko showed the novelist a number of acrylic works he had recently done, spoke of the devastating depression following his aneurysm and the difficulty he'd had working—until he'd seen a psychiatrist who'd given him a new drug which had lifted his depression, restored his vitality, and made it possible for him to work again.[54]

But Rothko's moods, at least as he communicated them to Dr. Grokest, continued to fluctuate. In March 1969—just after he had begun a relationship with Ad Reinhardt's widow, Rita—"I thought for the first time that he looked at ease."[55] His blood pressure was normal. But Rothko still could not stop drinking and smoking. He was taking the medications prescribed by Dr. Kline. And he was taking them Rothko-style. Sometimes, he didn't take them at all. Sometimes, as many friends attest, he'd swallow a handful of pills ("The doctor says take two of them, but who's counting?" he told Arthur Lidov). Sometimes, he combined the pills with scotch.[56] With the pills (or pills and alcohol), he sometimes *risked* suicide.

A treatment, like Kline's, promising relief from painful symptoms and involving no scrutiny of his private psyche by a removed professional held strong appeal for Rothko, an inward painter with "no tolerance for introspection."[57] With male authority, Rothko, for most of his adult life, had been assertive, wary of betrayal, quick to take angry offense. Now, on the one hand, as Motherwell saw, Rothko was stubbornly rejecting anyone else's judgment, so that no one could intervene, but leaving himself locked in an almost "metaphysical loneliness." On the other hand, Rothko grew passively dependent—relying on those, like Reis and Kline, whom many others found suspect.

"A painting was a real painting when it was full," Rothko told Anne-Marie Levine.[58] Stanley Kunitz sensed "a great vacuum at the center" of Rothko's being. In art, Rothko painted his emptiness—as full. In life, he had consoled himself with food, drink, cigarettes, now with antidepressants and tranquilizers. Rothko was the son of a pharmacist; he was the younger brother of pharmacists; he had grown up in a pharmacy. Dr. Kline was a psychopharmacologist. In the last year of his life, Rothko's medicine cabinet and bedside table were crowded with his prescriptions for gout, high blood pressure, anxiety, depression. On the night of his suicide Rothko took an overdose of the Sinequan prescribed by Dr. Kline.

Rothko recalled his own father as demanding and critical. When Jacob died in Portland, he left Marcus "in the lurch." He was the victimized son. Rothko thought of himself not as a mere painter but as the messianic bearer of a new vision, capable of transforming his sufferings, his losses, into a sensual and spiritual fullness that went "beyond painting." At the time of his death, one of the few books Rothko kept in his studio was a worn copy of Kierkegaard's *Fear and Trembling*. When he had drawn on that text for his 1958 lecture at Pratt, Rothko no longer identified with the son Isaac but with the patriarch Abraham: someone alienated from all those around him, even his wife, by his silent commitment to an act that went "beyond understanding."

When he ended his life, in a ritualized act of self-sacrifice, Rothko acted as both Abraham *and* Isaac, both the demanding father and the submissive son, memorably glorified by his suffering.

• • •

"My last memory of him is a happy one, when he was between his periodic bouts of depression a year ago," Bryan Robertson wrote soon after Rothko's death. "Separated from his wife and family, he had moved into his vast studio and told me that he had not felt so at ease, so optimistic and happy since he was a student. 'The studio is marvelous for music', he said, for he liked to play records, 'and I wake up every morning with something unresolved at hand to consider'."[59] Perhaps, when Rothko first moved into his studio, he felt relieved, emancipated from what had declined into an acrimonious marriage. Perhaps, with someone he didn't know all that well, he presented himself as transformed, returned to a romanticized version of his student days.

Soon after the end of his first marriage Rothko had felt himself "on the brink of a new life." This time, he had chosen to separate from Mell on January 1, as if he were symbolically asserting a desire for a new life. And when he had left, he had taken nothing with him. "He didn't pack, he just walked out," as if he were asserting a desire for a complete break with his old life.[60] But in January of 1969 Rothko was sixty-five; he had suffered a serious aneurysm; much of the time, he was depressed; he had two children, one of them just five; he was ending a *second* marriage, one that had lasted twenty-three years. In fact, the "new life" Rothko imagined in 1943 had finally repeated his old one, the past fatefully circling back on the present. Rothko had always had trouble finding ways of liberating himself that were not self-punishing, in part because liberation entails separation, something Rothko found very painful. He had withdrawn to his bed for three months after separating from Edith Sachar. Now, once again, he was alone, separated, this time surviving in the stark, cheaply furnished living area adjacent to his cavernous studio.

A few months after moving into the studio—one friend compared it to living at the bottom of an empty swimming pool—Rothko began a relationship with Rita Reinhardt.[61] She had been born in 1928 in Germany, as Rita Ziprkowski, the child of a Polish father and a Russian mother.[62] The family was Jewish. At the beginning of the Second World War, she was brought to England by a rescue organization. Her parents and a younger sister became victims of the Holocaust. When the war ended, she came to New York City, to live with an uncle. She studied painting with Norman Lewis at the Jefferson School, then at the New School, and at Columbia.

In 1953, she married Ad Reinhardt. She had first met Rothko through the Betty Parsons Gallery, saw him often during the 1950s, less so after Reinhardt and Rothko fell out, then more often again when the two men renewed their friendship in the last few years of Reinhardt's life.[63]

During the spring of 1969, Rita Reinhardt was forty, Rothko sixty-five. She had been a widow for eighteen months, he had been separated from his wife for three. Both were vulnerable. She had lost her husband, a painter who had never achieved much financial success, who was just beginning to be recognized at the time of his death, and who had left a large estate that she did not feel confident in managing on her own. Six months before his death, Ad Reinhardt, "feeling often these days like a new-born-babe in all my innocence and inexperience," had turned to Rothko for worldly advice.[64] In March of 1969, as Rita Reinhardt was negotiating an agreement to sell a number of her husband's paintings to Marlborough, she turned to Rothko, an older artist who was an experienced and powerful figure in the art world.

Rita Reinhardt was an orphan of the Holocaust, an exiled Jew, a "survivor." She was young. With jet black hair pulled straight back into a bun, very white skin and usually dressed dramatically in black, she impressed people as poised, refined—and very beautiful. Despairing, isolated, frightened by his own mortality, unable to control his drinking, his physical self-esteem damaged by illness and age, looking for a source of vitality and solace, Rothko turned to Rita Reinhardt. She thought he could take care of her; he thought she could take care of him.

Dr. Grokest observed that Rothko, just after he began seeing Rita Reinhardt, "looked at ease." She recalled that, during the rest of 1969, Rothko was often cheerful, steadily working, sometimes exhilarated by his work, able to spend hours studying his paintings. She and Rothko went to movies and plays, had dinner, talked politics, discussed his work, and often without any sense that Rothko was a deeply depressed person. She also recalled that there were agonizing times, that he had experienced a life-threatening illness, lost important friendships, been (he claimed) "kicked out by Mell," now found himself too tired and sick to enjoy his success, felt people were descending on him like vultures, felt that it wasn't right not to be taking care of his wife and that others would think that as well.

In 1943 Rothko had written his sister that although he found his new life both "exciting and sad," "the last thing in the world I would wish would be to return to the old one." Yet this time, despite dramatic gestures like moving out on January 1 and refusing to pack anything, Rothko felt pulled back, finding it difficult to draw a sharp boundary between his old life and his new one. To some friends, he complained that Mell drank too much, that she said she "hated" his paintings, that she had thrown him out.[65] Other friends he accused of spying on him *for* Mell. Yet, he also kept in daily contact with her by phone, usually calling her early in the morning and often talking with her for as long as thirty minutes. In fact, by taking nothing with him, Rothko had created a reason to return, so he would drop by the 95th Street house to pick up a shirt or a pair of pants. He also sometimes came for meals, though these visits often deteriorated into fights. Rothko had disapproved of Herbert Ferber's leaving his second wife for a much younger third wife. Was Rothko about to commit the same offense? Guilt inhibited him. So did the prospect of yet another loss.

At least according to Rothko, Rita Reinhardt was pressuring him to get a divorce and marry her; he resisted. Mell Rothko was urging him to return home; he resisted. One morning, about two weeks before his death, Rothko, agitated, burst into the Reis house. "Becky," he said, "if you knew what a liar I am, you wouldn't let me in this house. I lie to my wife. I lie to Rita."[66] Yet, despite his disgust with himself, Rothko could not act decisively.

Rothko felt trapped, paralyzed, impotent. During the Christmas season in 1969, two months before his death, he came with Rita Reinhardt to a party given by Katharine Kuh. "People were all over," Kuh recalled. "And he didn't talk to anyone; he just kept following me out to the kitchen." He was not drinking, but "he was very upset. He was at that point so completely caught up in and with himself that he was scarcely aware of the festivities around him." Katharine Kuh asked him why he didn't go back to Mell, if the break upset him so much. "He agreed that part of him did want to go back, but he realized that the past with its many bitter confrontations could no longer be bridged. 'It just wouldn't work', he claimed. And then he said, 'I've been thinking. They both would be better off if I got out of their lives'."

Ennobling suicide as a sacrifice *for* those closest to him, rather than an abandonment of them, Rothko could withdraw from this impossible situation.[67]

• • •

On May 28, 1968, Mark Rothko, while still recovering from his aneurysm, had been inducted into the National Institute of Arts and Letters.[68]

On June 9, 1969, he was awarded an honorary doctorate by Yale University, the college he had disdained and dropped out of in 1923. Kingman Brewster, the president of Yale, read Rothko's citation:

> As one of the few artists who can be counted among the founders of a new school of American painting, you have made an enduring place for

yourself in the art of this century. Your paintings are marked by a simplicity of form and a magnificence of color. In them you have attained a visual and spiritual grandeur whose foundation is the tragic vein in all human existence. In admiration of your influence, which has nourished young artists throughout the world, Yale confers upon you the degree of Doctor of Fine Arts.[69]

Rothko responded briefly:

I want to thank the University and the awards committee for the honor you have chosen to confer on me. You must believe me that the acceptance of such honors is as difficult as the problem of where to bestow them.

When I was a younger man, art was a lonely thing: no galleries, no collectors, no critics, no money. Yet it was a golden time, for then we had nothing to lose and a vision to gain. Today it is not quite the same. It is a time of tons of verbiage, activity, a consumption. Which is better for the world at large, I will not venture to discuss. But I do know that many who are driven to this life are desperately searching for those pockets of silence where they can root and grow. We must all hope that they find them.[70]

As Rothko had walked in the procession of Yale officials, faculty, and guests across the campus, he passed his cousin Ed Weinstein, who asked what he was doing there. Rothko pressed a finger to his lips and passed silently on. After the ceremony, Weinstein found Rothko removing his cap and gown and asked, "Aren't you going to have lunch with the rest of the recipients?" "Who needs their lunch. I'm going back to New York," Rothko declared, and the two men walked to the New Haven railroad station. Weinstein reminded Rothko of the time their "Uncle" Nathan had found Rothko drawing on some "N & S Weinstein" wrapping paper, shook his head, and commented, "Marcus, why are you wasting your time? You will never be able to earn a living that way." Rothko and his cousin laughed.[71]

By this time, Mark Rothko had decorated a room, or created an environment, with five of his murals at Harvard University. Fourteen of his works would soon fill the walls of a chapel in Houston. Nine of his Seagram paintings would soon be hung in a room of their own at the Tate Gallery in London. By April of 1969, Rothko had begun discussions with the UNESCO office in Paris about providing paintings for a room that would also contain sculpture by Giacometti.[72] In theory at least, these projects secured Rothko a lasting *place* in cultural history, a place outside time, uncorrupted *by* time—a recognition of his worth that would survive his death.

His 1968 inventory had established the presence of about eight hundred works in Rothko's "stock." What would become of *them* after his death? At least since 1960, Rothko had been considering a foundation, first in order to avoid taxes, later to control the dispersal of his paintings and to enhance his reputation after his death.[73] According to Rothko's 1968 will, the Mark Rothko Foundation would inherit the bulk of his estate. But the foundation had never been incorporated.

In the spring of 1969 Rothko had lunch with William Rubin, a curator at the Museum of Modern Art whom Rothko's will had named as a director of the foundation. In their conversation, "Mark Rothko was concerned about the preservation of his work," said Rubin. "He didn't want the work to be put on sale. He had enough money for his family. He felt, 'I want to protect the work'." In particular, Rothko spoke of his "deep desire to keep many or various groups of his paintings together permanently." Not long after, a first meeting of the foundation directors—Robert Goldwater, Morton Levine, Bernard Reis, Rubin, and Theodoros Stamos—was held at Rothko's studio. Rothko, "soused" from lunch, could barely walk, as if, said Rubin, "there was too much at stake." The meeting went forward anyway, Rubin proposing a small museum, like the Léger museum in France, to be located perhaps in a Manhattan brownstone, where a certain number of Rothko's works would always be on view. Reis dismissed this proposal as "preposterous," too expensive. Rubin then suggested loaning groups of Rothko works to museums unable to purchase his paintings but willing to set space aside for their long-term exhibition with proper lighting conditions. According to Rubin, the meeting also included a brief discussion of the foundation awarding grants to older artists in need.[74]

By the time the foundation was incorporated, in June 1969, Rubin had been removed as a director, and producer Clinton Wilder (a Reis client) and composer Morton Feldman (a friend of Rothko's) had been added. Rubin believes that Reis had persuaded Rothko to remove him.[75] The foundation, according to its certificate of incorporation, was to spend its funds "exclusively for charitable, scientific and/or educational purposes." Like Rothko's will (also drawn up by Reis), the certificate thus provided only the vaguest statement of purpose for a foundation likely, on Rothko's death, to receive a large number of very valuable paintings, about which the artist was well-known to have very protective feelings. Reis later stated that he'd deliberately left the language vague—it certainly doesn't seem accidental—in order not to "bind" the directors.[76]

Of course, from Rothko's point of view the function of such a foundation *was* to bind the directors to carry out his wishes. Reis should have solicited from Rothko, and included either in the will or the certificate of incorporation or both, some set of guidelines about the disposition of Rothko's works. In fact, in their letters to the Ferbers and Reis that had accompanied Mark and Mell Rothko's 1959 wills, they had formulated precisely such a set of policies for the posthumous distribution of Rothko's paintings. Such formal instructions were all the more imperative in the case of Rothko in 1969, when his depression and his drinking led him to say different things at different times.[77] Without such a statement, however, the executors of Rothko's estate and the directors of his foundation would necessarily rely on their own constructions of Rothko's wishes. As "The Matter of Rothko" would clearly demonstrate, these constructions were not always disinterested.

Several months after Rothko's death, in November of 1970, the directors voted to amend the certificate, with the foundation's sole purpose now "to provide financial assistance to mature creative artists, musicians, composers and writers."[78] When Robert Goldwater learned of the contemplated change, he objected. Reis told him that, in the last months of his life, Rothko had changed his mind about the foundation's purpose.[79] Clearly, Reis no longer objected to binding the directors; but that was because, when the charter was revised, the three directors who were also the executors of Rothko's will—Reis, Stamos, Levine—had already sold *all* of the paintings in Rothko's estate to Marlborough, and had concealed that agreement from their fellow directors.[80] Placement of Rothko's paintings could no longer be a concern; they—all 798 of them—had already been disposed of.

It is true that Rothko had often expressed concern for the plight of older, indigent artists. Younger painters were privileged; they had things too easy. "The young have everything done for them. All the awards, the prizes, the honors go to the young," Rothko complained. Besides, success and prosperity were distributed randomly, arbitrarily: "I paint the same way I did when I didn't have a dime and for the same reason," he said. "I don't know why this should be that I should suddenly have all this money. It has no reality."[81] While one part of Rothko battled to 'control the situation', another despaired of *any* stable, or enduring, form of order or control. His own success left him uneasy: he needed to protect it from the grasping young, and he wanted to share some of it with those members of his own generation who had never achieved much recognition but who—unlike, say, a Barnett Newman or an Ad Reinhardt—posed no threat to Rothko's own position. When Rothko looked at an older artist in need, he saw an image of what he himself—given his vision of a capricious marketplace—might well become at seventy-five.

Yet his worries about elderly artists were clearly secondary to his long-standing preoccupation with the placement of his works, however ambivalent this involvement had sometimes become in practice. Though not a close friend of Rothko's, Goldwater was (along with Dore Ashton) one of the few art critics Rothko respected, so much so that he had asked Goldwater to write a book about his work, gave him access to his papers, and, during 1969, met with him for several two- or three-hour discussions of his work. In Goldwater's view, the foundation had two purposes: the first being "to exhibit and disperse" Rothko's pictures "as to protect Mark Rothko's achievement and reputation, being especially conscious of his wish to have his paintings seen in groups rather than singly"; and the second being to sell "a portion of Mark Rothko's pictures, to make grants to mature artists" who "had displayed lifelong dedication to their art and were in need of financial assistance."[82] Rita Reinhardt, who was certainly close to Rothko during the last year of his life, said, "I am still convinced that Mark wanted his paintings kept, put in the Foundation for the purpose of showing his work in the best possible way. And he was not interested in selling off his paintings for anybody. That was furthest from his wishes."[83]

Yet, at the same time that he moved to protect his paintings by withdrawing them from the art market, Rothko continued to sell his works to Marlborough, again under the guidance of Reis.

Two months before his death, in December 1969, Rothko sold eighteen oil paintings to Lloyd for $396,000, in an arrangement once again involving long-term, interest-free, deferred payments.[84]

In February 1970, yet another Marlborough sale was being negotiated. On the morning of February 25, McKinney had an appointment to pick up Rothko at his studio and accompany him to the warehouse where his paintings were stored, so that Rothko could find some missing paintings he was looking for, and so McKinney could make a selection of works for the new Marlborough contract. McKinney sensed that Rothko attached some unique importance to their meeting, which he had twice postponed. "I think he felt that he had sold enough paintings. I think he felt that he had sold his . . . that he had sold his soul," said McKinney. "I think he wanted some privacy about his work, and I don't think he wanted us to know how much work was still available. I mean, any issue of selling to Frank Lloyd again, that was certainly an issue. But there were other issues, like he didn't want to disclose, to let us know what he still had."

On the evening of February 24, Rothko had dinner with Rita Reinhardt. "How dare Lloyd force his way into the warehouse to pick and choose from the long-treasured hoard of paintings?" Rothko asked. "Why had Bernard pressed him to do this? Whose side was Bernard on?" By this time—as he contemplated a third Marlborough sale within a year—Rothko felt "uneasy about what Bernard was doing," he was "questioning and doubting" him.

Rothko and Rita Reinhardt spent some time, as they had before, trying to make sense of the deal, why Rothko should do it, why Reis should push for it. But they could make no sense of it. Rothko felt devastated that Bernard was not taking care of him.

Rothko had warned Rita Reinhardt some time before, "Never cross Bernard." But the Rothko who had energetically battled with the art establishment for many years was now too weary to fight, and he seemed to fear that Reis, who for the past several years had involved himself intimately with Rothko's professional and personal life, had the power to "embarrass" or "disgrace" him. Still, Rita Reinhardt said, he did not have to complete the deal, go to the warehouse with McKinney the next morning. He could say she was ill, postpone the trip to the warehouse, put Marlborough off. But Rothko did not have the energy to resist.[85]

When, on the morning of February 25, McKinney arrived at the studio to pick him up for the trip to the warehouse, Rothko was dead.

• • •

Rothko's paintings of the 1950s and 1960s yearn toward a purified, transcendent space. Yet in the last eighteen months of his life all of those messy, confining, daily human realities which Rothko had sought to transcend in his work crowded in on him. His body was failing; his marriage was failing; his affair was failing; his artistic sanctuary was being opened to the agents of commerce. He felt trapped and helpless; he felt corrupted and doomed—doomed because corrupted. In a last grasp at some sense of dignity and control, he killed himself.

When Oliver Steindecker had called Arthur Lidov after discovering Rothko's body, Lidov, whose work as a commercial artist had given him some experience working with cadavers, came into the studio, walked up to Rothko's body, and stopped about four feet away—"I didn't touch it; I never touch a cadaver unless I'm paid for it"—observing that Rothko was (in Lidov's words) "utterly immobile."[86]

By taking his life in *his* way, Rothko had sacrificed his physical being in order to preserve the integrity of the "not-self." He left no note. As he had once remarked, "Silence is so accurate."

Afterword

I worked on this biography of Mark Rothko for seven years. During January and February of 1986 I lived in New York City, interviewing his family, his friends, his enemies, his neighbors, his doctors, his lawyers, his assistants, the widows of his friends, the widows of his enemies, the family of his first wife, the family of his second wife, curators of museums, critics of art, collectors of art, dealers of art. I've also traveled to Portland, Oregon, Los Angeles, San Diego, Washington, D.C., Cambridge, Mass., New Haven, Houston, Texas, London, and Daugavpils, Latvia.

Now, in the early 1990s, a literary critic can walk into the local paperback bookstore, buy, say, all the works of Jacques Lacan and all the novels of William Faulkner, return to his or her study, and be in business. But biography has a "material base." It costs money—to cover plane tickets, car rentals, hotel bills, meals, snacks, phone bills, postage bills, tape recorders, tapes, batteries, tips, and subway tokens. Once, when I was driving a rented car from Washington, D.C., to the eastern shore of Maryland to interview Rothko's nephew Kenneth Rabin, a large metal plate bounced off the bed of a truck in front of me, and as it hit the highway, I instantly formed a mental image of the plate bouncing up through my windshield and decapitating me. Instead it merely shredded all four of my tires as I ran over it. No Lacanian critics have ever lost their lives (or even their tires) in the line of duty.

Then there was my trip, in late March of 1991, to Rothko's birthplace in the Soviet Union. I had read that practically all the town's buildings had been destroyed during the Second World War, and I had been told that Russian census records were not available to foreigners, so I had little chance of finding an address for his family, much less of finding a building that corresponded to it. I knew of no family relatives that had remained in Dvinsk, and even if there had been any, they would have left or been killed during the First World War—or during the Second World War. Still, traveling to the birthplace of their subjects is something that biographers *do*. Going was a professional duty, to "soak up the atmosphere," even across the distance of eighty years.

During my childhood I had a recurrent dream of travelling to Russia, to Moscow, to the Kremlin. Why the son of Irish Catholics, living in a provincial and politically reactionary neighborhood in Flatbush, Brooklyn, should dream—ecstatically—of journeying to the Soviet Union is a question all too easy to answer. Eventually, I left my block, the borough, the city, the state, even the east coast—to end up teaching at the University of California, Berkeley—which, to my Irish relatives, was not much better than the Kremlin. But the dream continued long into adulthood, and as late as 1991 helped push me toward a Russian-Latvian journey.

At that time, to travel to Daugavpils, you needed an official invitation—which I obtained from Professor Harijas Marsavs, chair of the Philological Faculty at the city's Pedagogical Institute. So I would visit Mark Rothko's birthplace and give lectures (to students studying English) on Mark Rothko. Perhaps, I told my friends, I'd discover a ravine at the edge of town where, on certain evenings at sunset, the light broke into vibrating bands of color. I'd travel by way of Leningrad, see the Winter Palace, the Bronze Horseman, the Neva River, the Hermitage, then take an overnight train to Daugavpils. Justified as professional duty, my trip was actually conceived as romantic adventure.

Daugavpils, I discovered, has a museum, a Pedagogical Institute, a hotel (with a satellite dish on the roof), a theater (with a dramatization of "Viljams Folkners" *The Sound and the Fury* opening shortly), several movie houses, a large hospital, a small airport, and, just outside of town, alongside a large, beautiful lake, a synthetic fiber plant, which has completely polluted the lake. Though it contains many nineteenth-century buildings and no postmodern ones, Daugavpils is a late twentieth-century city; it is also small (population, 126,000) and provincial. No one I spoke with there had heard of Mark Rothko. When I showed a curator at the local museum some reproductions of his work, she examined one carefully for several moments, then murmured, "kon-struktee-veest." The students to whom I lectured about Rothko and showed slides of his work found it very amusing that anyone would pay thousands of American dollars for such pictures, and they were more interested in hearing about the legendary land of "Kal-lee-forn-ya" than their town's world-famous painter.

But the curator at the museum also showed me a copy of *Dvinchanin, A Reference Calendar of 1914,* a book produced by the town's Jewish community. Rothko's older brother, Moise, had told me that his family had lived near the Dvina River, on Shosseynaya Street, which he recalled as a cobbled road that became the main road to Petersburg. *Dvinchanin* listed Jews belonging to various professions; Rothko's sister, Sonia, a dentist, was listed at 17 Shosseynaya.

Afterword

The building—a three-story apartment—still stands, facing the earth dam and (visible from the upper floors) the Dauga River beyond.

To learn about the town and its history, I spoke with a physicist who is the town's unofficial historian, two members of the institute's history faculty, an Old Testament scholar, and three officials of the town's Latvian-Jewish Cultural Committee. Though no one had heard of Mark Rothko, everyone was willing to help me. I was given a detailed, turn-of-the-century map of the city, old photographs, old pamphlets describing the town and its history. I took long walks through the center of town. Standing on the bridge that crosses the river, I waited for sunset, observed the surrounding landscape (flat, with a strong horizon) and the region's diffused, northern light. I imagined Rothko as a boy living in a cramped, crowded turn-of-the-century flat, gazing out a window at visionary skies. I was taken for two long drives through the surrounding country. I was shown the cemetery where the remains of many of the approximately 120,000 people (most of them Jews) killed by the Germans during World War II have been reburied. I was taken to the site of one of these mass executions, in the woods north of town, along what appeared to be a rutted dirt road in a scrub pine forest, except that the soil was so white it looked bleached. Human bones—a jaw, a leg—were still pushing their way to the earth's surface. "Fifty years later, and no grass grows—like a monument from nature," one of my guides commented. I felt like weeping. I felt like taking some photographs. I wondered if I should. I asked. "Yes," said one of my guides, "they should see this."

Only as romantic adventure did my trip fall short. When I had arrived at the Leningrad airport, I discovered that the transportation from the airport to my hotel that I had paid for did not exist, and that my hotel room had been booked for the wrong night. Neither proved a calamity, but they made this aging, inexperienced traveler apprehensive. A few minutes after I got to my hotel room, someone knocked at the door; I opened it; a man spoke rapidly in Russian; I said, "Nyet," and closed the door. I went out for a walk. A few minutes after I returned, someone knocked at my door; he claimed he'd been sent to fix the TV, which was on. I should have said, "Hey, buddy, I grew up in New York; I *know* this scam." Instead, I slammed the door shut. Deciding that thieves were following me to my room, I made sure the door was locked, moved a table against the door, put a chair on top of the table. During the night, I woke up three or four times when someone turned the handle of my door to see if it were unlocked; I woke up three or four more times when the phone rang.

The following evening, I went to the Warsaw Station to get the train to Daugavpils. Fearing that I had been directed to the wrong station, or that I wouldn't be able to find my train, I arrived three hours early. The Warsaw Station is very old, very crowded, very loud, very dirty. I quickly saw (and so did the other 2,000 people there, it seemed to me) that I was the only American, the only member of a middle-class, apparently the only person carrying "luggage," certainly the only person wearing an Yves Saint Laurent coat. Being constantly stared at and openly discussed by strangers made me feel as if I were a Person of Coat. I wanted to explain that I'd bought the coat on sale at Macy's for $100, but in Russia $100 could be a year's income.

As I sat on an uncomfortable vinyl chair, pretending not to notice I was being stared at, time passed *very* slowly. Announcements of arriving and departing trains were made in *very* rapid Russian. I seemed to have the idea that if only someone would speak Russian slowly to me, I would understand it. A woman approached me, asked if I spoke English. I told her I did. She said, pointing, "those three men in fur caps over there are talking about robbing your suitcase." I moved to another vinyl chair, this one in the middle of an aisle, at the other end of the waiting room. I hooked one arm through my clothes carrier, the other through my leather overnight bag. Should I struggle with thieves, or let them have what are, after all, only my material possessions? Maybe I should concede the clothes carrier but fight for the smaller bag, which contained my lecture notes, slides, lists of questions I wanted to ask, my tape recorder? Do I still have my ticket? Where are my passport and visa? Filled with dread, suspiciously eyeing every adult (and some of the children) who passed down my aisle, I sat bent forward, hovering protectively over my worldly goods.

The young man sitting next to me asked if I spoke German. I said I spoke a little. He was a saxophone player and singer in an Estonian blues band; he was also a cocaine addict, vehemently sniffing every twenty seconds. It was hard to imagine that anyone in the Soviet Union could afford a cocaine habit—almost as hard as imagining an Estonian blues band. I had been a saxophone player too. "Sehr *gut*." In baby German, we critiqued Ornette Coleman, Charley Parker, Lester Young, each of them earning a "sehr gut." Time passed a *little* faster. Many sehr gut's later, he started to become a bit *too* freundlich, throwing his arm around my shoulders, grabbing my knee. Still watchfully tracking anyone passing down the aisle, and wracking my memory for German vocabulary forgotten since high school, I began to wonder if he were setting me up, killing time and plotting to swipe my smaller (and more valuable) bag when he left to get on his train. Or was I just misreading cultural difference? When he did leave, without lifting my bag, an elderly couple sitting behind us who had overheard our German, which they could actually speak, directed me to my train, the Leningrad-Warsaw Express.

Afterword

Sleeping berths on Russian trains consist of narrow leather seats, two lower, two upper to a compartment. You pay two rubles, ten kopeks to the conductor to rent a pillow, two sheets, a blanket. I stretched out on the hard leather as the train began to move "into the Russian night," I thought to myself, half seriously. Would one of the three men sharing my compartment rob me of my luggage or my vaunted overcoat? Would I sleep past my early morning stop and end up in Warsaw? Did I have my passport, my visa, my wallet, my plane ticket? Would Professor Marsavs—from whom I had not heard in two months (due to the chaos of the Soviet mails)—be waiting for me at the Daugavpils station? Would I ever get to sleep?

I did, for about forty-five minutes, and my host did meet me at the station, and then took me to my room in a student dormitory, on a floor reserved for visitors. I took a six-hour nap.

My first few days in Daugavpils were relaxed. On the third morning, however, a young man followed me out of the dorm, told me (in English) he was in town for a science conference, had no place to stay, had heard there was an extra bed in my room. Could he use it? I said no. He said he would return at the end of the day to ask again. I told the story to my host, who replied (not exactly reassuringly) with a story about a Swiss tourist in Estonia who had been killed for his suit. Would I be garrotted for my overcoat? He declared that under no circumstances should I let the young man into my room. That evening I returned with three people who had driven me through the countryside. I told them the story; they doubted there was a science conference. They walked with me into the building, talked with the dorm manager, who said that the young man really was attending a science conference, and he had been given another room on my floor.

I was safe, at least until I returned to the Warsaw station. I went up to my room, stretched out on my bed, picked up my copy of Charles Johnson's *Middle Passage*. Just as I started to read, the door handle turned, as someone tried to open it from outside. I moved a heavy table against the door; then I put another table on top of that one. Each night I barricaded myself in my room, then took a sleeping pill aptly named "halcyon." I had a recurring dream: heavily armed terrorists were holding me hostage in an airport.

• • •

Expensive, sometimes dangerous, sometimes scary, biographical research can also be fun and sometimes even glamorous. It can have a Robin Leach component, though it's more accurate to say—since many of the people I've interviewed for this book are neither rich nor famous—that, like a detective, I've had fragmentary glimpses of many different layers of contemporary American social life. When I stayed in New York, I lived at the Gramercy Park Hotel, at Lexington Avenue and 21st Street. Each morning I would descend from my room to the lobby, sometimes taking the back elevator with David Letterman's sidekick, Paul Shaffer. I would pretend not to know him; he would pretend not to know me.

At the desk I would exchange three or four singles for quarters, then spend about forty-five minutes on a pay phone (calls from my room cost $1.00), arranging appointments. Often, the bored permanent residents of the hotel would sit in the nearby cracked leather chairs to listen in on my efforts at biographical diplomacy. Occasionally they opened conversations with me; from one elderly woman who always came down to the lobby wearing a black dress and slippers, I received (and declined) two invitations to dinner at the "Artists' Club" on the other side of Gramercy Park. Once, the man using the phone next to me hung up, then simply leaned against the phone, listening to me. When I hung up, he identified himself as the driver of the car behind Jackson Pollock's car the night Pollock drove into a tree and killed himself; none of Pollock's biographers had gotten the story right, I was told, and the man volunteered an interview. But I decline *all* invitations extended in hotel lobbies.

Thursday, January 10, 1986, can stand as a typical day during my stay in New York. I had three appointments, the first with Sally Avery, the widow of Milton Avery, who lives on Central Park West. I rode uptown on the subway looking at the graffiti, memorizing my questions and sitting next to a conservatively dressed Japanese businessman who, sitting next to his conservatively dressed six-year-old son, was intently reading *Soldier of Fortune* magazine.

Mrs. Avery lives in a beautiful Art Deco building; her apartment is filled with Avery's work—portraits and landscapes with simple, flat shapes and lyrical colors. We sat on a couch, across from a large Avery seascape. Just as we were about to begin, my tape recorder refused to work, so, after several sweaty minutes of wrestling with it, I decided to take notes. Mrs. Avery is smart, articulate, and direct; she has a firm memory and an ironic sense of people—particularly of Rothko's first wife, Edith Sachar, who had once said of Milton Avery's work, "I wouldn't hang one in my bathroom." Edith, Mrs. Avery told me, had wanted Rothko to quit painting "because he didn't sell anything," so he could work for a jewelry business Edith had started. After they divorced, Rothko declared that living with Edith "was like living with a refrigerator." Yet in the later years of their marriage Edith, according to Mrs. Avery, would vacation by herself at Woodstock, where she was "openly unfaithful" to Rothko.

At noon I left these elegant surroundings, walked to a nearby Seventh Avenue coffee shop, drank coffee, and ate a toasted corn muffin while transcribing my notes. I found an electronics store, where the man behind the counter pronounced my tape recorder beyond repair. I bought a new one, slowly negotiating the price down to only a third more than what I had paid for the same, apparently faulty machine in Berkeley. My next appointment—with Ray ("Cowboy") Kelly, who had worked as Rothko's assistant in the mid-1960s—now took me from Central Park West to the Lower East Side. On the subway ride down I discovered that my original tape recorder hadn't worked because I had unconsciously pushed the "pause" button.

When I arrived at Kelly's walk-up on Broome Street, he wasn't there; a couple in their twenties were, like everyone else in New York City, eating Chinese takeout. The young man told me that Kelly was working "in the garden," and that he would take me around to him as soon as he finished his sweet and sour pork. I looked around the large, gray, one-room apartment. The couple were eating at a work table cluttered with art materials and food containers; there were a couple of mattresses on the floor; expressionistic paintings of political subjects—done in high-intensity yellows and reds—were hung on the walls; and across the room a TV, mounted on a tripod, played cartoons. When told that Kelly was "in the garden," I had imagined him on his hands and knees in the dirt working with a trowel, but I couldn't imagine where in this neighborhood a garden could be. Maybe on the roof? As it turned out, the "garden" was a neighborhood "sculpture garden," and "Cowboy" Kelly—tall, cheerful, wearing a ten-gallon hat and rimless spectacles—was presiding over its creation, out of old car parts, mattress springs, and other rusty metal junk, on an empty corner lot on Christie Street a few blocks away.

There, in my new Yves Saint Laurent overcoat, gray wool scarf, black leather gloves, and briefcase bursting with tape recorders, I felt only slightly less out of place than I had when I was earlier sized up by Mrs. Avery's doorman. Kelly was friendly, but not exactly loquacious. He introduced me to the work crew—one of whom did line drawings in sidewalk concrete with a hammer and chisel. I asked where I could see his work. He said, "You're standing on one." As Kelly showed me around the sculpture garden, a German shepherd ran up and peed on what appeared to have been the metal frame of a small greenhouse; I made a joke. Kelly didn't laugh. He refused to be taped. When I asked him about his memories of Rothko, all he would say was, "Man, he was a fucking genius."

For my last interview of the day—with the art critic Clement Greenberg—I took the subway back up to Central Park West. Greenberg offered me a drink; I declined. He drank some sherry. I turned one of my tape recorders on, then spent much of my time (as I usually do) bending over it, checking to make sure that it was still working. In his conversation, as in his essays, Greenberg likes to lay down definitive, slightly enigmatic pronouncements, delivered in a quiet, halting voice.

He began by observing that he "found Rothko sympathetic, but I also found him very square." This remark put me in the position of having to seem so square that I had to ask Greenberg what he meant by "square." He meant, he explained, that Rothko's ideas about art were "banal." Now, I had to ask what did Greenberg mean by banal? The answer was that Rothko's ideas about art were "the commonplaces of art talk" at the time. The following afternoon I asked the art historian Irving Sandler about this, to me, surprising characterization of Rothko; Sandler replied, "Oh, that's what he says about *all* the painters." Greenberg also told me about a confrontation in which Rothko "blew up" at him because he had not liked a show of Rothko's.

In fact, Greenberg went on, Rothko was "a great painter from '49 to '55," but "after '55 he lost his stuff." Greenberg expounded on other painters—Pollock, Picasso—who had lost their stuff. Suddenly Greenberg muttered something about "a real drink" and switched to bourbon; I switched off my tape recorder. We talked some more about lost stuff and I soon had the feeling that he might well go on sipping Jack Daniels and making pronouncements for several hours. So I packed away my tape recorder and headed back for the shabby gentility of the Gramercy Park Hotel. On the subway I sat across from a young woman wearing chartreuse sneakers, chartreuse socks, black chino pants, a black leather jacket, and spiked chartreuse hair; she was reading a book called *Are We Having Fun Now?*

But not all biographical research has the anecdotal richness of interviewing. I've put in hundreds of hours peering into the microfilm readers at the San Francisco office of the Archives of American Art, a branch of the Smithsonian Institution which collects the papers of American artists and which also has an extensive oral history program. Moreover, since I am Rothko's first biographer, I've had to compile records of his birth, his immigration, his residences, his school and college experiences, his marriages, his divorce, and his medical and employment histories. In New York, I'd fill in time between interviews by reading at the local branch of the Archives of American Art or by examining the old city directories and phone books at the 42nd Street branch of the New York Public Library. Most of the other people using these records, I gathered from overheard conversation on the library line, were either private detectives in search of missing persons or middle-aged Americans in search of their family histories. As it turned out, I was a little of both.

Rothko had lived in Brooklyn during the 1930s, and one night I was seated at a microfilm reader looking through old Brooklyn phone books. I had been born in Brooklyn in 1935, and I realized that I was reading the phone book for the year *before* my parents were married. I decided to look them up. As I was reading the page which listed my father's family, I suddenly became aware that I had lowered my face so close to the glass of the microfilm reader that my nose was almost touching it and that the fingers of both my hands were pressed to the glass—as if I were trying to break *through* it.

My experience illustrates two crucial characteristics of biography. In the first place, a biographer is always straining, by way of some verbal or visual sign, to recover a lost past; the glass of the microfilm reader is both the transparent means to that past and the hard obstacle separating us from it. In the second place, my experience dramatizes the truth that every biography is also, to some degree, an autobiography. In fact, it is only the force of this autobiographical involvement that can explain why anyone would undertake this costly, time-consuming, and frustrating labor.

When I read biographies, I often find myself asking, "Why did *this* biographer choose *this* subject?" So why, then, did I choose Rothko? Biographers want to ride into eternity on the coattails of the great; and many of them, while enjoying the ride, take an ungrateful look under the coat to check for torn or sweat-stained shirts, middle-age paunch, navel lint, or other hidden signs of human imperfection. Again like detectives, biographers are voyeurs who enjoy being privy to secrets. I don't deny any of these motives; I take great pleasure in knowing certain things about Rothko that only I know, and I'll admit to the fantasy that writing this book will make me sufficiently well-known so that, in New York City, someone will ask the journalist Jimmy Breslin if he's related to *me*.

But these motives are too abstract: they explain biography, but not a *Rothko* biography. As to my involvement with him, I can give you a specific date: January 2, 1979. I had been in New York City at the Modern Language Association convention and had stayed on because my hotel offered three extra days at a very low rate. Two years before, my mother and younger brother—both of whom lived in New York—had died. My mother died of cancer at sixty-seven. My brother died of a sudden heart attack at thirty-two. Two weeks after I had graduated from high school in 1953, my father, at forty-nine, had dropped dead of a heart attack while sitting, reading the morning paper, on the Flatbush Avenue IRT. Now I was the sole survivor of my original family. I felt as though I wanted to spend some time in New York but as though I no longer really belonged there. But I didn't want to return to Berkeley either, where I was about to end a sixteen-year marriage—and the thought of *that* gave me the same feeling I get when entering turbulence in a 727 jet.

January 2 was a brilliant sunny day but very cold. Being a fifteen-year resident of Berkeley, California, I did not then own an overcoat. Wearing a light

Afterword

sweater, I set out on a walk in ten-degree weather. From midtown Manhattan I walked all the way down to and across the Brooklyn Bridge; for some reason, whenever I'm in New York, I always end up walking across the Brooklyn Bridge, even though when I actually lived there I'd been mugged one morning on the bridge—by an elegantly-dressed young man wielding the biggest, shiniest knife I had ever seen. This time, failing to get mugged, I wandered back uptown, hoping to catch pneumonia.

I ended up at the Guggenheim Museum, where, I had been told, there was a Rothko retrospective. But I probably went in to the museum as much to get out of the cold as to see the Rothkos. I certainly had no particular sense of his work. At the age of forty-four I had put in a fair number of hours at museums, but this time had come more out of an idea of myself as a cultivated person than out of any emotional responsiveness to painting.

At the Guggenheim I took the elevator to the top level, then began walking down the museum's long winding ramp. I have no memories of looking at Rothko's figurative paintings of the 1930s or his surrealist works of the 1940s. What I *do* remember is being transfixed, swept up really, by the eloquent simplicity of the paintings that Rothko began to do in 1949. Empty and luminous, they seemed ebullient, ecstatic, a visionary alternative to the entanglements of my daily life. Yet their emptiness sometimes seemed a void, an annihilating vacancy that came from some profound sense of loss. Both Rothko's elation and his despair were moods I was particularly ready to experience in January of 1979.

I didn't leave the Guggenheim that day vowing to write this book. In fact, I didn't actually start working on it until seven years later; but my emotional response to his paintings was the beginning of my interest in Rothko. And one question that I did formulate that first day was how Rothko at forty-seven—just three years older than I was then—was able to re-form his work, his life, his *self*. I later learned that Rothko's second marriage in the mid-1940s and the birth of his first child in 1950 contributed to the elation of his new work, just as the death of his mother in 1948 contributed to its melancholy.

Yet Rothko did not sustain his exhilaration of the early 1950s for very long. By the end of that decade his colors had grown darker, his mood more somber, a movement that culminated in the "Black on Grey" works of the last year of his life. Circling down through the last few turns of the ramp at the Guggenheim exhibit was like a descent into a stark, airless hell.

My biography of Rothko began with my love of his paintings; but I was also moved to find out how Rothko, at mid-life, managed to liberate himself and his work and then, a little more than fifteen years later, how Rothko, now eminent, wealthy, and productive, felt trapped within his format, his marriage, his success. Since, in the seven years between seeing the Guggenheim show and beginning work on my book, I remarried and, at fifty, became the father of my third daughter, exploring how Rothko did it and then how he undid it was not, for me, a mere intellectual exercise. These and other issues from Rothko's life are not the only issues I've treated in this book; but they *are* the issues that originally activated me.

. . .

In writing the book itself, I have attempted to construct a detailed narrative of Rothko's life; to create a complex sense of the tensions, conflicts, and contradictions of his character; to suggest the changing network of social, historical, and cultural forces (especially art institutions) within which his life and work were shaped; to show how the life affected the work and the work, in turn, affected the life; and to exemplify a way of looking at and reflecting about Rothko's paintings.

My assumptions in writing about Rothko's paintings are expressivist, even though Rothko in 1958 declared himself "anti-expressionist." And my procedures in writing about his life have been empirical and narrative—i.e., biographical—even though Rothko's work strove to transcend the biographical (or historical) self. Rothko's resistance to my way of approaching him, in fact, created a tension that both stimulated me and kept me self-conscious about merely imposing my own methods on his life and work.

In my view, the ultimate justification of any critical method comes from what it *does,* and any readers who feel that this book has deepened or enriched or complicated their sense of Rothko's paintings can stop here.

But in the academic world, both expressive theory and biographical narrative have been called into question, and in an essay by J. R. R. Christie and Fred Orton, "Writing on a Text of the Life" (*Art History* 11, 4 [December 1988]:545–64), they have been called into question in relation to Rothko. For this reason, and because this essay reflects common attitudes among both literary critics and art historians, I want to examine its principal arguments.

Christie/Orton begin by taking up Richard Wollheim's assertion that "the greatness" of Rothko's *Red on Maroon* (1959) ultimately lies "in its expressive quality," which he defines as "a form of suffering and sorrow," "somehow barely or fragilely contained."[1] But according to Christie/Orton, "there is no way in which direct, unmediated feeling can be put into, and disinterestedly taken out of, the surface of a painting." "Inner experience only enters consciousness when it finds a language," they say, so Wollheim's expressive account of art omits those elements of "translation and rhetoric" which necessarily mediate between artist and painting, or painting and viewer. Then, subjecting Wollheim to a social critique, Christie/Orton place him in that "class of cultural managers which, because of its professional skills, cosmopolitanism and education, productive and distributive talents, has become responsible for the legitimation, ratification and validation of artistic culture." It is the prerogative of such authorities to "fix" the emotive meanings of paintings like *Red on Maroon* for less expert—i.e., nonprofessional—viewers.

But since expressive claims about a work are not easily justified by appeal to visual features on the surface of the painting, Christie/Orton continue, such claims must often be made credible by appeal to the personality and life of the individual artist. For "though paintings cannot be caused to be gloomy, suffering and sorrowful, people can." So biographies are produced, as a means of amplifying and justifying the views of cultural managers.

At this point, Christie/Orton discuss poststructuralist critiques which, asserting the priority of language, render obsolete the enabling assumptions of traditional biography—i.e., "persons as unitary identities, authors as producers of texts, contexts as relevant to texts, sources as access to lived history, 'beginnings' and 'origins' as explanatory foundation." If, for example, "the human subject attains its subjectivity in and through language," then it is "inevitably subjected," dominated by those "discursive forms" in cultural control at the moment. So what used to be thought of as persons are now themselves "signifiers," and once *that* happens, biography seems consigned to the trash heap of human history.

Yet, Christie/Orton are "loath to abandon" biography. Committed to "a Marxist history of art," they wish to preserve some hope of recovering the past. To this end, seeking to negotiate their way between Derrida and Marx, they propose a new form, the "biograph," which would represent the individual subject as plural. "Thanks to those aspects of critical theory which give us the pluralized subject we see that the biographies of the artist—biography must be indelibly plural—can be written as a pattern of possibilities." More broadly, they envision a new art history—"a discourse of the second order"—that would examine both paintings and art talk within the "discursive contexts" that produced them.

The notion of the biograph is a provocative one, resembling some of the possibilities suggested by James Clifford in "'Hanging Up Looking Glasses at Odd Corners': Ethnobiographical Prospects."[2] But what would biographies as patterns of possibilities actually look or read like? Christie/Orton don't say, and their proposal is so vague that it comes across as a wished-for rather than a genuine solution—the more so as it is contradicted by the biographical practice in their own essay.

Afterword

Christie/Orton close by returning to Wollheim, considering his statements about Rothko both in the context of Wollheim's own biography and as constructing a certain biography of Rothko. "In so doing we would still be studying the biographical, however problematized, and now in doubled form." Earlier, they have cited Wollheim's position as Grote Professor of Mind and Logic at the University of London, as the author of *Art and Its Objects,* and they identify the journal, *Studio International,* where his remarks about Rothko were originally published, as "the most important international journal of contemporary art published in the UK." At the end of their essay, they place Wollheim in art history—"at the moment of the demise of high Modernist painting"—and in relation to Rothko's life, since Wollheim's essay, published in December, 1970 "must" have been written in September or October of that year, "and in the knowledge of Rothko's suicide in March [sic]." In its "doubled form," biography turns out to be a simple, problem-free activity, allowing Christie/Orton not to represent Wollheim as a "pattern of possibilities," but, in a few sentences, to "fix" him as a cultural manager.

Moreover, throughout their essay, Christie/Orton continually hold on to some limited notion of human agency; and *that,* in the context of their essay, *is* problematical. For one thing, their critique of expressive theory assumes a linguistic determinism ("Inner experience only enters consciousness when it finds a language"), the same determinism they later attribute to critical theory and from which they then try to separate themselves. As Christie/Orton point out, "If Marx was correct, 'there is only one science: the science of history'. If Derrida is correct, there is only one science, the science of grammatology; and it is not a science, nor is it 'one'. Unless we opt outright for confrontation or simple stand-off, negotiation is enjoined." But this is equivalent to urging a treaty between Joseph Stalin and Pope Pius XII: there's no common space in which to negotiate.

Like many others, Christie/Orton end up logically trapped in the poststructuralist passageway they are trying to pass through and beyond. So they are forced simply to assume, to assert arbitrarily, a ground outside language, a Marxist position that grants subjects some limited but crucial power of agency.[3] "The project [of the biograph] would thus remain one of attaining historicity through the realization of human agency in the context of large-scale historical forces," they write. Described in these general terms, the biograph doesn't sound too different from the biography you have just read.

My purpose is not to fault Christie/Orton for their notion of human agency, but to agree with it, so I can fault their critique of expression in art, and specifically in Rothko's art. The model of expression they attack—feeling moving 'naturally' from artist to painting surface to viewer without resistance or complication from medium, convention, or cultural context—this simplified model is all-too-easy a target. One does not have to say that a painter is actually feeling emotion (or that feeling is all that's being expressed) as he or she paints, only that a complex of emotion and thought became available to him or her by the time the artistic process, its struggles with medium, conventions, contexts, was complete—and that that complex became available out of the artist's lived experience.

If it is possible for Marxist art historians to step outside the linguistic determinism assumed by critical theory—and provide "second"-order critiques of both painters and art critics—then, who knows, maybe it is possible for artists, too, to step outside and assert *some* human agency in an effort to express themselves on canvas. Christie/Orton's essay reveals one of the fundamental dilemmas of contemporary art and literary criticism: that it is very difficult, *in theory,* to argue for a prelinguistic self; and that it is equally difficult, in critical practice, to give up the idea.

Significantly, in their long essay Christie/Orton never offer any account of their own of Rothko's *Red on Maroon*. Like other left art critics—Serge Guilbaut in *How New York Stole the Idea of Modern Art* is an example—they do not have much to say about specific works of art, perhaps because they are engaged in a dispute *among* cultural managers. In writing the sections of this book dealing with Rothko's work, my own effort has been to provide a record of the transactions between these paintings and one patient and sympathetic viewer who carefully attempted to feel his way into the paintings, and to relate his reactions to the formal, visual properties of those paintings. I am less interested in fixing meanings than in encouraging others to spend time with these rich and moving works.

Berkeley
October 2, 1992

Documentation

I have tried to keep the notes to a minimum while also making my sources of quotation and information clear to my reader. Unless otherwise indicated, interviews were conducted by me. With my own interviews, after the first citation, I do not footnote if my source is named in the text. With interviews done by the Archives of American Art or by the Mark Rothko Foundation, I provide a full citation the first time I refer to a particular interview; thereafter I provide a shorter form. For untranscribed interviews done by the Archives of American Art, no page numbers are given.

In quoting from Rothko's unpublished writings I have corrected typographical and spelling errors.

ABBREVIATIONS

Archives and Collections

	AAA	Archives of American Art
	AIC	Art Institute of Chicago
	BNP	Barnett Newman Papers, AAA
	BPP	Betty Parsons Papers, AAA
	BRP	Bernard Reis Papers, AAA
	CSP	Clay Spohn Papers, AAA
	DSP	David Smith Papers, AAA
	ESP	Ethel Schwabacher Papers, AAA
	FM	Fogg Museum, Harvard University
	FMPSP	Federation of Modern Painters and Sculptors Papers, AAA
	FVOCP	Francis V. O'Connor Papers, AAA
	GMA	Guggenheim Museum Archive
	GKP	Gladys Kashdin Papers, AAA
	HFP	Herbert Ferber Papers, AAA
	KKP	Katharine Kuh Papers, AAA

Documentation

LKP	Louis Kaufman Papers, AAA
LSF	Lee Seldes Files, Lee Seldes, New York City
MOMA	Museum of Modern Art, New York
MRA	Mark Rothko Archive, Kate Rothko and Christopher Rothko
MRF	Mark Rothko Files
NGA	National Gallery of Art
PC	Phillips Collection
RMA	Robert Motherwell Archive, Greenwich, Conn.
TGA	Tate Gallery Archive
UWP	Ulfert Wilke Papers, AAA
WSP	William Seitz Papers, AAA

Published Sources

AACR	Gustave Harrow, *Art, the Artist, and the Consequences of Rothko* (Minneapolis, 1979).
AR	Dore Ashton, *About Rothko* (New York, 1983).
BN,SWI	*Barnett Newman, Selected Writings and Interviews,* ed. John P. O'Neill (New York, 1990).
"JL"	Letter, June 7, 1943, to Edward Alden Jewell of the *New York Times*; signed by Mark Rothko and Adolph Gottlieb, though Barnett Newman helped write the letter; published in the *Times* on June 13, 1943; reprinted in *MR,* pp. 77–78. Since the text is brief and easily available, I will not footnote quotations when I mention the title in my text.
LMR	Lee Seldes, *The Legacy of Mark Rothko* (New York, 1978).
MR	*Mark Rothko, 1903–1970* (London: Tate Gallery, 1987).
MR,AR	Diane Waldman, *Mark Rothko, 1903–1970: A Retrospective* (New York: Abrams, 1978).
MRHM	Marjorie B. Cohn, ed., *Mark Rothko's Harvard Murals* (Center for Conservation and Technical Studies, Harvard University Art Museums, 1988).
"MR:PAAM"	John Fischer, "Mark Rothko: Portrait of the Artist as an Angry Man," *Harper's Magazine,* 241 (July 1970):16–23.
MR,SMP	*Mark Rothko, The Seagram Mural Project* (Liverpool, England, 1988).
MR,WP	Bonnie Clearwater, *Mark Rothko: Works on Paper* (New York, 1984).
"PMA"	"The Portrait and the Modern Artist," typescript for a joint radio broadcast by Mark Rothko and Adolph Gottlieb on

WNYC (New York), October 13, 1943, reprinted in *MR*, pp. 78–81. Because this text is brief and easily available, I do not footnote quotations when I mention the title in my text.

RC   Susan Barnes, *The Rothko Chapel, An Act of Faith* (Austin, Texas, 1989).

"RWP"   Mark Rothko, "The Romantics Were Prompted," in *MR*, pp. 83–84. Originally published in *Possibilities* 1 (Winter 1947–48):84. Because this text is brief and easily available, I do not footnote quotations from it when I give its title in my text.

Unpublished Sources

"HN"   Hebrew Notebook; contains seven poems, a brief story, and a play, all written in Hebrew, by Rothko, sometime after his arrival in Portland (MRA).

"JC"   Alfred Jensen Conversations; conversations with Mark Rothko that were later transcribed by Alfred Jensen. Many of these were destroyed by Jensen after a falling out with Rothko; the surviving ones were transcribed by Katharine Kuh and provided to me by Regina Bogat.

"The Matter of Rothko"   Refers to the 15,000 pages of transcript, 5,000 pages of depositions, and approximately 1,000 exhibits in the trial of the suit over Rothko's estate. See *LMR* for a full account of this lawsuit. The record and exhibits can be found in the Records Room (402), 31 Chambers Street, New York City.

"ND"   Drafts of a talk or essay by Rothko on Nietzsche's *The Birth of Tragedy*, in MRA.

"PL"   Lecture given by Rothko at Pratt Institute in October, 1958; based on text in MRA. I quote the entire lecture—and the question-and-answer session that followed it—in Chapter 13. When I quote from it elsewhere, I do not provide a footnote if I mention the title in my text.

"SB"   "The Scribble Book," a notebook kept by Mark Rothko probably in the late 1930s (MRP, AAA). Since it is fairly short, and in order to avoid cluttering my text with citations, I have not provided page numbers for my quotations from this text.

Notes

Chapter One

1. "MR:PAAM":16.
2. Robert Motherwell interview, January 20, 1987; and *AR*, p. 155.
3. "MR:PAAM":22.
4. *AR*, p. 155.
5. Herbert Ferber interview, January 27, 1987.
6. Regina Bogat interview, February 5, 1986.
7. Dr. Albert Grokest interview, January 34, 1986.
8. Kenneth and Elaine Rabin interview, August 12, 1985; Stanley Kunitz, interview with Avis Berman, Part I, p. 24, AAA.
9. Regina Bogat interview.
10. Anne-Marie Levine interview, January 17, 1986.
11. *LMR*, p. 46.
12. Ibid., pp. 46, 50.
13. Dorothy Miller, interview with Avis Berman, May 4, 1981, p. 3, AAA.
14. "MR:PAAM":21.
15. Stanley Kunitz, interview with Avis Berman, Part I, p. 24, AAA.
16. Katharine Kuh, interview with Avis Berman, n.d., p. 9, AAA.
17. MRF, MOMA.
18. Ward Jackson interview, February 6, 1990.
19. Quotations from Stanley Kunitz in this paragraph are from his interview with Avis Berman, Part I, p. 23, AAA.
20. Kenneth and Elaine Rabin interview.
21. MRF, MOMA.
22. "MR:PAAM":18.
23. Ibid.

Chapter Two

1. W. Evans-Gordon, *The Alien Immigrant* (London, 1902), pp. 84–91.
2. Yudel Flior, *Dvinsk, The Rise and Decline of a Town,* trans. Bernard Sachs (Johannesburg, South Africa, 1956), p. 13.

As I indicate in my Afterword, the *Dvinchanin* book establishes that the Rothkowitz family lived at 17 Shosseynaya in 1913. Gesel Maimin, a former inhabitant of Dvinsk now living in Israel, told me that Jacob Rothkowitz is listed as living on Shosseynaya, in *Address-Calendar of the Town and Fortress-Depot of Dvinsk for 1902* (Dvinsky Listok, 1902), p. 53a. In 1902, the houses in Dvinsk didn't have numbers, but it seems quite likely that the family lived at the 17 Shosseynaya address all during the ten years Rothko lived in Dvinsk.

3. In *Dvinchanin,* Rothko's sister, Sonia, is listed as Rothkovitch, the family name also used by Rothko's brother, Albert Roth, in one of his interviews with Lee Seldes (LSF). Since Rothko's father came from a village in what is now Lithuania, the Germanic spelling, Rothkowitz (*rot kopf,* or red head), is more likely the original spelling, and it is the one the family used once they arrived in the United States.

4. My account of the town's history is based on *Latvia, Country and People,* ed. J. Rutkis (Stockholm, 1967), pp. 195–96; Moshe Amir (Bliach), "Dvinsk," in *The Jews in Latvia* (Tel Aviv, 1971), pp. 262–75; Flior, *Dvinsk;* and my interviews with Leo Truksans (March 25, 1991), Henriks Soms (March 26, 1991), Genovefa Barkovska (March 26, 1991) and Joel Weinberg (March 28, 1991), all of the Daugavpils Pedagogical Institute.

5. *Cross-Road Country—Latvia,* ed. Edgars Andersons (Waverly, Iowa, 1953), p. 88.

6. See Flior, *Dvinsk,* p. 24.

7. Yudel Flior describes the three railroad stations in *Dvinsk,* p. 12. The detail about the rooms for the czar comes from my interview with Mr. Leo Truksans of the Daugavpils Pedagogical Institute.

8. Professor Genovefa Barkovska interview.

9. In 1905 the population was 76,588; in 1913, 113,048 (Leo Truksans interview).

10. Flior, *Dvinsk,* p. 20.

11. Ibid., p. 17.

12. Interview with Ruth Cloudman, n.d., p. 4, AAA.

13. Flior, *Dvinsk,* p. 17.

14. Moise Roth interview, June 27, 1985.

15. Amir (Bliach), "Dvinsk," p. 268.

16. Flior, *Dvinsk,* pp. 98–115.

17. Ibid., p. 105. Flior describes the political situation in Dvinsk in chapters 8–12; the town's Jewish political parties are also discussed in Amir (Bliach), "Dvinsk," pp. 268–72.

18. Flior, *Dvinsk,* pp. 129–54.

19. Ibid., pp. 160–67.

20. Louis Greenberg, *The Jews in Russia* (New Haven, 1951), vol. 2, p. 87.

21. Flior, *Dvinsk,* pp. 142f.

22. Moise Roth interview.

23. Interview with Ruth Cloudman, p. 4, AAA.

24. Herbert Ferber, interview with Phyllis Tuchman, June 2, 1981, p. 5, AAA.

25. Rothko's father's real—or original—first name may have been Benjamin, the name Rothko gives on the certificates for both his marriages and the name that appears on some of Rothko's Portland school records. He is listed as Jacob in the *Address-Calendar of the Town and Fortress-Depot of Dvinsk,* and Jacob is the name that appears, for example, on his gravestone at the Ahavai Shalom cemetery in Portland. My date for Jacob Rothkowitz's birth is taken from this gravestone. Michalishek was first mentioned to me as Jacob's birthplace by Moise Roth and was confirmed by a number of family members. Moise Roth recalled that Jacob's father

"worked for the state or government keeping records." The *Address-Calendar* lists Jacob's father's name as Joseph.

26. Menke Katz, *Burning Village* (New York, 1972), pp. 12–14; this book of poems deals with Katz's memories of Michalishek and its destruction during the First World War.

27. Interview with Ruth Cloudman, pp. 12–13, AAA.

28. Kenneth and Elaine Rabin interview. The date of the marriage of Kate Goldin and Jacob Rothkowitz is not certain; I arrived at the year by adding sixteen years to her year of birth, but this method assumes that family memory of her as sixteen when she was married is correct. The date of Kate Rothkowitz's birth is taken from her gravestone at the Ahavai Shalom cemetery in Portland. The birth dates of Rothko's sister and brothers have been added by Milton Rabin to the interview with Sonia Allen, by Ruth Cloudman, n.d., p. 1, AAA.

29. Both Sonia and Moise remembered speaking Russian at home (Sonia Allen, interview with Cynthia J. McCabe, April 16, 1975, p. 10; Moise Roth, interview with Ruth Cloudman, p. 6, AAA).

30. Robert Olmos, "Mrs. Allen About Her Brother," "Northwest Magazine," *The Sunday Oregonian,* March 29, 1970, p. 7; Sonia Allen, interview with Ruth Cloudman, p. 6, AAA.

31. Sonia Allen, interview with Ruth Cloudman, p. 1, AAA; Sonia Allen, interview with Cynthia J. McCabe, p. 4; Dr. Sydney Weinstein interview, May 6, 1986; Moise Roth, interview with Ruth Cloudman, pp. 2–3, AAA.

32. Quoted in an essay on Rothko by Philippe Hosiasson, an excerpt from which I found in LSF, translated from the French by Lee Seldes.

33. Kenneth and Elaine Rabin interview.

34. Ibid.; on Jacob's role as local scribe, see also Sonia Allen, interview with Cynthia J. McCabe, p. 11. Time has Christianized the story of the Sabbath goy: Jews don't believe in "hell."

35. Kenneth and Elaine Rabin interview; Moise Roth, interview with Ruth Cloudman, p. 23, AAA; Moise Roth interview; interview with Richard and Johnnie Mae Roth, November 7, 1986.

36. Haskalah, the Jewish Enlightenment, which stressed secular education, including learning the national language and culture, seems the intellectual context which first shaped Jacob Rothkowitz. In Russia, however, haskalah, aiming at assimilation, was antirevolutionary; Jacob's combination of haskalah with dissident politics was highly unusual.

37. Quoted in *AR,* p. 5.

38. *AR,* p. 5; Sonia Allen, interview with Cynthia J. McCabe, p. 6; Moise Roth interview; Moise Roth, interview with Ruth Cloudman, p. 15, AAA; and *LMR,* p. 12.

39. Kate Rothko interview, February 25, 1986 and March 31, 1987; Robert Carleton Hobbs and Gail Levin, *Abstract Expressionism, The Formative Years* (New York, 1978), p. 119; Murray Israel interview, May 20, 1988.

40. Rothko told the quoted version of this story to Al Jensen; Jensen's account is quoted in "Budd Hopkins on Budd Hopkins," *Art in America* 61 (Summer 1973):92–93. Jensen also related the mass-grave story to Ulfert Wilke ("Diary," October 12, 1962, UWP,

AAA) and Wilke repeated the story to Rothko, who confirmed it (see Wilke's diary entry for March 6, 1963, UWP, AAA).

41. All of the historians I talked with in Daugavpils, as well as the officials with the local Latvian-Jewish Cultural Society, stated unequivocally that there had been no pogroms in Dvinsk, a view supported by Flior's memoir, *Dvinsk*; they also said that they had never heard of mass graves in connection with pogroms, though they would not rule it out as a possibility.

42. Kate Rothko interview; Joy Spalding interview, June 26, 1986; Sonia Allen, interview with Cynthia J. McCabe, p. 12; Sonia Allen, interview with Ruth Cloudman, p. 5, AAA.

43. Kate Rothko interview.

44. Ibid. Moise said that Rothko was tutored privately at home, both in my interview with him and his interview with Ruth Cloudman, p. 6, AAA. But Sonia stated that Rothko was sent to a parochial school (interview with Cynthia J. McCabe, p. 2). Rothko himself said that he had gone to *cheder*. Possibly, he attended both at different times.

45. Ulfert Wilke, "Diary," September 28, 1965, UWP, AAA.

46. "HN," MRA. The notebook itself was clearly manufactured in the United States, so the poems were written here, not in Dvinsk. Exactly when, it is impossible to say.

47. My description is based on a turn-of-the-century map of Dvinsk (provided to me by Professor Henriks Soms of the Daugavpils Pedagogical Institute) and on two 1903 postcard photographs of Shosseynaya sent to me by Gesel Maimin. Both map and postcards confirm the recollection of Rothko's brother Moise, who told his nephew, Milton Rabin, that the family "lived one block east of the river near a bridge" (Milton Rabin to author, June 11, 1987).

48. Flior, *Dvinsk,* pp. 87, 180; the rising rents are reported in *Dvinchanin,* n.p.

49. Interview with Lee Seldes, March 10, 1975, LSF.

50. Flior, *Dvinsk,* p. 11.

51. Ibid., p. 11; and Andersons, ed. *Cross-Road Country—Latvia,* p. 199.

52. Julian and Dorothy Roth interview, September 9, 1986; Moise Roth interview; Sonia Allen, interview with Cynthia J. McCabe, p. 3.

53. Moise Roth, interview with Ruth Cloudman, p. 4, AAA; Sonia Allen, interview with Cynthia J. McCabe, p. 11; Moise Roth, interview with Ruth Cloudman, p. 6, AAA; Sonia Allen, interview with Cynthia J. McCabe, p. 11; Moise Roth interview.

54. The information about Sam and Bessie Weinstein comes from the U.S. Census records, 1900, National Archives, Washington, D.C.; see also the Portland City directories starting in 1898 and William Toll, *The Making of an Ethnic Middle Class: Portland Jewry Over Four Generations* (Albany, New York, 1982); a photograph of Sam and Nate Weinstein appears on p. 114. See also my fig. 10. For further information about the Weinstein family, I've relied on my interviews with Dr. Sydney Weinstein and Arthur Gage, November 8, 1986. The "nephew" quoted is Mr. Gage.

55. List or Manifest of Alien Passengers for the United States, SS *Main,*

arrival January 16, 1913, National Archives, Washington, D.C. My account of Moise and Albert's journey is based on my interviews with Moise Roth, Julian and Dorothy Roth, Richard and Johnny Mae Roth, and Kate Rothko.

56. List or Manifest of Alien Passengers for the United States, SS *Czar*, arrival August 17, 1913, National Archives, Washington, D.C.

57. Ed Weinstein, interview with Barbara Shikler, June 14, 1983, p. 2, AAA; Sonia Allen, interview with Cynthia J. McCabe, p. 10.

58. Regina Bogat interview; Edith (Sachar) Carson, interview with Walter Hopps, October 19, 1972 (untranscribed), AAA.

59. "MR:PAAM":17.

60. A watercolor study for this painting shows a melancholy, ghostly figure in the gray area at the right, hovering beside and looking toward the three main figures. Rothko discarded the ghostly presence in the painting, perhaps because it made the point about being haunted by the past too explicitly and literally. The watercolor is Item 0.4 in Box 2/4, Mark Rothko, Prints and Drawings, NGA.

61. Sonia Allen, interview with Cynthia J. McCabe, p. 3.

62. Ibid., p. 6; the address comes from the *Portland City Directory*, 1914, and was confirmed by Moise Roth. It is important to know that Portland street numbers were changed in the early 1930s. The old 834 Front, for instance, was at the intersection of Front and Curry, quite far from the current 834 Front. My description of the house comes from *Insurance Maps of Portland, Oregon* (New York, 1909; corrected to 1926). The house no longer exists, apparently torn down when Front Street was widened in 1941. Both the city directories and the insurance maps are available at the Oregon Historical Society, Portland.

63. Moise Roth, interview with Ruth Cloudman, p. 8, AAA.

64. Moise Roth interview; Moise Roth, interview with Ruth Cloudman, p. 11, AAA. Notices of the death of Jacob Rothkowitz appeared in the *Oregonian*, March 28, 1914, p. 13, and March 29, 1914, section III, p. 8. Kate Rothko told me that the cause of her grandfather's death was colon cancer.

65. Minutes, March 27, 1914, Ahavai Shalom Synagogue, at the Jewish Historical Society, Portland, Oregon.

66. AR, p. 158.

67. Leon Grinberg and Rebecca Grinberg, *Psychoanalytic Perspectives on Migration and Exile* (New Haven, 1989), p. 125. My discussion of Rothko's migration is indebted to this rich study.

68. Albert Roth, interview with Lee Seldes, May 1975, LSF; Moise Roth, interview with Ruth Cloudman, p. 6, AAA.

69. Interview with Lee Seldes, February 1976, LSF.

70. "RWP," MR, p. 83.

71. Morris Calden interview, February 14, 1986; "PL," MRA.

72. Moise Roth, interview with Ruth Cloudman, p. 2, AAA.

73. Kenneth and Elaine Rabin interview; Joy Spalding interview.

74. The quotations about Kate Rothkowitz are taken from my interviews with Kenneth and Elaine Rabin, Milton and Joy Rabin, Joy Spalding, and Dorothy and Phil Reiter.

75. Kenneth and Elaine Rabin interview; Milton and Joy Rabin interview; Joy Spalding interview; Phil and Dorothy Reiter interview.

76. *AR,* p. 129.

77. David Anfam, who is working on a Rothko catalogue raisonné, informs me that the words "Rothkowitz" and "Family" are written on the back of this painting, and points out that reviews, probably referring to this painting, identify it as "Family." He suggests that "Family" is the title of the painting and that "Rothkowitz" is the name of the painter. The title "The Rothkowitz Family" was apparently arrived at by the Mark Rothko Foundation. Even if the title is "Family," Rothko drew on his own emotional past to create this symbolic depiction of mother, father, and child.

78. Sonia Allen, interview with Cynthia J. McCabe, p. 6; Moise Roth interview; Moise Roth, interview with Ruth Cloudman, p. 7, AAA; Arthur Gage interview; Gus Solomon interview, June 24, 1985.

79. Kenneth and Elaine Rabin interview; Julian and Dorothy Roth interview; Richard and Johnnie Mae Roth interview. Rothko's attendance at Failing is verified by both the school census forms for 1913–14 and the class lists for Failing's first grade. Class lists are available through the Records Management Department, Portland Public Schools; census forms are in the Oregon State Archives, Salem.

80. Interview with Cynthia J. McCabe, p. 11.

81. Alex and Sloan Tampkin interview, July 5, 1987; Rothko's memory of the wintry landscape is quoted in Ulrich Seelman Eggebert, *Badische Neuste Nachrichten* (Karlsruhe, Germany, 1962), collected in "Critical Reviews: Mark Rothko," in the MRF, MOMA.

82. Regina Bogat interview.

83. Max Gordon interview, August 9, 1985; Olmos, "Mrs. Allen About Her Brother," p. 4; Toll, *The Making of an Ethnic Middle Class,* p. 62; Manly A. Labby, interview, January 27, 1975 and February 7, 1976, Jewish Historical Society of Oregon, p. 4. Moise Roth also remembered the fighting for street corners (interview with Ruth Cloudman, p. 12, AAA); Sonia Allen, interview with Ruth Cloudman, p. 8, AAA.

84. Toll, *The Making of an Ethnic Middle Class,* p. 109; for accounts of the Portland Jewish community, see that text, passim; and E. Kimbark MacColl, *The Growth of a City: Power and Politics in Portland, Oregon, 1915–1950* (Portland, 1979), pp. 47–63.

85. *Portland City Directory,* 1915 and 1920; these addresses also appear on the school census forms from Rothko's time at Shattuck Elementary School and Lincoln High School.

86. Toll, *The Making of an Ethnic Middle Class,* p. 73.

87. Albert Roth, interview with Lee Seldes, May 1975, LSF. My information on Rothko's school career comes from class lists for Shattuck Elementary School and Lincoln High School and Rothko's transcript from Lincoln; his grades have been deleted from the copy of his high school transcript that was sent to me.

88. Aaron Director interview, July 2, 1985.

89. Rothko's early interest in music is mentioned by both Moise (interview with Ruth Cloudman, p. 13, AAA) and Sonia (interview with Ruth Cloudman,

p. 9, AAA). Rothko's ability to play the piano by ear was recalled by many of his relatives and friends.

My information about Rothko's Dramatic Art course comes from his high school transcript. Possibly, Rothko's interest in the theater went back to his time in Dvinsk, where there was a Russian theater, producing plays such as *Hamlet* and giving them "a Socialistic tinge" (Flior, *Dvinsk,* p. 148).

90. Mark Rothko, interview with Gladys Kashdin, May 4, 1965, GKP, AAA. Unfortunately, Rothko refused to let Kashdin tape their conversation, which has survived in the form of her notes; O[scar] C[ollier], "Mark Rothko . . . ," *The New Iconograph* 4 (Fall 1947):41; according to Rothko's Lincoln High and Yale transcripts, he did not study art in either high school or college; the Portland Art Museum told me there is no record of any Rothkowitz taking any of their children's art classes.

91. On the art program, see the annual reports of the Portland, Oregon, public schools, beginning with the *43rd Annual Report, 1915-1916.*

92. Edward Weinstein's recollections are quoted from his letter to Clair Zamoisky, February 24, 1978, MRF, GMA (Mr. Weinstein has his "uncle" addressing Rothko as "Mark," which I've corrected to "Marcus"). Arthur Gage also remembered Rothko drawing while working as a shipping clerk for a Weinstein uncle during the summer between his two years at Yale.

93. "MR:PAAM":17. Emma Goldman's forthcoming lectures were announced in the *Oregonian,* August 5, 1915; her arrest and fine were reported in the *Oregonian* for August 7, 8, 1915.

Rothko told Dore Ashton that he had attended some of these lectures (interview with Dore Ashton, February 24, 1986).

94. Cf. Rothko's Lincoln High transcript.

95. Kenneth Rabin remembered Rothko's distinction between Thucydides and Herodotus. Ernest Briggs recalled Rothko quoting Herodotus in one of his 1949 lectures at the California School of Fine Arts (interview with Barbara Shikler, July 12, 1982 and October 21, 1982, p. 6, AAA).

96. *The Cardinal* was Lincoln High's combination school newspaper, student literary magazine and, twice a year, school yearbook; my estimate of the Jewish population in the school is based on the admittedly imperfect (and stereotyping) method of using the names and photographs in the yearbook issues of *The Cardinal.* Max MacCoby's complaint appeared in *The Cardinal,* undated issue (between December 1920 and March 1921):75.

97. *The Cardinal* (June 1921)160; the "June Class Stock Show" lists Marcus Rothkowitz with "common name" as "Marcus," "reason for collection" as "his debating," and predicted profession as "pawn broker"; Max Naimark is listed with "common name" as "Max," "reason for collection" as "his similarity to Marcus," and his predicted profession as "Marcus' assistant." The anti-Semitism is clear.

98. Max Naimark to Clair Zamoiski, December 27, 1977, MRF, GMA.

99. *The Cardinal* (October 1920):33.

100. Ibid.:34-35.

101. On Pollock's adolescent rebellions, see B. H. Friedman, *Energy Made Visible: Jackson Pollock* (New York,

1974), pp. 8–11; Steven Naifeh and Gregory White Smith, *Jackson Pollock, An American Saga* (New York, 1989), pp. 132–36, 143–45; Deborah Solomon, *Jackson Pollock* (New York, 1987), pp. 41–42.

102. *The Cardinal* (May 1920):36.

103. Toll, *The Making of an Ethnic Middle Class,* pp. 58 and 102–3 and the oral histories at the Jewish Historical Society of Oregon, passim; Gilbert Sussman, interview with Jewish Historical Society of Oregon, 1976, p. 13.

104. John Higham, *Strangers in the Land: Patterns of American Nativism, 1900–1925* (New York, 1973), p. 215.

105. MacColl, *Growth of a City,* p. 138.

106. Ibid., pp. 139–58.

107. Ibid., pp. 156–62.

108. Richard and Johnnie Mae Roth interview.

109. Flior, *Dvinsk,* pp. 173, 175.

110. "Two Armies," in Katz, *Burning Village,* p. 33.

111. Flior, *Dvinsk,* pp. 179, 181.

112. Ibid., p. 183.

113. Portland, Oregon, Public Schools, *45th Annual Report, 1917–18* (Portland, 1918), p. 16.

114. *The Cardinal* (December 1918):25; (November 1919):36.

115. The MRA contains eight poems (and an untitled fragment), only two of which I would say were definitely written by Rothko: "Salutation" and "Walls of Mind: Out of the Past." One poem, "Beneath the Cypress," and the untitled fragment have the initials "M.B.F." at the end, suggesting they were written by Myrtle Forthun, a friend of Rothko's from Portland. In addition, there are five more poems, "They Who Had the Courage To Be Brave," "The Cypress Tree," and three gathered under the title "A Gallery of Portraits" ("The Lotus-Eater," "Sweet and Salt" and "The Bird of [Paradise]"). The MRA also contains a one-page fragment of a play, satirizing an acting company directed by a pretentious woman in a small provincial city; the subject probably derives from Rothko's experience with Josephine Dillon's acting company in Portland, in early 1924, so the play fragment was probably written during or after that time.

None of Rothko's poems are dated; nor do they contain any topical references which would help to date them. "Salutation," marked "Portland, Oregon" in the upper right corner of the typed page, could have been written while Rothko was a student at Lincoln High School or on a later visit to Portland, either when he returned for the summer at the end of each of his two years at Yale, or on one of his visits later in the 1920s.

Chapter Three

1. Toll, *The Making of an Ethnic Middle Class,* p. 77; Gus Solomon interview.

2. Stephen Steinberg, *The Academic Melting Pot: Catholics and Jews in American Higher Education* (New York, 1974), p. 9. On academic anti-Semitism in the 1920s, see also John Higham, *Send These to Me: Jews and Other Immigrants in Urban America* (New York, 1975), pp. 154–62; Marcia Graham Synnott, *The Half-Opened Door: Discrimination and Admissions at Harvard, Yale, and Princeton, 1900–1970* (Westport, Conn., 1979); and Dan A. Oren, *Joining The*

Club: A History of Jews and Yale (New Haven, 1986).

3. Oren, *Joining The Club,* p. 41, 43–45.

4. Papers of Frederick S. Jones, Yale Manuscripts and Archives Library, Yale University; Oren, *Joining The Club,* p. 41.

5. Thorstein Veblen, *The Higher Learning in America* (New York, 1957), pp. 88–89; Thomas Bergin, "My Native Country," in *My Harvard, My Yale,* ed. Diana Dubois (New York, 1982), p. 163; F. O. Matthiessen, *From the Heart of Europe* (New York, 1948), p. 71.

6. Oren, *Joining The Club,* p. 52.

7. Ibid., pp. 27–28; Max Naimark to Diane Waldman, February 14, 1978, MRF, GMA (emphasis in original); Aaron Director, interview with Lee Seldes, February 1976, LSF.

8. Rothko's yearbook entry for the Yale Class of 1925 mentions his cousins Jacob Weinstein, Yale 1908; Alexander Weinstein, Yale 1909; Isadore E. Weinstein, Yale 1923; and Daniel Weinstein, of the class of 1920.

9. *New Haven City Directory,* 1921; Sanborn Insurance Maps for New Haven; and Stan Tamarkin, "The Miracle of Oak Street: An Oral History of a Neighborhood," in Arthur A. Chiel, *Looking Back* (privately printed, 1975)—all at the New Haven Historical Society.

10. Rabbi Chiel liked to reprint in his column old newspaper articles about local Jewish families; on February 13, 1975, he reprinted a 1918 story about the Weinstein family. That Esther Weinstein was Jacob Rothkowitz's sister is confirmed by Albert Roth, interview with Lee Seldes, March 10, 1975, LSF. Ed Weinstein (interview with Barbara Shikler, p. 6, AAA) said that Abraham Weinstein's name was originally Hirsch. Other information based on the New Haven city directories, 1921 and 1922.

11. Interview with Barbara Shikler, pp. 12–13, AAA.

12. Max Naimark to Diane Waldman, February 14, 1978, MRF, GMA; Aaron Director interview; Max Naimark, interview with Lee Seldes, n.d., LSF. According to Naimark, Rothko worked in a dining hall (LSF). Aaron Director said that Rothko had worked in a dining hall and picked up and delivered clothes for a university cleaners. In his interview with Lee Seldes, Director added that Rothko also worked as a messenger for the university (LSF). In his February 24, 1978 letter to Clair Zamoiski, Edward Weinstein stated that Rothko worked at the Yale student laundry and at two cleaners, both near the old Yale campus (MRF, GMA).

13. Max Naimark and Aaron Director interviews with Lee Seldes, LSF; Max Naimark to Clair Zamoiski, December 27, 1977, MRF, GMA.

14. Naimark recalled seeing Rothko drawing and sketching while in New Haven (Max Naimark to Clair Zamoiski, December 27, 1977, MRF, GMA, and Naimark, interview with Lee Seldes, LSF).

Rothko's sister, Sonia, said that he went to Yale to study law ("Mrs. Allen About Her Brother":17). She also recalled that her mother hoped Rothko would become an attorney (interview with Cynthia McCabe, p. 10). Aaron Director, in his interview with Lee Seldes, remembered that Rothko wanted to be an engineer (LSF). Rothko later told at least two people that he had intended to become a labor organizer; see Wallace Putnam, "Mark Rothko Told Me," *Arts Magazine* 48 (April 1974):45; and *Current Biography Yearbook,* ed. Charles Moritz (New York, 1961), p. 398. But the Yale University of 1921 was an odd place to prepare for such a career.

15. See catalogue, Yale University, 1921–22, the section on "The Freshman Year"; Rothko's Yale transcript (LSF); for an account of the institution of the Ph.B. degree, see George W. Pierson, *Yale: The University College, 1921–1937* (New Haven, 1955), pp. 203–6; and Aaron Director, interview with Lee Seldes, recalled Rothko's loss of interest in Yale.

16. Max Naimark to Clair Zamoiski, December 27, 1977, MRF, GMA; Simon Whitney to Diane Waldman, June 11, 1978, MRF, GMA.

17. *The Yale Saturday Evening Pest* (February 17, 1923):1.

18. Pierson, *Yale: The University College,* pp. 71–99; *Yale Alumni Weekly* 32 (February 23, 1923):643, 646.

19. *Yale Alumni Weekly* 32 (February 16, 1923):619, and (March 2, 1923): 677.

20. *Pest* (April 7, 1923):1; (February 17, 1923):1; (March 3, 1923):1.

21. *Pest* (March 17, 1923):1–2.

22. *Pest* (February 17, 1923):1; (April 7, 1923):1.

23. *Pest* (March 17, 1923):2; (March 3, 1923):1; (March 17, 1923):1; (February 17, 1923):1; (April 7, 1923):1; (March 17, 1923):1.

24. *Pest* (March 10, 1923):1–2.

25. *Pest* (May 26, 1923):1; (March 24, 1923):1; and Pierson, *Yale: The University College,* p. 140.

Charles A. Bennett, a young assistant professor of philosophy, functioned as unofficial mentor for the *Pest.* Bennett's *A Philosophical Study of Mysticism* (New Haven, 1923) mounts a defense of the creative individual who, rejecting "timidity, conventionality and uniformity," "shakes himself free from the tyranny of all external requirements and utilitarian tests" (pp. 169–70). His *At a Venture* (New York, 1924) collects humorous essays directed at a variety of social, political, and literary targets: conservativism, modern science, economists, militarists, patriots, hypocritical clergymen, etc. No Emma Goldman or even an H. L. Mencken, Bennett wrote as a genteel insider, but his mixture of mysticism, liberalism, and irony, along with his support of the *Pest,* established at least one friendly faculty presence at Yale.

26. Sonia Allen, interview with Cynthia J. McCabe, p. 10; Julian and Dorothy Roth interview.

27. That Rothko listed in the 1925 Yale yearbook the college work done by Sonia and Moise and the Yale degrees achieved by four of his Weinstein relatives shows how fully he had internalized these values and expectations.

28. "A Certain Spell," *Time,* 77, 10 (March 3, 1961):75; and "MR:PAAM": 22.

29. Mark Rothko, interview with Gladys Kashdin, GKP, AAA.

30. Jack Flam, *Matisse, The Man and His Art, 1869–1918* (Ithaca, 1986), p. 27.

31. Mark Rothko, interview with Gladys Kashdin, GKP, AAA.

32. MR,AR, p. 22. Rothko's papers contain a one-page fragment of a play which satirizes Dillon's company (MRA).

33. On Gable in Portland, see Lyn Tornabene, *Long Live the King: A Biography of Clark Gable* (New York, 1976), pp. 55–65.

34. George and Shirley Climo interview, October 15, 1986; Aaron Director interview; Arthur Gage interview.

35. "RWP," *MR,* p. 83.

36. Rothko states in the Yale yearbook for the class of 1925 that he was then studying at the New School of Design; he also mentions having attended the school in his suit against Lewis Browne (see below, this chapter).

I have not been able to find out very much about the New School of Design. According to the entry in the *American Art Annual* 21 (1924–25), the school was located at 1680 Broadway, had been founded in 1923, had eleven instructors and taught classes in "drawing, commercial illustration, costume design, fashion illustration and interior decoration." Tuition was $75 a term.

37. Interview with Mark Rothko printed in Karlen Mooradian, *The Many Worlds of Arshile Gorky* (Chicago, 1980), pp. 197–98.

38. Registration records and class lists at the Art Students League; Carl Goreff to Diane Waldman, October 6, 1978; Leo Goreff to Diane Waldman, November 6, 1978 (both in MRF, GMA); Carl Goreff interview, January 12, 1990.

39. Ed Weinstein, interview with Barbara Shikler, p. 18, AAA.

40. Joy Spalding interview; Elizabeth Till interview, June 19, 1985; Sonia Allen, interview with Cynthia J. McCabe, pp. 4 and 9.

41. On the early careers of both Chagall and Soutine, see Kenneth E. Silver and Romy Golan, *The Circle of Montparnasse: Jewish Artists in Paris, 1905–1945* (New York, 1985). The Soutine story appears on p. 31.

42. Irving Howe, *The World of Our Fathers* (New York, 1976), p. 575.

43. Stanley Kunitz originally made the remark in conversation with Rothko. "When I said that to him once, he enjoyed it; it made him feel very good. I meant that there was in him a rather magisterial authority, a sense of transcendence as well, a feeling in him that he belonged to the line of prophets rather than to the line of the great craftsmen" (interview with Avis Berman, Part I, p. 12, AAA).

44. Alex and Sloan Tampkin interview; Arthur Lidov interview, May 15, 1988.

45. Quoted in Barbara Rose, *American Painting: The 20th Century* (Cleveland, n.d.), p. 13.

46. Rothko's self-description occurred in his interview with Gladys Kashdin, GKP, AAA.

47. Ibid.

48. Oscar Collier, "Mark Rothko," *The New Iconograph* 4 (Fall 1947):41.

49. Art Students League Catalogue, 1925–26, pp. 7–11, 17.

50. Barbara Haskell, *Milton Avery* (New York, 1982), p. 28.

51. Lawrence Campbell to the author, March 19, 1986.

52. Stuart Klonis, interview with Bruce Hooten, in "The Art Students League, Part I," *Archives of American Art Journal* 13, 1 (1973):6.

53. "Lloyd Goodrich Reminisces, Part I," *Archives of American Art Journal* 20, 3 (1980):7.

54. My account of Weber's life is based on Alfred Werner, *Max Weber* (New York, 1975); Abraham A. Davidson, *Early American Modernist Painting* (New York, 1981), pp. 28–34; Percy North, *Max Weber: American Modern* (New York, 1982); and Max Weber, interview with Carol S. Gruber, January–March 1958, Oral History Research Office, Columbia University. Weber's remark about literature is taken from the interview, p. 8.

55. The criticisms of Weber are quoted in Milton W. Brown, *American Painting: From the Armory Show to the Depression* (Princeton, N.J., 1955), p. 43, and in *Max Weber*, p. 40. Weber's sense of the Art Students League is stated in his interview with Carol S. Gruber, pp. 350 and 347.

56. Max Weber, interview with Carol S. Gruber, p. 2.

57. Goodridge Roberts, "Max Weber," *Canadian Art* 7 (Summer 1951):57.

58. Max Weber, interview with Carol S. Gruber, p. 34.

59. Joseph Konzal, interview with Barbara Shikler, October 25, 1983, MRF, NGA. Mr. Konzal was a student in Weber's class in November, December, and January, 1926–27.

Among Rothko's papers are ten typed pages titled, "MAX WEBER'S CRITICISMS (Given to Class of 1920–21)." That was not Rothko's class, but the comments—one of which is quoted as the epigraph to this section of my text—suggest that Weber was an active, often eloquent presence in the class who usually emphasized construction, but construction as emotionally or spiritually expressive (MRA).

60. Joseph Solman interview, January 15, 1986.

61. Joseph Solman, "The Easel Division of the WPA Federal Art Project," in *The New Deal Art Projects: An Anthology of Memoirs,* ed. Francis V. O'Connor (Washington, D.C., 1972), p. 118.

62. Interview with Avis Berman, Part I, May 6, 1981, p. 20, AAA.

63. Max Weber, *Essays on Art* (New York, 1916), pp. 11, 27, 48.

64. Kenneth and Elaine Rabin interview.

65. MR,AR, p. 22.

66. Ibid.

67. Rothko told Robert Motherwell that Soule had been his closest friend in the 1920s.

When Rothko's brothers Moise and Albert arrived at Ellis Island, they listed as the relative they were going to join a "cousin" named Weinstein at a New York City address (unreadable) (cf. Ship's Manifest Of Alien Passengers, SS *Main,* January 13, 1913).

68. MR,AR, p. 22; Gus Solomon interview; MacCoby testified in "Rothkowitz v. Browne"; see below, this chapter.

69. All four of these men testified on Rothko's behalf in "Rothkowitz v. Browne."

70. MR,AR, p. 22. Lewis Browne referred to Rothko's work painting signs in "Rothkowitz v. Browne."

71. *The Menorah Journal* 14, 3 (March 1928):246; in his November 16 deposition for "Rothkowitz v. Browne," Rothko claimed his advertising experience.

72. See Roland Marchand, *Advertising the American Dream* (Berkeley, 1985), p. 143.

73. "Rothkowitz v. Browne," New York State Supreme Court, 1928–29. I have not provided specific page numbers for the hearing transcript and depositions from this suit. My longer treatment of this episode, "The Trials of Mark Rothko," *Representations* 16 (Fall 1986):1–41, does provide such page references.

74. See "Lewis Browne," *Wilson Bulletin* 7, 6 (February 1933):334–48.

75. See *Who Was Who in American History: Arts and Letters* (Chicago, 1975), p. 60.

76. *New York Times,* January 5, 1929, p. 7; and January 8, 1929, p. 40; the *Times* also ran a story on the case on November 21, 1928, p. 9. The two January stories quote Browne describing Rothko's drawings as "monkey-doodles and jiggles." Browne actually spoke of Rothko's "little wiggles and jiggles and lines." "Monkey-doodles" were mentioned by Rothko's lawyer.

77. Both parties had to sign $1,500 bonds to cover possible court costs, for which the loser would be responsible. After the hearing there was further conflict (and an exchange of depositions) about whether Rothko should have to pay for the copy of the transcript supplied to the defendant. Again, Rothko lost; he owed $915.56. His bonding company would have paid the fee, but then would have tried to recover the money from him.

78. Browne testified that he had studied illustrating "at no school, excepting work in the studio of Hendrik Willem Van Loon, himself a noted historian and illustrator," and in the introduction to *The Graphic Bible* Browne mentions "my friend Dr. Hendrik Willem Van Loon, in which studio at Westport I first tried my hand at illustration.'" Some of Browne's drawings—e.g., the men on camels on p. 41 of *Stranger Than Fiction* (New York, 1925), which Browne claimed were copied in Rothko's men on camels on p. 34 of *The Graphic Bible*—are stylistically quite close to those of Van Loon. See, for example, Van Loon's *The Story of the Bible* (New York, 1923); possibly *The Story of the Bible* suggested *The Graphic Bible*.

79. Browne, *Stranger Than Fiction,* pp. 19–20.

80. Lewis Browne, "The Jew Is Not a Slacker," *North American Review* 207 (June 1918):857–62. Browne quotes, "The foreign born, especially the Jews, are more apt to malinger than the native born." He can understand "the prejudices of common people" (they derive from "ignorance"), but has a harder time with those "of more or less intelligent and fair-minded officials." Apparently, Browne had never heard of *institutional* anti-Semitism.

81. Arthur Garfield Hays, *City Lawyer* (New York, 1942), pp. 17, 19.

82. Arthur Garfield Hays, *Let Freedom Ring* (New York, 1928), p. x.

83. Ibid., p. xvi.

84. Hays, *City Lawyer,* p. x.

85. Rothko also offered to "draw or reproduce anything in *The Graphic Bible*" at the hearing to prove that it was his work, but the defense did not take up his offer.

86. In this context, Rothko pointed out that the religious painting of the past could be called illustrative, but what made it art was the creation of a formal wholeness: "If Raphael painted a picture, for a Christian Church . . . or

even Giotto—for instance the staircase of St. Francis of Assisi—to illustrate that particular thing—nevertheless, he would have to so order the various ingredients in the various parts, and the various portions of the picture into a sense of unity and harmony to make it a complete work."

87. At various points I will refer to the lawsuit over Rothko's estate ("The Matter of Rothko") and in my later chapters I will draw from some of the material from that suit (testimony, depositions, exhibits), but I have not included any direct account of the suit, since that has been provided by Lee Seldes in her *The Legacy of Mark Rothko.*

Chapter Four

1. Nathaniel Dirk is identified as the friend who accompanied Rothko in MR,AR, p. 266. Like Rothko, Dirk had studied with Max Weber (cf. *Who's Who in American Art,* ed. Alice Coe McGlauflin [Washington, D.C., 1935], vol. 1, p. 121). For my information about Hearthstone Point I am indebted to Frank W. Fuller, Chief, Bureau of Recreation, New York State Department of Environmental Conservation, Albany, New York.

2. Edith (Sachar) Carson, interview with Walter Hopps, AAA; Edith Carson, interview with Carol Carson, n.d., George Carson Papers; Andrea Hoffman, "Remembrance of Life as Artist's Wife," *Los Angeles Times,* n.d., clipping in George Carson Papers.

3. Edith Sachar to Marcus Rothkowitz, August 19, 1932, MRA.

4. Ibid., September 25, 1932, MRA.

5. Certificate and Record of Marriage, 23188, City Clerk's Office, New York City. This certificate supplies the only evidence of Rothko's address at 314 West 75th Street.

6. Sophie Tracy interview, February 11, 1986; Judith Eisenstein, interview with Barbara Shikler, January 16, 1985, MRF, NGA; Hoffman, "Remembrance of Life as Artist's Wife"; Edith (Sachar) Carson, interview with Walter Hopps, AAA.

7. Sophie Tracy interview; George Carson interview, June 2, 1986; Lilian and Milton Klein interview, April 9, 1987.

8. George Carson interview; Lilian and Milton Klein interview; William and Ann Sachar interview, March 4, 1987; Howard and Beverly Sachar interview, November 11, 1986.

611 Nostrand Avenue is listed as the family residence in the Brooklyn city directory for 1933–34; it is listed as the family business address in the Brooklyn phone books from winter 1934–35 until 1939–40.

9. Edith Sachar, transcript, Erasmus High School.

10. George Carson interview; William and Ann Sachar interview; Howard and Beverly Sachar interview.

11. Quotations from Edith Sachar, "Diary," 1931–37, n.p., George Carson Papers. Subsequent quotations will not be documented when this brief diary is named in my text as the source.

12. See William Henry Cobb, "Commonwealth College: A History," Ph.D. dissertation (University of Arkansas, 1963); William H. Cobb, "Commonwealth College Comes to Arkansas, 1923–1925," *The Arkansas Historical Quarterly* 23, 2 (Summer 1964): 99–122.

13. "Commonwealth College: A History," pp. 114–25, and 145–49.

14. Edith Sachar to Marcus Rothkowitz, August 19, 1932, MRA.

15. George Carson interview.

16. William E. Leuchtenburg, *Franklin D. Roosevelt and the New Deal* (Chicago, 1963), pp. 18, 2–3; "Winter of Despair" is the title of Leuchtenburg's second chapter.

17. Edith (Sachar) Carson, interview with Walter Hopps, AAA; "Rothkowitz v. Browne," p. 466.

18. Francis V. O'Connor, *Federal Support for the Visual Arts: The New Deal and Now* (Washington, D.C., 1968), pp. 60–63.

19. Ed Weinstein, interview with Barbara Shikler, pp. 18–20, AAA.

20. Edith (Sachar) Carson, interview with Walter Hopps, AAA.

21. George Carson interview; Hoffman, "Remembrance of Life as Artist's Wife."

22. George Carson interview.

23. Richard and Johnnie Mae Roth interview; Edith (Sachar) Carson, interview with Walter Hopps, AAA; Julian and Dorothy Roth interview; Kenneth and Elaine Rabin interview.

24. Stanley Kunitz, interview with Avis Berman, Part I, p. 8.

25. Julian and Dorothy Roth interview.

26. Albert Roth, interview with Lee Seldes, March 10, 1975, LSF; Richard and Johnnie Mae Roth interview; Julian and Dorothy Roth interview.

27. Julian and Dorothy Roth interview; Milton and Joy Rabin interview; Richard and Johnnie Mae Roth interview.

28. Moise Roth, interview with Ruth Cloudman, pp. 22 and 20, AAA; Sonia Newman interview, May 8, 1986; Dorothy and Phil Reiter interview; Julian and Dorothy Roth interview.

29. This address was first given to me by George Okum (George and Blanche Okun interview, February 11, 1986) and by Morris Calden (interview, February 14, 1986). Both Mr. Okun and Mr. Calden (in turn) rented a room in this apartment. Their memories are confirmed by Clark S. Marlor, *The Society of Independent Artists: The Exhibition Record, 1917–1944* (Park Ridge, N.J., 1984), p. 473, where Rothko's 1934 address is given as 1000 Park Place, Brooklyn.

30. George Carson interview; Lilian and Milton Klein interview.

31. The 724 Nostrand address appears in the Brooklyn telephone book for winter 1935–36; a list of their addresses later drawn up by Edith includes "two years on Park Place; one-half year on Nostrand Avenue" (George Carson interview).

32. George Carson interview.

33. Lilian and Milton Klein interview.

34. Louis Kaufman, interview with Ruth Cloudman, February 15, 1985, p. 5, AAA; Louis and Annette Kaufman interview, November 3, 1986.

35. Sally Avery, interview with Tom Wolf, Part I, February 19, 1982, p. 1, AAA. See also the Scrapbooks, Milton Avery Papers, AAA, which contain two reviews of this show, one by Murdock Pemberton, *Creative Art* (December 1928), n.p., which praises "the landscapes of M. Rothkowitz," and the other in the *New York Sun*, November 12, 1928, which declares that "M. Rothkowitz has a painter's vision." The *Sun* piece

also points out that Karfoil picked forty from two hundred submitted works.

36. Louis and Annette Kaufman interview; Sally Avery, interview with Tom Wolf, Part I, p. 10, AAA.

37. My account of Avery's life is based on Barbara Haskell, *Milton Avery* (New York, 1982). Though Avery was actually eighteen years older than Rothko, he took five years off his age at the time of his marriage, apparently to reduce the difference in age between himself and his younger wife. At some later point Avery took three more years off his age and began giving his birth date as 1893; Rothko thus would have thought that Avery was just ten years older—just about the difference between himself and his oldest brother, Moise.

38. Ibid., p. 17.

39. Louis and Annette Kaufman interview; Joseph Solman, interview with Avis Berman, May 6, 1981, Part I, p. 8, AAA; Haskell, *Milton Avery*, p. 13.

40. Haskell, *Milton Avery*, p. 26.

41. Wallace Putnam, interview with Avis Berman, July 13, 1982, p. 7, AAA.

42. Sally Avery, interview with Tom Wolf, Part I, pp. 2, 10, AAA.

43. Lilian and Milton Klein interview. Rothko lived at 137 West 72nd Street, according to the *New York City Directory* for 1933–34, where his profession is listed as teacher. The Averys were then living at 150 West 72nd Street.

44. Sally Avery to Clair Zamoiski, December 14, 1977 and April 5, 1978, Milton Avery Papers, AAA; Sally Avery, interview with Tom Wolf, Part I, pp. 6–9, AAA.

45. Sally Avery, interview with Tom Wolf, Part II, March 19, 1982, pp. 4–5, AAA; and Sally Avery, interview with Tom Wolf, Part I, p. 31, AAA.

Avery's *Portrait of Mark Rothko* (1933) is at the Museum of Art, Rhode Island School of Design, and is reproduced in color in Bonnie Lee Grad, *Milton Avery* (Royal Oak, Mich., 1981), color plate 2; a pencil sketch for the painting is reproduced in Haskell, *Milton Avery*, p. 30. An etching, *Rothko With Pipe, 1936*, is reproduced in Adelyn D. Breeskin, *Milton Avery* (Washington, D.C., 1969), illustration 11. Two other portraits of Rothko are reproduced in black and white in "Private Faces in Public Places," *Art News* 63, 10 (February 1965):36–38, 62. In addition, an Avery painting *Rothko in Profile* was sold in 1974 by the Knoedler Gallery in New York (Milton Avery Papers, AAA). The Avery portraits done of Rothko in the 1930s must have been titled later, since they use "Rothko," not "Rothkowitz."

46. Rothko's sketchbooks are in the Prints and Drawings Department, NGA. On his *Mother and Child*, see Sally Avery, interview with Tom Wolf, Part I, p. 23, AAA.

47. Rothko's "Commemorative Essay" was read by Rothko at the services for Milton Avery at the New York Society for Ethical Culture on January 7, 1965 (MR, p. 89). There are several drafts of the essay in MRA.

48. Sally Avery, interview with Tom Wolf, Part I, pp. 2, 30, AAA; Louis and Annette Kaufman interview.

49. Haskell, *Milton Avery*, p. 17; Sally Avery, interview with Tom Wolf, Part II, March 18, 1982, p. 4, AAA; Edith Carson, interview with Walter Hopps, AAA.

50. Haskell, *Milton Avery,* pp. 17, 26; Chris Ritter, "A Milton Avery Profile," *Art Digest* 27 (December 1, 1952):11; Louis and Annette Kaufman, interview with Ruth Cloudman, p. 12, AAA; Louis and Annette Kaufman interview.

51. Rothko quotations are from "Commemorative Essay," *MR,* p. 89; Louis Kaufman, interview with Ruth Cloudman, p. 5, AAA; Edith (Sachar) Carson, interview with Walter Hopps, AAA; Sally Avery, interview with Tom Wolf, Part I, p. 10, AAA. According to "Rothkowitz v. Browne," Rothko's address at the time he met Avery was at 10 East 15th Street.

52. Lilian and Milton Klein interview.

53. Quoted in Haskell, *Milton Avery,* p. 56.

54. Avery quotations from "'Modern' Art View Explained by Artists: Milton Avery and Aaron Berkman Discuss Own Paintings at Morgan Memorial," *Hartford Times,* January 3, 1931, p. 5 (Scrapbooks, Milton Avery Papers, AAA).

55. Quoted in Sanford Hirsch and Mary Davis MacNaughton, *Adolph Gottlieb, A Retrospective* (New York, 1981), p. 17.

56. Sally Avery, interview with Tom Wolf, Part I, p. 1, AAA.

57. "PMA"; the phrase "the human drama" was spoken by Rothko.

58. "RWP," *MR,* p. 84.

59. A copy of the catalogue for this show can be found in the MRF, MOMA, as well as in the Contemporary Arts Gallery Papers, AAA; a clipping of the review, author and place of publication unidentified, is in the Contemporary Arts Gallery Papers, AAA.

60. Joseph Solman, "The Easel Division of the WPA Federal Art Project," in *The New Deal Art Projects, An Anthology of Memoirs,* ed. Francis V. O'Connor (Washington, D.C., 1972), p. 122.

61. Contemporary Arts Gallery Papers, AAA; MR,AR, p. 267.

62. Edith (Sachar) Carson, interview with Walter Hopps, AAA.

63. Sally Avery interview, January 9, 1986.

64. Ilya Bolotowsky, interview with Paul Cummings, March 24, 1968, AAA; Robert Ulrich Godsoe, "The Art Marts," published in three New York newspapers on April 12, 1934 (clippings in Adolph Gottlieb Papers, AAA).

65. Joseph Solman, interview with Avis Berman, Part I, pp. 8, 15, AAA; Solman, "The Easel Division of the WPA Federal Art Project," pp. 123-24.

66. Interview with Avis Berman, Part I, p.4, AAA.

67. See Marchal E. Landgren, "A Memoir of the New York City Municipal Art Galleries, 1936-1939," in O'Connor, *The New Deal Art Projects, An Anthology of Memoirs,* pp. 269-79; and Press Release, December 30 [1935], Municipal Art Committee, City of New York, in LaGuardia Papers, Municipal Archives, New York City.

68. Joseph Solman interview, January 15, 1986; Robert Motherwell interview.

69. *New York Times,* January 7, 1936, p. 9; *New York World Telegram,* January 6, 1936, n.p. (clippings in Adolph Gottlieb Papers, AAA).

70. For a history of The Ten, see Solman, "The Easel Division of the WPA Federal Art Project," and Joseph Sol-

man, interview with Avis Berman, Part I, pp. 4–19, AAA.

71. Ben Zion interview, January 6, 1986; Joseph Solman interview; Joseph Solman, interview with Avis Berman, Part I, p. 5, AAA.

72. Interview with Avis Berman, Part I, pp. 4–5, AAA; Joseph Solman interview.

73. Interview with Avis Berman, Part I, p. 22, AAA; Joseph Solman interview.

74. Quoted in *Twentieth-Century American Art: Highlights of the Permanent Collection of the Whitney Museum of American Art* (Whitney Museum of American Art), n.p. My account of Mrs. Whitney and the museum is based on B. H. Friedman, *Gertrude Vanderbilt Whitney* (Garden City, N. Y., 1978), and D. Healy, "A History of the Whitney Museum of American Art, 1930–1954," Ph.D. dissertation (New York University, 1960).

75. *The Ten: Whitney Dissenters* (Mercury Galleries, 1938), Bernard Braddon Papers. According to Mr. Braddon and Sidney Schectman, in their October 9, 1981 interview with Avis Berman, p. 11, AAA, the catalogue was written by Braddon, Schectman, and Rothko.

76. "A History of the Whitney Museum of American Art, 1930–1954" lists all the participants in the biennials.

77. WPA, Adult Education Program, Art Tours for 7–12 November 1938, Bernard Braddon Papers.

78. Bernard Braddon and Sidney Schectman, interview with Avis Berman, p. 23, AAA.

79. Review of The Ten in the *New York Sun*, May 14, 1938 (clipping in Adolph Gottlieb Papers, AAA).

80. Bernard Braddon and Sidney Schectman, interview with Avis Berman, pp. 9, 20, and 11, AAA.

81. "Proposal by Mercury Galleries to The Ten," Bernard Braddon Papers.

82. Letter signed " 'The Ten,' M. Rothkowitz (Secretary)" to Mercury Galleries, December 26, 1938, Bernard Braddon Papers.

83. Solman, "The Easel Division of the WPA Federal Art Project," p. 128.

84. Joseph Solman to Jacob Kainen, February 26, 1939, Jacob Kainen Papers, AAA.

85. Joseph Solman interview; Solman, "The Easel Division of the WPA Federal Art Project," p. 122. On the American Abstract Artists, see Susan Larsen, "The American Abstract Artists Group: A History and Evaluation of Its Impact Upon American Art," Ph.D. dissertation (Northwestern University, 1974), and John R. Lane and Susan Larsen, eds., *Abstract Painting and Sculpture in America, 1927–1944* (Pittsburgh and New York, 1986).

86. Quoted in Solman, "The Easel Division of the WPA Federal Art Project," p. 126, and in Joseph Solman, interview with Avis Berman, Part I, p. 16, AAA. The phrase "silly smudges" was used by Edward Alden Jewell, who wrote in his review of The Ten's exhibit at the Montross Gallery in December 1936, "I do not believe I understand the American 'expressionists' so very well. Many of these paintings at the Montross I feel I do not understand at all. Often they look to me like silly smudges. And if a painting looks like a silly smudge, it is safe to conclude that you do not understand it" (*New York Times*, December 20, 1936, section x, p. 11).

87. Oskar Pfister, *Exressionism in Art* (New York, 1923); and Sheldon Cheney, *Expressionism in Art* (New York, 1934). Rothko quotes from Pfister's *Psycho-analysis in the Service of Education* (London, 1922) in "SB," where he later alludes to Pfister's work on expressionism. The source for Rothko's familiarity with the Cheney book is my interview with Morris Calden.

88. Pfister, *Expressionism in Art*, pp. 259, 245; Cheney, *Expressionism in Art*, p. 11.

89. Pfister, *Expressionism in Art*, p. 269.

90. "PMA."

91. The drawing is no. 1986.56.142, in Rothko no. W.25 in the Prints and Drawings Department, NGA. In this frontal sketch Rothko has long, thick, shapeless, animal-like legs, and he has wrapped his arms around himself, self-protectively, each hand clasping the opposite shoulder, the left arm unrealistically elongated. Except for his left thumb (or right, if he's looking into a mirror), his fingers are not delineated, making his hands look like paws. His glasses are blank circles, making his eyes into voids.

92. Morris Calden interview.

93. Among the many friends and family who remember Rothko as claustrophobic—he refused to fly for that reason—two with particular authority are his daughter, Kate, and his physician, Dr. Albert Grokest.

94. Letter from Bradley Walker Tomlin to "Earl," "March 1935" in Bradley Walker Tomlin Papers, AAA.

95. "The Brooklyn Jewish Center, Its Activities and Purposes," *Brooklyn Jewish Center Review* 14 (November 1933):11.

96. My account of Center Academy is mainly based on interviews with Judith Eisenstein (January 29, 1986) and Frieda Prensky (February 6, 1986), both of whom taught music there, as well as my interviews with Howard Adelson (October 11, 1988), Irene Dash (July 2, 1987), Martin Lukashok (January 20, 1986), Gerald Phillips (January 27, 1986) and Ruth Pomeranz (January 29, 1986)—all Center Academy students. In addition, I've relied on Fannie Neumann, "A Modern Jewish Experimental School—In Quest of a Synthesis," *Jewish Education* 4 (1932):26–36; "Center Academy Seven Years Old," *Brooklyn Jewish Center Review* 15 (March 1935):16; Irene Bush, "Ideal Education for the Jewish Child," *Brooklyn Jewish Center Review* 16 (June 1936):10; Sophia Soskin, "A Notable Anniversary," *Brooklyn Jewish Center Review* 19 (May 1938):7–8; and Lillis Rubee, "The Center Academy—Its Hebrew Program," *Brooklyn Jewish Center Review* 24 (May 1943):19, 21. See also Samuel P. Abelow, *History of Brooklyn Jewry* (Brooklyn, 1937), p. 132.

97. See Deborah Dash Moore, *At Home in America* (New York, 1981), especially her chapter "From Chevra to Center," which contains a section on the Brooklyn Jewish Center.

98. Neumann, "A Modern Jewish Experimental School":26–27, 33; Bush, "Ideal Education for the Jewish Child":10.

99. Neumann, "A Modern Jewish Experimental School":26.

100. Howard Adelson interview.

101. Neumann, "A Modern Jewish Experimental School":passim.

102. The *Brooklyn Jewish Center, An-*

nual Report, 1928 announces the opening of Center Academy on February 1, 1928.

103. Brooklyn Jewish Center Review 15 (January 1935):23 and 15 (February 1935):13.

104. Judith Eisenstein interview; Frieda Prensky interview; Frieda Prensky, interview with Barbara Shikler, April 3, 1985, MRF, NGA.

105. Judith Eisenstein interview; Frieda Prensky, interview with Barbara Shikler, MRF, NGA; Martin Lukashok interview.

106. Rothko scholars have not previously been aware of the existence of this essay, which appeared in the Brooklyn Jewish Center Review 14 (February–March 1934):10–11.

107. Three people—Juliette Hays (interview, January 28, 1987), Rebecca Soyer (interview, January 22, 1987) and Joseph Belsey (interview, December 17, 1987)—all have very strong and specific memories of Rothko teaching at a Jewish parochial school in Far Rockaway. Mr. Belsey, who lived there at the time, recalled Rothko stopping by for dinner after his day's work. I have been unable to identify the school.

108. Martin Lukashok interview.

109. Irene Dash interview, January 21, 1987; Frieda Prensky interview.

110. The tour is announced in the Brooklyn Jewish Center Review 17 (October 1933):17; Rothko's talk (February 9, 1933) is mentioned in the Brooklyn Jewish Center, Annual Report, 1933. Rothko also spoke to the school's PTA—e.g., on December 16, 1942 and April 16, 1943 (Brooklyn Jewish Center Review 24 [February 1943]:19–20).

111. Dates for the Brooklyn Museum show, held in the Library Gallery, were verified for me by Deborah Wythe, the museum's archivist. No catalogue was published and no clippings were saved. Information about the other exhibits is based on "A Notable Anniversary":8, where Soskin also states that "The Museum of Modern Art has bought several of our children's paintings for their permanent collection."

112. Brooklyn Jewish Center Review 14 (February–March 1934):10–11.

113. LMR, p. 12.

Chapter Five

1. WPA Papers, Roll DC 15, AAA.

2. Olin Dows, "The New Deal's Treasury Art Program: A Memoir," in O'Connor, The New Deal Art Projects: An Anthology of Memoirs, p. 26.

3. For the history of TRAP, see O'Connor, Federal Support for the Visual Arts: The New Deal and Now, pp. 25–26, 37–39; Richard D. McKinzie, The New Deal for Artists (Princeton, N.J., 1973), pp. 38–42; and Dows, "The New Deal's Treasury Art Program: A Memoir."

4. The letter, dated June 17, 1936, reads: "Artists who want to be considered for possible employment on the Treasury Relief Art Project are invited to send immediately photographs or other examples of their work to the Treasury Relief Art Project" in Washington, D.C. (WPA Papers, Roll DC 32, AAA).

5. "Notes for Mrs. [Alice] Sharkey, July 30 [1936]." "Rothcowitz [sic]—Called—wanted NR position—told him we could only use him on R" (WPA Papers, Roll DC 33, AAA) (R = Relief; NR = Nonrelief).

6. O'Connor, Federal Support for the

Visual Arts, pp. 43, 68–79; Gottlieb is quoted in FVOCP, Roll 1087, AAA.

7. WPA Papers, Roll DC 14, AAA; Olin Dows to Alice Sharkey, August 29, 1936, WPA Papers, Roll DC 14, AAA; Rothko's transcript of employment can be found in FVOCP, Roll 1088, frame 850, AAA; Solman, "The Easel Division of the WPA Federal Art Project," pp. 119–20.

8. An unidentified painting is recorded as received from Rothko on February 13, 1937, WPA Papers, Roll DC 31, frame 1389, AAA.

At least three additional Rothko WPA paintings have turned up— *Subway, Two Women at Window,* and *Women and Children.* The WPA project shut down in April 1943. Eight months later hundreds of unallocated works were sold from a warehouse in Queens, New York, for 4 cents a pound to a junk dealer who, in turn, sold them to Henry C. Roberts, owner of a Canal Street second-hand shop, where they were sold at $3–$5 a piece. Word spread of the availability of the works, and soon artists, dealers, and speculators were purchasing them. The three Rothko works were bought by a dealer and are now in the possession of Ira Smolin of New York City. See Josephine Gibbs, "End of the Project," *Art Digest* 18 (February 15, 1944):7; "End of WPA Art," *Life* 16 (April 17, 1944):85; and Joseph Solman to Jacob Kainen, "Saturday 1944," Jacob Kainen Papers, AAA.

9. McKinzie, *The New Deal for Artists,* p. 42.

10. Hugo Gellert, "The Artists' Coordination Committee," in *Art for the Millions: Essays from the 1930s by Artists and Administrators of the WPA Federal Art Project,* ed. Francis V. O'Connor (Boston, 1973), pp. 255–56.

11. WPA Papers, Roll DC 56, AAA. The list of those to be dismissed is dated May 16, 1937. The "Bulletin, Artists Union of New York" (n.d.) reported: "50 dismissed TRAP artists have been reinstated on the FAP. Intense activity by the Artists Union preceded these reinstatements. Are there still WPA workers who think they do not need a union?" (clipping in Harry Gottlieb Papers, AAA).

12. O'Connor, *Federal Support for the Visual Arts,* pp. 42–43; McKinzie, *The New Deal for Artists,* pp. 98–101.

13. Kainen is quoted in FVOCP, Roll 1089, AAA; on Rothko's termination, see his transcript of employment, FVOCP, Roll 1088, AAA.

14. So far as I have been able to determine Nahum Tschacbasov was not on the WPA.

15. Quoted in Solomon, *Jackson Pollock, A Biography,* p. 80.

16. Quoted in FVOCP, Roll 1087, AAA.

17. Interview with Irving Sandler, January 14, 1963, p. 16, AAA.

18. WPA Papers, Roll DC 112, AAA.

19. David Sylvester, "An Interview with David Smith," *Living Arts* 3 (April 1964):5.

20. Edith (Sachar) Carson, interview with Walter Hopps, AAA; Pollock quoted in "Unframed Space," *New Yorker* 26 (August 5, 1950):16; Kainen quoted in FVOCP, Roll 1089, AAA.

21. Quotations from Chet La More, "The Artists' Union of America," in O'Connor, *Art for the Millions,* p. 237. For the history of the union, see Gerald Monroe, "The Artists' Union of New

York," Ph.D. dissertation (New York University, 1971), and Gerald Monroe, "Artists on the Barricades: The Militant Artists' Union Treats with the New Deal," *Archives of American Art Journal* 18, 3 (1978):20–22.

22. Matthew Baigell and Julia Williams, *Artists Against War and Fascism: Papers of the First American Artists' Congress* (New Brunswick, N.J., 1986), pp. 3–44; the phrase "artists of all esthetic tendencies," taken from the congress's preamble, is quoted on p. 11. See also Serge Guilbaut, *How New York Stole the Idea of Modern Art* (Chicago, 1983), pp. 17–47.

23. Juliette Hays, interview with Dore Ashton, July 28, 1982, p. 3, AAA.

24. Milton Avery wrote to Louis Kaufman (December 20, [1936?]) that he "met a number of the gang, Rothkowitz, Harris, etc. Friday eve at the Artists' Congress"(LKP, AAA). "The Second Annual Membership Exhibition: American Artists' Congress" was held May 5–21, 1938, in the fifth-floor gallery at the John Wanamaker department store in New York City (ACA Gallery Papers, AAA). The art auction was held on Sunday, December 5, (1938?) at 85 Clark Street, Brooklyn (clipping in Ben-Zion Papers, AAA); Rothko exhibited *Street Scene, Restaurant, Landscape,* and *Figure Composition.*

25. Juliette Hays, interview with Dore Ashton, p. 3, AAA. David Margolis strongly recalled that Rothko was a member, though not a very active member, of the Artists Union who participated in some of the union's demonstrations (David Margolis interview, April 28, 1989).

26. H. R. Hays to Clair Zamoiski, December 27, 1977, MRF, GMA.

27. Rothko told his assistant Dan Rice of these arrests, though there is no record of them ("Dan Rice Interviewed by Arnold Glimcher," in *Mark Rothko: The 1958–1959 Murals: Second Series* [New York, 1978], n.p.).

28. Jacob Kainen, interview with Avis Berman, Part II, August 11, 1982, p. 3, AAA; Juliette Hays interview, January 28, 1987.

29. Juliette Hays interview; Gerald M. Monroe, "Art Front," *Archives of American Art Journal* 13, 3 (1973):15.

30. "MR:PAAM":17.

31. Based on Declaration of Intention (Portland, 1924), Declaration of Intention (New York, 1935), Petition for Naturalization (New York, 1937), and Oath of Allegiance (February 21, 1938), all obtained from the U.S. Naturalization and Immigration Service.

32. Rothko's first public use of his new name was in his show, with Marcel Gromaire and Joseph Solman, at the Neumann-Willard Gallery, January 8–27, 1940. By the following year he was listing himself as "Mark Rothko" in the Manhattan telephone book.

33. Sophie Tracy interview; Joseph Solman, interview with Avis Berman, Part II, p. 17, AAA. Buffie Johnson and H. R. Hays also tell the story that Neumann proposed the change to Rothko (Buffie Johnson to Clair Zamoiski, April 1978, and H. R. Hays to Clair Zamoiski, December 27, 1977; both letters are in MRF, GMA).

34. The letterhead for the Federation of Modern Painters and Sculptors—as well as their exhibition catalogues—lists "Marcus Rothko."

35. Both of Rothko's brothers were listed under the name "Roth" beginning

with the *Portland City Directory* for 1918. However, Rothko's self-naming may also have been influenced by an old family memory. Harry and Rebecca Rothkow lived in southwest Portland starting around 1912; they had two children, Benjamin and Morris, both of whom attended Shattuck School and Lincoln High with Rothko. Both Rothkow children, moreover, were born in Michalishek, the village where Jacob and Kate Rothkowitz had first lived. Harry Rothkow worked for Sam Weinstein's clothing business between 1912 and 1915 (cf. Portland city directories for those years). Harry Rothkow, then, was possibly the brother of Jacob and Sam or at least a relative. Rothko cut the *witz* ("son of") from his name as if severing himself from his father, but his new name still took him back to his family origins.

36. George Okun interview.

37. Among Rothko's papers are fifteen handwritten pages of quotes transcribed from and notes occasionally commenting on Freud's *The Interpretation of Dreams,* of which Rothko appears to have been an admiring reader. A Rothko note, making a cross-reference to Freud's *Introductory Lectures on Psychoanalysis,* reveals Rothko's familiarity with that text. He had also read Plato. At one point after noting Freud's dictum that "nothing is forgotten" in the unconscious, Rothko adds: "perhaps Plato's notion is correct that the child has a store of memories at birth already. Substantiated by the notion that man recapitulates archaic history, approved by Nietzsche and Freud"; later, commenting on Freud's assertion that for *judging* human character, a man's actions and conscious statements are enough, Rothko asks, "how about Plato's—that virtue must seem unvirtuous" (MRA).

38. As of the summer of 1992, David Anfam has found twelve of these subway paintings. A Rothko *Subway* was exhibited in The Ten's first show, at the Montross Gallery, December 16, 1935 to January 4, 1936, so the series began no later than December 1935. It is not clear how long Rothko continued to work on the series. He showed *Entrance to Subway* at Neumann-Willard in January of 1940; but there is some evidence that he had already begun his "myth" paintings by this time and may have been exhibiting older work that he had less doubt about. Four of the subway paintings are reproduced in *MR,AR,* plates 18, 20, 21, 22, and one other is reproduced in *The New Deal Art Projects,* plate 19. Rothko's later interest in *Subway Scene* was expressed to Dore Ashton (*AR,* p. 50).

39. Rothko has both simplified and distorted many of the actual features of the Nostrand Avenue station. He has eliminated decorative details (a geometric design along the top of the rear wall; an "N" at the left of the rear wall; the tiles on the rear wall and on the rear wall of the stairway leading down) and many functional details (lights on the ceiling; a fuse box on the rear wall; a pipe that runs along the ceiling; the handrails on the stairway to the street). He has eliminated the rectangular divisions of both the ceiling and the floor. The door at the left has been pulled around the corner, to the wall at the rear of the platform from the wall that runs between that rear wall and the stairs leading to the street. The two posts at the left have been moved to the right. The rear wall of the station has

been pulled several feet forward, and the floor pulled slightly upward. While the rectilinear architecture has been simplified and compressed, the human figures are diminished: the man in the change booth and the passengers (whose facial features ought to be quite distinct) have been distanced and reduced in size.

40. LKP, AAA. The letter is simply dated "June 20" but a reference to the publication the year before of Wallace Putnam's *Manhattan Manners* (1935) establishes the year as 1936.

41. My references to this talk are taken from a transcription provided to me by the Mark Rothko Foundation, now in the MRF, NGA.

42. The full and not exactly succinct title of this work is "A comparative analysis of the basic plastic elements, styles, and processes common to both the creative paintings of children and traditional art; and the application of this knowledge to the supervision of the creative art activity." The name on the title page, "Mark Rothko" (not Marcus Rothkowitz), and the address given, 29 East 28th Street, both suggest that this material was composed in the early 1940s (Rothko was listed at the 28th Street address in the June and December 1941 and June 1942 Manhattan phone books).

There's a strong possibility that this work on children's art and the book Rothko's friends remember are the same. Rothko read sections of a book-in-progress to Milton Avery as early as 1936; the notes in "The Scribble Book" date from the late 1930s; the outline and drafts of "comparative analysis" date from the early 1940s; and in 1941 Avery wrote to Louis and Annette Kaufman that Rothko "has eased up on his book," as if he were speaking of the same book he'd mentioned to the Kaufmans in 1936 (Milton Avery to Louis and Annette Kaufman, September 26, 1941, LKP, AAA).

To suggest the ambitious character of Rothko's project, I quote all of section I, C of his outline:

C. The definition and recognition of the plastic elements, their use, and their communicated effect.
  1. Kinds of shapes and what they represent or symbolize.
  2. Types of space and how they are achieved.
  3. Scale: size of objects in relation to the enclosing space, and psychological effects of its varied use.
  4. Line.
    1. As the definition of shapes.
    2. Its abstract function in the achievement of various types of space.
    3. Its function in design.
    4. Its character.
  5. Color.
    1. Its objective or subjective use.
    2. Decorative use.
    3. Sensuous use.
  6. Textures: sensuous, decorative or representational.
  7. Rhythm or repetition.
  8. Arrangements.
    1. Classicial.
    2. Emotional.
    3. Its function in arabesque or spatial composition.

In the few sections that have been drafted, Rothko stresses painting as "a biological activity," "a means of speech and communication as instinctive as speech itself," and he writes of the "ideal teacher" as someone with "the sensibility of an artist," though supplemented with knowledge—themes from "New Training For Future Artists and Art Lovers" and "The Scribble Book." One new idea, however, emerges in Rothko's conception of the teacher as an authority whose "very presence and manner create an atmosphere of ease and confidence." He will "react with sincere enthusiasm," "be able to understand the most obscure symbol" and will "make the child aware of his reaction." Indeed, the teacher, Rothko says, is "a co-creator." This teacher is an early version of Rothko's later wish for an idealized viewer whose quickening gaze would complete his works.

43. Quotes from Wilhelm Viola, *Child Art and Franz Cizek* (Vienna, 1936), pp. 12, 21, 26. This book was Rothko's source on Cizek (Viola is quoted in "SB," and all of Rothko's quotations from Cizek appear in Viola's text).

44. Ibid., p. 18.

45. Ibid., p. 21.

46. Rothko has taken this quotation from Pfister, *Psycho-analysis in the Service of Education,* pp. 64–65.

47. See Russell Lynes, *Good Old Modern* (New York, 1973), pp. 199–202, and Margaret Scolari Barr, "Our Campaigns," *The New Criterion,* Special Issue (Summer 1987):54–55. That *Playbill and Dollar Bill* was actually painted by N. A. Brooks, not Harnett, is convincingly argued by Alfred Frankenstein, in *After the Hunt* (Berkeley, 1953), pp. 148–50.

48. Lynes, *Good Old Modern,* p. 204.

49. Scolari Barr, "Our Campaigns": 55; Lynes, *Good Old Modern,* pp. 205–6.

50. Lynes, *Good Old Modern,* pp. 40–43.

51. Peter Collier and David Horowitz, *The Rockefellers, An American Dynasty* (New York, 1976), p. 146.

52. Ibid., pp. 145–47; Lynes, *Good Old Modern,* p. 5.

53. Lynes, *Good Old Modern,* p. 4.

54. Ibid., pp. 134–35.

55. "The Museum of Modern Art," *Fortune* 18, 6 (December 1938):128.

56. Lynes, *Good Old Modern,* p. 212.

57. Alice Goldfarb Marquis, *Hopes and Ashes* (New York, 1986), p. 175.

58. Larsen, "The American Abstract Artists Group," vol. 2, pp. 322–23.

59. Correspondence in MRF, MOMA.

60. Larsen, "The American Abstract Artists Group," vol. 2, pp. 325–29.

61. This is the address listed for Rothko in the TRAP papers, May 1937.

62. Joseph Liss, "Willem de Kooning Remembers Mark Rothko," *Art News* 78 (January 1979):41.

63. The show was held at the Hudson Branch of the New York Public Library, 10 Seventh Avenue South, New York City (clipping in Philip Evergood Papers, AAA).

64. George Okun interview.

65. On Rothko's petition for naturalization, he declared that he had begun living on Great Jones Street on December 1, 1935; he was still at that address in the spring of 1938, according to the catalogue for the 2nd Annual Exhibition of the American Artists' Congress (ACA Gallery Papers, AAA).

66. Edith (Sachar) Carson recalled working at Center Academy in her interview with Walter Hopps, AAA, a mem-

ory verified by several of the people connected with the school and by many of her and Rothko's friends and relatives.

67. Edith (Sachar) Carson, career summary, George Carson Papers.

68. Howard and Beverly Sachar interview; Dorothy Dehner, interview, January 18, 1986; George Carson interview; Edith (Sachar) Carson, interview with Walter Hopps, AAA.

69. Edith (Sachar) Carson, interview with Walter Hopps, AAA.

70. Edith Sachar to Marcus Rothkowitz (Summer 1937), MRA.

71. Ibid., August 5, 1937, MRA.

72. Ibid., August 5, 1937, MRA; ibid. (Summer 1937), MRA.

73. Ibid. (Summer 1937), MRA.

74. Judith Eisenstein interview; Frieda Prensky interview.

75. Edith (Sachar) Carson, interview with Walter Hopps, AAA; George Carson interview.

76. George Carson interview.

77. Ibid.; Morris Calden interview.

78. Howard and Beverly Sachar interview.

79. Ibid.; Lilian and Milton Klein interview; Morris Calden interview.

80. On September 26, 1941, Milton Avery wrote to Louis and Annette Kaufman: "saw Marcus he has eased up on his book and been acting as salesman for Edith his wife's efforts in jewelry designing" (LKP, AAA).

81. Interview with Tom Wolf, Part I, p. 11, AAA.

82. The 6th Street address appears in the Manhattan phone books for summer 1939, December 1940, and summer 1940. But it is given as Rothko's address on his letter (as secretary for The Ten) to the Mercury Galleries, December 26, 1938. Rothko told the synagogue story to Judith Eisenstein (interview with Barbara Shikler, MRF, NGA).

83. Probably as a result of Rothko's termination, and of their general economic straits, both Rothko and Edith entered federally funded competitions for art in public buildings around this time. Rothko submitted sketches for murals in two such buildings, a New Rochelle, New York, post office, and the Social Security Building in Washington, D.C. Neither work was commissioned.

The winner of the New Rochelle competition was announced on February 17, 1940 and Rothko entered as "Marcus Rothkowitz," so the New Rochelle sketch was probably done in late 1939. The winner of the Social Security competition was announced on November 12, 1940, with Rothko now "Mark Rothko," so that sketch was probably done in mid-1940.

Edith submitted clay sculptures for a federal building in New Orleans and for the Social Security Building, the New Orleans competition occurring probably in late 1939 or early 1940, and the Social Security sculpture competition occurring probably in mid-1940. Neither of her works was commissioned.

Photographs of Rothko's work are in RG 121 MS, Box 19, Entry 18 (New Rochelle) and RG 121 MS, Box 25, Entry 275 abc (Social Security Building) in the National Archives, Washington, D.C.; and photographs of Edith's work are in RG 121 MS, Box 26, Entry 199ab (Social Security Building) and Box 18, Entry 183ab (New Orleans) at the National Archives.

Both sets of Rothko's sketches treat American historical material ironically. The New Rochelle sketches are reproduced as figure 23; the Social Security Building project consisted of a series of images from the life of Benjamin Franklin. A pencil drawing of one section of the Social Security Building project can be found in Prints and Drawings, NGA, Mark Rothko, Box 3/4, W545A.

84. Henry Berman interview, February 14, 1986. Berman recalled that Rothko and Edith were at Trout Lake in the summers of 1936 and 1937. The quotation about the art classes is from a letter from Berman to Stephen Paine, who bought a painting Rothko did of Berman's first wife, Henrietta.

85. Geoffrey Perrett, *Days of Sadness, Years of Triumph: The American People, 1939–1945* (Madison, Wisconsin, 1985), p. 16.

86. Dore Ashton, interview with Joseph Liss, August 10, 1982, AAA.

87. Joseph Liss, "A Portrait by Rothko," *The East Hampton Star,* September 2, 1976; a copy of Liss's essay can be found in MRF, Whitney Museum of American Art.

Chapter Six

1. Eric von Manstein, *Lost Victories,* trans. Anthony G. Powell (Chicago, 1958), pp. 183–84.

2. Paul Carell, *Hitler Moves East, 1941–1943* (Boston, 1963), pp. 33–35.

3. Gerald Reitlinger, *The Final Solution: The Attempt to Exterminate the Jews of Europe, 1939–45* (London, 1961), pp. 212–13.

4. Shosseynaya had by now been named 18 November Street, the date of Latvia's independence from the Soviet Union.

5. Quotations from Martin Gilbert, *The Holocaust* (London, 1986), p. 179; my account also draws on Reuben Ainsztein, *Jewish Resistance in Nazi-Occupied Eastern Europe* (London, 1974), pp. 231–32, and my interviews with Leo Truksans, Henriks Soms, Genovefa Barkovska, Joel P. Weinberg of the Daugavpils Pedagogical Institute and my interview with Anatoly Fishel and Boris Volkovitsh of the Latvian-Jewish Cultural Committee.

6. *Portland City Directory,* 1941 and 1942; Richard and Johnnie Mae Roth interview; Julian and Dorothy Roth interview; Milton and Joy Rabin interview; Kenneth and Elaine Rabin interview.

7. Arthur Gage interview; Edith (Sachar) Carson, interview with Walter Hopps, AAA.

8. Interview with Barbaralee Diamondstein, in *Inside New York's Art World* (New York, 1979), p. 243.

9. John Morton Blum, *V Was for Victory* (New York, 1976); see the chapter "The Wartime Consumer," pp. 92–105; the active market for jewelry is mentioned on p. 98.

10. Perrett, *Days of Sadness,* p. 176.

11. Milton Avery to Louis and Annette Kaufman, January 13, 1941, LKP, AAA.

12. Mark Rothko to Joseph Liss, February 3, 1941, MRF, NGA. On the envelope for this letter, the return address is 29 East 28th Street, New York City, making it certain that Avery in his January 13, 1941 letter to Louis and Annette Kaufman is talking about the 28th Street apartment and making it probable that Rothko had moved there the

previous October, then the traditional beginning of the year for leases in New York City. The name on the return address is "M. Rothkowitz," as if "Rothko" at this point functioned mainly as a professional name.

13. From the FBI file on the American Artists' Congress, obtained under the Freedom of Information Act.

14. Quoted in Gerald M. Monroe, "The American Artists' Congress and The Invasion of Finland," *Archives of American Art Journal* 15, 1 (1975):17. My discussion of the congress is generally indebted to Monroe's essay.

15. *New York Times,* April 15, 1940, p. 19, and April 17, 1940, p. 25.

16. *New York Times,* April 17, 1940, p. 25.

17. Quoted from the catalogue statement for the federation's first annual exhibit (1941), FMPSP, AAA. Unless otherwise indicated, quotations from the federation's papers are from this source.

18. "No Blackout for Art," statement in the catalogue for the federation's second annual exhibit (1942), FMPSP, AAA.

19. Federation of Modern Painters and Sculptors file, MOMA.

20. Minutes for meetings of December 4, 1940 and January 3, 1941, FMPSP, AAA. On February 3, 1941, however, the federation did protest a move to make a military band being trained by Leopold Stokowski play "100% American" music (FMPSP, AAA).

21. Minutes, April 7, 1941, FMPSP, AAA.

22. Cecile Whiting, *Antifascism in American Art* (New Haven, 1989), p. 135.

23. Minutes, July 7, 1941, FMPSP, AAA.

24. Minutes, November 12, 1941 and January 29, 1942, FMPSP, AAA.

25. Minutes, September 15, 1941, FMPSP, AAA.

26. "No Blackout for Art," FMPSP, AAA.

27. As "SB" shows, keeping art separate from history had always been Rothko's position, one that he restated in a March 23, 1941, letter to Dean Joseph George Cohen, of Brooklyn College, with whom he had recently spoken about the possibility of a teaching position; there are four drafts of this letter in the MRA.

Cohen had put together a pamphlet "on the use of objective criteria in the measure of drawing ability." Rothko, given his commitments to the "universal," is not as unfriendly to such a project as he ought to be, but he *is* looking for a job, and he does show that there are basic differences among three authorities cited by Cohen: Auguste Rodin, Jean Metzinger, and Kenyon Cox (probably in his *Concerning Painting* [New York, 1917]). Both Rodin and Metzinger, for example, endorse "expressiveness," which, Rothko points out, they define differently. Rodin's "expressiveness involves the use of physical contortions for the representation of intense emotional states," whereas Metzinger "rejects this type of subjectivism, the better to achieve expressive formal relationships. Here we enter the world of morality and personal predilections whose antagonisms are difficult to resolve, indeed."

On the other hand, Cox, at least as interpreted by Cohen, holds that a drawing is "excellent in precisely the measure in which it was able to reflect a faithful imaging of the subject." As Rothko argues, this position requires that the artist "should not exhibit a drawing without posing his subject beside it, and under the precise conditions at the time of drawing. For without it, how could the spectator enjoy the full corroboration of its excellence?" Rothko then deftly shows that Cox's view "does not depend upon reference to a particular subject but rather on some abstraction, some ideal of proportion and appearance" and so is actually dependent on a notion of "expressiveness in relation to this ideal" for its judgments of value. Judgments of excellence, Rothko continues, "can refer only to the degree of success with which drawing has achieved the particular kind of expressiveness to which the artist is committed."

Modern art "can be of invaluable assistance" in thinking about these problems, Rothko says, since it "has been achieved thru the analysis and the recapitulation of man's known art experience." Picasso, for example, himself "a perpetrator of wholesale distortions, considers himself profoundly in debt to Ingres." He also "blessed" both Miró and Dali—"Miró, who imparts mass to space thru the movement of a line completely divorced from shape; Dali[,] who achieves vacuous space and peoples it with hyperphotographic mass"—and Picasso has "proceeded to combine these irreconcilable devices to his own ends. The fact that Miró, Cox and Dali can worship at a single shrine, be it Ingres, Titian or Piero della Francesca[,] is a compelling indication of the existence of a common denominator."

Here, Rothko endorses the value for their investigations of the "comparative and historical method," one he would later come to spurn, and which he now sees as corrupted by "many recent practices," by which he means Marxist practices. "To me, the comparative and historical viewpoint is essentially a demonstration of *the integrity of the plastic continuity of art;* of the logical inevitability of each step as art progresses from point to point" (my emphasis). What's happened recently is "the evolvement of a series of correlations between art and the social environment." Such correlations could illuminate both society and art, but they have been pursued with such "evangelism, that in many quarters art has become a minion, obsequious to society's whim, badgered from corner to corner by a succession of environmental concussions, changing its hues, chameleon like, in the interests of adaptability."

"These facile correlations," Rothko warns, "have a strong attraction for the popular mind, which still unconsciously yearns for the golden synthesis of 18th Century materialism." They "have been incorporated into our vernacular where they serve with the force of axiomatic fact" and "where they have erected a screen between art and the sensibilities to which it is addressed." Rothko concedes that "there is always a wide distance between the vernacular and the speech of contemporary truth." "It may be well argued that vulgarization is organic to the nature of the vernacular, must always attend it, and that its speech can never coincide with that of truth. Yet, such coincidence is a limit which we must strive to approach," particularly through education.

28. *New York Evening Sun,* February

2, 1942, p. 16; the letter also was the subject of a story in the *New York Times,* February 3, 1942, p. 21.

29. *The Nation* 156, 12 (March 20, 1943): 431.

30. FMPSP, AAA.

31. Letter, March 2, 1942, FMPSP, AAA.

32. Correspondence from the federation to the museum is in the Alfred Barr Papers, AAA; Greenberg's comment appeared in "Art," *The Nation* 158, 7 (February 12, 1944):195–6.

33. According to a press release for Rothko's one-man exhibit at Peggy Guggenheim's Art of This Century Gallery in 1945, he stopped painting for a year after his show at the Neumann-Willard Gallery in January of 1940 (quoted in Francis M. Celentano, "The Origins and Development of Abstract Expressionism in the United States," M.A. thesis, [New York University, 1951, p. 45]).

34. I discuss Rothko's notes on his reading of *The Interpretation of Dreams* in Chapter 5. Characterizing the threat posed to him by younger painters, Rothko told John Hurt Fischer in the early 1960s that "the kings die today in just the same way they did in Frazer's *The Golden Bough*" ("MR:PAAM":22). So he was familiar with Frazer, though it is not certain how or when. See below, on Rothko's reading of *The Birth of Tragedy*. Gottlieb discusses his reading of Jung in his interview with Dorothy Seckler, October 25, 1967, p. 17, AAA.

35. Mark Rothko to Joseph Liss, February 3, 1941, MRF, NGA.

36. A clipping of the *Times* ad is in the Samuel Kootz Papers, AAA.

37. Kootz's letter appears in Edward Alden Jewell, "The Problem of Seeing," *New York Times,* August 10, 1941, section 9, p. 7.

38. Sally Avery, interview with Tom Wolf, Part I, p. 23, AAA. While Rothko and Gottlieb explored ancient myths in quite different styles, they did collaborate on one painting, mysteriously marked "2092 Madison Avenue" on the back, now in the possession of the Adolph and Esther Gottlieb Foundation.

39. Esther Gottlieb, interview with Phyllis Tuchman, October 22, 1981, p. 1, AAA; Sally Avery, interview with Tom Wolf, Part I, p. 1, AAA.

40. My account of Gottlieb's life is based on Adolph Gottlieb, interview with Dorothy Seckler, October 25, 1967 (untranscribed), AAA; and Mary Davis MacNaughton, "Adolph Gottlieb: His Life and Art," in Hirsch and MacNaughton, *Adolph Gottlieb, A Retrospective.* Unless otherwise indicated, all the Gottlieb quotations in my text are taken from the Seckler interview.

41. Unlike the many women of their generation who stayed at home to raise children, Esther Gottlieb and Edith Sachar worked, thus reversing conventional familial roles. But like many women of their generation, they gave up their own ambitions to enable their husbands to realize theirs. Either way, patriarchy prevailed.

42. Interview with Tom Wolf, Part I, p. 2, AAA.

43. Ibid., Part I, pp. 2, 7, AAA.

44. Interview with Dorothy Seckler, p. 12, AAA.

45. Adolph Gottlieb to Howard Baumbach, January 3, 1938, Howard Baumbach Papers, AAA. Two days be-

fore, Gottlieb had written to Baumbach, recalling Avery's advice, "Don't try to paint a masterpiece." But, Gottlieb continued, "it seems to me now that this is the very thing to do—try to make a masterpiece—it probably won't be one anyway. Of course, from his point of view Milton's right, there are many pictures that would be pretty good if they weren't belabored and worked to death in trying for perfection. But right now I am sick of all the *pretty good* pictures and want a picture that is either *dam[n] good* or no good" (Adolph Gottlieb to Howard Baumbach, January 1, [1938], Howard Baumbach Papers, AAA).

46. Interview with Dorothy Seckler, p. 15, AAA.

47. Esther Gottlieb and Sanford Hirsch interview, July 1, 1987; letter from Edith (Sachar) Carson, January 5, 1978, quoted in MR,AR, p. 34.

48. Harold Rosenberg, *Barnett Newman* (New York, 1977), pp. 27–29; BN,SWI, p. 137.

49. Mark Rothko, interview with Gladys Kashdin, GKP, AAA; "Adolph Gottlieb: An Interview with David Sylvester," *Living Arts* 1, 2 (June 1963):4.

50. Paul Bodin interview, July 2, 1987; Morris Calden interview; Sanford Hirsch and Esther Gottlieb interview.

51. "Adolph Gottlieb: An Interview with David Sylvester":4.

52. One of them was Howard Baumbach (Howard Baumbach interview, June 28, 1987).

53. See *Bulletin, The Metropolitan Museum of Art* 1, 3 (November 1942):116, 141; and 1, 4 (December 1942):141–43.

54. Whitney is quoted in Lynes, *Good Old Modern,* p. 233; the list of exhibits is taken from the same source, p. 452.

55. BN,SWI, pp. 29–30; catalogue for the first exhibit of New York Artist-Painters, Louis Schanker Papers, AAA.

56. Letter from Joseph Solman to Jacob Kainen, n.d., Jacob Kainen Papers, AAA.

57. In "American Modern Artists" Rothko had exhibited *Seascape, Seated Figure, Sculptor* and *Nude.*

58. *Abstract and Surrealist Art in America* (New York, 1944), p. 118; reprinted in *MR,* p. 81.

59. In the early 1940s Rothko produced several works which represent (among other things) an eagle and a hare, usually with a hollow space at its center. A drawing in MRP, AAA, shows a large vulturelike bird clutching a woman. In the lower right, Rothko has drawn a swastika, suggesting his awareness of the political meaning of the eagle.

60. Drafts for "JL," in MRP, AAA; and "PMA."

61. "JL."

62. Perrett, *Days of Sadness, Years of Triumph,* pp. 210 and 255.

63. Hirsch and MacNaughton, *Adolph Gottlieb, A Retrospective,* p. 32.

64. Ernest Briggs, interview with Barbara Shikler, July 12 and October 21, 1982, p. 11, AAA.

65. Wallace Putnam, "Mark Rothko Told Me," *Arts Magazine* 45, 7 (April 1974):45.

66. Adolph Gottlieb, "Jackson Pollock: An Artists' Symposium," *Art News* 66 (April 1967):31.

67. "Clyfford Still," catalogue essay

for Still exhibit at Art of This Century, February 1946; reprinted in *MR*, p. 82.

68. "PMA."

69. *Vogue,* October 1, 1942, p. 30.

70. Juliette Hays interview; Juliette Hays, interview with Dore Ashton, pp. 6–7, AAA; Milton Avery to Louis and Annette Kaufman, September 26, 1941, LKP, AAA.

71. Joseph Belsey interview; Sophie Tracy interview.

72. Quoted by Buffie Johnson, in my interview with her.

73. Morris Calden, interview with Bonnie Clearwater and Barbara Shikler, June 30, 1982, MRF, NGA.

74. Interview with Walter Hopps, AAA; the studio was at 36 East 21st, first listed under "Edith Sachar" in the Manhattan phone book for December 1942.

75. Morris Calden interview; Sally Avery interview; Sally Avery, interview with Tom Wolf, Part I, p. 11, AAA.

76. Morris Calden interview.

77. Hobbs and Levin, *Abstract Expressionism, The Formative Years,* p. 119.

78. Prints and Drawings Department, NGA, Rothko H.6.5.

79. "PL," MRA.

80. Prints and Drawings Department, NGA, Rothko H.8.8.

81. Cecile Abish interview, May 20, 1988; George and Shirley Climo interview; *AR*, p. 52.

82. Preface, *AR*, n.p.

83. Regina Bogat interview.

84. "ND," MRA.

85. Dore Ashton interview; she said that Rothko told her he had attended some of these lectures.

86. *Pest,* April 28, 1923. Peter Selz recalled Rothko telling him that he'd read Nietszche while a student at Yale (Peter Selz interview, September 11, 1986).

87. "ND," MRA.

Chapter Seven

1. Press release quoted in Angelica Zander Rudenstine, *Peggy Guggenheim Collection, Venice* (New York, 1985), p. 771.

2. *New York Times,* October 20 and 21, 1942.

3. Hedda Sterne recalled that she first met Rothko at this opening (Hedda Sterne interview, January 22, 1986).

4. My account of Peggy Guggenheim's life is based on Jacqueline Bograd Weld, *Peggy: The Wayward Guggenheim* (New York, 1986), and Peggy Guggenheim, *Out of This Century: Confessions of an Art Addict* (New York, 1979).

5. Guggenheim, *Out of This Century,* p. 209.

6. Rudenstine, *Peggy Guggenheim Collection, Venice,* p. 771, note 2.

7. Robert Saltonstall Mattison, *Robert Motherwell: The Formative Years* (Ann Arbor, 1987), p. 53.

8. Aline B. Saarinen, *The Proud Possessors* (New York, 1958), p. 336; Guggenheim, *Out of This Century,* pp. 275–76.

9. *A Not-So-Still Life* (New York, 1984), p. 226.

10. My account is based on "A Selective Chronology of Avant-Garde Activities in America, 1925–1947," Appendix III in Melvin Lader's "Peggy Guggenheim's Art of This Century: the Surrealist Milieu and the American Avant-

Garde, 1942–47," Ph.D. dissertation (University of Delaware, 1981).

11. "Collector as Creator," *Saturday Review* 43 (November 12, 1960):30.

12. Minutes, November 21, 1941, FMPSP, AAA.

13. Guggenheim, *Out of This Century*, pp. 168–70; Weld, *Peggy*, pp. 276–77; Bernard Reis, interview with Paul Cummings, p. 32, AAA.

My account of Reis's life is based on two biographical resumés that are in the BRP, AAA; his interviews with Paul Cummings, June 3 and 10, 1976, AAA; Rebecca Reis, interviews with William McNaught, March 24, April 29, May 6, May 15, May 22, July 14, September 8, and September 9, 1980 [untranscribed], AAA; and my own interview with Rebecca Reis, November 8, 1986. Unless otherwise indicated, subsequent quotations from Rebecca Reis in this section are taken from her interviews with William McNaught.

14. Bernard Reis, *False Security: The Betrayal of the American Investor* (New York, 1937).

15. Bernard Reis, interview with Paul Cummings, p. 20, AAA.

16. Interview with Paul Cummings, November 24, 1971, p. 50, AAA.

17. Guggenheim, *Out of This Century*, p. 266.

18. Ibid., pp. 266–67.

19. *The Diary of Anais Nin, 1939–1944* (New York, 1969), p. 281.

20. Robert Motherwell to William Baziotes, September 6, 1944, William Baziotes Papers, AAA.

21. Weld, *Peggy*, p. 270; and Ernst, *A Not-So-Still Life*, pp. 226–27.

22. Jimmy Ernst, interview with Paul Cummings, September 30, 1974, p. 13, AAA. Ernst dates the party in 1947 or 1948.

23. Interview with Paul Cummings, p. 30, AAA.

24. Ibid., pp. 84, 47, 35.

25. Sally Scharf remembered that Rothko invited her to lunch to meet Matta (William and Sally Scharf interview, January 8, 1986).

26. Robert Motherwell interview; Sidney Simon, "Concerning the Beginnings of The New York School: 1939–43, An Interview with Robert Motherwell," *Art International* 11, 6 (Summer 1967):23.

27. Max Ernst, for instance, had painted *Oedipus Rex* (1922), *Oedipus II* (1934), and *Oedipus and the Sphinx* (1935). See Whitney Chadwick, *Myth in Surrealist Painting, 1929–1939* (Ann Arbor, 1980).

28. Mark Rothko, "Personal Statement" (1945), reprinted in *MR*, p. 82; Herbert Ferber, "Waldorf Panel 1," *It Is* 6 (Autumn 1965):8; Barbaralee Diamondstein, "An Interview with Robert Motherwell," reprinted in *Robert Motherwell* (New York, 1982), p. 228.

29. "Manifesto of Surrealism, 1924," reprinted in *Manifestoes of Surrealism*, trans. Richard Seaver and Helen R. Lane (Ann Arbor, 1969), p. 26. Among Rothko's papers there is a page on which he has transcribed a quotation from Breton. Headed "Automatism—Surrealism—Andre Breton," the passage reads: "We must search therefore for a link common to various modes of perception, enumerated above—its link is automatism. An appeal to automatism in all its forms, is our only chance of solving, outside the economic plane, all these contradictions of principle which,

since they existed before our social regime was formed, are not likely to disappear with it. These contradictions cry out for attention, since they make themselves cruelly felt and since they imply a servitude even more profound and even more final than a temporal servitude.— They are the contradictions of being [unreadable word] of objectivity and subjectivity of perception, and representation, of past and future, of collective and individual love, even of life and death."

30. Interview with James Johnson Sweeney, excerpted in *Theories of Modern Art*, ed. Herschel B. Chipp (Berkeley, 1968), p. 435.

31. Interview with William Seitz, January 22, 1952, WSP, AAA. Seitz noted that Rothko "insists that I write this down as a direct quote."

32. WP, pp. 27 and 20–21.

33. "Modern Painters Open Show Today," *New York Times*, June 2, 1943, p. 28.

34. "End-of-the-Season Melange," *New York Times*, June 6, 1943, section 2, p. 9.

35. FMPSP, AAA.

36. My account of this myth is indebted to Franz Cumont, *The Mysteries of Mithra*, trans. Thomas J. McCormack (New York, 1956).

37. The text of the Jewell letter, with two small changes of punctuation, is based on a copy of the original typescript in the MRF, MOMA.

38. "Clyfford Still," *MR*, pp. 82–83.

39. Hirsch and MacNaughton, *Adolph Gottlieb, A Retrospective*, p. 13.

40. Annalee Newman interview, January 26, 1987.

41. My account of Newman's life is based on Thomas B. Hess, *Barnett Newman* (London, 1972); Brenda Richardson, *The Complete Drawings, 1944–1969* (Baltimore, 1979); and introductory material provided in BN,SWI. Whenever possible I will quote from this text.

42. Hess, *Barnett Newman*, p. 9.

43. BN,SWI, p. 195.

44. Hess, *Barnett Newman*, p. 9.

45. BN,SWI, p. 45.

46. Hess, *Barnett Newman*, p. 12.

47. Ibid., p. 13.

48. BN,SWI, p. 45.

49. Ibid., pp. 4–8.

50. Mark Rothko to Katharine Kuh, July 14, (1954), KKP, AIC.

51. Hess, *Barnett Newman*, p. 14.

52. BN,SWI, p. 23.

53. Hess, *Barnett Newman*, p. 24. These quotations do not appear in the versions of this essay collected in BN,SWI.

54. BN,SWI, pp. 166–67.

55. BN,SWI, pp. 166–69.

56. Hess, *Barnett Newman*, pp. 22–25.

57. Ibid.

58. Annalee Newman interview.

59. Adolph Gottlieb, interview with Martin Friedman, August 1962, at the Adolph and Esther Gottlieb Foundation.

60. Interview with William Seitz, March 25, 1953, WSP, AAA. Seitz's note reads: "generally speaking there is nothing about the 1945 [sic] statement he would repudiate, although says neither he nor Gottlieb wrote it."

61. For an account stressing Rothko's participation, see Bonnie Clear-

water, "Shared Myths: Reconsideration of Rothko's and Gottlieb's Letter to *The New York Times*," *Archives of American Art Journal* 24, 1 (1984):23–25.

62. All quotes from Rothko's drafts for the letter are from the MRP, AAA.

63. The words in brackets are an addition or possible substitution Rothko inserted above the line with the words outside the brackets.

64. Bernard Malamud, "The Aquamarine Sunrise: A Memory of Rothko," in *MR,AR*, pp. 13–14. In the version of this story he told to Dore Ashton, Edith "was sitting on the stoop and when he came back, she said, 'What! They didn't take you?' or something like that, and Rothko was very angry. According to him that was the moment he decided to take off" (Dore Ashton interview).

65. David Margolis interview; he recalled that the two men—Boris Margo and Rothko—shared a two-room flat, with Rothko occupying the back room.

66. My account of the divorce is based on "Edith Sachar Rothkowitz v. Marcus Rothkowitz," Supreme Court, New York County, Index No. 30611, 1943, Office of the County Clerk, New York City. The separate home addresses for Rothko and Edith Sachar are taken from the divorce records. Rothko's 52nd Street address first appears in the Manhattan phone book for summer-fall 1945. Edith Sachar's business address on 21st Street first appears in the Manhattan phone book for summer-fall 1943. When they separated, they had moved, probably in October of 1942, from their 28th Street apartment to one at 36 East 21st Street.

67. Sally Avery interview; Howard Baumbach interview.

68. Jack Kufeld, interview with Avis Berman, October 5, 1981, p. 7, AAA.

69. Earle Blew interview, January 18, 1990; Arthur Gage interview; Louis and Annette Kaufman interview.

70. Milton Avery to Louis and Annette Kaufman, November 8, 1943, LKP, AAA.

71. Sophie Tracy interview.

72. Mark Rothko to Sonia Rabin (Fall 1943).

Chapter Eight

1. Hess's account appears in his *Barnett Newman*, p. 19, but this mythic generational biography began with Harold Rosenberg in his well-known "The American Action Painters": "With a few important exceptions, most of the artists of this vanguard found their way to their present work by being cut in two. Their type is not a young painter but a re-born one. The man may be over forty, the painter around seven. The diagonal of a grand crisis separates him from his personal and artistic past" (*Art News* 23 [December 1952]:48).

Rosenberg's notion of the "grand crisis" was first applied to Rothko by Elaine de Kooning in her "Two Americans in Action: Franz Kline and Mark Rothko": "The cleavage between the present and the past for certain artists is as drastic as it was for Saul of Tarsus outside the walls of Damascus when he saw a 'great light' and heard a great question, the popular version of which is '*Quo Vadis*?'. . . . Sometimes, [this question] is a shout and the artist jumps, like Saul, from his Past into his Present: he is no longer Saul, he's Paul, and he knows where he's going. He didn't make a decision; he had a revelation; he is a Convert. His present dates from the moment of his conversion. The work or actions that went before are part of his Past which no longer exists" (*Art News Annual* 27 [1958]:89).

2. Buffie Johnson interview; Buffie Johnson, interview with Barbara Shikler, November 3, 1982, pp. 1–3, AAA. Rothko was not Sophie Rosenstein's "nephew" but her cousin by her marriage to Arthur (Weinstein) Gage.

3. Hermine Benhaim, "Howard Putzel and the Beginnings of Abstract Expressionism," unpublished essay, n.p., Howard Putzel Papers, AAA. Ms. Benhaim is quoting Buffie Johnson. Peggy Guggenheim, however, did not remain a Rothko admirer. When, sometime in the 1950s or 1960s, Bernard Reis proposed a show of Art of This Century painters, she responded, "I can't bear the paintings of Barney Newman. I hate all that school of painting including Rothko's present work and would not want my name associated with it" (Peggy Guggenheim to Bernard Reis, March 20, [?], BRP, AAA).

4. Milton Avery to Louis Kaufman, June 10, 1944, LKP, AAA. By "the Guggenheim" Avery is referring not to the later Guggenheim Museum but to Peggy Guggenheim's Art of This Century.

5. Mark Rothko to Sonia Rabin, November 15, 1944.

6. David Porter, *A Painting Prophecy—1950* (Washington, D.C., 1945). Apparently, Porter was asked to write the catalogue essay for Rothko's Art of This Century exhibit, but his essay, which begins with the same general statements Porter used in his brochure for the "Painting Prophecy" show, was not used. In an undated letter Rothko thanks Porter "for your vehement interest in my pictures" (both Porter's essay and Rothko's letter are in David Porter Papers, AAA). Howard Putzel's statement for the "A Problem for Critics" show was reprinted by Edward Alden Jewell in "Toward Abstract Or Away?" *New York Times,* July 1, 1945, section X, p. 2. Rothko had exhibited in "40 American Moderns" at Putzel's 67 Gallery from December 4 to 30, 1944 (Melvin P. Lader "Howard Putzel: Proponent of Surrealism and Early Abstract Expressionism in America," *Arts* 56 [March 1982]:93).

7. Quoted in Jewell, "Toward Abstract Or Away?" p. 2.

8. "Personal Statement"; reprinted in *MR,* p. 82.

9. Jewell, "Toward Abstract Or Away?" p. 2.

10. *New York Times,* July 8, 1945, section X, p. 2.

11. Mark Rothko to Emily Genauer, January 15, 1945, in Emily Genauer Papers, AAA.

12. Mark Rothko to David Porter, n.d., David Porter Papers, AAA.

13. Mark Rothko to Barnett and Annalee Newman, July (31?), 1945, BNP, AAA.

14. As my account of the painting will subsequently show, *Slow Swirl* was painted after Rothko had met and fallen in love with his second wife in the fall of 1944. Thus, I date the painting *late* 1944.

15. Interview with Phyllis Tuchman, October 22, 1981, p. 16, AAA.

16. Bernard Reis kept the books for Art of This Century and his account sheets are in the BRP, AAA; they record sales and prices for Rothko's show at the gallery.

17. "Mr. Rothko would like to show the large canvas since he considers it his most important" (Peggy Guggenheim to Grace Morley, April 23, 1946, MRF, San Francisco Museum of Modern Art).

18. Anna Chave, *Mark Rothko, Subjects in Abstraction* (New Haven, 1989), pp. 108–10.

19. Mark Rothko, interview with William Seitz, March 25, 1953, WSP, AAA.

20. Letters from Peggy Guggenheim to Grace L. McCann Morley, director of the San Francisco Museum of Modern Art, on June 1, 1946, and February 13, 1947; and Grace Morley to Peggy Guggenheim on February 15, and December 4, 1946. On August 20, 1946 Rothko wrote to Morley, "I am delighted to hear that the Museum is to have the large painting permanently. It is my favorite of all those I have painted, and I hope it continues to wear well upon growing acquaintance" (all of this correspondence is the MRF, San Francisco Museum of Modern Art, along with the records of Rothko's exchange to get *Slow Swirl* back). My information about the painting's place in the Rothkos' living room and its nickname come from my interview with Kate Rothko.

21. Juliette Hays interview.

22. A show of "Italian Masters" seems a strange exhibit for a museum of *modern* art, and it was. The twenty-eight paintings had been at the San Francisco World's Fair; the Metropolitan refused the show partly on the grounds that accepting it would legitimatize the Italian Fascist regime. Alfred Barr's belief that great art was beyond politics freed him to accept the show (Alice Goldfarb Marquis, *Alfred H. Barr, Jr: Missionary for the Modern* [Chicago, 1989], pp. 192–93).

23. Aldarilla Shipley was born on February 13, 1896; Morton Beistle was born September 28, 1888. My information about Mell Rothko's life is taken from my interviews with her two sisters and their husbands: George and Shirley Climo, and Richard and Barbara Northrup, October 15, 1986; from my interviews with Ruth Moran, April 15, 1992, Barbara and Richard Morrow, January 12, 1990, and Betty Schoenfeld, April 16, 1992; and from my interviews with Kate Rothko and Christopher Rothko, February 6, 1986.

24. Information about Mell Beistle's high school career comes from her senior yearbook, *Caldron* (1939), provided to me by Barbara Northrup.

25. *Mr. Heinie* was followed by *Mr. Heinie and Mr. Scroot* (1939), *Just Puggy* (1939), *Open Daily* (1942), and *I Spy* (1944). In addition, Mell Beistle illustrated *Resolute* by Lima L. Henderson (1940). All the books were published by David McKay.

26. *Erondiks* (Skidmore College Yearbook) (1940), p. 54.

27. Ibid., (1943), n.p.

28. The address is from the Manhattan phone book for winter-spring 1945.

29. Kate Rothko interview; Aaron Siskind, interview with Barbara Shikler, September 28, 1982 and October 2, 1982, p. 31, AAA.

30. They were married in New Jersey because, as a stipulation to Rothko's divorce from Edith Sachar, he could not be married in New York. Both Rothko and his bride had to give false New Jersey addresses to be married there, a fact that made Rothko, according to Annalee

Newman, very nervous (Annalee Newman interview). The witnesses at the marriage were Mell's mother and a man named Morton M. Deutsch, then living at 19 West 16th Street, New York City (Record of Marriage, Office of the Registrar of Vital Statistics, Linden, New Jersey).

31. *LMR,* p. 19; Aaron Siskind, interview with Barbara Shikler, p. 31, AAA.

32. Mark Rothko to Kate Rothkowitz (1944); Aaron Siskind, interview with Barbara Shikler, p. 31, AAA.

33. Mark Rothko to Sonia Allen, November 15, 1944.

34. Sophie Tracy interview.

35. A letter from Rothko to Barnett and Annalee Newman—written from East Hampton, Long Island, August 10, 1946—states that "we have delayed our trip West until October, and that we will stay here in the country until then," making clear Rothko was no longer teaching at Center Academy (BNP, AAA). Referring to his show at the Mortimer Brandt Gallery (April 22 to May 4, 1946), Rothko wrote to Louis and Annette Kaufman that "I sold enough to be able to give up my teaching (thank God) and one person invested more than $1000 in the stuff" (May 17, [1946], LKP, AAA). Rothko's freedom from teaching was made possible in part by his wife's job, which she kept until their 1950 trip to Europe, when their daughter Kate was conceived.

36. George and Blanche Okun interview.

37. Elizabeth Till interview, June 19, 1985. See Till's "A Study in Retrospect" and "Mark Rothko at the Guggenheim," in *Northwest Magazine, The Sunday Oregonian,* for March 29, 1970 and December 17, 1978, respectively.

38. Sophie Tracy interview.

39. *AR,* p. 83.

40. Ruth Moran recalled that Rothko said he liked her husband because he, too, was a "supreme pessimist."

41. Juliette Hays interview; George and Blanche Okun interview.

42. Aaron Siskind, interview with Barbara Shikler, p. 31, AAA.

43. Earle Blew interview.

44. *Clyfford Still,* ed. John P. O'Neill (New York, 1979), p. 21. My account of Still's life relies on "Biographical Chronology" in this text, plus "Clyfford Still Biography" and "Notes by Clyfford Still" in *Clyfford Still* (San Francisco, 1976); Thomas Albright, "A Conversation with Clyfford Still," *Art News* 75 (March 1976):30–35; Thomas Albright, "The Painted Flame," *Horizon* (November 1979):24–27, 32–33; and Thomas Albright, *Art in the San Francisco Bay Area, 1945–1980* (Berkeley, 1985), pp. 20–35.

45. In a letter to Clay Spohn, November 23, 1955, Still wrote that "I have remained in almost total isolation from those friends we knew years ago such as Rothko, Ferren, Siskind, Gottlieb. Their interests are of a more practical nature than I am able to tolerate. Occasionally, I set a bomb adrift just to remind them I am on this planet" (CSP, AAA).

46. Letter from Mrs. Clyfford Still to the author, March 26, 1986. The correspondence between Rothko and Still was abundant enough for Still to propose to Rothko, on November 1, 1951, "that we gather together the letters we have exchanged over the last few years and read them again. It occurs to me that in them may be a better record of

our relation to our work, and the world we have touched, than can be provided by any other means." Still's motive, one he shared with Rothko, was to save the work from those cultural institutions that sought to "own" it: "If I accept the economic and moral responsibility for my acts, the least I can do is to follow through with a statement when the spokesmen for the status quo would presume to incorporate me or deny my right to exist" (*Clyfford Still* [1976], p. 115).

47. Ernest Briggs, interview with Barbara Shikler, July 12 and October 21, 1982, p. 7, AAA.

48. "Clyfford Still," in *MR*, p. 82. Rothko's essay, however, does make Still over into one of the "small band of Myth Makers who have emerged" in New York "during the war." Perhaps that is *one* reason Still later repudiated the essay.

49. Clyfford Still to Betty Parsons, September 20, 1946, BPP, AAA.

50. Clyfford Still to Betty Parsons, July 23, 1947, in LSF.

51. The catalogue for this show, September 9 to September 27, 1947, at Wildenstein's, is in the FMPSP, AAA.

52. For Still's account of this loan, see O'Neill ed., *Clyfford Still*, pp. 60 and 184. Both Diane Waldman, in "Mark Rothko: The Farther Shore of Art" (*MR,AR*, p. 52), and Michael Compton, in "Mark Rothko, The Subjects of the Artist" (*MR*, p. 49), identify the Still painting as *1947-8-W No. 2*. In *Clyfford Still* (1976), p. 114, Still gives simply *1947-8-W* as the painting loaned Rothko, but in O'Neill, *Clyfford Still*, p. 188, he gives *1947-48-W No. 1*. There, Still states that in a California School of Fine Arts studio which he loaned Rothko for the summer of 1949, "Rothko developed his final style after seeing Still's large black *1947-48-W No. 1 (PH-114)*." But Rothko's exhibit at Betty Parsons in March–April of 1949 establishes that Rothko had evolved his mature style before this summer trip to San Francisco.

53. Clyfford Still to Betty Parsons, April 11, 1951, BPP, AAA.

54. Quoted in Albright, "The Painted Flame":32.

55. Katharine Kuh, interview with Avis Berman, n.d., p. 14, AAA. Dore Ashton similarly remarked, "Mark was deeply impressed by this guy who condemned everything. And there was a certain timidity in Mark, of which Still had none."

56. Quoted in Albright, *Art in the San Francisco Bay Area, 1945–1980*, p. 30.

57. Quoted in Mary Fuller McChesney, *A Period of Exploration: San Francisco, 1945–1950* (Oakland, 1973), p. 33; Ernest Briggs, interview with Barbara Shikler, p. 5, AAA.

58. *AR*, p. 93.

59. Albright, "The Painted Flame": 26.

60. *Clyfford Still* (1976), p. 122.

61. Albright, "The Painted Flame": 32.

62. Ibid., 32; *Clyfford Still* (1976), p. 110.

63. Albright, *Art in the San Francisco Bay Area, 1945–1980*, p. 21.

64. Albright, "The Painted Flame": 26; Ti-Grace Sharpless, *Clyfford Still, October 18–November 29, 1963* (Philadelphia, 1963), n.p.

65. "A Statement by the Artist," in *Clyfford Still: 33 Paintings at the Albright-Knox Art Gallery* (Buffalo, N.Y., 1966), p. 17; letter from Clyfford Still to Gordon Smith, January 1, 1959, in *Paintings by Clyfford Still* (Buffalo, N.Y., 1959), n.p.

66. Albright, "The Painted Flame": 26.

67. The painting, now in the collection of the National Museum of American Art (Smithsonian Institution), is reproduced in Albright, *Art in the San Francisco Bay Area, 1945–1980*, p. 23.

68. Albright, "The Painted Flame": 32.

69. *Clyfford Still* (1976), p. 108; O'Neill, *Clyfford Still*, p. 178.

70. O'Neill, *Clyfford Still*, pp. 177–78.

71. Clyfford Still, "Cézanne: A Study in Evaluation," M.A. thesis, (Washington State College, 1935), pp. 4–5.

72. Ibid., pp. 8, 11, 16, 22.

73. Both of these paintings are reproduced in *Clyfford Still* (1976), plates 9 and 10, and Still explicitly identifies both as paintings shown to Rothko. *1944-G* is 69″ × 33″, and *1945-H* is 90″ × 69″.

74. Albright, "The Painted Flame": 32; "Review," *Magazine of Art* 41 (March 1948):16.

75. O'Neill, *Clyfford Still*, p. 180; *Clyfford Still* (1976), p. 119.

76. Quoted in Albright, *Art in the San Francisco Bay Area, 1945–1980*, p. 30.

77. On the resemblances (and differences) between the work of Still and Rothko, see AR, p. 95; Waldman, "The Farther Shore of Art," in MR,AR, p. 51; Stephen Polcari in "The Intellectual Roots of Abstract Expressionism," *Arts Magazine* 54, 1 (September 1979):129–30; David Anfam, "Clyfford Still," Ph.D. dissertation (Courtauld Institute of Art, 1984).

78. Interview with Barbara Shikler, p. 7, AAA.

79. O'Neill, *Clyfford Still*, p. 27.

80. Albright, *Art in the San Francisco Bay Area, 1945–1980*, p. 31; Ernest Briggs, quoted in McChesney, *A Period of Exploration*, p. 42.

Chapter Nine

1. Guggenheim, *Out of This Century*, p. 320; and Wald, *Peggy*, p. 356.

2. Milton Avery to Louis Kaufman, September 6, 1945, LKP, AAA; Calvin Tomkins, "A Keeper of the Treasure: Betty Parsons," *New Yorker* 51 (June 9, 1975):51–52; Betty Parsons, interview with Gerald Silk, June 11, 1981, p. 1, AAA; "A Keeper of the Treasure":52, 54.

According to Tomkins, Pollock was part of the group that wanted to remain together; but the problems of relocating Pollock were unique, partly because of his greater reputation, partly because of his reputation as a drinker, but mainly because a dealer had to be found willing to pay him the monthly stipend that Peggy Guggenheim was paying him. So it seems to me unlikely that Pollock would have joined the other three.

3. Rothko's agreement with Parsons, dated November 28, 1947 and lasting until June 30, 1949, can be found in BPP, AAA. The precise dates of the Rothko exhibits are in the "Chronology" in MR,AR, pp. 271–73.

4. The Whitney held annuals in painting and in sculpture, watercolors and drawings; Rothko, exhibiting in

both, thus took part in seven annuals in five years. For a list of the specific exhibits, see the "Chronology" in MR,AR, pp. 271–73. Rothko's letter to Lloyd Goodrich, December 20, 1952, refuses to submit paintings for the Whitney annual then being organized and also refuses any possible purchase by the museum. Two years later, Rothko, invited to take part in "The New Decade: 35 American Painters and Sculptors," declined, but was willing to sell a painting to the museum (John Baur to Mark Rothko, November 15, 1954, and memo from John Baur, December 22, 1954, MRF, Whitney Museum of American Art). Again in 1957 Rothko refused to enter a Whitney competition (Mark Rothko to Rosalind Irvine, April 9, 1957, MRF, Whitney Museum of American Art). Rothko's description of the Whitney as a "junkshop" is quoted in LMR, p. 27.

5. "Oils and Watercolors by Mark Rothko" was shown at the San Francisco Museum of Modern Art from August 16 to September 8, 1946, containing nineteen oils and ten watercolors. Eleven of the oils and all the watercolors traveled to the Santa Barbara Museum, where they were exhibited from October 1 to 15, 1946 (MRF, San Francisco Museum of Modern Art).

6. Based on material in BPP, AAA. Three of these paintings—*Vernal Memory, Geologic Memory,* and *Phalanx of the Mind*—had appeared in Rothko's Parsons show the previous year. (I am assuming that *Verdant Memory*, from the 1947 show, and *Vernal Memory* are the same painting.) *Gethsemane, Phalanx of the Mind, Agitation of the Archaic,* and *Intimations of Chaos* appear on a list of Rothko paintings at Art of This Century that came to the Betty Parsons Gallery when he moved there; and *Companionship and Solitude* is listed as in "the gallery," presumably Art of This Century, as of June 5, 1946 (BPP, AAA). *Intimations of Chaos* was included in the San Francisco Museum of Modern Art show.

7. At Art of This Century *Poised Elements* was listed at $450, and *Gethsemane* at $550. At Parsons in 1948 the paintings cost $600 and $750, respectively (BPP, AAA).

8. I use the term "multiform" to refer to all the "abstract" paintings Rothko produced between 1946 and 1949.

9. Mark Rothko to Barnett and Annalee Newman (July 31), 1945, BNP, AAA.

10. Mark Rothko to Clay Spohn, May 11, 1948, CSP, AAA.

11. The two Aaron Siskind installation photographs of Rothko's 1949 Parsons show make it clear that at least one of the multiforms was exhibited (see fig. 31); this painting, then titled *Number 1, 1949,* had already been purchased by Mrs. John D. Rockefeller III in January 1949. In 1955, the Rockefellers gave the painting to Vassar College. At the time of his 1961 MOMA show, in which Rothko exhibited eight of the multiforms, he requested that the title be changed to *Number 18, 1948.* So, either in 1961 Rothko wanted to place all the multiforms back in 1948, or in January of 1949 he wanted to present a 1948 painting as a very recent work—and then in 1961 corrected the date. The Siskind photographs are reproduced in MR,AR, p. 280. The Rockefeller sale is recorded in BPP, AAA. The subsequent history of the painting is given in a document titled "Number 18,

605

1948" in MRF, GMA. For the multiforms in the MOMA show, see Peter Selz, *Mark Rothko* (New York, 1961), p. 43.

12. Untitled statement, *Tiger's Eye* 1, 2 (December 1947):44; reprinted in *MR*, p. 83.

13. Mark Rothko to Sonia Rabin, November 15, 1944.

14. "RWP."

15. Fifteen of these paintings are reproduced in a Pace Gallery catalogue, *Mark Rothko, Multiforms* (New York, 1990); the one I am discussing (60" × 49½") is no. 15 in this catalogue.

16. "Historians['] unity is a unity of death. What we want is a live unity," Rothko told William Seitz (interview, January 22, 1952, WSP, AAA).

17. See, for example, *Untitled* (c. 1941), no. 3419 at the Guggenheim Museum. I'm indebted to Elizabeth Childs of the Guggenheim for pointing out to me the frequency with which the eagle/rabbit symbolism appears in Rothko's work.

18. Interview with Phyllis Tuchman, p. 9, AAA.

19. WP, p. 32.

20. "The article is pretty well formed and written," Rothko wrote to Robert Motherwell on December 8, 1946. "I shall want to go over it a time or two more; but to make it more specific, it will be in the mail on Thursday reaching you on Friday, unless I see you in town before then" (RMA). Since Motherwell was then an editor for *Possibilities*, the article Rothko refers to must be "The Romantics Were Prompted." The essay, then, was written about a year before its publication, just as Rothko was beginning to produce the multiforms.

21. Mark Rothko to Barnett Newman (August 1950), BNP, AAA.

22. Clement Greenberg, "Kafka's Jewishness," *Art and Culture* (New York, 1961), p. 268.

23. Interview with Phyllis Tuchman, February 17, 1981, p. 2, AAA.

24. Rothko misuses the word "ubiquitous," which means "omnipresent." I assume he means something like "all experience."

25. By 1949 both Jackson Pollock and Clyfford Still were already using similar "titles" for their work. On this question Still wrote to Betty Parsons: "The pictures will be without titles;— only identified by numbers. Risking the charge of affectation I am omitting titles because they would inevitably mislead the spectator, and delimit the meanings and implications latent in the work" (Clyfford Still to Betty Parsons, March 3, 1947, BPP, AAA); and later, "I want no allusions to interfere with or assist the spectator. Before them I want him to be on his own" (Clyfford Still to Betty Parsons, December 29, 1949, BPP, AAA). Identifying pictures by number and year, moreover, plays down their status as self-contained works of art and emphasizes their place in the artist's ongoing creative process.

Sometimes, however, Rothko seems to have been pulling his numbers out of a hat—e.g., *Number 117, 1961*. Is this the hundred and seventeenth painting Rothko produced in 1961? Not likely. Later, Rothko conventionally titled one post-1949 work *Homage to Matisse* (1954), while other titles allude to the painting's colors—e.g., *Yellow, Blue on Orange* (1955)—and still others verge on identifying literal subject matter—

e.g., *Light, Earth and Blue* (1954) or *Blue Cloud* (1954).

26. Untitled statement in *Tiger's Eye* 9 (October 15, 1949):114; reprinted in *MR*, p. 85.

27. M[argaret] B[reuning], "Fifty-seventh Street in Review: Mark Rothko at Parsons," *The Art Digest* 23, 14 (April 15, 1949):27; and T[homas] B. H[ess], "Reviews and Previews," *Art News* 43, 2 (April 1949):48. A clipping of the Moscanyi review can be found in MRF, NGA.

28. "Mark Rothko," *Magazine of Art* 42, 1 (January 1949):20–21. An essay by Oscar Collier, "Mark Rothko," had appeared in *The New Iconograph* in the fall of 1947, but the text, accompanied by seven reproductions of Rothko's work, is just two paragraphs long.

29. A letter from Rothko to Kenneth and Joy Rabin, June 2, 1948, indicates that the Rothkos were leaving the following morning for East Hampton; another letter from Rothko to the Rabins, July 28, 1948, reveals that Rothko has just returned from Provincetown. Rothko spent most of the summer in 1947 and in 1949 in San Francisco, teaching at the California School of Fine Arts, so 1948 must be the summer Rosenberg is remembering, but Rothko did not spend the entire 1948 summer in East Hampton, as Rosenberg recalled (Harold Rosenberg, interview with Joseph Liss, December 10, 1977, n.p.).

30. Interview with Joseph Liss. Ernest Briggs recalled that Rothko, in his 1949 lectures at the California School of Fine Arts, spoke of his search for "the personal image" (interview with Barbara Shikler, p. 6, AAA).

31. Murray Israel interview.

32. My account of Betty Parsons' life depends on Tomkins, "A Keeper of the Treasure"; Calvin Tomkins, *Off the Wall: Robert Rauschenberg and the Art World of Our Time* (New York, 1980), pp. 57–63; Rosalind Constable, "The Betty Parsons Collection," *Art News* 86, 3 (March 1, 1968):48–49, 58–60; Grace Lichtenstein, "Betty Parsons: Still Trying to Find the Creative World in Everything," *Art News* 78, 3 (March 1979):52–56; Betty Parsons, interview with Paul Cummings, June 4 and 9, 1969, AAA; and Betty Parsons, interview with Gerald Silk, June 11, 1981, AAA.

33. Interview with Paul Cummings, p. 3, AAA.

34. Tomkins, "A Keeper of the Treasure":48.

35. Mark Rothko to Louis and Annette Kaufman, May 17, 1946, LKP, AAA.

36. *BN,SWI*, p. 107.

37. Tomkins, "A Keeper of the Treasure":51.

38. Ibid., p. 52.

39. Lawrence Campbell quoted in ibid., p. 45; Clement Greenberg, quoted in Tomkins, *Off the Wall*, p. 58.

40. Tomkins, "A Keeper of the Treasure":52.

41. Ibid., p. 52.

42. "57th Street," *Fortune* 34, 3 (September 1946):145. The best-known account of the market in this period is Serge Guilbaut, *How New York Stole the Idea of Modern Art: Abstract Expressionism, Freedom, and the Cold War* (Chicago, 1983). Guilbaut's provocative work has been helpful to me at many points, but his basic historical narrative of the Abstract Expressionists' move from political commitments in the

1930s to a flight from history in the 1940s does not fit Rothko, who was never really political in the first place. On the issue of their acceptance on the market, a less melodramatic, more accurate account is provided in two essays by Deirdre Robson, "The Avant-Garde and the On-Guard: Some Influences on the Potential Market for the First Generation Abstract Expressionists in the 1940s and Early 1950s," *Art Journal* 47, 3 (Fall 1988):215–21; and "The Market for Abstract Expressionism: The Time Lag Between Critical and Commercial Acceptance," *Archives of American Art Journal* 25, 3 (1985):19–23. For a perceptive account of the sociology of the market, see Marcia Bystryn, "Art Galleries as Gatekeepers: The Case of the Abstract Expressionists," *Social Research* 45 (Summer 1978):390–408.

43. Robson, "The Market for Abstract Expressionism":19.

44. Aline B. Louchheim, "Who Buys What in the Picture Boom," *Art News* 43, 9 (July 1, 1944):12–14, 23–24.

45. "57th Street":148.

46. So, at least, Rothko asserted in his letter to Louis and Annette Kaufman, May 17, 1946, LKP, AAA. Of the eighteen works exhibited at Mortimer Brandt, two (*Archaic Idol* and *Olympian Play*) were on loan (from Kenneth MacPherson and Bill Davis, respectively). Of the sixteen remaining, ten (*Geologic Reverie, Gethsemane, Ancestral Imprint, Vessels of Magic, Implements of Magic, Omen, Tentacles of Memory, Omen of the Bird, Incantation,* and *Immolation*) were sold, though some of these were not sold until well into 1947. In addition, the copy of the catalogue for the Mortimer Brandt show that appears in BPP adds three additional titles in handwriting: *Entombment, Prehistoric Memory,* and *Votive Mood. Entombment* could refer either to *Entombment I* or *II*. In any case, all four of these paintings were also sold. There is no evidence in BPP that one person spent $1,000, but Parsons' records may be incomplete. Her books do not indicate a price for four of the fourteen sales listed above; the total for the ten that do have a price is $1,825; *Heraldic Dream* ($100), *Altar of Orpheus* ($75), and *Personages* ($100) were also sold in this period, bringing the total to $2,100, of which Rothko would have received (after Parsons' 33 percent commission) $1,400, plus his share of the four works for which no price is recorded, probably another three or four hundred dollars. My information about the rise in Rothko's prices comes from BPP, AAA.

47. See sales records BPP, AAA. Angelica Zander Rudenstine in her *Peggy Guggenheim Collection, Venice* (pp. 691–92) seems to confuse *Immolation* with an earlier Rothko watercolor, *Sacrifice,* bought by Peggy Guggenheim and dated by her first as 1945, then later as 1943. Rudenstine quotes Rothko's letter to the Brooklyn Museum, May 21, 1947, in which he dates *Vessels of Magic* (purchased by the Museum) in April 1946 and mentions "five paintings of the same size and shape which were painted almost on the eve of my watercolor exhibition in April 1946," one of which, he says, has "been acquired by Peggy Guggenheim." But Betty Parsons' records establish that Rothko here refers to *Immolation,* not *Sacrifice.*

48. E. W. Root purchased *Omens of Gods and Birds* on January 3, 1946; he also bought an unidentified oil painting

by Rothko on April 10, 1949, from Betty Parsons for $200 (BPP, AAA). On Root, see "One Man's Collection," *Art Digest* (March 1, 1953):13.

49. C. A. Blyth, *American Business Cycles, 1945–50* (New York, 1969); see especially the graph in his fig. 1.1, which shows the economic slowdown from late 1948 to late 1949 (p. 20). See also Robson, "The Market for Abstract Expressionism":20.

50. Rothko did sell three oil paintings during 1948—*Number 10, 1948* ($400), *Number 23, 1948* ($250), and *Number 24, 1948* ($250); they are presumably multiforms, which he did seem to exhibit privately. During 1948, he sold an unidentified gouache for $125, *Votive Mood* for $150, an unidentified watercolor for $250; one Parsons list of Rothko works sold includes three watercolors that are dated 1948, without indicating either the price or the date of the sale (BPP, AAA).

51. Quoted in Mattison, *Robert Motherwell, The Formative Years*, p. 130.

52. Samuel Kootz Papers, AAA.

53. Marcia Bystryn, "Art Galleries as Gatekeepers":405.

54. Tomkins, "A Keeper of the Treasure":45.

55. That address first appears as the return address on a letter from Rothko to Barnett Newman, July 31, 1945, BNP, AAA.

56. Mark Rothko to Kenneth and Joy Rabin, December 1947.

57. Dorothy Miller to Clair Zamoiski, January 9, 1978, MRF, GMA; Miller dates the purchase in 1950, but the records in the BPP, AAA, establish the date of purchase as January 4, 1949. Miller may be confusing this purchase with another made by the Rockefellers on December 28, 1950 (BPP, AAA).

58. In the 1949 show Rothko exhibited eleven paintings, ranging in price from $100 to $3,000, though the $3,000 price is apparently for the painting already bought by the Rockefellers for $1,000. The average price for a work at this exhibit was about $850, a figure pulled up by the $3,000 asked for *Number 1, 1949* (the next most expensive painting was $1,800). For the eleven paintings in the 1950 show, Rothko's prices ranged from $500 to $1,500, with the average price about $1,100 (BPP, AAA). My interviews both with members of Rothko's family and Edith Sachar's family—with whom he remained in some kind of contact—reveal that the Rockefeller sale assumed the status of a kind of mythical event in both families.

59. "After Three Years," *Magazine of Art* 39, 4 (April 1946):138.

60. "The Present Prospects of American Painting and Sculpture," *Clement Greenberg, The Collected Essays and Criticism* (Chicago, 1986), vol. 2, pp. 169–70.

61. Interview with Dorothy Seckler, p. 17, AAA.

62. My discussion here is indebted to Meyer Schapiro's "Nature of Abstract Art," in *Modern Art, 19th and 20th Centuries* (New York, 1982), pp. 185–211.

63. Interview with Gladys Kashdin, GKP, AAA.

64. Robert Motherwell and Ad Reinhardt, eds., *Modern Artists in America* (New York, 1952), p. 22.

65. Interview with Irving Sandler, April 22, 1968, p. 75, AAA.

66. "JC," February 8, 1955.

67. Robert Motherwell recalled a party at the Newmans' where, after drinking a couple of bottles of vodka, they began singing along with a record of *Don Giovanni*. "Mark sang *Don Giovanni* as if it were *Boris Godonov*. We were all singing at the top of our lungs and having a ball."

68. Mark Rothko to Clay Spohn, February 2, 1948, CSP, AAA.

69. In the 1947 summer session (June 23 to August 1) Rothko taught "Painting," "restricted to artists and advanced students," from 9–12 on Monday, Wednesday, and Friday; and he lectured on "Contemporary Art" on Friday, 1–2. In the 1949 summer session (July 5 to August 12) he taught the same "Painting" class at the same hours and lectured on "Views of Painting Today" on Thursday, 1–2 (Roy Ascott [Dean, San Francisco Art Institute] to Clair Zamoiski, August 10, 1977, MRF, GMA).

70. Fred Martin interview, July 3, 1985.

71. Smith and Hultberg quoted from McChesney, *A Period of Exploration*, pp. 32–33. Rothko's comment about painting eyes on a rock echoes the last sentences of his "Personal Statement" (1945): "Rather be prodigal than niggardly. I would sooner confer anthropomorphic attributes upon a stone, than dehumanize the slightest possibility of consciousness" (*MR*, p. 82).

Nature made the urban Rothko uncomfortable; so did machines. He was as bad a driver as he was a gardener. Rothko, in fact, was a painter who did not like to work with his hands—at least not to work carefully, precisely, methodically with them. The edges of his rectangles were fuzzy; but the stretchers on which he placed his beautiful canvases were often sloppily or hastily made. He had no affinity for that part of twentieth-century art (and literature) that celebrates or just confronts the "machine age." When he painted subways in the late 1930s, he was engaged not by the trains but by the platforms—or by the people on the platforms.

Rothko did not want to render the human as mechanical as, say, Léger does. This is the same Rothko who refused to represent the human figure once he could no longer do so without mutilating it. Wishing to think of himself as prodigal and creative, rather than as niggardly and cruel, he was preoccupied with humanizing the inhuman, be it natural or man-made, a landscape or a subway station.

72. Albright, *Art in the San Francisco Bay Area, 1945–1980*, p. 26; Ernest Briggs, interview with Barbara Shikler, pp. 6–7, AAA; McChesney, *A Period of Exploration*, p. 33.

73. Mark Rothko to Barnett and Annalee Newman, July 19, 1947, BNP, AAA.

74. Spohn drew up an elaborate set of questions (numbered and subdivided) to ask Rothko during one of his 1947 Friday lectures. On a separate sheet, Spohn identified a question (e.g., "2-B"), then recorded Rothko's answer. In my reconstruction I've simplified Spohn's questions and corrected his spelling (CSP, AAA).

75. Ernest Briggs, interview with Barbara Shikler, pp. 3–4, AAA; Fred Martin interview.

76. Mark Rothko to Betty Parsons, November (1947), BPP, AAA.

77. Mark Rothko to Barnett and Annalee Newman, July 24, 1947, BNP, AAA. Both summers in San Francisco Rothko lived at 2500 Leavenworth Street.

78. Clyfford Still to Robert Motherwell, January 3, 1948, quoted in O'Neill, *Clyfford Still,* p. 186. Motherwell, too, remembered that the idea for what became the Subjects of the Artist school originated with Still.

79. O'Neill, *Clyfford Still* (1979), p. 186. Still's diary entry records a meeting in June 1948.

80. On the history of the school, see Barbara Cavaliere and Robert C. Hobbs, "Against a Newer Lacoon," *Arts* 51 (April 1977):110–17; E. A. Carmean, Jr., Introduction, *American Art at Mid-Century: The Subjects of the Artist* (Washington, D.C., 1978), pp. 15–41; Mattison, *Robert Motherwell, The Formative Years,* pp. 185, 195–96; and Motherwell and Reinhardt, eds., *Modern Artists in America,* p. 9.

81. Bernard Reis, interview with Paul Cummings, p. 56, AAA; and Mattison, *Robert Motherwell, The Formative Years,* p. 185; Cavaliere and Hobbs, "Against a Newer Lacoon":111; and Motherwell and Reinhardt, eds. *Modern Artists in America,* p. 9.

82. Rothko spoke on November 18, 1949; admission was 59 cents (cf. a postcard announcement in MRF, MOMA Library).

83. Quoted in E. A. Carmean, Introduction, p. 15.

84. Max Kozloff, "An Interview with Robert Motherwell," *Artforum* 4, 1 (September 1965):37.

85. Quoted in *AR,* p. 104.

86. Mark Rothko to Katharine Kuh, July 28 (1954), KKP, AIC.

87. Quoted in Mattison, *Robert Motherwell, The Formative Years,* p. 185. Since 1938 Hofmann's school had been located at 52 West 8th St.

88. Cavaliere and Hobbs, "Against a Newer Lacoon":110; Yvonne Thomas interview, February 11, 1990.

89. O'Neill, *Clyfford Still,* p. 187.

90. See Kate Rothkowitz's obituary notice in the *Oregonian,* October 13, 1948 (the "Chronology" in MR,AR incorrectly dates her death in early 1950); Joy Spalding interview. Like Motherwell, Annalee Newman recalled "a lot of talk about whether or not to go to Portland," adding that Rothko "thought that by the time he got there she'd be buried."

91. The story is quoted—from Greenberg's account—in Peter Fuller, *Art and Psychoanalysis* (London, 1980), p. 224. A somewhat different version of the story is told by Harold Rosenberg in his interview with Joseph Liss, from which I've taken a few details. What's common to both versions, however, is Rothko's panicked paralysis as the boat sank.

It's not certain whether this incident occurred before, or after, the death of Kate Rothkowitz. If it happened after, the impact of her death may have been part of what made Rothko passive and despairing.

92. Ben Dienes interview, January 9, 1987; "JC," n.d. Hedda Sterne similarly recalled that there was a period of "one or two years, between his surrealist and transitional works, when he stopped

painting. He wrote, went to East Hampton."

93. Joy Spalding interview; George and Shirley Climo interview.

94. "JC," April 23, 1956 and June 17, 1953.

95. Stanley Kunitz, interview with Avis Berman, Part II, p. 7, AAA; Robert Motherwell, "On Rothko" (1967), RMA; Richard and Barbara Northrup interview; Mooradian, *The Many Worlds of Arshile Gorky*, p. 198.

Anna Chave points out Rothko's engagement with the composition of the pietà in his surrealist paintings of the mid-1940s (*Mark Rothko, Subjects in Abstraction*, pp. 149–55, 161–71).

I should say here that my book is indebted at many points to Professor Chave's rich and subtly argued study of Rothko. Her thesis is that "Rothko's pictures have subject matter insofar as they can be shown to implement traces of certain elemental and symbolically charged pictorial conventions" (p. 3). Here, she implies that pictorial codes are Rothko's subject. Elsewhere, she implies that these pictorial codes are his means of making his subject available to his viewers: "By creating his art with a structure of traces, he exploited the only available pictorial language for presenting the subjects that mattered so much to him, without being confined by the premises and terms of that language" (p. 186). I agree with the latter statement. My own interest—as here with the pictures in which Chave finds the pietà composition—has been intended to suggest *why* Rothko would become preoccupied with paintings in which the suffering of the son elicits maternal solicitude. See Chapter 12 below.

Chapter Ten

1. My account of this episode is based on B.H. Friedman, "'The Irascibles': A Split Second in Art History," *Arts Magazine* (September 1978):96–102; and on Irving Sandler, "The Irascible Eighteen," a catalogue essay for an exhibit "The Irascibles," at the CDS Gallery, February 4–27, 1988. Ten sculptors (Louise Bourgeois, Mary Callery, Herbert Ferber, Peter Grippe, David Hare, Ibram Lassaw, Seymour Lipton, Theodore Roszak, Day Schnabel, David Smith) also signed the letter of protest, but in the ensuing publicity, they literally dropped out of the picture.

2. Quoted in Calvin Tomkins, *Merchants and Masterpieces, The Story of the Metropolitan Museum of Art* (New York, 1970), p. 309.

3. *Time* 55 (June 5, 1950):54. On the publicity generated by the protest, see Sandler, "The Irascible Eighteen."

4. Sandler, "The Irascible Eighteen":n.p. Jimmy Ernst also recalled that Rothko, along with Still and Newman, at first opposed collaborating with *Life* (interview with Paul Cummings, p. 68, AAA).

5. Friedman, "'The Irascibles'":102.

6. Sandler, "The Irascible Eighteen":n.p.

7. *Number 11, 1950*, was sold to Mrs. John D. Rockefeller III for $1,000; *Number 9, 1950*, to Jeanne Reynal for $1,300; *Number 10, 1950*, to Mrs. Joseph Branston for $500 (the work *Number 10, 1950*, now owned by MOMA, was originally *Number 10, 1951*); *Number 13, 1950*, to Walter Bareiss for $600; *Number 22, 1950*, to Steve Burke for $900; and *Number 19, 1950*, to Hey-

wood Cutting for $750. These sales totaled $5,050, which gave Rothko, after the one-third gallery commission, and an $86.97 deduction for expenses, $3,279.69. According to his December 28 statement from Betty Parsons, however, Rothko was sent a check for $1,313.02, suggesting that Parsons had either advanced him some of the money or that she paid him in installments over the following year. Parsons' records also contain some indications that two other paintings—*Number 22, 1950* ($900), and *Number 4A, 1950* ($600)—may have been sold, so Rothko's income might have been slightly higher (BPP, AAA).

8. On October 29, 1950, Rothko wrote to Kenneth and Joy Rabin that he had not yet found a teaching position. On December 28, he wrote to them of waiting for the birth of the baby and reported his job at Brooklyn College, adding that he had just bought a DeSoto from the Averys.

9. Quoted in Harold Rosenberg, "Rothko," *New Yorker* 46, 6 (March 28, 1970):94.

10. "JC," April 22, 1956.

11. Interview with William Seitz, January 22, 1952, WSP, AAA; Sophie Tracy interview.

12. Mark Rothko to Katharine Kuh, July 14 (1954), KKP, AIC.

13. Interview, January 22, 1952, WSP, AAA.

14. Interview with Avis Berman, Part II, p. 8, AAA.

15. Statement, made at a MOMA symposium, "How to Combine Architecture, Painting and Sculpture," *Interiors* (May 10, 1951):104; reprinted in *MR*, p. 85.

16. William Seitz, *Abstract Expressionist Painting in America* (Cambridge, Mass., 1983), p. 102.

17. Rothko made this statement to Daniel Bell sometime in the mid-1950s; it is quoted by Teresa Hensick and Paul M. Whitmore, "Rothko's Harvard Murals," in *MRHM*, p. 15.

18. *AR*, p. 167; and "PL," MRA.

19. Interview with Avis Berman, Part I, p. 1, AAA.

20. *AR*, pp. 112–13; and Celina Trief interview, October 12, 1988.

21. "Rothko said he had never been particularly interested in Picasso. That Cézanne, and Picasso, too, had been fundamentally interested in the Renaissance. He said Picasso had not broken with the past really. That it was Miró who had done this" (Ethel Schwabacher, conversation with Mark Rothko, March 1, 1955, ESP, AAA).

22. *LMR*, p. 26.

23. Mark Rothko to Barnett and Annalee Newman, August 8, 1950, BNP, AAA.

24. Mark Rothko to Barnett Newman, April 17, 1950, BNP, AAA.

25. Mark Rothko to Richard Lippold, May 6 (1950), Richard Lippold Papers, AAA.

26. "JC," March 12 and April 22, 1956.

27. Regina Bogat interview. Hedda Sterne said that Rothko found European art "sadistic and brutal," complaining "if I see one more man's head held in arm. . . ." He pronounced Botticelli "design." "Here, he was not really looking," Sterne added. "He reacted in defense of what he was doing."

28. "On Rothko" (1970), RMA.

"When you go to Italy," Rothko told Ben Dienes, "you must see the Fra Angelicos," specifying that Dienes should see not the ones at the Vatican but those in Florence. "He felt everything was of one piece," Dienes said. "The division was of one piece. That's the way he put it. You saw the wholeness of it. He says he considered those cells a treasure." See also *AR*, pp. 137, 147–50. Dore Ashton speculates that Rothko may have seen Fra Angelico on his 1950 visit to Europe, but basically she locates Rothko's discovery on his 1958 visit. Writing on Rothko in the catalogue for the 1958 Venice Biennale, Sam Hunter says, "it is significant that in his first encounter with Italy, and Europe, some years ago, Mark Rothko was most deeply moved by the art of Fra Angelico" (*Lipton, Rothko, Smith, Tobey* [New York, 1958], n.p.). Since Hunter could have only gotten this information from Rothko, and since the catalogue had to have been produced before Rothko's second trip to Europe in the summer of 1958, Rothko discovered his enthusiasm for Fra Angelico in 1950.

29. "JC," January 24, 1956.

30. "JC," February 8, 1955.

31. Mark Rothko to Barnett and Annalee Newman, August 8, 1950, BNP, AAA.

32. "Kathy Lynn" was called "Kate" from the start, and in 1958, when Rothko legally changed his own name to "Mark Rothko," he legally changed his daughter's name to "Kate."

33. Mark Rothko to Barnett and Annalee Newman, June 30 (1950), BNP, AAA. On June 1, 1950 Rothko had written to Kenneth and Joy Rabin announcing that "today" he and Mell had learned of the pregnancy.

34. Mark Rothko to Barnett and Annalee Newman, July 26, 1950, BNP, AAA; Mark Rothko to Richard Lippold, May 6 (1950), Richard Lippold Papers, AAA.

35. Rothko's application for the position was supported by reference letters from Holger Cahill and Alfred Barr, whose December 11, 1950, recommendation can be found in the MRF, MOMA: "I have known Mr. Rothko for several years and his painting since the late 1930s when I used to notice it with special interest in various group exhibitions," wrote Barr, who expressed "enthusiasm" for Rothko's recent work, adding that "aside from his painting I guess that he would make an excellent teacher. He is not only clear in his ideas and gifted with words, but has a considerable knowledge of and interest in the art of the past."

36. Saul Fuerstein, interview with Barbara Shikler (telephone), November 2, 1983, MRF, NGA. Mr. Fuerstein was the monitor in a graphics class taught in January–February 1951 at the Art Students League by Will Barnet; Rothko briefly attended the class to prepare for a course he was about to teach at Brooklyn College. Mr. Fuerstein seems to date Rothko's remark about supporting his family from a later period, but the details he gives—"Mell quit job, was pregnant"—place it from his contacts with Rothko at the Art Students League.

37. *Broeklundian* (1953), n.p.

38. For an excellent history of the department, see Mona Hadler and Jerome Viola, "Introductory Essay," *Brooklyn College Art Department: Past and*

Present 1942–77 (New York, 1977), pp. 11–15. On the Bauhaus: "I do not live here"—i.e., his studio—"the same as I do at home," Rothko told William Seitz of his objection to the Bauhaus. "I do not want to admire a chair as art when I sit on it. This is a question of meaning versus craft" (interview with William Seitz, January 22, 1952, WSP, AAA).

39. *LMR,* p. 27; Milton Brown interview, July 1, 1987.

40. My account of the workings of the department mostly comes from my interview with Milton Brown. The course titles are taken from the Brooklyn College Catalogue, 1953, pp. 90–93.

41. Brooklyn College Catalogue, 1953, p. 93.

42. "He did some etchings at one time," said George Okun, recalling that sometime between 1933 and 1936, when he was working at a photoengraving shop, "I brought Mark some copper plates. Copper was very expensive then." Okun never saw the etchings, but Rothko "was very happy to get the plates." On Rothko's participation at Atelier 17, see Martica Sawin, "Stanley William Hayter at 84," *Arts Magazine* 60, 5 (January 1986):61. If Rothko did participate at Hayter's Atelier 17, none of the work has survived.

43. Rothko attended the class from January 29 to February 7, 1951, according to records at the Art Students League. He worked mainly with Saul Fuerstein, Barnet's class monitor, who remembered that Rothko "did raised ground etching, small, neat. His work had a spiral shape, simple, with swirling shapes" (interview with Barbara Shikler, MRF, NGA). A plate (and one impression) from Rothko's return to the Art Students League are now at MOMA.

44. Morris Dorsky (chairman, Department of Art, Brooklyn College) to Clair Zamoiski, February 1, 1978, lists the courses Rothko taught at Brooklyn College and gives his employment dates as February 1, 1951 to June 30, 1954 (MRF, GMA). Of Rothko's "Elements of Drawing" class, Murray Israel said, "He wasn't really good at teaching drawing. I don't think he knew how to draw. . . . But he was a spectacular teacher because he was a personality." Of Rothko's "Color" course, Celina Trief remembered: "he never did color charts or color wheels or anything of that sort, and we'd just work with color. In a way he wanted us to do little Matisses and little de Koonings and little anybodys, but just to understand what color was about through the use of it."

45. "We liked him. Some of us did. Others were, I think a lot of students, were afraid of him. He was such an imposing figure physically too. . . ." (Celina Trief interview).

46. Murray Israel interview.

47. "MR:PAAM":20; *LMR,* p. 31.

48. Murray Israel interview; also based on my own experience as a student at Brooklyn College from 1953 to 1957.

49. Ibid.

50. Milton Brown interview. Professor Brown remembered that Rothko was in competition only with Jimmy Ernst, who did get the position, but the drafts of a letter Rothko wrote to Dean Gaede of Brooklyn College reveal that there were two others (unnamed) involved in the competition (drafts in MRA).

51. Ruth S. Shoup to Mark Rothko, March 16, 1954, MRA.

52. "JC," February 14, 1956.

53. My quotations from the letter are taken from six pages of drafts in MRA; it is unknown whether Rothko ever completed or sent the letter.

54. *LMR*, p. 31.

55. Milton Brown interview. In one of the drafts of his letter to Dean Gaede, Rothko writes: "I wish to say to the committee as I have repeatedly expressed myself to P[rofessor] W[olff] during these years that I reject the philosophy of the Bauhaus on which our curriculum is based [as] being invalid to the proper ideas of the liberal arts" (MRA).

56. Milton Brown interview; Martin James interview, May 16, 1988.

57. Robert Jay Wolff to Dean Gaede, n.d., Robert Jay Wolff Papers, AAA. Wolff's letter deals with an Ad Reinhardt polemic, "The Artist In Search of an Academy: Part Two: Who Are the Artists?" (*College Art Journal* 13, 4 [Summer 1954]: 314–15), attacking (among others) Barnett Newman (who sued him over the piece) and Clyfford Still, then (like Reinhardt) teaching at Brooklyn College.

58. *LMR*, pp. 30–31.

Chapter Eleven

1. Parsons herself recalled only the presence of Newman, Pollock, Rothko, and Still; see Tomkins, "A Keeper of the Treasure":52–54. According to Alfonso Ossorio, "seven powerhouse artists" attended: Newman, Rothko, Bradley Tomlin, Herbert Ferber, Seymour Lipton, himself, and one other painter, whom he only specifies as not Clyfford Still (quoted in Jeffrey Potter, *To a Violent Grave, An Oral Biography of Jackson Pollock* [New York, 1985], pp. 146–47). At other times, however, Ossorio included Still (Naifeh and Smith, *Jackson Pollock, An American Saga*, p. 891; they also place Ad Reinhardt at the meeting, p. 677).

2. Naifeh and Smith, *Jackson Pollock, An American Saga*, pp. 684–85.

3. Constable, "The Betty Parsons Collection":59.

4. Clyfford Still to Betty Parsons, September 21, 1951, and Betty Parsons to Clyfford Still, December 4, 1953, BPP, AAA.

5. Hess, *Barnett Newman*, p. 57; Betty Parsons, interview with Gerald Silk, June 11, 1981, p. 2, AAA.

6. "As I had informed you at our last meeting in New York, my relationship with the Betty Parsons Gallery was terminated last spring," Rothko wrote to Katharine Kuh, September 27, 1954, KKP, AIC.

7. Mark Rothko to Kenneth and Joy Rabin, February 9, 1954.

Number 10, 1950, was exhibited at Betty Parsons in April 1951, then titled *Number 10, 1951*. The asking price was $1,500 and the selling price $1,250. For the story of its purchase, see *LMR*, p. 26, and Marquis, *Alfred H. Barr, Jr.: Missionary for the Modern*, p. 237. See also Lynes, *Good Old Modern*, pp. 298–99.

8. Thomas Hess, "Reviews and Previews," *Art News* 48, 10 (February 1950):46; M[ary] C[ole], "Fifty-seventh Street in Review: Mark Rothko," *The Art Digest* 25, 14 (April 15, 1951):18. In addition to the Hess and Cole pieces, the other five reviews are: Howard Devree,

"In New Directions," *New York Times,* January 8, 1950, section II, p. x; Belle Krasne, "Mark of Rothko," *The Art Digest* 24, 8 (January 15, 1950):17; Carlyle Burrows, "Final Works by Beckmann and a Group of Americans," New York *Herald Tribune,* April 8, 1951, section 4, p. 8; Stuart Preston, "Chiefly Abstract," *New York Times,* April 8, 1951, p. 18; and Paul Mocsanyi, "Art in Review," *United Press Red Letter,* News Feature Service, May 14–15, 1951.

9. Based on the list of group shows in MR,AR, p. 282, and a list of 1950–51 Rothko exhibits in the BPP, AAA. Dorothy Miller called abstraction the "dominant trend" in the show's catalogue, *Fifteen Americans* (New York, 1952), p. 5.

10. Mark Rothko to Herbert and Ilse Ferber, August 19, 1952, HFP, AAA.

11. BPP, AAA. I should say at this point that Parsons' books are incomplete and what we do have is fairly chaotic. Sometimes sales are recorded, but then not reflected in statements to Rothko, perhaps because the painting was returned (though this is not recorded). At other times payments are made to Rothko without any recorded indication as to what they are for. Sometimes known sales—Parsons' own purchase of three Rothko paintings, for example—are not recorded. My point is that I'm not confident that my account of Rothko's early 1950s sales in this paragraph is exact in detail, though I am confident that the overall picture is correct.

12. Jensen's transcriptions of several of his conversations with Rothko (including this one) take the form of a letter to a friend named Elise.

13. "One-Picture Wall or Many-Pictured Wall," *Vogue* (April 15, 1950):66–69.

14. Sally Avery, interview with Tom Wolf, Part I, p. 14, AAA.

15. Dorothy Miller to Clair Zamoiski, January 9, 1978, MRF, GMA; she also recounted her dealings with Rothko around the "Fifteen Americans" exhibit in her interview with Avis Berman, May 4, 1981, AAA; and in Gruen, "Dorothy Miller in the Company of Modern Art," *Art News* 75, 9 (November 1976):54–58.

16. Quoted in *AR,* p. 129.

17. Mark Rothko to Lloyd Goodrich, December 20, 1952, MRF, Whitney Museum of American Art; reprinted in *MR,* pp. 85–86; drafts in MRA. My quotations are from a copy of the letter (typed) in MRF, MOMA.

On June 8, 1953, Rothko made a similar statement to Frederick Wight, apparently in connection with the possibility of his participating in a show related to John Bauer's *The New Art in America:* "the problems raised by your visit are complicated, and I have had to give them long and serious thought; for they involve the preponderant pattern of museum activity around contemporary art produced in America, of which the projected book seems to me a typical instance. I am so convinced about the wrongness of this activity: that it is conceived without a real commitment to the pictures, and that it destroys their real meaning for the public; that I cannot willingly cooperate or lend myself to the project as I understand it. I say this with full knowledge of the seriousness of denying the most far-reaching machinery for the dissemination of one's name and work in this country. But from the point of view of my own feelings, I must hope and wait for those occasions when there is the possibility of the work being perceived in the terms of its real meaning, and avoid those when the opposite seems likely to be true. Should these occasions occur, I shall use them with gratitude" (Mark Rothko to Frederick Wight, June 8, 1953, John Bauer Papers, AAA).

18. Interview with Avis Berman, Part I, p. 22, AAA.

19. Ben Dienes interview.

20. James B. Byrnes, "Remembering Mark," in *Mark Rothko: Ten Major Works* (Newport Harbor, 1974), p. 30.

21. Herbert Ferber interview.

22. Robert and Elizabeth Morrow interview.

23. Wassily Leontief interview, February 13, 1986.

24. Donald Blinken interview, January 28, 1986.

25. Herbert Ferber interview.

26. Mark Rothko to Barnett Newman (August) 1950, BNP, AAA.

27. Katharine Kuh to Mark Rothko, April 22, 1954, KKP, AIC. Rothko accepted the show, he told Ethel Schwabacher, "as they were willing to show his works alone in proper setting" (interview with Mark Rothko, February 20, 1955, ESP, AAA).

28. Mark Rothko to Katharine Kuh, (1954), KKP, AIC; Katharine Kuh to Mark Rothko, April 22, 1954, KKP, AIC.

29. Katharine Kuh to Mark Rothko, June 3, 1954, KKP, AIC; Katharine Kuh to Mark Rothko, July 8, 1954, KKP, AIC; Mark Rothko to Katharine Kuh, July 14, 1954, KKP, AIC.

30. Mark Rothko to Katharine Kuh, July 14, 1954, KKP, AIC. When Kuh quoted the last three sentences of this letter in her announcement of the show ("Mark Rothko," *Art Institute of Chicago Quarterly* 48, 4 [November 15, 1954]:68), she changed the wording slightly; I have returned to Rothko's original language.

31. Robert Motherwell interview.

32. Rodman, *Conversations with Artists* (New York, 1957), p. 93; emphasis Rodman's.

33. Mark Rothko to Katharine Kuh, July 28, 1954, KKP, AIC.

34. Both passages are taken from Rothko's letter of July 14, 1954, KKP, AIC; see Kuh, "Mark Rothko":68.

35. Mark Rothko to Katharine Kuh, September 25, 1954, KKP, AIC.

36. Katharine Kuh to Mark Rothko, October 4, 1954, KKP, AIC.

37. Mark Rothko to Katharine Kuh, October 20, 1954, KKP, AIC.

38. "PL," MRA.

39. Rothko shipped nine paintings to the Chicago Art Institute: *Number 12, 1951; Number 14, 1951; Number 10, 1952; Number 7, 1953; Number 6, 1954; Number 9, 1954; Number 11, 1954; Number 4, 1953* and *Number 1, 1954* (Mark Rothko to Petronel Lukens, September 12, 1954, KKP, AIC). According to Rothko's letter to Kuh on October 20, 1954, only eight of the nine pictures were hung (KKP, AIC).

40. Mark Rothko to Katharine Kuh, October 20, 1954, KKP, AIC.

41. Rothko gives his new address in his letter to Katharine Kuh, April 22, 1954, KKP, AIC.

42. Ulfert Wilke, "Diary," August 7,

1963, UWP, AAA. Philip Guston, who brought up the subject of the Hilton in this conversation, mentioned, incorrectly, that Rothko had had a studio on the site. So I've changed "studio" to "flat" and "worked" to "lived" in Wilke's transcription of the conversation.

43. In a January 8, 1952, letter to Kenneth and Joy Rabin, Rothko reports that he may have found a 600' second floor loft, at 53rd and 6th, which needs to be partitioned to share and split costs. His letter to them of March 10, 1952, indicates that by then he'd already moved into the loft.

44. "JC," February 8, 1955; "JC," April 23, 1956.

45. Interview with Mark Rothko, January 22, 1952, WSP, AAA.

46. Celina Trief interview; Dan Rice interview.

47. See the two photographs of this studio in *MR,AR*, p. 275.

48. Sidney Janis, interview with Avis Berman, Part I, October 15, 1981, p. 19, AAA.

49. Dana Cranmer, conservator for the Mark Rothko Foundation, points out in her essay, "Conserving the Collection," that in examining the "140 works on canvas from all periods which had been removed from their stretchers," "the inadequacy of Rothko's original stretchers became apparent: most of the paintings were 'out-of-square.' The 'artist-built' stretchers—'strainers' actually—were so flimsy that they obviously had not remained rectangular if they ever had been" (*Eliminating the Obstacles Between the Painter and the Observer* [privately printed, 1986], p. 38).

50. Dana Cranmer, "Painting Materials and Techniques of Mark Rothko: Consequences of an Unorthodox Approach," *MR*, p. 189.

51. Regina Bogat interview.

52. "Concerning the Beginnings of The New York School: 1939–1943: An Interview with Robert Motherwell Conducted by Sidney Simon in New York in January 1967," *Art International* 11, 6 (Summer 1967):23.

53. Rothko's self-description as Apollonian comes from the Regina Bogat interview.

54. "Working With Rothko, A Conversation between Roy Edwards and Ralph Pomeroy," *New American Review* 12 (1971):111.

55. Oliver Steindecker interview, February 20, 1986.

56. Celina Trief interview; Stanley Kunitz, interview with Avis Berman, Part II, p. 12, AAA.

57. Interview with Avis Berman, Part I, pp. 26–27, AAA.

58. William and Sally Scharf interview; Sally Scharf, quoted in *LMR*, p. 37.

59. Interview with Avis Berman, Part I, p. 12, AAA.

60. James Murray Cuddihy, *The Ordeal of Civility* (New York, 1974), p. 9.

61. Interview with Avis Berman, Part I, p. 13, AAA; Stanley Kunitz interview; interview with Avis Berman, Part I, p. 2, AAA.

62. Interview with Phyllis Tuchman, August 27, 1981, p. 1, AAA.

63. Cuddihy, *The Ordeal of Civility*, p. 99.

64. Rothko's preference for flamboyant hats was recalled by Ethel Baziotes and can be seen in photographs; see, for example, *MR,AR*, p. 14, *LMR*, p.

193, and my fig. 29. Rothko spoke of his fondness for "funny hats" to James B. Byrnes; see Byrnes's "Remembering Mark," p. 4, and the photograph of Rothko on the same page.

65. Lee Seldes says that Rothko was angry because news of his refusal in 1958 of a Guggenheim award found its way into an art column, and that he became angry when he saw the critic Emily Genauer in the museum because he connected her with the news story (*LMR*, pp. 39–40). Katharine Kuh said that Rothko told her that he broke the window because one of his pictures could be seen through it (interview with Avis Berman, pp. 21–22, AAA).

66. Robert Motherwell, interview with Lee Seldes, n.d., LSF.

67. David Hare interview, January 9, 1986; Elaine de Kooning, interview with Phyllis Tuchman, p.11, AAA; Jane Lawrence interview, January 7, 1986.

68. Louise Bourgeois interview, January 7, 1986; Donald Blinken interview, January 28, 1986; Budd Hopkins interview, January 28, 1986.

69. Interview with Phyllis Tuchman, p. 3, AAA.

70. Ibid., pp. 3–4.

71. Rodman, *Conversations with Artists*, pp. 93–94; Regina Bogat interview; Robert Motherwell interview; Kate Rothko interview.

72. " 'Stand Up Close...,' " *Newsweek* 57, 4 (January 23, 1961):60.

73. Mark Rothko to Sonia Rabin (Fall 1943).

Chapter Twelve

1. Hedda Sterne, interview with Phyllis Tuchman, p. 4, AAA; Ida Kohlmeyer, "About Rothko," *Arts Quarterly* 4, 4 (October–November–December 1982):59.

2. Interview with Mark Rothko, January 22, 1952, WSP, AAA.

3. Yet, more ambivalently, Rothko told Seitz that Mondrian was a Calvinist who spent his life caressing canvas. See also Rothko's remarks on Mondrian in his June 17, 1953, conversation with Alfred Jensen, quoted in Chapter 11.

4. Rothko's papers contain an undated and incomplete draft of a letter to Sylvester expressing gratitude for his essay "Rothko," a review of the version of Rothko's MOMA show at the Whitechapel Art Gallery, October 10–November 12, 1961.

"First of all my gratitude," Rothko wrote, "not because it appeared, but because a person has seen so fully, has had such insight into the meaning and purpose of the pictures. I am grateful too for the fervor which you possess and the ability to think and formulate.

"Once a writer asked how the writing of art of today could be improved. My answer was that what is written is equal to the person who writes it.

"What I mean is that what is satisfying to me in putting on a show like this is that at least one person rise to the heights to which the pictures aspire."

David Sylvester's essay appeared in the *New Statesman* 20 (October 1961): 573–74; reprinted in *MR*, pp. 36–37.

5. All of these figures represent Rothko's share after the gallery's one-third commission had been deducted (based on sales records in MRF, NGA, and BRP, AAA).

6. Interview with Avis Berman, Part I, pp. 1–3, AAA.

7. My account of Sidney Janis is

based on John Brooks, "Why Fight It?: Sidney Janis," *New Yorker* 36 (November 12, 1960); Les Levine, "A Portrait of Sidney Janis on the Occasion of His 25th Anniversary as an Art Dealer," *Arts* 48 (November 1973): 51–54; and Gruen, *The Party's Over Now*, pp. 243–53.

8. Brooks, "Why Fight It?":71.

9. Gruen, *The Party's Over Now*, p. 244.

10. Levine, "A Portrait of Sidney Janis":53.

11. Janis "tried to grab my gallery away," said Betty Parsons. "I fought him one whole summer in the law courts and ended up by moving out myself. But it was a fierce fight we had. I couldn't stand being on the same floor with Janis, which is why I really left. The lawsuit ended up neutral—it ended up status quo. But when I moved out, Janis took over the whole floor" (quoted in Gruen, *The Party's Over Now*, pp. 238–39).

12. Levine, "A Portrait of Sidney Janis":51.

13. A Rothko painting was paired with one by Nicholas de Stael in the show of young French and American painters. Rothko commented to William Seitz: "Blobs vs. blocks. They both begin with 'b.' Comparisons are false!" (interview with William Seitz, January 22, 1952, AAA).

14. Brooks, "Why Fight It?":84.

15. Ibid.:62.

16. Quoted in Peter Deeley, "The Million-Dollar Art Wrangle," *Observer-Review*, December 30, 1973 (clipping MRF, TGA).

17. See Betty Parsons' angry letter to Clyfford Still, December 4, 1953, about his signing with Janis without telling her (BPP, AAA).

18. Tomkins, *Off the Wall*, pp. 184–85.

19. Gruen, *The Party's Over Now*, p. 248; Sidney Janis, interview with Avis Berman, Part I, p. 8, AAA.

20. Sidney Janis, interview with Avis Berman, Part II, November 18, 1981, p. 2, AAA; LMR, p. 34; Thomas B. Hess, "Mark Rothko, 1903–1970," *Art News* 69 (April 1970):29.

21. Interview with Avis Berman, Part I, pp. 18–19, AAA.

22. Mark Rothko, interview with Ethel Schwabacher, February 20, 1955, ESP, AAA.

23. Motherwell, "On Rothko" (1970), RMA.

24. Interview with Avis Berman, Part I, p. 6, AAA.

25. "MR:PAAM":21.

26. Sophie Tracy interview.

27. Motherwell, "On Rothko" (1970), RMA; and Sally Avery, interview with Tom Wolf, Part II, p. 11, AAA.

28. Mark Rothko to Robert Motherwell, July 1958, RMA; Mark Rothko to Clay Spohn, September 23, 1957, CSP, AAA; Sidney Janis, interview with Avis Berman, Part II, pp. 7, 3, AAA.

29. "The Great International Art Market: I," *Fortune* 52, 6 (December 1955):119. The second half of the essay appeared in *Fortune* 53, 1 (January 1956).

30. "The Great International Art Market: I":157, 150–52.

31. See Harold G. Vatter, *The U.S. Economy in the 1950s* (New York, 1963).

32. "The Great International Art Market: I":157.

33. Quoted in ibid.:169.

34. Ibid.:119.

35. Levine, "A Portrait of Sidney Janis":53.

36. "The Great International Art Market: II":122–23; Robson, "The Market for Abstract Expressionism":22; Levine, "A Portrait of Sidney Janis":53.

37. An account of the case, written by Norman Lipkind, who had been a fellow student of Newman's at CCNY and was later a special deputy clerk in the Supreme Court, New York County, can be found in the Alice Yamin Papers, AAA.

38. "JC," December 7, 1955, and February 8, 1955.

39. Clyfford Still to Sidney Janis, April 4, 1955, in Alfonso Ossario Papers, AAA. The letter is labeled "COPY" so Still probably circulated the letter.

40. Interview with Dorothy Seckler, June 10, 1965, p. 12, AAA.

41. Hess, *Barnett Newman*, p. 48.

42. Mark Rothko to Barnett and Annalee Newman, August 7 (1950), BNP, AAA.

43. Newman's letter to Sidney Janis, April 9, 1955, is reprinted in BN,SWI, pp. 200–202. The editor of the Newman collection, John P. O'Neill, suggests in a note that Newman may not have sent the letter but does not give his reasons for thinking that.

44. Mark Rothko to Herbert and Ilse Ferber, August 19, 1952, HFP, AAA.

45. Hess, *Barnett Newman*, p. 56; Sally Avery, interview with Tom Wolf, Part I, p. 21, AAA; *LMR*, p. 29; Regina Bogat interview; Annalee Newman interview.

46. Clyfford Still to Alfonso Ossario, December 18, 1953, Alfonso Ossario Papers, AAA. In a letter to Katharine Kuh, October 22, 1965, Still dates his disaffection with "the Parsons gang" from 1951: "When I took up residency in New York in 1950, I slowly discovered the range and depth of [Newman's] schemes. And during 1951 I began my repudiation of him and what I had to call the Parsons gang. However, much damage was done by that time and the violation continues to this day in spite of my efforts to separate the free and creative from the parasitical and authoritarian" (KKP, AAA).

47. In January of 1956 Still wrote to Rothko that he had just discovered a large red painting of Rothko's which had been sent to him in exchange for the Still black painting (apparently already returned). Still had already returned a smaller work with symbolic images, and he mentions that Rothko has at least three more of Still's paintings, implying he would like them returned (MRF, NGA). The Still letter to Rothko, quoted *LMR*, p. 36, has disappeared.

48. Ben Heller interview, January 27, 1987; Katharine Kuh, interview with Avis Berman, n.d., pp. 13–14, AAA.

49. Annalee Newman interview; *LMR*, p. 29. Robert Motherwell, whose break with Newman did not come until after Rothko's, similarly recalled that Rothko "would ask about Newman."

50. Katharine Kuh interview. On the morning of Rothko's suicide, Katharine Kuh received a phone call from Still, who had not heard of Rothko's death. When she informed him, Still replied: "I'm not a bit surprised. This was inevitable because of the way he lived" (interview with Avis Berman, p. 16, AAA).

51. Telegram from Joseph Piore to Mark Rothko, March 13, 1952, BPP, AAA.

52. Mark Rothko to Herbert and Ilse Ferber, (August 19, 1952), HFP, AAA.

53. Rothko discusses the trip to Woodstock in his letter to Herbert and Ilse Ferber, (September 2, 1952), HFP, AAA. Annalee Newman showed me an announcement for this, the "4th Annual Woodstock Art Conference," Friday, August 22, and Saturday, August 23, 1952, with John Ashford, George Boas, James Fitzgibbons, Harry Holtzman, Susanne K. Langer, George L. K. Morris, Robert Motherwell, Barnett Newman, David Smith, and Robert Wolff as the speakers. According to Robert Motherwell, about one hundred people attended the conference.

54. This is how Newman's remark is always quoted. His actual comments were less epigrammatic: "I have insisted on coming here as a citizen because I feel that even if aesthetics is established as a science, it doesn't affect me as an artist. I've done quite a bit of work in ornithology, and I have never met an ornithologist who thought that ornithology was for the birds" (BN,SWI, p. 247). In a 1970 interview with Emile de Antonio, however, Newman quoted himself as having said that "aesthetics is for me like ornithology must be for the birds" and this may be the source of the version usually quoted (BN,SWI, p. 304).

55. Mark Rothko to Herbert and Ilse Ferber, (September 2, 1952), HFP, AAA.

56. Edward Corbett to Clay Spohn, January 4, 1955, CSP, AAA. Corbett reports a conversation in which Rothko told him of the offer from the University of New Mexico.

57. Linda Abbott, administrative assistant, Department of Fine Arts, University of Colorado at Boulder, to Clair Zamoiski, August 25, 1977, MRF, GMA; Mark Rothko to Robert and Betty Motherwell and Herbert and Ilse Ferber, July 7 (1955), RMA, and HFP, AAA.

58. According to Kate Rothko, "my father, I understand from other people, was one of the worst drivers who ever hit the road. And didn't enjoy it either. My mother did not drive. He also did not have a very good sense of direction. I remember at age seven telling him how to get through Providence, which I remembered from the year before—which irritated him no end."

59. Byrnes, "Remembering Mark," pp. 6–7, 30.

60. Mark Rothko to Robert and Betty Motherwell and Herbert and Ilse Ferber, July 7, (1955), RMA, and HFP, AAA.

61. Mark Rothko to Herbert and Ilse Ferber, (July 14, 1955), HFP, AAA.

62. Mark Rothko to Robert and Betty Motherwell and Herbert and Ilse Ferber, July 7, (1955), RMA, and HFP, AAA; the Rothkos lived at 1255 19th Street, Boulder (cf. Mark Rothko to Herbert and Ilse Ferber, [July 14, 1955], HFP, AAA).

63. Mark Rothko to Herbert and Ilse Ferber, (July 14, 1955), HFP, AAA.

64. According to Pat Trivigno, then chairman of the art department, Rothko received the "modest" fee of $1,000 for his visit (Pat Trivigno interview, November 10, 1990).

65. Mark Rothko to Herbert and Ilse

Ferber, (March 14, 1957), HFP, AAA. He was then living at 510 Iona Street, Metairie.

66. Kohlmeyer, "About Rothko":34.

67. Pat Trivigno interview; Pat Trivigno to Clair Zamoiski, August 25, 1977, MRF, GMA; Pat Trivigno to the Mark Rothko Foundation, June 17, 1985, MRF, NGA.

68. "About Rothko":34.

69. Emily Genauer, "New Solos," *New York Herald Tribune,* April 17, 1955, in MRF, NGA; L[averne] G[eorge], "Fortnight in Review," *Arts Digest* 29, 15 (May 1, 1955):23; and T[homas] B. H[ess], "Reviews and Previews," *Art News* 54, 4 (Summer 1955):54.

70. E.C. Goossen, "The End of Winter in New York," *Art International* 2, 2–3 (1958):37; and Dore Ashton, "Art," *Arts and Architecture* 75, 4 (April 1958):8.

71. Rothko did write (but not sign) a statement for a young painter, Clinton Hill, for his show "Ladders and Windows: Recent Paintings" at the Zabriskie Gallery, November 21 through December 10, 1955:

"When looking at my pictures after they were painted, I decided they were windows and ladders. I saw them as an outsider, and began to ponder the idea meaning of these images. At first it occurred to me, windows were aperatures [sic] for seeing larger vistas, but later I realized that windows can be closed as well as opened and a man must decide how many windows his facade will have. The question of how many windows one opens, or how often one pulls down the blinds is a decision concerning self-revelation and reticence. (It involves not only one's biography, but one's relationship to other men.) It becomes an issue of what things should be said and what should be left unsaid.

"Jacob's ladder is again like the first thought, as it is used to climb high and higher. It occurs to me the cliff dwellers and the Pueblo Indians used their ladders, which were visible, to reach levels of every day living. Perhaps Jacobs [sic] ladder belongs to my earlier work, but now I feel that perhaps these ladders and windows are of my everyday habitat.

"In most lives windows are forever curtained and levels of living are well concealed within the interior. It is the artist who now and then attempts to pull back the blinds."

Mr. Hill told me of Rothko's writing the statement (and provided me with a copy of it) in my interview with him, January 28, 1986.

72. "Rothko's Wall of Light," *Art Digest* 29, 5 (November 1, 1954):5. Rothko did threaten lawsuits when angry, but after Lewis Browne, he never acted on the threat. Gus Solomon, a friend from Portland, remembered giving a party at the Hotel Pierre in the early 1950s, at which Rothko was "drinking, doing all the talking, vilifying his relatives because he had to work selling papers and piling pants. His relatives didn't do enough for him." At the end of his diatribe, a lawyer named George Levin turned to Rothko and said, "You're not as big a son of a bitch as you're making yourself out to be." The following day Rothko called Levin, threatening to sue him.

If Rothko did threaten to sue whoever wrote about his work, he must have spoken in anger, or to intimidate, since it's not clear—particularly after the failure of Newman's suit against Reinhardt—what Rothko could have sued for, how he could have hoped to win, and what (given the incomes of art critics) he could have hoped to collect.

73. Ibid.:19.

74. Mark Rothko, interview with Ethel Schwabacher, November 7, 1954, ESP, AAA. When Schwabacher asked about Crehan's statement "that the meeting of edges (edges of large planes) seemed to him to indicate border states between the conscious and the unconscious," Rothko said "this was the only hackneyed conception Crehan had. That the use of the words conscious, unconscious was outdated. That words have a 'dateline.' These words were appropriate to discussions of surrealism; but were exhausted now, and so did not fit the problem."

75. All quotations are from the seven typed pages of drafts for what appears to be an essay or talk on Rothko's relation to *The Birth of Tragedy* (MRA). Since there is no final copy, it is not clear whether Rothko ever completed the essay. In his sentence about his ambition for his pictures, he has typed the word "unmistakably" over the word "unequivocally."

76. Or, in another draft: "I have believed as long as I can remember that the nobility and the contemplative exaltation of art is a hollow shell unless it has as its core, unless it is filled to the point of bulging by the wild."

77. Above the word "thoroughly" in this sentence Rothko has typed the word "enough."

78. Motherwell, "On Rothko" (1970), RMA.

79. Mark Rothko to Clay Spohn, May 11, 1948, CSP, AAA.

80. Rothko's line of argument here provides the basis for a remark of his quoted in *Life*: "A painting is not a picture of an experience; it is an experience" (*Life* 42 [November 16, 1959]: 83.

81. *LMR*, p. 37.

82. Interview with Phyllis Tuchman, p. 5, AAA.

83. Interview with Joseph Liss, December 11, 1977.

84. Mark Rothko to Clay Spohn, September 23, 1957, CSP, AAA.

85. Mark Rothko to Robert and Betty Motherwell, August 3, 1954, RMA.

86. "JC," July 23, 1956.

87. Chave, *Mark Rothko: Subjects in Abstraction,* pp. 149–55, 161–71. Chave finds that "vestiges or traces" (p. 171) of these compositions continue into certain of Rothko's transitional and classic paintings.

88. Jackie Rice interview, February 21, 1986.

Chapter Thirteen

1. "Park Avenue To Get New Skyscraper," *New York Times,* July 13, 1954, 25.

2. Peter C. Newman, *Bronfman Dynasty: The Rothschilds of the New World* (Toronto, 1978), p. 166. My account of Phyllis Lambert's participation in the project relies on Newman's book, pp. 165–66; Franz Schulze, *Mies van der Rohe, A Critical Biography* (Chicago, 1985), pp. 270–72; and Phyllis Bronfman Lambert, "How a Building Gets

Built," *Vassar Alumnae Magazine* 44, 3 (February 1959):13–19.

3. For Sam Bronfman's life, I've relied on Newman, *Bronfman Dynasty,* and Stephen Birmingham, *"The Rest of Us"* (New York, 1985), pp. 156–57, 159–63, 213–16, 222–24, 241–52, 328–38, 361–69.

4. "Seagram's Bronze Tower," *Architectural Forum* 109 (July 1958):71.

5. Lambert, "How a Building Gets Built":18.

6. Phyllis Lambert interview, May 15, 1987; Philip Johnson interview, July 6, 1987; Sidney Janis to Phyllis Lambert, June 6, 1958, and purchase order, both in MRA; Philip Johnson to Ronald Alley, March 30, 1972, MRF, TGA. "There were no other conditions," Johnson wrote. "The commission was extremely informal and Mr. Rothko returned the amount paid to him when he became unhappy with placing these pictures in a commercial space."

7. Liss, "Willem de Kooning Remembers Mark Rothko":43.

8. Motherwell, "On Rothko" (1970), RMA.

9. Quoted in Roy Edwards, "Mark Rothko, A Personal Reflection," MRF, GMA.

10. Mark Rothko to Clay Spohn, February (2?), 1948, CSP, AAA.

11. Dorothy Miller, interview with Avis Berman, p. 23, AAA; Gruen, "Dorothy Miller in the Company of Modern Art":57; John Baur to Mark Rothko, November 15, 1954, MRF, Whitney Museum of American Art; Memorandum from John Baur to Mr. More, Mr. Goodrich, Miss Irvine, and Miss McKellar, December 22, 1954, MRF, Whitney Museum of American Art; and Mark Rothko to Rosalind Irvine, April 9, 1957, MRF, Whitney Museum of American Art.

12. Mark Rothko to James Johnson Sweeney, September 9 (1958), MRA. Rothko did not wish to make his refusal into a public gesture. In his letter to Sweeney, the Guggenheim's director, he said, "I am writing this in privacy. I have no desire to embarrass anyone, should you wish to substitute anyone else's painting."

13. Philip Johnson interview. "The space was always intended to be a restaurant and Mr. Rothko was thoroughly aware of this," Johnson wrote to Ronald Alley, March 30, 1972, MRF, TGA. Phyllis Lambert wrote to Johnson, "as I remember, Rothko absolutely knew it was a restaurant" (Phyllis Lambert to Philip Johnson, April 25, 1972, MRF, TGA).

14. "Dan Rice Interviewed by Arnold Glimcher," n.p.

15. *AR,* p. 154. Bernard Reis recalled attending a meeting with Rothko and the restaurant's architect (whom he misremembered as Edward Stone), who "started the conference by pointing out there would be two dining rooms—one for the caviar high-class trade, and one for the general public. He wanted Rothko to do something for the fashionable restaurant" (Bernard Reis to Norman Reid, February 21, 1974, MRF, TGA). Mell Rothko remembered that her husband had no idea that the room would be a restaurant; he "simply had the dimensions of the room to work from" (memorandum by Ronald Alley, May 28, 1970, MRF, TGA).

The architect's drawing reproduced in Olga Gueft, "The Four Seasons," identifies the larger room as "Dining Room" and the smaller one as "Private Dining

Room" (*Interiors* 119, 5 [December 1959]: 81). See fig. 39.

16. Mark Rothko, interview with Ethel Schwabacher, May 30, 1954, ESP, AAA; Michael Compton, Introduction, *Mark Rothko, The Seagram Mural Project* (London, 1988), p. 14.

Rothko told Mrs. Gifford Phillips that he didn't like large museums and suggested instead a number of one-man museums, "small, very simple buildings—made of cinder block, I remember that—scattered throughout the country in small towns. And each building would be an homage to a particular artist. One would contain Reinhardts, one Rothkos. . . ." (quoted in *RC*, pp. 25–26). On other occasions, Rothko favored an urban location for his private museum: "He wanted to find a sponsor who would build a little house in New York with Rothko's name on it where his paintings would be seen without having to confuse them with the works of other people" (Herbert Ferber, quoted in *RC*, pp. 25–26).

17. "MR:PAAM":16.

18. See, for example, the letter from Bernard Reis to Norman Reid, February 21, 1974, MRF, TGA.

19. Mark Rothko to Robert Motherwell, July 1958, RMA. The English artist Richard Arnell recalled hearing Rothko say that "he deliberately painted the 4 Seasons pictures to be out of key with the setting and to disturb the diners" (Richard Alley, memorandum, July 16, 1974, MRF, TGA).

20. Miró painted the mural in New York, using Carl Holty's studio in the East 90s, where it was shown to a number of New York artists. Rothko could have seen the mural there, or when it was shown briefly at MOMA before being installed. See Duncan Macmillan, "Miró's Public Art," in Barbara Rose, *Miró in America* (Houston, 1982), pp. 102–3, and Barbara Rose, "Miró in America," in ibid., pp. 34–35. It's also possible that Rothko saw the work after it was installed, when he was visiting his wife's family in Cleveland, although Cincinnati is about two hundred miles from Cleveland. Rothko discussed his admiration for the work with Pat Trivigno.

21. "Adolph Gottlieb—notes recorded by Dore Ashton, February 4, 1972," MRF, NGA. Esther Gottlieb said that when her husband, Ferber, and Motherwell agreed to produce works for the New Jersey synagogue, "Mark was furious. 'I would never do anything for any religious dogma. Religious—what's that got to do with art?' " (interview with Sanford Hirsh, pp. 21–22, AAA).

22. Sophie Tracy interview.

23. The room is 55' long, by 26' 1¼" wide and 15' ¾" high.

24. This doorway is hidden behind two movable partitions (about 4' wide and 9' high, covered with the same rawhide that covers the walls), one coming out from the east, one from the south wall. Like the box-shaped entrance from the Pool Room, these partitions intrude into the room's space. It is not clear when, if ever, Rothko knew of their existence.

25. These openings are 7' 10¼" high and 8' 11½" wide. The 9' 1" wide doorway, the same height as the openings, is a box shape which projects 4' 5¼" into the room.

26. The areas above the west wall's openings and door are divided into rectangular compartments by vertical beams

that continue the sides of the openings up to the ceiling. These compartments, then, are also just under 9' wide. The paintings that probably were intended for this wall—e.g., T 1167 and T 1169, two of the works Rothko gave to the Tate Gallery—were all 15' wide and thus would not have fit into these compartments. My guess is that Rothko was unaware of this division of the wall, which he would have objected to for some of the same reasons he objected to frames.

27. "Suggestions from Mr. Mark Rothko regarding installation of his Paintings at the Whitechapel Gallery 1961," MR, p. 88.

Rothko's statement that the murals should be hung 4' 6" above the floor because that was the height at which they were painted does not square with Dan Rice's strong memory that Rothko was very uncertain about the exact height at which he wanted to hang the paintings.

28. "Dan Rice Interviewed by Arnold Glimcher," n.p.; Liss, "Willem de Kooning Remembers Mark Rothko":43; Phyllis Lambert interview.

29. Mark Rothko to Robert Motherwell, July 1958, RMA. In a 1961 Statement of Net Worth for Mark and Mell Rothko prepared by Bernard Reis and Company, the estimated cost of the Bradford Street property was $10,075, with $2,023.49 in improvements and $1,500 in furnishings ("Resp. Ferber, Exhibit #1," in "The Matter of Rothko").

30. Mark Rothko to Clay Spohn, February (2?), 1948, CSP, AAA.

31. Interview with Avis Berman, Part I, p. 9, AAA.

32. Mark Rothko to Robert Motherwell, July 1958, RMA.

33. Ibid. The 1956–57 Manhattan phone book lists Rothko's studio at 104 West 61st Street; the building, now demolished and replaced by Fordham University buildings, was just west of Columbus Avenue. "I shall not be able to keep the studio much longer," he wrote to Clay Spohn. "It is destined to be wrecked by spring" (Mark Rothko to Clay Spohn, September 23, 1957, CSP, AAA).

34. Mark Rothko to Robert Motherwell, July 1958, RMA.

35. Regina Bogat interview.

36. While Rothko's old gymnasium was 2' wider than the small dining room at the Four Seasons, his 10' storage space along the north wall made his actual working space about 8' narrower than the restaurant space.

"The studio was a converted gymnasium in what had once been a YMCA on the Bowery," John Fischer writes. "Inside it he had erected a scaffold of the *exact dimensions* of that dining room in the Seagram building, for which he supposedly was painting murals" ("MR:PAAM":21; my emphasis). This description seems to be the origin of subsequent ones (see, for example, Bonnie Clearwater, WP, p. 46) which state that Rothko constructed an exact replica of the Four Seasons room in his studio; but the studio was not long or wide enough and its ceiling was too high for that.

37. The estimate of forty canvases comes from David Anfam, with the proviso that it is not always possible to distinguish Seagram paintings from individual paintings done around the same time.

38. Dan Rice interview; Dan Rice, conversation with Bonnie Clearwater

and Dana Cranmer, November 1983, MRF, NGA.

39. Compton, Introduction, p. 12.

40. "MR:PAAM":16.

41. The United States Pavilion exhibited two sculptors, David Smith and Seymour Lipton, and two painters, Mark Tobey and Rothko. The Biennale, whose catalogue contained an essay on Rothko by Sam Hunter, ran from June 14, to October 19, 1958.

42. René d'Harnoncourt, Foreword, *The New American Painting* (New York, 1959), p. 5. The other painters included in the show were William Baziotes, James Brooks, Sam Francis, Arshile Gorky, Adolph Gottlieb, Philip Guston, Grace Hartigan, Franz Kline, Willem de Kooning, Robert Motherwell, Barnett Newman, Jackson Pollock, Theodoros Stamos, Clyfford Still, Bradley Walker Tomlin, and Jack Tworkov. The show, having circulated from Basel to Milan, Madrid, Berlin, Amsterdam, Brussels, Paris, and London, was then exhibited at MOMA in New York, from May 28 to September 8, 1959.

43. Lynes, *Good Old Modern*, p. 384. On the relation between Abstract Expressionism and cold-war cultural politics, see Max Kozloff, "American Painting During the Cold War," *Artforum* 11, 9 (May 1973):43–54; Eva Cockcroft, "Abstract Expressionism, Weapon of the Cold War," *Artforum* 12, 10 (June 1974):39–41; David and Cecile Shapiro, "Abstract Expressionism: The Politics of Apolitical Painting," *Prospects* 3 (1977): 175–214; Annette Cox, *Art-as-Politics: The Abstract Expressionist Avant-Garde and Society* (Ann Arbor, 1982); and Serge Guilbault, *How New York Stole the Idea of Modern Art*. Most of these accounts, however, make the erroneous assumption that because the work of certain artists was appropriated for official political purposes, *that* exposes its real character, as if an object were identical with its uses. In the case of Rothko, moreover, to describe his paintings as celebrations of individual freedom—whether you are a functionary of the State Department or a leftist art historian—is to distort them.

44. *Partisan Review* 22 (Spring 1955):179–96; the essay (revised 1958) is reprinted in Clement Greenberg, *Art and Culture* (Boston, 1961), pp. 208–29. Subsequent references will be to *Art and Culture*.

I am not attempting to provide a full account of Greenberg's theoretical position in the mid-1950s; I am attempting to provide an account of the position staked out in one Greenberg essay, the one most likely to have caught Rothko's attention.

45. Clement Greenberg interview, January 9, 1986. Rothko was not the only painter-victim of Greenberg's crushing pronouncements. "To be an artist is to be pompous," he said. "He was fond of the phrase 'as stupid as a painter', and frequently lamented that 'all artists are bores.'" Rothko was "a clinical paranoid ... pompous and dumb," Gottlieb "a pantspresser," Kline "a bore," Still "pretentious," Newman "boring," and de Kooning "tedious beyond belief" (Naifeh and Smith, *Jackson Pollock, An American Saga*, p. 632; see also Gruen, *The Party's Over Now*, pp. 178–83).

46. Greenberg, *Art and Culture*, pp. 228–29.

47. Ibid., pp. 208–9.

48. Ibid., pp. 221, 228.

49. Clement Greenberg interview.

50. Greenberg, *Art and Culture*, p. 226.

51. Newman was angry enough to respond to Greenberg in a letter (August 9, 1955) recently published in *BN,SWI*, pp. 202–4. Newman described Greenberg's claim that "I am derived from Still" as "the most serious error" in his essay, and Newman is at great pains to show that "my concept and style had already been formed" before he ever saw Still's work. Newman was very sensitive about the issue of Still's influence, responding to some remarks (in an interview) by Robert Motherwell about Still's importance with a series of angry, insulting letters to *Art International* (see *BN,SWI*, pp. 225–33).

52. Greenberg, *Art and Culture*, p. 225.

53. "MR:PAAM":17.

54. Ibid. Rothko's estimate of Rosenberg had not been so negative when they first met while Rothko was living in East Hampton in 1946: "Harold Rosenberg has one of the best brains that you are likely to encounter, full of wit, humaneness and a genius for getting things impeccably expressed," he wrote to Newman, then inserted a between-the-lines sentence: "But I doubt that he will be of much use to us" (Mark Rothko to Barnett and Annalee Newman, August 10, 1946, BNP, AAA).

55. "MR:PAAM":17–18.

56. *Art News* 51 (December 1952): 22–23, 48–50; reprinted in Harold Rosenberg, *The Tradition of the New* (New York, 1959), p. 25. Subsequent references will be made to *The Tradition of the New*.

57. Rosenberg, *The Tradition of the New*, pp. 32, 34.

58. For an argument that Rosenberg is attacking Pollock here, see Naifeh and Smith, *Jackson Pollock, An American Saga*, pp. 704–5.

59. Rosenberg, *The Tradition of the New*, pp. 34, 24.

60. Barbara Rose, "Jackson Pollock et l'Art Américain," *Jackson Pollock* (Paris, 1982), p. 18.

61. *Art News Annual* 27 (1958): 86–97, 174–79.

62. Interview with Phyllis Tuchman pp. 1–2, AAA.

63. Interview with Phyllis Tuchman, p. 10, AAA. "Extremely myopic, [Rothko] could not move without his spectacles. But when he read or studied details, he would remove the glasses and hold the book or menu within inches of his eyes" (*LMR*, p. 100).

64. Interview with Phyllis Tuchman, pp. 6, 10, AAA.

65. De Kooning, "Two Americans in Action":174.

66. Elaine de Kooning, interview with Joseph Liss, December 11, 1977; see also Elaine de Kooning's interview with Phyllis Tuchman, p. 10, AAA.

67. Interview with Joseph Liss.

68. Interview with Phyllis Tuchman, p. 8, AAA.

69. "Editor's Letters," *Art News* 56, 8 (December 1957):8.

70. Dore Ashton's story about Rothko's lecture appeared in the *New York Times*, October 31, 1958, p. 26, headlined "ART: LECTURE BY ROTHKO," with the subhead: "Painter Dissociates Himself From the 'Abstract Expressionist' Movement." Some of Ashton's notes have been published—e.g., in *AR*, pp. 144–46, and *MR*, p. 86. (In

MR, as in *The New York School: The First Generation, Paintings of the 1940s and 1950s,* ed. Maurice Tuchman [Los Angeles, 1965], pp. 30–31, the first four paragraphs of the text have been mistakenly transcribed from some of Rothko's comments in "PMA.") A set of Ashton's notes can be found in the MRF, NGA, along with what appears to be a draft of her *Times* story. Some of Irving Sandler's notes are used in his "Mark Rothko," in *Mark Rothko, Paintings 1948–1969* (New York, 1983), pp. 11–12.

I will be quoting from the text in MRA, which I assume is a transcription of a taped recording of the talk because the text has been professionally typed, and because Ashton describes Rothko as speaking without notes (AR, p. 44).

71. AR, p. 44.

72. In Rothko's MOMA retrospective, all four of the paintings called *Sketch for Mural* (presumably from his second series for the Four Seasons) and four of five paintings titled *Mural, Section* (presumably from the third series) are 8'9" high, as is the *Mural for End Wall.*

73. The five gouache drawings are now in the estates of Kate Rothko and Christopher Rothko; they are reproduced in Compton, Introduction, p. 32, and in Thomas Kellein, *Mark Rothko: Kaaba in New York* (Basel, 1989), pp. 77–78.

Five sketches of the frieze have survived, two crayon sketches on maroon construction paper, two tempera sketches on maroon construction paper, and one tempera sketch on white paper stained red. All of the sketches (H. 24.1, H. 24.2, H. 25.1, H. 25.2, H. 25.3) are now in the Prints and Drawings Department, NGA, and all are reproduced in Kellein, *Mark Rothko: Kaaba in New York,* pp. 52–53. H.24.1 and H.25.2 are reproduced in WP, plates 43 and 44.

All of the sketches create a continuous frieze of five or six works along a strip of construction paper—H. 24.1, for example, is $3^{11}/_{16}''\times 18''$—leading Bonnie Clearwater to conclude that the sketches are not for specific works, but that they "reveal Rothko's initial intentions for the installation of the murals" (WP, p. 46). But since the individual "works" in these sketches at the NGA are all different from each other (rather than providing different orderings of the same "works"), the sketches seem to have been done prior to, and intended to generate, individual paintings. By the time he produced these sketches, Rothko had arrived at his new vertical column format, but he uses some yellows and blues that are much brighter than any of the colors in the paintings identified with what he later called the second "series." These sketches, then, were probably done between the first and second series.

74. "MR:PAAM":22; and Sir James George Frazer, *The Golden Bough,* abridged edition (New York, 1963), vol. 1, p. 1. This abridgement, first published in 1922, was the most likely source of Rothko's knowledge of *The Golden Bough.*

75. "MR:PAAM":22; and "ND," MRA.

76. Rothko's contrast between Brutus and Abraham is taken from Kierkegaard, who argues that Brutus's decision to execute his sons (for their part in an effort to restore a Roman king) was understandable, since his act violated one

631

ethical norm (the love of a father for his son) for the sake of a higher ethical norm (justice). Brutus is a "tragic hero," but Abraham, who "overstepped the ethical entirely and possesses a higher *telos* outside of it," is a "knight of faith" (*Fear and Trembling* [New York, 1954], pp. 68–9). In April 1956 Rothko told Alfred Jensen that he had first read *Fear and Trembling* about a year before, so he presumably read this Anchor paper edition shortly after it appeared ("JC," April 23, 1956). Friends recall seeing a well-worn copy of this book on a bedside table in Rothko's studio near the end of his life.

77. "JC," April 23, 1956.

78. Kierkegaard, *Fear and Trembling*, p. 97.

79. On Mies and the Nazi regime, see Elaine S. Hochman, *Architects of Fortune, Mies van der Rohe and the Third Reich* (New York, 1989). The stories about Philip Johnson were mentioned to me by Peter Selz and Robert Motherwell.

80. Kierkegaard, *Fear and Trembling*, p. 29.

81. "JC," July 23, 1956.

82. Kierkegaard, *Fear and Trembling*, pp. 31–32.

83. Mark Rothko to Kenneth and Joy Rabin, May 2, 1959; "MR:PAAM": 16; the agreement with Reis, dated May 18, 1958, can be found in BRP, AAA; the date of the name change (File No. 4641-1959, Superior Court, New York) was May 16, 1959, BRP, AAA; Rothko also mentions the name changes in his May 2, 1959, letter to Kenneth and Joy Rabin.

84. Rothko had been discussing providing for his family in case of his death with the collector Ben Heller at least since late 1957. In a letter to Rothko, Heller points out that Mell's position (particularly with regard to inheritance taxes) would be fine, but that by the time Kate would likely inherit the paintings, "they may have been driven up to a very high value which will then impose a high tax problem for her since you have, after all, a large amount of work available." Heller suggested that both Mark and Mell could each give Kate the $3,000 annual gift they were allowed, "and the establishing of some split Will which would leave directly to Katie a certain portion of your estate." Another possibility is a trust (Ben Heller to Mark Rothko, December 13, 1957, MRA).

Rothko's conversations with Heller continued, and a letter to Rothko from Heller in June 1960 reveals that Rothko had been considering setting up a foundation, some of the advantages of which Heller explained (Ben Heller to Mark Rothko, June 6, 1960, MRA). A Heller letter of December 8, 1960, expands on some of the possibilities for giving Kate gifts (Ben Heller to Mark Rothko, December 8, 1960, MRA).

85. Mark Rothko to Katharine Kuh, January 11, 1955, KKP, AIC; Katharine Kuh, interview with Avis Berman, pp. 8, 9, AAA.

86. *LMR*, pp. 42–43.

87. Mark Rothko and Mary Alice Rothko to Mr. and Mrs. Herbert Ferber and Bernard J. Reis, June 11, 1959, HFP, AAA.

88. Mark Rothko to Kenneth and Joy Rabin, May 7, 1959. John Fischer has Rothko sailing on the USS *Constitution*, but since Rothko's letter to the Rab-

ins was written close to the event, I'm assuming that Fischer misremembered the name of the ship.

89. "MR:PAAM":16–17.

90. Regina Bogat interview.

91. "MR:PAAM":22.

92. Kate Rothko interview; Kenneth and Elaine Rabin interview; Mark Rothko to Kenneth and Joy Rabin, May 2, 1959 (which mentions the return date and ship); Mark Rothko to Kenneth and Joy Rabin, May 7, 1959 (which gives some of the itinerary); and a postcard from Venice, n.d., Mark Rothko to Kenneth and Joy Rabin (which says that the Rothkos expect to arrive in Paris on July 15, and that they plan to proceed from Paris to Brussels).

93. Morton Levine, "Mark Rothko," in *Mark Rothko: Ten Major Works* (Newport Beach, CA, 1974), p. 5; Anne-Marie Levine, "A Nice Jewish Man" (unpublished poem).

94. Giulio Carlo Argan, *Fra Angelico and His Times* (Cleveland, 1955). See AR, pp. 147–50, for an account of Argan's book and its likely impact on Rothko. Argan stresses "the thoroughness with which, at San Marco, history, nature and myth have been ruled out in favor of rite and symbol" (p. 87).

95. Jacob Kainen, interview with Avis Berman, August 10, 1982, p. 18, AAA.

96. "MR:PAAM":16. Rothko mentioned Michelangelo's Medici Library as a source for the Seagram murals to many of his friends. "I know that Rothko admired the dark murals in the Medici library. He felt that these created just the kind of feeling he was after," Bernard Reis wrote to Norman Reid, February 21, 1974, MRF, TGA.

97. On this painting, see Richard Wollheim, *On Art and the Mind* (Cambridge, Mass., 1974), pp. 128–29.

98. Mark Rothko to Katharine Kuh, September 25, 1954, KKP, AIC.

99. "$4.5 Million Restaurant to Open Here," *New York Times*, July 16, 1959, p. 33; and "Food News: Dining in Elegant Manner," *New York Times*, October 2, 1959, p. 22. My description of the restaurant is based on these two articles, plus B. H. Friedman, "The Most Expensive Restaurant Ever Built," *Evergreen Review* 3, 10 (November–December 1959):108–16; "The Four Seasons: Collaboration for Elegance," *Progressive Architecture* 40 (December 1959):142–47; and Henry Russell Hitchcock, "The Current Work of Philip Johnson," *Zodiac* 8 (n.d.):70–72.

100. Michael Compton suggests that this meal "must have taken place in the spring of 1960. When Terry Frost came over to New York for the opening of his first exhibition there in April 1960, he was taken to dinner by Rothko, who said he had just finally cancelled the contract" (Introduction, p. 14).

101. Rothko's remark about restaurant prices was made to Robert Motherwell, in 1969, after Rita Reinhardt had taken Rothko, the Motherwells, and Bernard and Rebecca Reis to dinner at an expensive French restaurant near Greenwich, Connecticut.

102. G[ueft], "The Four Seasons":82, 86.

103. "Dan Rice Interviewed by Arnold Glimcher," n.p.; and interview with Avis Berman, Part I, p. 21. Kate Rothko also remembered that her father and mother went to eat at the Four Seasons "and that was the turning point—

when they actually ate there, they were totally turned off."

104. "MR:PAAM":16. Rothko gave a similar account of the evolution of the Seagram project to Norman Reid, director of the Tate Gallery. "Rothko told me he had made three sets of paintings and that the ones we were looking at were drawn from two of the series," Reid wrote in a November 3, 1969, memorandum after a five-hour talk with Rothko (in New York) about a possible gift of some of the panels to the Tate (MRF, TGA). Dan Rice similarly recalled that "there were, even given the exact dimensions, three separate sets of murals, two of which were rejected, plus a lot of individual paintings that were done almost in exact terms" ("Dan Rice Interviewed by Arnold Glimcher," n.p.).

105. Dan Rice drew a diagram of this three-one-three sequence in his interview with the Mark Rothko Foundation (MRF, NGA). As both Compton and Kellein point out, Rice's memory of seven paintings receives some support from Rothko's numbering of the *Sketches for Murals* and the *Mural, Sections* in his MOMA exhibit, where the highest number was 7 (see Selz, *Rothko*, p. 44). Yet this catalogue equally complicates this theory, since it lists *Mural, Section* nos. 2, 3, 4, 5, 7—plus an additional *Mural for End Wall*; this sequence raises the possibility that Rothko intended to hang eight paintings. Another problem: the end wall has to be the south wall (the north being all window). But if Rothko began his numbering at the north end of the east wall (the 6′ × 15′ size of sections 5 and 7 requires that they be hung on the narrow west wall), then the end wall panel should be no. 4. The width of no. 4 (8′9″ × 7′10″) suggests that it *may* have been intended for the south wall, since the two east-wall sections are much wider (both are 8′9″ × 15′). Neither Compton nor Kellein confront the problems raised by the *Mural for End Wall*.

106. Compton, Introduction, p. 13.

107. All quotations are from Haftmann's untitled essay in the catalogue for the 1971 exhibit of Rothko's work at the Kunsthaus, Zurich.

Haftmann dates his conversation with Rothko in the spring of 1959, before Rothko's trip to Europe, but after he had decided to refuse the commission. This can't be correct. Rothko's shipboard conversations with John Fischer indicate that he was then still working on the third series ("I think I can finish off the job pretty quickly after I get home from this trip"— "MR:PAAM":16); and since the Four Seasons did not open until after his return, and many people recall that Rothko decided to refuse only after eating there, the conversation with Haftmann must have taken place later (unless Haftmann's memory has conflated more than one studio visit). Possibly, Haftmann visited in the spring of 1960, when Michael Compton dates Rothko's final refusal of the commission.

108. As we have seen, Rothko told Fischer that he had sold panels from the first series "separately as individual paintings." It is not certain how many paintings were produced for the first series or how many were sold. There is, in fact, only one painting, *White and Black on Wine*, 1958, that has been generally accepted as from this first series, though even this attribution, first made

by Ronald Alley of the Tate Gallery, is somewhat speculative.

Mr. Alley writes, "The only picture from the first series that has been definitely identified is *White and Black on Wine*, 1958, formerly in the collection of William S. Rubin, New York, and now in that of Ben Heller, which has two horizontal soft-edged rectangular patches of white and black on a wine-coloured ground" (*Catalogue of the Tate Gallery's Collection of Modern Art* [London, 1981], p. 660). Mr. Alley offers no reasons for his "definite" identification; he is presumably basing it on the exceptional size of the painting (8'9" × 13'10"), particularly its height, that of many of the Four Seasons panels.

Yet in his instructions for the hanging of his one-man retrospective at the Whitechapel Art Gallery in 1961, Rothko says that at MOMA, the murals were hung as a "unit." "The only exception to this grouping of the murals is the picture owned by Mr. Rubin, 'White and Black on Wine' 1958, which could take its place, but with a raised hanging among the other works since it is a transitional piece between the earlier pictures of that year and the mural series" (*MR*, p. 88). Rothko's comment does not rule out the possibility that *White and Black on Wine* was part of the first set, but he does differentiate it from the "mural series."

109. See the descriptions of viewing the Seagram panels in Rothko's studio by Dore Ashton, in *AR*, pp. 154–56, and by Werner Haftmann in *Mark Rothko*, exhibition catalogue, trans. Margery Schaer, (Zurich: Kunsthaus, 1971, n.p.). Selz, *Rothko*, lists ten paintings (p. 44), but Thomas Kellein points out that a corrected copy of the catalogue, in the MOMA library, indicates that *Mural for End Wall* was not shown (*Mark Rothko, Kaaba in New York*, p. 40, note 27). On Rothko's gift to the Tate Gallery, see below, Chapter 18.

110. Jack Cowart, curator of twentieth-century art at the NGA, said of the exhibit of the six murals, "This installation is an opportunity to have a coherent environment as intended by Rothko instead of taking six disparate paintings and making a combination to our own taste" (quoted in *New York Times*, November 10, 1985, section I, p. 81).

111. Sir Alan Bowness, Preface, *Mark Rothko, The Seagram Mural Project*, p. 7.

112. Of course, museums, too, function inside history, and the room at the Tate devoted to Rothko's murals has changed twice since the first installation, which Rothko directed by using a cardboard model (18" × 19½" × 7½") of the original room. In the model he placed gouache on colored construction-paper models of the paintings. See records in MRF, TGA. Both the cardboard model and the gouache models can be found at the TGA. The present room is arranged quite differently.

Chapter Fourteen

1. Memorandum from Peter Selz to Monroe Wheeler, February 9, 1961, MRF, MOMA. Selz reports Rothko's request, based on the appearance of the reviews by Katharine Kuh, Robert Goldwater, and Thomas Hess during the following month, but Selz sees "no hope" for extending the show.

2. *MR*, p. 88. The document sent to

the Whitechapel consists of notes taken from a conversation with Rothko about the Whitechapel hanging, the notes taken by someone at MOMA.

3. "Art: Mark Rothko," *Spectator* 224 (March 7, 1970):314.

4. James Brooks to Ronald Alley, April 22, 1976, MRF, TGA.

5. These figures are based on a memorandum (January 26, 1972) from Bernard Reis to Irving Moskovitz, one of the three attorneys defending Marlborough A.G. (the Marlborough parent company, located in Liechtenstein) during the suit initiated (and won) by Kate Rothko over the mismanagement of her father's estate.

The memo lists each year from 1955 to 1963, gives the number of pictures sold and the "net" to Rothko (after commission), the figures coming from Sidney Janis reports (1955 to 1960) and from the annual statements of net worth done for Mark and Mary Alice Rothko by Bernard Reis and Company (1961–62). (The 1961 and 1962 reports are "Resp. Ferber Exhibits 1 and 2," "The Matter of Rothko.") I have not given an average figure for 1963, since Reis only lists for that year Rothko's sale of five of the Seagram murals to Count Giuseppe Panza at $20,000 each—an amount that presumably reflects a discount on the price of each painting because of the number of paintings purchased.

I've assumed that the Janis commission was $33^{1}/_{3}$ percent (although Reis's statement of net worth reports indicate that the commission was sometimes 20 percent and occasionally 10 percent). I've used the $33^{1}/_{3}$ percent to convert Rothko's share back into the amount received for the paintings prior to commission, then divided that amount by the number of paintings for that year to arrive at an average price.

The figures I've arrived at by this method are admittedly artificial, since an average blends together oils and watercolors, works on canvas and works on paper, large paintings and small paintings; nor does the average reflect the date of the painting. All of these variables would importantly affect the price of any individual painting. Here are some particular transactions that both complicate my figures and bear out my basic contention about Rothko's rising prices.

In 1957, Rothko sold *Earth Greens* (1955; $91^{3}/_{8}"$ × $73^{5}/_{8}"$) and *White Band* (1954; $81"$ × $86^{5}/_{8}"$) to Ben Heller for $2,000 and $2,500 respectively. In 1958, Rothko sold Heller *Browns* (1957; $91^{3}/_{4}"$ × $76^{1}/_{8}"$) for $4,000. In 1959, he sold Heller *Four Darks on Red* (1958; $102^{1}/_{8}"$ × $116^{3}/_{8}"$) for $8,000, and in 1960 Heller purchased *White, Pink and Mustard* (1954; $92"$ × $66^{1}/_{4}"$) for $7,000 ("Rothko Paintings Purchased and Sold By Heller," Petitioners' Exhibit 159, and Ben Heller to Gustave Harrow, January 9, 1974, "Resp. Exhibit 259," both from "The Matter of Rothko").

In 1957, Duncan Phillips purchased *Mauve Intersection,* 1948, and *Green and Maroon,* 1953; the asking price was $2,500 each and Phillips received a $100 discount for purchasing both paintings, so the sales price was $2,400 each (Sidney Janis to Duncan Phillips, February 12, 1957, MRF, PC). In 1960, Janis sent Phillips a price list for four paintings: *Blue and Green,* $9,000; *Green and Tangerine on Red,* $9,000; *Black and Red on Red,* $9,000; *Orange and Red on Red,* $7,000 (MRF, PC).

In 1961 Rothko sold three paintings

to Sidney Janis—*Maroon on Blue* (92" × 70½"), *Red and Orange* (71" × 56"), and *Yellow Stripe* (78½" × 70")—for $8,000, $5,333.34, and $6,000 respectively. (These prices presumably represent a discount, possibly as much as 33⅓ percent, that Rothko would have given his dealer.) That year, five paintings were sold *by* Janis—*Dark over Light* (1954; 90" × 50"), *Violet Bar* (1957; 66" × 69"), *Yellow Band* (1956; 86" × 80"), *Brown, Blue, Brown on Blue* (1953; 115" × 91¾") and *Black and Dark Sienna on Purple* (1960; 120" × 105")—for $9,000, $8,000, $12,000, $15,000, and $15,000 respectively.

In 1962, Janis sold three works—*White and Red* (1961; 101" × 89¾"), *Horizontal White over Dark* (56½" × 96½"), and *Reds Light and Dark # 6* (69¾" × 54½")—for $22,000, $12,000, and $12,500. That year Janis purchased two works (again presumably discounted)—*#5 Reds* (69¾" × 62¼") and *Red Maroons #2* (1961; 79" × 81")—for $10,600 and $14,000. Rothko also sold two paintings to the collector Mary Lasker, *Number 2, 1962* (81" × 76"), and *Number 1, 1962* (69" × 60") for $15,000 and $10,000.

Information on the Sidney Janis sales is taken from Mark and Mary Alice Rothko, Statement of Net Worth, for 1961 and for 1962, done by Bernard J. Reis and Co. ("Resp. Ferber Exhibit 1 and 2," "The Matter of Rothko"). (Note: in identifying these paintings I have only given the year when it was supplied in the documents I consulted.)

6. My information about Rothko's productivity comes from David Anfam.

Rothko's regularity of production undermines two contradictory stories that still circulate in the New York art world about him: that, after he became successful, he limited his yearly production to stay in a lower tax bracket; that he mass-produced "Rothkos" to satisfy the cravings of rich collectors.

7. Bernard Reis suggests another possible motive: "I always told Rothko, don't sell all your pictures in any one year because if they're any good they're your best investment" (interview with Paul Cummings, p. 52, AAA). From this point of view, Rothko himself would be viewing his paintings (partly) as investments.

8. Sidney Janis to René d'Harnoncourt, January 16, 1961, MRF, MOMA.

9. Ulfert Wilke, "Diary," January 30, 1966, UWP, AAA.

10. Quoted from the untitled talk that begins "there seems to be a profound parallel" (MRA).

11. Untitled statement, 1949; reprinted in *MR*, p. 85.

12. "Art: The Wild Ones," *Time* 72 (February 20, 1956):70–75 reproduces Rothko's *Orange Over Yellow,* with the caption: "Mark Rothko, 52, paints very big pictures of very little. This characteristic layer-cake canvas is more than 6 ft. high, looks something like a window on an odd sunset. 'I'm not interested in color,' Rothko insists. 'It's light I'm after'."

In 1959 *Life* did a two-part article on "Baffling U.S. Art: What It Is About" (*Life* 47, 19 [November 9, 1959]:68–77, 79–80 and *Life* 47, 20 [November 16, 1959]:74–83, 85–86). The first part dealt with Jackson Pollock, the second ("The Varied Art of Four Pioneers") with Clyfford Still, Franz Kline, Willem de Kooning, and Rothko. One untitled Rothko work is given a full-page reproduction (juxtaposed with a photograph of a sunset). An essay about Donald Blinken's collection, "How Young Collectors Live with Art," *House and Garden*, 122 (November 1962):216–17, includes a photograph of the two Rothko paintings hung in Blinken's living room.

Articles about Rothko's MOMA exhibit appeared in *Newsweek* 57, 4 (January 23, 1961):60 and *Time* 77 (March 3, 1961):74–75.

Reviews of the MOMA show included:

John Canaday, "Is Less More and When for Whom?: Rothko Show Raises Questions About Painters, Critics and Audience," *New York Times*, January 22, 1961, section x, p. 17.

Robert M. Coates, "The Art Galleries," *New Yorker* 36, 50 (January 28, 1961):78–81.

Irving Sandler, "New York Letter," *Art International* 5, 2 (March 1, 1961):40–41.

Katharine Kuh, "The Fine Arts: Art Without Isms," *Saturday Review* 44, 9 (March 4, 1961):37, 145.

Robert Goldwater, "Reflections on the Rothko Exhibition," *Arts* 35, 6 (March 1961):42–45.

T[homas] H[ess], "Reviews and Previews," *Art News* 60, 1 (March 1961):10.

Max Kozloff, "Mark Rothko's New Retrospective," *Art Journal* 20, 3 (Spring 1961):148–49.

13. The Statement of Net Worth, December 31, 1965, for Mark and Mary Alice Rothko from Bernard J. Reis and Co. ("Resp. Ferber Exhibit 4," "The Matter of Rothko") makes Rothko's implication in middle-class American life particularly clear.

By this time, Rothko had sold his Provincetown cottage, so he was receiving mortgage payments as well as making them (on the 95th Street house). He had made about $19,000 worth of improvements on the 95th Street house since purchasing it. During 1965, he had paid a little less than $2,300 for domestic help. He had major medical insurance on himself, his wife, and his daughter. He had a homeowner's insurance policy. He had a general liability policy on his studio, a fine arts floater-policy covering his unsold paintings, and a workman's-compensation policy. He was making contributions to a retirement fund for self-employed persons.

Because he generally took payment for works in the form of annual installments, he was also owed a lot of money and was thus assured of substantial income for the next several years—e.g., he would receive $81,000 in 1966, $73,000 in 1967, and $82,000 in 1968. Payments for the Houston chapel—$35,666.67 per year—would continue until 1973.

14. "JC," April 22, 1966.

15. Byrnes, "Remembering Mark," p. 30.

16. *LMR*, p. 66. The visit was to the home of Hope and Paul Makler. When the Maklers first visited Rothko's studio, he told them he had already promised to others the paintings he was willing to sell that year. For a few years, they called Rothko about a possible purchase; he put them off. In 1967, he told them, "It's your turn," and they bought an orange and red painting which they soon found too intense. "It was like sitting in a furnace," according to Hope Makler. They returned the painting, but in March 1968, they bought *Number 119, 1961*, from Marlborough, which

gave them an $8,000 discount from the $36,000 Rothko and the gallery had agreed upon. Rothko was enraged over the discount, and was mollified only after his trip to Philadelphia. For a record of the 1968 sale, see "Exhibit #235-A" in "The Matter of Rothko."

Sally Scharf recalled Rothko's "increasing sense that he was losing control, because there were too many paintings bought and brought out where he wouldn't even have visitation rights like you might have if you're divorced with a child. He did like to go and see where the work was and he didn't let go that way."

17. In October 1962 Rothko, along with Adolph Gottlieb, Philip Guston, and Robert Motherwell, left Janis to protest his "The New Realists" exhibition of Pop art. Rothko signed a contract with Marlborough Galleries on June 10, 1963 (BRP, AAA).

18. *LMR*, pp. 66–67.

19. Max Kozloff, "Mark Rothko (1903–1970)," *Artforum* 8 (April 1970):88; Stanley Kunitz, interview with Avis Berman, Part I, p. 17, AAA.

20. Ben Heller, interview with Paul Cummings, January 8, 1973, p. 12, AAA.

21. Bernard and Rebecca Reis, interview with Ralph Pomeroy, January 1971 (with Donald McKinney also present), p. 5, BRP, AAA; *LMR*, p. 66.

22. Blinken purchased *Three Reds* (1955; 68" × 38½"), in May 1956; six months later, he bought *Blue over Orange* (1956; 86" × 79"), and an untitled 1946 watercolor (38¾" × 25½"). In 1958 he obtained *Number 9, 1958* (101" × 82"), and in 1962 or 1963 he acquired *Number 117, 1961* (93" × 81")

(cf. Spencer Davidson, "After the Rothko Scandal an Old Friend Guards the Goods," *Avenue* [March 1982]:120–22, 124, 126, 128; interview with Donald Blinken, MRF, NGA; Donald Blinken interview. All of the paintings owned by Blinken are reproduced in *MR,AR* (plates 61, 123, 125, 149, 162).

23. *House and Garden* 122 (November 1962):216–17. The article includes a photograph of the two Rothko paintings then hung in Blinken's living room.

24. Interview with Paul Cummings, pp. 12–13, AAA.

25. Robert and Elizabeth Morrow interview.

26. This is the painting identified by Ronald Alley of the Tate Gallery as belonging to the "first series" of Seagram panels; it is reproduced in *MR,AR* (plate 150) with the title *Black, Maroons and White*.

27. Ben Heller interview, January 27, 1987. Heller gave William Rubin $25,000 plus Rothko's *Browns, 1957*, for the mural panel. At that time, Heller owned *Yellow, Green* (1953; 76½" × 67½"), bought in 1955 for $1,350, *Earth Greens* (1955; 91⅜" × 73⅝"), bought in 1957 for $2,000, *White Band* (1954; 81 × 86⅝"), bought in 1957 for $2,500, *Four Darks on Red* (1958; 102⅛" × 116⅛"), bought in 1959 for $8,000, *Browns* (1957; 91¾" × 76⅛"), bought in 1958 for $4,000, *White, Pink and Mustard* (1954; 92 × 66¼"), bought in 1960 for $7,000, and *Greens and Blue on Blue*, n.d. (79¼" × 69⅛"), bought in 1964 for $16,000 (cf. "Petitioners' Exhibit 159," "The Matter of Rothko").

On Heller's collection, see Henry Geldzahler, "Heller: New American-Type Collector," *Art News* 60 (September 1961):28–31, 58; and Cynthia Kellogg, "At Home With Art," *New York Times Magazine,* May 8, 1960, pp. 84–86.

28. Rothko sold *Earth, Green and White,* 1957, to the University of Arizona in 1957; *Red, White and Brown,* 1957, to the Kunsthalle Basel in 1958; *Olive over Red,* 1956, to the Baltimore Museum of Art in 1958; *Red, Brown and Black,* 1958, to MOMA in 1959; *Light Red over Black,* 1957, to the Tate Gallery (London) in 1959; *Number 1, White and Red,* 1961, to the Toronto Gallery of Art in 1962; *Number 2, Red Maroons,* 1961, to the Cleveland Museum in 1962.

He also sold *Orange and Red on Red,* 1957, and *Ocher, Red on Red,* 1954, to the Phillips Collection (in 1960 and 1964, respectively). My information on these sales comes from Sidney Janis material in MRF, NGA.

29. Nelson Rockefeller bought *White and Greens in Blue,* 1957, in 1958 (the painting was subsequently destroyed in a fire at the governor's mansion while Rockefeller was governor of New York); Mrs. John D. Rockefeller III purchased *Sienna, Black on Dark Red,* 1959, in 1959 (she had bought *Number 1, 1949,* in 1949); and David Rockefeller bought *White Center,* 1950, in 1960 (Janis Records, MRF, NGA).

30. John and Dominique de Menil bought *Number 10, 1957,* in 1957; Burton and Emily Tremaine purchased *Maroon on Blue,* 1957–60, in 1961 (they had bought *Number 8, 1952,* in 1953) (Janis Records, MRF, NGA, and BPP, AAA).

31. Quoted in *The Collector in America,* ed. Jean Lipman (New York, 1971), p. 14.

32. "Odd Ball In," *Newsweek* 60 (October 25, 1965):104.

33. Allene Talmey, "Art Is the Core," *Vogue* 144 (July 1964):116–23, 125; Jane Kramer, "Man Who Is Happening Now," *New Yorker* 42 (July 26, 1966):64–120; Tom Wolfe, "Bob and Spike," *The Pump House Gang* (New York, 1968), pp. 175–203; Robert C. Scull, "Re the *F-111:* A Collector's Notes," *Metropolitan Museum Bulletin* 26, 7 (March 1968):282–83.

34. Kramer, "Man Who Is Happening Now":64.

35. Ethel Scull, in Emile de Antonio and Mitch Tuchman, *Painters Painting* (New York, 1984), pp. 123–24.

Actually, Warhol did not use thirty-six different images; he chose only seventeen, then 'repeated' some of these, usually cropping them differently or reversing them or painting them a different color.

36. Kramer, "Man Who is Happening Now":64.

37. Ibid.:109–10, 112, 115–16, 118–20.

38. My account of the Sculls is based on the sources in note 33, this chapter, plus: "Scull, Robert C," *Current Biography,* ed. Charles Moritz (New York, 1974), pp. 356–59; John Duka, "Back on Top with the Mom of Pop Art," *New York* 19 (June 9, 1986):62–68; Doris Saatchi, "Keeping Up with the Johnses," *Vanity Fair* 251 (May 1987):52, 54, 56, 58, 61.

39. De Antonio and Tuchman, *Painters Painting,* p. 110; Kramer, "Man Who Is Happening Now":82.

40. Talmey, "Art Is the Core":118; Wolfe, *The Pump House Gang,* p. 181.

41. Duka, "Back on Top with the

Mom of Pop Art":65; *Current Biography*, p. 357.

42. Andy Warhol and Pat Hackett, *POPism, The Warhol Sixties* (New York, 1980), pp. 86–87; John Bernard Myers, *Tracking the Marvelous* (New York, 1983), pp. 216–17.

43. De Antonio and Tuchman, *Painters Painting*, p. 106.

44. Kramer, "Man Who Is Happening Now":66, 70; Warhol and Hackett, *POPism*, p. 86.

45. Saatchi, "Keeping Up with the Johnses":56.

46. Janis Records, MRA, NGA.

47. Richard and Johnnie Mae Roth interview; Milton and Joy Rabin interview; Phil and Dorothy Reiter interview; Julian and Dorothy Roth interview.

48. Hedda Sterne, interview with Phyllis Tuchman, pp. 2–3, AAA.

49. Richard and Johnnie Mae Roth interview.

50. Albert Roth, interview with Lee Seldes, May 1975, LSF; Kenneth and Elaine Rabin interview.

The story of Rothko selling paintings to cover Albert's medical expenses is told by just about everyone in the family. Kenneth Rabin recalled that Rothko sold paintings to a wealthy woman he hated who had long wanted one of his paintings and who had contributed lots of money to a New York hospital. According to Rabin, Rothko "called her up and said, 'You've got to get my brother in there, and you can have whatever painting you want.'"

The woman must be Mary Lasker, a collector, philanthropist, and a close friend of Bernard Reis; she and her husband, Albert, founded the Albert and Mary Lasker Foundation for Medical Research (Reis was its director for many years). Rothko did sell two paintings to Mary Lasker, *Number 1, 1962* ($10,300), and *Number 2, 1962* ($15,000), on May 17, 1962. Janis received $1,300 from the sale of *Number 1*, $1,500 from the sale of *Number 2*; payment to Rothko was made in four annual installments (1962–65), with the largest payment last. In 1962 he received $1,000 for *Number 1* and $1,500 for *Number 2* (cf. Mark and Mary Alice Rothko, Statement of Net Worth, December 31, 1962 by Bernard J. Reis and Co., ["Resp. Ferber, Exhibit 2," "The Matter of Rothko,"] and a sheet listing "Mark Rothko Paintings Owned by Mrs. Lasker," in BRP, AAA).

In addition, the sales records in Peter Selz Papers, AAA, list a transaction in which two "small abstractions" owned by Albert Roth were sold to Lawrence Rubin, for $2,667 each. Apparently Rothko gave the paintings to his brother, so he could sell them (presumably they'd be taxed less if sold by Albert). These paintings were likely used to raise money for Albert's treatment, and the ones sold to Mary Lasker may have been.

Another of Albert's surgeries took place in the winter of 1966–67. Sally Avery wrote to Louis and Annette Kaufman, "Rothko was here—he hasn't painted all winter because his brother was very sick in Memorial Hospital here" (Sally Avery to Louis and Annette Kaufman, April 19, 1967, LKP, AAA).

The detail about Albert Roth going to Memorial Hospital comes from my interview with Dr. Grokest and from documents assembled by Bernard Reis for his defense in the suit over Rothko's estate (BRP, AAA).

51. Vita Deming interview.

52. Mark Rothko to Herbert Ferber, (1962), HFP, AAA.

53. Victor Bockris, *The Life and Death of Andy Warhol* (New York, 1989), pp. 119–20.

54. Warhol and Hackett, *POPism*, pp. 34–35.

55. Al Held, interview with Paul Cummings, December 12, 1975, pp. 70–71, AAA.

56. William Rubin interview, January 9, 1986.

57. Tomkins, *Off the Wall*, pp. 96–97.

58. Calvin Tomkins, "Leo Castelli: A Good Eye and a Good Ear," *New Yorker* 56 (May 26, 1980):52.

59. Ibid.

60. Ibid.:57.

61. Quoted in William S. Rubin, *Frank Stella* (New York, 1970), p. 13.

62. Warhol and Hackett, *POPism*, p. 7. The story of Karp's visit is also told in Bockris, *The Life and Death of Andy Warhol*, pp. 98–100, where Victor Bockris places the incident in "the summer of 1960" (p. 98).

63. G. R. Swenson, "What Is Pop Art?—Part I" (interviews with Jim Dine, Robert Indiana, Roy Lichtenstein, Andy Warhol), *Art News* 62 (November 1963):25.

64. *Art as an Investment* (New York, 1961), p. 409.

65. Quoted in Barbara Rose, *Claes Oldenburg* (New York, 1970), p. 67.

66. "Something New Is Cooking," *Life* (June 15, 1962):115–16, 119–20.

67. Sidney Janis, *The New Realists* (New York, 1962), n.p.

68. Alan Jones and Laura de Coppet, *The Art Dealers* (New York, 1984), p. 39.

69. "Pop Art—Cult of the Commonplace," *Time*, 81 (March 5, 1963):69.

70. *Life*, 55 (September 20, 1963):123.

71. "Abstract Paintings/By Expressionists/ Sold for $284,000," *New York Times*, October 14, 1965, p. 52, and "Odd Ball In":104. The *Times* story provides the following prices: Still, *Painting—1951*, $29,000; Newman, *Tundra*, $26,000; de Kooning, *Police Gazette*, $37,000; Tobey, *Wild Field*, $14,000; Kline, *Shenandoah*, $19,000; Kline, *Initial*, $18,000, and Rothko, *Reds, Number 22*, $15,500—making Rothko a low man on the Abstract Expressionist totem pole. (*Reds, Number 22*, must be either *Reds* [1961] or *Reds* [1962], listed by Sidney Janis as sold to Rothko—Janis Records, NGA.)

72. BN,SWI, p. 260.

73. John-Franklin Koenig, "Abstraction *chaud* in Paris in the 1950s," in *Reconstructing Modernism*, ed. Serge Guilbaut (Cambridge, Mass., 1990), pp. 15–16.

74. Kate Rothko interview.

75. Vita Deming interview; George and Shirley Climo interview; Jean Bultman interview, January 13, 1986; Jane Lawrence interview.

76. "Is There a New Academy?" Part I, *Art News* (Summer 1959):34–37, 58–59; and "Is There a New Academy?" Part II, *Art News* (September 1959):36–39, 58–60.

77. Count Giuseppe Panza to Mark Rothko, October 19, 1960, MRA; September 7, 1961, MRA; October 21, 1961, MRA; November 11, 1961, MRA. In the correspondence, no titles for

the paintings, only dimensions, are given. Two of the paintings were owned by Kate Rothko, 15′ × 8¾′ and 14′ × 8¾′, and three by Rothko, 12′ × 8¾′, 8½′ × 8¾′ and 8½′ × 8¾′. Count Panza was to pay Mark Rothko $1,041.66 per month and Kate Rothko (with her father acting as her agent) $1,041.67 per month—both for forty-eight months. Count Panza also agreed not to resell the paintings for ten years (Mark Rothko to Count Giuseppe Panza, November 24, 1961, MRA).

78. Count Giuseppe Panza to Mark Rothko, November 25, 1963, MRA; January 31, 1964, MRA; December 13, 1963, MRA; and "Interview with Giuseppe Panza," in *Art of the Sixties and Seventies, The Panza Collection* (New York, 1987), p. 42. See also Tommaso Trini, "At Home With Art: The Villa of Count Giuseppe Panza Di Biumo," *Art in America* 58 (September–October 1970):103–9, where Count Panza attributes the pause both to the economic conditions and to his "feeling of uncertainty about the post-pop period" (p. 109).

79. According to *Art of the Sixties and Seventies*, p. 269, Count Panza owned *Red and Blue over Red* (1959); *Violet and Yellow in Rose* (1954); *Black and Dark Sienna on Purple* (1960); *Purple Brown* (1957); *Brown, Blue, Brown on Blue* (1953); *Black, Ocher, Red over Red* (1957); and *Red and Brown* (1957).

80. Count Giuseppe Panza to Mark Rothko, January 31, 1964, MRA; March 26, 1964, MRA. Originally, Count Panza wished to obtain two paintings he had seen when Rothko's one-man MOMA exhibit traveled to London in the fall of 1961 and to Rome in the spring of 1962: *Homage to Matisse,* 1954, and *Number 30, 1954*. But Rothko replied that these works "are not available because all of the pictures that were in the travelling show have been consigned to a foundation now being formed where they will remain intact as a group" (Mark Rothko to Count Giuseppe Panza, January 23, 1964, MRA).

81. In preparing for "The Matter of Rothko," Bernard Reis wrote a statement on his "Relationship to the art world" and in particular he listed various services he claimed to have performed for Rothko. Item 4 on his list was "Matters relating to Panza," where Reis describes Rothko's arrangement with the count, then writes: "In 1963, Dr. Panza reneged on the deal and this caused considerable distress to Mark.

"Mark did not want to continue with Sidney Janis, and Dr. Panza had made it clear to Rothko that he was no longer interested in abstract expressionist art but was developing an interest in pop art" (BRP, AAA).

After reneging on the deal, Count Panza never spoke to Rothko in person; his letters to Rothko insist on the economic reasons for his decision. What Reis may be remembering was what Rothko thought was the case, as opposed to what Count Panza said was the case.

82. Al Hirschfeld interview, January 4, 1986.

83. Karl Schrag interview, January 30, 1986.

84. Warhol and Hackett, *POPism,* pp. 20–21.

85. Ibid., p. 18.

86. Swenson, "What Is Pop Art?":61; Warhol and Hackett, *POPism,* p. 3.

87. Charles Baudelaire, "The Painter

of Modern Life," in *The Painter of Modern Life and Other Essays,* trans. Jonathan Mayne (London, 1964), p. 13.

88. *Time* 82 (November 22, 1963):72.

89. Diana Crane, *The Transformation of the Avant-Garde, The New York Art World, 1940–1985* (Chicago, 1987), pp. 2–5.

90. "For More Than Art's Sake," *Business Week* (May 15, 1965):158. My account of Frank Lloyd's life is based, in addition, on "Francis Kenneth Lloyd, A Biography"—an undated press release issued by Marlborough (in LSF); "Aggressive Giant," *Time* 82 (July 19, 1963):56; John Russell, "Swinging Art Dealers: The Marlborough Boys in New York," *Vogue* 142, 1 (January 1, 1964):102–5, 162; David L. Shirey, "Frank Lloyd and the Marlborough: Art and Success," *New York Times,* May 21, 1973, p. 40; "Artfinger: Turning Pictures into Gold," *Time* 101 (June 25, 1973):65–66, 71; "The Million-Dollar Art Wrangle," *Observer Review,* December 30, 1973, p. 17, in MRF, MOMA; Grace Glueck, "The Man the Art World Loves to Hate," *New York Times Magazine,* June 15, 1975, pp. 12, 15, 17, 20–22.

91. Shirey, "Frank Lloyd and the Marlborough," p. 40.

92. Glueck, "The Man the Art World Loves to Hate," p. 20.

93. The gas stations were transformed into "a successful oil business" in "Francis Kenneth Lloyd," n.p.

94. Russell, "Swinging Art Dealers":104.

95. "Francis Kenneth Lloyd," n.p; Glueck, "The Man the Art World Loves to Hate," pp. 21, 151.

96. Russell, "Frank Lloyd and the Marlborough":40; "For More Than Art's Sake":151.

97. "For More Than Art's Sake":152. Lloyd himself later became involved in a scandal when he purchased, then resold at considerable profit, works by Rousseau and van Gogh "deaccessioned" by the Metropolitan. He proved to be a little too pessimistic on the issue of masterpieces permanently disappearing into museums.

98. Shirey, "Frank Lloyd and the Marlborough," p. 40.

99. "I had met Frank Lloyd on a number of occasions before 1963 in New York and in Venice," Reis wrote in an account of his "Relationship to the art world" prepared for "The Matter of Rothko" (BRP, AAA).

100. Quoted in *LMR,* p. 59. Lee Seldes has Rothko asking for a show in Minsk (probably because either Lloyd or Guston misremembered the name of Rothko's birthplace); I've changed it to Dvinsk.

101. Ibid., p. 41.

102. The Reis collection is described (with several photographs) in "A Monumental Collection of Modern and Primitive Art," *Interiors* 110 (February 1951):80–85, 167. In addition, a six-page handout, produced for a MOMA tour of the collection, lists the works that were hung in the Reis home in April 1964 (BRP, AAA). The list contains one Rothko, a 1962 oil painting. By this time the Reises owned (or had owned) Rothko's *Number 47, 1957* (oil on paper), loaned to MOMA for Rothko's 1961 exhibit there. See Peter Selz to Mr. and Mrs. Bernard J. Reis, October 27, 1960, BRP, AAA, or the catalogue for the show, Selz, *Rothko,* p. 44.

A sheet in Reis's papers, probably compiled in 1968–70, lists six paintings by Rothko in the Reis collection. *Grey and Black* (1969; 68" × 60"); *Blue and Green* (1968; 39" × 26"); *Red Pink* (1961; 69" × 54"); *Sienna and Orange on Wine* (1962; 69" × 66")—all oils on canvas—were hanging in the Reis home. Two other works—*Brown Maroon Rust on Plum* (1959; 38" × 25"—tempera on paper mounted on masonite) and *Dark Picture* (1968; 47¾" × 40"—oil on paper mounted on linen)—were at the Marlborough Gallery.

Sienna and Orange on Wine is probably the 1962 painting on the list for the MOMA tour of the collection; by the time of the 1968–70 list, *Number 47, 1957*, must have either been sold or given as a gift. *Blue and Green,* inscribed on the back "to Bernard and Becky Reis in love and friendship" was a gift from Rothko. In "The Matter of Rothko," Reis testified that all of his Rothko paintings had been gifts from Rothko, received between 1955 and 1969. He also claimed that he had never sold any of these gifts, though *Number 47, 1957*, had disappeared from his collection by 1969 and two of the Rothko paintings on his 1968–70 list were at Marlborough, through which gallery Reis was selling off other works in his collection. See "Examination of Bernard Reis," p. 59, in "The Matter of Rothko."

103. Myers, *Tracking the Marvelous,* p. 237; *The Unharried Hostess: Thirty Memorable Dinners in Thirty Minutes* (New York, 1963); and Rebecca Reis, "Cook a Memorable Dinner in 30 Minutes," *The Evening Bulletin* [Philadelphia], February 12, 1964 (clipping in BRP, AAA).

104. Myers, *Tracking the Marvelous,* pp. 236–37.

105. At least some of the American painters complained that while Reis would accept their work as gifts (in return for his professional services), Reis did not buy their work. "His real interest was in the Europeans," Robert Motherwell said. "In fact, to this day if you look at his collection it's predominantly European. The best pictures are European. The only money was spent on Europeans. To the degree that he had any American paintings I'm sure we gave them to him. He was very conservative and snobbish that way without really knowing it" (interview with Paul Cummings, p. 84, AAA). To judge from the list of works for the 1964 tour of the Reis collection (n. 102, above), Motherwell's assertion that it was "predominantly European" is fair enough.

106. Quoted in *LMR,* p. 42.

107. Bernard Reis, interview with Paul Cummings, p. 27, AAA; Rebecca Reis, interview with William McNaught, April 29, 1980, AAA.

108. "Relationship to the art world," BRP, AAA.

109. In the Reises' interview with Ralph Pomeroy (p. 1), Rebecca Reis says that when Rothko was looking for a house to buy, he first wanted one on 84th or 85th Street, but "Bernard told Mark not to buy it" because it needed too much work, was badly located and overpriced. But "when we saw" the 95th Street house, "we told them immediately to buy it" (BRP, AAA). In this interview and in her own interview with William McNaught (AAA), Mrs. Reis unself-consciously reveals how in charge of Rothko she and her husband imagined themselves to be.

110. This estimate is based on the 1969–70 prices for works sold by Rothko of similar size to those owned by Reis. The prices are taken from "Appendix C" to "Post-Trial Memorandum of Marlborough Gallery, Inc. and Marlborough A.G.," in "The Matter of Rothko." See note 102, this chapter, for a list and description of the Rothko paintings in the Reises' collection.

111. Arthur Lidov, whose studio was in the same 69th Street building as Rothko's, recalled, "I felt that he should certainly know how to operate a thermostat, and with a little bit of instruction know how to turn the valves on the furnace so there was water in the boiler. But it turned out that these were manipulative challenges beyond him. He wasn't prepared to admit that they were beyond him. He liked to pretend that they were beneath him, but on certain occasions when he actually had to perform them, it turns out that he didn't quite remember what he should do and managed to do it wrong."

Bernard Reis's secretary, Ruth Miller, remembered that as it was "nearing the time for him to get Social Security, it was really troubling him. Not because he was becoming sixty-five, but the whole business of applying and what do you do and all of that. It just seemed an impossible thing for him to contemplate" (Ruth Miller interview, October 11, 1988).

112. *AACR*, pp. 10–11.

113. *LMR*, p. 41. Emphasis in the original.

114. A copy of Rothko's contract, dated June 10, 1963, can be found in BRP, AAA. Presumably because of the size of the sale, Rothko had given Lloyd a 40 percent discount. There were ten oils on canvas, two "large oil on paper," and three "small oil in paper." The paintings were divided into four lots, with Rothko to be paid $36,916.50 on January 2, for four consecutive years starting in 1965 (for a total of $147,666). The oil on canvas paintings included in the sale were *Red and Black* (1960; 69½" × 69"), *Mauve and Orange* (1961; 63" × 69"), *Brown Red Black* (1959; 72" × 45¼"), *Orange Brown* (1963; 69" × 90"), *Orange Red and Red* (1962; 80" × 93"), *Orange Red Yellow* (1956; 69" × 79½"), *Orange Red Yellow* (1961; 81" × 93"), *Blue Orange Red* (1961; 81" × 90"), *Green Red Blue* (1955; 77⅞" × 81⅝") and *Blue and Gray* (1962; 76" × 69"). The works on paper were not specified (cf. four memoranda, dated June 10, 1963, from Marlborough Galerie A.G. to Mark Rothko, in BRP, AAA).

115. Donald McKinney interview, May 19, 1988; *LMR*, p. 59; Shirey, "Frank Lloyd and the Marlborough":40.

116. "Janis abandoned abstract expressionism for Pop in the early 1960's," Motherwell said (interview with Paul Cummings, p. 105, AAA).

As late as 1960, Janis's own collection included works by de Kooning, Gorky, Kline, Pollock, and Still, but none by Baziotes, Gottlieb, Guston, Motherwell, Rothko. To an interviewer, Janis "conceded that the preponderance of Europeans in his private collection has led some people to conclude that his interest in Abstract Expressionism is chiefly a commercial one" ("Why Fight It?":98).

Janis did purchase Rothko's *Horizontals, White over Darks* (1961), in 1962, the year Rothko left the gallery (cf. *The Sidney and Harriet Janis Collection, A Gift* to the *Museum of Modern Art* [New York, 1968], p. 20). But Rothko would have perceived the European emphasis in Janis's collection, and his own absence from it, as revealing a disturbing lack of enthusiasm and commitment.

"I think most of the abstract expressionists felt that he really didn't have sufficient commitment," Robert Motherwell said. "He didn't buy any of our work, though, as you know, he had a great European collection. In a way he was like Bernard Reis, seemingly the friend and interested but not to the degree to buy" (interview with Paul Cummings, p. 107, AAA).

117. Shirey, "Frank Lloyd and the Marlborough":40.

118. But only apparently so, since after the suit over Rothko's estate, Frank Lloyd was convicted of tampering with evidence—i.e., for altering entries in Marlborough's stock book (*LMR*, p. 327).

The stock book was placed in evidence in "The Matter of Mark Rothko" at the time of Donald McKinney's testimony in November 1973. "But it soon became clear that, contrary to Lloyd's reputation as a stickler for detail when it came to money matters, the condition of the stock book was anything but meticulous." Many entries for Rothko works were missing; for many others, new slips, without price information, had been placed in the binder. When the book was produced again later in the trial, further changes appeared (*LMR*, p. 188). Either Marlborough kept sloppy books or had engaged in a sloppy cover-up.

Chapter Fifteen

1. In a March 19, 1962 letter to John Coolidge, director of the Fogg Museum at Harvard, Bernard Reis reports that Rothko has occupied his new studio and is working on the panels he will give to Harvard (MRF, FM). Rothko had left the 222 Bowery studio by January 1, 1962, the date on which Michael Goldberg moved into it (Michael Goldberg interview).

2. Nathan Pusey interview, February 24, 1986.

3. On Rothko's concern with the cycle of death and rebirth, see Chave, *Mark Rothko, Subjects in Abstraction,* esp. pp. 161–71; and Stephen Polcari, "Mark Rothko: 'In My Beginning Is My End'," *Abstract Expressionism and The Modern Experience* (New York, 1991), pp. 117–49.

4. John Coolidge to Eugene Kraetzer, Jr., November 28, 1962 (MRF, FM). Mr. Kraetzer was the recording secretary and assistant secretary to the Harvard Corporation. The deed of gift was signed January 16, 1963, but the basic arrangement with Rothko was spelled out in a memo written by Coolidge (December 12, 1961), after a conversation with Rothko (MRF, FM). For an account of the project and of the subsequent deterioration of Rothko's works, see *MRHM*.

5. Wilder Green, quoted in *MRHM*, p. 12.

6. Wilder Green interview, May 17, 1988.

7. John Coolidge to Nathan Pusey, October 3, 1962, MRF, FM.

8. Ibid., February 1, 1963, MRF, FM.

9. "MR:PAAM":16.

10. In the spring of 1956 Duncan Phillips visited the Janis Gallery and became interested both in purchasing and

showing Rothko's work (Duncan Phillips to Sidney Janis, May 8, 1956, MRF, PC). By late 1956, the Phillips Collection had already received four Rothko paintings to be exhibited in "Paintings by Mark Rothko, Bradley Tomlin and Kenzo Okada," at the museum from January 6 to February 26, 1957 (Duncan Phillips to Sidney Janis, October 25, 1956, and November 19, 1956, MRF, PC).

In February 1956, Phillips bought two of the Rothko works from the exhibition, *Mauve Intersection* (1948) and *Green and Maroon* (1953).

"We have to like our extra large pictures extra well because of our lack of space," Phillips wrote Janis in early 1958. "I often wish we had room for another Rothko. He wears so well and is definitely an artist after my own heart. For such a man I would make room if I found one with irresistible color" (Duncan Phillips to Sidney Janis, January 6, 1958, MRF, PC).

Two years later, from May 4 to 31, 1960, the Phillips gave Rothko a small one-man exhibition, showing the two works from its own collection, plus five on loan, of which Duncan Phillips bought two: *Green and Tangerine on Red*, 1956, and *Orange and Red on Red* (1957), MRF, PC.

In 1964 Phillips acquired *Ocher and Red on Red* (1954), which then became the fourth painting in the Rothko room.

The museum sold *Mauve Intersection* in 1971 through Parke-Bernet.

The annex that opened in 1960 is now the old annex, a new one having opened in September 1989. Previously the Rothko room, entered by a single small door, occupied a quiet corner on the first floor of the old annex. Now, a second door has been added, just across from the first, connecting two galleries exhibiting the permanent collection, so a lot of people pass through the room, right in front of one of the pictures. The room has lost its contemplative quiet.

11. John Coolidge to Nathan Pusey, December 13, 1961, MRF, FM.

12. John Coolidge to James R. Reynolds, February 13, 1962, MRF, FM.

13. The paintings could not be sold, loaned, moved or their sequence changed without the approval of Rothko or his representative. If the paintings were moved, they would be reinstalled under his supervision; and the triptych would always "be treated as a unit." If the paintings were moved and could not be located at an acceptable location at Harvard, they would be returned to the Mark Rothko Foundation. In an attempt, probably not too effectual, to make use of the room more egalitarian, the deed stipulated that interested persons could visit the room by contacting the appropriate university officials (MRF, FM).

14. Michael Goldberg interview.

15. One image was developed on pale-green construction paper. See Mary E. Schneider's excellent account of the relation between the studies and the paintings, in "Rothko's Studies for the Harvard Murals," *MRHM*, pp. 31–60. Two of the pen and ink drawings are reproduced in *WP* (plates 57 and 58); all three are now at the NGA. The studies—twenty-seven images on fifteen sheets on construction paper (twelve of which have images on both sides)—are reproduced with the Schneider essay; these studies are now at the Fogg Museum.

16. Schneider, "Rothko's Studies for

the Harvard Murals," p. 31. Four of the sketches consist of a colored square, three of these containing a smaller colored square inside; another study stacks horizontal rectangles in Rothko's classic format.

17. John Coolidge, memorandum after conversation with Rothko, December 12, 1961, MRF, FM.

18. My calculation assumes that he started work on the Seagram panels in September 1958, and decided to withdraw from the commission around April 1960. Rothko, of course, was traveling in Europe for about three months in the summer of 1959.

19. The Harvard panels were complete by Nathan Pusey's visit on October 24, 1962. After Rothko moved into the First Avenue studio around January 1, of that year, it would have taken some more time to build the partitions used to recreate the walls of the dining room before he actually began work on the project. A Bernard Reis letter to John Coolidge, March 19, 1962, reporting that Rothko was installed in his new studio and at work on the Harvard project, establishes that work had begun by that date (MRF, FM).

20. Rothko produced seven panels for the Harvard project; the two he did not hang are both now at the National Gallery: *Untitled (Harvard Mural)* (1961; 6006.60), and *Untitled (Harvard Mural)* (1961; 6007.60H). The first of these is 110½" × 92⅞", the second is 104¹³⁄₁₆" × 95¹¹⁄₁₆". All of the panels Rothko hung were slightly more than 105" high, so it's not clear where the first of the rejected panels was intended to hang, but it couldn't have been in the triptych, since it would have been 5" higher than the other two. The second of these two paintings is quite close in its measurements to *Panel Three*. The two paintings are listed as part of the gift from the Mark Rothko Foundation to NGA, in *Eliminating the Obstacles,* p. 52. A more accurate date for these two works would be 1962.

21. To protect the paintings from the chairs and from people, a dado was built just below them, and portable stanchions were built to be placed just in front of them. As Teresa Hensick and Paul M. Whitmore point out in "Rothko's Harvard Murals," "unfortunately both of these measures backfired: the stanchions were constantly moved about and the dado made an all too convenient shelf" (MRHM, p. 16).

22. Karyn Esielonis, "The History of Rothko's Harvard Murals," MRHM, p. 10.

23. Agnes Mongan to Elizabeth Jones, November 2, 1970, MRF, FM.

24. John Coolidge to Eugene Kraetzer, October 26, 1967, MRF, FM.

25. Elizabeth Jones to Agnes Mongan, November 3, 1970, MRF, FM.

26. Unsigned memo, probably by Agnes Mongan, November 17, 1970, MRF, FM; Agnes Mongan to Bernice Jones, November 18, 1970, MRF, FM; Agnes Mongan to Wassily Leontief, November 23, 1970, MRF, FM.

27. Agnes Mongan to Charles Coulson, March 29, 1971 and April 2, 1971, MRF, FM; *LMR,* p. 136.

28. John Coolidge to Eugene Kraetzer, October 26, 1967, MRF, FM; Elizabeth Jones to Agnes Mongan, November 3, 1970, MRF, FM; Elizabeth Jones, Rustin Levenson, David Rinne, memorandum ("Rothko Murals"), March 18, 1971, MRF, FM.

29. Hensick and Whitmore, "Rothko's Harvard Murals," pp. 15–30.

30. The white rectangles and their connecting bars in *Panel Five*, for instance, have faded.

31. Esielonis, "The History of Rothko's Harvard Murals," p. 11.

32. Ibid., pp. 10–11.

33. Hensick and Whitmore, "Rothko's Harvard Murals," p. 29.

34. Ada Bortoluzzi to Seymour Slive, May 3, 1977, MRF, FM; and Ada Bortoluzzi to Sydney Freedberg, April 25, 1979, MRF, FM.

35. Greta Anderson to Suzannah Doeringer, Sally Sachhauser, and Diane Headley, April 24, 1979, MRF, FM.

Chapter Sixteen

1. From April 9 to June 2, 1963, Rothko did exhibit five of the Harvard panels at the Guggenheim Museum. Max Kozloff writes that Rothko "refused to show in this country any of the work he had done since his 1961 retrospective at the Museum of Modern Art, for fear it would be hostilely received. No one could persuade him otherwise, though many tried" ("Mark Rothko [1903–1970]":88).

2. Katharine Kuh interview.

3. MRF, NGA.

4. My account of the de Menils is based on Anne Gruner Schlumberger, *The Schlumberger Adventure* (New York, 1982); Ann Holmes, "Dominique de Menil: From Jeune Fille to 'Renaissance Woman'," *Art News* 82, 1 (January 1983):80–85; Michael Ennis, "Mrs. de Menil's Eye," *Texas Monthly* 12, 7 (July 1984):116–21, 172–74; Eleanor Freed, "Dominique de Menil: Rare Vision in the Arts," *Texas Humanist* (September–October 1984):42–46; Grace Glueck, "The de Menil Family: The Medici of Modern Art," *New York Times Magazine*, May 18, 1986, pp. 28–113; Walter Hopps, Introduction, *The Menil Collection* (New York, 1987), pp. 9–13; and RC, especially pp. 31–35.

5. Schlumberger, *The Schlumberger Adventure*, p. 3. The author, Anne Gruner Schlumberger, is Dominique de Menil's sister, her book an "inside narrative" of the evolution of the family business into a vast multinational corporation.

6. Glueck, "The de Menil Family," p. 38.

7. *Who's Who in America*, vol. 46 (Wilmette, Illinois, 1990), p. 801.

8. *Who's Who in America*, vol. 35 (Chicago, 1969), p. 568; RC, p. 31. Mr. de Menil worked for the Banque National pour le commerce et l'industrie from 1932 to 1938; he changed his name from Jean to John when he was naturalized as an American citizen in 1962.

9. Glueck, "The de Menil Family," p. 42.

10. Ibid.

11. Quoted in Freed, "Dominique de Menil: Rare Vision in the Arts":46.

12. Glueck, "The de Menil Family," p. 66.

13. Ibid.

14. Ibid., pp. 66, 46.

15. The comparison has been made by Grace Glueck, in "The de Menil Family," and by Anna Chave, in a paper, "Rothko's Doubt," read at the Rothko Symposium, Yale Institute of Sacred Mu-

sic, Worship and the Arts, December 1, 1989.

16. "John de Menil," in "Four Tributes," *Art in America* 61, 6 (November–December 1973):42. According to Sidney Janis's records, the de Menils purchased *Painting, Number 10, 1957*, from Rothko himself on October 9, 1957 (MRF, NGA).

17. Freed, "Dominique de Menil: Rare Vision in the Arts":44. Rothko never owned any African sculpture, though he did have a sculpture by Herbert Ferber which he kept in the hallway between his studio and Arthur Lidov's.

18. Rothko's contract with St. Thomas University (January 1965), drawn up by Bernard Reis, stipulated that Rothko would be paid $250,000, plus an estimated $25,000 in expenses (studio rent, cost of building mock walls in the studio, travel expenses to Houston for installation, etc.). Rothko would be paid $1,000 a month for thirty-six months beginning January 1, 1965, and he would be paid about $35,000 a year for six years beginning January 1, 1968.

In return Rothko would "undertake to make a sufficient number of paintings to adequately illumine the interior of the new chapel at the University of St. Thomas under the supervision of Mr. Philip Johnson," Rothko then estimating that since the building would be "an octagonal shape with an apse," he would likely produce ten paintings— "1 to each of the sides, and 3 for the apse." He also agreed that "the sketches and trial paintings" made for the project would become the property of the University of St. Thomas (BRP, AAA).

19. Philip Johnson, "University of St. Thomas," *Architectural Record* 126, 3 (September 1959):180; and Philip Johnson, quoted in *RC*, p. 78.

20. On one of Philip Johnson's early architectural drawings, Rothko sketched in his paintings on a side wall, a priest standing behind an altar, and a space for the congregation. So Rothko was well aware of the uses to which the Catholic chapel would be put (see *RC*, fig. 28, and Susan Barnes's discussion of the drawing, pp. 51–52).

21. A January 2, 1969 letter from Rothko to the Institute of Religion formalizes the transfer of the contract for the chapel paintings from St. Thomas to the institute, which agreed to continue the annual $35,000 payments due Rothko until January of 1974. An accompanying document establishes that the institute's debt will be guaranteed by Mr. and Mrs. de Menil (BRP, AAA).

22. Mark Rothko, interview with Ethel Schwabacher, May 30, 1954, ESP, AAA; Compton, Introduction, p. 14; "MR:PAAM":20.

23. Phyllis Lambert interview; Budd Hopkins interview. "You have to make a pilgrimage to see his icons . . . it was very important to him that you make an effort to see them, that they not be just accessible. These were religious experiences that you had to bring yourself to" (Jonathan Ahearn interview, November 3, 1986).

24. A letter, March 10, 1971, from Dominique de Menil to Bernard Reis, discussing the problems of lighting the paintings (which had been installed just a few weeks before) indicates that Rothko had in mind placing a "diaper" under the skylight similar to the parachute he used in his studio (BRP, AAA).

25. Interview with Ralph Pomeroy, pp. 8–9, AAA.

26. Ulfert Wilke, "Diary," October 23, 1964, UWP, AAA.

27. See the version of the contract dated January 5, 1965 in BRP, AAA: "I have been working with Mr. Johnson during the past four or five months and he has approved the amount of space to be covered in the Chapel." Rothko may have received two checks in connection with the project as early as January 1964 (Dominique de Menil to Mark Rothko, January 15, 1964, BRP, AAA), though it may be that, since it was January, Mrs. de Menil accidentally wrote 1964 instead of 1965.

28. The distance between the two side walls of the chapel is 50′ 2½″; the rectilinear apse is pushed 6′ back from the main floor; and the distance from the rear wall to the front of the apse is 50′ 1½″. The north (front) wall is 29′ wide; the south (rear) wall is 20′ 8½″ wide, as are the two side walls; the four angled walls are 15′ wide. My figures come from the Barnstone and Aubry plan, reproduced in *RC*, p. 85.

29. By the time I visited the building in the summer of 1991, the space was occupied by the Urasenk Chanoyu Center, an organization devoted to perpetuating a traditional Japanese tea ceremony. Inside Rothko's former studio, they have built a series of low Japanese buildings and small gardens, so the space is now impossible to measure. My estimate of the floor size is taken from the March 15, 1970, lease ("Petitioners' Exhibit 176," "The Matter of Rothko"), as are my measurements for the two front areas; my estimate of the height was made during my visit to the Center.

30. My description of the studio is based mainly on my interview with Arthur Lidov, May 15, 1988, who drew a diagram of 157 East 69th Street for me; I've also taken some details from Lee Seldes's description, *LMR*, pp. 1–2. According to Mr. Lidov, the two sofas, the bed, and the bath were only installed after Rothko began living there in January 1969.

31. According to Rothko's 1965 U.S. tax return, his income that year was $68,828.79 ("Resp. Ferber," unnumbered, "The Matter of Rothko").

32. Hans Namuth photographs (see fig. 45 for one of them), taken as Scharf and Rothko were building the mock-up, show that there were windows across the rear (north) wall of the studio. According to Arthur Lidov, the mock walls were placed so that they blocked any light from these windows from entering the studio; this left the skylight as the only source of natural light for viewing paintings. Lidov's memory is confirmed by the Alexander Lieberman photograph of the studio that is reproduced on p. 54 of *RC*.

It is important to realize that Rothko fabricated only three walls, since many writers state that he built an exact replica of the chapel in his studio; but the studio was too small for that.

33. Pierre Scheider, *Matisse* (New York, 1984), p. 442.

34. "The Rothko Chapel," *Art Journal* 30, 3 (Spring 1971):249.

35. *RC*, p. 55.

36. It is very likely, as Susan Barnes suggests (*RC*, p. 56), that two peculiarly-shaped paintings now in the Menil Collection were produced during this early, experimental phase. Both are just

about 21" high and 180" long. They were given numbers 6027.59S (21" × 178⅝") and 6028.59S (21⅛" × 181⅞") by Rothko during his 1968–69 inventory. His numbering suggests he connected them with the 1959 Seagram project, but his numbering is often unreliable, and their palette—black forms on red, and black forms on maroon—resembles that of the chapel project. "Each painting has three loosely-brushed forms: two long rectangles flanking a central form with one side hollowed out in a rounded niche" (RC, p. 56). In 6027.59S, the form is hollowed at the bottom, whereas in 6028.59S the form is rounded at the top—as if the two paintings composed a top and bottom. My guess is that Rothko contemplated placing these two works above and below the apse triptych, which is just a bit wider (189") than these two paintings.

37. The de Menil Collection received seven of these sketches—the only surviving ones, so far as I know—from the Mark Rothko Foundation; five of the sketches are reproduced in RC, pp. 59, 60, 63.

38. The wooden architectural model—from an early design, since the chapel's floor is still recessed by three steps, a feature later discarded—is now at the Menil collection, as are two of the small paintings Rothko fashioned for it. Johnson's model is 5⅜" × 16½" × 16½"; a photograph of it appears on p. 58 of RC.

The amount of paste on the walls of the model suggests that many possibilities were tested. Jonathan Ahearn, Rothko's assistant in the fall of 1968, recalled that when he came to the studio one day, he discovered "a full set" of these small papers which Rothko had put in the trash. Ahearn took the papers out of the trash, inserted them in a book he had with him, brought them home with him, but felt so guilty that he brought them back to the studio and threw them out. So there were many more of these panels than the two that have survived at the Menil Collection.

Johnson later provided Rothko with a larger scale model (12¾" × 37¼" × 40½") which had a circular opening at the middle of the floor, so that Rothko could insert his head and look from inside the model. A photograph of this model can be found on p. 65 of RC.

39. Ulfert Wilke, "Diary," October 14, 1967 and May 6, 1967, UWP, AAA (emphasis in the original).

40. Oliver Steindecker told me that he'd worked for Rothko for about seventeen or eighteen months; that would place his hiring in the fall of 1968 (Oliver Steindecker interview, February 20, 1986). But he had earlier told his interviewers at the Mark Rothko Foundation (March 12, 1985, MRF, NGA) that he had started in February 1969, and this date fits better with Jonathan Ahearn's recollection that he left Rothko in the winter of 1968–69.

41. Marjorie Phillips, *Duncan Phillips and His Collection* (Boston, 1970), p. 288.

42. Ulfert Wilke, "Diary," October 14, 1967, UWP, AAA; Rothko made similar comments about the murals to a number of people, among them Dore Ashton: "In the fall after he had returned from an important sojourn in Europe [1967], he mused, 'You never know where your work will take you', adding that in the Houston cycle he was interested neither in symmetry or

asymmetry, but only in proportions and shapes" (*AR*, p. 179).

43. Bockris, *The Life and Death of Andy Warhol*, p. 147.

44. Interview with Ralph Pomeroy, p. 2, BRP, AAA.

45. Lee Seldes writes that Scharf's job as Rothko's assistant ended because of this incident (*LMR*, p. 65), but Mr. Scharf told me that he left the job when Rothko no longer wanted to have another painter in the studio.

46. Quoted in *LMR*, p. 92.

47. Edwards and Pomeroy, "Working with Rothko":116.

48. "The Rothko Chapel," *Art in America* 61 (January–February 1973):15.

49. Edwards and Pomeroy, "Working with Rothko":111.

50. As he had with the Seagram murals, Rothko interrupted his work on the chapel paintings to travel to Europe in the summer of 1966, staying two months, mostly (according to Kate Rothko) in Rome and London.

51. According to Susan Barnes, all the chapel paintings have the same ground, consisting of two coats. "The first layer consists of dry pigments, alizarin crimson and an ultramarine blue, mixed in rabbitskin glue," and the second "has the same pigments with the addition of bone-black dry pigment to make the color darker, but here the medium is synthetic polymer"(*RC*, pp. 58–59).

52. During 1964 Rothko had produced at least five paintings in which a single large *hard-edged* black rectangle has been placed on a darker black ground; the chapel paintings, while created for a specific place, appear to grow out of these earlier experiments.

53. These borders vary, both within and between the two side-wall triptychs, more than they at first seem to. For the east-wall triptych the top border for all three panels is 2", and the bottom 3"; the sides of the central panel are 6", with outside borders of the two side panels 4½" and the inside borders 5½". See below for my discussion of these "irregularities."

54. de Menil, "The Rothko Chapel":251.

55. And perhaps he did not do all of the interior forms. Ray Kelly recalled that Rothko painted the black areas in the first four or five canvases, then supervised Edwards and Kelly as they painted the rest (*RC*, p. 61).

56. A diagram of one side-wall triptych and the two adjacent angle-wall paintings, done by Dore Ashton during a November 1966 visit, shows the three triptych panels still evenly aligned (MRF, NGA).

Rothko's instructions, added to a Barnstone and Aubry drawing, indicate that the center panel for the west wall triptych is 10" higher than the side panels, while the center panel for the east-wall triptych is 8¾" higher. For a discussion of the ways in which these two works are neither as symmetrical nor as identical as they appear, see below, this chapter.

Mrs. de Menil recalled that Rothko told her that a friend (unnamed) had proposed the idea of raising the central panel (*RC*, p. 65). Whoever originated it, the idea derived from practical conditions (i.e., the pulley system) in the studio.

57. *RC*, p. 67.

58. Daniel Goldreyer interview, February 19, 1986.

59. All four of these paintings are now held by the Menil Collection.

60. The chapel opened on February 26, 1971, but as Mrs. de Menil's address that evening—copies are available at the chapel desk—makes clear, the dedication took place the following day.

61. More precisely, these canvases are each 18' high, the two side panels are 5' wide, and the central panel is 5'9" wide.

62. Rothko carefully considered these doorways, which he recreated on the mock-up walls in his studio; in fact, it was the dimensions of the doors in the two side walls that Rothko changed the day after his conference with Mrs. de Menil (RC, fig. 42, p. 68).

63. William Scharf stated that Rothko sought a "uniform" surface, but these traces of his gradual enlarging of the dark rectangles were apparent in the murals at least from the time they were hung. In "The Rothko Chapel," written not long after its opening, Mrs. de Menil observed that "a careful look at any of the black fields reveals successive stages. At first, the field occupied only the central part—an opening into the night. Step by step, the field was enlarged, leaving only a narrow margin of color. The night had invaded the wall" ("The Rothko Chapel":251).

64. On the west wall, the top borders are 2", the bottom border for the center panel is 3", the sides 2¾". On the east wall all three bottom borders are 3". All of my measurements are taken from the Barnstone-Aubry diagram, RC, p. 68.

65. On the west wall, the inside vertical borders for the side panels are 4½", the outside 3"; on the east wall, the inside vertical borders for the side panels are 5½", the outside 4½". The vertical borders for the west wall's center panel are 4½", for the east wall 6".

66. Ulfert Wilke, "Diary," October 14, 1967, UWP, AAA. What Rothko is quoted as saying about the differing shapes in the two triptychs is not quite right: both the vertical *and* horizontal borders of the east panel are wider than those of the west.

67. "Art," *Nation* 212, 11 (March 15, 1971):350. Dore Ashton wrote that "the downright Americanness of this great misunderstanding of simplicity is seen in the tasteless, low skylight with its cheap aluminum mullions, its naked I-beam supports and its exposed bolts. Ever so functional. But fundamentally disfunctional, for the searing Western light invades the entire chapel from its lowbrowed, shallow dome, and annuls the very essence of Rothko's work: its slow revelations in time" ("The Rothko Chapel in Houston," *Studio International* 181 [June 1971]:274).

68. In 1976, both Philip Johnson and Eugene Aubry were asked to help solve the problem of the skylight. A wooden replica of the chapel, one-half its size, was built on the lawn outside to serve as a kind of laboratory in seeking solutions (Ann Holmes, "The Rothko Chapel Six Years Later," *Art News* 75 [December 1976]:37).

69. The size and shape of the areas in shadow changes according to the amount of light admitted through the skylight. In the winter, after dark, rows of floodlights along the top of the baffle are sometimes turned on, creating their own lines of shadow along the bottoms

of the paintings, particularly the angle-wall and rear-wall paintings.

70. Dominique de Menil, Foreword, *The Menil Collection*, p. 8. On *Broken Obelisk*, see RC, pp. 90–99.

71. Dominique de Menil to Mark Rothko, January 15, 1964, BRP, AAA.

72. Rodman, *Conversations with Artists*, pp. 93–94; Edwards and Pomeroy, "Working with Rothko":121; de Menil, Foreword, p. 8.

73. Ibid., p. 7.

74. "Address by Mrs. John de Menil, Friday—February 26, 1971." In "The Rothko Chapel," Mrs. de Menil wrote: "The Chapel venture, which conjured his heart, his soul and his total energies, evokes the pursuit of mystics, entering into 'silent darkness'. It is beyond the support of words and images that God can be reached. Fulfillment rewards renunciation" ("The Rothko Chapel":251).

75. I was not able to make use of Mr. Nodleman's book which, as I was completing this one, had been announced by the University of Texas Press, but had not yet appeared. I am indebted, however, to his *Marden, Novros, Rothko: Painting in the Age of Actuality* (Seattle, 1978).

76. In a conversation about Ferber with Ulfert Wilke, Rothko praised Ferber's "desire to survive" (Ulfert Wilke, "Diary," August 7, 1963, UWP, AAA).

In an undated letter to Smith, apparently written around the time of Rothko's 1961 MOMA retrospective, Rothko declared that "I think I understand why you addressed it to Mark Rothko artist. It is the salute of one old man to another both of whom have managed to survive in this rat race on terms which are their own and also human, and I salute you in turn. That with it all we have families, kids and apples is indeed a miracle.

"Excuse me for being rhetorical, but I think your gift was a stroke of rhetoric of the highest form. There is too little of it, and I am grateful" (Mark Rothko to David Smith, n.d., DSP, AAA).

Chapter Seventeen

1. Ulfert Wilke to Mrs. John de Menil, April 7, 1970, UWP, AAA; the "Are you necking?" detail comes from Wilke's "Diary," April 22, 1968, UWP, AAA. The date of Rothko's illness comes from the the bill of Dr. Allen Meade, who treated Rothko in the Emergency Room, BRP, AAA.

2. Ulfert Wilke, "Diary," January 30, 1966, UWP, AAA.

3. LMR, pp. 70–71.

4. A folder of Rothko's hospital and medical bills in BRP, AAA, contains the diagnoses, "dissecting aortic aneurysm" and "gout," along with the prescribed treatment: Valium and allopurinol.

5. Dr. Allen Meade interview, February 17, 1986. So far as I can tell from the bills in BRP, AAA, Rothko was in New York Hospital from April 20, until May 3, 1968. He was certainly home by May 8, when Dr. Grokest made a house call.

6. Among others, Jacob Kainen recalled that Rothko was limited to works no more than 40″ high; see Kainen's "Self-destruction, the final, tragic act of a principled man driven into a corner," *The Washington Post, Potomac Magazine*, 127, April 11, 1971, p. 28, and his interview with Avis Berman, October 8, 1982, p. 20, AAA.

7. The psychological impact of the

aneurysm, the medications prescribed for him, heavy drinking, depression—any one or some combination of these could have caused the impotence.

8. Dr. Allen Meade interview.

9. Robert Motherwell to Herbert and Edith Ferber, July 24, 1968, HFP, AAA.

10. In October, 1968 Rothko weighed 167 pounds, compared with the "190 pounds heading toward 200" Dr. Grokest estimated for early 1961.

11. *LMR,* p. 71; Bernard and Rebecca Reis, interview with Ralph Pomeroy, pp. 1–2, BRP, AAA.

12. Quoted in Laurie Adams, *Art on Trial* (New York, 1976), p. 180.

13. Rothko, then still negotiating with Norman Reid for a gift of his paintings to the Tate Gallery left the museum its choice of five of the Seagram panels. For Rothko's gift to the Tate, see Chapter 18.

14. A copy of Rothko's will is "Petitioners' Exhibit 11" in "The Matter of Rothko." According to Lee Seldes, Rothko wrote at least one more will before his death: "Sometime during that last year of his life, Rothko reportedly had Reis execute another will. It was said to be witnessed by Rita Reinhardt, among others. Allegedly, when she later asked Reis about his will, he is said to have told her that he had destroyed it because it was unfair to the children. How it could have been more disadvantageous to the children than Rothko's previous will does not bear scrutiny" (*LMR,* p. 99). But if there were any later wills, they were destroyed or lost, and the will of September 13, 1968 was the one executed after Rothko's death.

15. See Jon Schueler's recollections of helping Rothko move in Chapter 14.

Ben Heller recalled his first visit to Rothko's studio, "and Mark brought out a bunch of paintings with his usual way of not treating them with maximal care, physical care, let's say." Donald McKinney said that Rothko "would treat his paintings not very well. He would just basically shove them. He'd have these big bins and he'd just pull them out, push them back in. You know, they meant a lot to him obviously, but at the same time he, I don't know, it was almost in a way that he hated them" (Donald McKinney interview, May 19, 1988).

16. In his testimony in "The Matter of Rothko" Dan Rice recalled that the inventory began in the latter part of November 1968. A letter from Morton Levine to the district director of the Internal Revenue Service, November 29, 1973 (in BRP, AAA), explains $5,000 paid from Mark Rothko to him in February 1969 as "payment in part for making a photographic inventory of the late Mr. Rothko's entire stock of paintings as of the fall of 1968–winter 1969. Some 800 paintings were involved. Each was measured, catalogued and photographed in 35 mm color slides over a period of several months beginning in the fall of 1968. I organized the system of cataloguing and did the photography." Both in his deposition and his examination in "The Matter of Rothko," Levine said that he had proposed the idea of the inventory to Rothko in Provincetown during the previous summer.

Rothko's letter of December 30, 1968 to Kenneth and Joy Rabin speaks of cataloguing and photographing "40 years of work."

17. *LMR,* p. 73.

18. Jonathan Ahearn interview.

19. Interview with Avis Berman, Part II, pp. 10–11, AAA.

Kate Rothko remembered: "It was a very difficult summer because he had just gotten out of the hospital and he was having difficulty getting started painting again and in addition he was supposed to be painting on a small scale; he wasn't supposed to be exerting himself too much. So I think it was a very frustrating summer for him. I don't think he'd been painting in almost four months. I think he had a lot of anxiety about his health."

20. Interview with Avis Berman, Part I, p. 26, AAA; Stanley Kunitz interview.

21. Kainen, "Self-destruction. . .":28. One night that summer, after a party for Stanley Kunitz, Katharine Kuh was driving home with the historian Richard Hofstadter, who related that Rothko "had confessed to him that night at the party that even the thought of pigment and brush was repulsive to him. He'd come to the point where he just hated painting. Mark told him that he continued to paint only because he was driven by habit and conscience. . . ."

22. Stanley Kunitz, interview with Avis Berman, Part II, p. 12, AAA; Jonathan Ahearn interview.

23. Since arriving at his signature format in the late 1940s, Rothko had mainly worked with oil on canvas. But he had used acrylic paints before. Bonnie Clearwater writes that "recent conservation analysis by the Mark Rothko Foundation's conservator, Dana Cranmer, has revealed that Rothko began to experiment with acrylic and Magna paint on his canvases as early as 1947. However, he usually combined these with oil paint, tempera, and rabbit-skin glue with powdered pigments" (*WP*, p. 61, note 54). *Untitled* (1949; plate 28 in *MR*), for example, mixes oil, acrylic, and powdered pigments on canvas. *MR,AR* reproduces two small acrylics on paper dated 1959 (plates 157 and 158).

During the 1950s and 1960s Rothko produced some work on paper, though until there is a catalogue raisonné, it won't be clear how much. The Marlborough sales records list eight works on paper sold prior to 1967, three undated, one dated 1959, two 1960, one 1962, one 1963 ("Legend to Appendix C, Proved Sales of Rothko Paintings," attached to "Post-Trial Memorandum of Marlborough Gallery, Inc. and Marlborough A.G." in "The Matter of Rothko"). *WP* reproduces four papers from 1949, two from the "early 1950s," and two dated "c. 1959" (plates 20, 27). *MR,AR* reproduces one small tempera on paper from 1953 (plate 135), two small acrylics on paper dated 1959 (plates 157 and 158) and one small oil on paper mounted on canvas from 1960 (plate 159). One oil on paper (owned by Bernard Reis) was exhibited in Rothko's MOMA retrospective. Three 1949 works are listed among the works on paper dated 1949–66 given to various institutions by the Mark Rothko Foundation (*Eliminating the Obstacles*, p. 47), and Rothko's estate holds two 1949, two 1952, seven 1959, and one 1960 works on paper. Again, Rothko may have done other works on paper which he sold privately or gave as gifts, but at this point it appears that between 1949 and 1966, Rothko did not do very many papers and did just a few works solely with acrylics.

24. *Eliminating the Obstacles*, pp. 47, 53–55, lists eight such works, all

mounted on Masonite, the largest of which is 30⅛″ × 22⅛″ × 1⅞″. Another acrylic on paper is listed (p. 48) as *Untitled* (1967), but its size (60⅛″ × 47¹¹⁄₁₆″) and its catalogue number (2104.69—the last two digits indicating the year of composition) suggest that the work is *Untitled* (1969). Three of these 1967 works—1255.67, 1267.67, and 1268.67—are reproduced in *WP* (plates 28–30).

Other works on paper from 1967 may have been included in Rothko's sale of sixty-one works on paper to Marlborough in February 1969. Unfortunately, the contract, though it does discriminate between "25 large papers" and "36 different papers," gives no list of specific works on paper included in the transaction.

Since Rothko began producing these works in 1967, it is possible that some of those dated 1968 were also done before the aneurysm.

25. Interview with the Mark Rothko Foundation, n.d., MRF, NGA.

26. According to David Anfam's catalogue, there are about ten.

27. Jonathan Ahearn interview; Oliver Steindecker, interview with the Mark Rothko Foundation, May 10, 1983 (untranscribed), MRF, NGA. Steindecker pointed out that before beginning a work Rothko was very concerned that the paper "was really stretched," and that he was also very concerned with the size of the edge, i.e., how much of the edge had been covered by the masking tape and would remain as a white border after the tape was removed.

A black and white photograph of one of Rothko's plywood easels appears in *MR,* p. 195, and a color photograph of the interior of the Mark Rothko Foundation's warehouse gives a partial view of the same easel in *Eliminating the Obstacles,* p. 26.

28. Interview with the Mark Rothko Foundation, MRF, NGA.

29. One of the sentences from Oskar Pfister's *Psycho-analysis in the Service of Education* that Rothko copied into "SB."

30. The Mark Rothko Foundation names seventy-six of these works on paper from the mid-1940s in its list of gifts to various institutions (*Eliminating the Obstacles,* pp. 44–56). Rothko used watercolor, gouache, tempera, ink, pencil, and chalk (in various combinations) to create these works.

31. Interview with the Mark Rothko Foundation, MRF, NGA.

32. Interview with Gerald Silk, n.d., pp. 3–4, AAA.

33. Because many of the works on paper from Rothko's last two years were sold to Marlborough in February 1969 (and have disappeared into private collections), judging the range, quality, and character of this work is not yet possible. Moreover, Rothko may have sold other of these works privately. Bernard Malamud describes his near purchase of one of these papers in his essay "The Aquamarine Sunrise," *MR,AR,* pp. 14–15. Rothko told Malamud, in the early winter of 1969, that "he'd had a prolific several months painting a flood of acrylics on paper. He said they had come to hundreds of paintings that summer and afterwards. He was in a period of wonderful productivity."

The first step in examining Rothko's late work would be a catalogue raisonné of these works on paper. Eighty-eight works on paper dated between 1967 and 1970, however, are listed among the gifts by the Mark Rothko Foundation to various institutions (*Eliminating the Obstacles*, pp. 44–56). Thirty-five late works on paper (three of them from Rothko's estate, the rest then still held by the Mark Rothko Foundation) were exhibited in Bonnie Clearwater's "Mark Rothko, Works on Paper." My sense of the late work on paper derives from this exhibit, supplemented by viewing some of the works at the NGA.

34. MR, p. 85. In his Pratt lecture, Rothko had similarly contended "that small pictures since the Renaissance are like novels; large pictures are like dramas in which one participates in a direct way" ("PL," MRA).

35. WP, p. 39.

36. *Night Studio, A Memoir of Philip Guston by His Daughter* (New York, 1988), pp. 69–70.

37. Interview with Gerald Silk, p. 3, AAA.

38. "Mark felt narrowed into a certain way of painting—one direction with a similar language of forms," said the painter Karl Schrag, who was also a 95th Street neighbor. During the 1960s Rothko told William Scharf he wished he could return to the kind of work he did in the 1940s (interview with the Mark Rothko Foundation, MRF, NGA).

39. Katharine Kuh, interview with Avis Berman, p. 15, AAA; Stanley Kunitz, interview with Avis Berman, Part I, p. 19, AAA.

40. Interview with Phyllis Tuchman, p. 2, AAA.

41. Phyllis Tuchman, "Chronology," in *Herbert Ferber, Sculpture, Painting, Drawing 1945–1980* (Houston, 1983), pp. 40–43.

42. Herbert Ferber interview. Ferber was married to Dr. Sonia Stirt, a psychoanalyst, from 1932 to 1943, to Ilse Falk from 1944 to 1967, to Edith Popiel from 1967 until his death (Tuchman, "Chronology," pp. 40–43).

43. Rebecca Reis, interview with William McNaught, May 22, 1980, AAA.

44. Ulfert Wilke, "Diary," July 18, 1965, and April 10, 1964, UWP, AAA.

Rothko's notion that Ilse was better known than her husband was incorrect. By the time Ferber married Ilse in 1944, he had—despite whatever pressures his dental practice placed on his time—accumulated an impressive record of exhibitions, in fact more impressive than Rothko's was in 1944; nor did these accomplishments diminish after he married Ilse (See Tuchman, "Chronology," pp. 40–43).

45. In his interview with me, Ferber said that he and Rothko had a "severe falling out temporarily." Two letters Rothko wrote to Ferber while Rothko was teaching at the University of California, Berkeley, in the summer of 1967, are quite friendly in tone and suggest that, by then, the falling out had ended, even if it had not been entirely forgotten. See Mark Rothko to Herbert Ferber, July 7, 1967, and Mark Rothko to Herbert and Edith Ferber, July 19, 1967, HFP, AAA.

46. Cf. the findings of Judge Millard L. Midonick (New York State Surrogate's Court) "In the Matter of the Estate of Mark Rothko," reprinted in *AACR*; see p. 117 and passim.

47. "ND," MRA.

48. Christopher Rothko interview.

49. Betty Schoenfeld interview; and Ruth Moran interview.

50. Ruth Moran interview.

51. David Todd interview, January 9, 1986; and Peter Selz interview.

52. *LMR*, p. 77; Georgio Cavallon interview, January 24, 1987; Anne-Marie Levine interview.

53. Dore Ashton, "Feb. 26, 1969," MRF, NGA.

54. Paul Gardner, "The Ordeal of Kate Rothko," *New York* 10, 6 (February 7, 1977):50.

55. Ibid.

56. Jane Lawrence interview.

57. Kate Rothko interview.

58. Jackie Rice interview; Anne-Marie Levine interview; David Todd interview.

59. *LMR*, p. 78.

60. Copies of the contract and the supplementary agreement can be found in BRP, AAA. In addition, the supplementary agreement allowed Rothko to draw from Marlborough, as an advance, up to $75,000 a year.

61. A letter of July 18, 1969, from Rothschild Bank AG (Zurich) to Rothko (BRP, AAA) confirmed the schedule of payments to Rothko:

January 3, 1970	$44,510
January 3, 1971	49,520
January 3, 1972	74,636
January 3, 1973	96,000
January 3, 1974	96,000
January 3, 1975	109,200
January 3, 1976	124,200
January 3, 1977	40,800
January 3, 1978	114,600
January 3, 1979	117,532
January 3, 1980	66,635
January 3, 1981	66,665
January 3, 1982	66,665
January 3, 1983	53,273

62. To make this estimate, I used the schedule of payments due to Rothko in my note 61, this chapter. The total accumulated by this schedule, by the way, is $1,120,866, not $1,050,000. Sticking to the schedule's total and allowing 6 percent annual interest on the unpaid balance, I calculated that the total interest due to Rothko at the end of the fourteen years was $439,023. Deducting that figure from the $1,120,866, I arrived at an actual selling price of $681,843.

Lee Seldes, without indicating how she arrived at it, estimates $615,000 to be the actual price paid by Marlborough. She says that Rothko received a $100,000 down payment, but neither the contract nor the schedule of payments mentions this figure (*LMR*, p. 78).

Arthur Lidov said that Rothko "confessed abashedly that he thought he had $700,000 in a Swiss bank account, but he was not sure. He wasn't sure what the amount was or where it was exactly, or so he affected." Rothko also mentioned Swiss bank accounts to Rita Reinhardt. According to Lee Seldes, Mell Rothko told one friend "there were two secret numbered accounts in Swiss banks. The first, she said, was in both their names, and the second was countersignable by Bernard Reis. Rothko had also mentioned Swiss accounts to Lidov and Daniel Goldreyer. To Goldreyer he specified that one was intended for Kate and the other for Topher" (*LMR*, p. 117). Secret bank accounts would have been in character for Rothko, but no evidence of them has ever been found.

63. See Ben Heller in his January 9, 1974 deposition for "The Matter of Rothko" ("Respondent's Exhibit 259"),

p. 6; Gustave Harrow also points out this alternative in *AACR,* pp. 8–9.

The supplementary agreement, which permitted Rothko to sell Marlborough as many as four paintings a year, did make it possible for him to take advantage of his rising prices (with only a 10 percent commission), but only after surrendering this possibility with eighty-seven of his works.

64. Kainen, "Self-destruction. . .":28.

65. Figures for the other years: 1962, $82,330; 1963, $53,062; 1964, $74,785; 1965, $88,812; 1966, $87,424; 1967, $119,990; 1968, $84,764. The 1963 income is based on the copy of Rothko's 1963 U.S. tax return in BRP, AAA; the 1968 income is based on the U.S. tax return marked "Resp. Ferber 16A" in "The Matter of Rothko." The other figures are taken from the financial statements prepared for Rothko by Bernard Reis in 1962, 1964, 1965, 1966, 1967 ("Resp. Ferber," Exhibits 2, 3, 4, 5, [6], in "The Matter of Rothko").

66. The principal source of this income was the Houston chapel, for which Rothko was still owed about $35,000 annually until 1974 (cf. the annual financial statement, 1967, prepared for the Rothkos by Bernard J. Reis and Co.—"Resp. Ferber [6]," "The Matter of Rothko"). Curiously, this statement lists only $9,000 a year (from 1968 to 1972) owed to Rothko by Marlborough, though Rothko's February 1969 contract arranged for much higher payments over a much longer period of time; see the schedule of payments in note 61, this chapter.

67. Cf. "Sales by Sidney Janis, Year Ended December 31, 1961" (Exhibit B, Schedule 2) in the annual financial statement, 1961, prepared for the Rothkos by Bernard J. Reis and Co. ("Resp. Ferber 1," "The Matter of Rothko").

68. All of these works are oils on canvas. The prices come from: "Professional Income, Year Ended December 31, 1962" (Exhibit B, Schedule 3—Purchases by Mary Woodward Lasker) in the annual financial statement, 1962, prepared for the Rothkos by Bernard J. Reis and Co. ("Resp. Ferber 2," "The Matter of Rothko"); and from "Legend to Appendix C," appended to "Post-Trial Memorandum of Marlborough Gallery, Inc. and Marlborough A.G." in "The Matter of Rothko." This appendix provides a list of "Proved Sales of Rothko Paintings," though information in Rothko's annual financial statements from Reis, from Rothko's tax returns, and from the list of Janis sales at the MRA, NGA reveals that this list is incomplete.

69. For a fuller account of Rothko's rising prices, see Gustave Harrow's "A Generation of Rothko's Rising Prices," "Petitioner's Post-Trial Reply Brief," pp. 335–48, in "The Matter of Rothko." Harrow writes that "from the start of this compilation in 1955 through the period immediately following Rothko's death, *December, 1970,*" there was "a continuous upward movement and then acceleration, of Rothko's prices" (p. 338), a rise Harrow dramatically illustrates with three graphs (one for the average price for all Rothko's works, another for oil paintings, and the third for works on paper).

70. Stanley Kunitz (among others) spoke of "numbers of cases in which while he was alive he helped persons and always anonymously," sometimes

giving a painting which the person could sell or giving them money (interview with Avis Berman, Part I, p. 21, AAA).

71. According to Kate Rothko: "He certainly didn't start to spend any more in the late 1960s. The most I could say, the second time [i.e., *her* second time, in 1967] we travelled to Europe, I'm not even sure I could say we travelled more luxuriously—the only thing I remember being shocked at is that we actually took the first class boat back. I was always told it was because we couldn't get a second class ticket. I wondered if that was true. And we also stayed in a very fancy hotel in London which I gather had been arranged by Bernard Reis. He seems to have arranged a fair amount of that trip so it may have influenced the way we travelled. I didn't really see any changes in the way we lived."

72. Cf. the annual financial statement, 1967, prepared for the Rothkos by Bernard J. Reis and Co. ("Resp. Ferber 6," "The Matter of Rothko"). That year Rothko's total income was $129,451.86. Reis subtracted $30,395.78 for professional expenses (including rent of Rothko's studio, commissions, restorations, assistants' pay, shipping and storage, fine arts insurance). That left $99,057.08 after professional expenses. The family spent $37,669, mostly on the 95th Street house mortgage, on their trip that summer to Europe, and in day-to-day living expenses. That left $61,387.71, minus $9,852.03 in taxes, for a remainder of $51,535.68.

In 1961, the excess of income over expenses was $31,913.88; in 1962, $12,350; (1963, no information); in 1964, the excess was $13,672.91; in 1965, $34,632.70; in 1966, $14,789.14. This information is, again, based on Bernard J. Reis and Co.'s annual financial statements ("Resp. Ferber," Exhibits 1, 2, 3, 4, 5, [6], in "The Matter of Rothko").

73. Some cash Rothko simply hid in envelopes around the studio. When Mell Rothko looked through the studio just after her husband's death, she found, "in the well behind the walls of the Houston chapel structure, in cubbyholes, and between the pages of books," a total of $1,800 (*LMR*, p. 113).

74. Cf. the annual financial statement, 1967, prepared for the Rothkos by Bernard J. Reis and Co. ("Resp. Ferber [6]" in "The Matter of Rothko").

75. At the time of his death, however, Rothko did have two $100,000 Treasury bills, plus one for $60,000 for Christopher and one for $30,000 for Kate. See "Respondents Reis and Stamos' Exhibit 76A" and their "Exhibit 94" (an accounting of Rothko's estate) in "The Matter of Rothko." While Rothko's estate would reside mainly in the value of pictures unsold at the time of his death, he did set up trust funds for his children: he would give them gifts of paintings, which were then sold, with money deposited (characteristically) in a savings account.

76. *LMR*, p. 42; Herbert Ferber, "The Rothko Case," *Partisan Review* 51, 1 (1984):105.

77. Dan Rice interview; conversation with Rita Reinhardt. Dan Rice spoke of "that insidious manner in which Reis interjected himself in the workings of all matters financial and this would drift into personal life."

78. Interview with William McNaught, September 8, 1980, AAA.

79. Deposition, January 9, 1974, p. 6, "The Matter of Rothko."

80. According to Bernard Reis's statement, "Relationship to the art world," Frank Lloyd met with Rothko in his studio on November 8, 1968 (BRP, AAA). The negotiations for the contract Rothko signed on February 21, 1969, would probably have extended over at least a few months, particularly given Rothko's caution in reaching such decisions, a caution that grew much stronger in the period after his aneurysm. So, it is *possible* that the entire time (or much of it) between the expiration of the first contract and the signing of the second may have been occupied with these negotiations. On the other hand, Jacob Kainen, who had known Rothko in the 1930s and saw him when both were in Provincetown in the summer of 1968, recalled a conversation that summer in which it was "quite clear" that Rothko "had no gallery commitment at that time. As a matter of fact, he mentioned the 1969 contract to me later, with considerable embarrassment, probably remembering his earlier defiance" (cf. the typescript of a letter to *Art News* [1973] in which Kainen is complaining that he has been misquoted about Rothko—BRP, AAA).

In the "Relation to the art world" document Reis also quotes from a February 10, 1969, letter from Lloyd to Rothko: "Pending our further negotiations, in case Mr. Baumgartner of Chicago or any other collector should come to you, please do not offer any paintings for sale.

"Mr. Baumgartner, a client of ours, came in last Saturday and was interested in a painting of yours. We told him we expect a number of important paintings of yours. Any negotiations with individuals can only ruin the price structure we expect to build for you" (BRP, AAA). On February 9, 1969, Rothko's first contract with Marlborough had expired and his second had yet to be signed, so it's not clear what basis Lloyd has for this request. Perhaps the second agreement had already been reached but not yet signed. If so, Lloyd's letter makes clear that with the second Marlborough contract, studio sales were ruled out (Donald McKinney recalled "a confrontation" in which "Lloyd tried to stop him from selling from his studio").

81. "He bent my ear a great deal about his dissatisfaction with the deal he had made with Marlborough," said Arthur Lidov. "He was very dissatisfied with his dealings with Marlborough."

82. In Bernard Reis's "Relationship to the art world" statement, he says of the June 1963 contract: "Rothko never turned over a single painting for sale in Europe." Reis then quotes from a February 9, 1968, letter from Lloyd: "I feel that Marlborough Gallery A.G. is entitled to enforce its agreement and, as this agreement has been assigned to the Marlborough-Gerson Gallery, we will have to have a serious talk with Rothko in the future. I do not want to create any difficulties but you will understand that something has to be done" (BRP, AAA). The passage from Lloyd's letter —I've quoted all that Reis quotes— does not make clear what part of the agreement Lloyd thinks that Rothko is not abiding by. But if Rothko never turned over paintings for Marlborough to sell in Europe, where did the paint-

ings in his 1964 Marlborough exhibit—many of them subsequently sold by Marlborough—come from?

83. Marlborough's small New London Gallery was located at the gallery's original space at 17–18 Old Bond Street.

A copy of the catalogue is "Exhibit 575" in "The Matter of Rothko." "Respondents' Exhibit 570" lists all the Marlborough one-man shows for Rothko, and the 1964 London exhibit is the only one before Rothko's death in 1970.

MR,AR, however, lists another Marlborough one-man exhibit at the New London Gallery (London) in the winter of 1965–66.

Of the works shown at the 1964 Marlborough show, five of the oil paintings on canvas and all of the works on paper had been sold by the time of Rothko's second Marlborough contract in 1969.

84. So Beyeler testified in "The Matter of Rothko" (quoted in LMR, p. 216).

Selling paintings out of his New York studio, Rothko in these years was doing better than Marlborough. According to an unnumbered document I found among "The Matter of Rothko" exhibits—"Appendix B—Sales of Rothko paintings prior to May 21, 1970"—which contains a fuller list of sales made by Rothko himself, he sold sixteen of his own works during the five years of the Marlborough contract, five of them to museums (Kansas City Museum, Dusseldorf Museum, Phillips Collection, St. Louis Museum, Museum of Fine Arts, Houston).

This appendix does not make clear which of these works were oils on canvas, which were works on paper; but the prices listed suggest that probably all but one were oils on canvas.

85. Rothko mentioned his suspicions to the Los Angeles collector Marcia Weisman; see her interview in *The First Show, Painting and Sculpture from Eight Collections, 1940–1980*, ed. Julia Brown and Bridget Johnson (Los Angeles, 1983), p. 130.

86. Cf. "Legend to Appendix C," in "The Matter of Rothko"—a document prepared by Marlborough itself.

This document also lists eight other sales of Rothko paintings made by Marlborough between 1963 and 1968, one of them made by Marlborough London, the other seven by Marlborough New York. It is not clear to me how the gallery obtained these paintings, which are not on the list of purchases made from Rothko in 1963.

87. Donald McKinney interview.

88. LMR, p. 67; Donald McKinney interview. Mr. McKinney pointed out that there might be various reasons for such a change—e.g., Lloyd might quote different prices to different clients. But these operations, common enough in galleries, were apparently going on without Rothko's knowledge.

Lee Seldes writes, "Several times during the last year of his life, Rothko stormed into Marlborough on Fifty-seventh Street and demanded to see their price lists. Somehow he had heard that their markup was much higher than they led him to believe. One Marlborough employee has reported that she was told to switch the prices while Rothko cooled his heels. His suspicions were justified, but it is not known whether they were confirmed" (LMR, p. 98).

89. Arnold Glimcher interview, January 29, 1986; *LMR*, p. 73.

90. *LMR*, p. 74.

On February 25, 1969, Glimcher wrote to Rothko, asking him to reconsider the Beyeler offer.

"As you probably know," Glimcher wrote, "Beyeler is the most respected dealer of twentieth century masterworks in the world. The respect he enjoys is based largely upon his knowledge, taste and astounding record of museum sales and influence. In the last fifteen years he has been involved in the placement of more works in museums than any other gallery or dealer. His integrity and reputation would most certainly have vast residual effects in the ultimate destination of your works.

"At this point in your career it is no longer difficult to sell paintings, however the judicious placement of works can only be offered by a rare gallery situation. Beyeler's interest in your work is long-standing and your financial requirements are no obstacle. Certainly, the careful and well-timed handling of your works in Europe should be a major consideration to you. . . .

"You have the added assurance that the dealer who has so large a commitment in your work has integrity, a sense of timing and adequate finances not to dissipate the value of these works through quick sale. He is also out of the class of merchant or 'department store' of fine art and represents only a few artists of your class, including Dubuffet, Toby and Picasso."

Emphasizing Beyeler's respectability, museum influence, integrity, judicious sense of timing of sales, Glimcher was clearly implying a pointed contrast between Beyeler and the unabashed merchant, Frank Lloyd. But Rothko had signed with Marlborough four days before Glimcher's letter (Arnold Glimcher to Mark Rothko, February 25, 1969, "Respondents' Exhibit 102," "The Matter of Rothko").

91. Reis, *False Security*, pp. 162–63.

92. Dore Ashton, "Feb. 26, 1969," MRA, NGA. I've added a few commas and capitals and corrected a few typos in Ashton's text.

Chapter Eighteen

1. Norman Reid, untitled memorandum, August 20, 1988, in MRF, TGA. On the subject of Rothko's view of Turner, Reid commented later in the memorandum: "As to Turner, I am sure Rothko felt a kinship with him and his gift was certainly influenced by Turner's presence at the Tate. At the opening of the show of late Turner paintings in New York, he jokingly said to me, pointing to one of the most abstract sky and sea watercolors, 'That chap Turner learned a lot from me!'" (The Tate was heir to Turner's estate, now shown in a separate building adjoining the main galleries.)

2. Mark Rothko to Norman Reid, October 16, 1965, MRF, TGA.

3. Ibid., December 8, 1965, MRF, TGA. Reid recalled Rothko's story of the offer to MOMA in an August 20, 1988, memorandum, MRF, TGA. The Rothko files at MOMA do not mention Rothko's offer, but it may have been made (if it was made) in conversation and then not recorded.

4. According to his 1963 federal tax return (BRP, AAA), Rothko deducted $35,000 (or one-fourth of the total $140,000 value of the five paintings) as

a contribution to Harvard. So the Harvard project gave him a $35,000 deduction for four years. Assuming the deduction began in 1962, it would have expired in 1966, and Rothko gave his first gift to the Tate, *Sketch for Mural, No. 6, 1958,* in 1967. A telegram from Bernard Reis to the Tate Gallery, December 18, 1967, advises Reid "ROTHKO DONATES LARGE PAINTING AS FIRST OF GIFTS. PLEASE CABLE AMERICAN FEDERATION TODAY SO THAT GIFT CAN BE ACCEPTED BEFORE THE END OF THE YEAR" (BRP, AAA). The Rothko paintings were actually given to the American Federation of Arts, which then gave them to the Tate, so he could receive the same tax deduction he would have received for a gift to an American museum. Reis wanted the gift accepted before the end of the year, so it could be declared on Rothko's 1967 tax return.

5. Mark Rothko to Norman Reid, August 24, 1966, MRA; Mark Rothko to Bernard and Rebecca Reis, n.d., BRP, AAA.

6. Norman Reid, memorandum, August 20, 1988, MRF, TGA. The room under discussion was Room 18, 30' square, the room in which Rothko's nine paintings were first installed in May 1970.

7. Norman Reid to Mark Rothko, August 22, 1966, MRA. This typed letter was sent to Rothko with a handwritten note on the back: "This note was written before the arrival of your letter (as you can see from the Date)[.] It was not sent because it was incomplete but I think you should see it now because it shows what I had . . . in mind." The handwritten addition is dated August 26 (1966), MRF, TGA.

About exhibiting a changing selection from Rothko's gift, Reid wrote "that there should be a Rothko room—where the pictures would be changed from time to time (*your* pictures, I mean) so there would be new arrangements, like music, playing a different tune. . . ."

8. Norman Reid to Mark Rothko, August 26 (1966), MRA.

9. Norman Reid to Mark Rothko, March 21, 1967, BRP, AAA; "Rothko Weighs Gift / Of 20 of His Works / To the Tate Gallery," *New York Times,* April 11, 1967, p. 50.

10. Memorandum, August 20, 1988, MRF, TGA. When asked by the *Times,* a few days later, to comment on the story, Rothko declared, "Premature!" "Though he acknowledges 'discussions between Norman Reid, the Tate's director, and myself,' he insists that 'nothing has been decided'." When asked whether he had ever made such offers to American museums, Rothko commented, "I've spoken with many museum people here, and the Tate seems to be the best place for my pictures. I'm interested in the paintings and naturally want to see them displayed to best advantage" (Grace Glueck, "Art Notes," *New York Times,* April 23, 1967, section 2, p. 32).

11. Rothko's letter, addressed to the trustees rather then Reid (perhaps because he was angry with Reid for talking to the press), has not survived. On April 21, 1967, Reid wrote to Rothko, "Our Trustees met yesterday and I read your recent letter to them. They were very distressed—as indeed I am—that the Press should have got hold of the fact that you were considering making a gift to Britain and were very sad to

think that it may have caused you worry and irritation.

"The newspaper reporter who spoke to me claimed that he had learned about our discussions in New York and, as he was clearly in possession of the salient facts, I thought the best course was to keep the story straight as he was determined to publish what he knew in any case. I took care to emphasize the fact that you had taken no decision and I hope the publicity which this received has not meant that you have been subjected to endless enquiries and proposals" (Norman Reid to Mark Rothko, April 21, 1967, MRA).

12. Board of Trustees, Tate Gallery, to Mark Rothko, April 14, 1967, MRA; Mark Rothko to Norman Reid, April 24, 1967, MRF, TGA; and Norman Reid to Mark Rothko, April 26, 1967, MRF, TGA.

13. Mark Rothko to Norman Reid, July 15, 1968, MRF, TGA. Reid had already heard about Rothko's illness and sent him a handwritten note hoping for Rothko's "complete recovery," and "I hope you may be able to give some thought to the room at the Tate which we so look forward to opening" (Norman Reid to Mark Rothko, May 24, [1968], MRF, TGA).

14. Mark Rothko to Norman Reid, September 12, 1968, MRF, TGA.

15. Norman Reid to Mark Rothko, October 12, 1968, MRF, TGA.

16. Mark Rothko to Norman Reid, March 10, 1969, MRF, TGA; and Norman Reid to Mark Rothko, March 24, 1969, MRF, TGA.

17. Norman Reid to Mark Rothko, June 17, 1969, MRF, TGA; and Mark Rothko to Norman Reid, [summer 1969], MRF, TGA.

18. Norman Reid, "Note on a Discussion With Mark Rothko in New York," August 1, 1969, MRF, TGA.

19. Reid's memorandum, August 20, 1988, states the role of the tax reform bill in bringing the negotiations to a conclusion (MRF, TGA).

On November 5, 1969, Reis had sent Rothko a memo, in which he estimated Rothko's income over the next five years ($178,000 per year), pointed out that the current tax law allowed Rothko a 30 percent contribution to a museum "and the amount which you give in 1969 if not used in that year can be carried forward for five years." But "this privilege will expire on December 31, 1969." Thus, Rothko could now make a gift of $267,900 (30 percent of the $893,000 income Reis projected for the next five years). If Rothko sold paintings for $267,900, he would keep only $53,580; but if he contributed $267,900 he would save $187,530 in income tax. "It is for this reason," Reis concluded, "that the gift which you are making to the Tate should be consummated as quickly as possible" (Bernard Reis to Mark Rothko, November 5, 1969, BRP, AAA).

20. Norman Reid, memorandum, August 20, 1988, MRF, TGA.

21. The cardboard model, $19^{5/8}'' \times 18'' \times 7^{1/2}''$, is in the TGA, as are the eight model works, tempera on colored construction paper.

When Rothko's Gallery 18 opened at the Tate in May 1970, all nine murals—from the 1967 and 1969 gifts—were hung in a room about 30' square. Two of the paintings were placed in a double hang, with T1167 above T1169, on one wall; Rothko had used a similar double hang in his MOMA exhibit (see the Tate's installation photograph in Reid, "The Mark Rothko Gift":29).

22. Quotations are from a memorandum by Norman Reid, "Mark Rothko Gift: New York," November 3, 1969, MRF, TGA.

23. Norman Reid, memorandum, August 20, 1988, MRF, TGA. Rothko's letter of agreement, November 7, 1969, is also in the MRF, TGA; it states that "a room has been created for me in the Tate Gallery next to and similar to the rooms now used for the exhibition of Picasso, Matisse & Giacometti works of art." Perhaps not all the paintings in the gift would be exhibited at one time, "but it is understood that there will be no other works of art of any kind except those created by me."

A letter (November 20, 1969) to Rothko from Sir Robert Sainsbury, chair, trustees of the Tate Gallery, states that because of extensive rebuilding, the museum could not promise that the paintings will remain in Gallery 18, but it could assure him that the pictures would never be sold (MRF, TGA).

In December 1969, Rothko also made a gift of three paintings—*Number 24, 1947/8, Untitled* (c. 1948), and *Number 22, 1950*—to the MOMA; the deed of gift, dated December 30, 1969 (just before the new tax law went into effect), culminated discussions over the previous nine months.

In early March, while William Rubin had been selecting Rothko works for the Modern's "The New American Painting and Sculpture: The First Generation" (June 18–October 5, 1969), he had first raised the subject of a gift to "round out" Rothko's representation at the museum, which had already been promised two paintings owned by Mell Rothko, *Slow Swirl at the Edge of the Sea* (1944), and *Magenta, Black, Green on Orange* (1949). Rothko "raised the question of a commitment on the part of the Museum of a 'room' of Rothkos which would be guaranteed to him in perpetuity." Rubin believed that no museum could make this kind of commitment. He and the art historian Robert Goldwater tried to flatter Rothko out of his desire: "Bob and I tried to explain to Mark that the real guarantor of the works remaining visible in the future is not any document which an institution would sign but the great quality of the works themselves. Museums do not put their Picassos and Matisses in the cellar, and they won't put their Rothkos there" (William Rubin to Bernard Reis, March 13, 1969, MRF, MOMA).

Rothko relented about the room, but he also wanted to stipulate that the paintings not travel, be loaned, sold, or exchanged. Should the museum decide that it was no longer "interested in retaining any one of them in its collection, that picture or pictures will be returned to the Mark Rothko Foundation," and lack of interest was defined as not exhibiting the work for two years, the one exception being during a major building program (Walter Bareiss to Mark Rothko, June 16, 1969, and William Rubin, memorandum to Nick Koch, April 7, 1969, both in MRF, MOMA). In the end, Rothko ceded "all right to possession, dominion and control" of the three paintings to the museum (MRF, MOMA).

Apparently out of gratitude for his one-man exhibit, Rothko had given *Number 19, 1958*, to the museum in December 1961; he had stipulated that the gift be anonymous, that "the picture not be lent or shipped for exhibitions," and that "the picture shall not be offered for sale, or given away by the Museum" (Mark Rothko to Alfred Barr, December 14, 1961, MRF, MOMA). The museum agreed, except for the stipulation against giving the painting away. In his response, Barr said the museum could not bind future trustees absolutely and suggested that Rothko name his choice of two institutions to which the museum should give the painting if it were no longer wanted (Alfred Barr to Mark Rothko, December 22, 1961, MRF, MOMA). Rothko later named (1) the Mark Rothko Foundation and (2) the Phillips Collection (Mark Rothko to Betty Jones, December 27, 1962, MRF, MOMA).

Near the end of his life, Rothko also raised the possibility of giving the Phillips Collection "first choice of a group" of his works. Here, again, Rothko wanted a *permanent* place for his paintings, "with the promise that they would never be moved even temporarily to another gallery." But as Marjorie Phillips wrote to Rothko, the Phillips's policy was to keep its "units" of artists always hanging, "but to be able to move them now and then if some contingency should arise such as a large loan exhibition" (Marjorie Phillips to Mark Rothko, December 1, 1968, MRF, PC). So nothing came of Rothko's offer.

Retrospective exhibits, gathering together work done over a given period of time, are the artist's equivalent of the poet collecting poems into a book—except that the exhibition is a (frustratingly) transient event. Partly for this reason, Rothko sought permanent homes for his paintings.

Chapter Nineteen

1. Sylvia Plath, "Lady Lazarus," *Ariel* (New York, 1965), p. 7.

2. My account here relies on *LMR*, pp. 1–2, and on my interview with Arthur Lidov, who corrected a few of Lee Seldes's details.

3. *LMR*, p. 106.

4. Paul Wilkes, *New York Times Magazine*, April 19, 1970, pp. 32–84.

5. Ibid., pp. 33–70.

6. *LMR*, p. 314.

7. Paul Wilkes interview (telephone), August 10, 1989.

8. Quoted in *LMR*, p. 109.

9. Ibid., pp. 105–6; Arthur Lidov interview.

10. *LMR*, pp. 106–7; Dr. Allen Meade interview.

11. *LMR*, pp. 317–18.

12. Ibid., p. 314.

13. A toxicological lab, however, later found no evidence of barbiturates. "According to the report by Dr. Charles Ungerberger, the chief of the laboratory at the time, there was no alcohol in Rothko's blood, no 'basic drugs' in the stomach, no traces of barbiturates in the brain tissue, and no acidic drugs in his stomach. His findings completely contradicted the autopsy and what was known of Rothko's habits and final hours" (*LMR*, p. 313).

14. Ibid., pp. 108–9.

15. Lee Seldes devotes a chapter of *LMR* to exploring the possibility that Rothko was murdered. "*Almost* certainly it was a suicide," she begins, but then adds, "but *almost* leaves the question finally unresolved. Investigation of the circumstances so long after the event have

proven inconclusive" (*LMR*, p. 308). By the end of the chapter, however, she asserts a somewhat different view. There are two possibilities: either Rothko was murdered or "if Rothko was not murdered, he was pressured into taking his own life. The circumstances—including the medication, the forced selection and sale of his paintings to Marlborough, the hypocrisy of his friends—ensnared him like a noose pulled taut by others. It was at best a kind of remote-control killing" (*LMR*, p. 317). Either way, Rothko was murdered.

Seldes cites what she regards as several suspicious features of Rothko's death:

1. He was found without his glasses on, but he was so myopic that it seems unlikely he could have cut his arms without them (*LMR*, p. 314).

2. He left no note—uncharacteristic in view of his usual need to "have the last word" (*LMR*, p. 110).

3. Since the sight of his own blood "upset him abnormally," it seems unlikely he would have chosen to bleed to death (*LMR*, p. 105).

4. "Given Rothko's slovenly personal habits, how to account for the neatly folded suit placed over a chair?" (*LMR*, p. 309).

5. No medicine vials were found in a studio that, in Rothko's last days, had contained a pharmacopeia of medications for gout, hypertension, depression, and so on (*LMR*, p. 312).

6. The autopsy concluded, citing the contents of Rothko's stomach, that Rothko had died of "acute barbiturate poisoning" as well as loss of blood from his wounds (*LMR*, p. 108); but a subsequent laboratory test found no evidence of barbiturates (*LMR*, p. 313). How explain this discrepancy?

Some of these features strike me as somewhat anomalous—i.e., Rothko's neatly folded trousers (not suit), assuming the pants *were* as neatly folded as Lappin perceived, and Wilkes recorded, them to be. The medicine vials may simply have been thrown away. If Rothko found the sight of his own blood upsetting, he may have removed his glasses either just before or just after cutting his arms, in order to avoid seeing the blood. Besides, a deliberate blood letting might be experienced quite differently from, say, an accidental cut with a razor blade.

Later on, at the very end of this chapter, I'll imply a rationale for the absence of a note. In many ways, the deliberate and silent acting out of a violent, self-destructive act seems to me entirely plausible for Rothko. The discrepancy between the autopsy and the laboratory reports is explained by Seldes, who was told by a Dr. Bastos in the medical examiner's office that "the lab test given for barbiturates was entirely different from the kind given to uncover chloral hydrate and Sinequan," the most likely drugs for Rothko to have used (*LMR*, p. 317).

16. Dr. Allen Meade interview.

17. Brian O'Doherty, "Rothko's Endgame," in *Mark Rothko: The Dark Paintings 1969–70* (New York, 1985), p. 5. Mr. O'Doherty misremembers the studio as a "firehouse," for which I've substituted "carriage house."

18. Robert Motherwell, "On Rothko" (1970), RMA. I've also quoted my transcription of a few additional remarks made by Mr. Motherwell as he was reading this essay at the Rothko Symposium

organized by the Yale Institute of Sacred Music, Worship and the Arts on December 3, 1989.

19. Anne-Marie Levine interview; Bernard Reis, deposition, pp. 715–16, for "The Matter of Rothko"; Bernard Reis, interview with Ralph Pomeroy, p. 10, BRP, AAA.

20. Oliver Steindecker, interview with the Mark Rothko Foundation (untranscribed), May 10, 1983, MRF, NGA.

21. He also produced at least two works with just ink on paper during 1969; see the untitled works catalogued as no. 1 and no. 3 among the Mark Rothko Foundation's gifts to the NGA in *Eliminating the Obstacles*, p. 44.

22. In 1968 Rothko produced one work 71¾" × 60" (1214.68), one 60¹⁵⁄₁₆" × 42⁵⁄₁₆" (1203.68), another 60" × 42⁹⁄₁₆" (1209.68) and another 60⁵⁄₁₆" × 42¼" (1211.68)—all listed as gifts to the NGA in *Eliminating the Obstacles*, pp. 46–47.

The progression in the size of Rothko's papers during 1969—I'm assuming the catalogue numbers reflect the actual sequence of composition, since these works were done during or just after his inventory—is not completely consistent but it is a strong trend; see the 1969 works on paper listed in *Eliminating the Obstacles*, pp. 46–47.

Eliminating the Obstacles (pp. 44–56) lists forty-five 1969 works on paper distributed to various museums by the Mark Rothko Foundation. There are about thirty in his estate. Others may have been included in his February 1969 sale to Marlborough. Rothko's last year was quite productive.

23. In her essay "Mark Rothko: The Brown and Grey Paintings," Eliza E. Rathbone writes that there are "approximately thirteen" of them (Carmean and Rathbone, *American Art at Mid-Century*, p. 245). The number thirteen will have to stand until we have a catalogue raisonné of Rothko's works on paper.

David Anfam provided me with eighteen as the number of "Black on Grey" works, though his catalogue is not yet complete and he may discover more.

William Scharf (among others) recalled that Rothko started the "Brown on Grey" paintings in the summer of 1968 (interview with the Mark Rothko Foundation, MRF, NGA). But all of those I have seen are dated 1969, and since they were done during or just after Rothko's inventory, I assume these dates are correct, though Rothko may have done some earlier that he discarded.

24. Kohlmeyer, "About Rothko":59.

25. Quoted in Kainen, "Self-destruction . . .":28.

26. Daniel Goldreyer interview; Jonathan Ahearn interview; Oliver Steindecker interview; see also Bonnie Clearwater's account of this process in *WP*, p. 43. Rothko had these works mounted in order to protect them. "Concerned over their fragility, he began to have the papers mounted on canvas [*sic*] and was glad when he was told that they would last longer and their colors change less than if directly painted on canvas" (Robert Goldwater, "Rothko's Black Paintings," *Art in America* 59, 2 [March–April 1971]:58).

The Pace Gallery exhibition catalogue for *Mark Rothko, Paintings 1948–69* reproduces five 1969 works on paper which are mounted on canvas, though these may have been mounted after Rothko's death.

27. Donald McKinney, "Mark Rothko," in Werner Haftmann, *Mark Rothko* (New York, 1971), p. xvi.

28. Ray Parker interview, January 25, 1986; Goldwater, "Rothko's Black Paintings":62.

29. Untitled statement; reprinted in *MR*, p. 85.

30. *AR*, p. 188.

31. McKinney, "Mark Rothko," p. xiii.

32. Dan Rice was present when Donald McKinney and Frank Lloyd came to the studio to select works for the December 1969 sale. "Watch these slanty-headed people, they don't know which end is up," Rothko commented. "And indeed Rothko and Rice watched wryly as Lloyd and McKinney passed up the new blacks on greys for more colorful works" (*LMR*, p. 98).

33. Conversation with Rita Reinhardt, October 10, 1991. Rita Reinhardt did not want to be formally interviewed for this book, but she did informally talk with me, read the sections of the manuscript where she is discussed, then talked with me again. I'm grateful for her help.

34. Stanley Kunitz, interview with Avis Berman, Part I, p. 16, AAA; *AR*, p. 179. Naomi Vine's essay on Reinhardt, "Mandala and Cross," persuasively argues for Reinhardt's mysticism, drawing on his private journals, which adopt a much less polemical (and formalist) stance than his published writings. She also points out that Reinhardt's black paintings seem to elicit actual touches from viewers, so that Reinhardt spent "considerable time" during the 1960s restoring their vulnerable surfaces (*Art in America* 79, 11 [November 1991]:131–32). So Rothko was right about their mysticism and half-right about their untouchability.

On the differences between Rothko and Reinhardt, see Rathbone, "Mark Rothko: The Brown and Grey Paintings," pp. 260–61.

35. The frequency of Rothko's visits to Dr. Grokest is documented in Grokest's bills (BRP, AAA); the visit to Dr. Meade's office—August 1969—while Grokest was on vacation is described by Lee Seldes in *LMR*, p. 92; the rest of my information comes from my interviews with Drs. Grokest and Meade.

36. *LMR*, p. 99. Dr. Grokest related the liver and hernia diagnoses to me during my interview with him; the diagnosis of Dr. Miller comes from his bill (BRP, AAA).

37. William Styron, *Darkness Visible* (New York, 1990), p. 37.

38. *LMR*, p. 92; Dr. Albert Grokest interview.

39. Bruce and Dorothy Ruddick, interview with the Mark Rothko Foundation, n.d. (untranscribed), MRA, NGA. The interviewer is not identified on the tape.

40. *American Psychiatric Association, Biographical Dictionary* (Washington, D.C., 1983), p. 638; *LMR*, p. 75. Rebecca Reis mentioned the grant from the Lasker Foundation to Kline in her interview with William McNaught, May 15, 1980, AAA.

Dr. Victor Reuss, of the Langley-Porter Institute in San Francisco, told me that Kline's main contribution was in "early chemical trials with beta-inhibitors (anti-depressants) and early lithium work." Dr. Kline's book, *From*

Sad to Glad (New York, 1974), according to Dr. Reuss, was "an important book, introducing the layman to new advances in the field of psychopharmacology" (Dr. Victor Reuss interview [telephone], April 14, 1992).

Reis's position with the Albert and Mary Lasker Foundation is listed on a three-page biographical statement apparently prepared in connection with his testimony in "The Matter of Rothko," in BRP, AAA. According to Lee Seldes, "Bernard Reis had also been Dr. Kline's accountant and had negotiated the lease and improvements made in Kline's offices" (LMR, p. 75).

41. Kline, *From Sad To Glad*, p. 162. In a later chapter on "Suicide," Kline argues that in Western culture, depression often leads to suicide because Judeo-Christian ethics condition us to think that we—not biochemical tides—are responsible for our despair. "The depressive is often quite consciously guilty, and what he feels guilty about is being depressed" (p. 195). "I sometimes tell my depressed patients that they are suffering from one of nature's forces—a kind of storm within the brain. They will ride out the storm far more easily if they do not try to dredge up reasons as to why they brought such trouble on themselves" (p. 197).

42. "The treatment period varies widely, but typically a substantial start toward recovery is made in some four to eight weeks with periods of progressive improvement back toward normality in subsequent weeks.

"For a small percentage of depressive patients the recovery is only partial. They show definite improvement but continue to experience some distress. And finally there is a small intractable core of all cases in which medications do not provide significant relief" (Kline, *From Sad to Glad*, p. 11).

Later, Dr. Kline declares that therapy is "usually completed in a matter of months at a typical cost of around $500" (p. 112).

43. Ibid., p. 10. "Once the treatment is well established," Kline writes, "the typical patient visit requires about fifteen minutes. For a good many it's even quicker. They are in and out of my office in five to ten minutes, pausing just long enough to report that all is going well" (pp. 161–62).

44. Though often stating that he does not oppose a "talking cure," Kline can't resist sardonic characterizations of it, and he insists that drug treatment must come first. "Of course, one does see patients whose problems can't be worked out in a handful of fifteen-minute visits. There are people who have remained enmeshed in the same basic problems all their lives, and they may or may not be able to talk it out in a hundred hours or more. They are the severe neurotics, and they present an entirely different case. For them neurosis often becomes a way of life rather than an illness" (Kline, *From Sad to Glad*, p. 163). By accusing patients not susceptible to *his* methods of making their problems into "a way of life," Kline reintroduces the notions of personal responsibility and guilt that he elsewhere criticizes.

45. Ibid., p. 151.

46. Ibid., p. 9; Mildred Sola Neely, "Dr. Kline Writes About Depression for Putnam," *Publishers Weekly* 205, 18 (May 6, 1974):48; Kline, *From Sad to Glad*, p. 78.

47. Interview with William McNaught, September 8, 1980, AAA.

48. In my interview with him, Dr. Grokest dated Rothko's first visit to Dr. Kline as "December of '69. . . . It was a Monday night, December 9." This date, just two-and-a-half months before Rothko's death, seems rather late, and does not conform with the memory of Dr. Meade, who recalled changing Dr. Kline's prescriptions for Rothko in August 1969 (see LMR, p. 92). December 9, moreover, was on Monday in 1968, not 1969, and I am adopting the 1968 date as much more likely.

49. Rebecca Reis, interview with William McNaught, September 8, 1980, AAA.

50. Kline, From Sad to Glad, p. 145.

51. Rothko saw Dr. Lision on August 11, 1969 (cf. bill in BRP, AAA); see also LMR, p. 92.

52. LMR, p. 92; Dr. Alan Meade interview. According to Dr. Victor Reuss, Sinequan is "not absolutely contraindicated" for patients with heart disease; in fact, it is sometimes used in cardiac wards. "Rothko might have seemed very agitated, anxious to Kline, and Sinequan is a strong sedative. There might have been a better alternative, but Sinequan is not manifestly a bad choice."

53. Dr. Victor Reuss interview; LMR, p. 97.

54. Interview with Bernard Malamud, February 19, 1986; LMR, p. 76. In January 1965, the FBI, at the request of the White House, had done a security check on Rothko, apparently to "clear" him for the Johnson inaugural. The FBI reported that Rothko had signed, in December 1962, a sixtieth-birthday salute to David Siqueiros "from the intellectuals in the United States," published in a Mexico City newspaper and urging Siqueiros's release from prison (cf. enclosure, "MARK ROTHKO," in memorandum from the FBI to Lee C. White, White House, January 14, 1965).

Six months later President Johnson initiated an FBI check of all the artists who had signed a telegram to Johnson protesting the war in Vietnam, among them Rothko. This report again mentioned the Sequeiros letter and added that, on April 5, 1965, the Bureau "received information that an individual by the name of Mark Rothko [had] signed a 'Writers and Artists Protest' against the continuation of the present American policy in Vietnam" (cf. enclosure "MARK ROTHKO," FBI memorandum, June 4, 1965).

55. Rothko mentioned his relationship with Mrs. Reinhardt to Dr. Grokest in March 1969.

56. "I have seen him on at least two occasions pour a quantity of pills into his palm and pop them. When I asked what the hell he was doing, how many he was supposed to take, he said, 'the doctor says take two of them, but who's counting?'" (Arthur Lidov interview).

57. LMR, p. 92.

58. Anne-Marie Levine interview.

59. Robertson, "Art: Mark Rothko": 314.

60. LMR, p. 78.

61. Jane Lawrence interview.

62. According to the license for her marriage to Ad Reinhardt (City Clerk's Office, New York City), Rita Ziprkowski was born October 18, 1928 in Germany to Isaac Ziprkowski (born in Poland) and Lisa Leiserson (born in Russia).

Mrs. Reinhardt, however, said that 1928 may not be correct—she may be a few years younger; the records of her birth were lost at the beginning of World War II.

63. Conversation with Rita Reinhardt, September 21, 1992.

64. Quoted from postcard, Ad Reinhardt to Bernard Reis, March, 1967, BRP, AAA.

65. Anne-Marie Levine interview; Arthur Lidov interview.

66. Rebecca Reis interview; the date comes from Mrs. Reis's interview with William McNaught, September 8, 1980, AAA. Rita Reinhardt said that she was not urging Rothko to divorce.

67. Dr. Grokest pointed out that Rothko killed himself as Christopher was approaching his seventh birthday—the age of Rothko when his father left Dvinsk. "To me it was a repeat of his own abandonment when he was seven," Grokest said. Christopher, however, would not be seven until August of 1970, six months after Rothko's death. On the other hand, since there is no documentary evidence with which to date Jacob Rothkowitz's departure from Dvinsk, we only have family memory to rely on for Rothko's age at the time. It is possible that one element (among many) in Rothko's suicide may have involved imposing on his son what had happened to him at roughly the same age.

68. Rothko had received a Creative Arts Awards Medal from Brandeis University in 1965 (*New York Times*, March 29, 1965, p. 43).

On his induction into the National Institute of Arts and Letters, see the *New York Times*, May 29, 1968, p. 60.

A letter from Hortense Zera, Librarian for the institute, to Clair Zamoiski, August 18, 1977, confirms Rothko's election; an attached copy of the program establishes that he did not attend the ceremony, probably because he was still recovering from his aneurysm (MRF, GMA).

69. Quoted in *Salute to Mark Rothko*, pamphlet for an exhibit at the Yale University Art Gallery, May 6–June 20, 1971.

70. Copy in BRP, AAA.

71. Based on Ed Weinstein to Clair Zamoiski, February 24, 1978, MRF, GMA, and Mr. Weinstein's interview with Barbara Shikler, pp. 16–17, AAA.

72. "Motherwell Muses" (1969), RMA. This two-page journal entry records a Motherwell visit to Rothko's studio. The typescript I have—prepared for publication of a collection of Motherwell's writings—is just dated 1969, but Dore Ashton, who also refers to this journal entry, provides a date: April 21, 1969 (*AR*, pp. 189 and 202, n. 97).

73. A June 8, 1960, letter from Ben Heller to Rothko discusses the tax advantages of a foundation, though the letter suggests that Rothko has other considerations in mind for the foundation (MRA).

74. William Rubin interview, January 9, 1986; *LMR*, pp. 85, 87–88.

75. According to Rubin, Reis had told Rothko that Rubin wanted to be curator of the Rothko museum he was proposing—an absurd idea, Rubin pointed out to me, because he was then a curator at MOMA. Lee Seldes writes, "Later, Mell told Rubin that Bernard Reis had influenced Rothko against him. But the other directors agree that Rothko was

angry because Rubin had suggested he be paid a fee as a consultant to the foundation" (*LMR*, p. 88).

In his deposition for "The Matter of Rothko," Reis recalled Rubin's proposal for a Rothko museum in New York and that Rubin wanted to be paid for his work. According to Reis, Rothko objected: "I don't want to have anything to do with that son of a bitch" (p. 501).

76. *LMR*, p. 88. Copies of the certificate can be found in BRP, AAA, and as "Petitioners' Exhibit 133" in "The Matter of Rothko." According to the copy in BRP, the document was signed (by the seven directors—Rothko, Goldwater, Levine, Stamos, Wilder, Feldman, and Reis) on June 12, 1969 and filed with the State of New York on July 21, 1969.

77. When William Rubin heard from Robert Goldwater that the foundation's charter was to be amended, he wrote to Bernard Reis, "As you yourself observed, [Mark] harbored frequently changing, frequently contradictory feelings about everything and everybody, especially toward the end" (*LMR*, p. 134).

78. Quoted in *LMR*, p. 135; see also Stanley Kunitz, letter to the editor, *New York Times Book Review* (April 30, 1978):20.

79. *LMR*, p. 133. In the letter he wrote to Bernard Reis when he heard of the planned change in the foundation's purpose, William Rubin said: "If Mark, in the disturbed last year of his life, could have dismissed his abiding concern about his work, it can only be explained as a function of his pervasive depression and despair. . . . Even if Mark at one point did dismiss his concern for the future of his work, he did it as a sick man, not far from suicide. Since he also expressed views to the contrary, you are faced with an ethical problem: which of his views to make operative. Certainly, these original purposes are what Mark wanted throughout his life and indeed during at least part of his terminal sickness" (*LMR*, pp. 134–35).

Of course, the exchanges between Goldwater and Reis or between Rubin and Reis about Rothko's intentions simply confirm my argument that Reis's writing of Rothko's will and/or of the foundation's certificate of incorporation should have included some unambiguous statement of Rothko's intentions for the foundation.

80. See *AACR*, pp. 6–7; see also Gustave Harrow's letter to the editor (his reply to Stanley Kunitz's letter to the editor) in the *New York Times Book Review* (June 25, 1978):49, 56.

The other directors did not learn of the two sales—one for a hundred paintings, the second for the rest of the estate—arranged by the executors in May 1970 (three months after Rothko's death) until June 1971 (*LMR*, p. 145–47).

81. Stanley Kunitz, interview with Avis Berman, Part I, p. 19, AAA; Vita Deming interview.

82. Quoted in *AACR*, p. 7.

83. Quoted in *LMR*, pp. 214–15. Lee Seldes is apparently quoting from a written statement made by Rita Reinhardt.

84. Three of the paintings were sold outright by Rothko and paid for immediately—$63,000 ($84,000 minus a $21,000 or 25 percent commission); six of the paintings were sold by Rothko for $114,000 ($152,000 minus a $38,000 or 25 percent commission), the amount to be paid in ten $11,400 in-

stallments beginning May 1, 1970; three were sold by the Mark Rothko Foundation for $75,000 ($100,000 minus a $25,000 or 25 percent commission), the amount to be paid in four $18,750 installments beginning February 15, 1970; and six paintings sold by his children (or their trusts) for $144,000 ($192,000 minus $48,000 or 25 percent commission), the amount to be paid in ten $14,400 installments beginning May 1, 1970 (Frank Lloyd to Mark Rothko, December 8, 1969 [plus six pages of attachments], BRP, AAA).

85. *LMR,* p. 103; Rita Reinhardt, two interviews with Lee Seldes (telephone), n.d., LSF; conversations with Rita Reinhardt.

86. Arthur Lidov interview.

Afterword

1. Wollheim's comments are quoted from "The Work of Art as Object," in *On Art and the Mind* (Cambridge, Mass., 1974), pp. 128–29. Christie/Orton also implicate Clement Greenberg and Michael Fried in expressivist thinking, though I won't be dealing with this part of their argument since it does not involve Rothko.

2. "'Hanging Up Looking Glasses at Odd Corners': Ethnobiographical Prospects," in *Studies in Biography,* ed. Daniel Aaron (Cambridge, Mass., 1978), pp. 41–56. As they acknowledge, Christie/Orton owe something to David Antin, "Biography," *Representations* 16 (Fall 1986):42–49.

3. Christie/Orton in part base their case for biography by describing it as "unavoidable," because "humans are irreducibly narratable, narrating beings." The scripts for these stories that are constantly going on in our heads are culturally specific, so at first it sounds as though such narratives are culturally determined; but then it turns out that selves somehow can appropriate these stories. "He or she gets the stories from other lives and what he or she learns of other lives, 'factual' or 'fictional,' and, having *decided* on their relevance, uses them existentially" (my emphasis).

Acknowledgments

I've dedicated this book to my wife, Ramsay. I will always be grateful to her for the many hours she spent looking at Rothko paintings, talking with me about them, giving me the benefit of her subtle feeling for and complex understanding of Rothko and his work. Her ideas, her actual words, are present on every page. Without her, without her generous support and love, without her deep intelligence, this book would not exist.

My daughters, Jennifer, Susannah, and Nora, have not only tolerated their father's involvement with Mark Rothko, they have encouraged it with their jokes and their love.

I want to thank two friends: Michael Rogin, for many stimulating ideas during many lunchtime conversations about Rothko, for his acute observations after reading parts of the book-in-progress, then after reading the whole; and Andrew Griffin, for making helpful suggestions after reading parts of the manuscript, and in particular for several ideas that now inform my section on Rothko's *Self-Portrait* of the 1930s.

I am indebted to David Anfam, of the National Gallery of Art, for opening the Rothko files at the gallery to me, for answering numerous questions, and for his generosity with the information he has gathered for his catalogue raisonné of Rothko's paintings; to Regina Bogat, for furnishing me with the conversations with Rothko transcribed by Alfred Jensen; to Bernard Braddon, for documents relating to The Ten; to George Carson, for providing me with photographs and papers of his late wife, Edith Sachar; to Bonnie Clearwater, of the Mark Rothko Foundation, for help with copying the transcript of "Rothkowitz v. Browne" and for making paintings then in the foundation's possession available to me; to Joseph Liss, for permitting me to use four interviews he conducted when he was considering writing a biography of Rothko; to the late Robert Motherwell, for generosity with his time and free access to his archive; to Kenneth Rabin, for providing me with letters written by Rothko to his sister

Acknowledgments

and mother; to Joy Spalding, for dates and brief quotations from letters that Rothko sent to her and Kenneth Rabin; and to Lee Seldes, for sharing her Rothko files with me.

It is a pleasure to remember my conversations with the many people who were willing to talk with me about Rothko, and I'm indebted to them all for their time and candor: Cecile Abish, Mina Abramowitz, Howard Adelson, Jonathan Ahearn, Emily and Newell Alford, Sally Avery, Dore Ashton, Armand Bartos, Carlo Battaglia, Howard Baumbach, Ethel Baziotes, Joseph Belsey, Ben-Zion, Howard Berman, Earle Blew, Donald Blinken, Paul Bodin, Regina Bogat, Louise Bourgeois, Albert Bowker, Bernard Braddon, Milton Brown, Sylvia Browne, Joan Bultman, Morris Calden, Nicholas Carrone, George Carson, Georgio Cavallon, George and Shirley Climo, Irene Dash, Dorothy Dehner, Vita Deming, Ben Dienes, Aaron Director, Morris Dorsky, Judith Eisenstein, Vica Emery, Herbert Ferber, Arthur Gage, Arnold Glimcher, Lloyd Goodrich, Carl Goreff, Esther Gottlieb, Michael Goldberg, Daniel Goldreyer, Max Gordon, Wilder Green, Clement Greenberg, Albert Grokest, David Hare, Juliette Hays, Clinton Hill, Theo Hios, Sanford Hirsch, Al Hirschfeld, Ben Heller, Budd Hopkins, Murray Israel, Martin James, Buffie Johnson, Philip Johnson, Barbara Kaminstein, Louis and Annette Kaufman, Ray Kelly, April Kingsley, Milton and Lilian Klein, Jack Kufeld, Katharine Kuh, Stanley Kunitz, Robert Langbaum, Phyllis Lambert, Jane Lawrence, Vassily Leontief, Anne-Marie Levine, Arthur Lidov, Martin Lukashok, Bernard Malamud, David Margolis, Fred Martin, David McKee, Donald McKinney, Alan Meade, Ruth Miller, Ruth Moran, Richard and Barbara Morrow, Robert Motherwell, Annette Nachumi, Sonia Newman, Annalee Newman, Richard and Barbara Northrup, Ned O'Gorman, George and Blanche Okun, Carla Panicali, Ray Parker, Gerald Phillips, Barbara Poe, Ruth Pomeranz, Ralph Pomeroy, Morris Pottish, Frieda Prensky, Nathan Pusey, Kenneth and Elaine Rabin, Milton and Joy Rabin, Rebecca Reis, Rita Reinhardt, Jackie and Dan Rice, Phil and Dorothy Reiter, Julian and Dorothy Roth, Moise Roth, Richard and Johnny Mae Roth, Christopher Rothko, Kate Rothko, William Rubin, Howard and Beverly Sachar, Willie and Ann Sachar, William and Sally Scharf, Karl and Ilse Schrag, Betty Schoenfeld, Jon Schueler, Lee Seldes, Peter Selz, Lily Sievan, Thomas Sills, Joseph Solman, Gus Solomon, Rebecca Soyer, Joy Spalding, Theodoros Stamos, Oliver Steindecker, Hedda Sterne, Claire Sykes, Alex and Sloan Tampkin, Yvonne Thomas, Elizabeth Till, David Todd, Sophie Tracy, Celina Trief, Pat Trivigno, Sydney Weinstein, Paul Wilkes, and Elizabeth Zogbaum.

I have benefited from a good deal of help from the Archives of American Art, particularly from Paul J. Karlstrom and his assistants in the San Francisco

Acknowledgments

office, but also from Garnett McCoy and his staff in Washington, D.C., and from William McNaught and his staff in New York City.

I was assisted, too, by Judith Cousins, in the Painting and Sculpture Department at the Museum of Modern Art; by Ward Jackson, archivist at the Solomon R. Guggenheim Museum; by the librarians at the Museum of Modern Art and the Whitney Museum of Modern Art; the staff at the YIVO Institute; and by Carlotta Owens, of the American Prints and Drawings Department at the National Gallery of Art.

I'm grateful to Karen Wilson, my editor at the University of Chicago Press, for her patience, her encouragement, and her suggestions.

I presented sections of this book to the Biography Seminar at New York University, and to a psychobiography group in San Francisco, and I'm grateful to both groups for their stimulating discussions of my work.

The Committee on Research, University of California, Berkeley, also provided me with a grant that enabled me to hire Sandra Gustafson to transcribe many of my taped interviews. I'm grateful to Ms. Gustafson for her scrupulous work, to Irene Tucker, for translating Rothko's Hebrew poems, and to Teresa Faherty for help in editing the manuscript.

I am indebted to the American Philosophical Society, the American Council of Learned Societies, the Travel to Collections Program of the National Endowment of the Humanities, and the Committee on Research, University of California, Berkeley, for grants that helped with the considerable costs of travel that this project entailed.

I am most grateful to the John Simon Guggenheim Memorial Foundation, the National Endowment for the Humanities, the President's Research Fellowships in the Humanities, University of California, and the Humanities Research Fellowship Program, University of California, Berkeley, for generous grants that provided me with the time in which I could pursue this project more carefully and thoughtfully (and more quickly) than would otherwise have been possible.

I am indebted, finally, to the John Simon Guggenheim Memorial Foundation for a generous grant which helped with the publication costs of this lengthy book.

Index

Abish, Cecile, 290–91, 322, 365
Adelson, Howard, 115
Aeschylus, 150, 166, 170, 175, 176, 236, 242, 359, 499
Ahearn, Jonathan, 469, 492–93, 494, 524
Alloway, Lawrence, 482
American Abstract Artists, 106, 122, 141, 186, 289
American Artists' Congress Against War and Fascism, 62, 123, 147, 148, 154–55, 156
American Laboratory Theater, 55, 64
"American Modern Artists," 164–65, 195
Angell, James R., 52
Angier, Roswell, 48, 49
Arensberg, Walter, 205
Argan, Guilio Carlo, 400
Arp, Jean, 209–10
Art Institute of Chicago, 264, 307–12, 356, 378, 397, 402
Artists' Coordination Committee, 120, 156
Artists for National Defense, 156
Artists for Victory, 156, 164
Artists Union, 122–23, 156
Art of This Century. *See* Guggenheim, Peggy
Art Students League, 60–63, 161, 196, 420, 469; Rothko sees nude model at, 55, 99, 174; Rothko attends, 56, 60–63, 64, 289
Ashton, Dore, 25, 173, 356, 389, 430, 440, 490, 542; on Seagram murals, 3, 4, 375, 405; on Houston murals, 460, 465, 466, 470, 484; 1969 conversation with Rothko, 511
Aubrey, Eugene, 466
Avery, Milton, 91–97; Rothko on, 93, 94, 303, 360; sketch classes, 93, 127, 197; gallery affiliation, 101; compared to Rothko, 102; exhibits at Whitney, 104; on WPA, 121; on Rothko's book, 130, 169; refuses to show work to Rothko and Gottlieb, 162; on masterpieces, 594 n. 45; on Rothko's apartment, 153; on Rothko's show at Art of This Century, 208; on death of Howard Putzel, 231; decline of friendship with Rothko, 347, 348; death, 490
Avery, Sally, 91–97, 162, 339, 346, 550; on Edith Sachar, 99, 145, 146, 170, 205; Rothko on Plato, 244; Rothko's hypochondria, 204, 347

Baker, George, 40, 42
Barnes collection, 196, 225
Barnes, Susan, 475, 485
Barnet, Will, 289
Barnstone, Howard, 466, 473

Barr, Alfred, 137, 139–41, 159, 427, 428; Rothko courts, 6; Rothko, purchases of, 254, 298; argues with Rothko over lighting, 303; recommends Rothko, 373, 614 n. 35
Battaglia, Carlo, 173
Baudelaire, Charles, 434
Baumbach, Howard, 204, 247
Baziotes, Ethel, 231, 318
Baziotes, William: Rothko on, 195; on WPA, 121; gallery affiliations, 181, 231, 250–51, 256, 336, 442; warned against Bernard Reis, 183; relation to Surrealists, 184; teaches at the Subjects of the Artist school, 223, 263; death of, 490
Beistle, Aldarilla, 216–18
Beistle, Barbara, 216, 398
Beistle, Morton James, 216–18, 220
Beistle, Robert Morton, 216, 220
Beistle, Shirley, 216–19, 398
Benton, Thomas Hart, 95
Ben-Zion, 101
Beyeler, Ernest, 508
Biddle, George, 154
Bischoff, Elmer, 227, 258
Black Mountain College, 348
Blew, Earle, 221, 223
Blinken, Donald, 306, 323, 417–18
Bliss, Lizzie P, 138–39, 250
Bogat, Regina, 6, 63, 288, 450, 471
Bolotowsky, Ilya, 101, 104, 155
Bonestall Gallery, 105
Bourgeois, Louise, 323
Braddon, Bernard, 104–5
Braque, Georges, 138, 208, 256, 257
Breton, André, 181, 183, 184, 185, 597 n. 29
Breuning, Margaret, 247
Bridgman, George, 60–61, 117
Briggs, Ernest, 222, 223, 227, 259–60
Bronfman, Samuel, 371–72
Brooklyn College, 287–94; Rothko appointed, 273; Rothko's salary at, 299; benefits of salary, 304, 314; Rothko as teacher at, 248, 290–91, 615 n. 44; Reinhardt votes against Rothko, 292, 347; on Rothko losing job at, 360; Kate Rothko attends, 503
Brooklyn Jewish Center, 86, 111–12, 114, 126
Brooklyn Museum, 116, 252, 254
Brooks, James, 121, 344, 412, 415
Brown, Milton, 255, 288, 290, 293
Browne, Lewis, 65–78, 85, 104, 113, 114, 145, 170, 217, 293, 408
Byrnes, James, 350–51

Cahan, Abraham, 54
Calden, Morris, 130, 142, 144, 169
Calder, Alexander, 180
California Palace of the Legion of Honor, 222, 227, 298
California School of Fine Arts, 222, 223, 227, 258–62, 263, 264, 265, 289, 350, 423
Carson, George, 90
Castelli, Leo, 421, 427–28
Cavallon, Georgio, 501
Cedar Street Bar, 257–58
Cézanne, Paul, 61, 62, 88, 139, 140, 161, 226; Rothko on, 283, 301, 613 n. 21
Chagall, Marc, 17, 57, 181, 320
Chamberlain, John, 422, 430
Charles Egan Gallery, 251
Chave, Anna, 213, 368, 612 n. 95
Cheney, Sheldon, 106
Christie, J. R. R., 555–58
Cizek, Franz, 130, 132–36, 167
Clearwater, Bonnie, 186, 237, 496
Clifford, James, 556
Climo, Shirley. *See* Beistle, Shirley
Commonwealth College, 83–84, 217
Compton, Michael, 382, 406
Contemporary Arts Gallery, 97–98
Coolidge, John, 446, 447–48, 450, 451, 452, 455, 456
Corbett, Edward, 258
Cornell, Joseph, 250, 263

Corwin, Robert, 48
Couturier, Fr. Marie-Alain, 461
Cox, Kenyon, 592 n. 27
Cranmer, Dana, 316
Crehan, Herbert, 356–57, 625 n. 74
Cubism, 61, 63, 147, 161, 194, 210, 214; Rothko on, 174, 330, 392, 394; "Cubism and Abstract Art," 139, 140, 147
Cuddihy, James Murray, 320–21
Curry, John Stuart, 164

Dali, Salvador, 137, 181, 592 n. 27
Dash, Irene, 115
David Porter Gallery, 209–10
Davis, Stuart, 154
de Antonio, Emilio, 470
de Chirico, Giorgio, 144, 185
Dehner, Dorothy, 145, 148
de Kooning, Elaine, 91, 282, 321, 322, 323, 324, 363–64; essay on Rothko, 386–89, 392, 599 n. 1
de Kooning, Willem: Rothko on, 314, 360; on WPA, 121; meets Rothko, 142; gallery affiliations, 251, 256, 336, 438–39, 442; goes abstract, 255; part of "downtown" group, 257; lecture by, 263; on Rothko's Seagram murals, 373, 378; relation to Bernard Reis, 397, 507; in Robert Scull collection, 420, 422, 430
de Menil, Dominique, 377, 418, 459–63, 468, 473–74, 482, 483–86
de Menil, John, 377, 418, 459–63, 464, 473, 483
Deming, Vita, 431
Dewey, John, 113
d'Harnoncourt, René, 303, 413
Diamond, Harold, 339, 367
Diebenkorn, Richard, 258
Dienes, Ben, 266, 305, 323
Diller, Burgoyne, 289, 290
Dillon, Josephine, 55
Dine, Jim, 429, 430

Director, Aaron, 26, 34, 36, 38, 46, 47, 51, 54, 65
Dirk, Nathaniel, 81
Downtown Gallery, 341
Dows, Olin, 119, 120
Duchamp, Marcel, 179, 181, 208
Dvinsk, 9–22, 25, 31, 45, 52, 150–52, 242, 320

Edwards, Roy, 469–70, 471, 472–73
Eisenstein, Judith, 115
Eliot, T. S., 53, 93
Ernst, Jimmy, 181, 184, 291–92
Ernst, Max, 180, 181, 182, 184, 185, 208
Evans-Gordon, Major W., 9–10

Federal Advertising Agency, 65
Federal Art Gallery, 122
Federation of Modern Painters and Scupltors, 155–59, 182, 186–87, 191, 196, 223, 498
Feldman, Morton, 540
Ferber, Herbert: Rothko's childhood stories, 13, 18; Rothko's theatricality, 18, 324; Rothko and Mozart, 173; Rothko and Surrealism, 185, 237; parties of, 257–58; Rothko's depressions, 265; Mell's pregnancy, 287; Rothko against group shows, 304; Rothko's attachment to his works, 305; refers Rothko to Dr. Grokest, 363; synagogue commission, 377; Rothko's will, 398; relation to Bernard Reis, 439, 506; sculpture of, 467; as survivor, 486; split with Rothko, 498–99, 538; Rothko letters to, 346, 349, 350–54, 425
Ferstadt, Louis, 64, 91
"Fifteen Americans," 299, 303, 314, 318, 338, 344, 348, 349, 374
Fischer, Harry, 437
Fischer, John Hurt, 7, 376, 382, 385, 391–92, 398–99, 400, 406, 449
Flior, Yudel, 10, 11, 12, 41

Ford, Gordon Onslow, 379
Ford, Ruth, 207
Fra Angelico, 285, 400, 614 n. 28
Francesca, Piero della, 134, 285
Frankenthaler, Helen, 431, 439, 493
Frank Perls Gallery, 298
Frazer, Sir James, 161, 187, 391–92
Freud, Sigmund, 174, 361, 475; *The Interpretation of Dreams,* 126, 161, 597 n. 37

Gable, Clark, 55, 56
Gage, Arthur, 58, 64, 205, 207
Galerie Bonaparte, 102
Gallery of Living Art, 138, 142
Gallery Secession, 100–101
Gauguin, Paul, 139, 140
Gellert, Hugo, 156
Genaur, Emily, 211, 355, 385
Georgette Passedoit Gallery, 104
Giacometti, Alberto, 539
Gideonse, Harry, 292–93, 330
Gitlitz, Morris, 46
Glimcher, Arnold, 509
Godsoe, Robert, 98, 100
Goldberg, Michael, 426, 431
Goldman, Emma, 35, 36, 40, 72, 174
Goldreyer, Daniel, 474, 527
Goldwater, Robert, 5, 331, 492, 528, 540, 541, 542
Goodrich, Lloyd, 61, 66, 103, 121, 303–4
Goodyear, Conger, 137, 198
Goosen, E.C., 356
Gordon, Max, 32, 39
Goreff, Mrs., 56
Gorky, Arshile, 56, 121, 142, 267, 335, 336
Gottlieb, Adolph, 161–64; in Milton Avery group, 92, 93, 162; on Avery, 96, 594 n. 45; in The Ten, 101; on WPA, 119–20, 121; in Federation of Modern Painters and Sculptors, 155, 158; theories of art, 161, 163–64; 168, 178, 184, 187; "Pictographs," 167; gallery affiliations, 181, 250, 251, 336, 337, 429; letter to Edward Alden Jewell, 191–203, 264; on Rothko in hospital, 204; on Surrealists, 256; part of "uptown" group, 257; lecture by, 263; writes protest letter, 271–72; decline of Rothko friendship, 347, 348; synagogue commission, 377; relation to Bernard Reis, 439; on Rothko's "Black on Grey" series, 528
Gottlieb, Esther, 93, 147, 211–12, 231, 379, 594 n. 41
Graham, John, 92
Green, Wilder, 435, 447, 449, 452, 454
Greenberg, Clement, 142, 159, 251, 255, 383–85, 386, 390, 551–52, 629 n. 45
Grodzinsky, Dr. Herman, 49
Grokest, Dr. Albert: first treats Rothko, 363–65, 367; Rothko's dependency on food and alcohol, 4; Rothko's distrust, 27; Dvinsk, conversation of, 325; treats Mell Rothko, 369; Rothko visits 1959, 381; Rothko visits 1961, 411; Rothko visits 1962, 424–25; Rothko not introspective, 471; Rothko's aneurysm, 489–90, 524; Rothko's marital problems, 491; on Bernard Reis, 507; Rothko visits 1968–69, 530, 533, 534–35, 537
Gropper, William, 95, 124
Guggenheim, Peggy, 179–81, 208–9, 211–12, 215, 221–22, 231, 250, 252, 399, 435, 459
Guggenheim Museum, 141, 147, 374, 454, 525, 554
Guilbaut, Serge, 384, 607 n. 42
Guston, Philip, 19, 121; Rothko on, 360; gallery affiliations, 336, 337, 397, 429, 438–39, 441, 442; on Rothko's lighting, 338

Haftmann, Werner, 407–8
Halpert, Edith, 341

Hare, David, 223, 263, 302, 322, 431
Harnett, William, 137
Harris, Louis, 64, 91, 94, 101, 104, 155, 203–4
Harrow, Gustave, 441–42
Hays, Arthur Garfield, 68, 72–78
Hays, H. R., 124, 159–60
Hays, Juliette, 123, 159–60, 169, 170, 217
Hayter, Stanley William, 289
Held, Al, 426, 431, 433
Heller, Ben, 347, 417–18, 459, 463, 507–8, 632 n. 84, 636 n. 5, 639 n. 27
Hess, Thomas, 206, 247, 298, 344–45, 355
Higham, John, 39
Hill, Clinton, 624 n. 71
Hirschfeld, Al, 433
Hofmann, Hans, 106, 142, 264–65
Holty, Carl, 289
Holtzman, Harry, 289
Hoover, J. Edgar, 154
Hopkins, Budd, 305–6, 323, 325, 337
Hopkins, Harry, 118
Howe, Irving, 57
Huelsenbeck, Richard, 263
Hultberg, John, 259

Indiana, Robert, 426, 429
Institute for Religious and Human Development, 464
"The Irascibles," 271–73, 288, 341, 383
Israel, Murray, 275, 290–91
Israels, Nathan, 64

James, Martin, 288
Janis, Sidney, 166, 315, 334–39, 348, 373, 413, 427, 436, 441; artists move from Parsons, 297–98; Rothko exhibitions at, 343, 355–56, 383; letter from Clyfford Still, 343–45; letter from Barnett Newman, 345–46, 347; submits Rothko painting to Guggenheim competition, 374; artists resign from, 429, 442; collection exhibited, 459

Jensen, Alfred, 95, 322, 326; conversations with Rothko quoted, 266, 276, 285, 292, 300–302, 313–14, 343, 359–61, 367, 392, 393, 415
Jewell, Edward Alden, 162, 191–95, 199–200, 210–11, 582 n. 86
Johns, Jasper, 421, 422, 427, 428, 430, 432, 434
Johnson, Buffie, 170, 207–8
Johnson, Philip, 254, 298, 299, 462; designs Four Seasons restaurant, 3, 371, 373, 375, 393, 405; designs Houston chapel, 463–66, 468, 469, 484–85
Jones, Cecil, 119
Jones, Elizabeth, 451, 454–55, 456
Jones, Frederick S., 48
Julian Levy Gallery, 181
Jung, Carl, 160

Kafka, Franz, 31, 65, 220
Kainen, Jacob, 105, 120, 121, 122, 124, 165, 494
Kandinsky, Wassily, 141, 147
Kant, Immanuel, 131
Karfoil, Bernard, 91
Karp, Ivan, 428
Katz, Menke, 14, 41
Kaufman, Annette, 169, 205
Kaufman, Louis, 91, 93, 94, 130, 169, 205, 208
Kawamura Museum, 409
Kellein, Thomas, 406, 409
Kelly, Ray, 469–70, 472, 551
Kierkegaard, Soren, 126, 378, 392–94, 408, 535
Kiesler, Frederick, 179, 180, 231
Klein, Lilian. See Sachar, Lilian
Kline, Franz, 249, 315, 316, 348, 420, 422, 439; lives in Greenwich Village, 142, 147; gallery affiliations, 251, 336, 397, 441, 442; part of "downtown" group, 257, 314; Elaine de Kooning essay on, 386, 388; death of, 431, 490
Kline, Dr. Nathan, 523, 524, 532–36

Koenig, John-Franklin, 430
Kootz, Samuel, 160–61, 231, 250–51, 253, 256, 335–36
Kozloff, Max, 416
Kraetzer, Eugene, 451, 455, 456
Krasner, Lee, 121, 142, 266, 341
Kufeld, Jack, 92, 101, 204
Kuh, Katharine, 223, 264, 380, 405, 495; curates Rothko exhibit, 307–12, 331, 338, 387, 397, 402; Rothko on Clyfford Still, 347–48; Rothko on mural commissions, 405, 459, 466; Rothko on Marlborough Gallery, 508; Rothko hints of suicide, 538
Kunitz, Stanley: on Rothko's MOMA exhibit, 2, 6; on Rothko's cultural origins, 8; Rothko as rabbi, 58; Rothko on nature, 87, 379–80; Mell's feeling for Rothko, 221; Rothko's need for companionship, 222, 234, 348; vacuum in Rothko, 267, 535; Rothko as friend, 321; Rothko's desire to create rooms, 279, 304, 408, 466; Rothko's rejection of Europe, 283; Rothko's dislike of teaching, 288; Rothko's need for admiration, 318, 416, 422; Rothko's impatience, 319; Rothko's will, 398; Rothko rejects Four Seasons, 406; Rothko in Provincetown, 1968, 493, 494; Rothko's hostility toward younger artists, 498; Rothko as parent, 502; Rothko's Marlborough contract, 505; Rothko's 1969 depression, 529

La Guardia, Fiorello, 101, 197
Lambert, Phyllis, 371, 372–73, 375, 376, 378
Lasker, Mary, 641 n. 50
Lawrence, Jane, 322, 323
Léger, Fernand, 161, 181, 208, 259
Lehotay, Dr. Judith, 523–24
Leontief, Wassily, 446, 455
Levine, Anne-Marie, 5, 367, 444, 500–501, 505, 507, 529; Rothko visits in Brussels, 399–400; Rothko's will, 492; day of Rothko's death, 529
Levine, Morton, 399–400, 441, 492, 523, 540, 541
Levy, Julian, 263
Lichtenstein, Roy, 428, 429, 433
Lidov, Arthur, 467, 473–74, 490, 521–22, 535, 543
Lipchitz, Jacques, 181
Lippold, Richard, 284, 287, 405
Lision, Dr. Arnold L., 534
Liss, Joseph, 148–49, 153, 160, 379
Lloyd, Frank, 78, 336, 422–23, 435–39, 442–43, 455, 505–10, 528, 542–43
Los Angeles County Museum, 298, 430, 463
Louis, Morris, 430
Lukashok, Martin, 115

MacAgy, Douglas, 247–48, 258, 261, 264
MacCoby, Max, 36, 37, 54, 64, 66, 81
MacColl, E. Kimbark, 39
McKinney, Donald, 442–43, 508–9, 527, 528, 542–43
Malamud, Bernard, 203, 534
Margo, Boris, 203
Marlborough Gallery. *See* Lloyd, Frank
Masson, André, 181
Matisse, Henri, 55, 60, 61, 95, 100, 103, 139; Rothko's interest in, 144, 283, 328, 360; *The Red Studio,* 283; chapel at Vence, 377, 462
Matta, Roberto, 147, 181, 182, 185
Matthiessen, F. O., 48
Mayer, Musa, 497
Meade, Dr. Allen, 490–92, 523, 530, 533, 534
Mercury Galleries, 103–5
Messer, Thomas, 525
Metropolitan Museum of Art, 103, 138, 140, 161, 164, 196, 224–25, 459; Rothko's knowledge of collections, 74–75, 283; protest against, 271–72

Metzinger, Jean, 592 n. 27
Michaleshek, 14, 21, 41, 45, 586 n. 35
Michelangelo, 400–401, 446
Miller, Dorothy, 6, 141, 142, 254, 299, 303, 383
Miller, Dr. Lawson E., 530
Miró, Joan, 181, 185, 208, 209–10, 404; Rothko's interest in, 283, 334–35, 377, 390, 592 n. 27, 613 n. 21
Mitchell, Joan, 431
"Modern Artists in America," 257, 263, 271
Mondrian, Piet, 129, 181, 198, 199, 208, 298, 384; Rothko on, 276, 300, 330, 355, 469
Monet, Claude, 87, 300
Mongan, Agnes, 454–55
Montross Gallery, 102, 138
Moran, Ruth, 218, 220
Morrow, Elizabeth, 221
Mortimer Brandt Gallery, 232, 252
Motherwell, Robert: on Rothko's childhood stories, 17, 21, 22, 171, 278; Rothko's desire for collective intimacy, 101; Rothko's temper, 33, 322; New York, World War II, 153; gallery affiliations, 180, 181, 208, 231, 251, 253, 256, 298, 336, 337, 429, 508; on Surrealists, 184, 185; begins "Elegy" series, 255; part of "uptown" group, 257–58; at the Subjects of the Artist school, 223, 262–65; death of Rothko's mother, 265–66; Rothko on objects, 267, 339; Rothko on Fra Angelico, 285; Rothko's trip to Europe, 286; Rothko against group shows, 304; Rothko's automatic drawing, 317; Rothko on art, 333, 357; Woodstock Conference, 349–50; Rothko's Bowery studio, 3; Rothko's self-doubt, 373–74, 459; relation to Bernard Reis, 183, 397, 439, 441, 442; Rothko in Provincetown, 1968, 491, 493, 494, 535; Rothko on money, 506; Rothko studio party, 525; Rothko's suicide, 521, 523; Rothko letters to, 340, 350–51, 365, 376–77, 380–81
Mozart, Wolfgang, 173, 258, 266, 279, 319, 396, 504, 610
Mumford, Lewis, 154
Municipal Art Gallery, 101
Museum of Modern Art: history of, 137–41, 250; Rothko visits, 116, 144, 283; protests against, 141, 158–59; World War II exhibits, 164; Surrealist exhibits, 181; ignores contemporary American painters, 208, 209, 254; shows "Italian Masters," 215; power of, 255, 256; denounced, 271; purchases a Rothko painting, 298; Rothko exhibits at, 4, 298–99, 383, 459; Sidney Janis's relation to, 335, 336; attitude to Robert Scull, 421; Jasper Johns purchase, 427; "Sixteen Americans," 428; Rothko gifts to, 513, 669 n. 23; Rothko calls junkyard, 514. *See also* "Fifteen Americans"
Museum of Non-Objective Art, 141, 147. *See also* Guggenheim Museum
Myers, John Bernard, 421

Naimark, Max, 34, 36, 37, 38, 46, 47, 49, 50, 54, 64, 65
Namuth, Hans, 385
National Gallery of Art, 277, 409
Neuman, J.B., 116, 125
Nevelson, Louise, 121
New Art Circle Gallery, 138
Newman, Annalee, 93, 196, 198, 200, 286, 287, 343, 346, 348
Newman, Barnett, 195–200; in Avery group, 92, 93, 162, 197; lives in Greenwich Village, 142; crisis of subject, 163, 197–98; theories of art, 198–99; friendship with Rothko, 202–3; gallery affiliations, 231, 232, 250, 286, 297; first "zip" painting,

Newman, Barnett (*cont.*) 255; part of "uptown group," 257–58; at the Subjects of the Artist school, 263–65; "The Irascibles," 271–73; patriarchal manner, 323; sues Ad Reinhardt, 342–43; attacks Rothko, 345–46; "invisible" to Rothko, 349; Clement Greenberg on, 384–85; Harold Rosenberg on, 386; in Robert Scull collection, 420, 422, 430; Rothko's loss of friendship with, 5, 498–99; Rothko letters to, 211, 260, 261, 284, 287, 306–7
"New York Artist-Painters," 164–65, 166, 195
Nietzsche, Friedrich, 224, 233, 349; *The Birth of Tragedy,* 126, 131, 160, 173–76, 198, 357–59, 369, 389, 473, 499–500, 587 n. 37
Nin, Anais, 183
Nodelman, Sheldon, 485
Noguchi, Isamu, 329
Noland, Kenneth, 430
Northrup, Barabara. *See* Beistle, Barbara
Novak, Barbara, 503

O'Doherty, Brian, 471, 525
O'Keeffe, Georgia, 138
Okun, George, 126, 156, 245
Oldenburg, Claes, 429, 430, 432, 433
Opportunity Gallery, 91, 161
Orton, Fred, 555–58

Paalen, Wolfgang, 181, 378
"Painting Prophecy—1950, A," 209
Panicalli, Carla, 438
Panza, Count Giuseppe, 432–33
Park, David, 258
Parker, Ray, 426, 431, 469, 480, 528
Parsons, Betty, 222, 249–54, 261, 273, 342, 386, 498, 537; Rothko exhibitions at, 223, 231–32, 233, 246–48, 307; Newman exhibitions at, 286, 346; artists leave, 296–300; legal dispute with Sidney Janis, 336

Patchen, Kenneth, 84
Pearson, Ralph, 154
Pfister, Oskar, 106, 108, 132, 136–37, 143, 245
Phillips, Duncan, 469, 636 n. 5, 647 n.10
Phillips, Gerald, 115
Phillips Collection, 449, 669 n. 23
Picasso, Pablo, 60, 61, 95, 141, 161, 256, 257, 404; exhibitions of, 139, 147, 208, 209–10; Rothko on, 102, 103, 136, 144, 200, 259, 283, 360, 361, 390, 592 n. 27, 613 n. 21
Pierre Matisse Gallery, 181, 231
Pierson, George, 54
Plato, 131, 244, 587 n. 87
Polcari, Stephen, 647 n. 3
Pollock, Jackson: adolescence, 37; on WPA, 121, 122; lives in Greenwich Village, 142; gallery affiliations, 181, 208, 211, 232, 250, 256, 297; Rothko on, 195, 314; begins drip paintings, 255; at Cedar Bar, 258; fishing trip with Rothko, 266; *Number 1, 1948,* 275; working methods, 274–75, 316, 385; *Autumn Rhythm,* 341; reputation of, 345; Clement Greenberg on, 384; *Blue Poles,* 404; Harold Rosenberg on, 386; death of, 431, 490, 524
Portland, Oregon, 24, 26–27, 31–42, 47, 56–57, 266; Rothko visits, 86–89, 205, 423; Rothko watercolor of, 87–88
Portland Art Museum, 88, 116, 232
Pousette-Dart, Richard, 195
Prensky, Frieda, 115, 116
"Problem for Critics, A," 209–11
Public Works of the Art Project, 121
Pusey, Nathan, 445–46, 447, 448, 450, 451
Putnam, Wallace, 92, 167
Putzel, Howard, 208–11

Rabin, Kenneth, 15, 28, 56, 324, 399, 423, 424, 545

Index

Rabin, Sonia. *See* Rothkowitz, Sonia
Rauschenberg, Robert, 419, 427–28, 429, 430, 432, 434
Reid, Norman, 513–18
Reinhardt, Ad, 121, 141, 250, 256, 263, 271–72, 346; at Brooklyn College, 288, 289, 290, 292, 293; attacks Newman and Rothko, 342–43, 347, 374; black paintings, 529; death, 490
Reinhardt, Rita, 499, 507, 529, 535, 536–38, 542–43
Reis, Bernard, 5, 157, 182–183, 377, 438–42, 466, 525; advisor to Peggy Guggenheim, 180; as collector, 182, 184, 439, 644 n. 102; meets Rothko, 263; represents Rothko with Sidney Janis Gallery, 397; role with Harvard murals, 448, 454–56; role with Houston chapel, 465; role with gift to Tate Gallery, 515; day of Rothko's aneurysm, 489–90; as Rothko's executor, 78, 183, 398, 499; Rothko's dependency on, 441–42, 507–8, 509–10, 535; brings Rothko to Dr. Nathan Kline, 532, 533; director of Mark Rothko Foundation, 78, 183, 492, 540–43
Reis, Rebecca, 182–83, 439–40, 470, 499, 501, 505, 507, 525, 533, 538
Rembrandt, 283, 291, 339, 410
Renoir, Auguste, 360
Reynal, Jeanne, 321, 386, 387–88
Reynolds, James, 448, 450
Rice, Dan, 368, 373, 492; on Seagram murals, 315, 316–17, 375, 378, 381–82, 391, 403, 405–6
Rivers, Larry, 435, 442
Robertson, Bryan, 412, 536
Robson, Deirdre, 341–42, 607 n. 42
Rockefeller, Abby Aldrich, 138, 250
Rockefeller, David, 418
Rockefeller, John D., Jr., 138–39
Rockefeller, Mrs. John D. III, 254–55, 418

Rockefeller, Nelson, 137, 141, 418–19
Rodin, Auguste, 592 n. 27
Rodman, Selden, 309
Roosevelt, Franklin D., 85, 207, 209
Root, Edward Wales, 252
Rosenberg, Harold, 248, 266, 368, 385–86, 388–89, 390, 599 n. 1, 630 n. 54
Rosenberg, May, 368–69
Rosenquist, James, 422, 429, 433
Rosenstein, Sophie, 205, 207
Roth, Albert, 14, 16; migration, 21, 22; in Portland, 24, 26, 32, 38; changes name, 125; drafted World War I, 40; Rothko visits, 86, 88, 89; translator, 153; cancer, 424–25, 446, 490, 641 n. 50; Rothko's relation, to, 398, 423–25, 442; quoted, 17, 20
Roth, Bella, 88
Roth, Clara, 89, 423
Roth, Dorothy, 262
Roth, Julian, 88, 262
Roth, Moise, 14, 16, 546; migration, 21, 22; Portland, 24, 32, 38, 54, 153; changes name, 125; Rothko's relation to, 27, 88–89, 398, 423–25, 442; quoted, 13, 15, 17, 18, 20, 21, 26
Roth, Richard, 88
Rothko, Christopher, 431, 460, 489, 492, 500, 501, 504–5, 531
Rothko, Kate: birth, 273, 286–87; childhood, 319, 349, 365–67, 368; name changed, 397; travels to Europe, 398–99; adolescence, 489, 502–5; quoted, 17, 27, 219, 326, 368, 379, 380, 415, 449, 490, 507, 525
Rothko, Mark, critical reception: 5, 97–98, 100, 186–87, 191–95, 247–48, 298, 355–57
———, exhibitions: 5–7, 88, 91, 97, 98, 101–5, 123, 142, 155, 160, 164–65, 186–87, 208–12, 222, 223, 232, 246, 248, 252–53, 256, 261, 298–99, 303, 306–12, 334, 336, 354, 355–56, 383, 411–12, 454,

693

Rothko, Mark (*cont.*)
459, 605n n. 5, 6, 11, 608 n. 46, 609 n. 58, 618 n. 39, 621 n. 13, 629n n. 41, 42, 647 n. 10, 650 n. 1, 665 n. 83

———, Jewishness: 9–45, 47–52, 54, 57–59, 60–63, 65–78, 101, 104, 106, 111–17, 154–55, 161–62, 202–3, 241–42, 258, 283, 320–27, 407

———, life: birth, 14; childhood illness, 17; memory of mass grave, 17–18, 109; attends *cheder,* 18–19; father migrates to Portland, 20–21; migrates to Portland, father dies, 21–28, 31–34, 39–42; elementary schools, 32, 33–34; high school, 34–38, 41–42; Yale University, 47–54; New School of Design, 56; Art Students League, 56, 60–63; illustrations for *The Graphic Bible,* 65–78; teaches at Center Academy, 86, 88, 89, 112–17, 130–31, 252; marries Edith Sachar, 81–91, 94–95, 143–46, 169–73; works for WPA, 119–23, 147; joins The Ten, 101–6, 141; becomes U.S. citizen, changes name, 125–26; founder of the Federation of Modern Painters and Sculptors, 155–59; divorce, 170, 203–5; marries Mary Alice Beistle, 209, 218–21; teaches at California School of Fine Arts, 258–62; founder of the Subjects of the Artist school, 262–65; mother dies, 265–68; travels to Europe, 282–87; daughter born, 286–87; teaches at Brooklyn College, 287–94; refuses Whitney Annual, 303–4; attends Woodstock Conference, 349–50; teaches at the University of Colorado (Boulder), 350–53; teaches at Tulane University, 353–55; refuses Guggenheim Museum award, 374; marital problems, 365–69; creates murals for Four Seasons restaurant, 370–409; writes will, 397–98; second trip to Europe, 398–401; one-man exhibit at Museum of Modern Art, 4–7; creates murals for Harvard University dining room, 445–57; signs contract with Marlborough Gallery, 442–43; birth of son, 431; creates murals for chapel in Houston, 458–86; third trip to Europe, 543 n. 50; suffers aneurysm, 489–92; makes new will, 492, 499; forms Mark Rothko Foundation, 492, 540–42; conducts inventory of his work, 492–93; separates from wife, 505, 532, 536–38; second contract with Marlborough Gallery, 505–10; honorary degree from Yale University, 538–39; gives paintings to the Tate Gallery, 512–18; relationship with Rita Reinhardt, 535, 536–38; third contract with Marlborough Gallery, 542–43; death, 521–25, 543

———, lighting of paintings: 303, 338, 412, 447, 448–49, 454, 479, 482–83

———, love for music: 34, 81–82, 126, 173–76

———, painting methods: 316–17, 382, 468–70, 472–73, 495–96, 526, 654 n. 51

———, political attitudes: 35–37, 113–14, 123–25, 148, 154–55, 156, 166–69

———, protectiveness toward works: 303–6, 317–18, 374, 397–98, 415–18

———, sales: 212, 251–53, 254–55, 297, 299–300, 334, 341, 342, 412–13, 417–18, 422, 432–33, 442–43, 505–6, 600 n. 16, 602 n. 35, 605 n. 11, 608n n. 46, 47, 609n n. 50, 58, 612 n. 7, 616 n. 7, 617 n. 11, 636 n. 5, 638 n. 16, 639n n. 22, 27, 640n n. 28, 29, 641 n. 50, 642 n. 71, 643 n. 79, 646n n. 114, 116, 647 n. 10, 651 n. 18, 658 n. 23, 665n n. 84, 86, 677 n. 84

Index

———, studios: 3–4, 313, 314–15, 318, 380–81, 451, 466–68, 469, 470, 525, 619 n. 43, 628n n. 33, 36, 649 n. 19

———, theories of art: 73–77, 114, 116–17, 130–37, 191–95, 200–203, 210–11, 233–34, 239–45, 246–47, 260–61, 307–12, 329–32, 389–97, 588 n. 42, 592 n. 27

———, writings, published: "Monday at Lincoln," 36–37; "False Gods," 51, 52; "New Training for Future Artists and Art Lovers," 114, 116–17, 131; Letter to Edward Alden Jewell, 191–95, 199–203, 241, 264; "The Portrait and the Modern Artist," 162, 163, 184, 191, 264; Letter to *New York Times,* 210–11; "Personal Statement," 210, 241; "Clyfford Still," 168, 222; Statement (1947), 233–34; "The Romantics Were Prompted," 58–59, 63–64, 99, 109–10, 111, 174–75, 189, 239–45, 257, 276, 278, 310, 357, 389, 525, 606 n. 20; Statement (1949), 246–47; Statement (1951), 280; Letter to *Art News,* 388–89

———, writings, unpublished: "Salutation" (poem), 42–45; "Walls of Mind: Out of the Past" (poem), 44–45; Center Academy talk, 130–31, 140; "The Scribble Book," 106, 113, 117, 124, 127, 128, 130–37, 142, 167–68, 171, 174, 238, 244, 245, 285, 332; Pratt Institute lecture, 28, 190, 276, 281, 282, 389–97

———, works: *Aeolian Harp,* 232; *Agitation of the Archaic,* 232, 605 n. 6; *Altar of Orpheus,* 608 n. 46; *Ancestral Imprint,* 608 n. 46; *Annunciation,* 100; *Antigone,* 160; *Archaic Idol,* 608 n. 46; *Beginnings,* 232; *Black and Dark Sienna on Purple* (1960), 636 n. 5, 643 n. 79; *Black and Red on Red,* 636 n. 5; *Black, Ocher, Red over Red* (1957), 643 n. 79; *Black on Grey* (1969), 528–29; *Blue and Green,* 636 n. 5; *Blue and Gray* (1962), 646 n. 114; *Blue and Green* (1968), 644 n. 102; *Blue Cloud* (1954), 606 n. 25; *Blue Orange Red* (1961), 646 n. 114; *Blue over Orange* (1956), 639 n. 22; *Brown and Black in Reds* (1958), 373; *Brown, Blue, Brown on Blue* (1953), 636 n. 5, 643 n. 79; *Brown Maroon Rust on Plum* (1959), 644 n. 102; *Brown Red Black* (1959), 646 n. 114; *Browns* (1957), 636 n. 5; *Ceremonial Vessel,* 232; *Companionship and Solitude,* 232, 605 n. 6; *Dance,* 232; *Dark over Light* (1954), 636 n. 5; *Dark Picture* (1968), 644 n. 102; *Drawing* (early 1940s), 171; *Drawing* (early 1940s), 171–72; *Dream Memory,* 232; *The Eagle and the Hare,* 165, 166; *Earth, Green and White* (1957), 640 n. 28; *Earth Greens* (1955), 636 n. 5; *Entombment I,* 252, 304, 608 n. 46; *Entombment II,* 608 n. 46; *Four Darks on Red* (1958), 636 n. 5; *Geologic Memory,* 232, 605 n. 6; *Geologic Reverie,* 608 n. 46; *Gethsemane,* 232, 244, 252, 605n n. 6, 7, 608 n. 46; *Green and Blue on Blue,* 639 n. 27; *Green and Maroon* (1953), 449, 636 n. 5; *Green and Tangerine* (1956), 449, 636 n. 5, 647 n. 10; *Green, Red and Blue* (1955), 333, 506, 646 n. 114; *Grey and Black* (1969), 644 n. 102; Harvard Murals, 445–57, 475, 649 n. 20; *Heraldic Dream,* 608 n. 46; *Homage to Matisse* (1954), 606 n. 25, 643 n. 80; *Horizontals, White over Darks,* 636 n. 5, 646 n. 116; Houston Murals, 458–86, 495, 652 n. 36; *Immolation,* 252, 608 n. 46, 47; *Implements of Magic,* 608 n. 46; *Incantation,* 608 n. 46; *Intimations of Chaos,* 232, 605 n. 6; *Iphigenia and The Sea,* 165, 166; *Last Supper,* 159–60, 165; *Light,*

Rothko, Mark (*cont.*)
Earth and Blue (1954), 606 n. 25; *Light Red over Black* (1957), 640 n. 28; *Magenta, Black, Green on Orange* (1949), 669 n. 23; *Maroon on Blue* (1957–60), 636 n. 5, 640 n. 30; *Mauve and Orange* (1961), 646 n. 114; *Mauve Intersection* (1948), 636 n. 5, 647 n. 10; *Mount Hood*, 97; *Mural Sketch* (c. 1939), 590 n. 83; *Mural Sketch* (c. 1940), 590 n. 83; *Number 24, 1947/48*, 669 n. 23; *Number 10, 1948*, 609 n. 10; *Number 18, 1948*, 605 n. 11; *Number 23, 1948*, 609 n. 50; *Number 24, 1948*, 609 n. 50; *Number 1, 1949*, 246, 254–55, 605 n. 11, 609 n. 58; *Number 8, 1949*, 302; *Number 14, 1949*, 298–99; *Number 4A, 1950*, 612 n. 7; *Number 9, 1950*, 612 n. 7; *Number 10, 1950*, 274, 276–79, 282, 298, 299, 314, 612 n. 7; *Number 11, 1950*, 612 n. 7; *Number 13, 1950*, 612 n. 7; *Number 19, 1950*, 612 n. 7; *Number 22, 1950*, 612 n. 7, 669 n. 23; *Number 12, 1951*, 28, 274, 618 n. 39; *Number 14, 1951*, 618 n. 39; *Number 8, 1952*, 640 n. 30; *Number 10, 1952*, 618 n. 39; *Number 4, 1953*, 618 n. 39; *Number 7, 1953*, 618 n. 39; *Number 18, 1953*, 299; *Number 1, 1954*, 618 n. 39; *Number 6, 1954*, 618 n. 39; *Number 9, 1954*, 618 n. 39; *Number 11, 1954*, 618 n. 39; *Number 30, 1954*, 643 n. 80; *Number 47, 1956*, 644 n. 102; *Number 10, 1957*, 640 n. 30; *Number 9, 1958*, 639 n. 22, 669 n. 23; *Number 16, 1960*, 420; *Number 1, White and Red* (1961), 640 n. 28; *Number 2, Red Maroons* (1961), 640 n. 28; *Number 117, 1961*, 606 n. 25, 638 n. 22; *Number 119, 1961*, 638 n. 16; *Number 1, 1962*, 636 n. 5., 641 n. 50; *Number 2, 1962*, 506, 636 n. 5, 641 n. 50; *Number 3, 1967*, 506; *#5 Reds*, 636 n. 5; *Number 22 (Reds)*, 430, 642 n. 71; *Ocher, Red on Red* (1954), 640 n. 28, 647 n. 10; *Oedipus*, 160; *Olive over Red* (1956), 640 n. 28; *Olympian Play*, 608 n. 46; *Omen*, 608 n. 46; *Omen of the Bird*, 608 n. 46; *The Omen of the Eagle*, 165–69, 171, 173, 175, 186, 188, 200, 214, 215, 236, 241, 244, 332; *Omen of the Gods and Birds*, 252, 608 n. 48; *Orange and Red on Red* (1957), 449, 636 n. 5, 640 n. 28; *Orange Brown* (1963), 646 n. 114; *Orange over Yellow*, 637 n. 12; *Orange Red and Red* (1962), 646 n. 114; *Orange Red Yellow* (1956), 646 n. 114; *Orange Red Yellow* (1961), 646 n. 114; *The Oregon Forest*, 97; *Personages*, 608 n. 46; *Phalanx of the Mind*, 232, 605 n. 6; *Poised Elements*, 232, 605 n. 7; *Portland*, 97; *Portrait of Rothko's Mother*, 29–30, 368; *Primeval Landscape*, 244; *Purple Brown* (1957), 643 n. 79; *Red and Black* (1960), 646 n. 114; *Red and Blue over Red* (1959), 643 n. 79; *Red and Brown* (1957), 643 n. 79; *Red and Orange*, 636 n. 5; *Red, Brown and Black* (1958), 333–34, 382, 640 n. 28; *Red Maroons #2*, 636 n. 5; *Red on Maroon* (1959), 401–3, 555–56; *Red Pink* (1961), 644 n. 102; *Red, White and Brown* (1957), 640 n. 28; *Reds* (1957), 422; *Reds* (1961), 422; *Reds Light and Dark #6*, 636 n. 5; *The Rothkowitz Family* (or, *The Family*), 30–31, 90, 109, 110, 192, 267, 367, 570 n. 77; *Sacred Vessel*, 232; *Sacrifice*, 608 n. 47; *The Sacrifice of Iphigenia* (1942), 211; *Sculptress*, 98–100, 109, 110, 171, 214, 368; *Seagram Murals*, 3–4, 5, 109, 133, 370–409, 411–12, 432–33, 451, 459, 513–18; *Self-Portrait*, 107–10, 126–27, 149, 190, 215, 234, 237–38, 273, 315,

324; *Sienna and Orange on Wine* (1962), 644 n. 102; *Sienna, Black on Dark Red* (1959), 640 n. 29; *Slow Swirl at the Edge of the Sea*, 211, 212–16, 235, 244, 261, 280, 287, 601 n. 20; *Street Scene*, 22–24, 26, 31, 53, 64, 107, 108, 123, 127, 130, 185, 192, 453, 569 n. 60; *Subterranean Fantasy*, 128; *Subway*, 585 n. 8; *Subway Scene*, 127–30, 185, 415, 587 n. 39; *The Syrian Bull*, 187–91, 192, 200, 201, 214, 218, 241, 244; *Tentacles of Memory*, 252, 608 n. 46; *Three Reds* (1955), 639 n. 22; *Two Women at Window*, 585 n. 8; *Untitled* (early 1930s), 87–88; *Untitled* (early 1930s), 96; *Untitled* (c. 1940), 172–73, 212, 214, 237–38; *Untitled* (c. 1948), 669 n. 23; *Untitled* (1948), 235–39, 246, 268; *Untitled* (1949), 658 n. 23; *Untitled* (1960), 215; *Untitled* (1962), 506; *Untitled* (1969), 658 n. 24; *Vernal Memory*, 232, 605 n. 6; *Vessels of Magic*, 252, 608 n. 46; *Violet and Yellow in Rose* (1954), 643 n. 79; *Violet Bar* (1957), 636 n. 5; *Votive Mood*, 609 n. 50; *White and Black on Wine* (1958), 418, 634 n. 108; *White and Greens in Blue* (1957), 355, 640 n. 29; *White and Red* (1961), 636 n. 5; *White Band* (1954), 636 n. 5; *White Center* (1957), 422, 640 n. 29; *White, Pink and Mustard* (1954), 636 n. 5; *Woman and Child*, 93; *Women and Children*, 585 n. 8; *Yellow Band* (1956), 506, 636 n. 5; *Yellow, Blue on Orange* (1955), 606 n. 25; *Yellow Green* (1953), 417–18; *Yellow Shine*, 636 n. 5

Rothko, Mary Alice ("Mell"): marries Rothko, 209; relation to *Slow Swirl at the Edge of the Sea*, 215–16; life before marriage, 216–19; early relation to Rothko, 219–21, 234–35; in San Francisco, 261–62; birth of daughter, 273, 286–87, 288, 317; her beauty, 274; travels to Europe, 283–84; returns to work, 298; domestic life, 319, 365; travels to Boulder and New Orleans, 350–55; relation to Rothko, late 1950s, 367–69; second trip to Europe, 398–99; will, 398, 441; dinner at Four Seasons, 404–5; birth of son, 431; Rothko's aneurysm, 489–92; relation to Rothko, mid-1960s, 493, 500–502; separation from Rothko, 467, 505, 507, 532, 536–38

Rothkowitz, Jacob, 14, 143, 245, 416, 431, 566 n. 25; character of, 15–17, 18–19, 58; migration to Portland, 20–21, 25, 45, 224, 393–94; death of, 24, 26–28, 31, 77, 267, 327, 363, 425, 535

Rothkwitz, Kate, 14–16, 22, 32, 88, 125, 152, 286; character of, 28–31, 109, 280; letter from Rothko, 219; death of, 265–68, 279, 423, 611 n. 90

Rothkowitz, Sonia, 14, 15–16; migration, 18, 22, 24, 25; life in Portland, 32, 37, 87, 88, 152–53; Rothko's relation to, 89, 398, 505; Rothko letters to, 208–9, 219, 327, 423, 497–98, 546; quoted, 17, 21, 24, 31, 57

Rubin, William, 492, 540

Ruddick, Dr. Bruce, 531–32

Sachar, Bella, 82, 89, 90

Sachar, Edith, 22, 122, 127, 163, 220, 274, 287; marries Rothko, 81–95, 594 n. 41; Rothko's model, 98–100, 109; jewelry business, 120, 143, 146, 153, 160, 169; marital troubles, 102, 141–49; divorce, 169–71, 203–5, 218, 327, 368, 536

Sachar, Howard, 82, 86, 89, 90, 124, 144–45, 146

Sachar, Lilian, 82, 89, 90, 145

Sachar, Meyer, 82, 89, 90

Sachar, Pauline, 82, 83, 90

Index

Sachar, Willie, 82, 83, 90
Saint Thomas University, 462, 463–64, 484
Sandler, Irving, 272–73, 389, 552
San Francisco Museum of Modern Art, 215, 222, 232, 252, 254, 261
Schanker, Louis, 92, 101
Schapiro, Meyer, 142, 154–55, 326
Scharf, Sally, 319, 466, 507
Scharf, William, 305, 313, 466, 467–69, 471, 474, 495, 496
Schectman, Sidney, 104–5
Schneider, Pierre, 467
Schoenberg, Dr. Bernard, 530–31
Schrag, Karl, 433, 505
Schueler, Jon, 426–27, 431, 433
Scull, Ethel, 419–22
Scull, Robert, 419–22, 430, 433, 462, 463
Segal, George, 419, 429
Seitz, William, 278, 281, 314, 326, 329–32, 391
Seligman, Kurt, 181
Selz, Peter, 326, 431
Sert, José Luis, 445, 447, 453
Seurat, Georges, 139, 140
Sharkey, Alice, 120
Shaw, Benjamin, 203–4
Shriver, Sargent, 417
Sievan, Maurice, 121, 527
Siskind, Aaron, 219
67 Gallery, 209–19, 231
Smith, David, 121, 122, 148, 155, 442–43, 486, 490, 524
Smith, Hassel, 258, 259
Smith, Jean Kennedy, 417
Smith, Tony, 251, 253
Soby, James T., 159
Solman, Joseph, 62–63, 92, 100–102, 105, 106, 115, 120, 124, 165
Solomon, Gus, 38, 54, 64, 624 n. 72
Sonnabend, Michel, 300
Soule, Gordon, 58, 64, 91
Soutine, Chaim, 57, 103
Spalding, Joy, 399

Spohn, Clay, 223, 228, 233, 258, 260–61, 264, 268, 340, 357, 365, 374
Stamos, Theodoros, 195, 250, 252, 271, 273, 469; Rothko's relation to, 325, 365, 499; director of Mark Rothko Foundation, 441, 492, 540, 541; day of Rothko's death, 523, 543
Stein, Gertrude, 137, 140
Stein, Hirsch, 64
Steindecker, Oliver, 469, 470, 493, 496, 521–22, 526, 543
Stella, Frank, 422, 428, 430, 432
Sterne, Hedda, 184, 204, 221, 243, 250, 271–72, 329, 339, 521
Stevens, Wallace, 93
Still, Clyfford, 221–28; on Cézanne, 226; meets Rothko, 205; Rothko on, 168, 195, 222–23, 227–28; praises Rothko, 222, 223; gallery affiliations, 181, 222, 231–32, 250, 297, 336; at California School of Fine Arts, 258, 259, 261; at the Subjects of the Artist school, 223, 262–63; on his correspondence with Rothko, 602 n. 46; ends friendship with Rothko, 5, 286, 622 n. 47; Clement Greenberg on, 384–85; Harold Rosenberg on, 386; denounces art scene, 342, 602 n. 45, 622 n. 46; letter condemns Rothko, 343–48; in Robert Scull collection, 420, 422, 430; on Rothko's suicide, 622 n. 50
Strega, Dr. Helen, 523–24
Styron, William, 530
Subjects of the Artist School, The, 223, 262–65, 288, 345, 440
Sullivan, Mrs. Cornelius J., 138–39, 250
Surrealism, 163, 180–86, 246, 252, 255–56; Rothko's relation to, 174, 185–86, 194, 208, 283, 334–35, 440
Sussman, Gilbert, 38
Sylvester, David, 330, 620 n. 4

698

Index

Taft, Henry W., 73–76
Tanguy, Yves, 180, 181
Tate Gallery, 409, 459, 512–18
Taylor, Francis Henry, 271
The Ten, 101–6, 122, 141, 147, 163
Thiebaud, Wayne, 429
Thomas, Yvonne, 265, 299, 321, 386, 426
Todd, David, 500
Tomlin, Bradley Walker, 184, 256, 299, 300
Treasury Relief Art Project, 119–21, 156
Tremaine, Burton and Emily, 418
Trief, Celina, 290–91, 319
Trivigno, Pat, 353, 354–55
Trottenberg, A. D., 447–48, 450
Tschacbasov, Nahum, 101
Turner, Joseph, 666 n. 1
291 Gallery, 138
Tworkov, Jack, 493, 496, 498

University of California, Berkeley, 423, 502–3
Uptown Gallery, 98, 100

Valentin, Curt, 231, 256
Valentine-Dudensing Gallery, 138
Valentine Gallery, 101, 147
van der Rohe, Mies, 371, 372, 393, 405
van Gogh, Vincent, 108–9, 139, 140, 211
van Loon, Hendrik Willem, 70
Ventgen, Frank, 522
Viola, Wilhelm, 132–33

Walkowitz, Abraham, 349
Warhol, Andy, 419, 421, 422, 426, 428, 429, 432, 433–35, 436, 470
Weber, Max, 59, 61–63, 76, 95, 102, 104, 122, 244, 316; Rothko in class, 56, 60, 83, 94, 576 n. 59
Weinstein, Abe, 21
Weinstein, Abraham, 49

Weinstein, Barbara, 81
Weinstein, Bessie, 21
Weinstein, Daniel, 49
Weinstein, Edward, 35, 49–50, 56, 85, 539
Weinstein, Esther, 49
Weinstein, Florence, 265
Weinstein, Harold, 64, 81, 153
Weinstein, Hazel, 21
Weinstein, Jacob, 49, 56
Weinstein, Joe, 21
Weinstein, Louis, 49
Weinstein, Moe, 21
Weinstein, Nate, 21, 24, 539
Weinstein, Sam, 21, 24, 35, 49
Weinstein, Sylvia, 21
Whitechapel Gallery, 378, 411–12, 432, 513, 514
Whitney, Gertrude, 101, 103
Whitney, John Hay, 138, 164
Whitney, Simon, 46, 51
Whitney Museum of American Art, 101, 141, 142, 144, 299; protest against, 103–5; exhibits Rothko, 232, 298; purchases a Rothko, 252, 254; Rothko refuses participation, 303–4, 374, 604 n. 4; Rothko breaks window, 322
Wilder, Clinton, 540
Wilke, Ulfert, 469, 480, 489
Wilkes, Paul, 522–23
Wise, Stephen, 38, 66, 69
Wolfe, Tom, 419, 420–21
Wolff, Robert Jay, 288, 289, 292, 293
Wollheim, Richard, 555–58
Works Progress Administration, 23, 62, 70–74, 119–23, 147, 155, 156, 197, 585 n. 8
Wright, Dr. Irving, 489–91

Yale Saturday Evening Pest, The, 51–54, 124, 174

Zorach, William, 154

699

Photo Credits

Color Plates

All color plates © 1993 by Christopher Rothko and Kate Rothko Prizel/ARS, New York.

All color plates are of works by Mark Rothko. 1: *Street Scene XX (Rothko number 3053.36)*, Gift of The Mark Rothko Foundation, © 1993 National Gallery of Art, Washington; 2: *Portrait of Rothko's Mother*, Kate Rothko Prizel; 3: *Family (Rothko number 3207.30)*, Gift of The Mark Rothko Foundation, © 1993 National Gallery of Art, Washington; 4: *Late 1920s (Landscape) (Rothko number 1083.25–27)*, Gift of The Mark Rothko Foundation, © 1993 National Gallery of Art, Washington; 5: *Untitled*, Gift of The Mark Rothko Foundation, © 1993 National Gallery of Art, Washington; 6: *Untitled (sculptress) (Rothko number 3107.30)*, Gift of The Mark Rothko Foundation, © 1993 National Gallery of Art, Washington; 7: Christopher Rothko; 8: Kate Rothko Prizel; 9: *The Omen of the Eagle (Rothko number 3223.40)*, Gift of The Mark Rothko Foundation, © 1993 National Gallery of Art, Washington; 10: (Estate #3086.39), Christopher Rothko; 11: Allen Memorial Art Museum, Oberlin College; Gift of Annalee (Mrs. Barnett) Newman in honor of Ellen H. Johnson, 1991. The two paintings, *Syrian Bull* by Mark Rothko and *Rape of Persephone* by Adolph Gottlieb, were given to Barnett Newman by Gottlieb and Rothko in appreciation for Newman's help in formulating the letter that Gottlieb and Rothko sent to Edward Alden Jewell, Art Editor of the *New York Times*, and which he published on June 13, 1943; 12: *Slow Swirl by the Edge of the Sea*, 1944, oil on canvas, 6′3 3/8″ × 7′3/4″, The Museum of Modern Art, New York, Bequest of Mrs. Mark Rothko through The Mark Rothko Foundation, Inc.; 13: (Estate #4008.48), Kate Rothko Prizel; 14: *Number 10*, 1950, oil on canvas, 7′6 3/8″ × 57 1/8″, The Museum of Modern Art, New York, Gift of Philip Johnson; 15: (Estate #5226.51), Christopher Rothko; 16: *Red, Brown, and Black*, 1958, oil on canvas, 8′10 5/8″ × 9′9 1/4″, The Museum of Modern Art, New York, Mrs. Simon Guggenheim Fund; 17: Tate Gallery, London/Art Resource, N.Y., T1165; 18: Courtesy of The President and Fellows of Harvard College, Gift of Mark Rothko; 19: The Menil Collection, Houston; 20: *1967 (Rothko number 1268.67)*, Gift of The Mark Rothko Foundation, © 1993 National Gallery of Art, Washington; 21: (Estate #5218.69), Kate Rothko Prizel.

Black-and-white photographs

Copyright © 1993 by Christopher Rothko and Kate Rothko Prizel: 14–17, 24–25, 27–30, 35–37.

1: Gesel Maimin; 2–5: Kenneth Rabin; 10: Oregon Historical Society, #PGE 130-82b; 11: Oregon Historical Society, #OrHi 11930; 12: Oregon Historical Society, #OrHi 6135; 13: Oregon Historical Society, #OrHi 26684; 18–22: George Carson; 23: National Archives; 24: Mark Rothko, *Two Abstract Figures Entwined*, Gift of The Mark Rothko Foundation, © 1992 National Gallery of Art, Washington; 25: Mark Rothko, *Untitled*, Gift of The Mark Rothko Foundation, © 1992 National Gallery of Art, Washington; 26: Elizabeth Schoenfeld; 31: Arnold Siskind Foundation courtesy the Robert Mann Gallery; 32: Nina Leen, *Life* Magazine, © 1951 Time Warner Inc.; 33–34: © Hans Namuth 1991; 38: Rudy Burckhardt; 39: Philip Johnson; 40–41: Regina Bogat; 43, 45: © Hans Namuth 1991; 46: Alexander Liberman; 47–48: Hickey and Robertson, Houston, Texas, courtesy of The Rothko Chapel; 49: Peter Selz; 50: Dr. Morton Levine; 51–52: Dr. Morton Levine, courtesy of the Smithsonian Institution.

All other photographs were taken by the author.